MONETARY AND FINANCIAL ECONOMICS

James L. Pierce
University of California, Berkeley

John Wiley & Sons
New York   Chichester   Brisbane   Toronto   Singapore

To Jonathan, Susan, and Samuel.

Cover design: Karin Gerdes Kincheloe
Cover illustration: Narda Lebo

Library of Congress Cataloging in Publication Data:
Pierce, James L.
     Monetary and financial economics.

     Includes bibliographies and index.
     1. Finance. 2. Money. 3. Banks and banking.
I. Title.
HG173.P53   1984   332   83-26073
ISBN 0-471-08757-2

Printed in the United States of America

10 9 8 7 6 5 4 3 2 1

PREFACE

During the several years that I have taught money and banking to undergraduates at Berkeley, I have become increasingly frustrated with existing textbooks. Several recent texts have demonstrated that modern macroeconomics can be presented successfully to undergraduates on a relatively rigorous and sophisticated level. I believe that this text does the same for modern monetary and financial economics.

This book contains a great deal of economics. The tools of modern economics are used not only in the macroeconomics and policy chapters, but also to explain institutional and historical factors, the behavior of individual depository institutions, the money "supply," and other subjects that occupy money and banking texts.

Great changes have occurred in the last several years in both the American financial system and in the economic analysis used to study that system. For that reason, this book is concerned not only with money and banking but with the broader issues that constitute monetary and financial economics. In addition, the topics of conventional money and banking texts are covered from a modern perspective. For example, I emphasize depository institutions rather than banks, and transactions accounts rather than demand deposit accounts. The role of money is covered in detail, but within the context of a world in which changes in demands and supplies of various assets are important.

Basic economic principles are discussed in detail. For example, the concept of the interest rate is defined and motivated by a Robinson Crusoe story that stresses the relationship between consumer preferences concerning current versus future consumption and the marginal productivity of capital. The tools of portfolio theory are developed and used to study the demand for assets and supply of liabilities for households, nonfinancial firms, and financial intermediaries (with emphasis on depository institutions). Portfolio theory is also used to analyze the determinants of the term structure of interest rates, showing, that interest rate expectations are important for thrifts, banks, and for the investment decisions of firms.

Financial innovation and deregulation have accelerated in recent years. These forces are probably beneficial for the financial system, but they certainly complicate the life of a textbook writer. Several chapters were rewritten to keep up with innovation and deregulation as they occurred. The text discusses both the Depository Institutions Deregulation and Monetary Control Act of 1980 and the Garn-St Germain Act of 1982. It also examines the effects of having money that pays a market rate of interest, and the effects of the virtually total decontrol of time deposit interest rates that occurred in October 1983.

Perhaps more important, the text stresses the economic forces that have produced financial innovation and deregulation. Armed with the appropriate economic tools, students can evaluate the consequences of the further innovation and deregulation that will occur after this book's publication.

Much of the sterile debate among the extreme members of the Keynesian and monetarist factions of economics has been replaced in recent years by a synthesis of views. This synthesis can be seen in the similarities of the models used by Tobin, and by Brunner and Meltzer. I have attempted to carry over that synthesis to the macroeconomic chapters of this book. The *IS-LM* framework is used, but attention is paid to the price level, inflation, inflationary expectations, and wealth. Some of the conclusions reached are appealing to monetarists and some to Keynesians. For example, Chapter 16 shows that sustained inflation is a monetary phenomenon and, therefore, is ultimately the responsibility of monetary policy. Furthermore, in Chapter 18, a balanced discussion is presented concerning the debate over the wisdom of monetary policy rules. Chapter 18 shows that there is an analytic basis for preferring rules, but that the basis may not be met in reality. For the Keynesians we have a role for fiscal policy and for supply-side shocks that can produce substantial periods of inflation and of unemployment. The inability of either monetary or fiscal policy to deal effectively with stagflation in the short run is discussed.

Chapter 18 is concerned with monetary policy in theory and practice, and Chapter 19 is concerned with the actual execution of policy 1965 through 1982. In writing those chapters, I have been able to draw on my "insider's" knowledge as a former senior staff member of the Board of Governors of the Federal Reserve System and former associate economist for the Federal Open Market Committee. These positions gave me an appreciation that is not available to outsiders for the difficulties of effectively executing monetary policy. To be sure that my knowledge of the policy process has not become dated, I interviewed current senior staff members, Federal Reserve governors, and Reserve bank presidents. These discussions helped me to understand the policy procedures and problems that developed after my departure from the Federal Reserve in 1975.

Some of the material presented in this text is more advanced than one typically finds in a money and banking text. For example, there are separate chapters on portfolio theory (Chapter 5) and on the term structure of interest rates (Chapter

6). There is also a chapter that introduces wealth into a conventional macromodel (Chapter 15); this allows monetary policy and government budget deficits to be studied in depth. Chapter 18, Monetary Policy in Theory and Practice, puts considerable emphasis on the effects of uncertainty concerning the current and future state of the economy, and of uncertainty concerning the timing and extent of effect of policy changes.

There are three reasons why the material in this book can be presented successfully to undergraduates. First, I have covered all the material in this text in my undergraduate course at Berkeley with considerable success. Second, reviewers from schools with undergraduate programs that are less demanding than Berkeley's have endorsed the approach. Third, the success of the newer intermediate macroeconomics texts indicates that undergraduates can handle relatively advanced material.

I realize that many users will not want to teach as intensive and exhaustive a course as is possible with this text. As a result, the book is written so that whole chapters, and parts of chapters, can be omitted without disturbing the flow of the text or the understanding of later material. For example, some instructors may want to skip Chapter 5 and 6. While it is important to understand portfolio theory and the determinants of the term structure of interest rates, enough is said about these topics in later chapters to allow the more formal material of Chapters 5 and 6 to be omitted. Similarly, Chapter 7 presents a model of bank behavior that allows one to analyze liability management, the relationship between the interest rates on liabilities and loans, and the effects of interest rate ceilings for liabilities. It is possible to cover the more conventional material on banks and thrifts in Chapters 8 through 10 while skipping Chapter 7. Chapter 15 presents a fairly sophisticated macromodel that introduces wealth. Some instructors may consider this material to be too advanced and this chapter can be omitted. Chapter 17 contains an extended discussion of international trade and finance. These topics have become increasingly important in recent years, but this material can be omitted without losing continuity. Finally, the historical discussions that appear as parts of Chapters 2, 9, and 10 can be omitted without loss of continuity.

In a nutshell, individual instructors have considerable flexibility to design their own course when using this text. The level of difficulty of the book depends on how much of the material from the more demanding chapters and sections is included. In all situations, however, material is developed assuming that students only have had an introductory course in economics and high school algebra.

Many people have helped me with this project. Earl Rolph and William Dudley read a draft of the entire manuscript and gave detailed and highly constructive comments. Richard Esposito, the economics editor for Wiley, recruited several reviewers who also read the entire manuscript and whose comments helped improve the final version of this book. Edward Ettin offered many helpful comments on monetary policy issues, institutionals, and data. Roger Craine, Jeffrey Frankel, and Spencer Krane made many excellent comments on various chapters. I thank all these people for their help.

I also thank the students in my Economics 136 class who acted as guinea pigs by using chapter drafts as their text. They uncovered several errors and their experience with the text drafts helped to improve the presentation. Janet Ceglowski and Phyllis Hallinan were teaching assistants for the course and they also contributed excellent suggestions. Jonathan and Susan Pierce (Sam is too young) read much of the manuscript and their thoughtful comments are appreciated, if not their glee in finding Dad's prose less than crystal clear at times.

William Dudley and Spencer Krane were my research assistants for this book. I appreciate the excellent work they did.

Last, and most, I thank Suzanne Edwards. Suzanne typed countless drafts of the book, became the world's expert on word processing, and took care of the administrative and procedural aspects of the book's production. Her skill and enthusiasm were all the more remarkable when one considers that she was pursuing a demanding, fulltime administrative job in the Berkeley Economics Department at the same time. By her good example, Suzanne kept my spirits up when they waned. Thanks, Suzy!

James L. Pierce

CONTENTS

Chapter 5: **PORTFOLIO THEORY   99**

THE FUNCTIONS AND DEFINITION OF MONEY

1

The quantity of money plays an important role in affecting national output, employment, and inflation. The description and explanation of this role occupy many chapters of this book. It is appropriate to begin the text by analyzing the functions of money and by presenting a practical definition of money that is in common use.

In this chapter, it is shown that money functions as a medium of exchange, as a unit of account, and as a store of value. A widely accepted definition of money is called *M1*. It is comprised of the public's holdings of media of exchange, currency and coin, plus its holdings of transactions accounts at banks and other depository institutions.

FUNCTIONS OF MONEY

Medium of Exchange

A *medium of exchange* is anything that is generally accepted and used by the public in payment for goods and services or for payment of debts. An easy way to appreciate the importance of a medium of exchange is to imagine an economy in which there is no money. In this economy, transactions take place in the form of exchanges of physical commodities or services. Such exchange is called *barter*. In a barter economy, workers make purchases by trading the commodities they produce for other commodities. For example, cobblers get hungry from time to time and want to trade some of the shoes they produce for food. Farmers in a barter economy are willing to trade food for shoes.

In an economy that produces only shoes and food, there is no problem with barter; but in economies with more than two commodities, an important defect of barter occurs. If cobblers want to exchange shoes for a number of different commodities, it is necessary to exchange shoes for each one of them. As the number of commodities increases, it becomes increasingly difficult for the cobblers to find individuals who happen to want shoes and happen to offer commodities the cobblers want to consume. Such happy matchups can occur, and they are called a *double coincidence of wants*. With a large number of products, however, it is unlikely that this coincidence occurs very often, and more roundabout methods of exchange are often necessary. Farmers may have to accept shoes in payment for corn even though they want new togas instead. They must then find toga sellers who are willing to exchange togas for shoes. The toga sellers may not want shoes so they have to find someone else with whom to trade. The shoes could be traded a number of times before they end up on the feet of someone who wants them.

Ancient economies developed markets at which many traders could meet to exchange commodities. These markets eased the problem of roundabout trading, but they did not eliminate it. Modern, complex economies are incompatible with the barter system because there are too many kinds of goods and services available to allow production and distribution to be conducted efficiently through barter. Think of the complexity and expense of Sears Roebuck's attempting to trade its thousands of products for other commodities. The hardware department might sell one screwdriver for a bushel of corn and another screwdriver for a banana cream pie. What is Sears to do with all the commodities it receives in trade?

As a result of the inefficiencies of barter, economies achieved substantial savings of time and effort by using a single commodity (or at least a small number of commodities) as a medium of exchange. This medium of exchange is called *money*. Money can be used for transactions when individuals are willing to accept it in payment for goods, services, or debts. Barter is no longer necessary when there is money. Workers are paid in money, and merchants sell their products for money. Money provides generalized purchasing power because it can be used to purchase any commodity or service.

Many items have been used as media of exchange (money) in various economies at different times. These items have ranged from livestock, clamshells, wampum, and gold to paper money and, most recently, to accounts where payments are made by checks or through electronic transactions. Some items are superior to others as media of exchange because an effective medium should be portable, easily divisible (to make change), relatively scarce, and difficult to counterfeit. These considerations rule out many candidates. Goats have been used as a medium of exchange, but they are difficult to carry around and even more difficult to make change with. However, they are relatively scarce and defy the efforts of counterfeiters. Sand is fairly easy to carry around and to make change with (except in a breeze), but sand is freely available and would not last long as money. No one would accept sand in exchange for goods and services because it can be obtained at the beach without giving up commodities. Though these considerations narrow the choice of items that can be used as media of exchange, the choice is still a wide one. Factors leading to the choice of media of exchange in modern economies are discussed in the next chapter.

Unit of Account

A second property of money is that it serves as a *unit of account.* A unit of account is an arbitrary common denominator or measuring stick for prices. For example, in the United States the dollar is the unit of account; prices are quoted in terms of dollars. The unit of account makes price comparisons far easier than would be the case if prices were quoted in terms of various commodities.

Consider the simple case of an economy without a unit of account that produces only shoes, corn, and togas. Assume that ten ears of corn purchase one shoe, five ears of corn purchase one toga, and two togas purchase one shoe. The cobbler thinks of the prices of corn and togas in terms of the number of shoes necessary to obtain them (1 for 10 and 1 for 2), the farmer thinks of the prices of shoes and togas in terms of corn (10 for 1 and 5 for 1) and the toga producer thinks of shoe and corn prices in terms of togas (2 for 1 and 1 for 5). When someone asks the price of shoes, the farmer responds, "ten for one," and the toga maker replies, "two for one"; the prices in terms of corn and togas. This might not create much confusion in an economy with only three commodities, but confusion would be massive for an economy with thousands of commodities.

A further complication of the situation is that not all the prices are independent of each other. In an economy with n commodities, there are only $n-1$ independent prices. For example, in a three-commodity economy there are only two independent prices. The third price is implied by the other two.

Table 1.1 shows exchange possibilities for a three-commodity barter economy. The figure in the numerator of each ratio is the number of shoes, ears of corn, or togas that a buyer has to give up in order to purchase the number of shoes, ears of corn, or togas shown in the denominator. For example, a person exchanging corn for shoes is buying shoes and selling corn. The rate of exchange is 10 ears of corn for 1 shoe or $10C/1S$. Similarly, a person exchanging togas for corn faces a price of 1 toga for 5 ears of corn or $1T/5C$.

The rates of exchange between shoes and togas have been indicated by a dash to illustrate the proposition that in a three-commodity economy, there are only two independent prices. If we know the price of corn in terms of shoes and the price of togas in terms of corn, the price of togas in terms of shoes is immediately determined. If this rate of exchange were not announced, it could be discovered by trading one shoe for ten ears of corn and the ten ears of corn for two togas. Thus, one shoe buys two togas, and two togas buy one shoe.[1]

---

[1] Algebraically, there are only two independent equations describing the prices of three commodities. From Table 1.1 we have (1) $1S = 10C$ and (2) $1T = 5C$. We can derive the expression relating S and T by solving (2) for C to give $1C = (1/5)T$ and substituting for C in (1) to give $1S = 10(1/5)T$ or (3) $1S = 2T$.

TABLE 1.1
RATES OF EXCHANGE IN A THREE-COMMODITY ECONOMY

Buying (denominator)	Selling (numerator)		
	Shoes(S)	Corn(C)	Togas(T)
Shoes (S)	$1S/1S$	$10C/1S$	—
Corn (C)	$1S/10C$	$1C/1C$	$1T/5C$
Togas (T)	—	$5C/1T$	$1T/1T$

If toga sellers try to get a higher price for their togas in terms of shoes, they will fail so long as the price of togas in terms of corn and the price of corn in terms of shoes are known. For example, if sellers try to get one shoe in payment for each toga, holders of shoes will exchange the one shoe for ten ears of corn and exchange the ten ears of corn for two togas. Because indirect trading is possible, toga sellers are prevented from charging more than one shoe for every two togas. If shoe sellers get greedy and try to get three togas for each shoe, they will be unsuccessful. Holders of togas can exchange togas for corn and corn for shoes. Thus, indirect trading prevents shoe sellers from getting more than two togas per shoe.

In a three-commodity economy, it is a relatively simple matter to figure out the third price given the other two. Indirect trading ensures that the third price will not differ from what is implied by the other two. In more complex economies, it is more difficult to make all the calculations to ensure that direct and indirect trading will result in the same rate of exchange between any two commodities. For example, in an economy with 1000 commodities, there are 499,500 prices, of which 9,999 are independent. It would be mind boggling for people to keep track of all trading possibilities for 1000 commodities.

Unless there is agreement within an economy on a convention by which prices are measured, great confusion can result. The problem was solved by establishing a unit of account. A unit of account can be a single commodity (e.g., corn) by which it is generally agreed to measure prices, or it can be an abstract measure that has no physical representation. In practice, the medium of exchange itself is usually denominated in the unit of account. For example, in the United States the unit of account is the dollar, and the media of exchange (coins, currency, and accounts upon which checks can be drawn) are denominated in dollars.

In principle, the unit of account need not be the same as the medium of exchange; it can be an abstract unit of measure. For example, the medium of exchange might be called "dollars"; and the unit of account, "bits." Such practice causes few problems so long as one knows how many bits there are in a dollar (for the uninitiated, the answer is eight). With this knowledge, it is possible to convert the price quoted in bits to the number of dollars that actually have to be expended.

There is nothing to be gained by separating the unit of account from the medium of exchange, so the practice is to combine them. Thus, prices are meas-

TABLE 1.2
DOLLAR PRICES IN A THREE-COMMODITY ECONOMY

	Item		
	Shoes	Corn	Togas
Price per unit	$2.00	$0.20	$1.00

ured in dollars, and transactions are carried out using media of exchange denominated in dollars. Because some people seem to enjoy variety, in the United States prices are occasionally quoted in bits, and in England prices are sometimes quoted in guineas. There are no longer physical bits or guineas; rather, they are abstract units.[2]

A unit of account greatly simplifies price comparisons. People do not have to know the rates of exchange among all commodities, only the price of each commodity in terms of the unit of account. A unit of account allows everyone to use a single language when talking about prices. Table 1.2 shows the prices of shoes, corn, and togas measured in terms of dollars as the unit of account. As the reader can verify, Table 1.2 implies all the rates of exchange shown in Table 1.1, but now price comparisons are easy.

Store of Value

Money as a medium of exchange provides generalized purchasing power; it can be expended on any collection of goods and services. If money is to carry out its function fully, it must also serve as a means of carrying that purchasing power into the future; it must serve as a *store of value*. A worker may get paid $100 a week but decide to spend only $20 on payday for consumption goods. The individual has decided to carry over the remaining $80 of purchasing power into the future in the form of money. If money could not be used as a store of value, it would be necessary for the worker to spend the entire $100 on payday, $20 on items for current consumption and $80 on commodities or other assets that are stores of value. It would be necessary to sell these assets in the future to obtain the money necessary to make other expenditures.

If money is to serve its function as a store of value, it must not be perishable. There are two forms of perishability. The most obvious form is physical perisha-

---

[2] The term *bit* is derived from the gold Spanish dollars or pieces of eight that circulated in the American colonies. There were eight bits in a dollar. When the United States adopted the dollar as its monetary unit, the term bit continued to be used as an abstract unit of account signifying eight to a dollar.

The guinea was an English gold coin that circulated in the seventeenth and eighteenth centuries. Its value was set at 21 shillings. Shilling coins are still used in Britain, but guineas are not. The guinea is used as an abstract unit of account signifying 21 shillings.

bility. It would be an unhappy worker, indeed, who got paid in peaches and decided to postpone a purchase for several months. Aside from the physical mess of carrying around the peaches, at some point they would simply cease to exist. It would not take society long to discover that peaches as money are the pits.

A second, more insidious form of perishability comes from *inflation.* Inflation is the rate at which the purchasing power of money is declining. Inflation means that over time a given amount of money buys fewer and fewer goods and services. An enterprising society might discover that it is better to use peach pits rather than peaches as money, only to discover that their purchasing power is rotting because of inflation.

Money serves its full function as generalized purchasing power only if it can be used for current and future consumption. If money is perishable, the public will want to convert it into commodities and other stores of value that are less perishable.[3]

The ability of money to serve as a store of value also allows it to be used as a standard for deferred payments. Many individuals make agreements to pay or receive money in the future. For example, when a person signs a lease for an apartment, there is an agreement to pay some specified amount of money each month for the apartment. Similarly, when a person borrows, there is an agreement to repay the principal plus interest to the lender in the future. Agreements of this kind are for deferred payment.

In a monetary economy, it is natural to state these agreements in terms of specified amounts of money to be paid at some later date. As long as money retains its purchasing power, there is considerable convenience in making and receiving these payments in the form of the medium of exchange. If the purchasing power of money varies, however, the use of money becomes less convenient. In this case, the apartment owner or lender must try to guess what the purchasing power of money will be when payments will be received in the future. If the purchasing power of money falls during the life of the agreement, those who receive payment are paid in depreciated money and are worse off than if the purchasing power of money had not declined. Payers of money in the future are made better off by being able to pay in depreciated dollars. If money appreciates in purchasing power over the life of the agreement, the losses and gains are reversed. Because many people do not like the risks involved, uncertainty about the future purchasing power of money makes money less attractive to them as a form of deferred payment.

MEASURING MONEY

Several forms of money are used in modern economies. Coins and currency (e.g., dimes and dollar bills) are the most familiar. Though they are used extensively to make transactions, coin and currency are not the principal media of exchange.

---

[3] We will see in later chapters that the costs and risks of holding other stores of value may induce the public to hold money even though it is perishable.

TABLE 1.3
THE QUANTITY OF MONEY (M1)
DECEMBER 1982 (Billions of dollars,
averages of daily figures)

Coin and currency	132.8
Transactions accounts[a]	345.4
M1	478.2

[a] Includes traveler's checks.
Source: *Federal Reserve Bulletin*, May 1983, Table 1.21.

Most money is held in the form of account balances at banks and other depository institutions. Payments are made by bookkeeping entries that transfer funds from one account to another. These payments are typically made by check. A check instructs a bank, savings and loan association, mutual savings bank, or credit union to deduct the amount written on it from the payer's account and transfer the funds to the account of the payee. For example, when you write a $100 check for tuition (don't you wish!), no coins or currency change hands. Instead, your school deposits the check in an account in its bank. That bank then sends the check to your bank, which reduces your account balance by $100. When the transaction is completed, your account balance is $100 lower, and your school's account balance is $100 higher.

Whereas checks are the most common method of transferring balances from one account to another, they are not the only means. Direct electronic transactions are becoming increasingly common where balances are transferred either by special encoded cards or by telephoned instructions. No matter how the balances are transferred, however, the crucial point is that these account balances are money. Accounts from which it is possible to make direct payments by check or other means are called *transactions accounts*.

We define money as coins and currency plus transactions account balances held by the public. This definition of money is called M1. Table 1.3 shows the amount and composition of M1 for the end of the year 1982. As the table indicates, about one third of M1 is coin and currency, and two thirds is transactions account balances.

Some economists use wider definitions of money called *M2* and *M3*. These definitions include assets that cannot be used as media of exchange but that can be quickly converted into M1 at low cost. These assets, which include savings and time accounts at depository institutions, are described in later chapters. We use M1 as the definition of money in this text because it is composed only of media of exchange.

SUMMARY

This chapter has discussed the functions of money and has argued that money plays a crucial role in complex economies. Money was invented to eliminate the substantial time and effort expended during barter on evaluating prices and on trading commodities. Because money is a unit of account, it allows easy comparisons of prices; because it is a medium of exchange, money allows transactions to be conducted much more simply than would be the case with barter. Because money provides generalized purchasing power, it also serves as a store of value. This latter function is not well performed, however, if the purchasing power of money varies.

This text uses a definition of money that includes only the media of exchange. This definition is called M1 and is composed of the public's holdings of coin and currency plus transactions account balances at banks and other depository institutions. Some economists favor M2 as the definition of money. M2 adds savings and time accounts at depository institutions and certain other liquid assets to M1.

SELECTED REFERENCES

Alchian, Armen, "Why Money," *Journal of Money, Credit and Banking*, February 1977, pp. 133–41.

Board of Governors of the Federal Reserve System, "The Redefined Monetary Aggregates," *Federal Reserve Bulletin*, February 1980, pp. 97–114.

Brunner, Karl and Allen Meltzer, "The Uses of Money in the Theory of An Exchange Economy." *American Economic Review*, December 1971, pp. 784–805.

THE EVOLUTION OF MONEY

2

Money has been used for thousands of years, and it has taken a wide variety of forms. The development of money coincides with the evolution of economies from simple to complex forms. Stones, goats, or cows may be acceptable forms of money in pastoral societies, but they are not too handy in modern economies. The money used in modern economies is the result of historical forces that led to gradual changes in monetary forms to meet new and more complex institutional arrangements.

Ideally, the use of money should always enhance economic development and expansion. Societies have learned, however, that this ideal is difficult to achieve. If money is too scarce, economic expansion can be stifled. Conversely, if money is too plentiful, inflation and economic dislocations can result. It is not possible in this chapter to develop in detail the reasons why monetary economies are sensitive to the quantity of money available. It is possible to provide examples, however, and to discuss briefly how forms of money have evolved that can facilitate economic expansion and development.

COMMODITY MONEY

Physical commodities were used as money in ancient societies. A commodity was the unit of account, the medium of exchange, and a store of value. The actual commodity varied from society to society, but seashells, animal teeth, livestock, corn, and tobacco are among the many forms used in rudimentary economies. All the items were relatively durable and difficult to counterfeit. Metals such as bronze, gold, and silver became popular because of their relative ease of transport, divisibility, and scarcity. Because of the convenience of money, it was not necessary to force individuals to accept the commodity as money. Self-interest led to commodity money.

When a commodity is adopted as money, its prices or rates of exchange relative to other commodities are altered. Consider the case of gold, which has been a popular form of money. Gold has been widely prized for ornamental and sacramental uses and, as a result, has enjoyed a relatively high value per unit. In a barter economy, the market value of gold is its rates of exchange relative to other commodities in the economy. There is no single price of gold; there are as many prices as there are commodities to exchange for it. For simplicity, however, we shall lump all the commodities together so that the price of gold is the rate of exchange between gold and all other commodities in the economy.

Panel I of Figure 2.1 describes the market for gold before gold is used as money. The figure shows the price of gold on the vertical axis and the total quantity of gold in the economy on the horizontal axis. The price of gold is the rate of exchange between ounces of gold and all other commodities. As the price of gold falls, people have to give up less and less of other commodities to get a given amount of gold. With a lower gold price, individuals desire to have more gold and less of other commodities; the demand curve slopes downward. The supply curve shows the responsiveness of gold mining and gold importation to a rise in the price of gold. The more commodities a gold miner or importer can get for an ounce of gold, the more gold will be supplied to the market; the supply curve slopes upward. The point at which the demand and supply curves intersect gives the equilibrium or market clearing price of gold in terms of commodities, P_0. At this price, the quantity G_0 of gold is used by the society.

Now assume that gold is adopted as money. In this case, gold is demanded as an ornament *and* as money. Panel II of Figure 2.1 shows the market for gold after it is used as money. The demand schedule for gold shifts to the right because society uses gold for money as well as for ornaments. At each price of gold, people want to have more gold than they did before. At the old price of gold in terms of other commodities, P_0, individuals now demand the quantity G_1 of gold. This demand is comprised of the original quantity demanded for ornamental purposes, G_0, plus the demand for gold as money, $G_1 - G_0$. There is no greater quantity of gold available (supplied) at P_0, so when people attempt to exchange other commodities for gold, they find that they can only induce others to give up gold if the price of gold rises. But the rise in price brings forth some increase in the quantity supplied. A new equilibrium occurs at price P_1. As long as the supply curve is upward sloping, the price must rise. At the price P_1, the society uses the quantity G_2 of gold. The quantity G_3 is used for ornamental purposes, and the quantity $G_2 - G_3$ is used as money. The rise in the price of gold induces the quantity supplied to increase by the amount of $G_2 - G_0$. This new supply is available for monetary purposes. But the increase in price also reduces the quantity of gold demanded for ornamental purposes from G_0 to G_3, so the total quantity of gold used as money is $G_2 - G_3$. The price of gold, P_1, must be paid for gold irrespective of whether it is used as an ornament or as money. The price of gold as money must be the same as the price of gold for alternative uses.

FIGURE 2.1
DETERMINING THE COMMODITY
PRICE OF GOLD.

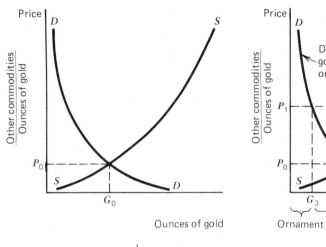

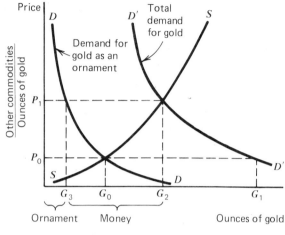

When gold is adopted as money, that commodity has generalized purchasing power over all the other commodities in the economy. The price of gold is the rate of exchange between money and all other commodities and, therefore, is the *purchasing power of money*. If the price of gold increases, an ounce of gold purchases more commodities than before, the purchasing power of money increases. If the price of gold decreases, the purchasing power of money declines because an ounce of gold purchases fewer commodities than before.

The *price level* is the amount of money (gold) that must be expended to acquire a given amount of commodities. The price level is the reciprocal of the purchasing power of money (i.e., the reciprocal of the price of gold). When the price of gold increases, less gold is required to purchase a given amount of commodities; the price level decreases. When the price of gold declines, more gold is required to purchase a given amount of commodities; the price level increases.

The purchasing power of money and the price level are affected by shifts in the demand and supply of gold. For example, if individuals' tastes change and the demand for gold as an ornament increases, the total demand for gold increases. In terms of Panel II of Figure 2.1, both demand curves shift to the right, and the price of gold increases.[1] At the existing price of gold, P_1, people want to hold more gold than before. They cannot obtain more gold at the existing price so they bid up its price. This means that they offer to exchange more commodities for

---

[1] The actual shifts in the demand schedules are not shown. It is left to the reader to verify graphically the conclusions in the text.

gold than before. The increase in price induces some increase in the quantity of gold supplied. The equilibrium price is established where the new higher demand curve intersects the supply curve. The price is higher than P_1, and the rise in price means that the purchasing power of money increases and, equivalently, that the price level decreases. Similarly, if individuals want to hold more gold as a store of value, the demand for gold as money increases. The total demand curve for gold shifts to the right, but the demand curve for gold as an ornament is unaffected. The price of gold increases, and the price level falls.

The supply of gold is also an important factor in determining the price of gold. Consider the case of a gold discovery. If a new source of gold is found, the supply curve shifts to the right as shown in Panel I of Figure 2.2. Gold miners produce a larger amount of gold at the price P_1 and use this new gold to purchase additional commodities. The increased demand for commodities pushes up the price of commodities in terms of gold. Thus, the purchasing power of gold declines; that is, the price of gold in terms of commodities falls. The price of gold must fall sufficiently to induce the public to hold additional gold. The new equilibrium occurs at the price P_2.

We conclude that an increase in the quantity of gold (money) supplied lowers the price of gold in terms of commodities. This means that the purchasing power of gold declines and the price level rises. The example given was in terms of a gold discovery, but the supply curve will also shift to the right if the demand of foreigners for commodities in our hypothetical economy increases. They bring in gold to purchase commodities, and the purchasing power of the gold declines as commodity prices rise. Other things being equal, an increase in the supply of gold (money) reduces its purchasing power.

Other things may not be equal, however. If the output of goods and services also expands, more money is demanded to facilitate the production and sale of the larger output. As shown in Panel II of Figure 2.2, both the supply and the demand schedules shift to the right, leaving the equilibrium price at P_1. In this case, a rise in the supply of gold does not lead to a bidding up of commodity prices. The output of commodities rises, and the public demands the increased quantity of gold to finance its greater transactions. When an economy grows, it needs an increased supply of money to finance its rising volume of transactions. In this situation, the quantity of money supplied must grow with the quantity demanded in order to keep the purchasing power of money unchanged. As we shall see in later chapters, however, individuals have methods of economizing on money holdings when money is scarce. The ability of individuals to vary the quantity of money demanded in response to the changes in money supply means that the relationship between the purchasing power of money and the quantity of money is not as simple as described in this chapter.

A major deficiency of commodity money is that there is no particular relationship between changes in the supply of the commodity and growth of the productive capacity of an economy. For example, an economy may experience a period of rapid growth of output at the same time that gold production is declining. In this case, there will not be enough money to conduct transactions for the growing volume of commodities unless there is deflation (i.e., the prices of commodities

FIGURE 2.2
RESPONSE OF THE COMMODITY
PRICE OF GOLD TO SHIFTS IN
SUPPLY AND DEMAND.

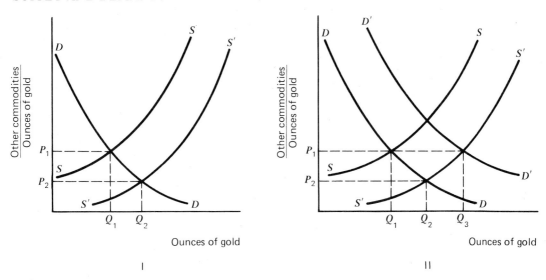

fall relative to gold) or unless there is a fall in real output. Alternatively, there may be periods of large gold discoveries that produce a growth of gold supply that outstrips the growth of production in an economy. In this case, inflation results. The lack of balance between the growth in supply of commodity money and growth in real economic activity created, in the past, an incentive for societies to develop forms of money whose supply would grow more in concert with real economic activity.

A COMMODITY STANDARD

Governments have played a crucial role in developing forms of money whose supply is responsive to the needs of the real economy. The motives of various governments were not always the best, but their actions helped lay the groundwork for modern monetary systems. To appreciate this role, let us consider the story of a king who wrestles with the problem of obtaining monetary flexibility under the "gold standard."

This story takes place in ancient times when gold had only begun to be used as a medium of exchange. The king observes that his subjects like to use gold as money, but they have difficulty obtaining accurate measures of the weight and purity of gold when exchanging gold for goods and services. The king hits on the idea of issuing gold coins bearing the royal stamp verifying the weight and purity of the gold in each coin. He decides to call the coins dollars and invents the symbol $ to denote dollars.

The public takes its gold to the king for conversion into dollar coins. This operation is called *minting*. The public finds the coins to be convenient for transactions, and the gold coins become the medium of exchange in the economy.

One day there is a significant gold discovery in the kingdom, and gold miners stand at the palace gates with large quantities of gold to exchange for gold coins. The king makes the exchange, and the miners go away with many bags of coin. They then spend these coins on goods and services. In the process, the miners bid up the prices of goods and services in terms of gold coins. They find that each gold coin, that is, each dollar, buys less than it used to. This decline in the purchasing power of the dollar displeases the gold miners, and they come to the king with their complaints. They demand their gold back, and the king is willing to oblige, but he wonders what the miners will do with the unminted gold. The miners inform him that they will use the gold to buy goods and services. The king points out that unminted gold is no longer accepted in transactions because of the inconvenience of dealing in unminted gold. But even if it were, unminted gold also would buy less than it did before. The price of pure gold in terms of commodities has also fallen. Each gold coin still contains one twentieth of an ounce of gold. If each gold coin now purchases fewer goods and services, each twentieth of an ounce of pure gold also purchases fewer goods and services.

The miners make a sad discovery. The king can fix the price between gold coins and pure gold, in our case 20 coins per ounce, but he cannot fix the price between gold and goods and services. There was an increase in the supply of gold that led to a bidding up of the prices of goods and services in terms of gold. A fixed "gold price," which is the rate of exchange between pure gold and dollar coins, does not provide fixed prices for goods and services in terms of either pure gold or gold coins.

During his discussions with the gold miners, the king has a great idea. Because coins have become so commonly accepted, he can reduce the gold content of each coin and still issue them. The king can *debase* the coin of the realm. An ounce of pure gold currently yields 20 one-dollar gold coins. The king can reduce the gold content of each so that one ounce of pure gold yields 25 one-dollar gold coins. Each ounce of pure gold that the king holds in his vault can be minted into 25 dollar coins rather than 20 coins. This seems to be such a profitable idea that the king decides to give it a try. He starts minting 25 coins from each ounce of pure gold rather than 20. The king realizes a profit because he can now purchase more goods and services with his gold than was previously the case. The profit that the king realized from reducing the gold content of these gold coins is called *seigniorage*.[2]

---

[2] King Henry VIII of England was an able practitioner of seigniorage. Coins had been 93 percent pure silver. From 1542 to 1547, Henry steadily debased English coins, so that by the end of his reign a silver coin was only 33 percent pure silver. Henry made a huge profit by tinkering with his coins. The result of this policy was inflation. In 1560, Queen Elizabeth called in the debased coinage and issued new coins of the old standard quality.

The king discovers that no one is willing to use the old gold coins for purchases of goods and services. Both they and the new coins have a price of one dollar, but an old gold coin contains more gold than a new coin. Holders of old coins withdraw them from circulation to be melted down for the raw gold they contain. For every 20 old one-dollar coins, holders reclaim an ounce of pure gold, which is exchanged for 25 new one-dollar coins. The disappearance of old gold coins is an example of *Gresham's law,* which states that "bad" money forces "good" money from circulation. In our case, the "bad" 25 coin-per-ounce money forces the "good" 20 coin-per-ounce money from circulation.

The king soon learns that his great idea has some unexpected consequences. Although he has increased the quantity of dollar coins, there is no increase in the economy's capacity to produce goods and services. Prices of goods and services are bid up further in terms of dollar coins.

Because the output of goods and services did not rise in the kingdom, an increase in the quantity of money only raised the price level. The king did discover a method of changing the quantity of money, that is, dollar gold coins, without there being a change in the quantity of pure gold, however. By varying the gold content of coins, the king could, in principle, make the money supply of his kingdom grow at a rate that is consistent with the rate of growth of output of goods and services. This discovery loosened the link between gold and money and thus provided flexibility to the quantity of money in the kingdom.

It might appear that when the king reduces the amount of gold in each dollar coin, he increases the price of gold. This is correct, but only in a very limited sense. Only the dollar price of gold rises from $20 for a pure ounce of gold to $25. The rate of exchange between pure gold and other commodities is not affected. Put the other way around, the price of a dollar coin declines because each coin buys less gold than it did before. This double relationship leads to the often confusing proposition that a reduction in the gold content of coins depreciates money. This proposition need not be confusing if one recalls that the appreciation of gold is in terms of dollars. If each ounce of gold purchases more dollars, then it must follow as a matter of arithmetic that each dollar buys less gold. A rise in the dollar price of gold may or may not reduce the value of dollar coins relative to goods and services in the economy. If output is not rising, the increased supply of coins is used to bid up dollar prices, and the value of dollars relative to goods and services declines. But if the level of real economic activity is growing, the increased supply of gold coins is used to finance the rising volume of transactions, and the dollar prices of goods and services do not rise.

The ability of the king to change the dollar price of gold provides him with a degree of flexibility in changing the money supply that would not be possible if the gold price were always fixed. If the king varies the gold content of coins with the objectives of promoting economic expansion and avoiding inflation, the flexibility is a blessing. He can reduce the economy's vulnerability to undesirable shifts in the supply of gold. If the king uses his powers to debase coins whenever he wants to create seigniorage profits, the economy is vulnerable to his whims and is cursed by the flexibility. Loosening the link between gold and money increases the flexibility of the money supply, but it also increases the vulnerability of the economy to poor government policies.

The parable of the king suggests that if a nation adopts a gold or other commodity standard and if its government is willing to vary the money price of pure gold, that nation can have control over its money supply. Any change in the supply of pure gold that has an undesired effect on the quantity of money can be offset by changing the money price of pure gold.

Historically, as trade among nations increased, this device proved not to be as useful as one might think. It was often politically difficult, if not impossible, to change the money price of gold. The analysis of the relationship between gold prices in two countries is a little tricky and is treated in the appendix to this chapter.

FULLY BACKED COMMODITY MONEY

Metallic coins were an important improvement over unminted metal as a medium of exchange, but they had disadvantages. Coins were often undesirable because of cost of transport and because coins can be shaved, that is, a little cut off of each coin until enough is available to produce a new coin. Because of these problems, individuals began to deposit their gold coins with governments or trusted individuals. The public received in return a piece of paper entitling the holder to redeem a specified amount of gold coins. These pieces of paper were promissory notes obligating the issuer to pay the amount of coins indicated. They were called notes. These notes often were used as money rather than coins.

Consider a country that is on the gold standard. The government mints coins containing one twentieth of an ounce of pure gold per coin. The government also issues gold-backed notes certifying that the notes can be exchanged for coins on demand. For example, a $20 note certifies that the government will exchange the note for $20 worth of gold coins. So long as the government has gold in its vaults that is equal in value to its outstanding notes, the public can always exchange notes for gold. The government's notes are fully backed by gold and are "as good as gold."

Governments are not the only issuers of gold-backed notes in the country. The public also leaves gold coins with merchants or goldsmiths for safekeeping, receiving in exchange notes certifying that their gold coins are on deposit. The merchant or goldsmith is paid a fee or other compensation for this service. The public can take the notes and exchange them for goods and services. The sellers of goods and services will accept these notes as long as they are confident that it is possible to exchange them for gold coins.[3]

---

[3] Many commodities other than gold have also been used as backing for money. For example, in the American colonies, tobacco certificates circulated as money. These certificates signified that so many pounds of tobacco were stored in warehouses.

Commodity-backed notes provided an important step in giving economies a convenient medium of exchange, but this paper money was not without its faults. Counterfeiting could be a problem, and recipients of certificates were vulnerable to fraudulent activities on the part of the storers of the commodity. Despite these difficulties, commodity-backed paper money became popular for transactions. Through elaborate printing, counterfeiting was difficult, and only the most trusted agents were used as depositories. Needless to say, strict laws and harsh punishments helped make these individuals trustworthy.

Commodity-backed notes were an alternative to coins as a medium of exchange, so the sum of coins and notes in circulation constituted the quantity of money in an economy. As long as notes were fully backed by a commodity, they did not alter the monetary system in any fundamental way. Both coins and notes were rigidly linked to a physical commodity, such as gold. The only flexibility in the link between the physical commodity and money lay in the ability of a government to vary the commodity content of coins. Once the commodity content of coins was fixed, the relationship between notes and the commodity was also fixed because notes could be fully redeemed for coins. When societies abandoned full-commodity backing of their money, however, their monetary systems were fundamentally altered.

FRACTIONALLY BACKED COMMODITY MONEY

There was little incentive for the public to exchange notes for coins as long as it was confident that the conversion could be made. At any time, redemptions of notes for coins were roughly offset by conversions of coins into notes. Because the inflows and outflows of coins were often roughly offsetting, the amount of coins stored by note issuers remained fairly constant. Note issuers discovered that they were holding more coins than were needed to meet note redemptions. They learned that it was not "necessary" to back their notes with an equal amount of gold because it was possible to expand note issues without expanding holdings of gold to back the notes.

Governments

Consider the case of a government that issues notes backed by gold. It originally issued a $100 note backed by $100 worth of gold coins. It now issues a second $100 note backed by the same gold. There is now $200 worth of notes backed by $100 of gold, so the notes have a 50 percent gold backing. Both notes certify that they can be redeemed for $100 worth of gold even though there is only $100 worth of gold in storage to redeem $200 worth of notes. As long as the public is confident that the notes can be redeemed, they will continue to circulate. The government can meet its obligations if $100 or less of redemptions occur.

The move to fractional backing of notes was appealing to governments. They could increase the amount of money in the economy without needing an increase in the amount of physical commodity to back the money. Furthermore, governments earned windfalls from seigniorage. By printing more notes, governments could purchase more goods and services without relying on increased tax receipts. In other words, governments could print notes to finance budget deficits.

By varying the percentage of commodity backing for notes, governments achieved significant flexibility in their ability to vary the quantity of money in the economy. This helped to stabilize the price level when the quantity of money was varied with the capacity of the economy to produce goods and services. It produced inflation when governments increased the quantity of money more rapidly than the growth in productive capacity and deflation when money grew less rapidly than productive capacity.

Banking

The invention of banking allowed the private sectors of economies to create additional variability in the percentage of money that was backed by a commodity.[4] The role of banks in the evolution of money is somewhat more complex than the role of governments, but the story can be told fairly simply by discussing why banks came to exist.

Many individuals were willing to use commodity-backed notes as money, but they were fearful of theft and needed a safe place to store their notes. Merchants and others who stored commodities or coins, or both, and who issued notes were natural recipients of the paper for safekeeping. These businesses soon discovered that, on average, for every customer who withdrew coins or paper from the vault, there was someone else who deposited coins or notes. Thus, there was always idle money in the vault. These businesses often made a practice of lending their own money to others in return for payment of interest. It was an easy matter to increase lending by issuing additional notes. The businesses had become banks; they accepted deposits of coin and notes and lent coins and notes to borrowers.

The mechanics of note issue for banks were somewhat different from those for governments. A bank had a certain amount of gold coins in its vault left by its customers on deposit. The customer received a bank note signifying that the gold coins were on deposit with the bank. That bank note circulated as money. Only rarely did anyone come to the bank's doors demanding the coins. The gold just sat there gathering dust. The banker learned that it was possible to expand loans by printing additional bank notes. These notes promised to pay out the same gold as backed the original notes.

---

[4] The sketchy description of banking in this chapter is intended to aid in the discussion of evolution of money and not to explain the complex activities of banks. Banking is discussed in detail in later chapters.

The notes that the banker issued to borrowers were indistinguishable from the notes it had issued to its original gold depositor. The notes issued to grant loans circulated as money in exactly the same way as the notes that had originally been backed by the gold. As loan activity expanded, each bank note was backed by less and less gold. The notes circulated as a medium of exchange as long as the recipients believed that the notes could be redeemed for coins.

Banking also allowed an important innovation that further weakened the link between the physical commodity and money. It was not unusual for individuals and businesses who had transactions with each other to have deposit accounts at the same bank. They discovered that it was often convenient to pay for transactions by instructing the bank to transfer funds from the account of the buyer to the account of the seller. A written order to a bank instructing it to pay a third party is called a check. Checks are not a new development in banking; they have been used for centuries to facilitate transactions. Checks often eliminated the need for individuals to conduct transactions with paper money or coins. Because transactions could be made by check rather than by requiring withdrawal of notes or coins, these *transactions accounts* became a medium of exchange and a new form of money.[5]

Banks often granted loans by increasing the transactions account balances of their customers rather than by issuing additional notes. The funds in these accounts would be withdrawn by check or redeemed for either notes or coins. Thus, funds in transactions accounts were money that was ultimately backed fractionally by a physical commodity.

With the invention of transactions accounts, banks could expand loans either by issuing additional bank notes or by increasing the transactions account balances of their customers. No matter how the bank dispensed funds to borrowers, the quantity of money rose when loans increased, and the increase occurred without any increase in the commodity that backed money. When a bank granted additional loans, it decreased the ratio of the commodity to money and diluted the commodity backing of money. Thus, the lending activities of banks affected the degree to which an economy's money was backed by a commodity.

Implications of Fractionally Backed Commodity Money for Economic Growth and Stability

Development of fractional backing of notes and deposits significantly weakened the links between a commodity, such as gold, and a nation's money. This step in the evolution of money had significant implications for economic growth and sta-

[5] Because depositors could obtain notes and gold coins on demand and because banks would make transfers from one account to another, the accounts were called demand accounts. For reasons that are explained in Chapter 8, these accounts are now called transactions accounts.

bility. In order to bring the various elements together, let us summarize the several links between the commodity and money. Consider a country whose government has established a gold standard by fixing the money (dollar) price of gold, that is, the rate of exchange between pure gold and gold coins. It stands ready to exchange coins for pure gold at the fixed price and to redeem coins for pure gold at the same price. The government also issues notes redeemable for coins. The country has banks that accept deposits in the form of coins, notes, or checks. The banks lend to borrowers in the form of coins, notes, or increases in transactions account balances.

This gold-based monetary system is depicted in Figure 2.3. The first linkage between gold and money is shown as arrow (a) indicating the minting of gold into coins. This link is not rigid because the government can change the gold content of coins, that is, the money price of gold. Though it was argued earlier that changes in the money price of gold can be politically difficult, these changes are a potential source of variability in the relationship between gold and money. The arrow labeled (b) shows the issuance of gold-backed notes by the government to the public. By reducing the amount of gold backing for notes, the government can issue more notes than there is gold to back them. Changes in the fractional gold backing of notes produce changes in the relationship of gold to the quantity of notes. Thus, the government controls two links between gold and money: the gold content of coins and the fractional gold backing of its notes.

The next links are between the public, as depositors, and banks. The public does not want to hold all the coins and notes that have been issued by the government, but, rather, deposits some of the money in banks for safekeeping and convenience. These deposits are redeemable for coins and, therefore, are ultimately redeemable for unminted gold. The deposits of coins and notes are shown as arrows (c) and (d). The public's use of bank accounts is important because these accounts provide banks with the resources necessary to grant loans and to expand the quantity of money. If the public did not deposit coins and notes with banks, the quantity of money in the economy would be the sum of coins and notes issued by the government. The public does use banks, however, and further expansion of the quantity of money is possible. The public controls the amount of coins and notes it deposits with banks and, consequently, affects the relationship between gold and money.

Banks take the public's deposits, set some funds aside to cover redemptions and deposit withdrawals, and lend the remainder. Banks grant loans in the form of coins, notes, and deposits shown as arrows (e), (f), and (g) respectively. The quantity of money is increased by the amount of bank loans.[6] For a given deposit base, the quantity of bank loans is determined by the behavior of the public as borrowers and by the behavior of the banks as lenders.

---

[6] Borrowers take the borrowed funds and spend them on goods and services. The sellers of goods and services redeposit some part of their receipts back in banks. Banks set aside part of these deposits and lend the rest. This process leads to a multiple expansion of loans and deposits. The factors limiting the process are discussed in Chapter 11.

FIGURE 2.3
LINKAGES FROM GOLD TO
MONEY.

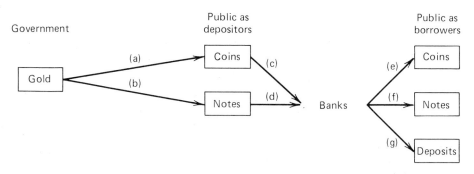

Once funds are lent by a bank, they are not available to meet deposit withdrawals or redemptions for coins. A prudently managed bank has sufficient funds available to meet its obligations to its depositors. In assessing the desirability of increasing the quantity of loans relative to deposits, a banker must balance the prospect of increased interest income against the risk that the bank will not be able to meet deposit withdrawals and note redemptions. This balancing act implies that banks will lend an amount that is less than their deposit and note liabilities. It also implies that if the demand for loans increases and interest rates rise, banks will increase loans to some extent and raise their exposure to deposit withdrawals and redemptions for coins.

These factors suggest that the quantity of bank loans does not bear a fixed relationship to the quantity of deposits. The level of loan demand and bankers' assessments of the likelihood of large account withdrawals and redemptions affect the quantity of loans for a given deposit base. These factors produce variability in the relationship between bank accounts and loans and, consequently, introduce a further slippage in the relationship between the quantity of money and the quantity of gold in an economy.

In summary, four factors loosen the linkages between gold and money. First, there are variations in the money price of gold. Second, there are variations in the fractional backing of notes. Third, there are variations in the fraction of the public's notes and coins that it deposits with banks. Fourth, there are variations in the fraction of deposits that banks lend. These four factors indicate that a country with fractional-commodity backing for money has achieved significant flexibility in its money supply. The quantity of money can be several times larger than the quantity of gold, and the ratio of money to gold can fluctuate widely.

Furthermore, the quantity of gold backing the monetary system can change. This quantity is called gold reserves because it is gold held in reserve by governments and banks to meet coin and note redemptions. The quantity of gold reserves rises when there is a gold discovery, when gold is imported from abroad, and when the public converts its holdings of unminted gold into gold coins or notes. The quantity of gold reserves declines when gold is exported to other countries and when the public redeems its holdings of notes and coins for unminted gold. Under a fractional system, the amount of money (coins, notes, and transactions accounts) is several times larger than the amount of gold reserves that backs it. This means that when the amount of gold reserves rises, there can be a multiple expansion of the quantity of money. When the amount of gold reserves declines, there is a multiple contraction in the quantity of money. Changes in the amount of gold reserves produce further fluctuations in the quantity of money.

The fractional system had the virtue of loosening the connection between gold and an economy's quantity of money. By varying the percentage of commodity backing for money, society could, in principle, achieve the quantity of money that it needed to carry on its transactions. Despite this virtue, the system was unstable. The fractional system was vulnerable to the public's fear concerning the redeemability of notes and deposits. At times people became concerned that they could not convert their money into gold, so they demanded gold. Under a fractional system the quantity of notes and deposits outstanding is larger than the amount of the gold or other commodity that backs the money. If enough people demanded gold, the gold reserves ran out before the paper and deposits did. Noteholders and depositors at the end of the line were left holding the bag. Their money became worthless when note issuers were unable to meet all of the redemptions. Under a fractional system, note and deposit redemptions reduced the amount of gold reserves and produced a multiple contraction in the quantity of money and credit.

Failures to convert notes and deposits into the commodity backing them inflicted losses on depositors and holders of worthless notes. Borrowers were hurt as well. When banks experienced large deposit withdrawals and redemptions, maturing loans were not renewed. Business and others who depended upon loans were injured.

The very elasticity of the supply of money provided by the fractional system could snap back on the economy and make it vulnerable to unsustainable booms followed by deep depressions. During periods of rising economic activity, bank loans and the quantity of money expanded, which further fueled expansion. As a result, the public prospered, and risks of large deposit withdrawals and redemptions for coin were slight. Banks responded by further increasing their loans relative to deposits and gold reserves. Prices increaseed as aggregate demand rose above the ability of the economy to produce goods and services. Eventually, some event, such as rapidly rising costs of materials and labor, slowed the growth of profits, and some firms were unable to repay their bank loans. These loan defaults weakened the condition of banks, and, as a result, depositors and noteholders became concerned about the safety of their money. Depositors withdrew their funds in the form of gold coins and noteholders demanded redemption for coin. Banks did not have sufficient reserves to meet redemptions and eventually had to suspend convertibility of notes and deposits into gold. Noteholders and depositors were injured, and the public abandoned banks as depositories. As a result, bank lending and the quantity of money fell. Solvent business firms were unable to obtain needed loans, and some failed. A downward spiral of falling aggregate demand and deflation developed. The spiral continued until the public's trust in banks returned.

The elasticity of money under a fractional commodity standard produced the ingredients for economic instability. The monetary system, which originally developed to aid economic expansion and to avoid the deficiencies of barter, took on a life of its own in which variations in the quantity of money could have adverse effects on real economic activity.[7] The tail could wag the dog.

Societies were aware of the problems with their banking systems and with the use of fractional backing of money by gold or other commodities. It was realized, however, that the growing complexity of their economies and the need for a flexible medium of exchange precluded turning back the clock to a simpler era of 100 percent backing of money with a commodity. Only if notes had a 100 percent commodity backing could the public be certain that issuers could always redeem their notes for the commodity. Only if banks never lent out their depositors' money could the public be assured that banks could always meet any deposit withdrawal. These remedies would solve the problem of instability, but the monetary system would lose its flexibility. Without some monetary flexibility, it would be difficult for economies to grow and prosper.

Instead of returning to the simpler, more inflexible monetary systems of earlier times, societies attempted to tame their existing monetary systems. Private banks pooled their resources to make funds available to banks that were experiencing panicked withdrawals and redemptions. It was hoped that when the public observed these banks meeting withdrawals and redemptions, panic would not spread to customers at other banks. The procedure worked as long as the panic was restricted to only a few banks. However, if a number of banks were hit at once, banks in total lacked the reserves to meet the demand. Wholesale failure could, and did, continue to occur. Governments also legislated minimum percentage for commodity backing of notes (e.g., 20 percent gold backing), and banks became increasingly subject to supervision and regulation. These efforts helped, but they could not eliminate the basic instability of a private banking system that promised to meet deposit withdrawals and currency redemptions on demand but then lent out most of the money to others. Such a banking system could never be able to survive a general monetary panic.

Societies gradually found solutions to their monetary problems in a series of reforms. These reforms allowed governments to gain better control over the quantity of money by totally eliminating commodity backing for currency and by guaranteeing the safety of the publics' deposits even during monetary panics. These changes came slowly, however, and were not completed until well into the twentieth century.

---

[7] Recall that changes in the amount of gold reserves through gold discoveries, imports and exports of gold, and changes in the public's holdings of unminted gold also produced fluctuations in money and credit.

One of the first steps was for governments to become the sole issuers of currency (notes). This currency was made legal tender. By law, *legal tender* must be accepted in payment for goods, for services, or in retiring debts. Initially, this legal tender was usually backed by some commodity, say gold. Governments usually had substantial stores of gold to meet demands for redemption, so their currency was less prone to panicked redemptions than were the notes issued by banks. Some governments even legislated minimum percentages for commodity backing of their currencies to assure the public, and perhaps themselves, that substantial demands for redemption could be met. However, over time the supplies of commodities like gold did not keep pace with economic growth. It was necessary for some governments to reduce the percentage of commodity backing for their notes or, as indicated earlier, to increase the money price of gold.

FIAT MONEY

Commodity-backed money could not expand with the growth of economic activity because of the political difficulties with increasing the money price of the commodities that backed money, because of the slow growth of the supplies of the commodities themselves, and because of the dangers of reducing the percentage of commodity backing. Furthermore, a fractional, commodity-backed system was unstable. Faced with these problems, societies eventually abandoned commodity-backed money. Governments issued currency (money) that was not backed by any commodity. The currency was declared to be legal tender and became money by *fiat* (Latin for "let it be done"); hence the term *fiat money*. It took societies a long time to reach this stage in the evolution of money, however.[8] For example, in the United States, a fractional commodity backing for currency was formally abandoned only in 1968.[9]

Fiat money is not backed by anything other than the trust of the public, as evidenced by its willingness to use the money in exchange for goods and services. Governments learned that money need not be backed by a physical commodity to be accepted as a medium of exchange. When money is declared to be legal tender, the public is legally required to accept the money in payment for goods and services or for the retirement of debts. With the development of fiat money,

---

[8] Countries did occasionally abandon commodity-backed money in favor of fiat money during wars and other national emergencies. For example, in the United States the federal government issued fiat "green backs" during the Civil War. Once the emergency passed, commodity-backed money was reimposed.

[9] In practice, beginning in 1934, gold had little practical significance as a backing for U.S. currency. A rather meaningless form of backing did stay on the statute books until 1968, however. U.S. currency could be redeemed for gold for international transactions until 1971.

economies were no longer beset with the panicked attempts by the public to redeem their currency and transactions account balances for the commodity reserve that plagued the fractional-commodity system. Under a fiat system, there is nothing to redeem the money for.

The introduction of fiat money demonstrated that money has value because it is money, not because it is a commodity. The value of any money, commodity backed or fiat, is determined by its purchasing power. That is to say by the quantity of goods and services that a given amount of money can buy. The purchasing power of money is determined by the quantity of money in an economy relative to the level of economic activity. In a fiat system, the quantity of money is not left to private markets but rather is affected by the government. The situation is complicated by the widespread use of transactions accounts, however. They are not legal tender, but the public accepts checks in payment for goods and services and for payment of debts. Despite this complication, modern governments exert considerable control over the quantity of money.[10]

The use of fiat money did not eliminate the potential instability caused by large withdrawals of currency from transactions accounts. Because banks do not hold sufficient currency to meet large withdrawals, their failure to meet currency withdrawals could trigger the same waves of bank failures and financial panics that occurred under commodity-backed monetary standards. The final step in perfecting the monetary system involved provision of currency by the government to banks during episodes of large deposit withdrawals. The provision of currency eased fears by the public that banks would not honor currency withdrawals. Once the fears were eliminated, withdrawals ceased, and currency was deposited back into banks.

Governments established central banks to control the quantity of transactions account balances and to provide currency to banks during period of panicked withdrawals by the public. These central banks, working closely with private banks, are able to provide stability to the financial system. In the United States, the activities of the central bank (the Federal Reserve System) are reinforced by the provision of government insurance for accounts at depository institutions. This insurance guarantees that depositors can always get their money out of depository institutions.[11] With these developments, monetary instability caused by banking panics was eliminated.

Although most economies have succeeded in eliminating monetary instability, success in eliminating recessions and avoiding inflation has been less frequent. The reasons for the successes and failures are discussed in later chapters. At this point, it suffices to observe that the primary virtue of a fiat system is that the quantity of money can, in principle, be set at a level consistent with achieving economic stability and growth. The shortcoming of the fiat system lies in the vul-

---

[10] The mechanics of this control are discussed in Chapters 11 and 12.

[11] Strictly speaking, only "small" depositors are totally protected. The details of deposit insurance are described in Chapters 9 and 10.

nerability of the economy to undesirable monetary policies of the government. Expansion in the quantity of money can lead to inflation when the quantity of money rises more rapidly than the productive capacity of the nation or to recession if the amount of money grows too slowly.

The ability of a government to print money without the discipline of a limited supply of a commodity to back the money is a great temptation. Modern governments are major purchasers of goods and services. Most governments like to spend, but many do not like to tax the public in an amount sufficient to cover the expenditures. The fiat system offers the temptation of a paper alchemy in which a government can make money out of paper simply by running the printing press. The money can finance expenditures in excess of tax receipts and lead to inflation. The usefulness of fiat money rests ultimately in the ability of a society to regulate the issuance of money in accordance with the needs of the economy and to control its government's urge to spend without taxation. A fiat system allows a country to set the quantity of money at a level consistent with achieving economic stability and growth. There is nothing automatic about the process, however. The ultimate control that a society has over the issuance of money in a fiat system rests with its willingness and ability to control its government.

The United States and other industrialized countries currently use fiat money. The national government issues fiat money in the form of currency and coin. The public holds most of its money in the form of transactions account balances at depository institutions, however.[12] Payments are made from these accounts by check, by telephone instructions to depository institutions, and by direct electronic transfers of funds from one party to another. These payments do not involve the exchange of legal tender (currency and coin), but they are the primary means by which transactions are conducted. Thus, the media of exchange (money) are coin and currency plus transactions account balances. As explained in Chapter 1, this definition of money is called M1. We will see during the course of this book that inflation and regulatory restrictions have recently produced a number of money substitutes that have made money difficult to define and to measure.

Many countries, including the United States, have experienced substantial problems with inflation and unemployment in recent years. Some of the problems were unavoidable, but some were caused by the inability of these countries to control the growth of money and credit. Frustration over recent economic performance has led to a renewed interest in a commodity (gold) standard as a means of achieving monetary "discipline." The discussion in this chapter indicates that a gold standard or other form of commodity backing is hardly a panacea for economic ills. The inflexibility of a full commodity standard and the potential instability of a fractional commodity standard make commodity backing a poor means of achieving control over modern monetary systems.

---

[12] In the United States, depository institutions are banks, savings and loan associations, mutual savings banks, and credit unions.

SUMMARY

Whereas the function of money is to simplify and ease economic transactions, societies initially adopted forms of money that could have undesirable effects on economic activity. The evolution of money over the centuries has been a process in which societies have gradually moved toward monetary systems that are both flexible and controllable.

It was natural for early societies to select a physical commodity as money. The commodity was already used in barter and had an intrinsic value in nonmonetary uses. With economic expansion, these societies discovered that the supply of the commodity used as money did not necessarily grow at a rate that was compatible with the needs of the economy. Sometimes the growth of commodity money was slower than the growth of economic activity, and sometimes the growth of money was more rapid than required to support real economic activity.

The inflexibility of commodity money led to a series of innovations that increased the flexibility of money supply. Fractional commodity-backed money was developed, banking was invented, and governments learned that they could vary the quantity of money by changing the money price of the commodity that backed money.

These developments increased the flexibility of money supply, but they also produced an unstable monetary system. The system worked as long as holders of paper money and bank accounts thought their money was safe. But if currency holders and depositors feared that their money was not safe, they tried to redeem their deposits and currency for the commodity that backed them. Under a fractional system, the quantity of outstanding currency and bank accounts was greater than the amount of gold or other commodity that backed them. Large redemption demands could not be met, and the public would be left holding worthless notes and deposits. Furthermore, banks were unable to continue to finance business activity. With bank loans unavailable, many firms were forced into bankruptcy. The fractional system permitted a boom-and-bust pattern of economic activity.

Societies sought to control their monetary systems through pooling of bank resources, through legislating minimum fractions for commodity backing of money, through bank regulation, and by allowing their governments to be the sole issuers of currency. These efforts helped, but did not solve the problem. The solution emerged in the twentieth century when fiat money was permanently established. By removing all commodity backing for money, societies were no longer saddled with redemption demands. It was discovered that money did not need to be backed by a physical commodity to be accepted as a medium of exchange. If coin and currency are made legal tender, people will use the money to conduct transactions. It was not necessary for money to have some alternative use as a commodity. Money has value because it is a medium of exchange.

Transactions accounts are also money, but they are not legal tender. Governments made transactions accounts safe by assuring the public that funds in these accounts could always be exchanged for coin and currency, that is, for legal tender. Without these assurances, the public would make massive withdrawals from banks at the first sign that currency withdrawals could not be met. These withdrawals could trigger the waves of bank failures and monetary panics that characterized earlier eras. Governments were able to ensure that deposits could be redeemed for coin and currency through operations of their central banks, through close working relationships between government and banks, and through the invention of deposit insurance.

With these developments came the maturation of the monetary system. The system is not an automatic one, however, because it requires governments to pursue monetary policies that are consistent with the economic needs of society. It is not always easy for governments to meet this objective.

APPENDIX

THE EFFECTS OF CHANGES
IN THE MONEY PRICE OF GOLD
ON INTERNATIONAL TRADE

It was asserted in the text that the international implications of changes in the money price of gold often made such changes impractical. The purpose of this appendix is to explain why this was the case.

Consider a country that raises the money price of gold as a method of increasing the supply of its money. Foreign governments often viewed an increase in the gold price as an unfriendly act because it adversely affected their economies. Assume that, in the United States, gold is priced by the government at $20 per ounce and in Great Britain gold is priced at £10 per ounce. These two gold prices imply that £1 buys $2 and that $1 buys £0.5. An American can take $20, in currency or check on a transactions account, exchange it for one ounce of gold in the United States, ship the gold to Great Britain, and purchase £10 with it.[13] A person in Great Britain can take £10, purchase an ounce of gold, ship the gold to the United States and buy $20 with it.

Now assume that the United States raises the price of gold to $40 per ounce and that the British retain the old price of £10 per ounce. A person in Britain now can exchange £10 for an ounce of gold, ship the gold to the United States and buy $40 rather than the former $20. In effect, £10 now buys $40 rather than $20. If domestic prices have not risen in the United States to offset the effects, the British have a strong incentive to buy goods and services in the United States. The

---

[13] In this example, the cost of shipping gold is neglected. Including shipping costs complicates the discussion without materially affecting the conclusions.

United States prices to the British have fallen by 50 percent. It formerly cost someone in Great Britain £10 to purchase $20 of American goods and services; now it only costs £5. Americans are in the opposite situation. It now takes $40 to buy £10 worth of goods and services from Britain rather than $20; the price of British goods to Americans has doubled, and U.S. demand for British products declines.

After the increase in the dollar price of gold, the British increase their imports of American goods and services, and the United States reduces its imports of British goods and services. The U.S. economy is stimulated by the increase in the purchases of its products, and the British economy is depressed by the decline in American purchases of its products. Furthermore, the British lose gold to the United States as its citizens exchange their currency for gold and ship it to the United States to buy dollars needed to acquire American products. The expansion of demand for U.S. products and the increase in the quantity of gold raise prices in the United States. At the same time, the lowered demand for British products and the shrinking quantity of gold reduce prices in Great Britain. Unless the British raise their price of gold to counteract the low demand for their exports, the process will continue until prices in the United States have doubled relative to prices in Great Britain. Because of the significant effects a change in the price of gold can have on other nations, such price changes have been used infrequently.[14]

SELECTED REFERENCES

Einzig, Paul, *Primitive Money*, London: Eyre and Spotiswoode, Ltd., 1948.

Carson, R.A.G. and Herman Kross, *Financial History of the United States* (2nd ed.), New York: McGraw-Hill, 1963.

Cipolla, Carlo, *The Monetary Policy of Fourteenth-Century Florence*, Berkeley, Cal: University of California Press, 1982.

Friedman, Milton and Anne Schwartz, *A Monetary History of the United States 1867–1960*, Princeton, N.J.: Princeton University Press, 1963.

Galbraith, John Kenneth, *Money: From Whence It Came and Where It Went*, Boston: Houghton Mifflin, 1975.

Melitz, Jacques, *Primitive Money*, Reading, Mass.: Addison-Wesley, 1974.

Studenski, Paul and Herman Kross, *Financial History of the United States* (2nd ed.), New York: McGraw-Hill, 1963.

---

[14] We will see in Chapter 17 that the same considerations often prevented countries from changing their exchange rates.

THE ACCUMULATION OF ASSETS, LIABILITIES, AND WEALTH

3

This chapter discusses the determinants of consumption and saving by households and of investment in productivity capacity by firms. It is shown that consumption, saving, and investment determine the accumulation of assets, liabilities, and wealth. It is necessary to study these issues in order to understand the role of the financial markets and institutions that comprise an economy's financial system. The financial system is discussed in the next chapter. This chapter is concerned with the basic economic forces that make a financial system necessary. The chapter begins with a simple analysis that isolates the basic economic forces that are at work in consumption, saving, and investment decisions. We then turn to more realistic and complex situations.

ROBINSON CRUSOE

The basic factors that determine consumption, saving, and investment can be identified by studying the economic decisions of Robinson Crusoe. Crusoe is trapped on a deserted island following a shipwreck of which he is the sole survivor. We will assume that he is able to salvage little from the wrecked ship except 365 pounds of potatoes, which are his only food. Crusoe knows that he will be rescued at the end of two years. By studying Robinson Crusoe's consumption, saving, and investment decisions over these two years, we can learn a great deal about the decisions of households and firms in more relevant settings.

With a two-year deadline, Robinson Crusoe has a relatively simple problem concerning how to allocate the consumption of potatoes over the two years. One obvious solution is to consume an equal amount of potatoes each day for two years.[1] Crusoe calculates that if he consumes one half of a pound of potatoes per day for 730 days, his wealth (i.e., his stock of potatoes) will be exhausted on the last day of the second year. Having little else to do, he also calculates other patterns of consumption of his wealth between the two years. Robinson quickly discovers that for every additional pound of potatoes consumed this year, he can consume one pound less next year. By similar calculation, he determines that for every additional pound of potatoes consumed next year, he can consume one pound less this year. The trade-off or *rate of exchange* between potatoes this year and potatoes next year is *one for one*.

Based on these calculations, Crusoe is faced with the question of how many potatoes to consume in each year. Robinson starts his deliberations by drawing a diagram in the sand showing his consumption opportunities between the two years. That picture is reproduced as line Q_I, Q_{II} in Figure 3.1. Consumption in the first year is shown on the horizontal axis, and consumption in the second year on the vertical axis. The diagram indicates that if all 365 pounds are consumed in the current year, no potatoes are available for the next year. If all the potatoes are consumed next year, no potatoes can be consumed this year. Keeping in mind the one for one rate of exchange between consumption this year and consumption next year, an equal split (point E) gives 182.5 pounds of consumption in each year. For every additional pound of potatoes consumed this year, Crusoe must forsake one pound of consumption next year. The slope of the line is minus one. The line Q_I, Q_{II} is called the *consumption opportunity line*.

The best that Crusoe can do is to have a combination of potato consumption in the two years that is represented by a point somewhere on the consumption opportunity line. He cannot have any consumption combination represented by a point above the line because that consumption requires more than the 365 pounds of potatoes. Crusoe can have a consumption combination such as point Z which is below the line. Point Z is inefficient for him, however, because it involves consuming only 140 pounds of potatoes in the first year and 100 pounds in the second for a total of 240 pounds. Thus, he would have 125 pounds of potatoes left over at the end of the second year. Crusoe wants to consume all the potatoes over the two years and concludes, therefore, that his maximum consumption opportunities between the two years are represented by the line Q_I, Q_{II}.

Crusoe realizes that he needs some method of expressing his preference for consumption this year versus consumption next year. He puzzles for a while and then decides to describe his preferences for consumption between the two years in general terms without regard to the real-world limitation of only having 365 pounds of potatoes. He will consider this constraint later. Robinson starts the task by describing his preferences for consumption this year versus next year in terms of all the combinations of consumption in the two years for which he is equally satisfied. He draws the relationship in the sand. That relationship is shown as the curve U_1 in Figure 3.2.

---

[1] On Crusoe's island, potatoes do not spoil.

FIGURE 3.1
CRUSOE'S CONSUMPTION
OPPORTUNITY LINE.

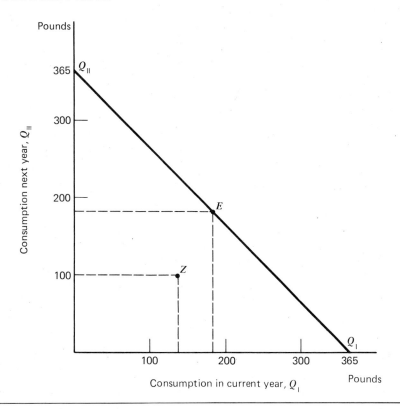

Clever fellow that he is, Robinson Crusoe has discovered the *indifference curve*! This curve shows all the combinations of consumption in the two years for which he is indifferent.[2] Crusoe derived the curve by considering initially an equal split of consumption between the two years, that is, 182.5 pounds in each year. This combination is labeled point *E*. From this point, Crusoe determines that if he reduces consumption by 100 pounds in the current year and increases consumption next year by 130 pounds (point *F*), he is as satisfied as at point *E*. Crusoe is indifferent between the consumption mix at point *E* and the mix at point *F*. He discovers this indifference by determining that if he reduces consumption this year by 100 pounds and if his consumption next year rises by less than 130 pounds next year, he is worse off than at point *E*. Alternatively, if he increases consumption

---

[2] Recall that, at this point of his analysis, Crusoe is not concerned about the amount of potatoes that is actually available for consumption.

FIGURE 3.2
CRUSOE'S PREFERENCE FOR
CONSUMPTION THIS YEAR VERSUS
NEXT YEAR.

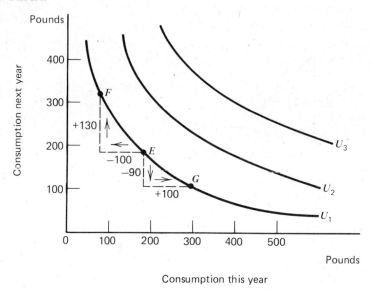

next year by more than 130 pounds, he is better off than at point E. At point F he is neither better off nor worse off than at point E. Crusoe next discovers that if he increases consumption this year by 100 pounds and reduces consumption next year by 90 pounds (point G), he is as satisfied as at point E. Thus, he is also indifferent between points E and G.

Crusoe goes through the same exercise for various combinations of potato consumption in the two years and discovers that the greater the amount of consumption this year, relative to consumption next year, the less willing he is to reduce further his future consumption in return for additional consumption this year. Thus, his indifference curve becomes flatter (more nearly horizontal) the greater the amount of current consumption relative to future consumption. Alternatively, the greater the amount of future consumption, relative to current consumption, the less willing he is to reduce further his current consumption in favor of additional consumption next year. Thus, his indifference curve becomes steeper (more nearly vertical) the greater the amount of future consumption relative to current consumption.

Crusoe next discovers that he can construct a number of indifference curves, each showing the various combinations of potato consumption in the two years for which he is indifferent. Higher indifference curves, such as U_2 and U_3, signify higher levels of satisfaction. If he can have more potatoes in each year, he is better off.

FIGURE 3.3
CRUSOE'S CONSUMPTION
DECISION.

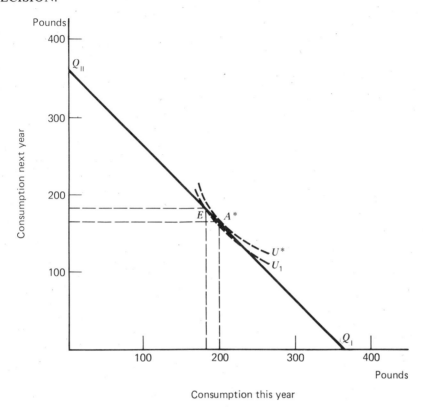

Crusoe realizes that this abstract description of his preferences is all well and good, but the fact of the matter is that he has only 365 pounds of potatoes. Furthermore, though the rate at which he is willing to substitute consumption in one year for consumption in the other year is given by the slope of his indifference curve, in reality, consumption of one more pound of potatoes this year always requires consumption of one less pound next year and vice versa. Thus, he is constrained by the consumption opportunity line. He next draws in the consumption opportunity line Q_I, Q_{II} from Figure 3.1 and discovers there is an indifference curve U^* that is tangent to the line. This situation is illustrated in Figure 3.3. At the point of tangency, A^*, Crusoe has achieved the highest level of satisfaction possible given the constraint of the consumption opportunity line. At point A^*, the slope of the consumption opportunity line is equal to the slope of his indifference curve. At point A^* the rate at which he can actually substitute consumption between the two years (the one-for-one slope of the consumption opportunity line) equals the rate at which his preferences (indifference curve) allow him to substitute consumption between the two years and still remain equally satisfied. The slope of the indifference curve, U^*, equals the slope of the consumption opportunity line at point A^*.

Crusoe concludes that he maximizes his satisfaction at point A^*, which involves consuming 200 pounds of potatoes in the current year and 165 pounds in the second year. He observes that he has a *positive time preference*. Even though the possible rate of substitution between the two years is one for one, Crusoe prefers to consume more than half of the potatoes in the current year.[3] With an equal split of consumption between the two years, Robinson would be at point E. At this point the highest indifference curve that Crusoe can achieve is U_1. At point E, the indifference curve U_1 is steeper than the consumption opportunity line. Thus, Crusoe is willing to give up more than one pound of potato consumption next year in return for one pound of additional consumption this year. The consumption opportunity line requires that he sacrifice only one pound next year for an additional pound this year. Crusoe moves down the consumption opportunity line. He increases his satisfaction by increasing consumption in the first year and decreasing consumption in the second year by the same amount. This substitution of current for future consumption continues until he reaches point A^* on indifference curve U^*. At this point, he is only willing to reduce consumption next year by one pound in return for one more pound this year. The slope of U^* at point A^* is equal to the slope of Q_I, Q_{II}.

After all the mental effort, Crusoe decides to examine the wreckage once more in the hope of finding more potatoes. There are no more potatoes, but while digging through the wreckage, Robinson finds a famous volume entitled *Elements of Potato Farming: An Application to Deserted Islands*. The book reveals that for every pound of potatoes planted this year, Crusoe can harvest two pounds next year. His eyes light up. If Robinson puts his wealth to work by planting the potatoes he does not eat this year, he can increase consumption next year. He calculates that for every pound of potatoes he does not eat this year and plants instead, he can eat two pounds next year. Alternatively, for every additional pound of potatoes he consumes this year, that is, does not plant, he reduces his potato consumption next year by two pounds.

The relationship between the amount of potatoes planted and the amount harvested is shown as the line Q_I^f, Q_{II}^f in Figure 3.4. Again we plot the amount of potatoes consumed this year on the horizontal axis and the amount of potatoes available for consumption next year on the vertical axis. The line Q_I^f, Q_{II}^f is called the *production possibility frontier*.[4] It shows the maximum amount of potatoes that

---

[3] Crusoe's positive time preference may be the result of impatience. It is possible for Crusoe to have a zero time preference, in which case he consumes the same amount in each year, or a negative time preference, where he consumes more in the second year than the first.

[4] You may be more familiar with curved (concave) production possibility frontiers. In Crusoe's case, such a frontier would indicate that as more and more potatoes are planted, the additional yield from planting one more potato declines. Thus, the slope of the frontier becomes increasingly flat as current production is reduced. We have not utilized such a frontier because it complicates the later analysis without changing the basic conclusions.

FIGURE 3.4
CRUSOE'S CONSUMPTION
OPPORTUNITIES: FARMING
VERSUS NOT FARMING.

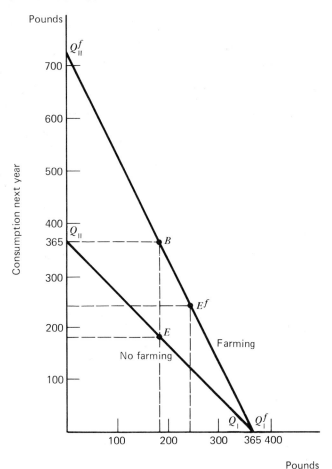

can be produced next year for varying amounts of potatoes planted (not consumed) this year. For example, if Crusoe consumes all his potatoes this year, none
can be planted. Consumption next year is still zero. If Crusoe consumes only half
of the potatoes this year, he can plant the remaining 182.5 pounds. This produces
365 pounds in the second year as shown by point B. If Crusoe plants the entire 365
pounds of potatoes (i.e., consumes nothing this year), he can obtain 730 pounds
next year.

By planting the potatoes that he saves, Crusoe can increase his consumption in both years. This can be seen by comparing the production possibility frontier, Q_I^f, Q_{II}^f in Figure 3.4 to the consumption possibility line Q_I, Q_{II} where there is no farming. For example, in the absence of farming, an equal split between the two years is shown by point E on Q_I, Q_{II} where 182.5 pounds are consumed in each year. With farming, an equal split is shown at point E^f. Here Crusoe consumes 243.33 pounds in the first year. This leaves 121.67 pounds to be planted, which yields 243.33 pounds next year. Thus, he can consume more in both years by planting the potatoes that he saves. The slope of the production possibility frontier is -2.0, indicating that for every pound of potatos not consumed, but planted instead, Crusoe obtains two pounds next year. Unless Robinson is a complete glutton and consumes the entire 365 pounds of potatoes the first year, he can plant what he does not eat and increase his consumption opportunities in both years. The productivity of farming allows Robinson to consume more over the two years than if the unused potatoes were stored rather than planted. The total output from farming depends upon the amount of potatoes that is not consumed, that is, saved, in the current year. The reward to Crusoe for not consuming his wealth in the current year is a higher level of consumption in the second year.

Crusoe's consumption decisions for farming versus not farming are shown in Figure 3.5. Point A^* on indifference curve U^* shows Crusoe's desired consumption in each of the two years when he does not farm. This is the same point as obtained in Figure 3.3, where he consumes 200 pounds in the first year and 165 pounds in the second year. When Crusoe farms, he can continue to consume 200 pounds of potatoes in the current year. Now, however, he can take the 165 pounds that are not consumed and plant them to yield 330 pounds by the end of the year. Thus, his consumption in the second year can rise from 165 pounds to 330 pounds. Crusoe can have the same consumption this year and more next year; that is, he can be at point B on line Q_I^f, Q_{II}^f.

Crusoe now determines whether he wants to be at point B. He answers this question by determining the point on the production possibility frontier Q_I^f, Q_{II}^f that provides him with the highest level of satisfaction. Robinson discovers that there is an indifference curve U^{*f} that is tangent to the production possibility frontier at point A^{*f}. This indifference curve represents the highest satisfaction he can attain and still have consumption consistent with the production possibility frontier. Robinson does not move to point B, therefore, but rather to point A^{*f}, where he consumes 240 pounds in the current year and 250 pounds next year. By planting the 125 pounds of potatoes he saves in the first year, Crusoe obtains 250 pounds in the second year. Farming allows Crusoe to consume more potatoes in each year.

The indifference curve U^{*f} has a slope of -2.0 at point A^{*f}. At the point of tangency, Crusoe is willing to exchange one pound of consumption this year for two pounds of consumption next year. This is exactly the rate that the production possibility frontier requires he substitute between current and future consumption.

It is instructive to determine why Crusoe selected point A^{*f} rather than point B or any other point on Q_I^f, Q_{II}^f. Farming has two effects on Crusoe's consumption

FIGURE 3.5
CRUSOE'S CONSUMPTION DECISION:
FARMING VERSUS NOT FARMING.

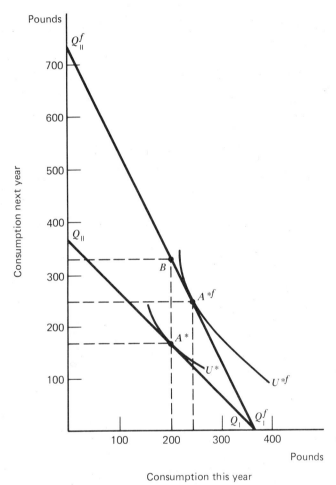

in the two years. First, it effectively increases his wealth, by allowing him to reach a higher level of satisfaction. This phenomenon is called the *income effect*. The income effect is measured by the amount of potatoes Crusoe would require in the absence of farming to achieve the level of satisfaction U^{*f} rather than U^*. This amount is determined by shifting the line Q_I, Q_{II} up and to the right until it is tangent to U^{*f}, as shown in Figure 3.6. This new line Q'_I, Q'_{II} is parallel to Q_I, Q_{II} and, therefore, has a rate of substitution between consumption in the two

FIGURE 3.6
CRUSOE'S INCOME AND
SUBSTITUTION EFFECTS.

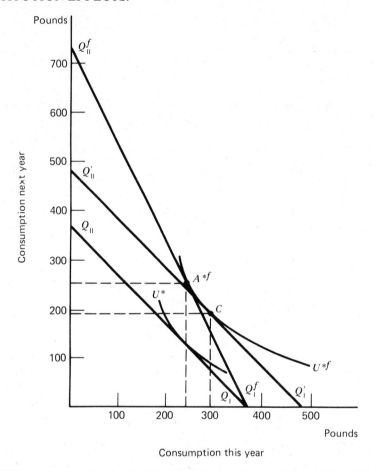

years of one for one. The point of tangency C on Q'_I, Q'_{II} indicates that if Crusoe had 480 pounds of potatoes to allocate between the two years rather than 365 pounds and if he did not farm, he would consume 290 pounds of potatoes in the first year and 190 pounds in the second year. Crusoe would consume more in each year, but his positive time preference would still favor current over future consumption.

The ability to farm not only increases Crusoe's effective wealth; it also alters the rate of exchange between current and future consumption. With farming, for every pound of potatoes that Crusoe does not consume this year, but saves and plants instead, he obtains two pounds of potatoes that can be consumed next year.

Farming changes the rate of exchange between current and future consumption and induces Crusoe to move from point C to point A^{*f}. With this move, he decreases current consumption and raises future consumption relative to point C. The rise in the rate of exchange between current and future consumption provided by the production possibility frontier induces Crusoe to substitute future for current consumption. This phenomenon is called the *substitution effect*. The rate of exchange between current and future consumption provided by the steeper production possibility frontier induces Crusoe to overcome his positive time preference and to consume more potatoes in the second year than in the first year. Crusoe favors current to future consumption when the rate of exchange is one for one. He is induced to postpone some consumption to the following year when faced with the opportunity to exchange one pound of consumption this year for two pounds of consumption next year at point A^{*f}.

To summarize the story to this point, farming allows Crusoe to achieve a higher level of satisfaction. The gain to Crusoe from planting rather than storing potatoes can be depicted as the equivalent of an increase in his original wealth from 365 pounds of potatoes to 480 pounds. If Crusoe had not found a book on potato farming, but rather had found 115 additional pounds of potatoes, he would have been able to achieve the level of satisfaction U^{*f} with this income effect. His preferences concerning current versus future consumption would lead him to point C on indifference curve U^{*f}. At point C, Crusoe increases his consumption in both years, but he still consumes more potatoes in the first year (290 pounds) than in the second year (190 pounds).[5]

Crusoe did not find additional potatoes, however; he found a book on potato farming instead. Knowledge gained from the book allows him to plant, rather than store, the potatoes he does not consume during the current year. Farming allows him to achieve indifference curve U^{*f}, but he does not select point C on

---

[5] The indifference curve U^{*f} was constructed to give this result. It is possible to construct indifference curves for which the income effect increases only current consumption or increases only future consumption. In fact, it is possible to construct Crusoe's preferences such that the income effect raises current consumption by so much that he *reduces* future consumption relative to point A^*. This phenomenon is called a *negative income effect* for the second year's consumption. Alternatively, it is possible that Crusoe increases his consumption in the second year so much that he reduces consumption in the first year relative to point A^*. This would entail a negative income effect for consumption in the current year. Economic theory does not allow one to exclude the possibility of a negative income effect for either current or future consumption. As a result, it is not possible to be sure that the income effect will induce Crusoe to increase his potato consumption in both years. For simplicity, however, we adopt the plausible assumption that the income effect is positive for both years. As we shall see later in this chapter, the income effect is important because it affects the extent to which a consumer increases saving when there is an increase in interest rates. If the income effect for consumption in the second year is negative and sufficiently large to offset the substitution effect, a rise in interest rates reduces current saving.

that curve. Because farming provides him with more than one potato for every potato he does not consume this year, Crusoe reduces his current consumption and increases his consumption next year relative to point C. His preferences lead him to point $A*^f$, where he consumes more potatoes in the second year (250 pounds) than in the current year (240 pounds). Thus, Crusoe substitutes future consumption for current consumption; that is, he increases the amount of potatoes that he saves (does not consume) during the current year.

SOME LESSONS FROM ROBINSON CRUSOE

The Robinson Crusoe story demonstrates that if households refrain from consuming all their wealth in any year, they liberate resources that can be used to produce more consumption goods in the future. For Robinson Crusoe, the link between current and future consumption is obvious. But in a complex economy, it is necessary to have some vehicle for encouraging the transfer of resources from present to future consumption. If households reduce current consumption, that is, save, and simply hoard the wealth, businesses will not have the resources for producing more consumption goods in the future. This would be the case for Crusoe if he stored the potatoes he wanted to consume in the second year rather than planting them. Only if wealth is diverted from current consumption *and* invested in physical capital, such as potato plants for Crusoe or machinery and other productive capacity for modern business, can more consumption goods be produced in the future.

THE ROLE OF THE INTEREST RATE

Businesses obtain resources from households by paying them interest. The role of interest can be seen by returning to the world of Robinson Crusoe. After the initial excitement over the wonders of farming, Robinson recalls that he is a terrible gardener. Somehow, his plants never grow. Fortunately, Crusoe by this time has befriended a native, who is an expert gardener. The native, whom Crusoe calls Friday, agrees to do the gardening. Though Friday likes to garden, he does not like to eat potatoes. He offers to return two potatoes for each one Crusoe lends to him for planting.[6]

Robinson Crusoe had already decided to consume 240 pounds of potatoes in the first year and to save 125 pounds for planting, as shown by point $A*^f$ in Figure 3.5. Robinson lends the 125 pounds to Friday, who promises to plant the

---

[6] We could be more realistic and have Friday keep some potatoes for himself. This would complicate the story, however, without adding any substance.

potatoes and to repay 250 pounds at the end of the year. The initial 125 pounds is called *loan principal,* and the difference in the amount of potatoes delivered in one year and the loan principal is called *loan interest,* in this case $250 - 125 = 125$ *pounds of potatoes. The interest rate* is loan interest relative to loan principal. For Crusoe, we have $(250 - 125)/125 = 125/125 = 1.00$, which in percentage terms is 100 percent.

The exchange between Robinson Crusoe and Friday can be stated more generally. Let Q_0 be the quantity of potatoes that Robinson lends at the beginning of the year, and let Q_1 be the quantity of potatoes that Friday repays at the end of the year. This transaction can be expressed as an interest rate, i, which is defined as the gain, relative to loan principal, to Crusoe from lending his potatoes for a year or

$$i = \frac{Q_1 - Q_0}{Q_0} = \frac{Q_1}{Q_0} - \frac{Q_0}{Q_0} = \frac{Q_1}{Q_0} - 1.$$

The interest rate measures the gain to Robinson Crusoe from exchanging potatoes today for potatoes next year. The number one is subtracted from the ratio Q_1/Q_0 to measure the gain. If $Q_1 = Q_0$, the ratio equals one, and there is no gain; that is, Robinson gets back only the principal, and the interest rate is zero.

Alternatively, we can rearrange the expression $i = (Q_1/Q_0) - 1$ to give $Q_1 = (1 + i)Q_0$. When Crusoe lends the quantity Q_0 to Friday, it grows to Q_1 by the end of the year. Note that $(1 + i) = (Q_1/Q_0)$. The term $(1 + i)$ is called the *interest rate factor.* It is a price showing the rate of exchange between potatoes today, Q_0, and potatoes in one year, Q_1. In effect, Crusoe sells (lends) the quantity of potatoes, Q_0, today in exchange for the quantity Q_1 next year. This price, or rate of exchange, is different from the prices discussed in Chapter 2 because it involves exchange of the same commodity at different times rather than exchange of different commodities at the same time. It is the dimension of time that makes the interest rate factor different from other prices and justifies giving it a special name. Note that the slope of the production possibility frontier equals the negative of the interest rate factor.

The role of the interest rate is twofold. First, it induces Robinson Crusoe to transfer his stored potatoes to Friday, who puts them to productive use. Second, the interest rate may induce Robinson to reduce consumption in the first year relative to the second year and supply Friday with a larger amount of potatoes for planting. Note that even if receipt of interest does not induce Crusoe to save more in the first year, it still induces him to lend his wealth to Friday so that it can be put to productive use. The higher the interest rate factor, the higher the price that Friday pays to Crusoe for transferring resources to him for planting. The interest rate that Friday is willing to pay is determined by the negative of the slope of the production possibility frontier. For example, if the slope were -3.0 rather than -2.0, each pound of potatoes planted yields three pounds next year. In this case, the interest rate factor is 3.0, and the interest rate is 2.0.

In complex monetary economies, physical commodities are rarely borrowed and lent. Rather, businesses borrow money from households that is used to purchase physical capital. This capital produces goods and services for future consumption. Sales of these goods and services to households generate income for businesses that allow them to repay the loans plus interest. The interest rate is the gain to the lender for transferring spending power to the borrower.

The use of money does not change the definition of the interest rate. A lender "sells" money today, M_0, in exchange for money to be received in the future, M_1. The loan principal is M_0, the loan interest is $(M_1 - M_0)$, the interest rate, i, is

$$i = \frac{M_1 - M_0}{M_0} = \frac{M_1}{M_0} - 1$$

and the interest rate factor is $(1 + i) = M_1/M_0$.[7] The interest rate factor, $(1 + i)$, is the rate of exchange between money today and money in the future. By convention, the interest rate is multiplied by 100 to give a *percentage rate of interest*. Because time is the crucial ingredient in the interest rate, it is expressed as percent per unit of time. By convention, the year is the common unit of time, and the interest rate is quoted as percent per year.

THE ROLE OF THE INTEREST RATE IN A MONETARY ECONOMY

Households differ in their willingness to reduce current consumption in return for higher consumption in the future, and they differ in the extent to which a rise in the interest rate induces them to transfer money to business. Businesses are faced with varying technological factors that determine the amount by which investment in physical capital produces consumption goods in the future. The additional output of consumption goods obtained by adding an additional unit of capital is the *marginal product of capital*. A fundamental role of the interest rate is to match consumer preferences with the productivity of capital. When the marginal product of capital is high, firms are willing to pay a high interest rate to households for loans. Firms bid up the interest rate, which induces households to provide more loans. Equilibrium is achieved when the interest rate rises to the point where the demand for loans by firms equals the supply from households. In equilibrium, the demand of households for consumption goods in the present and future is matched by the production by firms of consumer goods in the present and future.[8]

---

[7] The definition given here is for the nominal interest rate because we have not taken changes in the purchasing power of money into account. In Chapter 5, we do allow for these changes in defining the "real" interest rate.

[8] As we will see later, borrowing also occurs for purposes other than the purchase or production of physical capital. The interest rate, however, is still the rate of exchange between future and current consumption.

Referring back to Figure 3.5, recall that the slope of the indifference curve $U*$ at point $A*$ equals the slope of the consumption possibility line Q_I, Q_{II}. This slope is -1.00, which is the negative of the interest rate factor, $(1+i)$, when the interest rate is zero. When there is farming, the slope of the indifference curve $U*^f$ equals the slope of the production possibility frontier at $A*^f$. This slope is -2.00, which is the negative of the interest rate factor when the interest rate is 1.00. We conclude that the rate at which Robinson Crusoe is willing to exchange one pound of present potato consumption for future consumption equals the rate at which his economy (i.e., Friday the farmer) can physically convert an additional pound of potatoes planted this year into future consumption. This rate is the negative of the interest rate factor.

The matching of consumer preferences with the productivity of capital is easy for Robinson Crusoe. He can allocate his consumption between the two years such that the rate at which farming allows him to substitute current for future consumption (the productivity of capital) is equal to the rate at which he wants to substitute current for future consumption. Lending to Friday earns Robinson Crusoe an amount of interest plus principal that is equal to the quantity of potatoes he wants to consume in the second year. The interest income equals the additional quantity of potatoes that is available in the second year.

In complex economies, the matching of consumer preferences with the productivity of capital is more indirect than for Robinson Crusoe and Friday, but the same basic forces are at work. The interest rate is still the price that matches the preferences of households concerning current versus future consumption with the productivity of physical capital.[9] In complex economies, as with Crusoe, the act of saving does not ensure that there is investment in productive capacity. Investment occurs when households save *and* the resources are shifted to firms. We shall see in Chapter 4 that the financial system plays a crucial role in this process.

The interaction of consumer choices with the investment decisions of firms has a powerful effect on interest rates. There are many other forces that affect interest rates, however, particularly in the short run. Much of this book is devoted to discussing the financial factors that affect interest rates. In a discussion of these financial factors, however, it is important not to lose sight of the fundamental forces that are illustrated in the story of Robinson Crusoe.

THE RELATIONSHIP BETWEEN SAVING AND WEALTH

In this section, we examine the relationship between saving and wealth in more complex economies. We shall see that many of the same forces that affect Robinson Crusoe are at work in modern economies.

---

[9] In this chapter we talk about "the" interest rate as though there is only one interest rate. In fact, there are many interest rates depending on risk and other factors. Later chapters explain why there are many different interest rates.

Households commonly earn their incomes by providing labor services to businesses, and businesses earn their incomes by selling products to households. When households and businesses save from their incomes, their wealth accumulates over time.[10] A household saves when its flow of income exceeds its flow of expenditures on consumption. A business saves by retaining its flow of profits (revenue less costs) rather than paying out the profits to its owners.[11] When a household or firm saves, it adds to its wealth. Saving is a *flow*; it is the rate per unit of time at which economic units are adding to their *stock* of wealth.

When households or firms save, they are running a budget surplus; that is, they have a surplus of income over expenditures for consumption or production. They are called *surplus units*. A primary reason that a household runs a surplus (saves) is that it wants to postpone consumption to a later date. It uses the wealth accumulated from saving to support this later consumption.[12] A firm often runs a surplus because it wants to add to its production capacity.[13] When sufficient wealth is accumulated to support the purchase of a new plant or equipment, the wealth becomes embodied in new capacity.

A household has two sources of income: its labor income and the income earned from various assets that are held. Income from assets is composed of interest and dividend income plus any capital gains (appreciation in value) that occur when the prices of the assets rise. Asset income is reduced by any capital losses (depreciation of value) that occur when asset prices decline. A household also pays taxes, which reduces its *net* income.[14] Symbolically, household net income is defined as

$$Y_{NH} = L_H + DI_H + CG_H - CL_H - T_H$$

where

Y_{NH} : net household income

L_H : labor income

DI_H : dividend and interest income

CG_H : capital gains on assets whose prices have risen

CL_H : capital losses on assets whose prices have fallen

T_H : taxes paid.

---

[10] The form in which wealth is held is discussed in Chapter 4.

[11] Firms are owned by households, and profits retained by firms increase the wealth of their owners. It is useful for purposes of this chapter, however, to treat businesses as separate entities from households.

[12] There are other reasons that households save that are discussed later in this chapter.

[13] There are also other reasons for firms to save that are discussed later in the chapter.

[14] A household may also receive transfer payments from the government such as social security benefits. We handle this complication by defining taxes to be gross taxes less receipts of government transfer payments.

This definition of net household income is more inclusive than the definition of disposable income used in the national income accounts because it includes capital gains and losses on existing wealth. The national income approach is appropriate when one is studying the relationship between household income and currently produced output holding wealth constant. For reasons that are given as follows, the definition used in this chapter is more appropriate than disposable income for a discussion of the relationship between saving and wealth.[15]

A business also has three sources of income: receipts from sales of goods and services, interest and dividend income paid to it by others, and capital gains on the assets it holds. Net income is reduced when a business incurs costs of producing goods and services, when it has capital losses on its assets and when it pays taxes.[16] Symbolically, we have:

$$Y_{NB} = GR_B + DI_B + CG_B - CL_B - E_B - T_B$$

where

Y_{NB} : net business income

GR_B : gross receipts from sales of goods and services

DI_B : dividend and interest income

CG_B : capital gains on assets whose prices have risen

CL_B : capital losses on assets whose prices have fallen

E_B : expenses (costs) of producing goods and services

T_B : taxes paid.

We can now define saving and wealth and show the relationship between them. *Household saving,* S_H, is defined as the difference between net household income and household consumption of goods and services, C_H; thus $S_H = Y_{NH} - C_H$. *Business saving,* S_B, is defined as the difference between net business income and payment of dividends, DP_B to owners; thus, $S_B = Y_{NB} - DP_B$. Business saving is often called retained earnings.

The *wealth* (net worth) *of households,* W_H, is defined as assets held, A_H, less liabilities owed, L_H, or $W_H = A_H - L_H$.[17] *Business wealth* (net worth) is defined equivalently: $W_B = A_B - L_B$. With the definitions of saving and of wealth in mind, we can now show the relationship between the *flow* of saving and the *stock* of wealth held by households and business. When households and business save, they have two options, they can purchase additional assets, or they can reduce (payoff) outstanding liabilities. Using the Greek letter delta, Δ, to signify change, we have $S_H = \Delta W_H = \Delta A_H - \Delta L_H$ and $S_B = \Delta W_B = \Delta A_B - \Delta L_B$. By definition,

---

[15] The national income approach is adopted in Chapter 13, but we show in Chapter 15 that capital gains and losses on existing assets affect consumption and saving.

[16] As with households, taxes are net of transfer payments.

[17] For reasons given later in this chapter, we do not include future household earnings in wealth.

when households and businesses save, they increase their wealth. The increase in wealth can take the form either of increasing assets or of decreasing liabilities; there are no other options. The total stock of wealth held by households and business is simply the accumulation of their previous and current saving.

Dissaving

Saving for a household or business can be negative. If a household's saving is negative, current consumption exceeds current net income. If a business has negative saving, either losses are being incurred (rather than profits) or dividends and interest exceed net income. When households or businesses have negative saving, they are *dissaving*. Dissaving reduces wealth. The decline in wealth can take the form of either reduced assets or of increased liabilities. In either case, dissaving involves a reduction of wealth.

Many consumers and businesses want to dissave or to acquire assets in excess of their net worth. We shall call both of these economic units *deficit units*. The ability of these two groups to incur deficits is affected by their ability to borrow.[18] Unless dissavers can borrow, they can support their deficits only as long as they have assets that they can draw down (sell). Furthermore, without borrowing, it is impossible for economic units to hold assets in excess of net worth.

It is important to note that borrowing (increased liabilities) does not necessarily reduce the wealth of the borrower. A household or business can borrow, that is, incur a liability, and use the proceeds to purchase an asset. In this case, both assets and liabilities rise by an equal amount, and wealth is unaffected.

Debt allows economic units to finance total expenditures in excess of current wealth and income. If the debt-financed expenditure is for an asset, wealth is unaffected, and borrowing enables an economic unit to hold an amount of assets that is greater than its wealth (net worth). If the debt-financed expenditure is for household consumption or is used to cover losses and dividend payments for business, the wealth of the economic unit is reduced. We conclude that increased debt only makes a household or a business poorer if the debt is incurred because the economic unit is a dissaver.

Capital Gains Versus Other Sources of Income

It is now possible to explain why the definitions of household and business income include capital gains and losses on the assets held by the two groups. Consider the case of a consumer who experiences a capital gain on an asset. Net income rises by the amount of the capital gain.[19] The consumer has three options available for

---

[18] Businesses can also sell ownership shares.
[19] Assuming that all other components of net income are unchanged.

the disposition of this increased income. One option entails continuing to hold the asset and not changing consumption. In this case, net income, saving, and wealth rise by the amount of the capital gain. All the increased saving is embodied in the asset whose price appreciates.[20] The second option also entails continuing to hold the asset, but, in this case, the consumer increases consumption relative to labor income. In this case, saving and wealth rise by less than the capital gain on the asset. The third option entails selling the asset to "realize" the capital gain. If the asset is sold, the money received can be used either to purchase other assets (alternatively pay off liabilities) or to finance increased consumption.

It should be noted that the options available for capital gains income are the same options available from any other source of income. When labor income is received, the consumer has more money than before. The consumer's assets, in the form of money, rise. At this point, the holder has the option of continuing to hold the money or of selling it. One sells money by purchasing something. The money can be used either to purchase some asset (pay off a liability) or to finance increased consumption. Thus, the receipt of labor income has the same consequences for the consumer as a capital gain on an asset.

There is a difference between labor and capital gain income, however. If the consumer wants to "realize" a capital gain, it is necessary to sell part of the asset.[21] The money received can be used to purchase another asset or to increase consumption. Labor income is already in the form of money, so one transaction, that is, the sale of an asset, is avoided. This makes capital gain income different from labor income, but a capital gain is still income.[22] An identical argument can be made for why capital losses on assets reduce income.

THE ACCUMULATION OF ASSETS, LIABILITIES AND WEALTH BY BUSINESS AND HOUSEHOLDS

We now consider the economic decisions that lead business and households to save or dissave and, thereby, to change their holdings of wealth.[23] In order to

---

[20] Note that if the national income definition of disposable income is used, wealth rises, but saving and disposable income are unchanged. Because the increase in wealth equals saving, we have a contradiction. The national income approach implicitly measures wealth at book (original purchase price) rather than at current market prices.

[21] We will see in Chapter 4 that some assets, such as houses, are indivisible. It is necessary to sell the entire holding of the asset to realize the capital gain. This inhibits realization of capital gains for these assets. This problem is reduced by the extent that the holder can borrow using the appreciated asset as collateral.

[22] An individual's capital gains income is also taxed at a lower rate than his or her labor income.

[23] Government saving and dissaving is discussed in Chapter 14.

understand the role of the interest rate in determining the accumulation of assets and liabilities by a firm or a household, one must consider the concept of discounted present value.

Discounted Present Value

Discounted present value is a convenient method of comparing incomes and expenses that are realized at different dates. The sooner income is received, the better because the funds can be put to work earning interest. Similarly, the longer payment of expenses is postponed, the better because the funds can be invested until the expenses are paid.

The key to understanding discounted present value lies with the concept of *opportunity cost*. Any decision involves the weighing of alternatives. When one alternative is selected, the opportunity cost of that decision is the lost opportunity of selecting some other alternative. The opportunity cost of receiving money in the future is not receiving it now. The receipt of money today, however, does *not* prevent an economic unit from receiving money in the future. Money received today can be lent and thereby converted into money received in the future. When an economic unit receives money in the future or receives money today and lends it, the unit does not have access to the money until a future date. Receipt of money today allows the economic unit to consume goods and services today. Thus, the opportunity cost either of receiving money in the future *or* of lending money is the lost opportunity to consume today. Because receiving money in the future and lending money have the same opportunity cost, they should have the same value to an economic unit. That value is measured by discounted present value.

Consider the case of a baseball player who is negotiating the bonus he will receive for signing a contract. The owner of the team offers him the alternative either of receiving $100,000 today or of receiving various sums in the future. For example, the owner offers $100,000 today versus $110,000 at the end of the year or $120,000 at the end of two years. How can the ballplayer compare the alternatives? The ballplayer's business agent knows that there is a convenient way to compare current versus future receipt of income and explains the formulas to her client. The agent shows that for any interest rate, i, a sum of money M_0 received today can be lent for one year. At the end of the year, an interest income of iM_0 is earned and the principal, M_0, is repaid for a total at the end of the year of $M_1 = iM_0 + M_0 = (1+i)M_0$. The rate of exchange between money today and money next year is the interest rate factor $(1+i) = M_1/M_0$. Using this expression, the agent illustrates that at the prevailing interest rate of 10 percent, $100,000 received today is the equivalent of $110,000 received one year in the future. In this case, $M_0 = 100,000$, and $i = 0.10$, so $M_1 = (1.10)\$100,000 = \$110,000$. Conversely, $110,000 received one year in the future is worth $100,000 today. Thus, the *discounted present value* of $110,000 received in one year is $\$110,000/(1.10) = \$100,000$. It is the amount that can be lent now at 10 percent interest to end up with $110,000 one year from now. The offer of $110,000 payable in a year is no better than receiving $100,000 today. The ballplayer can receive $110,000 in one year either by lending $100,000 for a year or by receiving his bonus in a year. The owner of the baseball team is simply offering to give the player money next year, rather than money this year, at the going rate of exchange of $(1+i) = 1.10$.

The agent observes that if the ballplayer could get $115,000 next year rather than $100,000 this year, then the deal is appealing. She calculates the discounted present value (DPV) of $115,000 received one year in the future is DPV = $115,000/(1.10) = $104,545.45. In this case, $115,000 received one year in the future is worth more than $100,000 received today. In fact, only if the baseball player received $104,545.45 today would this sum be equivalent to receiving $115,000 next year. Investment of this amount grows to $115,000 by year's end: (1.10)104,545.45 = $115,000. Thus, paying the ballplayer $115,000 in one year is equivalent to receiving $104,545.45 today. Since the owner of the team is only offering $100,000 today, receiving $115,000 payable in one year is an appealing offer.

More generally, the discounted present value of an amount of money M_1^* received one year in the future is given by DPV = $M_1^*/(1+i)$. If the DPV of M_1^* is less than $100,000, the baseball player should accept the $100,000 today. If the DPV of M_1^* equals $100,000, then the two offers are equivalent. If the DPV of M_1^* exceeds $100,000, the ballplayer should consider receiving the payment in the future.[24]

The business agent next turns to the alternative of receiving $100,000 today versus $120,000 payable two years in the future. She observes that $100,000 received today can be invested for two years. If the funds are lent for two years, the ballplayer has $M_0 + iM_0$ at the end of the first year and lends this sum in the second year. For the second year, the ballplayer receives interest income on the original M_0, iM_0, plus interest income on the interest earned during the first year, $i(iM_0)$. Total interest income for the second year is $iM_0 + i(iM_0)$. The ability to earn additional interest income by reinvesting the interest earned in the previous year is called *compound interest*. At the end of the second year, the ballplayer has a total amount of money, M_2, of

$$M_2 = [M_0 + iM_0] + [iM_0 + i(iM_0)] = (1+i)^2 M_0 .$$

The expression for M_2 can be obtained more directly:

$$M_1 = (1+i)M_0,$$

$$M_2 = (1+i)M_1 = (1+i)(1+i)M_0 = (1+i)^2 M_0 .$$

---

[24] Whether the ballplayer wants to receive an amount of money at the end of the year whose DPV exceeds $100,000 depends upon his preference for current versus future consumption. If he has a high rate of time preference, he might still prefer to consume $100,000 today rather than $115,000 in one year. As we will see later, however, if the ballplayer can borrow against his future income, he may prefer the $115,000.

This expression allows the ballplayer to compare the receipt of $100,000 today versus receiving $120,000 from the owner two years in the future. In this case, M_0 = $100,000 and $(1+i) = 1.10$, so $M_2 = (1.10)^2 \$100,000 = \$121,000$. He is better off receiving immediate payment of $100,000 and lending it for two years, rather than receiving a payment of $120,000 in two years. When lent at 10 percent interest, $100,000 received today will grow to $121,000 at the end of two years. This is more than the $120,000 offered by the owner of the team. Compounding of interest is a powerful factor in making money received today grow into larger sums in the future.

The discounted present value of an amount of money, M_2^*, received two years in the future is given by DPV $= M_2^*/(1+i)^2$. For the ballplayer, we have $M_2^* =$ $120,000, so DPV $= \$120,000/(1.10)^2 = \$99,173.55$. This calculation indicates that $120,000 received in two years is the equivalent of receiving $99,173.55 today. We can check that this is correct by calculating the sum of money into which the $99,173.55 will grow by investing it for two years at 10 percent interest: $(1.10)^2 \$99,173.55 = \$120,000$. The ballplayer is better off receiving $100,000 today rather than $120,000 two years in the future.

The business manager is tiring of the negotiations and decides to present the ballplayer with the general formula for discounted present value so that any offer, no matter for how many years in the future, can be compared with the receipt of money today. She points out that an amount M_0 received today grows into the amount M_n after investment for n years, where $M_n = (1+i)^n M_0$. The amount M_n can be compared to an amount offered to be paid in n years, M_n^*. Alternatively, the discounted present value of M_n^* can be compared to M_0, where DPV $= M_n^*/(1+i)^n$. If the DPV of M_n^* is less than M_0, it is better to receive M_0 immediately and lend it for n years. If the DPV of M_n^* equals M_0, receiving M_n^* payable n years in the future is equivalent to receiving the amount M_0 immediately and lending it for n years. If the DPV of M_n^* exceeds M_0, the baseball player should consider receiving payment in the future. In this case, investment of M_0 for n years grows into an amount that is less than M_n^*. She instructs the ballplayer never to accept an amount M_n^* whose DPV is less than M_0.

The business manager points out that all the calculations of DPV were based on the assumption that the interest rate is constant over the time period considered. For example, in the calculation of the discounted present value of a payment received at the end of two years, it was assumed that the interest rate was 10 percent for both the first and second years. It is possible to calculate DPV when the interest rate is different in the two years.[25] Let i_1 be the interest rate in the first year, and let i_2 be the interest rate in the second year. At the end of the first year an amount M_0 grows to $M_1 = (1+i_1)M_0$. The amount M_1 is then lent for the second year at the interest rate i_2, and M_1 grows to

$$M_2 = (1+i_2)M_1 = (1+i_1)(1+i_2)M_0.$$

[25] The interest rate in the second year is not known with certainty. The implications of this uncertainty are discussed in Chapter 5.

The DPV of M_2 is $M_2/(1+i_1)(1+i_2)$. More generally, for investment over n years, we have $M_n = (1+i_1)(1+i_2)...(1+i_n)M_0$. For a sum of money M_n^* received n years in the future, we have:

$$DPV = M_n^* /(1+i_1)(1+i_2)...(1+i_n).$$

As before, M_0 can be compared to the DPV of M_n^*.

Changes in the interest rate from year to year can have an important effect on the discounted present value. Consider the case of receiving $120,000 two years in the future. If the interest rate is 10 percent in both years, it is better to receive $100,000 today rather than $120,000 in two years because the DPV of the $120,000 is $99,175.55. If the interest rate is 5 percent in the second year, however, DPV = $120,000/(1.10)(1.05) = $103,896.10. If the interest rate is 5 percent in the second year, the baseball player may prefer $120,000 in two years to $100,000 today.

As mentioned earlier, money received immediately has one crucial advantage over money received in the future. Money received today can be spent today; money received in the future cannot. The opportunity cost of either lending money today or of receiving money in the future is the lost opportunity to consume today. If the baseball player can borrow, however, it is possible to convert money received in the future into money that is available immediately for consumption. Consider the case where $M_1^* = \$115,000$, and assume the interest rate at which the ballplayer can borrow is 10 percent. The concept of discounted present value tells us exactly how much money he can borrow against this $115,000. At a 10 percent interest rate, a lender is willing to provide $115,000/(1.10) = $104,545.45 immediately in return for $115,000 payable in one year. At the end of the year, the ballplayer repays $104,545.45 of principal plus $10,454.55 of interest for a total of $115,000. Thus, an offer of a $115,000 bonus payable in one year is preferable to receiving a $100,000 bonus immediately because the $115,000 can be converted into $104,545.45 that is available immediately. Even if the baseball player wants immediate consumption rather than future consumption, he is better off by receiving his bonus in the future and borrowing against it. The baseball player should always accept a bonus M_n^* payable n years in the future whose DPV exceeds a bonus M_0 that is paid immediately. If the DPV of M_n^* is less than M_0, he should take M_0, and if the DPV of M_n equals M_0 he is indifferent.

If the ballplayer cannot borrow against future income or if the interest rate for borrowing exceeds the rate for lending, the analysis is more complex and is not considered here. Some of the implications of not being able to borrow against future income are discussed later in this chapter. At this point, however, we shall assume that borrowing is possible at the same interest rate as lending. In this case, DPV is the appropriate guide to determining the choice between immediate consumption and consumption in the future.[26]

---

[26] DPV is always the appropriate guide in deciding between money received in the future and money received immediately and then lent.

Discounted present value was implicit in our earlier story of Robinson Crusoe. There it was shown that Crusoe maximized his satisfaction when the rate at which he was willing to substitute consumption in the first year for consumption in the second year equaled the rate at which he could exchange consumption between the two years. That is to say, he maximized satisfaction when the slope of his indifference curve equaled the slope of the production possibility frontier. At that point, both slopes equaled $-(1+i)$. The rate of exchange between consumption in year two and year one is the interest rate. When Crusoe maximizes his satisfaction, he is indifferent between the mix of consumption between the two years at point A^{*f} in Figure 3.5 and a situation where he reduces consumption in the first year by one unit and increases consumption in the second year by $(1+i)$ units. If he could obtain more than $(1+i)$ units the second year, he increases satisfaction by decreasing current consumption in favor of consumption in the future. If he could obtain less than $(1+i)$ units, he increases satisfaction by increasing current consumption and reducing future consumption. Let ΔQ_I be the amount Crusoe changes consumption in the current year, and let ΔQ_{II} be the amount he changes consumption in the second year. Crusoe maximizes his satisfaction when $\Delta Q_{II}/\Delta Q_I = -(1+i)$, or $\Delta Q_I = -\Delta Q_{II}/(1+i)$. He is guided by discounted present value.[27]

Using Discounted Present Value to Explain the Demand by Firms for Capital Goods

The examples presented to this point have all involved the DPV of a receipt of money at a single date in the future. Discounted present value can also be used to evaluate different patterns of income realized over a number of years. This is important because a firm can use DPV to evaluate alternative investment projects. One project may involve equipment with a long life that earns relatively little in early years, because of start-up costs or excess capacity, but earns high income in later years. Some other projects may offer higher income in early years but little or no income in later years. It is possible to compute the DPV of the future net income streams for various investment projects to determine the one or ones that have the highest discounted present value.

Consider a firm that is considering the purchase of equipment that will wear out at the end of 10 years. The equipment is expected to add an amount y_1 to net income in the first year of operation, y_2 to net income in the second year, and so on up to y_{10} in the tenth year. The total net income, TNY, for the project over the ten years is

$$TNY = y_1 + y_2 + ... + y_{10}.$$

---

[27] A formal analysis that considers consumer choice over n periods is beyond the scope of this book. Later on in the chapter we do discuss consumption and saving behavior over a household's lifetime.

Using the Greek letter sigma, Σ, to indicate summation and using the letter j to indicate a counter that runs from 1 to 10, the expression for total net income can be written as

$$TNY = \sum_{j=1}^{10} y_j.$$

This gives us a compact way to express total net income over the 10 years. But income earned in later years is not worth as much today as the same income earned in earlier years. It is necessary, therefore, to compute the discounted present value of the total net income stream:

$$DPV = \frac{y_1}{(1+i_1)} + \frac{y_2}{(1+i_1)(1+i_2)} + \dots + \frac{y_n}{(1+i_1)(1+i_2)\dots(1+i_n)}.$$

If the interest rate is constant over the 10 years, we have:

$$DPV = [y_1/(1+i)] + [y_2/(1+i)^2] + \dots + [y_{10}/(1+i)^{10}], \text{ or}$$

$$DPV = \sum_{j=1}^{10} [y_j/(1+i)^j].$$

Table 3.1 shows net income streams from three alternative investment projects. Project I has a life of 10 years, during which time it incurs a loss in the first year, earns relatively low net incomes for the next several years, and earns high incomes in later years. Project II earns a constant $100 a year for 10 years. Over its entire life, Project II earns less total net income than project I. The third project has a life of 5 years and earns a net income of $175 in each year. Project III has the lowest total net income of the three alternatives. For each project, the DPV of the net income in each year is shown assuming interest rates of 0, 5, and 10 percent. The discounted present values of the total net income streams are shown as the sums of the DPVs in the individual years.

At a zero interest rate, the discounted present value of net income in each year equals the net income for that year. The sum of the incomes earned over the life of the project is the total net income, TNY, for that project. Project I has the highest TNY followed by projects II and III.

At a 5 percent interest rate, the DPV of the net income stream from project I is the lowest of the three projects. This move from first to last place for project I occurs because in the early years, net income is low relative to the other projects. These low incomes are not as heavily discounted as are the high net incomes in later years. For example the $50 loss in year 1 has a DPV of $-$47.62 at 5 percent interest, but the $350 income in year 10 has a DPV of only $214.87. The net income stream for project II has the highest DPV. That project earns a net income of $100 a year for ten years. Even though the net incomes in later years are relatively heavily discounted at 5 percent interest, these incomes still make a sufficient contribution to the DPV of the income stream for project II to place it ahead of project III.

TABLE 3.1
DISCOUNTED PRESENT VALUES OF NET INCOMES FROM THREE PROJECTS

Year (j)	Project I $y_i/(1+i)^j$			Project II $y_i/(1+i)^j$			Project III $y_i/(1+i)^j$		
	0%	5%	10%	0%	5%	10%	0%	5%	10%
1	-$50	-$47.62	-$45.45	$100	$95.24	$90.91	$175	$166.67	$159.09
2	0	0.0	0.0	100	90.70	82.64	175	158.73	144.63
3	20	19.05	15.03	100	86.38	75.13	175	151.17	133.53
4	50	41.14	34.15	100	82.27	68.30	175	143.97	119.53
5	75	58.76	46.57	100	78.35	62.09	175	137.12	108.66
6	100	74.62	56.45	100	74.62	56.44			
7	150	106.60	76.97	100	71.07	51.32			
8	200	135.37	93.30	100	67.68	46.65			
9	250	161.15	106.02	100	64.46	42.41			
10	350	214.87	134.94	100	61.39	38.55			
Sum (Σ)	$1,145	$692.00	$517.98	$1,000	$772.16	$614.44	$875	$757.66	$663.39

When the interest rate is 10 percent, however, the net income stream for project III has the highest discounted present value. That project has the lowest total net income of the three, but all the income is earned in 5 years. The other two projects have a life of 10 years, and the net incomes in the later years are heavily discounted when the interest rate is 10 percent. For example, the DPV of the $100 earned during year 10 for project II is $61.39 at 5 percent interest but only $38.55 at 10 percent interest. Because the income for project III is earned over 5 rather than 10 years, the discounting is not so heavy, and its net income stream earns the highest discounted present value.

Table 3.1 demonstrates the importance both of the time path of income and of the level of the interest rate for determining discounted present value. At low interest rates, income earned in the distant future is worth almost as much as income earned in the near future. At high interest rates, income earned in the distant future is worth substantially less than income earned in the near future, and, therefore, the time path of income is crucial for DPV. The net income stream for project III has the lowest DPV when the interest rate is zero, but it has the highest DPV when the interest rate is 10 percent. High interest rates discourage investment projects with slow payoffs and encourage projects with rapid payoffs.

The Use of External Funds to Finance Capital Expansion

The concept of discounted present value can be used to isolate the factors that motivate a firm to borrow in order to expand its capital stock. In order to keep the discussion manageable, the analysis that follows is highly simplified. It is assumed that a firm can predict future revenues, costs, profits, and interest rates with perfect accuracy. It is also assumed that a firm can borrow as much as it wants at the prevailing interest rate. Though these assumptions take us a long ways from reality, they allow the discussion to focus on some basic issues concerning why a firm borrows to increase its capital stock. The role of uncertainty about the future and of related factors is discussed in later chapters.

Consider a firm that is planning the purchase of a $1 million machine that wears out at the end of two years of operation. Assume that use of the machine will add $535,000 to net income in the first year of operation and $572,450 to net income in the second year for a total net income of $1,107,450.[28] The interest rate is 5 percent, so the discounted present value of the machine is $535,000/(1.05) + 572,450/(1.05)^2 = $1,028,753$.

The firm does not have sufficient current earnings plus accumulated wealth to purchase the machine. It considers becoming a deficit unit by borrowing the full

---

[28] For simplicity it is assumed that the firm knows with certainty that this future net income will be realized. In reality, future income from investment projects is subject to uncertainty, and so are future interest rates. The role of uncertainty is discussed in Chapter 5.

$1 million for two years at the going interest rate of 5 percent a year. The firm wants to determine whether the machine will add enough to net income to support the interest cost of the loan plus repayment of the loan principal at the end of the second year. We can make this calculation by deducting interest expense from net income earned in the first year and interest expense plus repayment of the loan from net income earned in the second year.[29] In the first year of operating the machine, the firm has the interest expenses of 5 percent on $1 million or $50,000. In the second year, it again pays 5 percent on the $1 million, and it also repays the $1 million. In the first year, the firm earns $535,000 and pays interest of $50,000 to give a net figure of $485,000. In the second year, the project earns $572,450, but the firm pays interest of $50,000 and principal of $1 million to give a net figure of $-477,550$ in the second year. The firm can assess the profitability of borrowing to purchase the machine by calculating the discounted present value of net income less interest and loan repayment for the two years. Let us call this calculation *net* discounted present value, NDPV. The NDPV of the two-year income stream is $485,000/(1.05) - $477,550/(1.05)^2 = $28,753$. A $1 million machine operated for two years will produce a net income less interest costs and loan repayments whose discounted present value is $28,753 at 5 percent interest. Because the NDPV is greater than zero, it is profitable for the firm to borrow the money and purchase the machine.[30]

After we go through these calculations, it is important to observe that there is a more direct method of assessing the profitability of the project. Before deduction of loan interest and principal, the project generates a net income over the two years whose DPV is $1,028,753. The machine cost $1 million to buy. The difference between the DPV and the purchase price is $28,753, which is exactly what we obtained for NDPV. An investment project is profitable whose discounted present value exceeds the purchase price of the equipment.[31] The concept of NDPV was used in the example to demonstrate that the DPV implies that sufficient net income is earned from the project to pay interest on the loan and loan principal. When these payments are made, the firm earns a net discounted present value of $28,750.

The profitability of the project depends crucially on the interest rate that is paid for borrowed funds. If the firm borrows at 10 percent interest rate rather than at 5

---

[29] Interest costs may be deducted from income for tax purposes. Technically, we should use the aftertax interest rate. This and other tax complications are not discussed here.

[30] As we will see in Chapter 4, the firm may sell ownership shares (stock) rather than borrow.

[31] The comparison of the DPV of the net income from a project with its purchase price is similar to the calculation of the marginal efficiency of investment (MEI) as described in many textbooks. It can be shown, however, that MEI is not always a reliable measure of profitability. For a discussion of DPV versus MEI, see William Baumol, *Economic Theory and Operations Analysis*, 3rd ed. (Englewood Cliffs, N.J., Prentice-Hall, 1972), pp. 463–69.

percent, the project is no longer profitable. The discounted present value is $535,000/(1.10)+$572,450/(1.10)^2 = $959,463, which is less than the $1 million purchase price.[32]

To summarize the discussion, a firm will use external funds (borrow) if the discounted present value of the net income from the project exceeds its purchase price. A rise in the interest rate reduces the DPV of a given stream of future net income and penalizes projects that earn more in later years than in early years. We reach the important conclusion that a rise in the interest rate discourages investment and borrowing.

The Use of Internal Funds to Finance Capital Expansion

Up to this point we have discussed a firm that is a deficit unit. In this section we examine a firm that is in a surplus position. This firm must decide what to do with the wealth it is accumulating. It can, of course, distribute this wealth to its owners through increased dividends. Many owners prefer to retain accumulated wealth in the firm, however, because it can use the wealth at least as profitably as they can. Wealth that is retained in a firm can be used to finance internal expansion, or, alternatively, the wealth can be lent to others. Discounted present value guides a surplus firm in determining how to invest its wealth.

Assume that a surplus firm, like the deficit firm discussed earlier, is considering the purchase of a $1 million machine, with a life of two years, that contributes $535,000 to net income in the first year and $572,450 to income in the second year.[33] As before, at a 5 percent interest rate the net income stream from the investment project has a discounted present value of $535,000/(1.05)+ $572,450/(1.05)^2 = $1,028,753. The firm's alternative is to lend the $1 million to another firm for two years at 5 percent interest. It will invest the funds internally only if the DPV from the machine exceeds the DPV from the loan. Calculation of the discounted present value of the two-year loan is straightforward. Recall from the earlier discussion of discounted present value that $(1+i)^2 M_0 = M_2$, so $(1.05)^2$ $1,000,000 = $1,102,500, and the discounted present value, M_0, is $1,102,500/(1.05)^2 = $1,00,000. The present value of $1 million lent at interest is $1 million.

If the firm uses its internal wealth to buy the machine, it obtains a DPV of $1,028,753. Alternatively if the firm lends the funds, the DPV of the loan is $1 million. The firm can add $28,753 more to its DPV by investing in a machine than by lending. Therefore, it will purchase the machine rather than lend its funds.

---

[32] The reader should confirm that the NDPV = − $40,537. The reader should also verify that the DPV equals the purchase price when the interest rate is 7 percent.
[33] As before, we are neglecting uncertainty about this future income and future interest rates.

The opportunity cost to a surplus firm of pursuing an internal investment project is the income it forgoes by not making a loan.[34] The firm must determine whether it is more profitable to invest a given amount of money internally or to grant a loan. The amount of money that is relevant for the comparison is the amount that must be expended to purchase the capital goods (i.e., their purchase price). Thus, the firm compares the purchase price of the capital goods to the discounted present value of the net income stream that they will generate. If the DPV exceeds the purchase price, it is more profitable to invest internally than to lend. If the DPV from the project is less than the purchase price of the equipment, it is more profitable to lend. When the DPV equals the purchase price, the firm is indifferent between internal investment and granting a loan. When the interest rate rises, internal investment declines and lending increases.

HOUSEHOLDS

In this section, we explain why households accumulate assets and why they issue liabilities (borrow). In order to understand why a household acquires assets and issues liabilities and why it changes the composition of its wealth, it is necessary to analyze the motives for saving and dissaving. There are several reasons why a household saves or dissaves. A major factor is the difference in timing between the receipt of income and the expenditure of that income on consumption. Just as Robinson Crusoe spread the consumption of his potatoes over the two years spent on the island, a household also spreads the consumption of its income over time.

For virtually all households, there is a difference in the timing of receipts of income and expenditures on consumption. For example, most households are paid at regular monthly or weekly intervals. They make some expenditures immediately, but they save most of the income payment in order to spend during the time interval until the next payday. This initial saving constitutes wealth that allows households to smooth out the difference in timing between receipts of income and expenditures on consumption between paydays.

Figure 3.7 shows a simple pattern of wealth for a household that is paid $1000 on the first day of each month.[35] Consumption expenditures are spread evenly during the month. At the instant the household is paid, there is no time to spend any of the money yet. Initially, the entire $1000 is saved, that is, added to wealth. As the month progresses, the household gradually spends the wealth on consumption. By the middle of the month, wealth has been reduced to $500, and by the end of the month no wealth remains. The process is repeated each month.

---

[34] It also has the opportunity to pay additional dividends. Owners of the firm prefer this alternative when they can invest the funds more profitability (higher DPV) than the firm can.

[35] Here we are assuming no dividend income, capital gains and losses, or taxes. Net income per month is $1000.

FIGURE 3.7
THE USE OF WEALTH TO SMOOTH
CONSUMPTION.

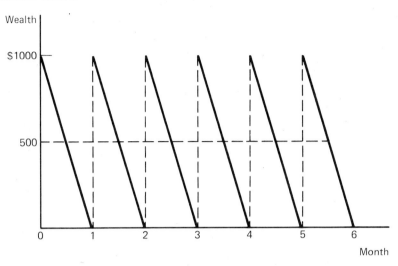

Some households behave in this hand-to-mouth fashion, but most do not. Some households consume less than their incomes between paydays, so their wealth grows from one payday to the next. Others consume more than their incomes and use either previously accumulated wealth or borrowing to cover their deficits. For them, accumulated wealth declines from payday to payday.

The Life Cycle Theory of Consumption

Households smooth out differences in the timing of income receipts and consumption over much longer periods than between paydays. An important factor determining whether wealth grows or shrinks over time is the household's expectation of the pattern of future income relative to the pattern of future desired consumption. Most households go through a fairly regular *life cycle* for labor income. In their early years, their labor income is low relative to what they can reasonably expect to earn in later years. During their middle years, peak income is achieved, and then labor income disappears as retirement age is reached.[36]

This life cycle of earnings produces an imbalance between the pattern of income and the desired pattern of consumption over a lifetime. By varying the rate of saving over its lifetime, a household achieves a pattern of consumption that

[36] Many persons continue to work part time after retirement. This behavior does not significantly alter the story given as follows.

accords with its preferences. In early years a household wants to purchase durable goods, such as cars and refrigerators; perhaps have children; and engage in other expensive activities. Yet during the early working years, income is low relative to what it will be in the future. There is often an incentive, therefore, to run a deficit during these early earning years. Because higher income is expected in the future, a household finances its deficit by running down assets, if it has any, or by borrowing against future income.[37]

In the middle years of the life cycle, as earnings rise to a peak, a household saves in order to repay any accumulated debts plus interest and also to accumulate assets that will be used to maintain consumption during later retirement years. During retirement, a household has no labor income. Its only income comes from earnings on previously acquired assets.[38] During this period, a household dissaves and finances its deficit by running down the assets accumulated during earlier years.[39]

When the ratio of saving to income varies over the life cycle, consumers can maintain a relatively steady rate of consumption despite large variations in income over their life cycles. Though the time dimension is much longer for the life cycle than for households that smooth out difference in timing between income and consumption from one payday to the next, the principle is the same. In both cases, variations in saving and wealth are used to insulate the flow of consumption from variations in income.

Figure 3.8 shows a simple pattern of income and saving over a household's life cycle. In the diagram, it is assumed that the household wants to maintain a constant rate of consumption over its lifetime and that there is zero accumulated savings (wealth) and zero debt at death. As indicated earlier, in early earning years, the household wants to dissave, that is, spend more than current income. This dissaving can take the form either of drawing down any assets that the household already has or of borrowing. In either case, the household spends more than current income and uses the income of later years to replenish assets or to repay debt. From point A to B in Figure 3.8, the household dissaves. From point B to C, the household saves, first to repay debts, if any, and then to accumulate wealth that is used to maintain consumption during the period of retirement. This latter period goes from point C to point D, during which time the household is again in a deficit condition. The deficit is financed by consuming the wealth accumulated during high income years. In the simple world of Figure 3.8, the household saves only during the middle years and dissaves early and late in life. The diagram is drawn in such a way that saving is exactly equal to dissaving so that at the end of the life cycle the household has saved nothing and has paid off all debts.

---

[37] We will see in the next section that borrowing may be impossible.

[38] These earnings include income from interest, dividends, and capital gains as well as pension fund and social security benefits.

[39] We argue in the next section that this dissaving does not occur for many retired persons.

FIGURE 3.8
INCOME AND CONSUMPTION
OVER A LIFE CYCLE.

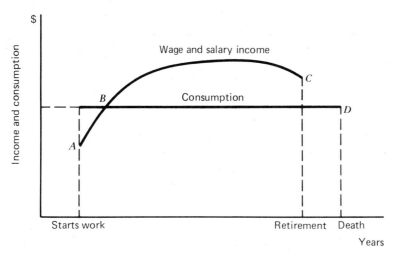

The pattern of saving over a household's life cycle described in this section is plausible, and it accords roughly with observed behavior. As with any theory, however, the life-cycle theory is incomplete. We shall now turn to some complications that have important effects on a household's consumption and saving.

Inherited Wealth

Many households leave estates, that is, they have positive wealth at point D of Figure 3.8. There are several reasons for this behavior. First, it is impossible to predict point D with certainty. Because a household does not know when judgment day will arrive, it is prudent to err on the side of conservatism. Most households do not attempt to end up with zero wealth at time of death but rather to have a cushion of wealth on the chance they may enjoy longevity.

In addition, many households accumulate estates that they leave to their heirs. They are willing to consume less over their lifetimes in order to build up this financial legacy to be left to others. One motive for providing an inheritance is to enable one's children to sustain a relatively high level of consumption during their early years as wage earners. In the absence of an inheritance, it might be difficult or impossible for the children to borrow sufficiently to maintain that level of consumption.[40]

[40] Some parents transfer wealth prior to death through gifts.

The difficulty in borrowing substantial sums during early years represents a serious problem for young households. In Figure 3.8, it was assumed that the prospect of higher income in the future allowed a household to borrow in order to maintain a relatively high level of consumption between points *A* and *B*. Such borrowing does occur in the real world, but it is limited in nature and size by the risks to lenders. In practice, if young persons want to borrow, they must demonstrate to lenders that they earn sufficient income currently to make loan payments, and they often have to demonstrate successful repayment of debt in the past. The second condition can create a "catch-22" situation in which persons have difficulty obtaining credit because they have not had credit in the past. Even when this hurdle is passed, households often find that credit can only be obtained for certain purposes. Credit is often available only to purchase some durable good, such as a car or a house, that the lender can seize and sell should the consumer default on the loan. It is difficult for households to obtain credit that is not secured by some marketable asset.[41] Lenders also often require that the borrower make a down payment when purchasing a durable good. For example, a household often cannot borrow the full amount of money required to purchase a car, but only a fraction (e.g., 80 percent) of the full amount. By investing some of its own wealth in the item, the household has a stake in not defaulting on the loan. Contrary to the life-cycle story told earlier, the need to make down payments on durable goods implies that young households often must actually reduce consumption relative to income (save) in order to accumulate the down payment.

The life-cycle theory asserts that young households incur debts because they expect their incomes to rise in the future. The discounted present value of a household's future labor income is its "human wealth." In principle, a household should be able to borrow using this wealth as collateral. Lenders do not use the prospects of high future income as an important factor in their decision to extend credit.[42] This occurs because the lender has no means of forcing the borrower to earn the higher income in the future. A young person might decide to change life styles and earn relatively little in the future. If this happens, the person might default on the loan. As a result, lenders are not guided by the human wealth of borrowers.[43] They use current income and past performance in debt repayment as criteria for extending credit, and they often tie the loan to the purchase of an asset for which a down payment is required.

---

[41] There are forms of unsecured credit available to households, such as through credit cards. They have to meet a minimum income requirement to obtain credit cards, however, and the amount of credit is limited. Credit unions are also an important source of unsecured credit to households. These institutions are discussed in Chapter 10.

[42] The baseball player in our earlier story about discounted present value may be able to borrow against future income because a bonus payable in the future is guaranteed by the owner of the team.

[43] It is this problem that led us to omit human wealth from our definition of total household wealth given earlier in this chapter.

It should be noted that by tying loans to the purchase of durable goods, lenders are not only financing consumption, but they are also financing the acquisition of assets in excess of the borrowers' net worth. Durable goods, such as refrigerators, cars, and houses are assets that provide a flow of consumption services over their lives. Because of their relatively long lives, these durable goods have a value, when new, that exceeds the value of the flow of services they provide during a relatively short time interval, such as a month or a year. The only *consumption* that a lender is financing is this flow of services. The remainder of the loan is financing the purchase of an *asset*. The value of a durable good as an asset is reduced only as it depreciates with age and use.[44]

The practices of lenders prevent many young households, which will have significantly higher incomes in the future, from borrowing and consuming as much as they would like in their early years. The problem can be reduced or eliminated if these households receive wealth from their parents in the form of inheritance or gifts. Thus, parents have an incentive to save enough over their lifetimes to accumulate funds for their offspring. To the extent that inheritance and gifts are not available, young households are unable to achieve the extent of dissaving predicted by life-cycle considerations.

The Saving Behavior of Retired Persons

The life cycle theory implies that retired persons dissave by running down the assets that they have accumulated during earlier years. This behavior does occur, but there are many persons who continue to save part of their interest and dividend income after retirement. There are several reasons for this behavior. Concern over prolonged illness induces many elderly households to continue to save after retirement. Furthermore, many households are so accustomed to saving that they do not change this lifelong habit at retirement. Finally, some households appear to find pleasure in amassing wealth. They like having wealth quite separate from the consumption opportunities that the wealth provides. These considerations explain why many households continue to be surplus units even after retirement.

Other Reasons for Saving by Working Households

There are several additional reasons that working households save. For example, it is not only young households that save in order to make a down payment on a house or a car. Furthermore, some households do not borrow for major items, but

---

[44] As many homeowners have learned, house prices can rise in value faster than inflation and provide capital gains income.

accumulate the needed funds through saving. In either case, households have to save until enough wealth is accumulated for a down payment or outright purchase of a major item.

In addition, few households' incomes are as regular or predictable as depicted in Figure 3.8. Households use their wealth to cushion the effects on consumption of *transitory* movements in income. For example, households reduce wealth (dissave) during periods of unemployment in an effort to maintain consumption. Conversely, the same households might save most, if not all, of an unexpected increase in income in the belief that what goes up might go down. Thus, transitory fluctuations in income produce fluctuations in saving and wealth.

Finally, the rate of interest may affect saving behavior. As shown in the Robinson Crusoe story, an increase in the interest rate will, under certain circumstances, induce a household to reduce current consumption in favor of increased consumption in the future.[45] That is to say, a rise in the interest rate induces the household to increase saving relative to current income. It was shown in the Crusoe story that the response of current consumption and saving to a change in the interest rate depends upon two effects. First, there is the substitution effect that induces the household to reduce current consumption (raise current saving) for given current income when the interest rate rises.[46] Second, there is an income effect because a higher interest rate increases the interest income on present and future wealth.[47] This higher interest income can be spread over the household's life cycle of consumption. Economic theory does not allow one to predict how the increased interest earnings will be allocated between current and future consumption. It appears plausible to assume, however, that the increased interest income will be spread relatively evenly between increased current consumption and increased future consumption. Thus, the income effect will probably raise current consumption and offset the substitution effect to some degree. The size of the offset cannot be predicted theoretically, and so the issue is an empirical one. Unfortunately, there is little reliable empirical evidence upon which to draw a conclusion. Despite the lack of firm empirical confirmation, we shall assume that an increase in the interest rate increases the current rate of saving relative to current income.

---

[45] Under other circumstances, a rise in the interest rate produces no change in saving and could even produce a decline in saving.

[46] The direction of this effect can be predicted on theoretical grounds.

[47] For reasons that will be made clearer in the next two chapters, an increase in the interest rate reduces the value of households' current wealth. This reduction may lead households to increase current saving in order to replenish the lost wealth. A decrease in the interest rate increases the value of current wealth. This rise in wealth may lead households to reduce current saving because part of their wealth-accumulation objectives have been met by the capital gain on their assets.

SUMMARY

This chapter has described the fundamental economic forces affecting the accumulation of assets, liabilities, and wealth in an economy. The desire of households to maintain a relatively smooth level of consumption over their life cycles is an important factor affecting this accumulation. When households save, they are consuming less than their current incomes. Saving adds to wealth. The assets in which the wealth is embodied provide stores of value that allow households to consume more than their incomes in the future. Thus, the decision to save is the decision to reduce current consumption below current income in return for greater consumption in the future. Just as Robinson Crusoe saved his potatoes to eat later, households save from their incomes and use their accumulated wealth to support consumption in the future.

When households dissave, they are consuming an amount that exceeds their current incomes. In the absence of borrowing, dissaving is possible only if households have wealth (assets) that can be liquidated. When borrowing is possible, a household can borrow to support consumption in excess of income and accumulated wealth. Borrowing is also used to acquire assets in excess of wealth. Thus, households accumulate liabilities, in part, so that they can accumulate assets. This accumulation of assets does not constitute saving, however, because the addition to assets equals the addition to liabilities and wealth is unaffected.

The decision to save or to dissave is influenced by the stage of a household in its life cycle of earnings. Young households tend to have high levels of consumption relative to their incomes. Young households often dissave if they have wealth or if they can borrow. As a household's income rises over time, saving rises relative to income. During the middle years of their life cycles, households save in order to accumulate wealth that is used to support consumption during retirement. When retirement occurs, some households dissave and use their previously accumulated wealth to support consumption in excess of current income.

There are other reasons for saving or dissaving. For example, many households save in order to accumulate a down payment for a major asset such as a car or a house. Furthermore, many households save in order to build a nest egg that can be used to maintain consumption when there are temporary declines in income. When the declines occur, households dissave and use the wealth to support a level of consumption in excess of current income. Finally, many households save in order to build estates that can be left to their children, and many retired households continue to save for a variety of reasons.

The story of Robinson Crusoe illustrates that if wealth is embodied in productive capacity, more consumption can be achieved in the future than if the wealth is held in nonproductive form. Just as Robinson Crusoe could increase his total consumption by lending potatoes to Friday for planting rather than storing them, an economy can increase its total consumption by "planting" its wealth in productive capacity. If wealth lies fallow, it will only support an increase in future consumption that is equal to the reduction in current consumption. If the wealth is invested in productive capacity, however, the amount of future consumption exceeds the reduction in current consumption.

In modern economies, wealth holders usually do not invest directly in productive capacity. Rather, they lend to firms who invest in productive capacity. Wealth holders are willing to lend their wealth because they receive interest on the loans. Receipt of interest adds to the net income of wealth holders and allows them to support additional consumption in the future. The increased productive capacity of firms allows them to produce the additional consumption goods in the future. The interest rate that is received on loans measures the gain in future consumption that is achieved by reducing current consumption. It is impossible to determine theoretically the effect of an increase in the interest rate on consumption and saving. We shall assume that an increase in the interest rate raises current saving and reduces current consumption. In the absence of firm empirical evidence, this behavior cannot be viewed with much confidence, however.

When bidding for loans, firms must have a method for measuring the profitability of adding to productive capacity. The discounted present value of the net income stream earned from the additional capacity provides the measuring stick. The interest rate plays a crucial role in determining discounted present value. The higher the interest rate, the lower the discounted present value of a project. It is profitable for a firm to add to capacity when the discounted present value of the net income from a project exceeds its purchase price. When the interest rate rises, the discounted present value falls, and firms reduce their investment in productive capacity.

Not all firms borrow in order to add to productive capacity. Some firms use their own accumulated wealth to acquire additional capacity. Firms with accumulated wealth have the opportunity to lend their wealth to others or to pay dividends to their owners. The opportunity cost of using wealth for internal expansion of capacity is the inability to lend the funds or to pay dividends. Surplus firms also compute the discounted present value of their investment projects, and they add to capacity only if the discounted present value exceeds the price of the project. The interest rate affects the investment decisions of deficit and surplus firms in the same way.

The next several chapters of this book describe how the decisions of households concerning the accumulation of assets, liabilities, and wealth are coordinated with the decisions of firms. We shall see that the primary function of the financial system is to channel resources from wealth holders to deficit units. Without a financial system, much of wealth would lie fallow, and the economy could not grow and prosper.

SELECTED REFERENCES

Hirshleifer, Jack, *Investment, Interest, and Capital*, Englewood Cliffs, N.J.: Prentice-Hall, 1970.

Modigliani, Franco and R. Brumberg, "Utility Analysis and the Consumption Function," in Kenneth Kurihare (ed.), *Post-Keynesian Economics*, New Brunswick, N.J.: Rutgers University Press, 1954.

THE FINANCIAL SYSTEM

4

The financial system is comprised of markets and institutions that channel funds from wealth holders to deficit units. This chapter explains why there is a financial system and describes the various markets and institutions in the system.

In the absence of a financial system, wealth holders can only hold their assets in the form of money,[1] durable commodities, physical capital, or funds placed directly with deficit units. Each of these alternatives has advantages and disadvantages to wealth holders. Holding money usually requires the least effort. Most income is received as money, so savers can simply let their savings accumulate in this form. As we saw in Chapter 1, money is not an ideal form of wealth when there is inflation that erodes its purchasing power. Uncertainty about the future price level makes money an uncertain store of value. Some wealth holders attempt to avoid declines in the purchasing power of money by acquiring durable commodities. When the price of a commodity rises at the same rate as prices in general, its purchasing power is maintained. Uncertainty about the future price of commodities plus the costs of purchasing, storing, and selling them can make commodities unattractive to many wealth holders, however. Physical capital is an attractive asset for business because it is a factor of production, but direct ownership of physical capital is not a feasible form of wealth for most households.[2] The final option available to wealth holders involves transfers of funds to deficit units. These transfers can take two forms. Wealth holders can either grant loans to

---

[1] In a world without a financial system, there are no transactions accounts, so all money is currency and coin.
[2] Here we are excluding durable consumer goods from capital. Factors determining the demand for capital goods by firms were discussed in Chapter 3.

deficit units or purchase ownership shares in businesses. Loans and ownership shares are attractive to some wealth holders, but the costs of acquiring and selling these assets, along with the risks they present, can make them unattractive forms in which to hold wealth.

In the absence of a financial system, wealth holders and deficit units must make direct contact and negotiate the terms on which loans are granted or ownership shares are purchased. There are several factors that make this direct contact costly and, in many cases, infeasible. Firms often want to raise substantial sums of money to finance additions to productive capacity. The size of the transactions are often beyond the means of an individual wealth holder. Thus, firms must go through the costly process of locating and dealing directly with a number of wealth holders. Furthermore, wealth holders may want to invest their funds for a different length of time than desired by firms. For example, a household that wants to make a consumption expenditure in the relatively near future is willing to grant only a short-term loan. The borrowing firm may need to retain the funds for a longer period than is consistent with the household's preferences. If the firm borrows for a short period of time, it has to bear the costs of arranging a new loan to replace the one it repays. This practice can be costly and, at times, impractical. Furthermore, many wealth holders are not willing to place their savings with a firm that might be incapable of repaying the agreed-upon interest and principal or incapable of paying dividends. Other wealth holders are willing to provide funds, but they demand such a high interest rate or such a high return on their ownership shares to compensate them for the risk that firms cannot use the funds profitably.

Consumers as deficit units face even greater problems. It is difficult and often impossible for them to find wealth holders who are willing to grant them loans. An extraordinary amount of time and effort must be expended to find a potential lender, and a loan often can be obtained only at a very high interest rate.

Problems of achieving direct contact between wealth holders and deficit units led to the development of a number of financial markets and institutions that specialize in bringing these two groups together. Specialization has produced a complex, refined, and effective financial system that has greatly reduced the costs of channeling funds from wealth holders to deficit units. This chapter describes the financial system, but does not attempt to provide an exhaustive list of all markets or of all institutions in the system. Rather, the major elements in the financial system are discussed and the economic forces that create specialization are analyzed.

PROPERTIES OF FINANCIAL INSTRUMENTS

A great deal can be learned about the financial system by examining the properties of *financial instruments,* defined to be money, loans (debts), and ownership shares. We use the term *securities* to denote loans and ownership shares.

Financial instruments differ in divisibility, transactions costs, liquidity, and price predictability and, thus, differ in their attractiveness to wealth holders and deficit units.

Divisibility

Divisibility of an asset refers to the size of the units in which it can be purchased or sold. Many wealth holders prefer assets that are highly divisible so that they can make purchases or sales of any desired magnitude. If an asset is highly divisible, either small or large transactions can be conducted. If the asset is not divisible, only large transactions are possible, and wealth holders lose flexibility in adjusting their asset holdings.

There are significant differences in the divisibility of various assets. For example, it is rarely possible to purchase or sell a fraction of a car or a house. Money is divisible down to the last penny, and some other financial assets are highly divisible.[3] Wealth holders are not able to purchase securities that are as divisible as money, however, and many securities are available only in relatively large denominations.

Securities lack the divisibility of money because it is too costly for deficit units to issue highly divisible debts or ownership shares. For example, it would be very costly for a firm to borrow $1 million in the form of one million bonds of $1 each. Rather, it issues bonds in minimum denominations of $1000 per bond.

Most wealth holders prefer highly divisible financial assets, and most deficit units prefer to issue relatively indivisible securities. Financial institutions developed to bridge the gap between the preferences of these two groups.

Transactions Costs

Transactions costs for wealth holders are the costs of purchasing and selling assets. Transactions costs for deficit units are the costs of selling securities to wealth holders.

Wealth holders can usually avoid transactions costs if they are willing to hold their assets as money. For income that is received in the form of money, saving is automatically in the form of money.[4] Thus, if wealth holders are willing to accumulate wealth as money, transactions costs are avoided. If they want to hold any

---

[3] We shall see later in this chapter that savings accounts and money market funds are highly divisible.

[4] We saw in Chapter 3 that capital gain income occurs as an increase in the price of an asset. This income can be "realized" only if the asset is sold, which involves a transaction cost.

other kind of assets, however, transactions costs must be incurred. In the absence
of a financial system, transactions costs are often high. For transactions to occur,
purchasers and sellers of an asset must locate each other and then negotiate the
terms at which it changes hands. Aside from the costs of searching for someone
with whom to do business and the costs of direct negotiation, there are also costs
of obtaining relevant information. For example, when a wealth holder is considering making a loan to a firm, costs are incurred in obtaining and evaluating
information on the firm's future profitability. This information is crucial to determining the riskiness of the loan. Similar costs are incurred in evaluating the riskiness of a security that is purchased from another wealth holder.

Deficit units also incur transactions costs when issuing securities. Costs must be
incurred in searching for and negotiating with potential purchasers of their securities and in obtaining the information required to offer a security whose maturity
and earnings are attractive to wealth holders. A large firm is likely to incur less
cost in issuing a security than is a small firm because it is known to many wealth
holders. A large firm is also likely to have a substantial quantity of securities outstanding, and its success in meeting interest and other payments on these securities
will be known to wealth holders. Because wealth holders are likely to know more
about a large firm than a small firm, they also incur less cost in assessing the riskiness of the securities issued by a large firm.

In the absence of a financial system, transactions costs are substantial, even for
large firms, and they are often prohibitive for small firms and for households.
Financial markets and institutions developed that have reduced transactions costs
for everyone.

Liquidity

Liquidity is the ability to convert an asset quickly into money without experiencing a significant reduction in its value. Assets vary significantly in their degree of
liquidity. Most physical assets are not very liquid. Consider the case of a person
who wants to sell a house. Houses are bought and sold every day, but they differ
from each other, and a given house is sold infrequently. When a house is put up
for sale, time is required to inform prospective purchasers of the house's availability. Even then, home buyers can inspect only a limited number of houses in a day.
Often only a few prospective buyers are in the market at any one time for the particular kind of house being offered. The market for a house is "thin."

A seller discovers that time is required to get the "full" price for a house. *Full
price* is the price that a house can fetch in the market if sufficient time is taken to
find a buyer. The more quickly the owner attempts to sell the house, the more
likely it is that a price below the full price will have to be accepted. For example,
a person who decides one morning to sell a house and insists that it be sold that
day will probably discover that a buyer can be found on such short notice only if
the price is very low. In fact, it may be impossible to find a buyer. If the seller
allows more time to elapse between the decision to sell and the actual sale of the

house, a higher price is likely to be realized. There is an upper limit to the price that can be realized, however. Prospective buyers will not pay a higher price for this house than for another one like it. With the passage of time, a number of buyers have done their comparison shopping, and the seller cannot expect to receive a higher price by keeping the house on the market for a longer period of time. The full price has been reached.

It should be noted that the relationship between the realized price and the full price holds only "on average." A seller might be lucky and find on the first day a purchaser who will pay the full price. But the seller might also be unlucky and need more time than usual to obtain the full price. The point, however, is that a significant amount of time typically must elapse between the decision to sell a house and the actual sale if the full price is to be realized.

The relationship between elapsed time and the price realized on an asset can be stated more generally. Assume that some asset has a known full price that can be realized if sufficient time is allowed to elapse between the time when the asset is put up for sale and the time of its actual sale. Call this price $P*$. If the owner attempts to sell the asset more quickly, a price lower than $P*$ will, on average, have to be accepted. The shorter the time between the decision to sell and the actual sale, the lower the realized price of the asset.

Figure 4.1 shows the relationship between elapsed time and the percentage of $P*$ that is realized for a house. If the seller is truly compulsive and attempts to sell the house the instant after deciding to sell it, there is no price at which the house can be sold; the realized price as a percentage of $P*$ is zero. As more and more time elapses between the decision to sell and the actual sale, the percentage rises until 100 percent is reached at time t_F. After that time, the full price is realized, and the seller can expect to do no better.

It is now possible to give a better explanation of liquidity. The shorter the amount of time that elapses before an asset's full price is realized, the more liquid the asset. For a perfectly liquid asset, the full price is realized immediately. That is to say, it can be converted immediately into money at its full value. Money is, of course, perfectly liquid in this sense. Other assets are less liquid than money. A house is an illiquid asset. Securities are more liquid, but in the absence of a financial system, a substantial amount of time may be required to find a buyer who is willing to pay the full price for securities. Furthermore, the larger the amount of securities to be sold, the longer it is likely to take to sell them at their full price. For large sales, it might be necessary to spread the sales out over time to avoid forcing down their price. Finally, some securities (loans and ownership shares) cannot be sold prior to maturity. In this situation, short-term securities are more liquid than long-term securities because less time must elapse before they mature. If securities can be sold prior to maturity, their degree of liquidity is measured by the time required to realize their full market price.

Other things being equal, wealth holders prefer liquid assets because of the flexibility these assets afford. They can be induced to hold relatively illiquid assets if the income from these assets is sufficiently high relative to the income from more liquid assets. Most wealth holders do not want to commit all their

FIGURE 4.1
LIQUIDITY.

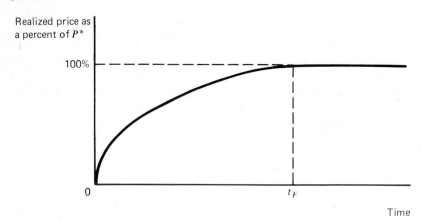

wealth to relatively illiquid assets, however, even if these assets offer high returns. They want to hold at least part of their wealth in liquid form to meet unforeseen contingencies. If illiquid assets must be sold to meet these needs, the price that is realized from a quick sale can be sufficiently low to wipe out the higher incomes that illiquid assets might offer.

The desire of wealth holders for liquidity can come into conflict with the preferences of deficit units. Deficit units often want to raise funds by issuing securities with long-term maturities in order to save the costs and uncertainties of frequently refinancing. These securities are often relatively illiquid. The conflicting objectives of surplus and deficit units are largely reconciled by financial markets and institutions.

Price Predictability

The final property of financial instruments concerns the accuracy with which their future prices can be predicted. Any asset is a store of value that carries purchasing power into the future. Wealth holders must be concerned, therefore, about the price at which the asset can be sold in the future and about the purchasing power of the money that is received when the asset is sold. A person who holds a security may be able to sell it quickly prior to maturity, but the price is uncertain. Even if the seller allows for the time required to achieve $P*$, it is impossible to know with certainty what $P*$ will be. The price of a security depends upon the demand by others for it and upon the amount of the asset being supplied by others. These demand and supply conditions depend upon a variety of factors, and the price of the security in the future cannot be predicted perfectly. A security may be highly liquid, but unattractive to many wealth holders because the holder does not know the full price at which it can be sold in the future. Assets differ in the predictability of their price. The less predictable the price, the riskier and less attractive an asset is to many wealth holders.[5]

Summary

Every asset has a particular degree of divisibility, liquidity, and price predictability. Every asset also has its own transactions costs of purchase and sale. It is the combination of these characteristics that is relevant to wealth holders. A financial instrument that appears attractive in terms of one characteristic may be unattractive in terms of other characteristics. For example, a security may be highly liquid, but it may be available only in large denominations. Similarly, a security that is highly liquid and is available in small denominations might have high transactions costs, or its future full price might be difficult to predict. The financial system has succeeded in reducing transactions cost and in increasing liquidity, divisibility, and price predictability for many financial instruments.

SECURITIES MARKETS

An early step in the evolution of the financial system was the development of organized markets for securities (debts and ownership shares) issued by large firms. A market offers the advantage of bringing a number of buyers and sellers together. Transactions costs are reduced because both sellers and purchasers save substantial time and effort in finding each other. Furthermore, with a number of purchasers and sellers, the price of a security is less likely to move erratically than if individual transactions are conducted outside the market. Holders of securities can sell them at any time without having to worry about the possibility that a better price might have been realized if more time had been spent searching out buyers. Thus, the development of organized markets significantly reduced transactions costs and increased the liquidity of securities.

Deficit firms also benefit from securities markets. Because holders of debt can sell the securities in the market, firms do not have to be so concerned about tailoring the maturity of their debt instruments to meet the liquidity needs of individual wealth holders. In the absence of markets, firms have to pay a relatively high interest rate to induce wealth holders to purchase their illiquid, long-term debt. Alternatively, they have to issue short-term debt and bear transactions costs of refinancing the debt. Thus, without markets, borrowing is more costly and capital

---

[5] The concept of risk and the attitudes of investors concerning risk are discussed in Chapter 5.

formation is inhibited. With markets, firms can issue long-term debt at lower interest rates because they do not have to compensate wealth holders for illiquidity. The market provides the liquidity. Long-term borrowing expanded significantly when bond markets developed and capital formation was encouraged.

Securities markets also allow firms to issue ownership shares in significant quantities. Ownership shares have no maturity; they exist so long as the issuing firm stays in business or until the firm buys them back. Relatively few wealth holders are interested in permanently locking their savings into ownership shares. The development of stock markets, which are markets in which shares are purchased and sold, made ownership shares attractive to many wealth holders. The shares became more liquid. When stock markets were established, deficit units greatly increased their issuance of ownership shares.

Market Specialists

Wealth holders and deficit units usually do not participate directly in securities markets; they engage the services of specialists who execute actual transactions and provide other services. Activities of various specialists increase the efficiency of securities markets by reducing transactions costs, increasing liquidity, and limiting fluctuations in security prices.

Brokers and Dealers

Security brokers are agents who are commissioned to buy or sell securities. Just as one retains a real estate broker to sell a house, one commissions a broker to buy or sell securities. Transactions can be accomplished by a telephone call to a broker, who executes the purchase or sale of securities for a fee.

Brokers spend their time making contact with a number of potential purchasers and sellers of securities. As a result of this contact, they can accomplish a transaction more easily than almost any individual wealth holder. Brokers also ease the problem associated with matching the needs of buyers and sellers. For example, a particular seller of securities may have a large block of securities to sell that could preclude sale to most individual wealth holders. The broker, who knows several wealth holders wishing to purchase smaller amounts of these securities, can put together the small purchases to accommodate the sale of the block of securities.

Market transactions are also conducted by security dealers. The primary difference between a dealer and a broker is that a dealer holds an inventory of securities from which purchases and sales are made. By contrast, a broker does not hold an inventory, but is simply an agent who purchases and sells securities for others. A dealer brings buyers and sellers together indirectly by purchasing securities that are then held in the dealer's inventory and by selling securities from the inventory. Dealers receive an income for their services by having a lower purchase price than sales price for securities. There is nothing unusual in this activity. It is in principle little different from the activities of a dealer in art or in used cars. By varying their inventories of securities, dealers help reduce the volatility of prices in many markets. The mechanics of how this is done is discussed in the appendix to this chapter.

Securities Analysts

The next type of specialist is the securities analyst. These specialists spend their time analyzing the financial reports of various firms, conducting interviews with management, and generally obtaining information about the earnings prospects and riskiness of various firms. The analysts, in turn, communicate this information to potential investors for a fee.[6]

Securities analysts can obtain information on a number of firms at a relatively low cost. Each wealth holder does not have to go through the process of performing a financial analysis of the various firms whose securities might be purchased. Sophisticated financial analyses can be obtained from specialists. It is efficient to have a small number of highly trained analysts do this work. Thus, analysts reduce transactions costs and uncertainty in securities markets.

Investment Bankers

Firms typically issue new stocks and bonds in relatively large quantities. There is a substantial amount of fixed cost in issuing new securities, so firms spread the cost over a large number of securities. This reduces the transactions costs per security.

A firm wants to sell its new securities for as high a price as possible, but it is often difficult to sell a large block of securities without depressing their price. Faced with this problem, a firm often enlists the services of an *investment banker*. Investment banking is not banking in the sense of accepting deposits and granting loans. An investment banker finds buyers for *new* securities issued by deficit firms. Some investment bankers sell newly issued securities for a fee, and others purchase the securities from the issuing firm and sell them to the public.

Issuers often have investment bankers bid against each other for the right to distribute new securities. Bids take the form of the price at which an investment banker is willing to purchase the security. When an investment bank purchases newly issued securities for resale to the public, it is said that it *underwrites* the issue. The investment banker earns profits by purchasing the securities at a lower price than they are sold.

Investment banking reduces transactions costs for both issuers and purchasers of securities. A firm can often issue new securities at lower cost through an invest-

---

[6] Securities analysts are frequently employed by brokers who offer financial advice to their customers. The costs of the analysts' services are included in the overall charge for securities transactions. Other brokers do not offer financial advice, and their charges are lower. They are commonly called discount brokers.

ment banker than through direct sale in the market. It is often less costly for an investment banker to obtain information concerning the availability of purchasers of new securities because investment bankers have continuing contact with a number of potential buyers of securities. Investment bankers also have knowledge of the current situation in securities markets, so they can aid the issuing firm in setting a price on its security that is competitive with other securities. Investment bankers can often provide this information at lower cost than if the firm itself tried to keep abreast of market conditions.

Investment bankers also reduce transactions costs for potential purchasers of new securities. Wealth holders often do not find it worthwhile to become experts on a particular firm or industry. Investment bankers can provide information on a number of firms and save the wealth holders a great deal of time, effort, and expense. Thus, investment bankers offer the services of securities analysts to both purchasers and issuers of new securities.

Virtues and Deficiencies of Securities Markets and Specialists

In the United States there are organized markets for thousands of different securities, and billions of dollars change hands in these markets each day. Some markets handle short-term debt issued by the government and major corporations. These debts are issued with maturities ranging from one day to one year.[7] Other markets handle longer-term debts issued by governments and business, and still others handle purchases and sales of corporate stock.[8] It is an easy matter to obtain price quotations for securities in any of these markets and to arrange a purchase or sale. The markets function smoothly and well and, in the process, serve the needs of many wealth holders and deficit units.

Despite their many virtues, securities markets exclude many participants. For example, some wealth holders are too small to participate. Firms typically issue securities in minimum denominations that are too large for many wealth holders. Furthermore, transactions costs can be prohibitive for small wealth holders. A broker, for example, may have to spend as much time arranging a security purchase for a $10 investor as for a $10 million investor. As a result, brokers charge small investors higher fees per dollar of transaction. These higher fees can make securities unattractive to small investors.

Furthermore, many wealth holders find securities too risky. Because of high transactions costs and indivisibilities of securities, they can only afford to purchase the securities of one firm or, at most, a few firms. Small investors often find that holding securities of one firm, or even a few firms, is too risky a venture. They have to put all their securities eggs in one basket. For many investors this lack of diversification is unattractive. Large investors buy the securities of many firms so they have their eggs in a number of baskets. Large wealth holders can stumble in

---

[7] The market for these short-term debt instruments is called the *money market*.

[8] The market for longer-term securities is called the *capital market*.

appraising the profitability of a particular firm, but if they hold securities of a number of firms, a stumble will not break all the eggs.[9]

Small firms also encounter high transactions costs when operating in securities markets. Small firms issue small amounts of securities, and they find it difficult to obtain investment banking services at low cost. Investment bankers have fixed costs that make the handling of a small issue of securities almost as costly as a large issue. They charge relatively high fees to small issuers in order to cover these costs. These fees can be too high to make security issues by small firms profitable. Even if the small firm does find it worthwhile to issue securities, other specialists, such as stockbrokers and securities analysts, do not find it worth their while to develop expertise and detailed knowledge in the operation of small firms. Thus, it is difficult for the investing public to obtain information at reasonable costs on the future prospects for small firms. The market for the securities of a small firm is limited.

Despite the significant contributions of securities markets and specialists, there is still scope for additional methods of increasing the efficiency of the financial system. These methods involve the operations of financial intermediaries. These intermediaries solve many of the problems of indivisibilities, transactions costs, and risk that make securities markets an incomplete vehicle for serving wealth holders and deficit units.

FINANCIAL INTERMEDIARIES

Financial intermediaries are firms that gather funds from wealth holders and distribute them to deficit units. Wealth holders hold part of their wealth in the form of ownership shares or debt instruments issued by the intermediaries. The financial intermediaries take the funds obtained from wealth holders and purchase ownership shares and debt instruments issued by deficit units. Thus, financial intermediaries bring wealth holders and deficit units together indirectly.

Financial intermediaries range in form from insurance companies and pension funds to banks and credit unions. They all have the common characteristic of pooling the savings of a number of wealth holders for investments in the securities issued by a number of deficit units. Because financial intermediaries differ in the ways that they channel funds from wealth holders to deficit units, it is probably best to describe some of the major methods by which this is accomplished. In the description, it is useful to distinguish between those financial intermediaries that do not accept deposits and those that do accept deposits.

Nondepository Institutions

One important vehicle for bringing wealth holders and deficit units together indirectly is a *mutual fund*. A mutual fund sells relatively small denomination

---

[9] The benefits of asset diversification are discussed in a less folksy manner in Chapter 5.

securities to wealth holders and uses the proceeds to purchase the market securities of deficit units. A mutual fund earns interest or dividend income, or both, from the securities it holds. It deducts operating expenses and a management fee, and then passes the remainder of the income to wealth holders through dividends on the mutual fund's shares. These dividends fluctuate with the income on the mutual fund's investments.

Mutual funds differ in the kinds of securities that they acquire and in the properties of ownership shares that they sell. Some mutual funds purchase only ownership shares that are traded in the stock market. Among these mutual funds there are differences in the kinds of stocks acquired. Some purchase stocks with stable earnings and prices whereas others buy stocks with more variable earnings and prices. Other mutual funds purchase both stocks and long-term debt, and some buy only debt instruments. A number of mutual funds purchase debt instruments with maturities of under one year. They are called *money market mutual funds.* These mutual funds are in direct competition with depository institutions for the public's liquid assets. They are discussed in greater detail later in this chapter.

Some mutual funds issue ownership shares that are traded on the stock market, and some distribute their shares through advertising campaigns and salespersons. Mutual funds whose shares are not traded on the stock market often agree to buy back, that is, redeem, their securities from holders. The prices of mutual fund shares, both in the stock market and in direct redemptions, are affected by the income performance of the mutual fund and by general market conditions.

The next major form of financial intermediary is the *insurance company.* There are many different kinds of insurance companies, but a popular and simple kind offers life insurance policies coupled with a savings plan. The purchaser of a life insurance policy buys not only insurance but also makes additional payments into a savings plan. The plan allows the individual eventually to accumulate savings that are equal to the original amount of life insurance.

Life insurance companies invest these savings in stocks, bonds, and real estate. They earn income on the assets they hold and pay an interest return on their customers' savings. Insurance companies offer wealth holders an investment that often yields a fixed rate of return. Many wealth holders prefer a fixed rate of return and find it advantageous to place their savings in insurance companies rather than participate directly in securities markets or purchasing mutual fund shares.

Individuals often save for retirement by participating in *pension funds.* Pension funds, like mutual funds and life insurance companies, invest the savings of wealth holders primarily in marketable securities. Many employers offer pension plans as a fringe benefit to employees. Employees often prefer pension plans to mutual funds or insurance policies because contributions to pension plans are not included in their taxable income. Taxes are only postponed, however, because taxable income is increased during retirement by an amount that is based, in part, on withdrawals from pension funds. Individuals are often in lower tax brackets, however, during retirement than when they are working. Thus, contributions to pension funds not only postpone the time when taxes are paid, but they also often reduce total taxes paid.

Mutual funds, insurance savings plans, and pension funds all pool the savings of a large number of relatively small wealth holders and use these funds to purchase securities issued by a number of deficit units. These financial intermediaries offer several advantages to wealth holders over direct participation in securities markets. A wealth holder may not have sufficient resources to purchase securities that are issued in large denominations. When the resources of many wealth holders are pooled, it is possible to purchase large denomination securities. Furthermore, high transactions costs and indivisibilities often prevent individuals from buying the securities of a number of different deficit units. With limited diversification, the investments of wealth holders are vulnerable to the performance of one, or only a few, securities. By pooling the resources of many individuals, financial intermediaries can buy the securities of a number of different firms, allowing the financial intermediaries to obtain the benefits of diversification. This diversification reduces the volatility of earnings for financial intermediaries. They, in turn, offer less risky assets to small wealth holders than are available from direct participation in securities markets.

Finally, the scale of operation for financial intermediaries allows them to employ analysts who assess the profitability and risk of purchasing the securities of various firms. Wealth holders who place their savings with these intermediaries do not have to evaluate the profitability and risk of purchasing securities of various firms; they only need to assess the profitability and risk of the financial intermediary itself. These wealth holders can save transactions costs in terms of time, effort, and broker or dealer fees by placing their savings with a financial intermediary rather than by participating directly in securities markets. Financial intermediaries offer a higher return or lower risk, or both, to many wealth holders than they can achieve by operating directly in securities markets.

Financial intermediaries also benefit deficit units by reducing the cost of the direct sale of securities. These intermediaries are so large that it can pay the issuer to make a direct sale of securities to them rather than use an investment banker. Even if an investment banker is used, the existence of financial intermediaries still reduces the cost of sale because investment bankers can deal directly with the intermediary rather than with a number of smaller purchasers.

The activities of mutual funds, insurance companies, and pension funds meet the longer-term needs of many wealth holders and deficit units. Wealth holders who deal with these financial intermediaries are often looking for relatively long-term investments and plan to retain their savings with the intermediaries for substantial periods of time. This behavior, in part, allows these financial intermediaries to make long-term investments. Furthermore, because the financial intermediaries pool savings of a large number of individuals, they have a relatively stable and predictable source of funds. Though some wealth holders may withdraw their savings from a financial intermediary, they are likely to be replaced by others. Thus, these financial intermediaries can commit funds for relatively long periods of time even though individual wealth holders may come and go. The ability of the financial intermediaries to make long-term investments often matches the needs of deficit units who are looking for long-term commitments of funds.

The three types of financial intermediaries differ significantly in the ability they offer individuals to withdraw their savings. The instruments issued by mutual funds, for example, are themselves traded in a market or are easily redeemable. Mutual fund shares provide, therefore, a high degree of liquidity to the investing public. There are transactions costs in selling mutual fund shares, however, and the value of the shares does fluctuate with the profitability of the fund and with general market conditions. Transactions costs and uncertainty about the price of the shares can reduce the attractiveness of many mutual funds as short-term investments. Shares in money market mutual funds can be purchased and sold at a very low cost, and their prices are highly stable. They are held extensively as short-term investments.

It is more difficult for individuals to withdraw from insurance and pension arrangements. Typically, for an insurance policy, the savings function represents a commitment over the life of the insurance policy although insurance companies do allow their customers to borrow against accumulated savings. Pension funds represent the least liquid form of investment. It is often difficult to withdraw funds from a pension program prior to retirement. If funds are successfully withdrawn, the employee may be liable for taxes on the accumulated savings. Participants in pension funds typically view these funds as a long-term commitment of savings.

The various financial intermediaries described so far serve an important function in financial markets, but their activities do not meet all the needs of wealth holders and deficit units. Wealth holders typically want to devote part of their savings to highly liquid and divisible investments with low transactions costs and limited price fluctuations. With the exception of money market mutual funds, nondepository financial intermediaries do not meet these needs.

Deficit units also are not completely served by mutual funds, insurance companies, or pension funds. These financial intermediaries typically do not supply funds to firms with short-term borrowing needs.[10] The intermediaries are geared to make long-term investments because it is costly for them to reinvest continually the funds from the repayment of short-term loans. Furthermore, neither securities markets nor nondepository financial intermediaries channel funds to households that are deficit units.[11]

Other financial intermediaries exist to serve the remaining needs of wealth holders and deficit firms and to meet the needs of households as borrowers. Many of these financial intermediaries are called depository institutions.

---

[10] Money market mutual funds do specialize in short-term loans.

[11] Nondepository financial intermediaries do purchase consumer mortgage loans. These activities are discussed in Chapter 8.

Depository Institutions

Depository institutions are financial intermediaries that accept the savings of wealth holders in the form of deposit accounts and lend the funds to deficit units. Commercial banks, savings and loan associations, mutual savings banks, and credit unions are depository institutions. Historically, each type of institution arose to meet a particular kind of financial need of wealth holders or deficit units. Currently, depository institutions specialize in various activities, and this specialization is encouraged, and sometimes required, by government regulation. Each type of institution is discussed in detail in later chapters, but a short summary of their activities is useful at this point.

Commercial banks are the banks described in Chapter 2. The adjective commercial is used to distinguish these banks from other banks, such as mutual savings banks. The adjective also indicates that businesses are heavy users of commercial banks both as borrowers and depositors. Commercial banks have the widest range of depository and lending powers of any type of depository institution.[12]

By custom and law, the other depository institutions are more specialized than commercial banks. *Savings and loans associations* (S&Ls) are primarily in the business of offering deposit accounts to consumers and in financing their purchases of housing. S&Ls provide a limited amount of credit to consumers for purposes other than housing, and they engage in a small amount of lending to business. *Mutual savings banks* (MSBs) are also primarily in the business of providing deposit accounts to consumers and financing the purchases of homes. The powers of MSBs are somewhat less restricted than those of S&Ls. *Credit unions* also offer savings accounts to consumers, but most of their loans are made to consumers for purposes other than the purchase of a home. Credit unions provide relatively short-term loans that are used by consumers for a variety of purposes. Credit unions do provide a limited amount of longer-term loans to finance the purchase of homes, however. A consumer must be a member of a credit union in order to use its services. Membership is restricted to individuals with a "common bond" established by such factors as place of employment, age (retired persons), profession (school teachers), or geography (neighborhood).

Although the various depository institutions have different powers and specializations, they all share the common functions of accepting deposits and granting loans. When funds are deposited with these institutions, they have, in essence, borrowed from the depositor. Customers lend funds to the institution when they make deposits to their accounts. They receive a promise from the institution that the funds will be returned (repaid) in the form of a withdrawal from the account under certain preestablished conditions.

Depository institutions offer various deposit accounts that differ in the conditions under which funds may be withdrawn. All institutions promise to repay

---

[12] In this book, when the term *bank* is used without an adjective to describe the type of bank, the term refers to a commercial bank.

funds deposited in transactions accounts on demand.[13] Having funds available on demand provides perfect liquidity, and transactions accounts offer other advantages as well. Funds in these accounts can be used directly for transactions and, therefore, are a form of money. Furthermore, customers can make a deposit or withdrawal of any size from transactions accounts provided the account is not overdrawn.[14] In contrast, when funds are placed with or withdrawn from securities markets or nondepository institutions, the transactions are for fixed denominations (e.g., $1000 per security). These fixed denominations obviously offer less flexibility than that offered by transactions accounts. Finally, deposits and withdrawals from transactions accounts can be made at low cost. Depository institutions rarely charge for the deposit of funds or for cash withdrawals. Many institutions do charge for processing checks, but these charges are modest compared to the costs of adding or withdrawing funds from securities markets or from mutual funds, insurance companies, and pension funds. Thus, transactions accounts offer almost perfect liquidity, perfect divisibility, and low transactions costs.

There is a second type of deposit account from which customers, in effect, can make withdrawals on demand. This account is called an ordinary savings or passbook account. These accounts are offered by all types of depository institutions. Savings accounts are different from transactions accounts, however, because funds cannot be withdrawn by check or telephone instruction. The customer must appear at the depository institution and receive payment. In December 1982 depository institutions were allowed to offer special savings accounts from which a limited number of transactions could be conducted by check, telephone, or preauthorization. This type of savings account is described in Chapter 8.

Savings accounts have the same flexibility as transactions accounts in terms of the ability to make cash withdrawals on demand and the ability to make deposits and withdrawals of any size. Furthermore, for savings accounts, there are rarely charges for deposits or withdrawals. The only cost to the depositor is the trip to and from the depository institution and the hassle of waiting in line to make a transaction. Savings accounts are less flexible than transactions accounts in the one important respect that checks cannot be written against ordinary savings accounts, and only a limited number of checks can be written against special savings accounts. Thus, savings accounts are not as liquid as checking accounts, but they are equally divisible and have low transactions costs.

Other types of deposits at depository institutions are less liquid because they have fixed, enforced maturities. Withdrawals cannot be made unless the deposi-

---

[13] A transactions account is an account for which cash withdrawals are payable on demand and payments can be made to third parties via checks or by a telephone or other authorized instruction.

[14] Many countries do allow accounts to be overdrawn, and their banks charge interest on these *overdrafts*. The overdraft is simply a form of a loan. Overdrafts generally are not allowed in the United States, but holders of bank credit cards can have overdrawn accounts covered by loans through their credit cards.

tor is willing to pay a substantial penalty. Accounts of this type are called time deposit accounts, and they range in maturity from seven days to eight years. With only a single exception noted further on, there is no market for these accounts, so a customer cannot sell a time deposit prior to maturity. Time deposit accounts also have minimum denominations that are set by depository institutions.[15]

Time deposit accounts are less flexible than transactions or savings accounts because they effectively require that the depositor lend funds to the depository institution until the maturity date of the deposit has been reached. Minimum denomination requirements also reduce flexibility and availability to many depositors. These accounts often offer less liquidity and divisibility and, when withdrawals are made prior to maturity, they have higher transactions costs than do mutual fund shares or direct market securities.

Large depository institutions have an additional means of attracting funds. These institutions issue *large denomination negotiable time deposits* with fixed maturities called certificates of deposits (CDs).[16] Because CDs are negotiable, it is not necessary for purchasers to hold them to maturity. They can be sold in an organized market. This feature makes CDs highly liquid. Other types of time accounts are not negotiable, and they are not so liquid. The maturity of CDs is typically for two to six months, but other maturities are also issued. Certificates of deposits are "deposits" in name only. They are, in fact, debt instruments issued by large depository institutions in competition with securities traded in various markets. The certificates have a minimum denomination of $100,000, but denominations of $1 million are common. Only large depository institutions have need to raise funds in such large chunks, and only large institutions have sufficient reputation to issue instruments that can be traded in an organized market. Certificates of deposit are highly liquid assets that are attractive to large investors, including nondepository financial intermediaries. Commercial banks are the primary issuers of these certificates, but the largest S&Ls and MSBs also issue them.

Interest income is an important inducement that depository institutions use to attract depositors. Until recently in the United States, it was against the law to pay interest on transactions accounts. Recent legislative and regulatory changes have altered this situation. The interest rates paid on many of these accounts move with market interest rates. The interest rates paid on most kinds of saving and time accounts have also been deregulated, and they move with market interest rates. Interest rates on large certificates of deposit do not have government-imposed ceilings.

Safety is the third advantage of the various deposit accounts offered by depository institutions. Federal deposit insurance guarantees safety for the first $100,000

[15] Federal regulation requires a minimum denomination of $2500 for seven to thirty-one day time accounts if the accounts are to pay a market rate of interest.
[16] Depository institutions also issue small denomination non-negotiable time accounts that they call CDs. These should not be confused with the CDs discussed in the text.

deposited in an institution by each customer. Deposit insurance is an important reason that accounts at depository institutions are so popular.

Depository institutions offer deposit services and pay interest on their accounts in order to attract funds that are lent to deficit units. These loans typically have a longer maturity than the deposits that support them. By pooling the accounts of many depositors, depository institutions find that their deposits are relatively stable. Pooling the deposits of various customers allows depository institutions to make loans that have a longer maturity than the maturity of the deposits themselves. For example, commercial banks, which have large transactions account liabilities, are able to make loans that have maturities ranging from a few days to several years. Similarly, savings and loan associations and mutual savings banks are able to make mortgage loans that have maturities of twenty to thirty years.

Depository institutions provide a significant service to many deficit units. It is difficult for relatively small deficit units to issue securities that are attractive to direct investors or to nondepository financial intermediaries. Depository institutions specialize in providing loans to them. These institutions have developed procedures for lending to relatively small deficit units at low cost. For example, depository institutions have developed methods of evaluating the credit worthiness of households who want to finance the purchase of houses, cars, and other durable goods. These borrowers cannot go to an organized securities market, issue their own securities, and obtain the needed funds. They can go to a depository institution and, if they meet the criteria of credit worthiness, obtain the funds from these institutions.

Finance Companies

Finance companies lend to consumers. These companies do not accept deposits, but instead issue securities directly in securities markets. They use the funds raised in these markets to make loans to consumers. Consumers to whom they lend cannot issue securities directly, but the finance company can issue its own security backed by a pool of consumer loans. Finance companies, like some depository institutions, have developed low-cost methods of evaluating credit worthiness and of processing consumer loans. Finance companies can obtain funds in securities markets and process loans at sufficiently low cost to allow them to charge consumers lower interest rates than many consumers would have to pay for alternative sources of credit. Finance companies limit the risk of many loans by requiring the borrower to secure the loan with an asset such as a car or house that can be sold should the borrower default on the loan. Depository institutions also use the same method of limiting risk.

Some finance companies are independent entities, but the largest ones are owned by major manufacturing and retailing firms and are called "captives." For example, automobile manufacturers like General Motors and Ford have their own finance companies that help finance the automobiles that they sell. The automobile companies use their captives to channel funds from wealth holders to the deficit units that are purchasing their cars.

Money Market Mutual Funds

Money market mutual funds issue shares to the public and invest the proceeds in money market instruments. These instruments include short-term government securities, large denomination CDs issued by depository institutions, and short-term debt issued by businesses, including finance companies. The details of money market mutual fund operations are given in Chapter 8. For purposes of this chapter, it is sufficient to observe that these mutual funds offer many of the same advantages as accounts at depository institutions. The shares of these mutual funds are highly liquid. They can be sold by writing a check, by making a telephone call, or by writing a letter. Furthermore, the shares pay a market rate of interest, and they offer low risk.[17] Money market mutual funds invest in safe assets such as government securities and debt issued by stable and profitable depository institutions and business firms. Risk is further reduced by diversification of the mutual funds' investments in the debt of many separate companies.

FINANCIAL ASSETS AND LIABILITIES OF HOUSEHOLDS, NONFINANCIAL BUSINESS, AND FINANCIAL INTERMEDIARIES

In this section, we put the pieces of the financial system together to examine the financial assets and liabilities of households, nonfinancial business, and financial intermediaries. By looking at these three elements together, we can see how various elements of the financial system perform the crucial task of channeling funds from wealth holders to deficit units.

Table 4.1 shows the major financial assets and liabilities of households at the end of 1982. For ease of comparison, both dollar and percentage figures are shown. In total, the household sector has $5384 billion (i.e., $5.384 trillion) of financial assets and $1741 billion of financial liabilities. The financial wealth (total assets less total liabilities) of the household sector is $3643 billion. This financial wealth is the net contribution of households to deficit units.

Households have only 6 percent of their total financial assets in currency and transactions accounts (money). A sizable 27 percent of total financial assets is in savings and time accounts, however. When these accounts are combined with transactions accounts, households have one third of their total financial assets with depository institutions. The next three items are assets held with mutual funds, life insurance companies, and pension funds. These account for 6, 5, and 17 percent of total financial assets, respectively. In total, 28 percent of total household financial assets are held with these nondepository financial intermediaries. When

---

[17] As will be explained in detail in Chapter 10, the popularity of money market mutual funds was a major factor in eliminating government-imposed interest rate ceilings at depository institutions.

TABLE 4.1
FINANCIAL ASSETS AND LIABILITIES OF HOUSEHOLDS[a]
(YEAR END 1982)

	Assets		Liabilities	
	Billions of $	Percent of total	Billions of $	Percent of total
Currency and transactions accounts	$ 307	6		
Saving and time accounts	1,469	27		
Mutual fund shares	297	6		
Life insurance reserves	247	5		
Pension funds	933	17		
Government securities	506	9		
Corporate and foreign bonds	64	1		
Corporate stock	1,232	23		
Mortgage loans	186	3	$1,137	65
Cosumer credit			431	25
All other	143	3	173	10
Total	$5,384	100	$1,741	100

Total financial assets less total financial liabilities: $3,643

[a] Includes households, personal trusts, and nonprofit organizations.
Source: *Flow of Funds Accounts, Assets and Liabilities Outstanding 1957–82,* Board of Governors of the Federal Reserve System, Washington, D.C., August 1983.

depository and nondepository institutions are combined, households have over 60 percent of their total financial assets with financial intermediaries of various kinds.

The remaining items in Table 4.1 are financial instruments that are held directly or issued directly by households. Nine percent of total financial assets is in the form of government securities. These are debts issued both by the federal government and by the states and their political subdivisions. Directly held corporate and foreign securities constitute only 1 percent of total household financial assets. In contrast, 23 percent of financial assets is in directly held corporate stock. Households hold $186 billion of mortgage loans as direct loans to other households and to business. This is swamped by the $1137 billion of mortgage debt of households. Mortgage loans are the largest liability of households, constituting 65 percent of total financial liabilities. Consumer borrowing is also large. It is 25 percent of total household financial liabilities. The final entry in the table is "all other" assets and liabilities. Here the assets are roughly offset by liabilities.

Table 4.2 shows the financial assets and liabilities of nonfinancial business. Here we see that nonfinancial business is in a deficit position. Total financial assets are $1174 billion, and total financial liabilities are $2178 billion. Thus, the nonfinancial business sector has a net deficit position of $1004 billion.

In the interest of brevity, the financial asset and liability categories for nonfinancial business are not shown with much detail. Currency and transactions accounts are 8 percent of total financial assets, and saving and time accounts are 8 percent. This gives a total of 16 percent of total financial assets held with deposi-

TABLE 4.2
FINANCIAL ASSETS AND LIABILITIES OF NONFINANCIAL BUSINESS
(YEAR END 1982)

	Assets		Liabilities	
	Billions of $	Percent of total	Billions of $	Percent of total
Currency and transactions accounts	$ 99	8		
Saving and time accounts[a]	99	8		
Credit market instruments	104	9	$1,685	77
Trade credit	489	42	389	18
All other	383	33	104	5
Total	$1,174	100	$2,178	100

Total financial assets less total financial liabilities: − $1,004

[a] Includes foreign accounts and repurchase agreements.
Source: *Flow of Funds Accounts, Assets and Liabilities Outstanding 1957−82,* Board of Governors of the Federal Reserve System, Washington, D.C., August 1983.

tory institutions. Nonfinancial business also holds 9 percent of total financial assets in the form of credit market instruments. Trade credit is the largest single financial asset, accounting for 42 percent of all financial assets. Trade credit arises because businesses often do not require immediate payment for sales. It is common for payment to be due several days (e.g., fifteen days) after delivery. The category "all other" financial assets includes loans and other financial assets not included in other categories.

Debt issued in credit markets is the major liability of nonfinancial business. This debt, which includes marketable debt and direct loans from financial intermediaries, is $1685 billion. Credit market instruments comprise 77 percent of all financial liabilities. The next category is trade credit liabilities of nonfinancial business. Most of trade credit is loans from one business to another. Thus, nonfinancial business has trade-credit assets of $489 billion and trade credit liabilities of $389 billion. Assets exceed liabilities because trade credit is extended to households and financial business.

Although credit market instruments are the major liability of nonfinancial business, households do not hold a substantial amount of this debt directly. Nonfinancial business issues the instruments to financial intermediaries. Households hold assets that are claims on these intermediaries.

Assets and liabilities for all financial intermediaries combined are shown in Table 4.3. The total asset figure of $4530 billion for financial intermediaries indicates their quantitative importance in channeling funds from wealth holders to deficit units.

Financial intermediaries hold currency and deposit accounts with depository institutions. These assets constitute 5 percent of all assets held. Financial intermediaries also hold a substantial amount of government securities (federal plus state and local). The $874 billion of government securities is 19 percent of all

TABLE 4.3
ASSETS AND LIABILITIES OF FINANCIAL INTERMEDIARIES [a]
(YEAR END 1982)

Assets	Billions of $	Percent of total
Currency and deposit accounts	$ 234	5
Government securities	874	19
Corporate and foreign debt securities	449	10
Business and other loans	843	19
Corporate stock	411	9
Mortgage loans	1,069	24
Consumer loans	375	9
Other assets	280	6
Total assets	$4,530	100
Liabilities		
Transactions accounts	$ 370	9
Saving and time accounts	1,868	43
Credit market debt	298	7
Mutual fund shares	297	7
Insurance and pension reserves	1,072	25
Other	409	9
Total liabilities	$4,314	100

[a] Depository and nondepository institutions.
Source: *Flow of Funds Accounts, Assets and Liabilities Outstanding 1957–82,* Board of Governors of the Federal Reserve System, Washington, D.C., August 1983.

assets held. Financial intermediaries provide funds to business through purchasing their debt securities, by granting direct loans, and by purchasing corporate stock. These assets comprise 10, 19, and 9 percent of total assets, respectively. When combined, the holding of business debt and corporate stock is 38 percent of the total assets of financial intermediaries. Substantial sums are also channeled to households by financial intermediaries. Mortgage loans are 24 and consumer loans are 9 percent of total assets, respectively. The total amount of credit extended to households is 33 percent of total assets. This represents roughly the same amount of funds as provided to business.

The liabilities of financial intermediaries also tell an interesting story. Transactions accounts are only 9 percent of total liabilities. Savings and time accounts are 43 percent, however. These accounts are a primary means by which financial institutions channel funds to deficit units. When we combine transactions accounts with savings and time accounts, the sum comprises 52 percent of all liabilities of financial intermediaries. Thus, depository institutions are quantitatively the most important type of financial intermediary.

Credit market debt is primarily the liabilities of finance companies. This debt is $298 billion, which is 7 percent of the total liabilities of financial intermediaries. Mutual fund shares are $297 billion, which is 7 percent of the total liabilities of financial intermediaries. Insurance companies and pension funds are quantitatively second only to depository institutions as financial intermediaries. Their $1072 billion of liabilities constitutes 25 percent of total liabilities issued by financial intermediaries.

SUMMARY

This chapter discussed the role of the financial system and described the major markets and institutions in the system. The function of the financial system is to transfer funds from wealth holders to deficit units. The efficiencies that the financial system achieves in transferring funds from wealth holders to deficit units is comparable in importance to the role of money in eliminating the inefficiencies of barter. In the absence of a financial system, firms and households wanting to finance expenditures in excess of their income and wealth encounter considerable difficulty in locating and striking bargains with wealth holders.

Securities (loans and ownership shares) issued by deficit units are attractive to wealth holders if they are divisible, have low transactions costs, and are liquid. Deficit units are also interested in issuing securities that have low transactions costs. They often prefer to offer securities that are illiquid and indivisible, however. The financial system lowers transactions costs and increases price predictability for securities. The system also enhances liquidity and divisibility for wealth holders while serving the needs of deficit units.

In the discussion of the financial system a distinction was made between securities markets and the activities of financial intermediaries. Securities markets allow purchasers and sellers of securities to transact their business at low cost. Equally important, wealth holders are able to find purchasers for securities when they want to sell them. The high liquidity and low transactions costs provided by securities markets make the debts and ownership shares issued by deficit units attractive to many wealth holders. Furthermore, market specialists, such as brokers and dealers, securities analysts and underwriters, have helped lower transactions costs, raise liquidity, and improve price predictability.

Financial intermediaries allow funds to be transferred from wealth holders to deficit units indirectly. Financial intermediaries issue their own securities to wealth holders and use the proceeds to purchase securities in various markets. This indirect procedure can be beneficial to both wealth holders and deficit units. Wealth holders benefit because financial intermediaries can reduce risk through diversification by pooling the resources of many customers to purchase the securities of many issuers. Intermediaries also deal in large volumes and incur lower transactions costs per security than do many individual wealth holders. Furthermore, financial intermediaries can engage in sophisticated financial analyses that are impossible for many wealth holders. Finally, intermediaries offer securities to the public that are more highly divisible and whose prices are more predictable than the securities offered by most firms.

Deficit units also benefit from the activities of financial intermediaries. They incur lower transactions costs when issuing new securities because intermediaries often purchase large blocks of securities. Furthermore, deficit units can issue securities in large denominations because financial intermediaries are less concerned about indivisibilities than are individual wealth holders. Finally, many intermediaries are willing to purchase long-term securities because they are less concerned about maturity and price certainty than are individual wealth holders.

In total, financial intermediaries have greatly enhanced the transfer of funds from wealth holders to deficit units. Their success is indicated by the huge amount of assets and liabilities that they command. There are many types of financial intermediaries, but two major types were described. Nondepository institutions (such as mutual funds, insurance companies, and pension funds) are primarily in the business of meeting the longer-term investment needs of wealth holders. They invest in long-term bonds and ownership shares of business. Depository institutions are primarily in the business of meeting the short-term investment needs of wealth holders. Commercial banks have the most flexible investment authority among depository institutions, and they lend to both business and households. Much of their lending is short-term, but they are also important suppliers of longer-term credit as well. Savings and loan associations, along with mutual savings banks, devote most of their resources to financing the purchase of housing. Credit unions are primarily in the business of extending relatively short-term loans to consumers.

Depository institutions fill an important gap in the financial system by offering a safe, divisible, and highly liquid form in which to hold wealth. They are also important lenders to businesses and households that lack access to securities markets. The liabilities of depository institutions are attractive to wealth holders, and the institutions are able to channel a substantial amount of funds from wealth holders to deficit units.

The case of transactions accounts illustrates the importance of depository institutions. One might think that if wealth holders retain their wealth in the form of money, there is no way that these funds can be transferred to deficit units. This is not necessarily the case, however. To the extent that the public is willing to hold its money in the form of transactions accounts rather than currency, the funds do get transferred. Depository institutions take the funds deposited in transactions accounts and lend them to deficit units.

APPENDIX

THE ROLE OF DEALERS IN SECURITIES MARKETS

Dealers provide an important service by smoothing out erratic fluctuations in securities prices and by increasing the liquidity of securities. Security dealers are particularly valuable in this respect when a market is "thin," that is, when it has relatively few transactions per day. When a market is thin and there are no dealers, large imbalances can develop in the market, and security prices can fluctuate widely. Furthermore, anyone who attempts to sell a relatively large quantity of securities quickly is likely to depress their price. To avoid depressing the price, the seller has to spread sales over several days; hence, the liquidity of the securities is reduced.

The role of dealers can be shown by considering a market that is subject to wide fluctuations in the demand and supply of a security from day to day. The market is described graphically in Figure 4A.1. Assume the market begins the day in balance with demand schedule D_0 and supply schedule S_0. The price is P_0, at which demand (purchases) equals supply (sales) at quantity Q_0. This balance of demand and supply is shown in panel I. Assume that, during the day, holders of the security want to sell more than Q_0 securities at price P_0, but investors still want to purchase Q_0 at price P_0. There is a shift in the supply schedule to the right to S_1, but the demand schedule stays at D_0. After the shift in supply, more securities are offered for sale than are purchased at price P_0. If the market is served by brokers, they inform their selling customers that all the securities offered for sale cannot be sold at P_0. If the customers want to sell the securities, they must accept a lower price. Some customers will decide not to sell at a lower price, but others will sell. As the price declines, more customers want to purchase securities; that is, there is a downward movement along the demand curve D_0. During the day, price declines until demand and supply are in balance at P_1, and the quantity of securities traded is Q_1.

The situation for the second day is shown in panel II. Assume that, during the second day, the supply schedule shifts back to S_0, but the demand schedule happens to shift to the right to D_1. Now the situation is the reverse of day 1; there are more orders to buy securities than to sell at the initial price P_1. During the second day, price rises until demand and supply are in balance at P_2.

In this example, price started at P_0 and then fluctuated between a low of P_1 and a high of P_2. If the market is subject to wide fluctuation in price from day to day, there is an opportunity for security dealers to make a profit and to reduce price fluctuations in the process. Dealers can smooth fluctuations in price by varying their inventories of securities. Assume that the same market is served by dealers. During day 1, dealers receive more orders to sell the security than to buy it at price P_0. The dealers must make a decision at this point. They can either lower the price at which they are willing to purchase and sell securities to P_1, where purchases meet sales, or they can maintain the price above P_1 by purchasing more securities than they sell and adding to inventory. If the dealers believe that the rightward shift in supply is relatively permanent, they will go along with the market and reduce the price to P_1. If they believe the shift in supply is temporary, so that supply is likely to be back at S_0 on the second day, the dealers will absorb some of the increased supply of securities into their inventories on day 1.

Assume that the dealers believe that the shift in supply is temporary. They cannot be sure that this is the case, however, so they will let price fall in day 1, but not all the way to P_1. The dealers limit the decline in price by adding their purchases

FIGURE 4A.1
THE ROLE OF DEALERS IN LIMITING PRICE FLUCTUATIONS.

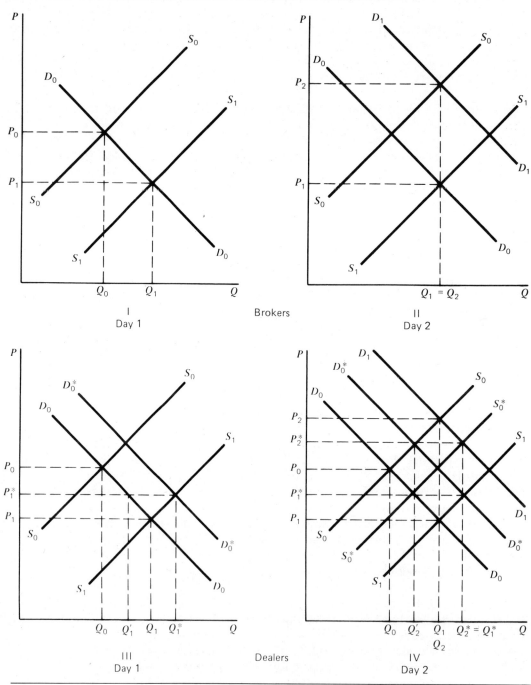

of securities to those of their customers. The situation on day 1 with dealers in the market is shown in panel III. The total demand for securities on day 1 shifts to the right by the amount of purchases by dealers to give a demand of D_0^*. Now the price declines only to P_1^* rather than to P_1. At price P_1^*, total sales of securities are Q_1^*. The dealers' customers purchase Q_1' of this total, and the dealers purchase $Q_1^* - Q_1'$. Dealers add these purchaes to their inventories.

Now consider the situation in day 2. The dealers were correct; supply does shift back to S_0. But there is a new surprise; demand has shifted rightward to D_1. In the absence of dealer intervention, the price rises to P_2. Dealers can make a trading profit by taking the securities they purchased in day 1 from their inventories and selling them in day 2. The situation in day 2 is shown in panel IV. When dealers sell securities from inventory, their sales are added to those of their customers. Total market supply shifts to the right by the amount of dealer sales to S_0^*. The shift in market supply limits the rise in price in day 2 to P_2^* rather than to P_2. At the price P_2^*, the public supplies the quantity Q_2', and the dealers supply the quantity $Q_2^* - Q_2'$. The quantity supplied in day 2 by dealers equals the amount that they purchased (demanded) in day 1, that is, $Q_2^* - Q_2' = Q_1^* - Q_1'$. Dealers make a profit in day 2 because they take the quantity of securities $Q_1^* - Q_1'$ purchased on day 1 at price P_1^* and sell them at price P_2^* on day 2. Dealer profits are $(Q_1^* - Q_1')(P_2^* - P_1^*) = (Q_2^* - Q_2')(P_2^* - P_1^*)$.

By varying their inventories of securities, dealers smooth out short-term fluctuations in the prices of securities.[18] Prices fall by less the first day and rise by less the second day. When dealers smooth out price fluctuations, they earn trading profits. Wealth holders benefit because they prefer stable security prices. Activities of dealers also increase the liquidity of securities held by large wealth holders by limiting price declines produced by large sales. Limiting the price declines allows the full price to be achieved more quickly, and, therefore, liquidity is increased.

Price volatility is likely in markets with relatively few transactions, and it is in these markets that dealers make the greatest contribution. In the United States, brokers *and* dealers are used in many markets. The brokers act as agents for wealth holders, and the dealers buy and sell securities on the order of brokers.

---

[18] Any participant in a market willing to vary its inventory of securities in the manner described here in the text performs the same price stabilizing functions as dealers do. Because of the large size of their inventories and their constant contact with the market, dealers are often in a better position than other participants to carry out this function.

SELECTED REFERENCES

Benston, George, "A Transactions Cost Approach to the Theory of Financial Intermediation," *Journal of Finance*, May 1976, pp. 215–232.

Board of Governors of the Federal Reserve System, *Introduction to the Flow of Funds*, Washington, D.C., 1975.

Dougall, Herber and Jack Gaumnitz, *Capital Markets and Institutions* (4th ed.), Englewood Cliffs, N.J.: Prentice-Hall, 1980.

Goldsmith, Raymond, *Financial Institutions*, New York: Random House, 1968.

Gurley, John and Edward Shaw, *Money in a Theory of Finance*, Washington, D.C.: Brookings Institution, 1960.

Stigum, Marcia, *The Money Market: Myth, Reality, and Practice*, Homewood, Ill.: Dow Jones-Irwin, 1978.

PORTFOLIO THEORY

5

The modern financial system allows wealth holders to balance the desirability of holding a variety of financial instruments against the benefits of holding physical assets. Similarly, deficit units choose among various maturities for their debts, and firms compare the implications of issuing debt versus ownership shares. Financial intermediaries also choose among various liabilities to offer to the public, and they acquire a variety of financial instruments.

The theory of portfolio selection describes how these economic units determine the composition of their assets and liabilities and, therefore, the composition of their wealth. These choices affect interest rates and the prices of assets and, in the process, affect real output, employment, and the price level. This chapter describes the basic elements of the theory of portfolio selection and shows how the theory explains the demand for various assets and the supplies of liabilities.

The material in this chapter is relatively difficult, but mastery of the elements of portfolio theory pays high dividends. The theory was developed by Harry Markowitz and James Tobin of Yale University as a means of explaining why investors hold diversified portfolios and how they respond to changes in asset returns and risks. They showed that uncertainty about the future is a crucial element in portfolio selection. The introduction of uncertainty complicates the analysis, but it also allows portfolio selection to be discussed fruitfully. One of the great contributions of Markowitz and Tobin was to analyze the role of uncertainty in economic decision making in a manner that was relatively simple but still yielded important conclusions concerning economic behavior. The tools developed here to study portfolio selection have a far wider use. For example, consumption and saving decisions by households and investment decisions by firms are made in an uncertain environment. Similarly, monetary and fiscal policies have to contend with uncertainty about the future. The tools of portfolio theory are valuable for understanding these and other issues in economics.

RATES OF RETURN ON ASSETS

The first step in developing the theory of portfolio selection is to determine how wealth holders can compare the returns available on various assets. For simplicity, we shall consider four different assets: money, bonds, ownership shares (stock), and physical assets. These assets differ in their divisibility, transactions costs, liquidity, and price predictability. They also differ in the flow of net income that they offer to wealth holders. Money held in the form of currency pays no interest, but many transactions accounts do earn interest. Bonds pay a fixed interest income, ownership shares pay dividends that vary with the profitability of firms, and many physical assets pay no interest or dividend income. The prices of bonds, ownership shares, and physical assets vary over time with changes in their demands and supplies. These price changes produce capital gains and losses that affect the net income from the assets. Furthermore, inflation (or deflation) affects the purchasing power of the returns earned on all assets. Confronted with all these factors, wealth holders must find a means of comparing the attractiveness of holding money, bonds, ownership shares, and physical assets. The rates of return on these assets provide the method of comparison.

We shall first define the rate of return in terms of an example and then provide a general definition. Consider the case of a wealth holder who purchased one year ago a twenty-year bond at a market price of $1000. The bond pays 10 percent interest at the end of each year and $1000 at maturity. Because of current demand and supply conditions in the bond market, the market price of the bond has risen to $1200. The wealth holder wants to determine the net income earned from the bond over the year. Interest income is 10 percent of $1000 or $100, but there has also been a capital gain. A brokerage fee of $25 had to be paid when the bond was purchased at the beginning of the year, so the net price of the bond when purchased was the market price ($1000) plus the brokerage fee, or $1025. Another $25 brokerage fee must be paid if the bond is sold. The net price upon sale is the current market price ($1200) less the brokerage fee, or $1175. The capital gain is net sales price less net purchase price, which is $1175 − $1025 = $150. Combining the interest income and the capital gain, we have a net income over the year of $100 in interest plus $150 capital gain for a total of $250. The *rate of return* on the bond for the year is defined as the *net income over the year divided by the initial net price*, or $250/$1025 = 0.244. The wealth holder has earned a 24.4 percent rate of return on the bond for the year.

This example leads us to a general definition of the net income and rate of return for any asset. The annual net income from any asset is comprised of any money income earned during the year, such as interest on a bond or dividends from stock, plus any change in the net price of the asset over the year. The rate of return on any asset is net income divided by the net price of the asset at the beginning of the period.[1] Thus,

$$r_a = \frac{\text{net income}}{\text{net initial price}} = \frac{c^a + (p_1^a - p_0^a)}{p_0^a}$$

where

r_a is the rate of return on an asset

c^a is the money income received on the asset over the period

p_0^a is the initial net price of the asset, that is, initial market price plus transactions costs

p_1^a is the net price of the asset at the end of the period, that is, market price less transactions costs.

Using the Greek letter delta, Δ, to signify a change in net price, we have $(p_1^a - p_0^a) = \Delta p^a$. Thus, if Δp^a is positive, a capital gain has occurred; if Δp^a is negative, a capital loss has occurred; and if Δp^a is zero, the net price of the asset has not changed. The expression for the rate of return can be rewritten as

$$r_a = \frac{c^a + \Delta p^a}{p_0^a} = \frac{c^a}{p_0^a} + \frac{\Delta p^a}{p_0^a}.$$

This definition can be used to determine the rate of return on any asset. Consider the case of a bond. When a bond is issued, the issuer agrees to make periodic payments of interest and to repay the principal at maturity. The holder of the bond receives interest payments by cutting off a *coupon* from the bond and presenting it to the issuer's bank at the end of each year.[2] When a bond is issued, its selling (market) price is typically equal to the amount of loan principal that the holder will receive at maturity. This price is called the *par value* of the bond.[3] The ratio of the annual coupon payment to the par value of the bond is called the

---

[1] The rate of return can be calculated for any time period such as a day, week, month, year, or decade. For ease of comparison, it has become customary to convert all returns into annual rates of return. For simplicity, we shall not consider time periods shorter than a year in this chapter. Annual rates of return for assets held longer than a year are discussed in Chapter 6.

[2] Strictly speaking, coupon payments are typically made twice a year. We shall abstract from this complication by assuming that a single payment is made at the end of each year.

[3] Recall from Chapter 3 that the discounted present value of a loan is the amount of the loan. As we shall see in the discussion of the term structure of interest rates, however, a bond cannot be issued at par if its coupon payments are out of line with market interest rates.

coupon rate. The coupon rate is simply the interest rate that a bond issued at par is paying when first issued.[4]

Once issued, the price of the bond varies as the demand and supply for it changes over time. Irrespective of any changes in the market price of the bond, however, the bond continues to make periodic and constant payments of interest in the amount indicated on its coupons. Thus, the ratio of coupon payments to the price of the bond changes when its price changes. This ratio is called the *current yield* on the bond.

With these details in mind, we can now describe the rate of return on a bond, r_b.[5] Let c be the annual coupon payment on a bond where the payment is made at the end of the year, and let p_p^b be the par value of the bond. The coupon rate, i_c, is defined as $i_c = c/p_p^b$, so $c = i_c \cdot p_p^b$. Consider the case where a bond is purchased at a net price that is not necessarily equal to its par value. The annual rate of return on a bond purchased at the net price p_0^b and whose net price after one year is p_1^b is given by

$$r_b = \frac{c + \Delta p^b}{p_0^b} = \frac{i_c \cdot p_p^b + \Delta p^b}{p_0^b} .$$

If the bond is purchased at its par value, $p_p^b = p_0^b$, so

$$r_b = \frac{i_c \cdot p_0^b + \Delta p^b}{p_0^b} = i_c + \frac{\Delta p^b}{p_0^b} .$$

In this case, the rate of return on the bond is the coupon rate plus the change in its net price relative to the net purchase price. In the special case where the price of the bond does not change and there are no transactions costs, the rate of return equals the interest (coupon) rate on the bond, that is, $r_b = i_c$.

When the net purchase price of the bond is not equal to its par value, we have:

$$r_b = \frac{c}{p_0^b} + \frac{\Delta p^b}{p_0^b} = i_c \cdot \frac{p_p^b}{p_0^b} + \frac{\Delta p^b}{p_0^b} .$$

The term $c/p_0^b = (i_c \cdot p_p^b)/p_0^b$ is the current yield on the bond. If p_0^b is less than the par value, p_p^b, the current yield exceeds the coupon rate, i_c, and if p_0^b is greater than p_p^b, the current yield is less than the coupon rate. We can think of the current

---

[4] Debt instruments that are issued with a maturity of less than a year typically do not have coupons. These instruments are issued at a price below par and pay par at maturity. The difference between the price when issued and the price at maturity constitutes the interest payment. Because our shortest time frame is one year, these instruments are not considered here, but their interest rate can be calculated easily.

[5] These details are important for understanding the rate of return on bonds and are essential for the later discussion of the term structure of interest rates.

yield on the bond as the interest rate that it currently pays. Defining the current yield, i_y, as $i_y = c / p_0^b$, we have:

$$r_b = i_y + \frac{\Delta p^b}{p_0^b} \ .$$

Thus, the rate of return on the bond is comprised of its current interest rate (yield) plus the change in its net price relative to the net purchase price.[6]

We can see from the expression that if the price of the bond does not change and if there are no transactions costs, the rate of return on the bond equals its current interest rate. The rate of return exceeds the current interest rate when the net bond price rises, that is, Δp^b is positive. The rate of return is less than the interest rate when the net bond falls, that is, Δp^b is negative. Furthermore, the higher the transactions costs, the lower the rate of return on the bond. The relevant measure of the return from a bond is *not* its current interest rate, but rather its rate of return. The current interest rate, changes in market price, and transactions costs all affect that return.

The general expression for the rate of return on a bond can be applied to other kinds of assets. Ownership shares, that is, common stock, do not pay a fixed coupon rate as do bonds. They pay dividends that vary with the profitability of the firm. The expression for the annual rate of return for common stock, r_s, is given by

$$r_s = \frac{d + \Delta p^s}{p_0^s}$$

where

r_s is the annual rate of return on common stock

d is the dividends earned during the year

Δp^s is the change in net price of the stock over the year

p_0^s is the net price of the stock at the beginning of the year.

Even if a firm does not pay dividends, a positive rate of return could be earned on the stock. If a firm saves its profits for internal use rather than pay dividends, the net price of the stock may rise if the savings generate sufficient additional profits. A positive rate of return is earned on the stock in this case.

Physical assets, such as gold or houses, also earn a rate of return.[7] In the case of these assets, all net income is in the form of changes in their prices. Gold, for example, pays no interest or dividends, but changes in its price can make holders

---

[6] For example, a bond yielding 10 percent that is purchased for a net price of $100 at the beginning of the year and has a net selling price of $110 at the end of the year has a rate of return of $.10 + \$110/\$100 = .10 + .10 = .20$, or 20 percent.

[7] Machinery and other physical assets used by businesses are not discussed here because their returns were described in detail in Chapter 3.

richer or poorer. The expression for the rate of return on a physical asset, r_f, is given by $r_f = \Delta p^f / p_0^f$. In the case of physical assets, transactions costs include any costs of storage.

Finally, we come to the rate of return on money. Assume that an individual holds an amount M_0 of money for one year. The money is in the form of currency, so it earns no interest. From the definition of the interest rate presented in Chapter 3, we know that the interest rate is $i_m = (M_1 - M_0)/M_0$. When no interest is paid, the holder has the same amount of money at the end of the year as at the beginning of the year, that is, $M_1 = M_0$, so $i_m = (M_0 - M_0)/M_0 = 0$. When money is held in the form of an interest-bearing transactions account, M_1 exceeds M_0 and $(1 + i_m) = M_1/M_0$. Because there are no capital gains or losses from holding money and transactions costs are zero, the rate of return on money always equals its interest rate, that is, $r_m = i_m$.

Up to this point, the rates of return on various assets have been defined in *nominal* terms; that is, they have not allowed for the effect of inflation or deflation. We shall now show the effect of changes in the price level on real interest rates and real rates of return.

When the price level rises (inflation), the purchasing power of money is reduced.[8] For example, if $1.05 buys today what $1.00 bought a year ago, the purchasing power of money has fallen by 5 percent; that is, 5 percent more money is required to purchase the same quantity of goods and services. The *price level* is an index that measures the number of dollars required to purchase a particular quantity (basket) of goods and services. The initial value of the price index is arbitrary, and we set it at 1.0 for some initial date. Changes in the price index measure changes in the purchasing power of money. In the example given earlier, the initial value of the index is 1.0 at the beginning of the year, and by the end of the year it is 1.05. At the end of the year, $1.05 is required to purchase what $1.00 buys at the beginning of the year. The percentage change in the price level over the year is 5 percent, which is the percentage *inflation rate* for the year.

The general expression for the inflation rate is

$$IR = \frac{P_1 - P_0}{P_0}$$

where

    IR is the annual inflation rate

    P_1 is the price level at the end of the year

    P_0 is the price level at the beginning of the year.

By convention, the inflation rate is multiplied by 100 to give the percentage inflation rate. Note that

$$IR = \frac{P_1 - P_0}{P_0} = \frac{P_1}{P_0} - 1$$

---

[8] A parallel analysis can be made for a decline in the price level (deflation), but this is so rare that it is ignored here.

and

$$(1+IR)=\frac{P_1}{P_0}.$$

Thus $(1+IR)$, which is called the inflation factor, is the ratio of the price level at the end of the year to the price level at the beginning of the year. The inflation factor is a price showing the rate of exchange between the purchasing power of money at the beginning of the year and at the end of the year.

With the definition of the inflation rate and the inflation factor in mind, we can now show how inflation affects the real rates of return on assets. First, let us examine the effect of inflation on the rate of return for money. At the beginning of the year, the wealth holder has M_0 of money, whose purchasing power is measured by the price level P_0. The *real quantity of money,* that is, money in terms of purchasing power, at the beginning of the year is M_0/P_0. For example, the wealth holder starts the year with $1000 of money, and the price index is 1.0, so $M_0/P_0 =$ $1000/1.0 = \$1000$. When no interest is paid, the individual still holds $1000 of money at the end of the year, but the price level has risen to 1.05. The real amount of money at the end of the year, M_0/P_1, is $1000/1.05 = \$952.38$. In terms of purchasing power, the individual's money holdings have declined from $1000 to $952.38. In real terms, that is, in terms of purchasing power, the individual has received a negative interest income of $952 $-$ \$1000 = -\$48$ on the money over the year. The *real interest rate* for money, ir_m, is real interest income for the year divided by the initial real money holdings, $ir_m = -\$48/\$1000 = -.048$ or -4.8 percent. The real rate of return on money, rr_m, equals the real interest rate on money, so the real rate of return on money in the example is -4.8 percent. Thus, the nominal interest rate and the nominal rate of return on money are zero, but because of the rise in the price level, the real interest rate and the real rate of return are -4.8 percent.

The general expression for the real interest rate (and real rate of return) for money, when no nominal interest is paid, is given by

$$ir_m = rr_m = \frac{(M_0/P_1)-(M_0/P_0)}{M_0/P_0} = \frac{M_0/P_1}{M_0/P_0} - 1$$

$$= \frac{1/P_1}{1/P_0} - 1 = \frac{P_0}{P_1} - 1.$$

The real interest factor is $(1+ir_m)=\dfrac{P_0}{P_1}$. Thus, the real interest factor is the ratio of the price level at the beginning of the year to the price level at the end of the year. We saw earlier that the inflation factor $(1+IR)= P_1/P_0$, so $(1+ir_m)= 1/(1+IR)$. The real interest factor for money is the reciprocal of the inflation factor. Furthermore, because $rr_m = ir_m$, we also have $(1+rr_m)= 1/(1+IR)$. The higher the inflation rate, the lower the real interest rate and the lower the real rate of return on money. The expression shows that if the inflation rate is zero, then $ir_m = rr_m = 0$; if the inflation rate is 5 percent, then $ir_m = rr_m = -4.8$; and if the inflation rate is 10 percent, then $ir_m = rr_m = -9.1$ percent.[9] If there is deflation, IR is negative, so the real interest rate and the real rate of return on money are positive. The greater the rate of deflation, the greater the real interest rate and the greater the real rate of return for money.

Now let us consider forms of money that do pay interest. If money is held for a year in an interest-bearing transactions account, a nominal interest income is earned that makes the initial amount of M_0 grow to M_1 by year's end.[10] The nominal interest rate, i_m, on the account is $i_m = (M_1 - M_0)/M_0$. Although the individual has a larger nominal quantity of money at the end of the year than at the beginning, the purchasing power of that quantity is eroded by inflation. To determine the real interest rate earned, one must calculate M_1 relative to the price level, P_1, prevailing at the end of the year. If, for example, the nominal interest rate is 5 percent and the inflation rate is also 5 percent, the interest income has just compensated the individual for the erosion of purchasing power and the real interest rate is zero. For a $1000 initial money balance, the wealth holder has $1050 in principal plus interest at the end of the year, but $1050 is required to buy what $1000 would purchase at the beginning of the year. In real terms, the individual has just broken even.

The general expression for the real interest rate and the real rate of return is

$$ir_m = rr_m = \frac{(M_1/P_1) - (M_0/P_0)}{M_0/P_0} = \frac{M_1/P_1}{M_0/P_0} - 1 = \left[\frac{M_1}{M_0} \cdot \frac{P_0}{P_1} \right] - 1$$

and

$$(1 + ir_m) = (1 + rr_m) = \frac{M_1}{M_0} \cdot \frac{P_0}{P_1}.$$

The greater the inflation rate, the more P_1 exceeds P_0, and the smaller the ratio P_0/P_1. Thus, inflation reduces the real interest rate and the real rate of return on the transactions account. If the nominal interest rate is less than the inflation rate, the wealth holder has less purchasing power in the account at the end of the year than at the beginning of the year. The real interest rate and the real rate of return are negative. If, however, the interest rate exceeds the inflation rate, there is more purchasing power in the account at the end of the year, so the real interest rate and the real rate of return are positive.

We conclude this section with a brief discussion of the effect of inflation on the real rates of return on nonmonetary assets such as bonds, common stocks, or physical assets. Only the case of bonds is discussed, but similar expressions can be obtained for other kinds of assets. Recall that the annual net income for a bond is

---

[9] It is sometimes stated that the real interest rate on money is the negative of the inflation rate; that is, $ir_m = -IR$. This is an approximation that is only accurate at low inflation rates. For example, if $IR = 1$ percent per year, $ir_m = -0.99$ percent per year, which is very close to -1 percent.

[10] The same analysis can be applied to a savings or time deposit account as well.

interest income plus any capital gain (or minus capital loss) net of transactions costs. The rate of return on the bond is net income divided by the price of the bond at the beginning of the year. Thus,

$$r_b = \left[i_y + \frac{\Delta p^b}{p_0^b} \right].$$

The *real rate of return* on a bond adjusts for changes in the purchasing power of money. We want to know if the nominal net income earned on the bond has exceeded, just kept up with, or is below the inflation rate.

The real rate of return factor for a bond, $(1 + rr_b)$, is the nominal rate of return factor $(1 + r_b)$ times P_0/P_1. Thus,

$$(1 + rr_b) = (1 + r_b) \cdot \frac{P_0}{P_1}.$$

If there is no inflation, $P_0/P_1 = 1$, and $rr_b = i_y + \Delta p^b/p_0^b$, which is the expression for the nominal rate of return on bonds, r_b. Thus, in the absence of inflation, the nominal and real rate of return are the same. The greater the rate of inflation, the smaller is P_0/P_1, and the lower is the real rate of return on the bond relative to the nominal rate of return. This can be seen directly by recalling that $(1 + IR) = P_1/P_0$, so

$$(1 + rr_b) = \frac{(1 + r_b)}{(1 + IR)}$$

and

$$rr_b = \frac{(1 + r_b)}{(1 + IR)} - 1.$$

The expressions for the real rates of return on common stock and on physical assets all involve multiplying the nominal rate of return factors by P_0/P_1. This is equivalent to dividing the nominal rate of return factor by the inflation factor $(1 + IR)$.[11] In all cases, given the nominal rates of return, the higher the inflation rate, the lower the real rates of return on the assets. This does not imply that inflation affects the real rates of return on all assets in the same way, however. For example, general inflationary pressures tend to push up the prices of physical assets and create capital gains for their owners. These capital gains can offset declining purchasing power. Other assets, such as money, do not offer similar protection, and inflation reduces their real rates of return.

We can now draw some conclusions from the discussion of rates of return. When wealth holders choose among the various assets that are available to them, they must have a standard of comparison. The nominal rate of return provides a

---

[11] It is conventional practice to define the real rate of return on any assets, rr_a, as the nominal rate of return less the inflation rate; that is, $rr_a = r_a - IR$. This is a convenient approximation for low rates of inflation.

common measuring stick that can be applied to all assets, but it does not allow for changes in the price level. In the calculation of the real rates of return on their assets, wealth holders take into consideration not only interest or dividend income, capital gains or losses, and transactions costs, but also the effects of inflation.

It is important to note that any asset is a store of value. An asset retains its real value only if its nominal value grows with the rate of inflation. The growth in nominal value can occur as a result of reinvestment of interest and dividend income or as a result of appreciation in the net price of the asset. The real rate of return allows a wealth holder to assess how the growth in the nominal value of an asset compares with the rate of inflation.

THE THEORY OF PORTFOLIO SELECTION

The discussion up to this point has been in terms of calculating real or nominal rates of return that are actually realized, for example, from last year to this year. These calculations provide useful information, but they are inadequate for making investment decisions. These decisions involve estimating the rates of return that will be earned in the *future*. When a wealth holder purchases an asset, the real rate of return that the asset will earn cannot be predicted with certainty. The theory of portfolio selection is concerned with how wealth holders choose among alternative assets whose real rates of return are uncertain.

The degree of uncertainty about the real rates of return that will be earned on alternative assets has an important effect on asset selection. We can see from the definitions of the real rates of return on assets how pervasive the uncertainty is. Currency, for example, might appear to be the safest asset to hold. Barring theft, the holder is assured by the government that the nominal value of the asset will not change. The holder cannot be sure that the real value of currency will remain constant, however, because there may be changes in the price level. The wealth holder might believe, for example, that there will be no inflation. If the expectation proves to be correct, all is well and good. If the expectation is wrong, however, and there is inflation, the currency holder has lost part of his or her purchasing power. Inflation picks the pockets of money holders just as surely as does a more conventional thief.[12] Other assets also have unpredictable rates of return. Government insurance makes transactions, savings, and time deposit accounts free from default risk, but the real rates of return on these assets are also affected by inflation. Rates of return on all bonds are uncertain because capital gains and losses are notoriously difficult to predict and even transactions costs are not completely predictable. Variations in the rate of inflation also contribute to the uncer-

---

[12] Deflation is like finding money on the sidewalk.

tainty concerning the real rates of return on bonds. Furthermore, bonds issued by state and local governments and by firms are subject to varying degrees of uncertainty concerning the ability of the issuer to meet interest and principal payments. Real rates of return on ownership shares are uncertain because dividend payments and stock prices are uncertain and because inflation affects the real rate of return on stocks. Finally, rates of return on physical assets are uncertain because their nominal returns depend upon the future behavior of their prices and their real returns are affected by the rate of inflation and the state of the economy.

Because uncertainty is so pervasive, it is important to determine how economic agents deal with uncertainty in deciding on the form in which to hold their wealth. The theory of portfolio selection takes the fascinating issues involved in human response to uncertainty and reduces the problem to issues that lend themselves to the application of mathematical statistics. This approach may or may not be productive for wider applications, but it does provide insights into economic behavior. The theory of portfolio selection helps explain economic behavior, but it is important to bear in mind that actual behavior is more complex, but less precise, than suggested by the theory. With this qualification in mind, we can now turn to the theory itself.

Wealth holders need some method of making comparisons among the possible real rates of return that might be earned on various assets. Consider a wealth holder who wants to compare the returns that might be earned on various assets over the next year.[13] Assume that, for each asset, the investor can list all the possible returns that might be earned next year and can assign a probability to each outcome. For present purposes, these probabilities may be viewed as the subjective beliefs of the investor. These "probability beliefs" may be the result of previous experience, of deep financial analysis, or of blind faith.

Table 5.1 lists the possible rates of return, r, for three different assets along with the probability, p, of each return occurring.[14] To keep the notation simple, the letter r is now used to denote the real rate of return on an asset. For simplicity, it is assumed that only four possible outcomes are available for each asset. For example, asset I has four possible outcomes, each of which is viewed by the investor as equally probable. Thus, a probability of .25 is assigned to each. With four possible outcomes that are equally probable, there is one chance in four, that is, 1/4, or .25, that a particular outcome will occur. It clearly makes a difference which outcome materializes because the possible outcomes range from a high of 20 percent to a low of 4 percent. Asset II has different characteristics from those of asset I. For this asset, outcome c is viewed as most probable. The investor believes that the chances are 7 out of 10 or .7 that a return of 10 percent

---

[13] From this point on, the term *return* is taken to mean the real rate of return unless otherwise stated.

[14] Because the investor is assumed to list all possible outcomes for the rate of return on an asset and because only one rate of return will materialize, the sum of the probabilities for each asset must be one.

TABLE 5.1
PROSPECTIVE RATES OF RETURN FOR THREE ASSETS

Outcome	Asset					
	I		II		III	
	r	p	r	p	r	p
a	20%	.25	100%	.05	40%	.10
b	14%	.25	60%	.20	20%	.30
c	10%	.25	10%	.70	5%	.40
d	4%	.25	−100%	.05	0%	.20
	$Er_1 = 12\%$		$Er_2 = 19\%$		$Er_3 = 12\%$	

will be earned. The second most probable outcome is b; the investor believes that the chances are 2 in 10 or .2 that a 60 percent return will be realized. There is also a .05 probability that the investment will double in a year as indicated by the 100 percent return under alternative a, and a .05 probability that the investment will be wiped out as indicated by the −100 percent return under d. Possible outcomes and probabilities of occurrence are also shown for asset III.

The three assets of Table 5.1 are different from each other both in terms of possible rates of return and in terms of the probabilities of various returns. How is the investor to compare the three assets? One natural method of comparison is to compute the "average" return for each asset. We can think of the Great Return Selector in the Sky (GRSS) as having three boxes. The first box has 100 pieces of paper in it, 25 of which have 20 percent written on them, 25 have 14 percent written on them, 25 have 10 percent, and 25 have 4 percent written on them. The GRSS stirs up the pieces of paper and picks one out and records the number written on it. The piece of paper is returned to the box, the pieces of paper are stirred up, and again a piece of paper is picked out and its message recorded. After this process is repeated a large number of times, the average return is computed. The average return is simply the sum of the returns that are recorded divided by the number of selections. The GRSS then moves on to the second box, which also contains 100 pieces of paper. Of the 100 pieces, 5 have +100 percent recorded on them, 5 say −100 percent, 20 have 60 percent, and 70 have 10 percent written on them. The same process of stirring, selection, recording of return, and replacement of the piece of paper is performed for box II. Again, after a large number of selections have been made, an average is computed. The third box also contains 100 pieces of paper, 10 with 40 percent written on them, 30 showing 20 percent, 40 showing 5 percent, and 20 with 0 percent written on them. The GRSS tirelessly repeats the sampling procedures and, when it is completed, computes the average outcome.

Assume that the GRSS actively stirred the 100 pieces of paper in each box before making a selection and never peeked while making a selection. After a large number of selections is made, we expect 25 percent of the selections from box I to be pieces of paper on which a return of 20 percent is recorded, 25 percent to be for 14 percent, and so on. The average return can be calculated much more easily than by adding all the numbers recorded by the GRSS. For asset I, the average is .25(20 percent) + .25(14 percent) + .25(10 percent) + .25(4 percent) = 12 percent. The average return can also be written more generally as $\sum_{j=1}^{4} p_j r_j$, where the r_j are the four possible returns and the p_j are the four probabilities of occurrence. The average return is the sum of the four possible returns, each weighted by its probability of occurrence, where the sum of the weights is one. Averages can also be calculated for assets II and III. The three averages are called the *expected values* of the returns for assets I, II, and III and are shown at the bottom of Table 5.1 as Er_1, Er_2, and Er_3. The expression "expected value of the return" for an asset is usually shortened to *expected return* on an asset.

On the basis of expected return, asset II is preferable to the other two assets because it offers an expected return of 19 percent as opposed to 12 percent for assets I and III. Expected return is a reasonable method of comparing uncertain outcomes because it is the average return that is obtained by the GRSS if a large number of selections are made from each box. It is also natural in the sense that it accords with how people seem to deal with uncertainty.

An investor who is guided by expected return prefers asset II to assets I and III. But how can an investor choose between two assets that have the same expected return? Though assets I and III have an expected return of 12 percent, they are not obviously equivalent. Asset III has a greater dispersion of possible outcomes than does asset I.

The greater dispersion of possible returns for asset III suggests that it is more risky than asset I. This designation may seem inappropriate because common usage only applies the term *risk* to unfavorable outcomes. Favorable possible outcomes are not commonly considered risky; rather, terms such as good fortune or great potential are usually applied to these outcomes. Thus, by common usage, the chance of a return of 0 percent on asset III is a risk; the chance of earning a return of 40 percent is a possibility of good fortune. The difficulty with distinguishing risk from good fortune is that most choices in a world of uncertainty involve situations in which favorable and unfavorable outcomes are both possible. Alternative assets may vary in the degree to which they offer favorable and unfavorable outcomes, but no one will choose an alternative that has unfavorable possible outcomes unless it also offers favorable possible outcomes as well. For this reason, the term *risk* is applied to situations that have both favorable and unfavorable possible outcomes. An asset is called more risky than another if it has a greater dispersion of possible returns relative to its expected return.

An asset's risk involves deviations of possible returns from its expected return. One measure of risk that seems appropriate is the sum of the differences between the expected return and each possible return weighted by its probability of occurrence. This measure, $\sum_j [(Er - r_j)p_j]$, is not useful, however, because it always equals zero![15] This bothersome problem can be avoided by squaring the

---

[15] See Table 5.2 for confirmation of this assertion.

deviations from the expected value to give $\sigma^2 = \sum_j [(Er - r_j)^2 p_j]$ where σ is the Greek letter sigma and σ^2 is called the *variance* of return.[16] The variance is a commonly used measure of dispersion, but it has "inflated" the actual deviations by squaring them. The measure of dispersion can be deflated by taking the square root of the variance to give

$$\sigma = \sqrt{\sum_j [(Er - r_j)^2 p_j]} = \left[\sum_j [(Er - r_j)^2 p_j] \right]^{1/2}.$$

This measure, σ, is called the *standard deviation* of return and is used as the measure of risk.

Table 5.2 shows the calculations of the variance and standard deviation of return for assets I, II, and III. These calculations indicate that asset I has an expected return of 12 percent and a standard deviation of return of 5.83 percent; asset III has the same expected return of 12 percent but a standard deviation of return of 12.08 percent. Thus, the dispersion of returns is greater for asset III than for asset I. Asset II has the highest expected return, 19 percent, and the greatest risk, 37.80 percent.

The investor is now in a position to choose among the three assets. Any investor prefers a high expected return to a lower one when the risks are equal. On the basis of expected return, asset II is the most attractive alternative. To obtain this expected return, the investor has to bear substantial risk, however. Whether asset II is selected or not depends upon the investor's preferences concerning risk. Assuming our investor does not like risk, asset III will not be selected, however, because it has the same expected return as asset I, but a higher standard deviation of return. If the investor likes risk, asset III is still not attractive because asset II offers more risk than asset III and more expected return. The choice boils down to asset I with its relatively low expected return and risk versus asset II with its higher expected return and higher risk. Without knowledge of the investor's preferences concerning the trade-off between expected return and risk, we cannot determine which asset will be chosen. Investor preferences and asset choices can be discussed more productively after we analyze the returns and risks for *collections* of assets rather than for single assets.

Before turning to this topic, however, it might be helpful to introduce a note of realism into the analysis. The concepts of expected return and standard deviation of return for an asset were developed by using a statistical approach that involved obtaining a list of all possible rates of return and their probabilities of occurrence. This approach is convenient for developing the concepts of expected value and standard deviation, and it is used by some investors. Other investors do not go

---

[16] The problem could also be avoided by obtaining the sum of the absolute deviations weighted by the probability of each outcome. This measure lacks desirable statistical properties and is not commonly used.

TABLE 5.2
CALCULATION OF VARIANCE AND STANDARD DEVIATION OF
RETURN FOR THREE ASSETS

Outcome	p	r	$p \cdot r$	$(Er - r) \cdot p$	$(Er - r)^2 \cdot p$
			Asset I		
a	.25	20%	5.0%	−2.0%	16.0%
b	.25	14%	3.5%	−0.5%	1.0%
c	.25	10%	2.5%	0.5%	1.0%
d	.25	4%	1.0%	2.0%	16.0%
Σ	1.00	$Er_1 = 12.0\%$		0.0	$\sigma_1^2 = 34.0\%$
					$\sigma_1 = 5.83\%$
			Asset II		
a	.05	100%	5.0%	−4.05%	328.05%
b	.20	60%	12.0%	−8.2 %	336.20%
c	.70	10%	7.0%	6.3 %	56.7 %
d	.05	−100%	−5.0%	5.95%	708.05%
Σ	1.00	$Er_2 = 19.0\%$		0.0	$\sigma_2^2 = 1429.0\%$
					$\sigma_2 = 37.80\%$
			Asset III		
a	.10	40%	4.0%	−2.8%	78.4%
b	.30	20%	6.0%	−2.4%	19.2%
c	.40	5%	2.0%	2.8%	19.6%
d	.20	0%	0.0%	2.4%	28.8%
Σ	1.00	$Er_3 = 12.0\%$		0.0%	$\sigma_3^2 = 146.0\%$
					$\sigma_3 = 12.08\%$

through the statistical exercises described in the text. Rather, they attempt to predict (forecast) the return they will earn on an asset and to form judgments concerning its risk. This is done in a variety of ways. Some investors use elaborate models to predict interest or dividend income (if any), capital gains or losses, and the rate of inflation in order to predict the real rate of return that will be earned on an asset. Other investors use the past behavior of the real rate of return on an asset as a predictor of its future rate of return without predicting the components of the return. Some investors dispense with any formal techniques and simply follow their instincts. No matter what method is used, predictions are made. Investors are aware that their predictions are subject to error, so they also form judgments concerning risk. Some investors try to estimate the risk of various assets statistically, and other investors make qualitative estimates. The theory of portfolio selection can accommodate these more realistic considerations by interpreting an investor's predictions of the return on an asset as the expected return and the investor's estimates of risk as the standard deviation of return.

Portfolios

Wealth holders must decide upon the proportion of their wealth to devote to such assets as money, bonds, corporate stock, and physical assets. A portfolio is simply a particular collection of assets. Each portfolio offers an expected return and risk of return. This section provides a formal definition of a portfolio and then goes on to discuss the expected return and risk for various portfolios.

For simplicity, we shall assume that wealth holders do not borrow to acquire assets, so wealth equals total assets for each wealth holder.[17] Symbolically, we have $W = A_1 + A_2 + \cdots + A_n = \sum_{i=1}^{n} A_i$, where W is total wealth and A_1, $A_2, \ldots, A_n$ are the amounts held of various assets. If we compute the share of each asset in total wealth, that is, $A_1/W, A_2/W, \ldots, A_n/W$, and take the sum, it follows that $A_1/W + A_2/W + \cdots + A_n/W = \sum_{i=1}^{n} \dfrac{A_i}{W} = \dfrac{W}{W} = 1$. Defining $w_1 = A_1/W$, $w_2 = A_2/W, \ldots, w_n = A_n/W$, we have $\sum_{i=1}^{n} w_i = 1$. A portfolio, P, is defined as $P = w_1 W + w_2 W + \cdots + w_n W = (w_1 + w_2 + \cdots w_n)W = (\sum_{i=1}^{n} w_i)W$.

Thus, given total wealth, a portfolio is defined by the set of w's. When the shares of individual assets in total wealth (the w's) change, then there is a different portfolio. This means that when wealth holders change the composition of their wealth, for example, less money and more bonds, they select a new portfolio.

If an investor's wealth rises and if the increase is invested in various assets in the same proportion as initial wealth, the w's do not change, but the size of the portfolio increases. If wealth remains unchanged, however, and the individual decides to hold more of one asset, then the holdings of other assets must decline by the same amount. In this case, the size of the portfolio does not change, but its composition changes. A portfolio whose size remains unchanged, but whose composition has changed is considered to be a new portfolio. For simplicity, we shall hold investors' wealth constant; thus, alternative portfolios involve varying the shares of various assets in total wealth.

An example illustrates the definition of a portfolio. Assume an individual has total wealth of $1000 and is considering alternative portfolios. Initially, the individual considers only a savings account, A_1, and government bonds, A_2, as components of various portfolios. One portfolio involves holding the entire $1000 in the savings account. In this case $w_1 = 1.00$ and $w_2 = 0.0$, so $P = w_1 W + w_2 W = 1.00(\$1000) + 0.0(\$1000) = \$1000$. Another portfolio involves holding the entire $1000 in government bonds. In this case, $w_1 = 0.0$, and $w_2 = 1.00$, so $P = 0.0(\$1000) + 1.00(\$1000) = \$1000$. The size of the portfolio does not change, but its composition does. A third alternative portfolio involves placing $500 in the savings account and $500 in government bonds, giving $w_1 = .5$ and $w_2 = .5$. Thus, $P = .5(\$1000) + .5(\$1000) = \$1000$. Again, the composition of the portfolio

---

[17] The case of borrowing is discussed in the appendix to this chapter.

changes. In general, assuming that government bonds are perfectly divisible, a continuum of portfolios $P = w_1 W + w_2 W$ is available using the two assets. Note that because $w_1 + w_2 = 1$, we can write $w_2 = 1 - w_1$. Thus, the available portfolios are given by $P = w_1 W + (1 - w_1)W$. The continuum of portfolios is obtained by reducing the proportion of wealth devoted to the savings account, w_1, from 1.00 to 0.0. With only two assets, a decision to increase the holdings of one asset implies a reduction in the holdings of the other asset by the same amount.

If the individual now considers a third asset, for example, corporate stock, A_3, we have $P = w_1 W + w_2 W + w_3 W$. The \$1000 can now be allocated among the three assets in varying proportions.[18] For portfolios with three assets, w_1, w_2, and w_3 are all allowed to range from zero to one, subject, of course, to the constraint that $w_1 + w_2 + w_3 = 1.00$. Thus, all combinations of w_1, w_2, and w_3 that satisfy this constraint involve different feasible portfolios. The constraint implies that there are only two independent w's because $w_3 = 1 - (w_1 + w_2)$. Thus, the expression for the portfolio can be written $P = w_1 W + w_2 W + [1 - (w_1 + w_2)]W$. In a three-asset portfolio, an increase in one asset implies a reduction in the sum of the other two assets by an equal amount.

In the general case, currency and transactions accounts, savings and time deposit accounts, various kinds of stocks and bonds, as well as a variety of physical assets, are all potential elements in a wealth holder's portfolio. A large number of potential portfolios is available because all combinations of $w_1, w_2 \cdots w_n$ involve different portfolios. There are only $n - 1$ independent w's, however, because

$$w_n = 1 - \sum_{i=1}^{n-1} w_i .$$

Portfolio Expected Return

An investor needs some way to compare all the potential portfolios that are available. One method is to compare the expected returns on alternative portfolios. The expected return on a portfolio is the expected real rate of return on total wealth when that wealth is invested in a particular collection of assets.

Assume that an investor has total wealth of \$1000 that is to be allocated between assets I and II, whose expected returns are 12 and 19 percent respectively as shown in Table 5.2. The investor wants to determine the expected returns from alternative portfolios involving varying proportions of the \$1000 invested in the two assets. The expression for the expected return on a portfolio, E_p, is given by $E_p = w_1 Er_1 + w_2 Er_2$, where w_1 and w_2 are the proportions of the \$1000 invested in assets I and II, and Er_1 and Er_2 are the expected returns for the two assets. Recalling that $w_1 + w_2 = 1$, we can rewrite the expected return for a portfolio as $E_p = w_1 Er_1 + (1 - w_1)Er_2$. From this expression it is clear that if $w_1 = 1.00$, the entire \$1000 is invested in asset I, so $E_p = 1.00(12 \text{ percent}) + 0.0(19 \text{ percent}) =$

---

[18] The two-asset case considered earlier in the text can be thought of as a special case of three-asset portfolios in which w_3 is always zero.

12 percent, which is the expected return on asset I. At the opposite extreme, if the entire \$1000 is invested in asset II, $w_1 = 0.0$ and $(1 - w_1) = 1.00 = w_2$, so $E_p = 0.0(12 \text{ percent}) + 1.00(19 \text{ percent}) = 19$ percent. In general, as the proportion of the \$1000 invested in asset I declines and hence the proportion of wealth invested in asset II increases, the expected return on the portfolio rises steadily (linearly) from 12 percent to 19 percent. The higher the proportion of asset II in the portfolio, the higher the expected return on the portfolio.

For an investor who is considering a number of different assets, the general expression for the expected return on a portfolio is given by

$$E_p = w_1 Er_1 + w_2 Er_2 + \cdots + w_n Er_n = \sum_{i=1}^{n} w_i Er_i$$

where

$$\sum_{i=1}^{n} w_i = 1.$$

Thus, the expected return on the portfolio is a weighted average of the expected returns on the various assets using the proportion of each asset in total wealth as the weights. By changing the w's and, hence, the portfolio, the investor can calculate the expected returns on alternative portfolios.

The significance of portfolio expected return depends upon a wealth holder's attitude concerning risk. Investors who are unconcerned about risk will invest all their wealth in the asset with the highest expected return; that is, they will select a portfolio composed of the asset with the highest expected return. Thus, the portfolio will contain only one asset, and the expected return on the portfolio equals the expected return on that asset.[19] In this situation, the concept of portfolio expected return adds nothing to our earlier analysis.

The concept of a portfolio is meaningful, however, for investors who are concerned about risk. If the portfolio with the highest expected return is a risky portfolio, investors may not want to hold it. Investors may not want to maximize the expected rate of return on their wealth because of the risks involved in such an investment strategy. In order to determine the role that the riskiness of individual assets plays in determining the riskiness of a portfolio of assets, it is necessary to define and discuss portfolio risk.

Portfolio Risk

Portfolio risk is measured by the standard deviation of the rate of return on the portfolio. Calculation of the standard deviation of portfolio return, σ_p, is not as straightforward as for the expected return on a portfolio, however.

---

[19] If there is more than one asset with this expected return, the wealth holder is indifferent among portfolios containing various combinations of these assets.

Let us start with the simplest case where the returns on assets are uncorrelated. Lack of correlation is perhaps most easily described by discussing how returns behave when they are correlated. Assume that the returns on two assets are positively correlated. In this case, there is a tendency for the return on one asset to be high when the return on another asset is high and for the return on one asset to be low when the return on the other asset is low. Except in the extreme case of perfect positive correlation, however, there is only a tendency in this direction. When two assets have perfect positive correlation, every time the return on one asset increases, the return on the other asset also increases. Every time the return on one asset declines, the return on the other asset decreases. In the more usual case, of less than perfect positive correlation of returns on two assets, sometimes the returns move in opposite directions, and sometimes the return on one asset changes, and the return on the other does not, but on average the two returns move in the same direction. The returns on General Motors (GM) and Ford stock are examples of positive correlation. The return on both assets rises when the demand for cars is high and falls when demand declines. Yet sometimes the return on GM stock rises when Ford stock declines and vice versa.

Negative correlation occurs when rates of return tend to move in the opposite direction. In this case, the return on one asset tends to be low when the return on another asset is high and to be high when the return on the other asset is low. Again, unless the returns have perfect negative correlation, the returns move in opposite directions only on average. The behavior of the return on oil company stock and automobile company stock is an example of negative correlation. High energy prices raise the profits of oil companies and increase the return on their stock. Rising gasoline prices reduce the demand for many kinds of U.S. autos and depress the return on the stock of their producers. There have been times, however, when the returns on the stock of oil companies and auto producers have moved in the same direction.

When returns on various assets are uncorrelated, there is no tendency for the returns to move in either the same or the opposite direction. Sometimes the returns move up together, but no more often than when the returns move in opposite directions or when the return on one asset changes and the return on another asset does not. When the returns on two assets are uncorrelated, it can be shown that the variance of the return on a portfolio composed of the two assets is given by $\sigma_p^2 = w_1^2\, \sigma_1^2 + w_2^2\, \sigma_2^2$ and the standard deviation of return is

$$\sigma_p = \sqrt{w_1^2\, \sigma_1^2 + w_2^2\, \sigma_2^2} = [w_1^2\, \sigma_1^2 + w_2^2\, \sigma_2^2]^{1/2}\,.$$

In general, for n uncorrelated assets we have

$$\sigma_p = [w_1^2\, \sigma_1^2 + w_2^2\, \sigma_2^2 + \cdots + w_n^2 \sigma_n^2]^{1/2} = [\textstyle\sum w_i^2 \sigma_i^2]^{1/2}$$

where

$$\Sigma w_i = 1\,.$$

This formula describes portfolio risk when the returns on the individual assets in the portfolio are uncorrelated. When asset returns are uncorrelated, portfolio risk can be reduced by spreading the portfolio over a number of assets rather than investing in a single asset. This is true even when all the individual assets have the same expected return and the same risk. Assume that there are two assets with the same expected return of 10 percent and the same standard deviation of return of 6 percent and that the returns are uncorrelated. If an investor initially holds the entire $1000 in one asset, then $E_p = 10$ percent and $\sigma_p = 6$ percent. If the investor equally divides the $1000 between the two assets that is, $500 each, we have

$$E_p = .5(10\%) + .5(10\%) = 10\%$$

and

$$\sigma_p = [.5^2(6\%)^2 + .5^2(6\%)^2]^{1/2} = 4.24\% .$$

By investing the $1000 in two assets with the same expected return and the same standard deviation of return, the investor can still have a portfolio with an expected return of 10 percent, but portfolio risk is reduced from 6 percent to 4.29 percent. The reduction in risk occurs because the investor has lessened the chance that the entire $1000 will be subject to an unusually large deviation from the expected portfolio return. If one asset experiences a low return, then the $500 invested in that asset will earn a low return. But it is unlikely that the $500 invested in the other asset will experience a low return at the same time. Thus, it is less likely with two assets than with one that the entire $1000 will be subjected to a large deviation from the expected return. A diversified portfolio reduces risk when asset returns are uncorrelated.

If there are three assets with an expected return of 10 percent and standard deviation of 6 percent, investment of one third of the $1000 in each still gives E_p of 10 percent, but now

$$\sigma_p = \left[(1/3)^2(6\%)^2 + (1/3)^2(6\%)^2 + (1/3)^2(6\%)^2 \right]^{1/2} = 3.46\% .$$

Portfolio risk is reduced further by spreading the $1000 over three assets whose returns are uncorrelated. Note that the expression for σ_p in the two asset case can be written as

$$\sigma_p = [(1/2)^2(6\%)^2 + (1/2)^2(6\%)^2]^{1/2} = [2(1/2)^2(6\%)^2]^{1/2}$$
$$= \sqrt{1/2(36\%)} = 6\%/\sqrt{2} .$$

For the three-asset case,

$$\sigma_p = [3 \cdot (1/3)^2(36\%)]^{1/2} = \sqrt{1/3(36\%)} = 6\%/\sqrt{3} .$$

In general, for n assets of equal risk, σ, we have $\sigma_p = \sqrt{\dfrac{1}{n}\sigma^2} = \sigma/\sqrt{n}$. As the number of assets in the portfolio rises, portfolio risk, σ_p, declines.

Table 5.3 shows the decline in σ_p as n increases. Having a portfolio of only five assets of which one fifth of total wealth is committed to each asset reduces the standard deviation of portfolio return by over 50 percent relative to investment in only one asset. By adding more and more assets and, thus, devoting a smaller and smaller share of total wealth to each asset, an investor can effectively eliminate risk.

TABLE 5.3
PORTFOLIO RISK AS THE NUMBER
OF ASSETS WITH UNCORRELATED
RETURNS AND EQUAL STANDARD
DEVIATIONS INCREASES
(ASSUMES FIXED PORTFOLIO SIZE)

Number	σ_p
1	6.00%
2	4.24
5	2.68
10	1.90
100	0.60
1,000	0.19
10,000	0.06

The principle of reducing total risk through pooling a large number of independent risks is most in evidence for insurance companies. An insurance company has a large number of life or fire insurance policies outstanding. Each policy has a risk associated with it. By spreading the risk over a large number of policies, the total risk is greatly reduced. Insurance companies must take care that the events are independent, however. Disasters that hit a particular locality or area of the country can produce many losses for the insurer. In these cases, the events are not independent, but are positively correlated because they are all affected by the disaster.

The returns on some assets are uncorrelated, and wealth holders can reduce risk by including them in their portfolios. It is often the case that asset returns are correlated, however. When returns are correlated, calculation of portfolio risk is more complicated, and only a verbal account is given here.[20] If asset returns are positively correlated, the gains from diversification are reduced. The higher the degree of positive correlation, the more likely it is that when one asset experiences an unusually low return, the returns on other assets will also be low. Similarly, the higher the degree of positive correlation, the more likely it is that when one asset experiences an unusually high return, the other assets in the portfolio will also have a high return. The higher the positive correlation, the smaller the reduction in portfolio risk from diversifying. As shown in the appendix to this chapter, when asset returns have perfect positive correlation, there is *no* gain from diversification. It does not reduce risk to put eggs in many baskets if the carrier falls off a cliff.

Negative correlation of asset returns actually enhances the advantages of diversification. With negative correlation, if the return on one asset is unusually

---

[20] The formula for portfolio risk when asset returns are correlated is given in the appendix to this chapter along with a more rigorous version of the story that follows.

low, the return on another asset is likely to be unusually high. Thus, the deviations of each asset's return from its expected return tend to offset the deviations of the return on another asset from its expected return. The greater the degree of negative correlation, the greater the reduction of portfolio risk. As shown in the appendix to this chapter, in the special case of perfect negative correlation, portfolio risk can be totally eliminated through diversification.

Efficient Portfolios

A basic tenet of the theory of portfolio selection is that investors only choose among *efficient portfolios*. A portfolio is efficient if there is no other collection of assets that provides the same risk at higher expected return. The concept of efficient portfolios can be described by considering two assets. Assume that asset 1 has an expected rate of return of 3 percent and a risk of 5 percent whereas asset 2 has an expected return of 6 percent and a risk of 10 percent. The expected return on portfolios comprised of these two assets is given by the expression $E_p = w_1(3\%) + w_2(6\%)$ where w_1 and w_2 are the proportions of the total wealth devoted to asset 1 and asset 2 respectively. Column (a) of Table 5.4 shows the response of portfolio expected return as w_1 is reduced from 1.0 to 0.0 and w_2 is increased from 0.0 to 1.0. If all wealth is invested in the original asset, that is, $w_1 = 1.0$ and $w_2 = 0.0$, then $E_p = 3$ percent, which is the expected return on asset 1. By decreasing w_1 and increasing w_2, the investor can increase portfolio expected return until at $w_1 = 0.0$ and $w_2 = 1.0$, $E_p = 6$ percent, which is the expected return on asset 2.

We now must determine what happens to portfolio risk when the investor increases the share of wealth devoted to the second asset. Asset 2 offers twice the expected return of asset 1, but it is also twice as risky. Assume that the returns on assets 1 and 2 are uncorrelated. In this situation, portfolio risk is given by $\sigma_p = [w_1^2 \sigma_1^2 + w_2^2 \sigma_2^2]^{1/2} = [w_1^2 (5\%)^2 + w_2^2 (10\%)^2]^{1/2} = [w_1^2 (25\%) + w_2^2 (100\%)]^{1/2}$. Column (b) of Table 5.4 shows portfolio risk as the share of asset 1 in the total portfolio is decreased and the share of asset 2 is increased. Even though asset 1 has a risk of 5 percent and asset 2 has a risk of 10 percent, moving from a portfolio composed exclusively of asset 1 to one with 90 percent of wealth in asset 1 and 10 percent in asset 2 actually reduces portfolio risk form 5 percent to 4.6 percent. If 80 percent of wealth is devoted to asset 1 and 20 percent to asset 2, portfolio risk is further reduced to 4.5 percent. This portfolio has an expected return of 3.6 percent as compared to 3 percent when all wealth is invested in asset 1. Thus, by holding a diversified portfolio, an investor can have higher expected return and lower risk than is available from holding all of wealth in asset 1. When more than 20 percent of wealth is devoted to asset 2, portfolio risk rises, but only when 60 percent is invested in asset 1 and 40 percent in asset 2 does portfolio risk rise back to 5 percent. This is the same risk as the investor confronts when all wealth is invested in asset 1. With the 60–40 mix of wealth between assets 1 and 2, the expected return on the portfolio is 4.2 percent as compared to an expected return of 3 percent when all wealth is invested in asset 1.

The relationship between portfolio expected return and portfolio risk for different blends of assets 1 and 2 is shown in Figure 5.1. At point *A*, all of wealth

TABLE 5.4
PORTFOLIO EXPECTED RETURN AND RISK FOR DIFFERENT
COMBINATIONS OF ASSETS 1 AND 2

Asset 1	Asset 2	Portfolio Expected Return	Portfolio Risk
w_1	w_2	(a)	(b)
1.0	0.0	3.0%	5.0%
.9	.1	3.3	4.6
.8	.2	3.6	4.5
.7	.3	3.9	4.6
.6	.4	4.2	5.0
.5	.5	4.5	5.6
.4	.6	4.8	6.3
.3	.7	5.1	7.2
.2	.8	5.4	8.1
.1	.9	5.7	9.0
0.0	1.0	6.0	10.0

FIGURE 5.1
PORTFOLIO EXPECTED RETURN AND RISK FOR DIFFERENT
COMBINATION OF ASSETS 1 AND 2.

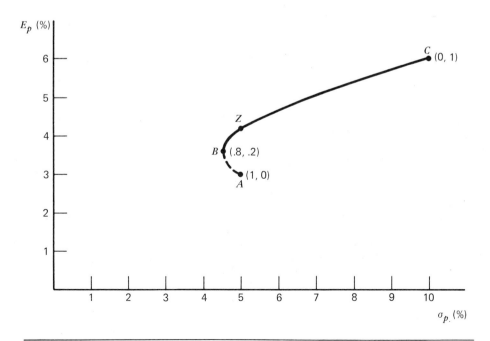

is invested in asset 1. The values of w_1 and w_2 are shown in parentheses as (1,0). From point A to point B, portfolio expected return rises, and portfolio risk declines as the share of asset 2 in wealth rises to 20 percent. From point B to point C, portfolio expected return and risk both rise as the share of asset 2 in wealth increases from 20 percent to 100 percent. Portfolios represented by the broken line between points A and B are inefficient because it is possible to achieve a higher portfolio expected return and simultaneously reduce risk. Any investor prefers a higher expected return if it can be achieved with no change in risk. All investors prefer point B to any point on the curve below B, so no investor will hold a portfolio indicated by a point on the broken line $A-B$.

It is important to note that the inefficiency of portfolios on the broken line $A-B$ has nothing to do with investors' preferences concerning risk. Even investors who like risk will not find portfolios on line $A-B$ to be efficient. Of all the points on $A-B$, point A is most risky, but there is another portfolio at point Z that offers the same risk but higher expected return. Any investor prefers more to less expected return and prefers a portfolio with the expected return and risk of point Z to a portfolio at point A. Investors who like risk prefer point Z to any point between B and Z, but point A is inefficient for them and for all other investors. The same argument can be made about the inefficiency of portfolios at any point between A and B.

If the returns on assets 1 and 2 are negatively correlated, the reduction in risk through diversification is even greater than indicated by Table 5.4. As shown in the appendix, if the negative correlation is perfect, it is possible to eliminate portfolio risk by holding a suitable mix of the two assets. If returns on the two assets are positively correlated, the reduction in risk through diversification is reduced. It is shown in the appendix to this chapter that some reduction is still possible as long as there is not perfect positive correlation.

In order to keep the discussion simple, we considered the case of only two assets, but the principal of portfolio efficiency applies to portfolios that contain many assets. With portfolios containing many assets, it may be possible to reduce portfolio risk below the 4.5 percent minimum reported in Table 5.4. Whether or not this is possible depends upon the extent of the risks on the other assets and the correlations between the returns on the assets.

The relationship between portfolio expected return and risk for a world of many assets is illustrated in Figure 5.2. We start with the asset that has the lowest risk of all individual assets. The expected return and risk for a portfolio that consists only of that asset is shown as point A. The investor adds assets to the portfolio that reduce risk and increase expected return until a minimum risk point is reached at point B.[21] From this point, the investor can achieve a higher expected portfolio return only by also increasing portfolio risk. Beyond point B, increased E_p is achieved by reducing the shares of assets with relatively low expected return

---

[21] Recall that wealth is fixed, so adding more assets indicates that the relative share of each asset in the portfolio declines.

FIGURE 5.2
THE INVESTMENT OPPORTUNITY LOCUS.

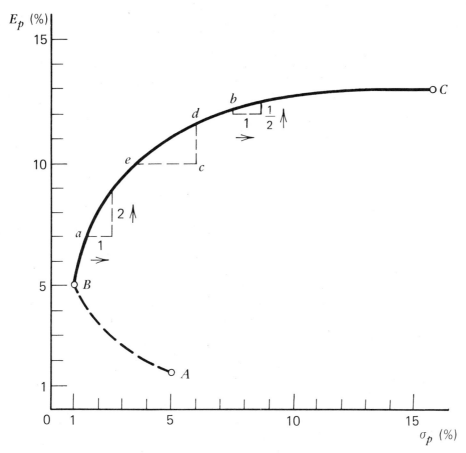

and risk and by increasing the shares of assets with higher expected return and higher risk. Diversification still pays, however, because the risk on portfolios containing relatively risky assets is less than the risk on these assets themselves.

The curve starts out from point B with a steep slope indicating that it is possible to obtain a large increase in E_p with only a small increase in σ_p. It is possible to add assets to the portfolio that have relatively high expected return and risk, but whose returns are negatively correlated or uncorrelated with the returns of other assets in the portfolio. As we move from point B toward point C, however, the curve becomes flatter, indicating that further increases in E_p are accompanied by larger and larger increases in σ_p. This worsening trade-off between portfolio expected return and risk occurs because to achieve further increases in E_p, one must reduce the degree of portfolio diversification by concentrating an increasing share of the portfolio in relatively few assets with high expected return and high risk. If the returns on these assets are positively correlated, risk is increased even further. Finally, at point C, all of wealth is held in the single asset with highest expected return. There is no diversification at point C because the portfolio contains only one asset. All benefits of diversification in reducing portfolio risk are eliminated, and σ_p equals the risk of the single asset with highest expected return.

By moving from point A to point B, the investor has exploited all the "freebies" from diversification, and any further increase in expected return is accompanied by increased portfolio risk as indicated by the curve $B-C$. The curve $B-C$ indicates that, when selecting a portfolio, the investor is faced with a trade-off between expected return and risk. An increase in expected return comes at the price of increased risk. The curve $B-C$ is called the *investment opportunity locus*.[22]

A particular point on the line, such as a, indicates the actual expected return and risk associated with a particular portfolio. The slope of the line indicates the additional expected return that the investor receives by selecting a more risky portfolio. For example, at point a, if the investor selects a new portfolio that increases portfolio risk by 1 percentage point, expected return on the portfolio increases by 2 percentage points. If the investor holds a portfolio that provides the expected return and risk indicated by point b, a further increase in portfolio risk by 1 percentage point increases expected return by only one half of 1 percent. Thus, as the investor selects riskier and riskier portfolios, the additions to expected return are smaller for a given increase in risk.

It is important to note that every point on $B-C$ represents an efficient portfolio. It is not possible to achieve a higher expected return without being subjected to increased risk. Any point below the line, such as point c, is not efficient. At point c, the investor can either increase expected return for a given risk by moving to point d or reduce risk for a given expected return by moving to point e. No rational investor will hold a portfolio providing the expected return and risk of point c.

Investor Preferences and Portfolio Selection

The investment opportunity locus describes the options available to an investor with respect to holding alternative portfolios. We must now examine how an investor determines what portfolio to hold. To answer this question, we must examine investor preferences.

Investors who do not like risk are said to be *risk averse*. These investors can be induced to forsake some of their aversions to risk, however, if sufficiently compensated by increased expected return. The preferences of a risk-averse investor con-

---

[22] Calculation of the investment opportunity locus for portfolios containing many assets is complicated and is not discussed here. The interested reader should consult Harry Markowitz, *Portfolio Selection* (New York: John Wiley, 1959), and William Sharpe, *Investments* (Englewood Cliffs, N.J.: Prentice-Hall, 1978).

FIGURE 5.3
INDIFFERENCE CURVES FOR A
RISK-AVERSE INVESTOR.

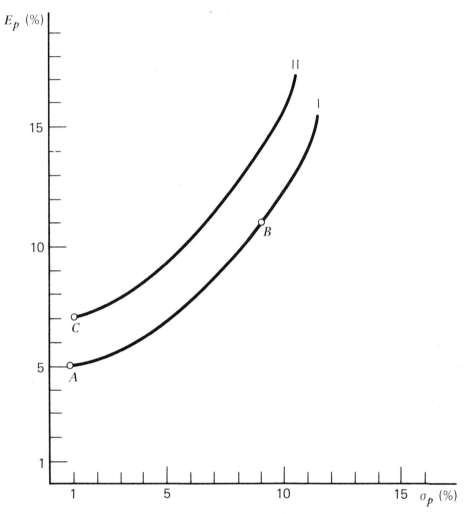

cerning the trade-off between expected return and risk on alternative portfolios
can be described with the aid of indifference curves. In Figure 5.3, indifference
curve I shows the combinations of portfolio expected return and risk for which an
investor is indifferent. The investor is indifferent between a portfolio at point A
offering an expected return of 5 percent and a standard deviation (risk) of 1 percent and a portfolio at point B that offers an expected return of 11 percent and a
standard deviation of 9 percent. As we move up the curve, the indifference curve

becomes steeper, indicating that larger and larger additions to expected return are required to compensate the investor for a given increase in risk. Thus, as the amount of portfolio risk increases, the investor is less and less willing to assume additional risk and must be compensated by larger and larger amounts of expected return.

If it is possible to have a higher expected return for a given amount of risk, the wealth holder is better off. Thus, every point on indifference curve II is preferred to every point on indifference curve I. In general, there is a family of indifference curves where each curve indicates the combinations of portfolio expected return and risk for which the investor is indifferent. Higher indifference curves indicate higher levels of satisfaction for the investor.

A wealth holder wants to achieve the highest level of satisfaction possible. The highest attainable indifference curve is dictated by the investment opportunity locus. Figure 5.4 combines the investor's indifference curves with the investment opportunity locus to determine the optimal portfolio. Point E^* is the combination of expected return and risk from a portfolio that maximizes the investor's satisfaction. We can see that point E^* is the point of tangency between the indifference curve U^* and the investment opportunity locus. This is the highest indifference curve attainable.

It is instructive to determine why the investor selects point E^*. Consider point F. At point F, the slope of the investor's indifference curve, U_1, is less than the slope of the investment opportunity locus. The slope of the indifference curve indicates the additional expected return that the investor requires in compensation for an increase in risk. The slope of the investment opportunity locus indicates the actual increase in expected return that is available from choosing a portfolio with additional risk. When the slope of the investment opportunity locus exceeds the slope of the indifference curve, the investor is willing to assume more risk to obtain additional expected return than the investment opportunity locus requires. Thus, the investor can increase satisfaction by moving up the investment opportunity locus. Point G indicates the opposite situation. Here the investor's indifference curve is steeper than the investment opportunity locus. At point G, the investor is assuming so much risk that he or she is willing to sacrifice a larger amount of expected return for a decrease in risk than the investment opportunity locus requires. A move to a less risky portfolio does not entail as large a reduction in expected return as the indifference curve through point G indicates. Thus, the investor increases satisfaction by moving down the investment opportunity locus from point G. At point E^*, the slopes of the investor's indifference curve and the investment opportunity locus are equal. At point E^*, the rate at which the investor is willing to substitute expected return for risk is equal to the rate at which the investor can actually substitute expected return for risk.

The more risk averse the investor, the less risky the actual portfolio selected. Figure 5.5 shows indifference curves for investor I and investor II. Investor I is highly risk averse, so his indifference curve rises sharply, indicating that at relatively low levels of risk he must be compensated with large increases in expected return for any further increases in risk. This investor selects a portfolio that pro-

FIGURE 5.4
THE OPTIMAL PORTFOLIO.

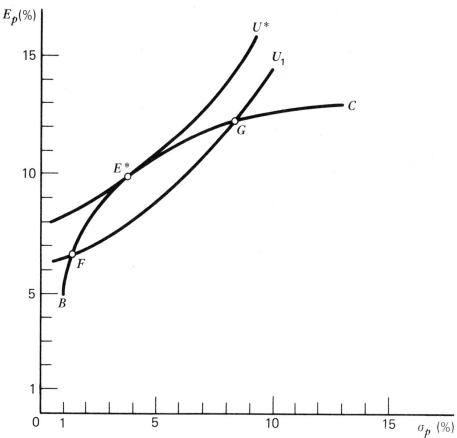

vides the low expected return and low risk of point *a*. Investor II is not as risk averse as investor I, so her indifference curve rises less sharply. Even at the relatively high risk level of point *b*, investor II does not require as much compensation with additional expected return for an increase in risk as investor I requires at point *a*. Investor II selects a portfolio that provides a higher expected return and higher risk than the portfolio of investor I. Despite the differences in risk aversion between the two investors, however, they both select diversified portfolios.

The less risk averse the investor, the flatter the indifference curves. If an investor is not concerned about risk at all, the indifference curves become horizontal lines indicating that all portfolios with the same expected return are equally attractive irrespective of their risks. Such an investor is called *risk neutral*. As shown in Figure 5.6, the indifference curves for a risk-neutral investor are horizontal lines where the higher the line, the greater the level of satisfaction. The

FIGURE 5.5
PORTFOLIO SELECTION FOR INVESTORS WITH
DIFFERENT DEGREES OF RISK AVERSION.

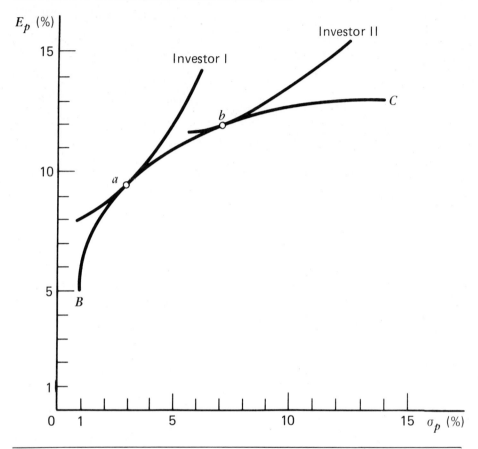

investor maximizes satisfaction on indifference curve 4 because this is the highest
indifference that can be achieved given the investment opportunity locus. A risk-
neutral investor always selects the portfolio with the highest expected return. This
portfolio is comprised solely of the asset with highest expected return. A risk-
neutral investor does not select a diversified portfolio.

There are investors who actually welcome risk because it offers the chance to
make a "killing." The fact that high risk also implies a chance of a large loss is not
so important to them. These investors are called *risk lovers,* and their indifference
curves slope downward indicating that they are actually willing to forsake
expected return if compensated by sufficient additional risk. Risk-loving investors
do not select a diversified portfolio, but rather invest their wealth in the riskiest
asset signified by the end point of the investment opportunity locus.

FIGURE 5.6
PORTFOLIO SELECTION FOR A
RISK-NEUTRAL INVESTOR.

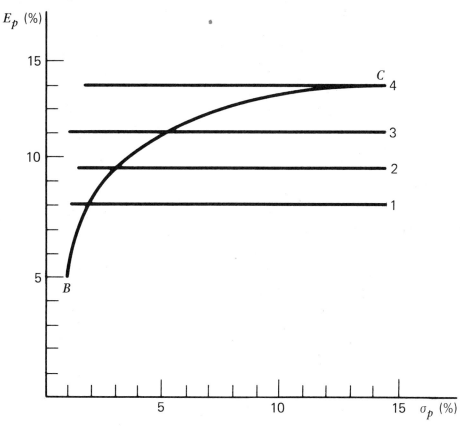

SUMMARY

The theory of portfolio selection describes how wealth holders choose among assets when the real rates of return that will be earned on these assets are uncertain. This uncertainty is described by the expected return and standard deviation of return for each asset. When individual assets are combined, a portfolio is created that has its own expected return and standard deviation of return. The expected return for a portfolio is simply a weighted average of the expected returns for the individual assets in the portfolio where the weights are the share of each asset in total wealth. The standard deviation of return for a portfolio depends not only upon the risk of each asset and its share of total wealth, but also upon the correlations between asset returns. The smaller the positive correlation between asset returns, the greater the reduction of risk through diversification. When asset returns are negatively correlated, portfolio return can be reduced even further; and, in the special case of perfect negative correlation, risk can be totally eliminated.

The expected returns and standard deviations of return for different portfolios allow us to construct an investment opportunity locus showing the trade-off between the expected return and risk for alternative portfolios. This locus indicates that, by changing the composition of their wealth holdings, investors can increase the expected return on their portfolios only by increasing portfolio risk.[23]

The degree of portfolio diversification that an investor achieves depends upon his or her attitudes toward risk. Risk-averse investors choose diversified portfolios, and, for extreme risk aversion, the portfolio with minimum risk and lowest expected value is selected. The smaller the amount of risk aversion, however, the greater the amount of risk that an investor is willing to assume and the greater the expected return on the portfolio. Risk-neutral and risk-loving investors represent an opposite pole from extreme risk aversion because they are not interested in portfolio diversification at all. These investors simply hold the asset with highest expected return and highest risk.

The theory of portfolio selection can describe the behavior of investors with radically different preferences concerning the trade-off between expected return and risk, but the theory offers most insights into the behavior of risk-averse investors. These investors hold diversified portfolios, and they can be induced to alter their portfolios as the expected returns and risks for individual assets change. In contrast, risk-neutral and risk-loving investors are only interested in the asset with highest expected return. These investors do not respond to changes in the expected returns and risk on other assets unless some other asset achieves the highest expected return.

For risk-averse investors, the expected return and risk of many assets are important for portfolio selection as well as the correlation of asset returns. If risk and correlation of returns on all assets are held constant, as well as the expected returns on all other assets, an increase in the expected rate of return on an asset induces the wealth holder to increase the share of total wealth devoted to that asset and to decrease the shares of other assets.[24] If expected return and correlation of returns are held constant, an increase in the riskiness of an asset induces

---

[23] It was shown that no rational investor selects a portfolio on the downward sloping portion of the investment opportunity locus.

[24] The increase in the expected return on an asset allows the investor to achieve a higher indifference curve. Thus, there is an income effect from the increased expected return. It is possible to have a negative income effect for the asset that exceeds the substitution effect. In this case, a rise in the expected return on an asset reduces the demand for that asset. This possibility is not considered in this text.

the investor to hold less of that asset and more of other assets. Finally, the greater the degree of positive correlation of return on various assets, the smaller the proportions of wealth devoted to these assets and the greater the proportion devoted to other assets.

We conclude that the demand for a particular asset varies positively with its expected return but negatively with its risk and negatively with the extent of its positive correlation with the return on other assets. We also conclude that the demands for various assets are interconnected. Given wealth, if an investor wants to hold more of a particular asset, he or she must also be willing to hold less of other assets. Thus, an investor may decrease the holdings of a particular asset not because its expected return declines or its risk increases, but rather because some other asset becomes more attractive.

These conclusions concerning the response of asset demand to changes in the expected return, risk, and correlation of returns for individual assets are only valid for risk-averse investors. Risk-neutral and risk-loving investors do not hold diversified portfolios, and they do not substitute among assets unless some asset ceases to have the highest expected return. This complication is not very important in most instances, however, because so many investors are risk averse. We know this is true because if most investors were not risk averse, it would be difficult to explain how assets in the economy come to be held. Most assets do not offer the maximum expected return sought by risk-neutral and risk-loving investors; these assets are held because investors are averse to risk.[25]

The theory of portfolio selection is a valuable aid in studying the demand for various assets, and the theory is applied extensively in subsequent chapters. For example, the theory is used to explain why banks and other depository institutions hold diversified portfolios. It is also used to explain changes in the composition of these institutions' portfolios when there are changes in the expected returns or risks (or both) for individual assets. These portfolio considerations are crucial for understanding the role of depository institutions in determining the amount of money and credit in the economy. The theory of portfolio selection also helps us understand the public's demand for money and other assets. These demands in conjunction with the asset demands of financial intermediaries have important macro-economic effects. We shall show that the portfolio decisions of the public and of financial intermediaries affect interest rates, real output, employment, and the price level.

---

[25] Transactions costs and indivisibilities may prevent a risk-averse investor with a small amount of wealth from diversifying. The best this investor can do is hold money or some similar asset.

APPENDIX:

MORE ON THE THEORY OF PORTFOLIO SELECTION

PORTFOLIO RISK WHEN ASSET RETURNS ARE CORRELATED

In Chapter 5, much of the discussion of portfolio risk assumed that the rates of return on assets are uncorrelated. The assumption simplified the discussion, but it is unrealistic. This section describes portfolio risk when asset returns are correlated.

The general expression for the standard deviation (risk) of return for a two-asset portfolio is

$$\sigma_p = [w_1^2 \, \sigma_1^2 + w_2^2 \, \sigma_2^2 + 2w_1 w_2 \rho \sigma_1 \sigma_2]^{1/2}$$

where the Greek letter rho, ρ, is the correlation coefficient for the returns on assets 1 and 2. It can be shown that the correlation coefficient cannot be less than -1.0 or greater than $+1.0$.[26] When two assets have perfect negative correlation of return, $\rho = -1.0$; when they have perfect positive correlation of return, $\rho = +1.0$.

If the returns on the two assets are uncorrelated, $\rho = 0.0$, and the general formula for portfolio risk simplifies to the expression used in Chapter 5:

$$\sigma_p = [w_1^2 \, \sigma_1^2 + w_2^2 \, \sigma_2^2 + 2w_1 w_2 \rho \sigma_1 \sigma_2]^{1/2}$$

$$= [w_1^2 \, \sigma_1^2 + w_2^2 \, \sigma_2^2]^{1/2} \, .$$

Furthermore, if the returns are positively correlated, that is, $0.0 < \rho \leqslant 1.0$, the standard deviation of portfolio return is greater than if the returns are uncorrelated. In the case where $\rho = 1.0$, we have:

$$\sigma_p = [w_1^2 \, \sigma_1^2 + w_2^2 \, \sigma_2^2 + 2w_1 w_2 \sigma_1 \sigma_2]^{1/2} \, .$$

If the returns on the two assets are negatively correlated, that is, $-1.0 \leqslant \rho < 0.0$, the standard deviation of portfolio returns is less than if the returns are uncorrelated. In the case of perfect negative correlation, we have $\rho = -1.0$ and

$$\sigma_p = [w_1^2 \, \sigma_1^2 + w_2^2 \, \sigma_2^2 - 2w_1 w_2 \sigma_1 \sigma_2]^{1/2} \, .$$

---

[26] Symbolically $-1.0 \leqslant \rho \leqslant 1.0$.

PORTFOLIO RISK WHEN THERE
IS PERFECT POSITIVE CORRELATION
OF RETURNS

If there is perfect positive correlation of asset returns, diversification does not reduce portfolio risk. When $\rho = +1.0$, the variance of portfolio return, σ_p^2, is

$$\sigma_p^2 = w_1^2 \sigma_1^2 + w_2^2 \sigma_2^2 + 2w_1 w_2 \sigma_1 \sigma_2 \,.$$

Note that

$$(w_1\sigma_1 + w_2\sigma_2)^2 = w_1^2 \sigma_1^2 + w_2^2 \sigma_2^2 + 2w_1 w_2 \sigma_1 \sigma_2$$

so

$$\sigma_p^2 = (w_1\sigma_1 + w_2\sigma_2)^2$$

and the standard deviation of portfolio return is

$$\sigma_p = w_1\sigma_1 + w_2\sigma_2 \,.$$

The standard deviation of a portfolio composed of two assets whose returns have perfect positive correlation is a weighted average of the standard deviation of return for each asset. Thus, when $\rho = +1.0$, portfolio risk is a linear combination of the risks on each asset; all an investor can do is average the risks on the two assets. Recalling that $w_1 = 1 - w_2$, we can write the expression for portfolio risk as $\sigma_p = w_1\sigma_1 + (1 - w_1)\sigma_2$. If all of wealth is held in asset 1, $w_1 = 1.0$ and $\sigma_p = \sigma_1$. If all of wealth is held in asset 2, $w_1 = 0.0$ and $\sigma_p = \sigma_2$. By varying w_1 between 1.0 and 0.0, the investor can achieve any linear combination of the risks on the two assets.

It should be noted that this risk averaging is different from the risk reduction that occurs when the two assets have less than perfect positive correlation of returns. Consider the case where asset 1 has a standard deviation of return of 3 percent and asset 2 has a standard deviation of 5 percent. Assume one half of wealth is invested in asset 1 and one half in asset 2. If the returns are uncorrelated, we have:

$$\sigma_p = [(.5)^2(3\%)^2 + (.5)^2(5\%)^2]^{1/2} = 2.9\% \,.$$

In this case, holding a diversified portfolio *reduces* portfolio risk below the risk on either asset. Now consider the case when the two returns are perfectly correlated. Here we have, $\sigma_p = .5(3\%) + .5(5\%) = 4\%$. Diversification produces a portfolio risk that is the *average* of the risks on the two assets. When there is perfect correlation of asset returns, diversification simply averages the risks on the two assets.

We have described the effect of perfect positive correlation on portfolio risk for two assets, but the argument generalizes. For a portfolio comprised of n assets, all of which have perfect positive correlation of returns, we have:

$$\sigma_p = w_1\sigma_1 + w_2\sigma_2 + \cdots + w_n\sigma_n \,.$$

Thus, the risk for a portfolio comprised of n assets is a weighted average of the risks for the individual assets. Again, a diversified portfolio does not reduce risk, it averages risk.

PORTFOLIO RISK WHEN THERE IS A PERFECT NEGATIVE CORRELATION OF RETURNS

When there is perfect negative correlation between the returns on two assets, it is possible to eliminate risk totally. For perfect negative correlation, we have:

$$\sigma_p^2 = w_1^2\,\sigma_1^2 + w_2^2\,\sigma_2^2 - 2w_1 w_2 \sigma_1 \sigma_2\,.$$

Note that

$$w_1^2\,\sigma_1^2 + w_2^2\,\sigma_2^2 - 2w_1 w_2 \sigma_1 \sigma_2 = (w_1 \sigma_1 - w_2 \sigma_2)^2$$

so

$$\sigma_p^2 = (w_1 \sigma_1 - w_2 \sigma_2)^2$$

and

$$\sigma_p = w_1 \sigma_1 - w_2 \sigma_2\,.$$

When $\rho = -1.0$, it is possible to select a portfolio for which $\sigma_p = 0.0$. This means that there is a value of w_1 and w_2 for which portfolio risk is zero. Setting portfolio risk equal to zero and solving for w_1, we obtain $\sigma_p = w_1 \sigma_1 - w_2 \sigma_2 = 0.0$, and $w_1 = w_2 \sigma_2 / \sigma_1$. The expression for w_1 can be rewritten as $w_1 \sigma_1 = w_2 \sigma_2$, or $w_1 / w_2 = \sigma_2 / \sigma_1$. Thus, when the relative shares of the two assets are the reciprocal of the ratio of their standard deviations, portfolio risk is totally eliminated.

The case of perfect negative correlation does not generalize as easily to portfolios with n assets as did perfect positive correlation. Perfect negative correlation means that the returns on any two assets always move in opposite directions. It is impossible for the returns on three assets always to move in opposite directions. If the return on asset 1 is always greater (less) than its expected value when the return on asset 2 is less (greater) than its expected value, asset 3 cannot have perfect negative correlation with both assets 1 and 2. If the return on asset 3 is always below (above) its expected value when the return on assets 1 is above (below) its expected value, asset 3 has perfect negative correlation with asset 1 but perfect *positive* correlation with asset 2. This problem does not arise for perfect positive correlation of asset returns because it is possible for the returns on all assets to be above their expected values at the same time or to be below their expected values at the same time.

It is possible for *pairs* of assets to have perfect negative correlation of returns, however.[27] The only zero risk portfolio that is efficient for an investor is the pair of assets among all pairs with perfect negative correlation that have the highest expected return. This pair of assets gives the greatest expected return among all portfolios with zero risk.

PORTFOLIO RISK WHEN THERE IS A RISK-FREE ASSET

The analysis of investment opportunities is simplified when there is a risk-free asset. In fact, many texts emphasize this case. The discussion of the role of a risk-free asset has been relegated to an appendix in this book because there are no risk-free assets. Despite this problem, it is useful to look at a world in which an asset exists for which there is no risk.

Money would be such an asset if the price level were always constant. Unexpected changes in the price level make the real rate of return on money uncertain, so money is, in fact, a risky asset. In this section, we shall assume that money is risk free. Thus, we are describing a world in which the purchasing power of money is always constant. In this situation, the real rate of return on money is completely certain.

Let us begin by considering two assets. One asset is money that has a known and riskless rate of return $\bar{r}_M$ and, therefore, has a standard deviation of return that is exactly zero. The other asset is a bond that has an expected rate of return of Er_B and a standard deviation of return, σ_B. For portfolios composed of these assets we have:

$$E_p = w_M \bar{r}_M + w_B Er_B$$

and

$$\sigma_p = [w_M^2 \sigma_M^2 + w_B^2 \sigma_B^2 + 2w_M w_B \rho \sigma_M \sigma_B]^{1/2},$$

where w_M and w_B are the relative shares of money and bonds in wealth and $w_M + w_B = 1$. Because the return on money is riskless, $\sigma_M = 0.0$ and $\rho = 0.0$, so the expression for portfolio risk simplifies to $\sigma_p = [w_B^2 \sigma_B^2]^{1/2} = w_B \sigma_B$. Portfolio risk is proportionate to the risk on bonds, where the factor of proportionality is the share of bonds in total wealth, w_B.

---

[27] These can be pairs of groups of assets.

Noting that $w_B = (1 - w_M)$, we have:

$$E_p = (1 - w_B)\bar{r}_M + w_B \, Er_B$$
$$= \bar{r}_M + w_B (Er_B - \bar{r}_M)$$

and

$$\sigma_p = w_B \, \sigma_B .$$

Thus, both expected return and risk vary linearly with the share of bonds in the total portfolio, w_B. Assuming that the expected return on bonds is greater than the return on money, the greater w_B, the higher E_p. Portfolio risk, σ_p, also varies positively with w_B. The linear dependence of E_p and σ_p on w_B implies a linear relationship between portfolio expected return and portfolio risk. Because $\sigma_p = w_B \sigma_B$, we observe that $w_B = \sigma_p / \sigma_B$. Substituting this expression for w_B into $E_p = \bar{r}_M + w_B (Er_B - \bar{r}_M)$, we obtain

$$E_p = \bar{r}_M + (Er_B - \bar{r}_M) \frac{\sigma_p}{\sigma_B}$$

so

$$E_p = \bar{r}_M + \left[\frac{Er_B - \bar{r}_M}{\sigma_B} \right] \sigma_p .$$

This expression shows that there is a linear relationship between portfolio expected return and portfolio risk.[28] When $w_B = 0$, all of wealth is invested in money, so $\sigma_p = 0.0$ and $E_p = \bar{r}_M$. When $w_B = 1.0$, $\sigma_p = \sigma_B$ so

$$E_p = \bar{r}_M + \left[\frac{Er_B - \bar{r}_M}{\sigma_B} \right] \sigma_B = Er_B .$$

The term $Er_B - \bar{r}_M / \sigma_B$ indicates the additional portfolio expected return that can be obtained by assuming additional portfolio risk. Er_B, $\bar{r}_M$, and σ_B are all constants, so the slope of the relationship is a constant. For a given value of risk for bonds, the greater the excess of Er_B over $\bar{r}_M$, the greater the increase in expected portfolio return for a given increase in portfolio risk.[29] For a given value of the differential $(Er_B - \bar{r}_M)$, the greater the riskiness of bonds, σ_B, the smaller the increase in portfolio expected return for a given increase in portfolio risk.

When one of two assets is risk free, the investment opportunity locus is a straight line. Panel A of Figure 5A.1 shows the investment opportunity locus for this two-asset case.[30] When $w_B = 0$, all of wealth is invested in money, so $E_p = \bar{r}_M$

---

[28] Note that if $\bar{r}_M = 0$, as it does for currency and some transactions accounts, the expression simplifies to $E_p = [Er_B / \sigma_B]\sigma_p$.

[29] Recall that increased portfolio expected return and risk are achieved by increasing the share of bonds in the total portfolio, w_B.

[30] This locus should be compared to the one described in Figure 5.1, where both assets are risky.

FIGURE 5A.1
THE INVESTMENT OPPORTUNITY LOCUS AND
PORTFOLIO CHOICE FOR MONEY AND BONDS.

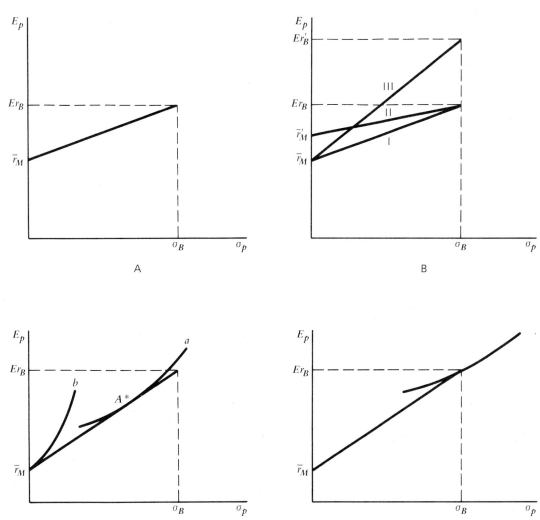

A

B

C

D

and $\sigma_p = 0.0$. It is possible to increase expected portfolio return above $\bar{r}_M$ by increasing w_B. When the share of bonds in wealth increases, portfolio risk also rises. Thus, the locus is upward sloping, and the slope equals $ER_B - \bar{r}_M / \sigma_B$. When all of wealth is invested in bonds, $E_p = Er_B$ and $\sigma_p = \sigma_P$.

Panel B shows three different investment opportunity loci. Recall that an investment opportunity locus is given by

$$E_p = \bar{r}_M + \left[\frac{Er_B - \bar{r}_M}{\sigma_B} \right] \sigma_p .$$

Line I is the same as the locus shown in Panel A. Line II shows a new locus when $\bar{r}_M$ is increased to $\bar{r}'_M$, but Er_B and σ_B are unchanged. This locus is higher than line I except at the point (Er_B, σ_B) where the entire portfolio is invested in bonds. For portfolios that contain money, a higher expected return is obtained when the return on money rises from $\bar{r}_M$ to $\bar{r}'_M$. The investment opportunity locus is also flatter, indicating that there is less favorable trade-off between expected return and risk when the return on money rises relative to the expected return on bonds. A shift in the portfolio from money to bonds produces the same increase in risk as before, but now there is a smaller increase in portfolio expected return because the gain is $(Er_B - \bar{r}'_M)$ rather than $(Er_B - \bar{r}_M)$. Line III shows what happens when Er_B is increased to Er'_B while $\bar{r}_M$ and σ_B are left unchanged. In this case, the locus becomes steeper, but it does not shift up. When Er_B rises, the trade-off between portfolio expected return and risk becomes more favorable. A shift from money into bonds produces the same increase in risk, but now there is a larger gain in portfolio expected return.

Panel C shows investor a, who moves along the linear investment opportunity locus until the highest possible indifference curve a is achieved at point $A*$. At this point, the slope of the indifference curve equals the slope of the investment opportunity locus. Even with a linear investment opportunity locus, this risk averse investor holds a diversified portfolio comprised of money and bonds.

There are two important exceptions to this result. When there is extreme risk aversion, only the riskless asset (money) is held. Panel C also shows investor b, who is so risk averse that only money is held. This investor's indifference curve b is so steep that satisfaction is maximizing by holding a zero-risk portfolio that earns a return of $\bar{r}_M$.

It is also possible that a risk-averse investor holds only bonds. Such a situation is shown in Panel D. Even at the point where all of wealth is held in bonds, this risk-averse investor has an indifference curve whose slope is less than the slope of the investment opportunity locus. This means that the investor requires a smaller increase in expected return for an increase in risk than can be obtained by actually increasing the holding of bonds and decreasing the amount invested in money. The best that this investor can do is hold all of wealth in bonds, that is, hold an undiversified portfolio. The investor would prefer, however, to have more expected return and risk than are allowed by the investment opportunity locus.

This investor can achieve a higher indifference curve if borrowing is allowed. Assume that the investor borrows money at the risk-free interest rate $\bar{r}_M$. The money is invested in bonds that have an expected return of Er_B and risk of σ_B. Recalling that wealth is the difference between assets and liabilities, that is, $W = A - L$, we can treat the borrowed money (liability) as a negative asset. This implies that w_M can be negative and w_B can be greater than one.

Consider the case where an investor has $1000 of wealth. In the absence of borrowing, the maximum value for w_B is 1.0 where the entire $1000 is held in bonds. Assume that the investor borrows an additional $1000 and uses the funds to purchase bonds. The investor now holds $2000 of bonds and has a $1000 liability, so wealth remains $1000. The ratio of bonds to wealth, w_B, is $2000/$1000 = 2.0, and the ratio of money to wealth, w_B, is $-$1000/$1000 = -1.0. We see that $w_M + w_B = -1.0 + 2.0 = 1.0$. If the investor borrows an additional $1000 and buys bonds, we have $w_M = -2.0$, and $w_B = 3.0$; so again $w_M + w_B = 1.0$.

If we assume that the investor can borrow at the risk-free interest rate of $\bar{r}_M$, it is possible to extend the investment opportunity locus beyond the point at which all wealth is held in bonds. Figure 5A.2 shows the investment opportunity locus when borrowing is possible. At point A, all of wealth is held as money, so $w_M = 1.0$, and $w_B = 0.0$. From point A to point B, the share of bonds in wealth rises from 0.0 to 1.0. As that share increases, both the expected return and risk of the portfolio increase linearly. At point B, all of wealth is held in bonds, so $w_M = 0.0$, and $w_B = 1.0$. From point B to point D, the investor borrows and invests the funds in bonds. This allows the investor to obtain additional expected return, and it also increases risk. As before, expected return and risk increase linearly with the ratio of bonds to wealth, w_B.[31] Point C^* shows the desired combination of portfolio expected return and risk for a risk-averse investor who borrows. This is the investor who in panel D of Figure 5A.1 invests all of wealth in bonds but who would like to hold even more bonds. At point B, the slope of the indifference curve is less than the slope of the investment opportunity locus. By borrowing and investing in additional bonds, the investor can move along the investment opportunity locus beyond point B. At point C^*, the investor maximizes satisfaction, and at this point the slope of the indifference curve equals the slope of the investment opportunity locus. Borrowing allows the investor to hold bonds in excess of wealth and to achieve a portfolio whose expected return and risk best accords with his or her preferences.

THE ROLE OF A RISK-FREE ASSET WHEN THERE ARE MANY ASSETS

Up to this point we have considered portfolios with only two assets. We can now extend the argument to portfolio with many assets. This extension yields some surprising results.

Figure 5A.3 shows an investment opportunity locus when there are only risky assets. Point A denotes a portfolio of several risky assets, and the portfolio has an

---

[31] Borrowers usually have to pay an interest rate that is higher than the risk-free rate. For them, the market opportunity locus past point B is flatter than for the segment from point A to point B.

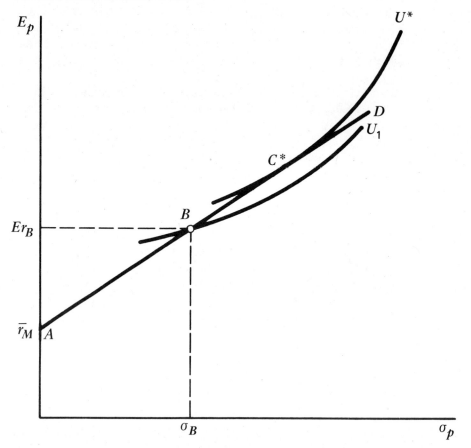

FIGURE 5A.2
PORTFOLIO SELECTION WHEN
BORROWING IS ALLOWED.

expected return of E_p^a and a risk of σ_p^a. Now assume that money is risk free and the investor is considering how to combine money with the portfolio of risky assets whose expected return and risk are shown at point A. The portfolio at point A contains n assets whose shares of total wealth are $w_1, w_2, \cdots w_n$. The investor can take part of total wealth and hold it as money. The *remaining* wealth can be held in the n assets in the same proportion to remaining wealth as they bear to total wealth at point A. For example, assume that at point A wealth is held in four assets, with 25 percent of total wealth devoted to each. The investor can use part of total wealth to hold money. The remaining wealth is divided equally among the four risky assets, that is, 25 percent in each.

The collection of risky assets can be thought of as a single composite asset with expected return E_p^a and risk σ_p^a. This asset can be blended with money to form a

FIGURE 5A.3
THE INVESTMENT OPPORTUNITY
LOCUS FOR MONEY AND A
COMPOSITE OF RISKY ASSETS.

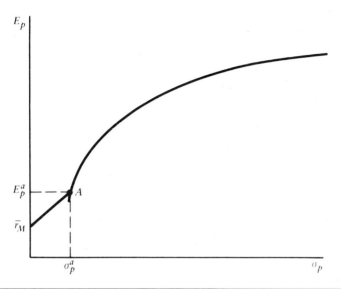

total portfolio composed of money and the composite asset. The expected return on the total portfolio is $E_p^T = w_M \bar{r}_M + w_a E_p^a$, where w_M is the share of money in *total* wealth and w_a is the share of the composite asset in total wealth. Because $w_M + w_a = 1$, the expression can be written as $E_p^T = (1 - w_a)\bar{r}_M + w_a E_p^a$. Because money is assumed to be risk free, the standard deviation of the total portfolio is $\sigma_p^T = w_a \sigma_p^a$. Thus, the expected return and risk for the total portfolio vary linearly with the share of the composite portfolio in total wealth, w_a.

By fixing the shares of the assets in the wealth that is not devoted to money, we have reduced the problem to the relationship between a single risky asset and a risk-free asset. The investment opportunity locus is a straight line starting at $\bar{r}_M$, where all of wealth is invested in money, and ending at point A, where all of wealth is invested in the composite asset. The slope of the line is $E_p^a - \bar{r}_M / \sigma_p^a$.

It should also be noted that the linear investment opportunity locus can be extended beyond point A by borrowing money at the risk-free interest rate and investing the funds in the composite asset. Thus, in terms of our earlier example, 25 percent of the borrowed money is invested in each of the four assets. This extended investment opportunity locus is shown as line I in Figure 5A.4.

Similar linear investment opportunity loci can be obtained by selecting other points on the original locus that contains only risky assets. Thus, point B in Figure 5A.4 shows a linear locus that combines the risk-free asset (money) with a composite asset comprised of the risky assets that provide the portfolio expected

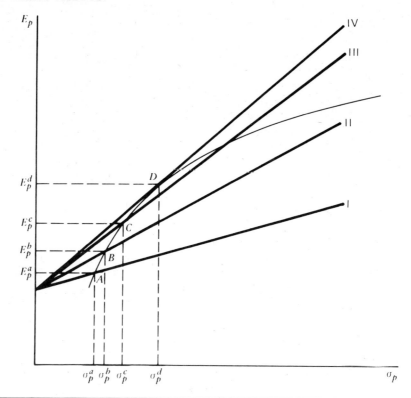

FIGURE 5A.4
INVESTMENT OPPORTUNITY LOCI
FOR ALTERNATIVE COMPOSITES
OF RISKY ASSETS.

return and risk of E_p^b and σ_p^b. As before, the wealth that is not devoted to money is invested in risky assets in the same proportions as at point B. The proportions at point B are different than at point A, however.

Note that as we move from point A to point B to point C, the linear investment opportunity loci become steeper. Finally, the locus IV that is tangent to the locus for risky assets at point D is the steepest linear locus that is feasible. The investment opportunity locus IV dominates all others because it allows investors to reach the highest indifference curve. It is preferred by all investors. For investors who prefer a lower risk than is available at point D, it is possible to move down line IV. They are better off blending money with the composite asset of point D rather than with composites of point A, B, or C because line IV offers the highest expected return for a given risk. For investors who are willing to bear more risk than σ_p^d (at point D), it is more efficient to move along line IV than either to move along any of the other linear loci or to move along the locus containing only risky assets. Again, line IV dominates because it gives the greatest expected return for given risk. Thus, line IV constitutes the set of efficient portfolios, and it is the only relevant investment opportunity locus.

We are led to the result that when there is a risk-free asset, the investment opportunity locus is linear. Furthermore, we reach the striking conclusion that *all* investors hold individual risky assets in the proportions to their total holdings of risky assets as implied by point *D*. The total amount of risky assets that an investor holds depends upon the investor's preferences. Some investors choose portfolios with expected returns and risks indicated by the segment of line IV between $\bar{r}_M$ and point *D*. Thus, they hold a combination of money and the composite portfolio of *D*. The more risk averse they are, the greater the share of money in the total portfolio and the smaller the share of the composite asset of *D*. Investors who are less risk averse do not hold money but borrow instead in order to achieve a position on line IV to the right of point *D*. The less risk averse these investors are, the greater the amount of borrowing and, therefore, the greater the excess of composite asset over wealth.

SOME CONCLUDING COMMENTS

If there is a risk-free asset, the analysis of portfolio selection is greatly simplified because the investment opportunity locus is a straight line. Furthermore, all investors hold individual risky assets in the same proportion to total holdings of risky assets as at point *D*. The only decision in this world is between the composite asset and the risk-free asset or, for those investors who borrow, how much to borrow.

The assumption of a risk-free asset has been used to develop an elegant theory of the market valuation of assets. A discussion of this theory is beyond the scope of this book, but the theory has attracted considerable attention among academics and market participants.[32]

Unfortunately, we do not live in a world with a risk-free asset. As a result, it is necessary to use the more cumbersome investment opportunity locus described in the body of Chapter 5. The discussion of the role of a risk-free asset has helped to highlight some of the important elements of the theory of portfolio selection, however. It has also provided a convenient vehicle for discussing the role of borrowing.

It is possible to introduce borrowing into the theory when there is no risk-free asset. The analysis is complex, however. There are risks to borrowing, and many market participants can borrow only at a higher cost than they can lend. These complications are considered in the more advanced literature. By treating borrowing as a negative asset in the derivation of the investment opportunity locus, this literature explains why many investors hold assets in excess of their wealth.

[32] For a lucid description of the theory, see Chapter 6 of William F. Sharpe, *Investments* (Englewood Cliffs, N.J.: Prentice-Hall, 1978).

SELECTED REFERENCES

Markowitz, Harry, *Portfolio Selection*, New York: Wiley, 1959.

Sharp, William, *Investments*, Englewood Cliffs, N.J.: Prentice-Hall, 1978.

Tobin, James, "The Theory of Portfolio Selection" in Hahn and Brechling (eds.), *The Theory of Interest Rates*, London: Macmillan, 1965.

THE TERM STRUCTURE OF INTEREST RATES

6

The *term structure of interest rates* is defined as the relationship that exists among "interest rates" on debts with different maturities, but the same risk of default. By studying the term structure of interest rates, we can learn a great deal about how the expectations of market participants about the future affect interest rates. We will show that the term structure of interest rates can, under certain circumstances, actually reveal the interest rates that market participants expect to prevail in the future. We will also show that because the future is uncertain, substantial errors are often made concerning the future behavior of interest rates. There are large gains to those who guess correctly and large losses to those who guess incorrectly. Studying the term structure of interest rates also reveals why depository institutions bear considerable risk by issuing short-term liabilities to finance the acquisition of long-term assets, such as mortgage loans.

EQUATING RATES OF RETURN FOR DIFFERENT HOLDING PERIODS

A key to understanding the term structure of interest rates is the *holding period*, that is, the period of time over which an investor might hold a debt instrument. Because there are organized markets for debt instruments, there is no necessary relationship between the maturity of a debt instrument and the holding period of an investor. For example, an investor can purchase a thirty-year bond, hold it for one year, and then sell it. Similarly, an investor can purchase a one-year bond and, when it matures, purchase another one.

The choice among various maturities of debt is determined by the rate of return that an investor expects to earn on the different maturities and by the investor's preferences concerning the trade-off between expected return and risk. Current interest rates, expected future interest rates, and transactions costs determine the expected rates of return for bonds of different maturities. These expectations coupled with the risks of different investment strategies determine whether an investor with a thirty-year horizon purchases a single thirty-year bond to hold to maturity interest rates, expected future interest rates, and transactions costs determine the expected rates of return for bonds of different maturities. These expectations coupled with the risks of different investment strategies determine whether an investor with a thirty-year horizon purchases a single thirty-year bond to hold to maturity versus holding a sequence of one-year bonds for thirty years. The same issues affect the decision to hold a one-year bond for one year versus holding a thirty-year bond for a year.

The basic issues involved in the choice among bonds with different maturities can be analyzed by considering a simple example of a one-year and a two-year bond. Assume that it is the first of the year and the government issues at par (i.e., $100) a one-year bond paying $10 of interest plus $100 of principal at the end of the year.[1] Thus, the current interest rate on one-year bonds is 10 percent.[2] The bond can be sold at par because at a 10 percent current interest rate the discounted present value (DPV) of $110 received in one year is $110/1.10 = $100. Assume that the government also wants to offer a two-year bond that pays $8 of interest (coupon) at the end of each year plus $100 at maturity. With the information available it is not possible to establish the price at which the two-year bond can be sold. Its price is the DPV of the coupon and principal payments over the two years; that is, $\text{DPV} = [\$8/(1+i_1)] + [\$108/(1+i_1)(1+i_2)]$. The interest rate factor for the first year, $(1+i_1)$, is known because i_1 equals 10 percent, but the one-year interest rate that will prevail in the second year, i_2, is not known. Assume for the moment that investors are clairvoyant and that they *know* that the interest rate on one-year bonds next year, i_2, will be 10 percent. In this case, the price of the two-year bond issued at the beginning of the first year, P_2^1, is $P_2^1 = \$8/(1.10) + \$108/(1.10)^2 = \$96.53$. If the interest rate on one-year bonds is going to be 10 percent in both the first and second years, no one will pay $100 par value for the two-year bond; it can only be sold at a discount from par, that is, for $96.53.

Now let us compute the rate of return that an investor earns in the first year by holding the one-year versus the two-year bond. For the one-year bond, the rate of return is simply 10 percent. The situation for the two-year bond is more compli-

---

[1] The example is in terms of government securities so that we can abstract from risk of default. The term structure of interest rates can be analyzed for bonds with default risk, and the basic conclusions are not affected.

[2] It may be useful to review the discussion of coupon rates, par value, current interest rates, and rates of return presented in Chapter 5.

cated. To compute its rate of return over the first year, we must determine the price of the bond at the *beginning* of the second year so that any capital gain or loss can be taken into account. At the beginning of the second year, the bond has one year left to maturity so, in effect, it becomes a one-year bond. We know that the interest rate on one-year bonds in the second year is 10 percent and that the old one-year bond pays $8 of interest plus $100 of principal at the end of the second year. Thus, the price of the two-year bond at the beginning of the second year, P_2^2; is given by $P_2^2 = \$108/(1.10) = \$98.18$. Now, we can calculate the rate of return from holding the two-year bond for the first year, r_2^1. The bond is purchased at the beginning of the first year for $96.53, and it can be sold after a year for $98.15, so there is a capital gain of $1.65.[3] There is also a coupon payment of $8 at the end of the year. Recalling that the rate of return on a bond is its net income, including capital gains or loss, divided by its purchase price, we have $r_2^1 = (\$8 + \$1.65)/\$96.53 = \$9.65/\$96.5 = .10$ or 10 percent. Thus, the rate of return on the one-year and the two-year bonds for the first year are both 10 percent.

The rates of return for the one-year and two-year bonds must be equal because the interest rate on one-year bonds is known for both years and there are no transactions costs. In this situation, no one will buy the two-year bond unless it offers the same rate of return as the one-year bond during the first year. Since the one-year bond pays $10 of interest and the two-year bond pays only $8 of interest, the price of a new two-year bond must be priced sufficiently far below par when issued to provide a capital gain plus interest income that produces a rate of return of 10 percent during the first year.

By a similar argument, the rate of return on the two-year bond during the second year is also 10 percent. The interest rate on new one-year bonds in the second year is 10 percent. We know that the two-year bond with one year to maturity pays $100 of principal at maturity, so its price at the end of the second year is the par value of $100. The price of the bond at the beginning of the second year is $98.18 so the holder obtains a $1.82 capital gain during the second year plus a coupon payment of $8. The rate of return for the second year, r_2^2, is $r_2^2 = (\$8 + \$1.82)/\$98.18 = \$9.82/\$98.2 = .10$, or 10 percent. The prices and rates of return for the one-year and two-year bonds in each year are summarized in Table 6.1.

We conclude from this example that if the interest rates on one-year bonds are known in advance for both the first and second years, the rate of return for each one-year holding period must be the same for one-year and two-year bonds. Given the coupon payments of $10 each year for one-year bonds and $8 each year for the two-year bond, one-year and two-year bonds can only be sold if their prices equal their DPV. If, for example, the price of the two-year bond exceeds its

[3] For simplicity, it is assumed that there are no transactions costs for buying or selling bonds. As we shall see later, however, transactions costs play an important role in determining the demand and supply of bonds with different maturities.

TABLE 6.1
COMPARISONS OF PRICES AND RATES OF RETURN
ON 1-YEAR AND 2-YEAR BONDS

	1-Year Bond			2-Year Bond		
Year	Coupon	Price at Beginning of Year	Rate of Return	Coupon	Price at Beginning of Year	Rate of Return
1	$10	$100	$10/$100 = .10	$8	$96.53	[$8+($98.18-96.53)]/96.53 = .10
2	$10	$100	$10/$100 = .10	$8	$98.18	[$8+($100-98.18)]/98.18 = .10

DPV of $96.15 when issued, no one will buy it because the two-year bond will earn a lower rate of return in the first year than a one-year bond. Similarly, if the price of the two-year bond is lower than $96.15, no one will buy a one-year bond the first year because it will earn a lower rate of return during that year than a two-year bond. Thus, the prices of one-year and two-year bonds must equal their discounted present values. At these prices, investors are indifferent between one-year and two-year bonds. Thus, abstracting from transactions costs and uncertainty about i_2, any investor is indifferent between one-year and two-year bonds when their prices equal the DPV of their future payments of interest and principal. When the interest payment for the two-year bond is less than the interest payment for the one-year bond, the two-year bond must sell for a discount when issued, and its price appreciation over the two years makes up for the lower interest payment.[4]

Up to this point we have assumed that the interest rate on one-year bonds in the second year is known in advance. This assumption is convenient for showing how the price of the two-year bond adjusts to equate rates of return on one-year and two-year bonds, but it is obviously unrealistic. The interest rate on newly issued one-year bonds, i_1, is known at the beginning of the first year, but the interest rate on one-year bonds in the second year, i_2, cannot be known with certainty until the second year begins. Thus, investors must choose between one-year and two-year bonds when i_2 is uncertain. The next step in the analysis of the term structure of interest rates is to examine investor behavior when future interest rates are uncertain.

RISK-NEUTRAL INVESTORS

When investors are risk neutral, there is no trade-off between expected return and risk because they are only interested in maximizing the expected rate of return on

---

[4] It is left to the reader to demonstrate that if the interest payment on the two-year bond exceeds the interest payments on the one-year bonds, the two-year bond will sell for a premium when issued, and it will sustain capital losses over the two years.

their portfolios. Based on their expectations (predictions) of future short-term interest rates,[5] risk-neutral investors select the bond maturity that offers the highest *expected* rate of return. They know that their expectations may not be realized, but these investors act on these expectations without regard to risk. This implies that risk-neutral investors act as if expected future interest rates are known with certainty. This is known as *certainty equivalence*. In our example, if investors expect the interest rate on one-year bonds to be 10 percent in the second year, they are willing to pay $96.53 for the two-year bond at the beginning of the first year, which is the same price that we obtained under the assumption that i_2 is known with certainty. Thus, the expected rate of return in each year from holding a two-year bond is the same as the expected return from holding two one-year bonds, and a risk-neutral investor is indifferent between the two investment strategies.

If the interest rate on one-year bonds is not 10 percent in the second year, then the realized rates of return from holding one-year versus two-year bonds will not be the same, but a risk-neutral investor is unconcerned about this risk. The price of the two-year bond at the beginning of the first year is $P_2^1 = [\$8/(1+i_1)] + [\$108/(1+i_1)(1+i_2)]$. The interest rate of 10 percent on one-year bonds in the first year is known (certain) but the interest rate in the second year is not. Risk neutral investors replace i_2 with its expected value, i_2^e, of 10 percent and compute $P_2^1 = \$96.53$. If the interest rate in the second year is 10 percent, then the price of the two-year bond at the beginning of the second year is $P_2^2 = \$98.18$. Thus, if expectations are realized, the two-year bond will actually earn a rate of return of 10 percent in each year, which was the expected rate of return for each year. If, however, the interest rate for one-year bonds in the second year is 15 percent rather than 10 percent, holders of two-year bonds will suffer. The price at the beginning of the second year is $P_2^2 = \$108/(1.15) = \$93.91$ rather than the $98.18 that was expected. An investor who purchases a two-year bond at the beginning of the first year for $96.53 sustains a capital loss of $93.91 - \$96.53 = -\$2.62$ and realizes a rate of return over the first year of $r_2^1 = (\$8 - \$2.62)/\$96.53 = .056$, or 5.6 percent. Thus, the investor would have been better off purchasing a one-year bond the first year because it returned 10 percent.

It should be noted that in the second year the two-year bond with one year left to maturity earns the same rate of return as a new one-year bond issued at the beginning of the second year. At the beginning of the second year, the interest rate of 15 percent on new one-year bonds is known. The old two-year bond pays $100 at the end of the year, so it realizes a capital gain of $100 - \$93.91 = \$6.09$ for a rate of return of $(\$8 + \$6.09)/\$93.91 = .15$, or 15 percent. Once the interest rate on new one-year bonds is known, a two-year bond with one year to maturity must earn the same rate of return as the one-year bond. No one will buy the old two-year bond unless it offers a return of 15 percent. This is precisely why the price is depressed to $93.91 once the 15 percent interest rate is known.

---

[5] In this chapter, the shortest bond maturity is assumed to be one year. Thus, the "short-term" interest rate is the interest rate on one-year bonds.

The argument presented so far might give the impression that because of uncertainty it is always better to purchase one-year bonds. This is not the case. Assume that the interest rate on one-year bonds in the second year is expected to be 10 percent but ends up being 5 percent. In this case, it would have been better to purchase a two-year bond in the first year. The price of the two-year bond at the beginning of the second year is $P_2^2 = \$108/(1.05) = \$102.86$. The original purchase price based on i_2^e of .10 is $96.53, so the capital gain is $102.86 - \$96.53 = \$6.33$. The realized rate of return for the first year is $(\$8+\$6.33)/\$96.53 = .148$ or 14.8 percent. Investors expected to earn a 10 percent return on two-year bonds over the first year, but they end up earning 14.8 percent. Investors in two-year bonds did better than those who purchased one-year bonds in the first year.[6]

Inferring Expected Future Interest Rates

If all investors are risk neutral, it can be shown that their expectations concerning future interest rates are embedded in the term structure of interest rates. This can be demonstrated by considering a new example. Assume, as before, that the government issues a one-year bond paying $10 of interest plus $100 of principal at the end of the year. It also issues a two-year bond paying $8 of interest at the end of each year and $100 at the end of the second year. In this example, however, both bonds are sold for $100 each. In light of our earlier discussion, how can both bonds sell for $100? The answer lies in investor's expectations concerning what the interest rate on one-year bonds will be in the second year.

If all investors are risk neutral, they will buy the bond with the highest expected rate of return over any holding period. The government can sell one-year and two-year bonds at the same price only if they both offer the same expected return to investors. Consider a two-year holding period. Investors equate the expected rate of return over two years from holding a two-year bond for two years to the expected return from holding a one-year bond in each year.

It is possible to calculate the value of the interest rate on one-year bonds in the second year that gives the same expected rate of return from purchasing a one-year bond in each of the two years as can be earned from purchasing a two-year bond and holding it to maturity. For an initial investment of $100, the purchaser of a one-year bond has $100(1.10) = \$110$ at the end of the first year and $\$110(1+i_2^e)$ at the end of the second year. For a two-year bond investment of $100 earns $8 of interest income by the end of the first year. Assume this $8 is invested during the second year in a one-year bond at the interest rate i_2^e.[7] During

---

[6] It is left to the reader to verify that if the interest rate on one-year bonds is 5 percent in the second year, two-year bonds with one year to maturity also earn a return of 5 percent.

[7] For bonds, interest income does not compound automatically the way it does in a savings account. Rather, the holder receives an actual interest (coupon) payment each year. This payment must then be invested in some other asset. For simplicity, it is assumed that interest payments are invested in one-year bonds or equivalently in a two-year bond with one year to maturity.

the second year, the two-year bond produces another $8 of interest income, and $100 is paid at maturity. The purchaser of the bond receives over the two years $8 of first-year interest plus $8 of second-year interest plus $8 $\cdot i_2^e$ of interest from the investment of the first-year interest income. The total payment to the purchaser over the two years, including the $100 of principal, is $8 + $8 + $8i_2^e$ + $100. We can now solve for the value of i_2^e that equates the expected rate of the return over two years from purchasing two one-year bonds to the rate of return on a two-year bond. For the two one-year bonds, we have a total over the two years of $100(1.10)(1 + i_2^e) = 110(1 + i_2^e)$; and for the two-year bond, we have a total over the two years of $8 + $8 + $8i_2^e$ + $100 = (1 + i_2^e)$8 + $108. Setting the two totals equal to each other and solving for i_2^e we get $110(1 + i_2^e) = (1 + i_2^e)$8 + $108, or $110 + $110i_2^e = $8 + $8i_2^e$ + $108, so $102i_2^e = $6, and $i_2^e = .0588$. If the interest rate on one-year bonds is 5.88 percent in the second year, the rate of return from purchasing a one-year bond at 10 percent interest followed by a second one-year bond at 5.88 percent interest gives the same (expected) rate of return over the two years as purchasing a two-year bond and holding it to maturity.

Over the two years, investment of $100 in two one-year bonds grows to $100(1.10)(1.0588) = 116.47, and investment of $100 in a two-year bond grows to the same value. We can define the *two-year rate of return* as the annual (constant) rate of return that makes $100 grow to $116.47 at the end of two years. This rate of return is often called the *yield to maturity*.[8] Let R_2 be the two-year rate of return. We can calculate R_2 from

$$(1 + R_2)(1 + R_2)\$100 = 116.47, \text{ or } (1 + R_2)^2 = \$1.1647$$

so

$$(1 + R_2) = \sqrt{1.1647} = 1.0792, \text{ and } R_2 = .0792.$$

Thus, the annual rate of return over the two years is 7.92 percent. The two-year rate of return is less than the 8 percent coupon interest quoted for the two-year bond. This occurs because the first year's interest income of $8 paid at the end of the year is invested in a one-year bond at 5.88 percent. If the interest income could be invested at 8 percent interest, the rate of return over the two years would be 8 percent.

Computation of the two-year rate of return leads us to an important observation. Because the two-year rate of return equals the rate of return from holding two one-year bonds, we have:

$$\$100(1 + i_1)(1 + i_2^e) = \$100(1 + R_2)^2, \text{ or } (1 + R_2)^2 = (1 + i_1)(1 + i_2^e)$$

and

$$1 + R_2 = \sqrt{(1 + i_1)(1 + i_2^e)} = [(1 + i_1)(1 + i_2^e)]^{1/2}$$

[8] Strictly speaking, we should use the terms expected two-year rate of return and expected yield to maturity.

The two-year rate of return is a sort of average of the two one-year interest rates. R_2 lies between i_1 and i_2^e, but it is not the simple average of the two interest rates. The two-year rate of return factor $(1 + R_2)$ is a *geometric average* of the one-year interest rate factors.

We conclude that the expected interest rate on one-year bonds in the second year, i_2^e, makes the two-year rate of return from holding a two-year bond equal to the rate of return from holding two one-year bonds. At the beginning of the first year, i_2^e is not known. It is the interest rate that will have to prevail on one-year bonds next year for the two-year rates of return from two one-year bonds and one two-year bond to be the same. The interest rate i_2^e is often called the *implicit forward interest rate* to denote that it is the one-year interest rate that must be expected to prevail next year if a one-year bond at 10 percent and a two-year bond at 8 percent are to have the same expected rate of return over the two years.[9]

If investors' expectations are correct concerning the interest rate that will prevail on one-year bonds in the second year, they will earn the same rate of return over two years either by purchasing a two-year bond and holding it to maturity or by purchasing a one-year bond in each year. Some investors have only a one-year horizon, however. In this case, we can also show that the expected one-year rate of return from holding a one-year bond and from holding a two-year bond for one year are the same. The one-year bond earns $10 during the first year, and the two-year bond earns $8 of interest income plus any capital gain or loss. In order to calculate the gain or loss, we have to determine the expected price of the two-year bond at the beginning of the second year. Investors expect the interest rate on one-year bonds in the second year to be 5.88 percent. At the end of the second year, the old two-year bond pays $8 of interest plus $100 of principal. A one-year bond is expected to pay $5.88 of interest plus $100 of principal. The two-year bond is expected, therefore, to pay out more money during the second year than a one-year bond and, therefore, is expected to sell for more than $100. In particular, investors expect the price of the two-year bond at the beginning of the second year to be $108/1.058 = $102. Thus, an investor who purchases a two-year bond at the beginning of the first year for $100 expects its price to appreciate to $102 by the end of the year for a capital gain of $2. The expected rate of return on the bond for the first year is $(\$8 + \$2)/\$100 = .10$, or 10 percent. We conclude that investors expect to earn the same rate of return in the first year from holding either a one-year bond or a two-year bond. Furthermore, at the end of the second year, the price of the two-year bond must be $100, so an investor expects to realize a capital loss of $2 in the second year and earn an expected return of $(\$8 - \$2)/\$102 = .0588$, or 5.88 percent. This equals the return expected for one-year bonds in the second year.

The various examples demonstrate how in the absence of transactions costs, risk-neutral investors expect to earn the same rate of return for any holding period

---

[9] The reader should verify that when $i_2^e = 10$ percent, the two-year bond cannot be sold at par. Rather, it can only be sold for $96.53 as shown in the earlier example.

irrespective of the maturity of the bond they hold. The equality of expected returns is achieved because risk-neutral investors always prefer the bond with the highest expected return. If a bond of a particular maturity has a higher expected return than a bond of another maturity, investors only want to hold the bond with the highest expected return. A bond with a lower expected return cannot be sold, so its price depreciates sufficiently to raise its expected return to that of the other bond. Thus, the expected returns on all bonds must be equal when investors are risk neutral and there are no transactions costs.

Transactions costs and risk aversion of wealth holders can change this result, but before turning to these considerations, we must discuss an important implication of the risk-neutrality case. The examples in the text have only involved one-year and two-year bonds, but the results generalize. For example, the expected yield to maturity for a three-year bond (three-year rate of return) must equal the expected return from investing in one-year bonds in each year. Thus, an investor with \$100 expects to earn $\$100(1+i_1)(1+i_2^e)(1+i_3^e)$ from investing in one-year bonds each year. The yield to maturity on a three-year bond, R_3, must provide the same expected income, so $\$100(1+R_3)^3 = \$100(1+i_1)(1+i_2^e)(1+i_3^e)$ and $(1+R_3) = [(1+i_1)(1+i_2^e)(1+i_3^e)]^{1/3}$. Thus, the yield to maturity factor for a three-year bond is a geometric average of the factors for the current one-year interest rate and the expected future one-year interest rates (implicit forward interest rates) in the second and third years.

In general, for a bond with n years to maturity, we have $(1+R_n) = [(1+i_1)(1+i_2^e)(1+i_3^e)\cdots(1+i_n^e)]^{1/n}$. This expression for the yield to maturity allows us to deduce all the expected future interest rates. For example, the yield to maturity for a one-year bond, R_1, is simply the interest rate on that bond, and the yield to maturity for a two-year bond, R_2, is given by $(1+R_2)^2 = (1+i_1)(1+i_2^e)$.[10] We can form the ratio

$$\frac{(1+R_2)^2}{(1+R_1)} = \frac{(1+i_1)(1+i_2^e)}{(1+i_1)} = (1+i_2^e)$$

so

$$i_2^e = \frac{(1+R_2)^2}{(1+R_1)} - 1.$$

For the case of a bond with two years to maturity and a bond with three years to maturity, we can construct the ratio

$$\frac{(1+R_3)^3}{(1+R_2)^2} = \frac{(1+i_1)(1+i_2^e)(1+i_3^e)}{(1+i_1)(1+i_2^e)} = (1+i_3^e)$$

and

$$i_3^e = \frac{(1+R_3)^3}{(1+R_2)^2} - 1.$$

[10] The yields to maturity can be obtained from the financial pages of the newspaper or from calling a broker or dealer.

Thus, the relationship between the yields to maturity of one-year and two-year bonds allows us to deduce the interest rate that investors expect to prevail for one-year bonds one year in the future. The implicit forward interest rate on one-year bonds two years in the future can be obtained by comparing the yields to maturity for three-year versus two-year bonds. In general, we can deduce the implicit forward interest rate for n years in the future by comparing the yields to maturity for bonds with n years to maturity and $n - 1$ years to maturity:

$$\frac{(1+R_n)^n}{(1+R_{n-1})^{n-1}} = \frac{(1+i_1)(1+i_2^e) \cdots (1+i_{n-1}^e)(1+i_n^e)}{(1+i_1)(1+i_2^e) \cdots (1+i_{n-1}^e)} = (1+i_n^e)$$

so

$$i_n^e = \frac{(1+R_n)^n}{(1+R_{n-1})^{n-1}} - 1.$$

By considering the yields to maturity for bonds whose maturities differ by one year, we can calculate the continuum of one-year interest rates expected for each year in the future. Thus, the current yields to maturity for bonds of different maturities divulge the markets' *current* expectations concerning future interest rates. If market expectations change, however, the yields to maturity also change to reflect the changes in expectations concerning future interest rates.[11]

To summarize the argument to this point, market participants attempt to predict future interest rates. Based on these predictions, bonds of various maturities are bought and sold, and bond prices change until the rates of return that risk-neutral investors expect to earn from any maturity are the same over all holding periods. An implication of this result is that the current pattern of yields to maturity for bonds of different maturities reveals the market's current predictions of future short-term interest rates. For example, if the current yield on new two-year bonds is below the interest rate on new one-year bonds, market participants predict that the interest rate for one-year bonds will decline in the second year. Similarly, if the current yield to maturity on new three-year bonds is above the yield on new two-year bonds, market participants predict that the interest rate on one-year bonds will rise in the third year. If expectations are correct, the rates of return earned from holding bonds of any maturity over any holding period will equal the rates of return from holding bonds of any other maturity. This leads us to the striking conclusion that aside from transactions costs, if future interest rates

[11] For simplicity, it is assumed throughout this chapter that all investors have the same expectations concerning future interest rates. In fact, investors often disagree about the future course of interest rates. In this case, implicit forward interest rates can be thought of as the interest rates expected to prevail in the future by a consensus of market participants.

could be predicted accurately, it would not make a particle of difference what maturity of bond an investor purchases.[12]

It is possible to obtain qualitative evidence on implicit forward interest rates by looking at what is commonly called a *yield curve*. A yield curve plots the current yields to maturity (the rates of return to maturity) on bonds with the same risk of default but different maturities. All yields to maturity are measured at the same point in time. Figure 6.1 illustrates four different yield curves. In Panel A, the yield to maturity rises as the maturity of bonds increases and then levels out at 10 percent for bonds of fifteen years maturity and over. This pattern implies that market participants believe that short-term interest rates will rise in the future from their current low value of 4 percent, reach a peak of 10 percent after fifteen years, and then remain at that value thereafter.

Panel B shows the opposite kind of pattern. Short-term yields are above longer-term yields. This pattern implies that market participants believe that current short-term interest rates will decline over the next five years and then remain constant at 7 percent. Panel C shows a "humped" yield curve in which wealth holders anticipate that short-term interest rates will rise for the next three years, then decline for nine years before leveling out at 6 percent after twelve years. Finally, Panel D shows the opposite pattern. Here, it is expected that short-term interest rates will first decline and then rise again. If future short-term interest rates are not expected to change in the future, the yields on all bonds will be the same; that is, the yield curve is flat.

It is important to note that our analysis of the term structure of interest rates simply assumes that market participants attempt to predict future interest rates. We have not assumed that the predictions are always accurate. All that a market participant can do is take whatever information is available about the future and make a guess about future interest rates. Interest rates are affected by a variety of influences, including unexpected movements in economic activity and inflation. As a result, actual short-term interest rates in the future often depart significantly from implicit forward interest rates. Furthermore, as events develop, participants in the bond market revise their forecasts of future interest rates. With these changes in forecasts come changes in the yield curve. Yield curves can, and do, change sharply as economic events lead market participants to revise their forecasts of future interest rates.

When investors are risk neutral and when there are no transactions costs, yields on bonds of different maturities differ only because market participants expect short-term interest rates to change in the future. This explanation of the relationship among yields on bonds of different maturities is often called the *expectations approach* because it uses expectations of future short-term interest rates to explain the term structure of interest rates. Expectations do play a central role, but transactions costs and the behavior of risk-averse investors prevent expectations of future interest rates from being the sole determinant of the term structure of interest rates.

[12] If interest rate forecasts are always correct, there is no risk, so risk aversion is not relevant.

FIGURE 6.1
ALTERNATIVE YIELD CURVES

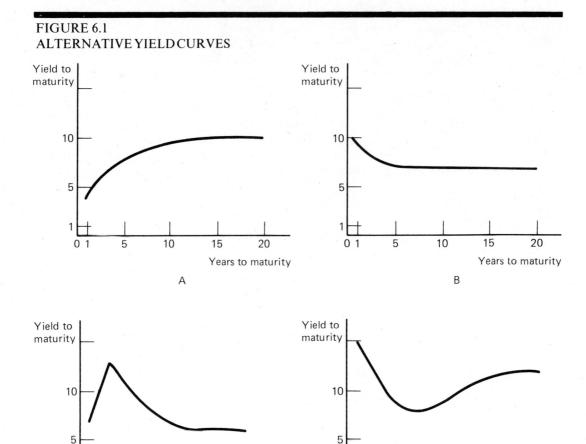

RISK-AVERSE INVESTORS
==

Because market participants are not clairvoyant, implicit forward interest rates are often not the actual interest rates that materialize. As a result, the actual rates of return earned on bonds of different maturity are, in fact, not all the same. Market participants who are risk neutral attempt to equate the rates of return, but forecast errors prevent them from being successful. Forecast errors introduce risk and can influence the decisions of risk-averse investors concerning the choice among bonds with different maturities. Risk-averse investors are willing to sacrifice expected return for a reduction in risk.[13] If bonds of one maturity are less risky than bonds of another maturity, these investors may be willing to accept a lower expected return on the less risky maturity. This consideration suggests that risk-averse investors do not always purchase the bond with the highest expected return and that their purchases and sales of bonds will not necessarily bring about equality of the expected returns on all maturities of bonds. Thus, the relationship among the yields on bonds with different maturities not only reflects expectations of future short-term interest rates but also the demand for less risky bonds by risk-averse investors.

In assessing the effect of risk on the term structure of interest rates, we must examine the nature of the risk. It is often asserted that long-term bonds are more risky than short-term bonds because an unexpected change in interest rates has a larger effect on the price of long-term bonds than short-term bonds. This assertion may or may not be true depending upon the expected duration of the change in interest rates. Consider the case where short-term interest rates are currently 10 percent and they are not expected to change in the future. Now assume that there is an unexpected rise in inflation that propels current short-term interest rates to 20 percent. The rise in the current short-term interest rate affects the prices and rates of return on existing bonds. The interest (coupon) income on these bonds is fixed, so their price has to fall. The rise in the current short-term interest rate may also induce market participants to revise upward their expectations of future short-term interest rates. If this occurs, there will be a further decline in the prices of existing bonds. How much bond prices change depends upon the period of time that short-term interest rates are expected to remain at 20 percent and upon the maturity of the bond.

The factors involved can be seen by considering the price of a bond with n years to maturity. When investors are risk neutral, that price is the discounted present value of the coupon payments plus the principal that is paid at maturity:

$$P_n = \frac{c_1}{(1+i_1)} + \frac{c_2}{(1+i_1)(1+i_2^e)} + \cdots \frac{c_n + p_p^b}{(1+i_1)(1+i_2^e)\cdots(1+i_n^e)} ,$$

where $c_1, c_2 \cdots, c_n$ are the coupon payments received at the end of each year and p_p^b is the bond principal received at maturity. Consider the case where short-term interest rates are expected to remain at 20 percent indefinitely. Here the current interest rate i_1 and all the expected future interest rates, $i_2^e, i_3^e \cdots, i_n^e$, rise to 20 percent. The degree of the effect of this revision of expectations on bond prices depends upon the maturity of the bond. For a bond with one year remaining to maturity with an initial price of $100 and a coupon payment of $10, the price falls to approximately $92. For a two-year bond the price falls to approxi-

---

[13] The risk being discussed here arises from errors made in predicting future short-term interest rates. We are not discussing default risk.

mately $85, and the price of a ten-year bond falls to $58. In general, if short-term interest rates are expected to rise permanently, the longer the maturity of a bond, the greater the decline in its price. The prices of existing bonds must fall sufficiently to induce potential purchasers to buy them rather than a succession of short-term bonds that are expected to return 20 percent per year. Current holders of bonds suffer capital losses, and they earn a lower rate of return than initially anticipated. The longer the maturity of the bond, the greater the capital loss to its holder when current and expected future interest rates increase. Similarly, if short-term interest rates are suddenly expected to be permanently lower than 10 percent, the prices of existing bonds rise, and the prices of long-term bonds rise by more than for short-term bonds. Current holders of bonds earn capital gains and the rate of return is higher than initially anticipated. The longer the maturity of the bond, the greater the capital gain. We conclude that long-term bonds are more risky than short-term bonds because they experience larger price adjustments when there are unexpected and permanent revisions in the level of expected future interest rates.

It is important to note, however, that the prices of longer-term bonds are not always affected more by revisions in interest rate expectations than are short-term bonds. If short-term interest rates are expected to rise or fall only temporarily, the prices of longer-term bonds are not affected very much. Consider the case where current and future short-term interest rates are initially expected to be 10 percent and where a temporary surge of inflation raises the current short-term interest rate to 20 percent. Assume that market participants expect the short-term interest rate to return to 10 percent after one year and remain at that value. Thus, only i_1 is affected, and all the expected future interest rates do not change. In this case, the price of a one-year bond again falls to $91.67, the price of a two-year bond is $91.74, and the price of a ten-year bond falls only to $92.66. In this situation, the longer the maturity of the bond, the smaller the decline in its price. Similarly, if there is a temporary, unexpected decline in the short-term interest rate, the prices of short-term bonds rise more than the prices of long-term bonds. Thus, if unexpected changes in short-term interest rates are viewed by market participants as temporary movements with no implications for future short-term interest rates, then short-term bonds are more risky than long-term bonds.

The riskiness of holding long-term versus short-term bonds depends upon the kind of forecasting errors that are most important to market participants. Risk-averse investors who want protection against errors in predicting the average level of future short-term interest rates will prefer to hold short-term bonds. Risk-averse investors who think they can accurately predict the average level of future short-term interest rates but who worry about errors in predicting the short-term interest rate from year to year, will prefer long-term bonds.

It is not possible on purely theoretical grounds to determine whether risk-averse investors prefer short-term bonds or long-term bonds. It does appear in practice, however, that there is a preference for short-term bonds. Over the last two decades, investors have made significant errors in predicting the average level of short-term interest rates that were to prevail in the economy. These errors arose primarily because inflation and short-term interest rates have on average been much higher than seemed imaginable when long-term bonds were initially purchased. For example, in the early 1960s, long-term bonds and mortgage loans that paid six percent interest were attractive to many investors. These investors did not anticipate the sharp increase in the average level of short-term interest rates that was to occur. By the 1970s and 1980s, these bonds and mortgage loans had sustained huge capital losses.[14] With the passage of time, long-term interest rates did rise as market participants raised their forecasts of expected future short-term interest rates. These upward revisions were often not sufficiently large, however, and long-term debt instruments continued to sustain capital losses as new waves of inflation hit the economy.

The lessons learned from misjudging the average level of future short-term interest rates induced risk-averse investors to demand a *risk premium* for holding long-term debt instruments.[15] The observed yield on a long-term bond equals its expected rate of return (risk neutrality) plus a risk premium. This implies that the price of a long-term bond is less than its discounted present value. The lower price allows the bond to earn a higher expected rate of return to maturity than the expected return from holding a sequence of short-term bonds. With a risk premium, the yields on long-term bonds exceed the yields on short-term bonds when investors do not expect future interest rates to change.

The existence of a risk premium requires that the expectations approach to the term structure of interest rates be modified. That approach asserts that the yield curve is flat when investors do not expect future short-term interest rates to change. It also asserts that when yields on long-term bonds exceed yields on short-term bonds, that is, an upward sloping yield curve, market participants expect short-term interest rates to rise in the future. With risk-averse investors, an upward sloping yield curve may simply reflect the fact that these investors must be compensated with a greater expected return if they are to hold long-term bonds. It is perfectly possible to have an upward sloping yield curve and for market participants to expect no rise in future short-term interest rates.

These considerations do not destroy the expectations approach, however. Sometimes the yield curve is upward sloping, sometimes it is flat, and sometimes it is downward sloping. *Changes* in the slope of the yield curve usually represent changes in expectations of future short-term interest rates rather than changes in the risk premium. Risk-averse investors require a premium to hold long-term bonds, but if there is a consensus that short-term interest rates will fall in the future, the yield curve becomes downward sloping. In this case, market expectations have overpowered the risk premium. The expectations approach must be modified to allow for a risk premium, however. Both expectations of future interest rates and the existence of a risk premium for long-term bonds affect the term structure of interest rates.

---

[14] As we shall see in Chapter 10, these losses had serious consequences for mutual savings banks and savings and loan associations.

[15] This is sometimes called a *liquidity premium*. This terminology is not used here because the premium concerns risk, not liquidity as we have defined it.

PREFERRED HABITATS FOR BOND HOLDERS AND BOND ISSUERS

The term structure is also affected by the behavior of market participants who attempt to minimize transactions costs by having their bonds mature at the times that the funds are needed for other uses. The desire to save transactions costs and to avoid price uncertainty induces these investors to acquire bonds that mature on the date that the funds will be put to alternative use. For example, consumers purchase bonds that mature when the funds are needed to support consumption during retirement, and businesses hold bonds that mature when the funds are needed to purchase equipment. These same considerations also affect the behavior of financial intermediaries. Insurance companies and pension funds, for example, are primarily interested in long-term investments because their own liabilities are long-term. These financial intermediaries can save transactions costs by purchasing long-term bonds rather than purchasing a succession of short-term bonds. Furthermore, they typically hold long-term assets to maturity, so price uncertainty is not relevant. Other financial intermediaries, such as commercial banks, have short-term liabilities and tend, therefore, to favor shorter-term bonds.

Issuers of bonds also attempt to have their debts mature when the funds can be repaid at least cost. Issuers attempt to avoid the transactions costs of refinancing short-term debt or of prepaying longer-term debt.

The preferences of market participants concerning the maturity of debt held and of debt issued can effect the term structure of interest rates and, therefore, modify the conclusions based on the expectations approach. Some investors and debt issuers have *preferred habitats*. Other things being equal, investors with short-time horizons tend to purchase short-term bonds, whereas investors with longer time horizons tend to purchase longer-term debt. Similarly, borrowers who need funds for a short period of time tend to borrow short-term, and borrowers with longer-term needs tend to issue long-term debt.

The term structure of interest rates is affected by the demand and supply of these market participants. If the demand of market participants whose preferred habitat is short-term bonds exceeds the demand of those who desire long-term bonds, or if borrowers prefer to issue long-term rather than short-term bonds, the prices of short-term bonds rise relative to long-term bonds. As a result, even if interest rates are not expected to change in the future, the yields on short-term bonds will be less than the yields on long-term bonds; that is, the yield curve is upward sloping. If borrowers prefer to issue long-term rather than short-term bonds, the effect is magnified because the supply of short-term bonds is less than the supply of long-term bonds. Conversely if preferred habitats are such that the demand for long-term bonds exceeds the demand for short-term bonds or if borrowers prefer to issue short-term rather than long-term bonds, the yields on short-term bonds will exceed the yields on long-term bonds (i.e., the yield curve will be downward sloping). Thus, preferred habitats can affect the term structure of interest rates. It is impossible to determine theoretically whether preferred habitats impart a positive or a negative slope to the yield curve.

Preferred habitats do not appear to have a major effect on the term structure of interest rates, at least in the short run, because there is a group of large investors who have no preferred habitat. These investors simply "play" the market in the hope of profiting from the mistakes of others in predicting future interest rates. Market participants with little or no inclination toward a preferred habitat, and participants who are willing to stray from their habitats if the anticipated profit is high, help keep the term structure of interest rates roughly consistent with expected future short-term interest rates. Based on the information that is available to them concerning the future state of the economy, these market participants form expectations concerning future short-term interest rates. After allowing for a risk premium, these participants buy and sell bonds, which affects prices and yields, until the expected rates of return from holding bonds of different maturities are equal.

So long as there are market participants with no habitat and participants with habitats who are willing to deal in somewhat longer-term or shorter-term bonds when expected profits are high, it is not necessary for all market participants to "play" the term structure of interest rates. Many market participants can remain within their preferred habitats and feel confident that the market made the right decisions. That is to say, they can be confident that the activities of others have equated the expected rates of return on all maturities of debt after allowance for a risk premium. All that is required for this confidence is the existence of enough market participants who do play the term structure of interest rates.

Available evidence suggests that the markets for debt instruments in the United States are *efficient* because they tend to equate the expected rates of return for different maturities after allowance for a risk premium. In an efficient market, most participants can safely stay within their preferred habitats and leave interest rate forecasting and the playing of the term structure to others. Debt markets appear to be *segmented* in the sense that many investors and debt issuers deal only in a particular maturity of debt. This segmentation does not make the market inefficient, however, because there are other participants who are willing to play the term structure of interest rates.

SUMMARY

The theory of portfolio selection sheds considerable light on the factors that determine the term structure of interest rates. The relationship among yields on bonds with different maturities is determined by the portfolio decisions of market participants. Wealth holders determine the expected rates of return and risks of holding bonds of different maturities and select the maturities that best accord with their preferences. Over any holding period, the expected rate of return on a bond of a particular maturity is affected by current and expected future interest rates and by transactions costs. The risk for the bond depends upon uncertainty concerning future interest rates and upon the maturity of the bond.

If market participants are risk neutral and if there are no transactions costs, the expected rates of return will be equal for bonds of all maturities for all holding periods. This does not mean that realized rates of return are equal, only that the *expected* returns are equal. According to the expectations approach, the relationship among yields on bonds of different maturities reveals expectations concerning expected future interest rates. For example, if the yields on short-term bonds are less than the yields on long-term bonds, market participants expect short-term yields to rise in the future. If the yields on short-term bonds are greater than the yields on long-term bonds, short-term interest rates are expected to fall in the future. Stated another way, yields on bonds with various maturities differ *because* market participants expect interest rates to change in the future. Only if interest rates are not expected to change in the future will the yields on bonds of all maturities be equal.

When allowance is made for risk aversion and transactions costs, the conclusions of the expectations approach are modified. Risk-averse investors balance expected rate of return against risk. If they determine that bonds of various maturities have different risks, these investors require a higher expected return on the bonds with greater risk. Historical experience indicates that long-term bonds are more risky than short-term bonds. This greater risk occurs because unexpected revisions in the market expectations concerning the *level* of future short-term interest rates have a greater effect on the prices of long-term bonds than on the prices of short-term bonds. Revisions in these interest rate expectations generate large capital gains and losses for long-term bonds, so the standard deviation of returns for these bonds is greater than for short-term bonds. Risk-averse investors can be induced to hold longer-term bonds only if they offer a higher expected return than for shorter-term bonds. This risk premium implies that if interest rates are not expected to change in the future, the yield to maturity on long-term bonds exceeds the yields on short-term bonds.

When risk aversion is taken into account, the expectation of future interest rates is not the only explanation of why yields on bonds of various maturities differ. If we observe that the yields on long-term bonds exceed the yields on short-term bonds, the cause may be the actions of risk-averse investors rather than the expectation by the market that short-term interest rates will rise in the future. Unless the degree of risk aversion has risen, however, *changes* in the shape of the yield curve may still be caused by shifts in expectations. For example, if the yields on long-term bonds suddenly rise relative to the yields on short-term bonds, it is likely that the market expects a rise in short-term interest rates in the future. Similarly, if yields on long-term bonds fall below yields on short-term bonds, it is likely that the market expects short-term interest rates to fall in the future. We can never be sure that a change in the shape of the yield curve is caused by a shift in expectations rather than a shift in the degree of risk aversion in the market.

The existence of transactions costs also complicates the explanation of the term structure of interest rates. Transactions costs are an important component of the expected rate of return on bonds of different maturities. Some market participants expect to put their funds to alternative use in the near future. If they hold long-term bonds, these investors have to bear the transactions costs of selling them. Transactions costs can be saved by holding short-term bonds that mature when the money is needed. Other participants do not plan to put their funds to alternative use in the near future, so they prefer long-term bonds. By holding long-term bonds, these investors can avoid the transactions costs of buying new short-term bonds when the old ones mature. Issuers of bonds are also affected by similar factors.

These considerations produce preferred habitats for market participants concerning the maturities of bonds they hold or issue. If preferred habitats are such that investors prefer short-term bonds to long-term and if interest rates are not expected to change in the future, they can be induced to hold long-term bonds only if their yield exceeds the yield on short-term bonds. If there is a preference for long-term bonds, yields on these bonds will be less than for short-term.

As was the case for risk aversion, it is unlikely that shifts in preferred habitats are an important factor in affecting changes in the shape of the yield curve. Preferred habitats change slowly, but the yield curve changes frequently and often sharply. These changes are probably caused by market expectations concerning future interest rates.

We are left with the conclusion that shifts in market expectations concerning future short-term interest rates are probably the major cause of changes in the shape of the yield curve. Risk-averse investors and market participants with preferred habitats do play a role, however. In particular, if interest rates are not expected to change in the future, the yields on long-term bonds exceed the yields on short-term bonds because of the higher risk of long-term bonds and the dominance of investors whose preferred habitat is short-term bonds.

After allowing for risk premiums and natural habitats, many market participants attempt to "play" the term structure of interest rates when existing yields are out of line with expectations. For example, firms that believe that the market has overreacted to some economic information by sharply raising yields on long-term bonds relative to short-term, will issue short-term bonds to finance long-term investment in the expectation that they can issue long-term bonds in the future at lower cost. This activity tends to raise short-term interest rates and lower yields on long-term bonds. Similarly, households may borrow heavily currently to finance expenditures if they expect interest rates to rise in the future. This tends to raise current short-term interest rates and to lower future short-term interest rates.

Financial intermediaries are also in the business of playing the term structure of interest rates. For example, depository institutions typically issue liabilities with maturities that have a shorter maturity than the assets they hold. This means that the liabilities mature before the assets do and that institutions have to reissue liabilities in the future to support their existing assets. When setting the interest rate that they charge for loans, these institutions must predict what the interest rate will be in the future when they replace their maturing liabilities. If they expect interest rates to rise in the future, they will charge a higher interest rate on their loans to compensate for the expected increase in borrowing cost. If they expect interest rates to fall, they will charge a lower interest rate.

As we shall see in later chapters, the risk associated with borrowing "short" and lending "long" has increased in recent years because of the sharp and unexpected changes that have occurred in short-term interest rates. This increased risk has induced depository institutions and other financial intermediaries to demand a risk premium for their loans, and it has induced them to strive for a closer matching of the maturity of their assets and the maturity of their liabilities.

SELECTED REFERENCES

Malkiel, Bert, *The Term Structure of Interest Rates*, Princeton, N.J.: Princeton University Press, 1966.

Modigliani, Franco and Richard Sutch, "Innovations in Interest Rates," *American Economic Review*, May 1966, pp. 178–197.

Nelson, Charles, *The Term Structure of Interest Rates*, New York: Basic Books, 1972.

A MODEL OF BANK BEHAVIOR

7

This chapter studies the basic factors determining the quantity of liabilities that a bank issues and the quantity of loans that it grants. It is shown that the interest rate on loans adjusts to equate the bank's supply of loans to the public's demand. Furthermore, in the absence of interest rate ceilings, the interest rate on bank liabilities adjusts to equate the public's supply of funds to the bank to the bank's demand for funds. The relationship between a bank's supply of loans and its demand for funds from the public is also studied. This relationship links the interest rate on bank liabilities to the interest rate on loans.

We then turn to an analysis of the effects of a government-imposed ceiling on the interest rate that a bank can pay for its liabilities. This is an important topic because interest rate ceilings for bank liabilities are being phased out. It is shown that an interest rate ceiling breaks the link between the interest rate on loans and the interest rate on bank liabilities. The effect of eliminating the ceiling is to raise the interest rate on bank liabilities while lowering the interest rate on loans.

The relationship between bank liabilities and bank loans, and the relationship between the interest rates on liabilities and loans, are studied using a model of bank behavior. This model is highly simplified and abstracts from much of the complexity of banking. Though this chapter is concerned with bank behavior, the same model can be used to study the behavior of other depository institutions such as savings and loan associations and mutual savings banks.

BANK LEVERAGE AND RISK

A bank issues liabilities so that it can hold assets in excess of its net worth. This means that a bank's willingness to issue liabilities is derived from its demand for assets. Just as a manufacturing firm uses labor, raw materials, and capital goods to produce its output, a bank uses liabilities as its raw materials, which, in conjunction with its labor force and capital goods, allow it to acquire assets.

In determining the quantity of assets to hold and, therefore, the quantity of liabilities to issue, a bank is guided by the desire to earn a profit for its owners. A bank's profit is the difference between its income and its costs. Income is generated from assets in the form of interest receipts and capital gains (less capital losses). Banks also earn income from fees charged for various services. For simplicity, these fees are neglected here. Costs take many forms, but the most important are interest payments on liabilities, costs of processing customers' accounts, and costs of granting and servicing loans.

It might appear that if the marginal (added) revenue from additional assets exceeds the marginal cost of additional liabilities, a bank would always want to increase its liabilities in order to expand its assets. However, this is not necessarily the case. Even if a bank could expand its liabilities without increasing their marginal cost and even if it could expand its assets without reducing their marginal revenue, a bank will experience additional risk as its asset size increases. The increased risk limits the expansion in assets.[1]

The increased risk takes two forms. First, there is the possibility that the bank can expand its asset holdings only by acquiring more risky assets. Though this possibility exists, particularly when it comes to granting additional loans, for simplicity we do not consider it. Rather, we shall concentrate on the increased risk to the owners of the bank that results from expanding assets without increasing net worth.

When a bank, or any other investor for that matter, borrows in order to hold assets in excess of net worth, it is using *leverage*. The greater the amount of borrowing, the greater the excess of assets over net worth and, therefore, the greater the amount of leverage. A bank with a net worth-to-asset ratio of 7 percent is holding $14.29 of assets for every $1 of net worth. Thus, the bank is holding 14.29 times as much assets as net worth. This multiple, which is the reciprocal of the net worth-to-asset ratio, that is, $1/.07$, is called the *leverage factor*.[2] Banks with a net worth-to-asset ratio of 4 percent have a leverage factor of 25; they hold $25 of assets for every $1 of net worth.[3]

The owners of a bank care about the rate of return that they receive on their investment in the bank. The *rate of return on net worth* is defined as profits (net income less interest expense) divided by net worth. It is the rate of return on the funds invested in the bank by its owners. For simplicity, we shall omit the effects of inflation and, therefore, not distinguish between nominal and real rates of return.

---

[1] We could adjust marginal cost and revenue for risk. In this case, the bank would equate risk-adjusted marginal cost to risk-adjusted marginal revenue.

[2] Let TA be total assets and NW be net worth. The ratio of net worth to total asset is NW/TA, and the reciprocal of this ratio, $[1/(NW/TA)] = TA/NW$, is the leverage factor.

[3] The largest banks in the country have ratios of net worth to total assets of 3.5 to 5 percent; small banks have rates of 7 percent or more.

Consider a bank that holds $1 million of assets that are supported by $930,000 of liabilities and $70,000 of net worth. Assume that revenue for the year less costs gives an annual profit of $10,000. The *rate of return on assets,* defined as profits divided by total assets, is $10,000/$1,000,000 = .01, or 1 percent. Thus, each dollar of assets produces 1 cent of profit. The rate of return on net worth is $10,000/$70,000 = .1429, or 14.29 percent. Each dollar invested in the bank by its owners produces 14.29 cents of profit for the owners. Now assume that the bank doubles its size to $2 million by issuing another $1 million of liabilities. Further assume that profits also double from $10,000 to $20,000. In this situation, the rate of return on assets is still 1 percent. Now, however, the rate of return on net worth is $20,000/$70,000, or 28.57 percent. Each dollar invested in the bank by its owners produces 28.57 cents of profits.[4] Banks are excellent examples of why wealth holders borrow in order to hold assets in excess of net worth.

Leverage is a mixed blessing because an increase in leverage also raises risk for the owners of the bank. Consider the case where the owners of the bank expect the rate of return on assets to be 1 percent but they realize that it may be as high as 1.5 percent or as low as $-.5$ percent. This dispersion of possible rates of return on assets means that there is risk for the owners of the bank. For a ratio of net worth to total assets of 7 percent, the leverage factor is 14.29, and the rate of return on net worth could be as high as 1.5%(14.29) = 21.44 percent or as low as $-0.5\%(14.29) = -7.14$ percent. For a ratio of net worth to total assets of 3.5 percent, the leverage factor is 28.57. This means that the rate of return on net worth could be as high as 1.5%(28.57) = 42.86 percent or as low as $-.5\%(28.57) = -14.29$ percent. We can see from this example that the dispersion of possible rates of return on net worth is proportional to the leverage factor.

In Chapter 5, we gave the rationale for using the standard deviation of the rate of return as the measure of risk (dispersion). It can be shown that the standard deviation of the rate of return on net worth equals the leverage factor times the standard deviation of the rate of return on assets. For example, if the return on assets has a standard deviation of 0.25 percent and if the net worth-to-asset ratio is 7 percent, the standard deviation of the return on net worth is 0.25%(14.29) = 3.57 percent. If the net worth-to-asset ratio is 3.5 percent, the standard deviation of the return on net worth is 0.25%(28.57) = 7.14 percent.

When asset size is doubled by issuing additional liabilities, the rate of return on net worth doubles, but so does the risk. The importance of an increase in risk depends upon bankers' attitudes toward risk. As explained in Chapter 5, risk-neutral investors maximize expected return without regard for risk. If bankers are risk neutral, they do not care about the increased risk that accompanies a rise in

---

[4] The rate of return on net worth is the rate of return on assets times the leverage factor. Let Π be profits. The rate of return on total assets (TA) is Π/TA, and the rate of return on net worth is Π/NW. We see that the rate of return on net worth is the rate of return on assets times the leverage factor: $\Pi/NW = (\Pi/TA)TA/NW$, where TA/NW is the leverage factor.

the expected return on net worth. They want to expand assets and liabilities as long as there is an increase in the expected return on net worth. This is a dangerous strategy when leverage is high. Consider the example of a bank with a standard deviation of the return on assets of 1.0 percent and a ratio of net worth to assets of 3.5 percent. This gives a leverage factor of 28.57 and a standard deviation of return on net worth of 1.0%(28.57) = 28.57 percent. With a little bad luck, the return on total assets could be −3.5 percent in a year. With any additional losses, the bank would fail. With a leverage factor of 28.57, this translates into a return on net worth of −100 percent. Thus, the −3.5 percent return on total assets totally wipes out the bank's net worth.

This prospect leads bankers to be concerned about risk. They limit risk by limiting leverage. In considering the desirability of increasing assets through issuing additional liabilities, a bank balances the increased expected return on net worth against the higher risk.

There is an additional reason that banker's practice risk aversion. As will be explained in Chapter 9, the government regulates the activities of banks in an effort to limit their risk taking. This occurs, in part, because the government insures the deposit liabilities of banks. In order to control the losses to the government's insurance fund, regulators limit leverage. Even a risk-neutral banker will limit leverage in order to avoid regulatory sanctions.

A SIMPLE MODEL OF BANK BEHAVIOR

With the important role of leverage in mind, we now can discuss the basic factors determining the amount of assets a bank holds and the amount of liabilities that it issues. To keep the story simple, we examine the behavior of a bank whose only liability is transactions accounts and whose only asset is business loans. It is assumed that the bank's net worth is fixed and that there is no legal limitation on the interest rate that the bank pays for its transactions accounts. Later on in this section we will examine the effects of interest rate ceilings. We will also consider the behavior of a bank that holds securities as well as loans.

The demand for loans by businesses and the supply of loans by the bank are shown in Panel I of Figure 7.1. The demand schedule for loans, LD, is downward sloping indicating that when the bank charges a low interest rate for its loans, its customers demand a large quantity of loans. Shifts in the loan demand schedule are discussed later. The supply of loans schedule, LS, is upward sloping, indicating that when the interest rate on loans is high, the bank wants to supply a large quantity of loans. The loan supply schedule is upward sloping because, given net worth, when loans increase, risk also rises. The bank will expand its loans only if

FIGURE 7.1
THE QUANTITY OF LOANS AND
TRANSACTIONS ACCOUNT
LIABILITIES AT A BANK.

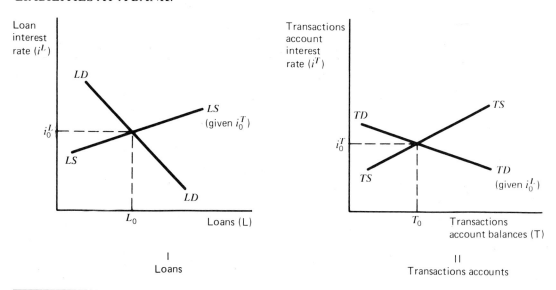

it is compensated for the increased risk by a higher interest rate on loans.[5] The
loan supply schedule is drawn under the assumption that the interest rate on
transactions accounts is given and is below the interest rate on loans. For a given
value of the interest rate on transactions accounts, a higher interest rate on loans
implies a higher expected profit and a higher expected return on net worth. When
the interest rate on transactions accounts increases, the loan supply schedule shifts
to the left. When the interest rate declines, the supply schedule shifts to the right.
These shifts and the relationship between the interest rate on transactions
accounts and the interest rate on loans are discussed later.

The intersection of the loan demand and supply schedules determines the quantity of loans, L, and the interest rate for loans, i^L. At this intersection, the quan-

[5] The loan supply schedule is shown in this and later diagrams as an upward-sloping
straight line. Because it is assumed that the owners of the bank are risk averse, the supply
schedule should become steeper, the greater the quantity of loans. Given net worth, the
greater the quantity of loans, the greater is the risk. Thus, ever larger increases in the loan
interest rate are required to induce the bank to supply additional loans. Eventually the
loan supply schedule becomes vertical. Allowing for nonlinearities would not change the
basic conclusions of our analysis, so it is assumed for simplicity that all demand and supply schedules, including the loan supply schedule, are straight lines.

tity of loans that businesses demand is equal to the quantity of loans that the bank supplies. This occurs when the interest rate is i_0^L and the quantity of loans is L_0.

Given net worth, when the bank changes the quantity of loans that it holds, it must also change the quantity of its liabilities by the same amount. The willingness and ability of the bank to lend is affected by the cost and availability of liabilities. Panel II of Figure 7.1 shows the demand and supply schedules for transactions accounts, which, for simplicity and ease of exposition, are assumed to be the bank's only liabilities. The supply schedule, *TS*, shows the amount of transactions account balances that the public supplies to the bank at different interest rates. The supply schedule is upward sloping, indicating that when the interest rate on transactions balances is high, the public supplies a large quantity of transactions accounts. Given income, wealth, and the expected returns on alternative assets, the public can be induced to hold greater balances if the interest rate on the accounts increases. When income and wealth increase or when the returns on alternative assets decrease, the supply schedule for transactions account balances shifts to the right. The schedule shifts to the left when income and wealth decline or when returns on alternative assets increase.

The demand schedule, *TD*, shows the bank's demand for transactions account liabilities at alternative interest rates. The demand schedule is downward sloping, indicating that the lower the interest rate that the bank pays on these liabilities, the more liabilities it wants to have. It is important to note that the bank's demand for transactions account liabilities is a *derived demand* emanating from its desire to supply loans. The bank's demand schedule is drawn under the assumption that the interest rate on loans is given and is above the interest rate for transactions accounts.[6] If the interest rate on transactions accounts declines, given the interest rate on loans, the expected profit from each loan increases. Under this situation, the bank supplies more loans and, therefore, demands more transactions account liabilities. Put another way, when the bank increases its lending, risk also rises. Given the interest rate on loans, the bank can be induced to increase its lending only if the interest rate on transactions accounts decline. This decline raises the expected return on net worth and compensates the bank for the increased risk when it increases its loans. Thus, given the interest rate on loans, the lower the interest rate on transactions accounts, the greater is the amount of these liabilities that the bank wants to issue.

The intersection of the demand and supply schedules for transactions accounts determines the quantity of these accounts, *T*, and the interest rate, i^T. At this interest rate, the quantity of transactions account balances supplied by the public is equal to the quantity demanded by the bank. The intersection occurs at the interest rate i_0^T and the quantity T_0.

---

[6] We assume that the loan interest rate is given when we draw the bank's demand schedule for transactions account liabilities, and we also assume that the interest rate on transactions accounts is fixed when we draw the bank's loan supply schedule. It is shown later that the interaction between the supply of loans and the demand for transactions accounts determines the interest rates on loans and on transactions accounts.

In Figure 7.1, the interest rate on transactions accounts, i_0^T, is less than the interest rate on loans, i_0^L. The interest rate on loans exceeds the interest rate on transactions accounts in order to provide revenues to cover labor and other costs and to provide an expected return to the owners of the bank that compensates them for risk. The quantity of loans also exceeds the quantity of transactions account liabilities. The difference between the quantity of loans and the quantity of transactions account liabilities is the net worth invested in the bank by its owners. This is also a source of funds used to acquire loans. As shown in Chapter 8, the net worth of owners allow banks to hold 7 percent more assets than their total liabilities.

It is instructive to analyze the effects of shifts in the demand for loans and of shifts in the supply of transactions account balances. First, consider the case of an expansion in economic activity that raises the expected net income streams from business investment projects. Given interest rates, the discounted present values of the net income streams also rise. This causes the loan demand schedule to shift to the right from LD to LD', as shown in Panel I of Figure 7.2. It should be noted that the loan demand schedule also shifts to the right as the result of an increase in the interest rate charged to businesses for alternative sources of credit. In this situation, loans from the bank become more attractive to borrowers relative to alternative sources of credit, and a larger quantity of loans is demanded from the bank at the interest rate i_0^L. As explained in Chapter 5, a change in relative interest rates leads borrowers to substitute bank credit for other liabilities.

Irrespective of the source of the shift in loan demand, at the initial interest rate on loans, i_0^L, firms increase the quantity of loans that they demand from L_0 to L'. Because the quantity of loans demanded at i_0^L now exceeds the quantity supplied, the bank raises its loan interest rate. Assuming that the interest rate for transactions accounts stays at i_0^T, the bank increases the interest rate on loans and increases the quantity of loans supplied by moving up the supply schedule, LS_0. The interest rate on loans rises until the quantity of loans demanded equals the quantity supplied. The loan interest rate rises from i_0^L to i_1^L and the quantity of loans rises from L_0 to L_1.

Panel II indicates that we cannot stop the story here. Because net worth is assumed unchanged, the bank must support the expansion in loans by increasing its liabilities by the same amount. Thus, when the interest rate on loans rises to i_1^L the bank's demand schedule for transactions accounts shifts to the right from TD_0 to TD_1.[7] At the initial interest rate for transactions accounts, i_0^T, the quantity of transactions accounts demanded by the bank increases by $T_1 - T_0$ which equals the expansion of loans, $L_1 - L_0$. But it is impossible for the bank to increase its liabilities if it continues to pay the interest rate i_0^T. At that interest rate, the public is willing to supply only the quantity T_0. In order to increase its liabilities, the bank must raise the interest rate. As the interest rate rises, the public supplies

---

[7] The subscript indicates that this is the bank's demand schedule for transactions accounts when the loan interest rate is i_1^L.

FIGURE 7.2
THE EFFECTS OF AN INCREASE IN
THE QUANTITY OF LOANS
DEMANDED.

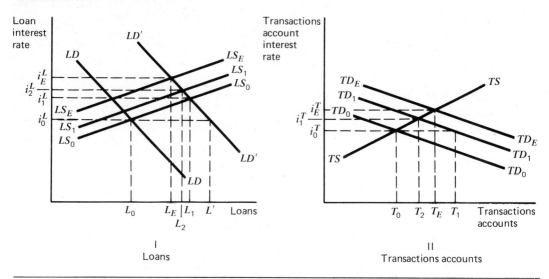

I
Loans

II
Transactions accounts

more transactions account balances according to the supply schedule TS. Given the interest rate on loans i_1^L and the interest rate on transactions accounts i_0^T, the bank demands T_1 of transactions account liabilities. As the interest rate on these accounts rises, however, it reduces the quantity of liabilities demanded below T_1 as it moves along the new demand schedule TD_1. The interest rate on transactions accounts rises until TS intersects TD_1 at the interest rate i_1^T. At this interest rate, the quantity of transactions accounts demanded by the bank equals the quantity supplied by the public at the quantity T_2.

The bank demands a smaller quantity of transactions accounts at the higher interest rate i_1^T than at i_0^T. Thus, the expansion in the quantity of transactions accounts, $T_2 - T_0$, is less than the expansion in loans $L_1 - L_0$. Because the bank can increase its loans only by the amount that its liabilities increase, the expansion of loans and of transactions account liabilities must be brought into balance. This is accomplished by an interaction between the interest rate on loans and the interest rate on transactions accounts. Increases in the interest rate on transactions accounts shift the loan supply schedule to the left, and increases in the interest rate on loans shift the demand schedule for transactions accounts to the right. These shifts reduce loans relative to L_1 and increase transactions account liabilities relative to T_2. The interest rates on loans and transactions accounts continue to rise, and the schedules continue to shift until the expansion of loans equals the expansion of transactions account liabilities.

The process is difficult to depict graphically, but it can be described in words. The loan supply schedule, LS_0, is drawn under the assumption that the interest rate on transactions accounts is i_0^T. When the interest rate on these accounts rises, lending becomes less profitable for the bank, and the loan supply schedule shifts to the left. Thus, when the interest rate on transactions accounts rises from i_0^T to i_1^T, the loan supply schedule shifts left to LS_1.[8] This leftward shift in loan supply produces a further increase in the loan interest rate from i_1^L to i_2^L and a reduction of loans from L_1 to L_2. The bank's demand schedule for transactions account liabilities, TD_1, is drawn under the assumption that the interest rate on loans is i_1^L. At the higher loan interest rate, i_2^L the bank's demand schedule for transactions account liabilities again shifts to the right (not shown). This produces a further increase in the interest rate on transactions accounts and an additional expansion in transactions account balances. The rise in the interest rate on transactions accounts produces a further leftward shift in the loan supply schedule (not shown), which produces a further increase in the loan interest rate and a decline in the quantity of loans relative to L_1.

As the loan interest rate rises, the quantity of loans declines relative to L_1. As the interest rate on transactions accounts rises, the quantity of these liabilities rises relative to T_2. Eventually, the quantity of loans comes into balance with the quantity of transactions account liabilities. As indicated in Panel I of Figure 7.2, in the final equilibrium the loan interest rate rises from i_0^L to i_E^L, and the quantity of loans is L_E. As shown in Panel II, the interest rate on transactions accounts rises from i_0^T to i_E^T and the quantity of these accounts is T_E.

We have the bank reach the final equilibrium through a step-by-step (iterative) process. The bank's demand schedule for transactions accounts shifts to the right in response to a rise in the loan interest rate, and its loan supply schedule shifts to the left in response to a rise in the interest rate on its liabilities. The description of this process helps explain the movement from one equilibrium to another, but the reader should not infer that banks actually follow this step-by-step process. In practice, banks raise the interest rate on loans and on liabilities simultaneously. However, the final outcome is the same.

We conclude that a rightward shift in the demand for loans produces an increase in the interest rate on both loans and transactions accounts. It also produces an increase in the quantity of loans held by the bank and an increase in its liabilities.[9] When the demand for bank loans increases, the loan interest rate rises, but so does the interest rate on liabilities. It is the increase in the interest rate on transactions accounts that induces the public to increase its account balances.

[8] The subscript indicates that this is the supply schedule when the interest rate on transactions accounts is i_1^T.
[9] If the demand schedule for loans shifts to the left rather than to the right, interest rates for loans and transactions accounts decline, and the quantity of loans and of liabilities also declines.

These increased balances are needed if the bank is to increase its lending in response to an increase in loan demand.

Note that in Figure 7.2, the interest rate on loans has increased by more than the interest rate on transactions accounts. A wider spread between the loan interest rate and the interest rate on liabilities is required to induce the bank to bear the additional risk of expanding its loans when its net worth is unchanged.

Now, let us consider the case of a rightward shift in the public's supply schedule of transactions accounts. This shift could occur as the result of an increase in income (saving) or a decline in the expected returns on alternative assets. As shown in Panel II of Figure 7.3, the shift in the supply schedule from TS to TS' means that at the initial interest rate, i_0^T, the quantity of these accounts supplied by the public increases to T'. Given the interest rate on loans i_0^L, the bank is not willing to accept more liabilities at the interest rate i_0^T. Thus, at the interest rate i_0^T the quantity of transactions accounts supplied by the public exceeds the quantity demanded by the bank by the amount $T' - T_0$. Given the loan interest rate, the bank is willing to accept more transactions account liabilities only if their interest rate declines. The interest rate on transactions accounts falls to i_1^T, and the quantity of account balances rises to T_1.

As shown in Panel I of Figure 7.3, at the lower interest rate on transactions accounts, i_1^T, the loan supply schedule shifts right to LS_1. At the loan interest rate i_0^L, the bank wants to supply the quantity of loans L'. The schedule shifts by the amount that transactions account liabilities increase, that is, $L' - L_0 = T_1 - T_0$. As before, this is not the end of the story because a rightward shift in loan supply reduces the loan interest rate. This makes lending less profitable given the interest rate on transactions account balances, i_1^T, so the bank's demand schedule for transactions accounts shifts to the left (not shown). This produces a further decline in the interest rate on transactions accounts. As a result, the loan supply schedule again shifts to the right, producing another decline in the loan interest rate. The loan supply schedule continues to shift to the right, the bank's demand schedule for transactions accounts continues to shift to the left, and the interest rates on transactions accounts and loans continue to decline. The process stops when the expansion of loans equals the expansion of transactions accounts. The final equilibrium is shown where the interest rate on loans falls from i_0^L to i_E^L and the quantity of loans increases from L_0 to L_E. The interest rate on transactions accounts declines from i_0^T to i_E^T, and the quantity rises from T_0 to T_E. As before, the expansion in loans is matched by an increase in liabilities, so $L_E - L_0 = T_E - T_0$.

We conclude that an increase in the public's supply of transactions account balances reduces the interest rate on these accounts and reduces the interest rate on loans. The quantity of loans and the quantity of transaction accounts increase.

The Effects of a Ceiling on the Interest Rate for Transactions Accounts

When the government imposes a ceiling on the interest rate that a bank can pay on its liabilities, the effects of shifts in loan demand or of shifts in the public's sup-

FIGURE 7.3
THE EFFECTS OF AN INCREASE IN
THE SUPPLY OF TRANSACTIONS
ACCOUNTS.

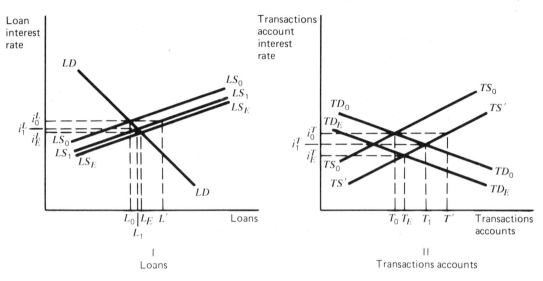

ply of account balances are not the same as when ceilings are absent. This section describes the effects of interest rate ceilings.

It is important to study the effects of interest rate ceilings because, until recently, they were imposed on most of the liabilities that banks issue.[10] Even today, ceilings continue to be imposed on some kinds of liabilities. Furthermore, the analysis of the effects of ceilings helps explain why they were removed.

In this section, we will continue to assume that transactions accounts are the bank's only liability. Until 1983, all kinds of transactions accounts were subject to interest rate ceilings. Currently, some are subject to ceilings, and some are not.

In order to see the effects of interest rate ceilings, let us return to the case of an increase in loan demand. Assume that prior to the shift in loan demand the interest rate on loans is i_0^L, and the interest rate on transactions accounts is i_0^T. Now assume that the government imposes an interest rate ceiling, $\bar{i}^T$, equal to the existing interest rate on transactions accounts, i_0^T. Thus, it is illegal for the bank to pay an interest rate on its transactions accounts that is greater than $\bar{i}^T$. The bank is only allowed to pay an interest rate that is equal to or lower than $\bar{i}^T$. The initial equilibrium for the bank is shown in Figure 7.4. Prior to the shift in loan demand, the interest rate on loans is i_0^L, and the interest rate on transactions accounts is

---

[10] The rationale for the interest rate ceilings for the liabilities of banks and other depository institutions is discussed in Chapters 9 and 10.

FIGURE 7.4
THE EFFECT OF AN INCREASE IN
LOAN DEMAND WHEN THERE IS
AN INTEREST RATE CEILING.

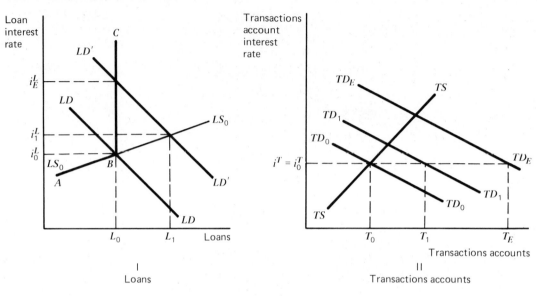

|
Loans

II
Transactions accounts

$i_0^T = \bar{i}^T$. The quantity of loans and of transactions accounts are L_0 and T_0 respectively. Since $\bar{i}^T$ is the interest rate that the bank wants to pay for transactions accounts, its actions are not constrained by the ceiling. In this situation, the interest rate ceiling, $\bar{i}^T$, is *not binding*.

Now, assume that the demand for loans shifts to the right from LD to LD', as shown in Panel I of Figure 7.4. Recall that the loan supply schedule, LS_0, is drawn under the assumption that the interest rate on transactions accounts is i_0^T. Because this is also the ceiling interest rate, we know that the interest rate on transactions accounts cannot rise. Given the interest rate $i_0^T = \bar{i}^T$, the bank wants to move up its loan supply schedule LS_0. If this were possible, the loan interest rate would rise to i_1^L, and the quantity of loans would rise to L_1. The bank can only expand its loans if it can expand its liabilities.[11] Because the bank cannot raise the interest rate on transactions accounts, it cannot attract the additional account balances from the public that are needed to support increased lending.[12] This means that the quantity of loans cannot rise.

---

[11] We assume that the bank does not have securities or other liquid assets that it can sell in order to expand its loans. The role of securities and other liquid assets is discussed later.
[12] The bank could use "nonprice" competition as a method of attracting additional account balances. The effect of nonprice competition is discussed later.

If the bank could move up its loan supply schedule, LS_0, the loan interest rate would rise to i_1^L. Recall that the bank's demand schedule for transactions account liabilities, TD_0, is drawn under the assumption that the loan interest rate is i_0^L. If the loan interest rate rises to i_1^L, the bank's demand schedule for transactions accounts shifts right to TD_1. At the interest rate $i_0^T = \bar{i}^T$, the bank increases its demand for transactions account liabilities by $T_1 - T_0$. This equals the increase in loans, $L_1 - L_0$, that the bank would like to hold.

Although the bank wants to increase its transactions account liabilities, the public does not want to hold any more transactions account balances as long as the interest rate is fixed at $i_0^T = \bar{i}^T$. As we saw earlier, in the absence of an interest rate ceiling, this would lead the bank to raise the interest rate it pays on transactions accounts. The bank would like to raise the interest rate on transactions accounts so it could increase its liabilities and its loans. The interest rate ceiling prevents the bank from raising the interest rate. Now the ceiling is a *binding constraint* on the bank.

At the interest rate i_E^L, the bank's demand schedule for transaction accounts is TD_E. This demand schedule indicates that given the loan interest rate i_E^L, the bank demands the quantity T_E of transactions accounts when the interest rate on these accounts is $\bar{i}^T$. This demand has no effect on the quantity of transactions accounts, however, because the public only supplies the quantity T_0.

As long as the interest rate ceiling is $\bar{i}^T$, the bank cannot increase its liabilities. This means that it cannot expand its loans. Because the demand for loans exceeds the fixed supply, L_0, the loan interest rate rises until the quantity of loans demanded on the schedule LD' equals the fixed supply L_0. This occurs at the interest rate i_E^L.

Because the quantity of transactions accounts is T_0, the bank's loan supply schedule is a vertical line at the quantity L_0. This indicates that so long as the quantity of transactions accounts is T_0, the quantity of loans cannot rise above L_0. The supply schedule is upward sloping for loan interest rates less than i_0^L and for quantities of loans less than L_0. This occurs because until the interest rate ceiling becomes binding, the bank is free to expand its liabilities and, therefore, its loans by raising the interest rate on transactions accounts. Thus, if the loan supply schedule had shifted to the left rather than to the right, the loan interest rate *and* the interest rate on transactions accounts would have declined. The quantity of loans and of transactions accounts would also have declined.

As long as the interest rate ceiling on transactions accounts is not binding, shifts in loan demand have the effect described in Figure 7.2. As shown in Figure 7.4, when the interest rate ceiling is binding, the loan supply schedule is vertical. The bank's loan supply schedule is upward sloping from point A to point B, and it then becomes vertical. Thus, the supply schedule is the heavy line ABC.

Given the interest rate ceiling on transactions accounts, $\bar{i}^T$, the quantity of loans is determined by the amount of transactions account balances that the public wants to hold (supplies) at the interest rate $\bar{i}^T$.[13] When the demand for loans shifts

---

[13] Strictly speaking, loans equal transactions accounts plus net worth. We assume net worth is fixed.

to the right, the bank cannot expand its liabilities; therefore, it cannot increase its loans. As a result, when the interest rate ceiling is binding, an increase in the demand for loans produces *no* increase in the quantity of loans. There is only an increase in the loan interest rate.[14] There is also no increase in the quantity of transactions accounts[15] and, of course, no increase in the interest rate on these accounts.

Now let us turn to the effects of a shift in the public's supply schedule for transactions account balances. This time we shall start with the situation where the interest rate ceiling is binding. This is done most easily by starting with the equilibrium that was established in Figure 7.4 after a shift in loan demand. This equilibrium becomes the initial situation in Figure 7.5, where the loan interest rate is i_0^L, the quantity of loans is L_0, the quantity of transactions accounts is T_0, and the interest rate on these accounts is $\bar{i}^T$. Neglecting net worth, $L_0 = T_0$. Given the loan interest rate i_0^L, the bank's demand schedule for transactions accounts is TD_0. At the ceiling interest rate $\bar{i}^T$, the bank demands the quantity T^b of transactions accounts, but the public supplies only the quantity T_0. Thus, the bank's demand exceeds the public's supply by the amount $T^b - T_0$. When the bank's demand for transactions accounts exceeds the public's supply, there is an *excess demand* for transactions accounts. In this situation, it is the public's supply schedule that determines the quantity of transactions accounts. The public is holding exactly the amount of transactions account balances that it wants at the interest rate $\bar{i}^T$. The bank wants to have a larger amount of transactions account liabilities than T_0, but it cannot increase its liabilities as long as the interest rate is $\bar{i}^T$.

Now assume that the public's supply schedule for transactions accounts shifts to the right from TS to TS'. Thus, at the interest rate ceiling, $\bar{i}^T$, the public increases its supply of transactions account balances from T_0 to T_1. There is still an excess demand for transactions accounts because the bank's demand still exceeds the public's supply. This means that the bank will accept the increased quantity of transactions accounts without reducing the interest rate on these accounts. Thus, the quantity of transactions accounts at the bank rise from T_0 to T_1.

The bank accepts all the additional transactions account balances when the supply schedule shifts from TS to TS'. The bank's liabilities rise by the full amount of the shift, that is, by $T_1 - T_0$. These liabilities are invested in loans. Thus, the loan supply schedule shifts to the right from LS to LS', which is the amount $L_1 - L_0 = T_1 - T_0$. The interest rate on loans falls to i_1^L. We conclude that an increase in the supply of transactions accounts by the public produces a decline in the loan interest rate and an increase in the quantity of loans when there is a binding interest rate ceiling.

---

[14] The bank may not raise the loan interest rate sufficiently to equate loan demand with supply. It might restrict credit by refusing loans to its less good customers or use other forms of credit rationing. We abstract from credit rationing here.

[15] Here we assume that the bank does not use nonprice methods of attracting more transactions balances such as giving away toasters. Nonprice competition is discussed later in this chapter.

FIGURE 7.5
THE EFFECT OF AN INCREASE IN
THE PUBLIC'S SUPPLY OF
TRANSACTIONS ACCOUNTS WHEN
THERE IS A BINDING INTEREST
RATE CEILING.

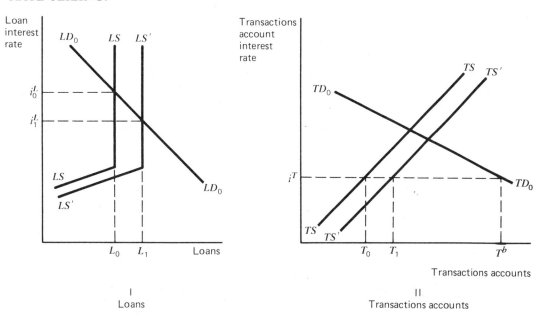

I
Loans

II
Transactions accounts

We saw in Figure 7.3 that when there is no interest rate ceiling, the loan interest rate also falls, and the quantity of loans also rises when the public's supply schedule for transactions accounts shifts to the right. However, the decline in the loan interest rate is less, and the expansion in the quantity of loans is smaller when there is no binding interest rate ceiling than when there is a ceiling. In the absence of a ceiling, the interest rate on transactions accounts declines when TS shifts to the right. This induces the public to reduce the quantity of balances supplied to the bank below T_1. Thus, the quantity of transactions accounts rises by less than the shift in the supply schedule. With this smaller increase in bank liabilities, the loan supply schedule shifts less to the right, and the interest rate on loans does not decline as much as when there is an interest rate ceiling. Because the decline in the interest rate is less, there is a smaller expansion in the quantity of loans.

When the interest rate ceiling is binding, the bank stands ready to accept any funds that the public will leave with it. This means that, in effect, the bank's demand schedule for transactions accounts is a horizontal line. Panel II of Figure 7.6 shows the bank's demand schedules for transactions accounts as downward

FIGURE 7.6
THE EFFECTS OF AN INTEREST
RATE CEILING FOR TRANSACTIONS
ACCOUNTS WHEN THERE ARE
SHIFTS IN THE PUBLIC'S SUPPLY OF
TRANSACTIONS ACCOUNTS.

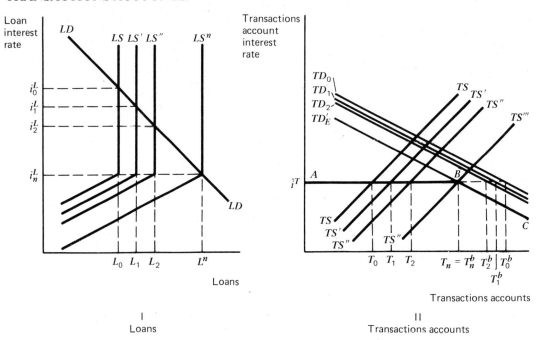

sloping. These schedules indicate the amount of transactions accounts that the bank would like to have, given the interest rate on loans. For example, the schedule TD_0 indicates the bank's demand for transactions accounts given the loan interest rate, i_0^L. Given the interest rate for loans, i_0^L, shown in Panel I, the bank will accept any quantity of transactions accounts up to T_0^b at the ceiling interest rate $\bar{i}^T$. For a quantity of transactions accounts greater than T_0^b, the bank will reduce the interest rate on transactions accounts below $\bar{i}^T$. The amount of transactions accounts the bank actually gets, however, is determined by the public's supply schedule TS. Thus, the quantity of transactions accounts is T_0.

Figure 7.6 shows that each time the supply of transactions accounts shifts right from TS to TS' to TS'', the quantity of transactions accounts increases by the amount of the shift in supply. The loan supply schedule shifts to the right by the amount that the quantity of transactions accounts increases. Each time the loan supply schedule shifts to the right, the loan interest rate declines. With lower loan interest rates, the bank's demand schedule for transactions accounts shifts left from TD_0 to TD_1 to TD_2. With the rightward shifts in the public's supply schedule for transactions accounts and the leftward shifts in the bank's demand schedule for these accounts, the bank's excess demand for transactions accounts is declining. Its initial excess demand is $(T_0^b - T_0)$. When the supply schedule shifts to TS', the loan interest rate declines to i_1^L, and the bank's demand schedule for transactions accounts shifts to TD_1. Given the interest rate ceiling, $\bar{i}^T$, the bank demands the quantity T_1^b, and the public supplies the quantity T_1. There is still an excess demand for transactions accounts, but the amount of the excess demand has declined to $(T_1^b - T_1)$. When the public's supply schedule shifts to TS'', the public supplies the quantity T_2 of transactions accounts. The bank lends the additional funds, and the loan interest rate falls to i_2^L. At this lower interest rate, the bank's demand for transactions account liabilities is T_2^b. Now the bank's excess demand has fallen to $(T_2^b - T_2)$.

With the supply schedule for transactions accounts shifting right and the demand schedule shifting left, the bank's excess demand for transactions account liabilities declines. Finally, at the loan interest rate i_n^L the quantity of transactions accounts demanded by the bank, T_n^b, equals the quantity supplied by the public, T_n. The bank's excess demand for transactions accounts is eliminated. Any further rightward shift in the supply of transactions accounts will produce a decline in the interest rate on these accounts. The bank will accept only additional transactions account liabilities beyond T_n if the interest rate on these accounts is reduced. Thus, beyond T_n, the interest rate ceiling is no longer binding, and the bank will move down the segment of its demand schedule BC.

We conclude that, given the ceiling interest rate $\bar{i}^T$, the bank will accept any quantity of transactions accounts that the public supplies up to the quantity T_n. Thus, the bank's effective demand for transactions accounts is the horizontal line AB. As long as the quantity of transactions accounts is not larger than T_n, the actual quantity of transactions accounts at the bank is determined by the public's supply. The bank is completely passive.

If the public's supply of transactions accounts is so great that it wants to hold a quantity of account balances greater than T_n at the ceiling interest rate $\bar{i}^T$, the bank ceases to be passive. With such a large quantity of transactions accounts, the bank is holding a large quantity of loans. Given the loan demand schedule LD, the public will borrow the amount that the bank wants to lend only at a low interest rate. When the loan interest rate falls below i_n^L, the bank is no longer willing to accept transactions accounts at the ceiling interest rate. It can be induced to accept transactions accounts in excess of T_n only if the interest rate on these accounts declines. Thus, for a quantity of transactions accounts in excess of T_n, the interest rate ceiling is no longer binding. When the interest rate ceiling is not binding, the bank's demand schedule for transactions account liabilities is downward sloping.

We conclude that the bank's effective demand schedule for transactions accounts is a horizontal line up to the quantity T_n. For quantities of transactions accounts larger than T_n, the demand schedule is downward sloping. The bank's demand schedule is shown as the heavy line ABC in Figure 7.6.

When the regulatory authorities raise the interest rate ceiling on bank liabilities, but the ceiling remains a binding constraint, the effect on the quantity of liabilities and loans is determined by the behavior of the public. Panel II of Figure 7.7 shows the effect on the quantity of transactions accounts when the ceiling interest rate is raised from $\bar{i}_0^T$ to $\bar{i}_1^T$. When the interest rate ceiling is $\bar{i}_0^T$, the bank's effective demand schedule is TD_0. When the ceiling is raised to $\bar{i}_1^T$, the effective demand schedule shifts up to TD_1 indicating that the bank will accept any quantity of transactions accounts up to T_1^b at the new ceiling interest rate $\bar{i}_1^T$.[16] With the higher interest rate, the public moves up its supply schedule TS and increases the quantity of transactions account balances at the bank from T_0 to T_1. The increase in liabilities, $T_1 - T_0$, is invested by the bank in loans so the loan supply schedule shifts by the amount $L_1 - L_0 = T_1 - T_0$, as shown in Panel I. The shift in loan supply produces a reduction in the interest rate on loans. We conclude that an increase in the interest rate ceiling on bank liabilities increases the quantity of liabilities and loans, and it decreases the interest rate on the bank's loans.

This is an important result because it contradicts the common assertion that a rise in the interest rate ceiling increases loan interest rates. This assertion is based on the observation that an increase in the interest rate on a bank's liabilities raises its costs. It is argued that the higher costs are passed on to borrowers through an increase in the interest rate on loans. This argument is defective because it disregards the increase in the bank's liabilities that occurs when the interest rate ceiling rises. The public supplies a larger amount of liabilities to the bank, which causes the loan supply schedule to shift to the right. This produces a decline in the loan interest rate. When there is a lower loan interest rate and a higher interest rate for transactions accounts, $(i^L - \bar{i}^T)$ declines. Thus, the bank's expected profit per loan is reduced. We cannot determine whether total profits fall or rise. This depends upon the interest rate elasticity of the public's supply of transactions accounts and upon the interest elasticity of loan demand.

It might be helpful at this point to summarize the analysis for the case of a binding interest rate ceiling. The reason that the bank is willing to accept all transactions account liabilities at the interest rate ceiling is that loans are sufficiently profitable that it would like to expand its lending. The ceiling prevents the bank from attracting additional account balances, so the best that it can do is pay the ceiling interest rate and accept all the balances it can get.

The expected return from additional lending is determined by the difference between the interest rate on loans and the interest rate on transactions account liabilities, that is, by $(i^L - \bar{i}^T)$. This interest rate differential is affected by the public's supply of transactions accounts and by the public's demand for loans. The differential is also affected by the level of the interest rate ceiling that is set by the government. When there is a rightward shift in the supply schedule of transactions accounts or a leftward shift in the demand schedule for loans, the interest

---

[16] For a quantity of transactions accounts greater than T_1^b, the bank's excess demand for liabilities is eliminated, and the new interest rate ceiling $\bar{i}_1^T$ is not binding.

FIGURE 7.7
THE EFFECTS OF AN INCREASE IN
THE INTEREST RATE CEILING ON
TRANSACTIONS ACCOUNTS.

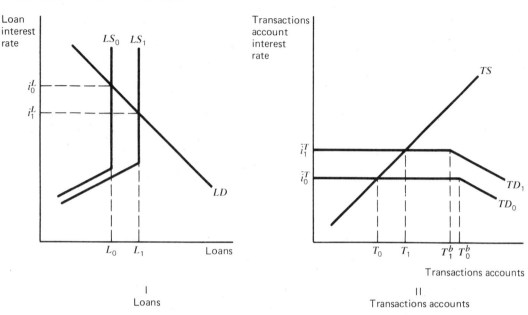

rate on loans declines, and, therefore, $(i^L - \bar{i}^T)$ is reduced. When there is a rise in the interest rate ceiling on liabilities, $\bar{i}^T$ rises and i^L falls, so the profitability of additional lending is reduced. The differential, $(i^L - \bar{i}^T)$, can be reduced to the point that additional lending is not profitable as long as the bank continues to pay the ceiling interest rate on its transactions accounts. At this point, the bank will expand its transactions account liabilities and loans only if the interest rate it pays on its liabilities is below the ceiling. When this occurs, the bank's demand schedule for transactions accounts becomes downward sloping, and its loan supply schedule is no longer vertical. We are back in a world without a binding interest rate ceiling.

The existence of an interest rate ceiling has several important implications for bank behavior. When the ceiling is binding, a bank is prevented from using an increase in the interest rate as a method of competing for additional account balances. This inability to compete means that a bank cannot affect the quantity of its liabilities. Thus, the quantity of liabilities is *exogenous* to the bank. The bank passively accepts new deposits into its customers' accounts and honors withdrawals without being able to determine the total size of its liabilities. Contrary to the case of no interest rate ceiling, a bank cannot affect its leverage because it cannot control the quantity of its liabilities. This situation makes the bank dependent on the public's willingness to hold account balances at the ceiling interest rate. It is the public's supply of balances to a bank that determines the size of its liabilities and, hence, its leverage.

The inability of a bank to control the size of its liabilities through changing the interest rate makes it vulnerable to shifts in the public's supply of account balances. Consider the case where the interest rate ceiling is binding and the expected rates of return for alternative assets, such as government securities or money market mutual funds, rise. The public now wants to hold more of these assets and less transactions account balances. The supply schedule for transactions accounts shifts to the left as the public reduces its holdings of these balances and increases its holdings of alternative assets. When the quantity of liabilities declines, the bank must decrease its loans by the same amount.

The reduction in liabilities and loans that occurs when market interest rates rise above interest rate ceilings for bank liabilities and *TS* shifts to the left is called *disintermediation*. This rather cumbersome term means that the role of banks as financial intermediaries is reduced when bank liabilities and assets decline. When interest rates on alternative assets fall below interest rate ceilings for bank liabilities, *TS* shifts to the right. Funds flow back into banks, and they increase their role as financial intermediaries. This is *reintermediation*. Until interest rate ceilings were largely dismantled in the early 1980s, disintermediation and reintermediation were important in determining the role of banks in the financial system.[17]

ADDITIONAL FACTORS AFFECTING BANK BEHAVIOR

So far we have considered a world in which a bank only holds business loans and only issues transactions account liabilities. Net worth is assumed to be fixed, so there is a one-to-one relationship between changes in the quantity of loans and changes in the quantity of transactions account liabilities at the bank. This one-to-one relationship holds irrespective of whether there is a binding interest rate ceiling or not. If loans rise, transactions account liabilities must increase by an equal amount. If these liabilities decline, loans must be reduced by an equal amount. When there is a binding ceiling on the interest rate for transactions accounts, the quantity of these accounts and of loans cannot be controlled by the bank; these quantities are determined exogenously by the public's supply of transactions balances.

This simplified world has allowed us to isolate some basic factors determining bank behavior, but we must now consider more realistic conditions. This section

---

[17] As we shall see in Chapter 10, disintermediation and reintermediation also had powerful effects on savings and loan associations and mutual savings banks.

studies the behavior of a bank that holds securities as well as loans; it also uses "nonprice" methods of attracting transactions account liabilities, and it issues other liabilities for which there is no ceiling on the interest rate paid.

The Role of Securities

A bank holds securities issued by the U.S. Treasury and other governmental units because they have lower risk than loans and greater liquidity.[18] Securities have a particularly important role when there is a binding ceiling on the interest rate for liabilities. In this situation, the quantity of liabilities is determined by the public's willingness to supply funds to the bank. If the quantity of liabilities falls, the bank must reduce its assets by the same amount. Because of their low transactions costs and high liquidity, it is less costly to reduce assets by selling securities than by selling loans or waiting for them to mature. Similarly, if there is an expansion in liabilities, a bank saves transactions costs by investing the proceeds in securities rather than loans if the rise in liabilities is expected to be temporary. Securities also give the bank flexibility in adjusting to shifts in the demand for loans. When loan demand increases, a bank can sell securities and expand its loans. When loan demand declines, a bank can expand its holdings of securities.

When deciding how to divide its total assets between loans and securities, a bank must balance the liquidity, low risk, and relatively low expected return on securities against the illiquidity, higher risk, and higher expected return on loans. The desired mix between securities and loans is determined by the principles of portfolio selection described in Chapter 5. The choice between loans and securities is affected by the interest rate and risk on loans relative to the interest rate and risk on securities. For simplicity, we assume that the interest rate and risk on securities are constant. This implies that a bank can be induced to increase its lending and, therefore, reduce its holdings of securities if compensated by an increase in the interest rate on loans. Thus, if the loan interest rate rises, a bank sells securities and increases its holdings of loans. If the interest rate on loans declines, a bank reduces lending and increases its holdings of securities.

When a bank adjusts its holdings of securities in response to changes in the loan interest rate, there is no longer a one-to-one relationship between changes in the quantity of loans and changes in the quantity of liabilities. When the loan interest rate increases, the bank sells securities and expands loans, so the ratio of loans to liabilities rises. When the loan interest rate declines, the bank increases its holdings of securities and decreases its loans, so the ratio of loans to liabilities declines. This implies that the loan supply schedule is upward sloping, rather than vertical, when there is a binding ceiling on the interest rate for liabilities.

---

[18] Banks hold relatively short-term federal and municipal securities. These securities experience relatively small price fluctuations, and, in the case of federal securities, there is no risk of default. There is default risk for municipals, but it is small compared to the default risk for loans.

FIGURE 7.8
LOAN SUPPLY WHEN A BANK CAN
SELL SECURITIES.

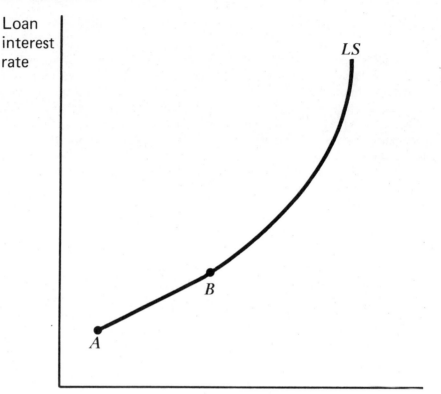

The loan supply schedule for a bank that holds securities is shown in Figure 7.8. Between points *A* and *B* the interest rate ceiling on its liabilities is not binding. The loan supply schedule is upward sloping over this range because as loans expand, risk increases. To the extent that the bank issues additional liabilities, leverage increases and risk rises. Risk also increases if the bank sells securities in order to expand loans. Because loans are more risky than securities, risk rises when loans replace securities in the bank's portfolio. This increase in risk occurs even though there is no rise in leverage. Beyond point *B*, the interest rate ceiling is binding, and the bank cannot issue additional liabilities. This means that any further increase in loans is the result of sales of securities. As loans rise, the share of securities in total assets falls. This produces larger and larger increases in risk. Thus, the loan supply schedule becomes increasingly steep. Eventually, there are no securities left, and the loans supply schedule becomes vertical.

We conclude that holdings of securities make it possible for a bank to expand its loans even when there is a binding ceiling for the interest rate on its liabilities. This expansion in loans is limited, however, by the amount of securities the bank has available to sell. Eventually, all the securities are sold, and the loan supply schedule is vertical.

Nonprice Competition for Liabilities

When interest rate ceilings are binding, banks use "nonprice" methods of competing for liabilities. Nonprice competition takes the form of advertising campaigns, "give-aways" of items such as toasters, low or zero service charges for processing account transactions, and the establishment of convenient locations to capture accounts. All these techniques are designed to make a bank's liabilities more attractive to the public.

These methods increase the rate of return on bank liabilities to the public. As a result, there is a movement up the supply schedule beyond the interest rate ceiling. Thus, the supply of liabilities increases, and, therefore, bank assets expand. The effects of nonprice competition are slow and relatively unpredictable, however. Nonprice competition is costly for banks, and it tends, over time, to drive operating costs upward. Thus, any excess profits that may accrue to banks from interest rate ceilings tend to be eroded over time by rising costs from nonprice competition for liabilities.

Avoiding Interest Rate Ceilings

Binding interest rate ceilings not only induce banks to use nonprice competition, but they also induce them to circumvent the ceilings. This is accomplished by issuing liabilities that are not subject to interest rate ceilings. In the 1960s and 1970s, banks invented an impressive array of liabilities that were exempt from interest rate ceilings. These liabilities, which are discussed in detail in Chapter 8, allowed banks to determine the total size of their liabilities by varying the interest rate paid.

As explained in the next chapter, through the use of large denomination certificates of deposit and other marketable liabilities, large banks have been more successful in "managing" their liabilities than have small banks. Large banks can determine the total quantity of liabilities they issue and, therefore, they can determine the quantity of assets held. As a result, large banks can determine the extent of their leverage. Small banks do not have access to the market for certificates of deposits and similar liabilities, so they cannot manage their liabilities as closely.

SUMMARY

In this chapter, a model was used to describe the interaction between a bank's supply of loans and the public's demand for loans along with the interaction between the bank's demand for funds and the public's supply of funds to the bank. These demands and supplies determine the total quantity of assets for a bank and the quantity of liabilities it issues to support its assets.

A bank's demand for funds is derived from its demand for assets. In the absence of ceilings on interest rates for liabilities, the amount of assets that a bank holds depends upon the interest rate it earns on assets relative to the interest rate it pays for liabilities. As long as the interest rate for loans exceeds the interest rate for liabilities, expected profits rise when liabilities and assets increase. Given net worth, leverage also increases, and, therefore, risk to the owners of the bank rises. A bank faces a trade-off between rising expected return and rising risk when it increases its assets and liabilities. The bank's preferences for expected return versus risk determine the amount of assets that it holds and the amount of liabilities that it issues. Thus, the bank determines its leverage.

When there is a binding ceiling on the interest rate that a bank can pay for liabilities, it cannot issue as many liabilities as it would like. In this situation, the quantity of assets and of liabilities is constrained by the amount of funds that the public is willing to supply the bank. In this case, a bank cannot determine its leverage. Removal of the interest rate ceiling raises the interest rate on liabilities and lowers the interest rate on loans.

Interest rate ceilings also affect the degree to which a bank can fulfill its role as a financial intermediary. When there is an increase in the demand for bank loans, the interest rate on loans rises, which induces the bank to expand its loans. In the absence of interest rate ceilings, it attracts additional funds by raising the interest rate paid for liabilities. Thus, an increase in the demand for bank loans leads to an increase in liabilities and an increase in loans. In this situation, the bank expands its role as a financial intermediary by borrowing more from surplus units and lending more to deficit units. When there is a binding interest rate ceiling for liabilities, the bank cannot attract additional funds. In this situation an increase in loan demand produces a rise in the loan interest rate, but there is no expansion of loans. The banks cannot increase its role as a financial intermediary. Furthermore, a rise in market interest rates above the ceiling rate for bank liabilities induces the public to withdraw funds from the bank in favor of market investments. In this case, disintermediation occurs; both liabilities and assets decline.

Banks hold liquid assets as well as loans, and they engage in nonprice competition for liabilities. Allowing for these factors does not alter the basic conclusions from the model. As long as there are no ceilings on interest rates, the size of a bank is an economic decision involving a trade-off between its quest for profit and its aversion to risk. When there are binding ceilings, the size of a bank is constrained by the availability of funds from the public. Securities and nonprice competition allow a bank some flexibility in adjusting to shifts in loan demand or in the supply of funds provided by the public, but these methods are poor substitutes for interest rates as the means of competing for the public's funds.

The model of bank behavior presented in this chapter omits much of the detail that makes banking such an exacting business. The model does isolate some basic factors that condition bank behavior, however, and it provides a useful framework for the more detailed discussion of the banking industry that follows in the next chapter.

THE COMMERCIAL BANKING INDUSTRY

8

The commercial banking industry plays a crucial role in the financial system. The activities of commercial banks touch virtually every segment of the economy. As a result, banks play a key role in transmitting the effects of monetary policy to the economy. The role of commercial banks cannot be fully described until the relationship between the Federal Reserve System and depository institutions is discussed and until we link the financial system to the rest of the economy. These subjects occupy many chapters of this book. The current chapter describes and analyzes the banking industry.

AN OVERVIEW OF COMMERCIAL BANKING

Historically, banks specialized in serving the depository and short-term credit needs of commerce. This specialization earned them the title of *commercial* banks. Over the past several decades banks have expanded their activities to the point that they now issue liabilities to virtually all elements of society, and they extend about as much credit to households as to business.[1] Furthermore, banks have moved increasingly toward providing long-term credit. Despite these changes, the term *commercial* is still used to differentiate these banks from other types of banks, such as mutual savings banks.

---

[1] Federal, state, and local governments also hold account balances at banks, and their securities are held by banks.

Commercial banks offer under one roof such a wide variety of depository, loan, and other services that many customers can conduct all their financial transactions through their bank. Banks are prevented by law, however, from offering certain kinds of financial services such as acting as full service stockbrokers and underwriting corporate securities. These restrictions prevent banks from becoming complete financial centers. Government regulation also limits the interest rates that can be paid on certain types of bank liabilities, and it limits the interest rates that can be charged on some loans. Regulation controls the chartering of new banks, it limits the locations at which existing banks can operate, and it limits bank mergers. Government regulation also subjects banks to various restrictions concerning the kinds of liabilities they can issue and the types of assets they can hold. Government regulation is discussed in detail in Chapter 9, but the implications of regulation are touched upon at various points in this chapter.

There presently are over 15,000 commercial banks operating in the United States. This is many times the number of banks that operate in other countries. Government policies toward mergers and branching are the primary reason for such a large number of banks in the industry.[2] There are rules limiting bank mergers, and many states require that banks within their borders operate out of only a limited number of locations. Other countries do not have similar branching and merger laws, and they have far fewer banks.

Although the United States has a large number of banks, most of them are very small. For example, of the more than 15,000 banks operating in the country, approximately 13,000 have total assets of $50 million or less. The combined assets held by the 13,000 smallest banks in the country total approximately $200 billion, which is less than the combined assets of the two largest banks in the country. As we will see later, size is an important determinant of bank behavior. A multibillion dollar bank has many options available to it concerning the liabilities it issues and the assets it acquires that are unavailable to a small bank.

The Aggregate Balance Sheet

Banks have three sources of funds to support their holdings of assets: deposit liabilities, other liabilities, and the net worth invested by their owners. Table 8.1 shows an aggregate balance sheet on December 31, 1982, for all insured banks operating in the United States. To keep the table simple, we have combined various items into general categories. For example, all types of loans are lumped into a single category, and time deposit accounts of all maturities and denominations are also combined.[3] The table shows both the total dollar value of each category and the category as a percentage of total assets.

---

[2] Banks that accept deposits and grant loans from various locations are said to have *branches* at these locations.

[3] The components of the various categories are discussed later.

TABLE 8.1
COMBINED BALANCE SHEET FOR ALL INSURED COMMERCIAL BANKS[a]
(DECEMBER 31, 1982)

	Billions of Dollars	Percentage of Total Assets		Billions of Dollars	Percentage of Total Assets
Assets			Liabilities		
Cash assets	$ 207	11	Transactons accounts	$ 453	24
Securities	373	20	Savings accounts [b]	220	12
Loans and related assets	1,281	69	Time accounts and other liabilities	1,060	57
Total assets	$1,861	100	Total liabilities	$1,733	93
			Net worth	128	7
			Total liabilities and net worth	$1,861	100

[a] Domestic offices.
[b] Other than those authorized as transactions accounts.
Source: *Federal Reserve Bulletin*, April 1981, pp. A76–A77.

A striking feature of the dollar figures is their size. The commercial banking industry holds over $1.8 *trillion* of assets. Three categories of assets are shown in the table. Cash assets include cash in banks' vaults, as well as deposit balances held with other banks and with the Federal Reserve. These assets earn no interest, and some are perfectly liquid. The securities held by banks are mainly securities issued by the U.S. government and by state and local governments. Most of the securities are highly liquid. The major asset category is loans and related assets, which constitute 69 percent of total assets held by banks. This category is composed of loans to businesses and households and to other financial institutions.

The liability side of the balance sheet reveals that despite the fact that virtually all the transactions account balances in the United States are held at commercial banks, only 24 percent of total asset holdings are supported by transactions accounts.[4] Furthermore, savings accounts, which historically have been an important source of funds to banks, now support only 12 percent of total assets. Quantitatively, the most important source of funds is time accounts and other liabilities, which support 57 percent of total assets.

Table 8.1 shows that only 7 percent of total assets is supported by net worth, that is, by funds invested in banks by their owners. Thus, 93 percent of total assets is supported by borrowed money of various kinds.[5]

---

[4] As of September 1983, over 90 percent of all transactions account balances in the country were held at commercial banks.

[5] The balance sheet data reported in this chapter are for the domestic offices of U.S. banks. If the assets and liabilities of foreign offices of U.S. banks are consolidated with the assets and liabilities of their domestic offices, only 5.7 percent of total consolidated assets is supported by consolidated net worth. For large banks, 3.5 to 5.0 percent of consolidated total assets is supported by net worth.

BANK ASSET AND LIABILITY MANAGEMENT

A bank must balance the costs and availability of its liabilities against the income and risk on its assets. The trick to banking is to hold assets whose liquidity, rates of return, and risk are compatible with the maturity and costs of its liabilities. The basic principles involved in selecting assets and liabilities were discussed in Chapters 5 and 7. In the remainder of this chapter, we apply those principles to explain the asset and liability management of banks.

LIABILITIES

It is useful to begin the discussion of bank liabilities by showing the amounts of the major liabilities that the banking industry has outstanding. As shown in Table 8.2, transactions accounts comprise 26 percent of total liabilities; savings accounts, 13 percent; and small denomination time accounts, 22 percent of total liabilities. The total of these categories, which comprises total liabilities over which a bank lacks close control, is 61 percent of total liabilities for the banking industry as a whole. The remaining liabilities are large denomination CDs and other market instruments. Banks have close control over these liabilities, which constitute 39 percent of total liabilities.

Liabilities Over which Banks do not have Close Control

Though banks vary interest rates to the extent possible and use nonprice competition in an effort to affect the quantity of transactions, savings, and small denomination time accounts, these liabilities fluctuate with the public's supply of funds for these account balances. The nature of these fluctuations have important implications for the kinds of assets that banks hold.

Banks attempt to predict fluctuations in these liabilities, and to some degree they are successful. Various methods are used, but past fluctuations in the levels of various types of accounts often help banks to predict future fluctuations. For example, there are seasonal fluctuations in the quantity of transactions and savings accounts. Banks are aware that these accounts tend to be drawn down during the summer vacation period or before holidays and to be built back up at other times. Similarly, banks in farming communities know that their liabilities fluctuate with the planting and harvesting seasons.

Many banks have also learned that the behavior of income in their localities and the movement of interest rates on various assets that compete with their accounts in their customers' portfolios affect the quantity of liabilities. Thus, many banks attempt to predict income and interest rate fluctuations as a guide for

TABLE 8.2
LIABILITIES ISSUED BY ALL INSURED COMMERCIAL BANKS
(MAJOR CATEGORIES: DECEMBER 31, 1982)

	Billions of Dollars		Percentage of Total Liabilities	
Transactions accounts	$ 453		26	
Savings accounts [a]	220		13	
Time accounts	720		41	
Small denomination		387		22
Large denomination		333		19
Other liabilities	340		20	
Total liabilities	$1,733		100	

[a] Other than those authorized as transactions accounts.
Source: *Federal Reserve Bulletin*, April 1983, p. A75.

setting the interest rates on their accounts and for making predictions of the future levels of their liabilities. The accuracy of these predictions is important because it affects the kinds of assets that banks hold.

To the extent that banks can predict fluctuations in their transactions, savings and small time account liabilities, they can smoothly adjust their assets in response. Consider the example of a bank that experiences a decline in its transactions account liabilities. If the decline is anticipated sufficiently far in advance, the bank can reduce its portfolio of assets with low cost. Transactions costs and price uncertainty from asset sales are eliminated by having assets in the portfolio that mature at the time that the liabilities decline. The funds obtained from maturing assets are used to pay off customers who are withdrawing funds from the bank.

The shorter the interval of time between the date when a bank knows it will lose liabilities and the actual loss, the more important liquid assets become. When a decline comes as a surprise, liquidity is essential. This helps explain why banks hold substantial amounts of highly liquid assets even though these assets often pay a lower interest rate than less liquid assets. A less liquid asset can be sold quickly only if its price is reduced relative to its "full" price.[6] The price reduction can reduce the realized rate of return on the less liquid asset below the return on a liquid asset.

Increases in liabilities can also pose problems for bank portfolio management. The shorter the lead time between the date when a bank knows its liabilities will increase and the date when the increase occurs, the more costly it is to acquire many kinds of assets. For example, a bank often can expand its loans quickly only if it is willing to reduce the interest rate substantially. Furthermore, it may be impossible to grant new loans quickly because of the need to process loan applications or to advertise the increased availability of loans. When an increase

[6] Liquidity was discussed in Chapter 4.

in liabilities comes as a surprise, a bank usually does not expand loans immediately, but, rather, it holds the funds idle or acquires securities. These assets are then reduced as loans are expanded.

The degree of stability and predictability of liabilities has important implications for bank portfolio management. The greater the fluctuations and the less predictable the fluctuations in a bank's liabilities, the greater its holding of liquid assets relative to its total assets. Because liquid assets have a lower rate of return than loans and other illiquid assets, a bank with volatile and unpredictable liabilities cannot earn as high a rate of return as would be possible if the level of liabilities were predictable and stable.

There are several factors that affect the degree of volatility and predictability of liabilities. It is convenient to discuss these factors in terms of the major types of liabilities that banks issue.

Transactions Accounts

The public holds most of its money in the form of transactions account balances.[7] If a bank only had one depositor, its transactions account liabilities would fluctuate with the transactions made by that customer. Banks are able to limit the fluctuations in their transactions account liabilities by having many customers. For a given average quantity of transactions account liabilities, as the number of accounts increases, the standard deviation of total liabilities declines. The reason for this phenomenon is the same as for the reduction of portfolio risk through diversification discussed in Chapter 5. If each depositor is an isolated entity, fluctuations in the balances in one account are independent of fluctuations in other account balances. In this situation, banks can be like insurance companies and reduce the risk of large fluctuations in their total transactions account liabilities to low levels by having a large number of customers.

Fluctuations in individual transactions account balances are often not independent of each other, but this lack of independence can, in many cases, actually reduce the variability of total transactions account liabilities. Consider the case of a business that has a transactions account at a bank in a small community. As that business pays wages, it reduces its account balance. If the firm's employees also have transactions accounts in the same bank, they increase their account balances. If these employees then purchase products from the firm, their expenditures reduce the account balances of the employees and increase the balance of the firm. The bank's total transactions account liabilities are steady because funds are transferred from one account to another within the bank.

In the case just described, there is negative correlation between fluctuations in the account balance of the firm and the balances of its employees. This negative correlation reduces the standard deviation of the bank's transactions account lia-

---

[7] Approximately 70 percent of money (M1) is transactions account balances, and 30 percent is currency.

bilities. If the fluctuations in the transactions account balances of various customers are positively correlated, however, the value of diversification is reduced.[8]
Banks located in communities where a particular firm or industry is dominant
often have accounts whose fluctuations are positively correlated. For example,
when there is a recession in the automobile industry, banks in Detroit lose account
balances from automobile manufacturers, from their suppliers, and from workers.
Because of this problem, banks attempt to attract accounts over a wide geographic
area and to have customers that represent many different economic groups. To
the extent that these efforts are successful, positive correlation of individual
account balances is reduced.

Even banks with a large number of transactions accounts cannot eliminate
fluctuations in their total transactions account liabilities. These fluctuations place
constraints on the ability of a bank to acquire illiquid, longer-term assets even
though these assets have attractive expected returns and acceptable risks. Fluctuations in transactions account liabilities induce banks to hold liquid assets.

Before 1983, all transactions account liabilities were subject to interest rate ceilings. Beginning in January of that year, transactions accounts held by individuals,
nonprofit organizations, and governmental units were exempted from interest rate
ceilings. Transactions accounts of business pay no interest.[9] This regulatory situation means that a bank can use the interest rate as a means of competing for the
balances of households and other nonbusiness entities, but not for the transactions
account balances of business.

Nonbusiness accounts are an important part of total transactions accounts for
most banks. This suggests that by varying the interest rate, a bank can gain some
control over these liabilities. Though the ability to move the interest rate
improves control, there is still a substantial amount of variability in these
accounts. Even though the accounts pay a market rate of interest, the public uses
them for transactions purposes. This means that the amount of these liabilities
still fluctuates with the seasons and with economic conditions. Furthermore,
many account holders do not reallocate their portfolios of assets every time there
is a fluctuation in relative interest rates. Thus, if a bank raises its interest rate relative to market interest rates and relative to interest rates paid at other banks, for a
short period of time, it does not receive a large increase in deposits. If the interest
rate remains high, however, a substantial amount of funds eventually flows into
the bank. The use of the accounts for transactions purposes and the slow response
of the public to a change in the interest rate prevent a bank from controlling
interest-bearing transactions accounts closely over short periods of time such as
week-by-week or month-by-month.

---

[8] The effect of positive correlation is discussed in the appendix to Chapter 5.

[9] Individuals, nonprofit organizations, and governmental units are allowed to hold special
accounts that have no interest rate ceiling as long as a minimum balance of $2500 is main-
tained. Businesses are not allowed to hold these accounts. They must use demand deposit accounts that pay no interest. The details of the special accounts are discussed in Chapter 10.

Savings Accounts

As explained in Chapter 4, savings account liabilities are similar to transactions accounts in that banks are willing to honor withdrawals on demand. They differ from transactions accounts because they cannot be used directly to conduct transactions. It is necessary to make a withdrawal from the account before funds can be used for expenditures. Holders of savings account balances tend to use the accounts more as a financial investment and less as a transactions balance than they do transactions accounts. Thus, bank customers vary their savings account balances in response to changes in wealth and changes interest rates and risks on alternative assets, but they do not use their savings accounts as an active transactions balance the way that they do transactions accounts.

The relatively low activity of savings accounts suggests that the greater the proportion of savings account liabilities in a bank's total liabilities, the less concerned it has to be about asset liquidity and maturity. Banks with a high proportion of savings account liabilities have a relatively stable source of funds that can be invested in relatively illiquid assets whose maturities, expected returns, and risks provide a higher expected return or lower risk, or both, on the asset portfolio.[10]

There are times, however, when savings account liabilities fluctuate widely. As long as the interest rate ceiling for savings accounts allows them to be competitive with other assets, bank customers continue to hold savings account balances. If, however, the expected returns on alternative assets rises above the interest rate ceiling, holders of savings account balances withdraw their funds and purchase assets with more attractive returns. Withdrawals from savings accounts are paid on demand, so if banks have not anticipated the withdrawals sufficiently far in advance, they can find themselves in a liquidity squeeze.

If the returns on alternative assets fall below the interest rates paid on savings accounts, banks experience large inflows of savings account balances. Because these balances begin to earn interest immediately, banks must quickly invest the funds in income-earning assets if they are to generate a profit. It may be costly or infeasible to increase loans rapidly. This induces the bank to purchase securities and other liquid assets initially, which reduces the profitability of the newly acquired savings account liabilities.

In the second half of the 1960s, market interest rates fluctuated around the interest rate ceiling for savings accounts, and, as a result, savings account liabilities fluctuated widely. In the 1970s, market interest rates remained above the interest rate ceiling, and savings accounts liabilities declined dramatically. In December 1982, banks were allowed to offer a new kind of savings account called a money market account. As the name suggests, these are designed to be competitive with

---

[10] This does not necessarily imply that banks with a high proportion of savings accounts in total liabilities are more profitable than banks with high proportions of transactions accounts. Profitability is also affected by the costs to banks of providing savings and transactions accounts. These costs are discussed later.

the accounts offered by money market mutual funds.[11] A money market account has no interest rate ceiling. It can be used to make up to six transactions a month by check, telephone, or preauthorization. The account has a minimum balance requirement of $2500. A money market account is technically a savings account, but it is functionally a limited transactions account. The limitation on the number of transactions prevents the account from being used actively as a transactions account by many customers, but the money market account has substantial liquidity. Unlike the interest-bearing transactions account, the money market account is available to business.

Money market accounts revitalized savings accounts for banks. By September 1983, the accounts grew to $215 billion. Money market accounts also allowed banks to gain closer control over their liabilities because there is no interest rate ceiling. The accounts cannot be closely controlled over short periods of time, however, for much the same reasons that interest-bearing transactions accounts cannot be controlled.

Nonprice Competition for Transactions and Savings Accounts

A bank can exercise some control over the size of its transactions and savings account liabilities by engaging in nonprice competition for the public's account balances. Convenient locations, longer banking hours, speedy deposit and check cashing services, and advertising campaigns are all popular methods of increasing the attractiveness of bank accounts relative to other assets.

Aside from providing convenience to their customers, banks also compete for transactions accounts by not charging the full costs of maintaining accounts. Some banks do not charge at all, some charge a fixed sum per transaction, and others assess a scale of charges that declines with the size of the account. It is rare for a bank to charge the full cost of maintaining its transactions accounts. By not charging the full cost of maintaining transactions accounts, banks do make the accounts more attractive to the public. This form of competition is costly to banks, however, because the public has little incentive to limit the number of transactions conducted through these accounts.

Banks have also developed other methods of making their accounts more attractive. They often offer their customers preferred treatment for loans and provide various advisory services at low cost as a method of encouraging new business. Finally, some banks have resorted to elaborate "giveaway" programs as methods of enticing new customers. For example, banks offer toasters, television sets, and even stuffed animals as inducements for new accounts.

By using nonprice inducements and by advertising the virtues of the inducements, banks do compete for transactions and savings account liabilities.

---

[11] These mutual funds were discussed briefly in Chapter 4, and they are covered extensively in Chapter 10.

Nonprice competition affects the public's demand for various accounts, but the effects are slow and difficult to predict. Nonprice competition is not a feasible method of quickly changing the size of transactions and savings accounts.

Small Denomination Time Accounts

Banks offer small denomination (less than $100,000) time accounts with fixed maturities ranging from seven days to eight years. When the account matures, the bank pays the holder the amount of money initially placed in the account plus any accumulated interest. Typically, the holder can withdraw interest payments as they are made or allow the interest to accumulate in the account. A holder can withdraw the money invested in a time account prior to maturity, but the bank assesses a substantial penalty for early withdrawals. This penalty discourages most customers from "cashing in" their time accounts prior to maturity. Furthermore, small denomination time accounts are nontransferable (not negotiable), so it is impossible for a holder to sell a time account to someone else. Thus, time accounts are less liquid than transactions and savings accounts. The longer the maturity of the time account, the lower its liquidity.

The existence of a fixed maturity for time accounts makes them fundamentally different from transactions and savings accounts. Though banks honor withdrawals on demand from transactions and savings accounts, the accounts themselves do not have a predetermined and fixed life. The size of a transactions or savings account varies over time as the customer makes deposits and withdrawals, but the account itself stays in existence until the customer closes it out. In contrast, a time account has a fixed maturity, and the size of the account does not change during its life except for the growth of accumulated interest. For example, a customer who acquires a $10,000 time account with a six-month maturity has lent the bank $10,000 for six months. The interest rate on the account is fixed for the six months. Once the time account is issued, the customer cannot increase the amount invested in it. Increased investment can be accomplished only by acquiring a new time account that will mature six months after it is purchased. Funds can be withdrawn from a time account, but the holder must pay a penalty upon withdrawal.

Because small denomination time accounts lack the liquidity of transactions and savings accounts or even of market securities, the public will hold them only if compensated for the illiquidity. Thus, these time accounts tend to pay a higher interest rate than transactions or savings accounts, and the longer the maturity of the account, the higher its interest rate tends to be. There are no interest rate ceilings for small denomination time accounts.[12]

Despite their higher cost, time account liabilities are often attractive to banks because funds invested in them are usually not withdrawn prior to maturity.

---

[12] The single exception is for time accounts with initial maturities of seven to thirty-one days and denominations of less than $2500.

Unlike transactions and savings accounts, time account liabilities are not subject to rapid decline when rates of return on alternative assets rise relative to the interest rate paid on the account. Time account liabilities decline as the accounts mature. Thus, banks have time to reduce their assets in an orderly manner when rates of return on alternative assets rise above the interest rate ceilings on time accounts. The amount of advance warning of a loss of time account liabilities depends upon the time to maturity of these liabilities.

Time account liabilities also allow banks to match the maturities of their assets and liabilities. For example, a bank issuing time account liabilities with a maturity of three years can use the funds to grant loans that mature in three years. If at the end of three years the holders of these time accounts want to withdraw their funds, the maturing loans provide the funds to meet the withdrawals. If the bank had supported the three-year loans with time accounts that mature in one year, it incurs transactions costs of "rolling over" the one-year time accounts. By matching the maturity of its time accounts to the maturity of its loans, these costs are avoided. Matching the maturity of time accounts to the maturity of loans also "locks in" a rate of return on bank assets. For example, if three-year time accounts cost the bank 8 percent interest and if three-year loans earn an interest return of 10 percent, the bank has assured itself a 2 percentage point return on the loans for three years.[13]

Time accounts have an important additional advantage over transactions and savings accounts. Because of the fixed maturity of time accounts, a bank can increase its time account liabilities by increasing the interest rate on new time accounts without having to pay a higher interest rate for existing accounts. This is not the case for transactions and savings accounts. When a bank raises the interest rate on transactions or savings accounts, it must pay the higher interest rate on both new and old accounts. If a bank attempted to attract new transactions or savings account balances by paying a higher interest rate for new accounts than for existing accounts, holders of existing accounts would withdraw their funds and open new accounts. Banks honor withdrawals from transactions and savings accounts on demand, so all accounts would become new accounts, and the higher interest rate would be paid on all accounts. Some customers might be slow to make the transfer because of ignorance or inertia, but most customers would make the switch quickly. Because there is no effective way to separate new from old accounts, it is costly to raise the interest rate on transactions and savings accounts as a means of issuing additional liabilities.

This situation has led to the active use of time deposit liabilities by many banks. If a bank wants to issue additional time account liabilities, the increased interest rate is only be paid on new time account liabilities. The penalties for early withdrawal inhibit the holders of old time accounts from cashing them in, so a bank

---

[13] For simplicity, this calculation assumes that loan principal is paid at maturity, and it neglects noninterest costs of maintaining the time accounts and the loan. It also neglects the risk that the borrower will fail to make interest and principal payments.

can effectively pay two different interest rates for time accounts liabilities of the same maturity.[14]

The flexibility of time accounts can be very important. Consider, for example, a bank that is considering a new one-year loan of $100,000 at 15 percent interest. The bank does not want to sell securities to finance the loan, so its only alternative is to increase its liabilities. The bank considers increasing the interest rate it pays on savings accounts as a method of attracting $100,000 of new savings account liabilities. The bank estimates that if it raises the interest rate paid on these accounts from 7 percent to 7.25 percent, it will receive an additional $100,000 of saving account balances. Because the bank must also pay 7.25 percent interest on its existing savings account liabilities, all savings accounts now cost 7.25 percent. The bank has $10 million of savings account liabilities outstanding, so its interest cost for existing liabilities rises by $25,000, that is, from .07($10 million) = $700,000 to .0725($10 million) = $725,000. The $100,000 of new saving liabilities have an interest cost of $7250, that is, .0725($100,000), so the total cost of savings account liabilities, both old and new, rises by $25,000 + $7250 = $32,250. Thus, it costs the bank $32,250 to obtain $100,000 of additional time deposit liabilities. This is a marginal interest cost of $32,250/$100,000, or 32.25 percent. Because the $100,000 is to be invested in a loan that earns an interest income of 15 percent, it is a losing proposition to finance the new loan with new savings account liabilities.

The bank discovers, however, that it can issue $100,000 of new, one-year time account liabilities at 10 percent interest. It does not have to raise the interest rate on old time deposits. In this case, it costs the bank $10,000 of interest to attract $100,000 of additional time account liabilities for a marginal interest cost of 10 percent. The loan earns 15 percent interest, so it is profitable to issue new time accounts.

Though small denomination time accounts can offer advantages over transactions and savings accounts, there are impediments that prevent banks from controlling the total quantity of these accounts with much accuracy. Small time accounts lack the flexibility to be closely controlled. Banks attract additional time accounts through intensifying advertising activities and by raising interest rates. They are willing to accept all the time accounts supplied by the public at the announced interest rate. The actual quantity of time account balances they receive cannot be accurately predicted. Furthermore, the degree of response of the public to changes in the interest rate on small time accounts is small in the short run. A large change in the interest rate is required to change the quantity of these accounts quickly.

We conclude that a bank's control over its small denomination time account liabilities is not very tight. Virtually total control is available for a number of liabilities issued by large banks. These liabilities are the subject of the next section.

---

[14] The size of the penalty does affect the maximum amount that the interest rate on new time accounts can exceed the interest rate on old accounts. If the difference exceeds the penalty, customers will switch to new accounts. Even in this case, banks have gained, however, because they receive the penalties for early withdrawals.

TABLE 8.3
MANAGED LIABILITIES ISSUED BY ALL INSURED COMMERCIAL
BANKS (DECEMBER 31, 1982)

	Billions of Dollars	Percentage of Total
Large denomination time accounts	$333	50
Federal funds purchased and securities sold under repurchase agreements	179	27
All other	158	23
Total	$670	100

Source: *Federal Reserve Bulletin*, April 1983, p. A75.

Liabilities Over which Banks have Close Control: Managed Liabilities

Over the last twenty years, large banks have developed an impressive array of financial instruments that allow them to practice active liability management. At the end of 1982, banks had nearly $700 billion of *managed* (closely controlled) *liabilities* outstanding. These liabilities supported approximately 36 percent of the assets held by the banking industry. Aside from their sheer size, these managed liabilities give large banks great flexibility in adjusting to changes in the quantity of nonmanaged liabilities and to fluctuations in loan demand.

In order to put the discussion that follows in perspective, Table 8.3 lists the three major categories of managed liabilities. Large-denomination ($100,000 or more) time accounts are the largest category; they provide 50 percent of all the funds raised by liability management. The category "federal funds purchased and securities sold under repurchase agreements" represents very short-term borrowing from banks, other financial institutions, and large customers. This short-term borrowing provides 27 percent of managed liabilities. The third category, "all other," includes borrowing from overseas, borrowing from the Federal Reserve, long-term debt, and other types of liabilities that are discussed later.

Large Denomination Certificates of Deposit

Quantitatively, the most important instrument developed by banks for active liability management is the *large certificate of deposit* (CD). These certificates are time accounts issued in minimum denominations of $100,000 that are sold by banks on an organized market. Unlike ordinary time accounts, ownership of CDs is transferable, so they can be sold prior to maturity. These instruments are issued for various maturities, but maturities of six months or less are most common. By a cruelty of terminology, many banks give the name certificates of deposits to some types of conventional (small) time accounts. These should not be confused with the negotiable CDs described here. Some large denomination CDs are non-transferable. These certificates are like jumbo versions of ordinary time accounts.

Because of their large denominations, CDs are held by large businesses, financial intermediaries, state and local governments, and wealthy individuals. Certificates of deposit are attractive to these investors because they are highly liquid and have low risk of default, and they pay a rate of return that is competitive with similar instruments issued by business and government.

The short-term maturities of CDs provide a substantial degree of liquidity to investors. Large banks have further increased the liquidity of their instruments by establishing an active market in which holders can sell their CDs prior to maturity. This kind of market is called a *secondary* market.

Smaller banks do issue large CDs. These instruments cannot be sold on a national market, however, because the reputations of small banks are not widely known. Regional markets have developed to handle the CDs of relatively large, but not nationally known, banks. Though ownership of the certificates issued by small banks may be transferable, lack of access to an organized secondary market limits their liquidity to the holder. Smaller banks usually have to pay a higher interest rate on their CDs to compensate their holders for the lower liquidity of these instruments.

Certificates of deposit allow large banks to engage actively in liability management. These banks can decide on the amount of CDs that they want to issue and sell that quantity on the market at the interest rate required for sale. For example, if a large bank loses $1 million in transactions account liabilities or if it wants to grant a new $1 million loan, it can offer $1 million of CDs for sale. These CDs can be sold quickly. The bank, of course, does not know exactly the interest rate it has to pay, but current quotations in the market give a good guide.[15]

Certificates of deposits allow banks to determine the size of their total assets. If a bank wants to grow, it issues additional CDs and purchases assets. If it wants to shrink, it does not replace all its maturing CDs. Thus, CDs allow banks to behave in the manner described by the model presented in Chapter 7. A bank balances the interest cost of adding to CD liabilities against the expected return and risk of expanding its loans. By being able to determine its size effectively, a bank can achieve whatever degree of leverage is consistent with its trade-off between expected return and risk.[16]

With the invention of CDs, large banks grew very rapidly. Currently, some of the largest banks support over one half of their assets with CDs. As indicated in Table 8.3 earlier, the total quantity of CDs outstanding is in excess of $300 billion.

Interbank Debt

Transactions and savings account liabilities at a bank fluctuate with the deposits and withdrawals of the public. Much of the short-term variation in these

---

[15] It is often difficult for smaller banks to sell CDs quickly because they do not have access to the national market.

[16] Subject, of course, to maximum leverage allowed by regulators.

accounts, that is, from day to day and week to week, tends to be self-correcting. For example, a bank may experience a decline in its liabilities on one day and an increase the next day. The same sort of variation often occurs from week to week. Thus, a bank can be in a situation where the average level of its transactions and savings accounts is highly predictable from month to month or from year to year, but the level fluctuates unpredictably from day to day or from week to week about this average.

Short-term fluctuations in transactions and savings account liabilities can require costly changes in a bank's portfolio of assets. For example, if a bank experiences a decline in these liabilities on any given day, it must pay out funds on that day. The funds can be obtained by drawing down any cash (currency and balances with other banks) the bank is holding, by selling assets, or by issuing new liabilities. The next day, the bank might have an inflow of account balances. The proceeds from the increase in these balances can be used to add to the bank's cash, to purchase assets, or to retire other liabilities.

Prior to the development of active liability management in the 1960s, banks had only two practical methods of adjusting to short-term fluctuations in liabilities. They could hold cash balances that fluctuate with liabilities; that is, when liabilities increase, a bank adds to cash, and when liabilities decline, it reduces cash. Alternatively, banks could hold liquid assets other than cash, such as market securities, that fluctuate with their liabilities.[17] Both methods have their drawbacks. Because neither currency nor account balances with other banks earn interest income, if banks hold cash, they forgo the interest income available on other assets. If banks hold securities, they earn an interest income, but the transactions costs of frequent purchases and sales of these assets can exceed the interest income. As a result of the transactions costs of frequent purchases and sales of market securities, banks often found it most profitable to hold idle cash that fluctuated from day to day and from week to week with liabilities. For longer-term variations in liabilities, such as from month to month or from one season to another, it was more profitable to use market securities and short-term loans.

Though it was often most profitable to use cash as the method of adjusting to short-term liability fluctuations, bankers discovered that they could increase profits by engaging in interbank lending. It often occurs that on any given day, when one bank is experiencing a decline in its liabilities, some other bank is experiencing an increase. Thus, one bank is reducing its cash balance to meet withdrawals at the same time that another bank is receiving additional account balances and adding to its cash. In this situation, both banks can benefit by arranging an interbank loan in which the bank that receives new account balances lends to the bank that loses balances. Because the lending bank does not know

---

[17] Payments of interest and principal provide a substantial flow of cash receipts into a bank. These receipts are highly predictable, however, and banks have already lined up new assets into which they place these funds. Thus, this source of cash is usually not available to meet short-term fluctuations in liabilities.

what its liabilities will be the next day, it usually wants the loan repaid the next day.[18] The borrowing bank is willing to repay the loan the next day because it may receive new balances or, if the new liabilities do not materialize, it can borrow again. Because the interbank market uses the services of the Federal Reserve to transfer funds quickly, the market is called the *federal funds market.*[19]

The federal funds market is beneficial to both lender and borrower. In the absence of interbank loans, the bank that receives an increase in liabilities will hold the funds idle if it expects its liabilities to decline in the near future. The transactions costs of buying a security one day and selling it the next day exceed the interest income earned for a day. Thus, without a federal funds market, there is no profitable investment outlet for funds that are available only temporarily. Transactions costs are very low in the federal funds market, so it is almost always profitable for a bank to lend funds overnight rather than hold them idle.

The borrowing bank is also made better off by the federal funds market because on average it does not need to hold so much cash. If the bank can borrow when it needs funds to meet a temporary decline in liabilities, it does not need to hold a cash balance for this purpose. The cash can be used to purchase assets that earn an interest income. Interest expense is incurred only on the days that the bank borrows.

The federal funds market offers low transactions costs and low risks to both lenders and borrowers. Transactions costs are low because a telephone network exists through which borrowers and lenders are brought together quickly and inexpensively. Default risk is low in the market for interbank loans because borrowing banks tend to be large and safe and because the risk of default on such a short-term loan is very small. There is risk in the sense that the interest rate on these loans is highly volatile. The interest rate on interbank loans is determined by the daily interaction of supply and demand. The demand and supply for interbank loans can change quickly, and the interest rate often fluctuates sharply from day to day and within a day from hour to hour. Banks face substantial uncertainty concerning what the interest rate will be on any given day in the future.[20] The implications for bank profits of unusually high or low interest rates are not very great, however, because the interest rate is paid only for one day. Daily interest rate fluctuations tend to cancel each other out, and on average the interest rate on interbank loans is no more difficult to predict than other interest rates.

As the market has developed, borrowers have tended to be large banks; and lenders, to be small banks. This structure arose for several reasons. First, a minimum denomination of $1 million prevents small banks from using the market

---

[18] Most interbank loans are repayable the next day, that is, they are overnight loans. Loans with larger maturity do occur, however.

[19] By convention, a borrowing bank is said to purchase federal funds, and a lending bank is said to sell federal funds.

[20] As we shall see in Chapter 18, the monetary policy actions of the Federal Reserve have an important effect on this interest rate.

for liability management. They can act as lenders, however, because market specialists arrange for small banks to share in a loan to a large bank. In addition, small banks are not sufficiently well known in the market to be able to borrow. Lenders prefer to lend to large and well-known banks. Finally, large banks are very much in the liability management business. Overnight borrowing is just another tool of the trade. Small banks do find it profitable to manage their assets through lending in the interbank market, however. The market for interbank loans developed quickly in the 1960s, and the total quantity of interbank loans is currently in excess of $100 billion.

It is important to note that though the federal funds market primarily involves overnight loans, many banks are in the market every day. Large banks use funds raised in this market to acquire relatively long-term assets. The choice between federal funds and other managed liabilities, such as CDs, is determined by transactions costs and by a bank's expectations of future short-term interest rates. Similarly, many small banks lend funds every day in the federal funds market. Their choice between federal funds and longer-term loans is determined by expectations of future interest rates and by the risks on alternative assets.

Repurchase Agreements

The interbank market has expanded in recent years into a general market in which holders of liquid assets, other than banks, make overnight loans to banks. This feat is often accomplished by the use of *repurchase agreements*. Under a repurchase agreement, a bank that wants to obtain additional funds sells a U.S. government security to a corporate customer or other investor overnight with the agreement to repurchase the security the next day.[21] A repurchase agreement is attractive to many investors because it offers low transactions costs and high liquidity. The investor deals directly with a bank rather than purchasing a security on the market. Liquidity is also high because the money is available the next day.

As a result of repurchase agreements, corporate treasurers and other large holders of liquid assets do not have to hold balances in a bank; they can lend their excess funds overnight. The arrangement is attractive to banks because they use repurchase agreements to attract additional funds as well as to retain their existing customers.[22] Large banks have been very active in using repurchase agreements, and they currently borrow over $75 billion in this market. Dealers in government securities also offer repurchase agreements to corporations and other large holders of liquid assets. Furthermore, small banks have recently begun to offer repurchase agreements to their larger customers. When repurchase agreements are

---

[21] As is the case with interbank loans, some repurchase agreements are for longer periods than overnight.

[22] As explained in Chapter 12, repurchase agreements also allow banks to avoid reserve requirements.

combined with the interbank market, banks have a total quantity of short-term borrowing of approximately $180 billion.

By entering into repurchase agreements, banks are able, in effect, to pay interest on demand deposit accounts. Banks and other depository institutions are allowed to pay interest on transactions accounts issued to individuals and nonprofit organizations, but it is illegal to establish these special accounts for businesses.[23] Business transactions accounts must be demand deposits. Because banks are prohibited by law from paying interest on demand deposit accounts, they pay interest indirectly by swapping a government security for the funds in a demand deposit account. Legally, interest is not being paid on the demand deposit account because the business reduces its account balance to pay for the government security. The demand deposit account is reduced, and the interest is earned on the security, not on the account. Repurchase agreements are an excellent example of how the marketplace develops means of circumventing artificial legal restrictions on payment of interest for accounts.

Other Forms of Liability Management

The third major category of managed liabilities listed in Table 8.3 (shown earlier) is a catchall. In total, this borrowing amounted to over $150 billion at the end of 1982 and accounted for 23 percent of the total funds raised through liability management.

Eurodollars

An important method of liability management available to large banks is the *Eurodollar market*. To understand the Eurodollar market, one must realize that many large banks are, in fact, multinational firms with offices located all over the world. These banks offer deposit accounts and issue other liabilities through their offices located outside the United States. These offices receive deposits in the form of the money used in the country where they are located (e.g., British pounds or Swiss francs), and they also receive dollar deposits. Many of the dollar liabilities of the bank offices located outside the United States are similar to CDs in that they are liabilities with fixed maturities issued in established markets. Other dollar liabilities are interbank borrowing. Because the market originated in London, these dollar liabilities are commonly called Eurodollars. The term *Eurodollar* is now a misnomer because dollar liabilities are issued all over the world.

The Eurodollar market allows banks to borrow dollars anywhere in the world.[24] These Eurodollar liabilities are used to support dollar loans both outside and

---

[23] Because it is impossible to distinguish personal transactions accounts from business accounts for sole proprietors, interest-bearing transactions accounts can be issued to sole proprietors.

[24] Banks also borrow in other currencies, but only dollar liabilities are discussed here.

inside the United States. Most important for our purposes, banks with offices in the United States use their foreign offices to issue Eurodollar liabilities that support loans granted in the United States.

The widespread use of the Eurodollar market to support domestic (U.S.) lending originally arose as a method used by large U.S. banks to circumvent the interest rate ceilings applied to large CDs. These ceilings have been eliminated, but Eurodollar liabilities continue to be an important method of liability management for large banks. The quantity of funds borrowed in the Eurodollar market and returned to offices in the United States fluctuates widely, but it has averaged about $90 billion in recent years.

With recent developments in the electronic transmission of funds, many banks use dollar liabilities of their non-U.S. offices as a means of circumventing the prohibition of interest on demand deposits. A large account holder can switch funds from the bank's U.S. office to an offshore office overnight. The offshore office pays a market interest rate for the funds, which are returned the next day. This arrangement is much like a repurchase agreement, but the bank does not have to hold securities during the day to sell overnight. The use of offshore offices for purposes of circumventing the prohibition of interest on demand deposits has grown dramatically in recent years. It helps explain, for example, the remarkable growth of bank activity in the Caribbean.

Borrowing from the Federal Reserve

Banks can, under certain circumstances, borrow from Federal Reserve Banks. When banks borrow from the Federal Reserve, they are said to use the *discount window*.[25] These loans are used primarily to help meet short-term unexpected withdrawals from deposit accounts. Borrowing from the discount window can be extremely important to a bank that has encountered difficulty in borrowing elsewhere. Furthermore, when many banks suffer large declines in liabilities as a result of temporary loss of public faith in banks, the Federal Reserve may be the only source of sufficient credit. In this situation, the Federal Reserve is the *lender of last resort* to banks.

The discount window is a crucial weapon in the government's arsenal for protecting the stability of the banking system and the nation's payment system.[26] As a practical matter, however, the discount window is rarely a substantial source of funds for banks and is not used for purposes of liability management. It is mainly an "insurance reserve" that is available should emergencies arise. Short of emergencies, the Federal Reserve is highly restrictive in its willingness to lend to banks, and total borrowing rarely exceeds $3 billion to $4 billion.

---

[25] Federal Reserve Banks used to have a window like a teller's window where commercial banks obtained funds by discounting their loans.

[26] The role of the discount window is discussed in detail in Chapter 12.

Subordinated Debt

Banks issue subordinated notes and long-term bonds in securities markets as an additional method of managing the size and maturity of their liabilities. With *subordinated debt,* should the bank fail, all depositors are paid off before holders of subordinated debt receive any payment. Because of the higher risk to holders of this debt, banks have to pay a relatively high interest rate. Many banks do issue subordinated debt, however, as a method of borrowing at longer maturities than is possible with time accounts. The amount of subordinated debt is relatively small and at the end of 1982 was approximately $7 billion for all insured banks.

Debt Issued by Bank Holding Companies

Corporations that own banks, called *holding companies,* and corporations that are affiliates of banks often issue liabilities in the market and use the funds to lend to the banks with which they are affiliated.[27] This source of funds was developed by large banks when there were binding interest rate ceilings for CDs. Since the elimination of these ceilings, the use of this source of credit has diminished, but it is still used as a method of liability management.

Some Conclusions Concerning Liability Management

The description of the methods used by banks to manage their liabilities does not do full justice to their scope, but it does give a flavor of their complexity and flexibility. Large banks have come a long way from the old days in which they passively accepted deposits and withdrawals from accounts and then invested whatever funds were available. These banks now actively borrow money at competitive interest rates in virtually every part of the U.S. financial system as well as in the financial systems of other countries. Smaller banks are not able to manage their liabilities with such flexibility. They are still basically passive agents that accept deposits and withdrawals as they come along. With the elimination of interest rate ceilings, smaller banks have improved their liability management. But they will still lack access to national and international markets for their liabilities. As a result, the degree of control over liabilities will remain qualitatively different for small than for large banks.

Despite the difference between large and small banks, the banking industry in the United States no longer relies on transaction accounts as its primary source of funds. With the growing reliance of banks on managed liabilities, the relative importance of transactions accounts has declined dramatically as a source of funds to banks. Figure 8.1 shows the percentage of total assets in the banking industry supported by transactions accounts from 1951 through 1982. In 1951, 70 percent of total assets was supported by transactions accounts. This percentage declined by 10 percentage points from 1952 to 1960 as banks increased their reli-

---

[27] Bank holding companies and nonbank affiliates are described in Chapter 9.

FIGURE 8.1
PERCENTAGE OF TOTAL ASSETS
SUPPORTED BY TRANSACTIONS
ACCOUNTS FOR ALL INSURED
COMMERCIAL BANKS
(DECEMBER 31, 1952–1982).

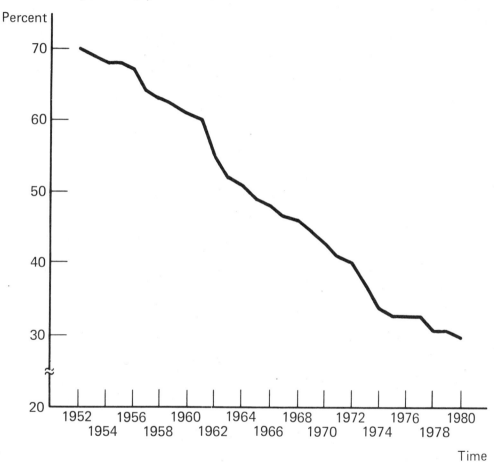

ance on savings and time accounts. In the 1960s as the markets for interbank loans, CDs, and Eurodollars developed, the percentage of total assets supported by transactions accounts fell from 60 percent to about 42 percent. Reliance on managed liabilities continued in the 1970s and early 1980s. By the end of 1982, only 24 percent of total assets was supported by transactions accounts. Small denomination time accounts and managed liabilities of various kinds have taken the place of transactions accounts as the major sources of funds to banks.

ASSETS

Commercial banks are unique among depository institutions in terms of the quantity and variety of assets that they hold. Banks in the aggregate hold a massive quantity of assets, and the banking industry lends funds in virtually every sector of the economy.

An overview of bank asset holdings is provided by Table 8.4, which gives a somewhat more detailed account than was provided by Table 8.1. The composition of the various categories is discussed later, but the figures reported in Table 8.4 give some indication of the extent of bank asset diversification. The figures in Table 8.4 indicate that the aggregate asset portfolio of the banking system is diversified with total assets divided fairly evenly among the various categories. Asset diversification has made banks substantial lenders to governments, business, and households. The extent of diversification is masked by the aggregate figures, however, and it is useful to look at the composition of the major asset categories.

Cash Assets

The composition of cash assets for all insured commercial banks on December 1982 is shown in Table 8.5. The first component of cash assets is vault cash. A bank must have sufficient currency and coin in its vault to meet its customers' cash withdrawals. Because of the danger of theft and because vault cash does not earn interest, banks try to hold a minimum quantity of currency and coin consistent with the need to meet withdrawals. A bank is able to limit the amount of vault cash that it holds by making withdrawals or deposits of currency and coin from its account at the Federal Reserve. Many small banks do not manage their vault cash by dealing with the Federal Reserve; rather, they use the services of larger, *correspondent banks*. These larger banks maintain accounts for smaller banks through which they receive deposits and withdrawals of currency and coin. The correspondent banks then make deposits and withdrawals of currency and coin at the Federal Reserve.

The second component of cash assets is balances held at the Federal Reserve. These are reserve accounts established by the Federal Reserve for purposes of imposing reserve requirements and for clearing checks presented by banks for payment.[28] Because reserve accounts earn no interest, banks usually seek to hold the minimum amount allowed by the Federal Reserve in this asset.

The third component of cash assets is balances held at depository institutions. Most of the balances are held at commercial banks, but some funds are held with other kinds of depository institutions. Funds held at banks and other depository institutions are called *correspondent balances* and are used to manage vault cash, to clear checks, and to make purchases of assets. Some proportion of these balances

---

[28] Holdings of vault cash also satisfy reserve requirements.

TABLE 8.4
ASSET HOLDINGS OF ALL INSURED COMMERCIAL BANKS
(MAJOR CATEGORIES: DECEMBER 31,1982)

	Billions of Dollars	Percentage of Total Assets
Cash assets	$ 207	11
Federal funds sold and securities purchased under repurchase agreements	103	6
Securities	373	20
Commercial and industrial loans	380	21
Real estate loans	298	16
Consumer loans	191	10
Other loans	157	8
All other assets	152	8
Total assets	$1,861	100

Source: *Federal Reserve Bulletin*, April 1983, p. A74.

TABLE 8.5
HOLDINGS OF CASH ASSETS BY ALL INSURED COMMERCIAL BANKS
(DECEMBER 31,1982)

	Billions of Dollars	Percentage of Total
Vault cash	$ 20	10
Balances at the Federal Reserve	27	13
Balances at depository institutions	92	44
Cash items in process of collection	68	33
Total	$207	100

Source: *Federal Reserve Bulletin*, April 1983, p. A74.

are held idle as *compensating balances* that are used to compensate correspondent institutions for the services they perform. No interest is paid on correspondent balances. Compensating balances are invested by the correspondent in earning assets.

The final item in cash assets is cash items in process of collection. This asset is the dollar value of checks that banks have received from their customers as deposits, but for which payment has not been yet received from the institutions upon which the checks are written. Banks receive new deposits every day, so there are always funds that are in the process of collection. This asset earns no interest and, in fact, is illiquid in the sense that banks cannot put the funds to alternative use until payment is received. Banks incur considerable expense to speed up check collection and, therefore, to reduce cash items in the process of collection.

We can see from the various components of cash assets why banks hold such a relatively large percentage of their total assets (11 percent) in these noninterest-bearing forms. For the most part, they have little choice. Banks must hold vault cash to meet cash withdrawals. They attempt to minimize the holdings of currency and coin, but in the aggregate $20 billion of vault cash is held. Banks have balances at the Federal Reserve in order to meet reserve requirements. Only about three or four percent of these balances are funds held in excess of required reserves. Banks hold balances with depository institutions in order to handle cash transactions, to clear checks, and to compensate correspondent institutions for their services. There are no data indicating the proportion of balances held at private depository institutions that are held in excess of those required to handle cash transactions, to clear checks and to compensate correspondents. It appears, however, that only a small proportion of balances held at depository institutions represent idle funds. Finally, assets must be held in the form of cash items in the process of collection because it takes time for checks and other transactions instruments to clear.

What emerges from this analysis is that only a small proportion of total cash assets represent idle balances held at the discretion of banks. Most of the funds are held as a necessary part of the banking business of handling customer transactions and as required reserves. Very little represents funds that are available to meet unexpected liquidity needs.[29] This does not mean, however, that banks are highly vulnerable to unexpected declines in liabilities and other unanticipated needs for liquidity. It simply indicates that many banks invest their idle funds in the market for interbank loans. These loans are highly liquid, *and* they earn interest. Furthermore, other banks meet liquidity needs by borrowing in the interbank market. As a result, they do not hold idle funds. In the absence of the markets for interbank loans and security repurchase agreements, banks would probably hold substantially more cash assets.

Securities

The composition of the aggregate holdings of securities is shown in Table 8.6. The two major categories are securities issued by the U.S. government and securi-

---

[29] Required reserves are not a very liquid asset. As long as a bank's deposit liabilities remain unchanged, it cannot reduce its reserve account at the Federal Reserve below the amount held as required reserves. Thus, only the funds held in excess of required reserves are available to meet loan demand or other increases in assets. Furthermore, only a fraction of required reserves is available to meet a reduction in liabilities. For example, if a bank must hold 10 percent of its liabilities as required reserves, its required reserves are reduced by only $10 for every $100 decline in liabilities. The remaining $90 must come from the reduction of other assets or from issuing new liabilities.

TABLE 8.6
HOLDINGS OF SECURITIES BY ALL INSURED COMMERCIAL BANKS
(DECEMBER 31,1982)

	Billions of Dollars	Percentage of Total
U.S. government	$194	52
States and subdivisions	154	41
Other	25	7
Total	$373	100

Source: *Federal Reserve Bulletin*, April 1983, p. A74.

ties issued by states and their political subdivisions.[30] Securities earn interest income, and most securities are highly liquid. Approximately one half of total holdings of securities is debt issued by the U.S. government. A substantial share of U.S. government securities held by banks is in the form of short-term securities, for which there is a highly organized and efficient market. These securities, which include three- and six-month Treasury bills, can be sold quickly at low transactions costs. Though not as liquid as interbank loans, these securities provide banks with an important source of liquidity. Banks hold longer-term U.S. government securities, which are also relatively liquid. Most of these securities have a maturity of under five years. Government securities are attractive to banks because there is no risk of default. The only risk comes from variations in prices of these securities.

The second major category is holdings of securities issued by states and their political subdivisions, which account for 41 percent of the total holdings of securities by banks. Securities of states and political subdivisions are exempt from federal income tax. These securities allow banks to avoid taxation on their interest income while retaining a significant amount of liquidity. The rate of return on securities of states and political subdivisions is competitive with other securities on an aftertax basis. These securities are subject to default risk, but defaults are rare.

Commercial and Industrial Loans

Banks extend credit to business primarily through commercial and industrial (C&I) loans. In the aggregate, these loans constitute 21 percent of total assets held by banks. C&I loans range from short-term loans used to finance holdings of inventories to long-term loans that finance major investment projects. The bank-

[30] U.S. government securities are mainly the obligations of the Treasury but include securities issued by various federal agencies as well.

TABLE 8.7
PERCENTAGE DISTRIBUTION OF C&I LOANS AMONG INDUSTRIES
FOR LARGE COMMERCIAL BANKS
(DECEMBER 31,1980)

	Industry Classification
Durable goods manufacturing	16
Nondurable goods manufacturing	13
Mining	11
Trade	17
Transportation and communication and public utilites	14
Construction	4
Services	15
All other	10
Total	100

Source: *Federal Reserve Bulletin*, April 1981, p. A22.

ing industry lends to virtually every type of business ranging from large manufacturing firms to small retailers.

Table 8.7 shows the percentage distribution of commercial and industrial loans among various industrial groups. Data on the composition of C&I loans are not available for all commercial banks in the United States, so the figures in the table are for C&I loans held by banks with assets in excess of $1 billion. Commercial and industrial loans held by these large banks constitute over 55 percent of the C&I loans held by all insured commercial banks.

The figures reported in Table 8.7 illustrate that the banking industry holds a diversified portfolio of C&I loans.[31] The largest percentage of C&I loans, 17 percent, is in credit extended to the trade sector, which is composed of both wholesale and retail trade. Banks lend nearly as much to manufacturers of durable goods, however. Finally, loans to service industries; to mining firms; and to transportation, communication, and public utilities also constitute a substantial share of total C&I loans.

Characteristics of C&I loans

Commercial and industrial loans differ substantially in size, maturity, risk, and the interest rate charged. In the model presented in Chapter 7, it was implicitly assumed that business loans are homogeneous and that a single interest rate is charged for all business loans. This simplified the analysis and allowed us to focus on the fundamental factors determining the quantity of loans that a bank holds and the interest rate that it charges on loans. The model is useful for examining

---

[31] Many banks cannot achieve the degree of loan diversification suggested by Table 8.7. Most banks do achieve substantial diversification, however.

the relationship between the quantity of liabilities and the quantity of loans at a bank, and it allows us to isolate the effects of interest rate ceilings. The model is not useful, however, for studying differences among loans. Though basic supply and demand factors are at work in determining the total quantity of loans and the average interest rate charged, each loan is the result of negotiation between a bank and its business borrower.

Commercial and industrial loans range in size from a few thousand dollars to billions of dollars and their maturities range from less than a month to loans with maturities of several years. C&I loans with initial maturities in excess of one year are called *term loans.* The interest rate charged on a particular loan is determined by the bank's perception of its risk and by the bargaining power of the bank and its customer.

Loan Risk Commercial and industrial loans include some of the riskiest assets that banks hold. An important form of risk arises from the possibility that a borrower will be unable to make interest payments or repay the loan at maturity. This kind of risk is called *default risk.* Banks are able to limit default risk in various ways. A primary method is through diversification of loans. Banks avoid having a large proportion of their loan portfolio in loans to a particular borrower or to a particular industry.[32] Furthermore, banks attempt to exploit any negative correlation in the rates of return for loans to different borrowers. For example, banks lend to both oil companies and to chemical manufacturers. A boost in the price of petroleum raises the costs of manufacturing chemicals that use petroleum as a raw material. This reduces the profits of chemical manufacturers, so the default risk of these loans increases. The rise in petroleum prices increases the profitability of oil companies, however, and reduces their default risk. Thus, the increase in default risk for chemical manufacturers is offset by the decline in default risk for oil companies.[33]

Banks also reduce default risk through provisions in loan contracts. They often write loan agreements in which the borrowing firm is required to secure the loan by specific assets, such as machinery. Furthermore, the borrower may be required to meet certain balance sheet requirements such as limiting the amount of accounts receivable or maintaining a minimum amount of liquid assets. In some cases, the loan agreement allows the bank to take part in management decisions or even to replace management personnel should the borrower encounter difficulty in making its interest or principal payments.

Much of the risk in commercial and industrial lending involves late payment of interest or principal rather than nonpayment. When loans are *delinquent,* a bank often incurs costs in collecting the late payments. These costs include involve-

---

[32] Bank regulations also limit the amount that can be lent to any one borrower.

[33] In 1982 and 1983, one bank failed and several others nearly failed as the result of concentrating in loans to oil companies. Several of these companies defaulted on their loans when oil prices fell. This is an example of the dangers of not diversifying loans.

ment of bank personnel in the operations of a delinquent firm as well as collection costs. It is the chance of incurring these costs, as well as the risk that the borrower will be unable to repay the loan, that lead banks to charge relatively high interest rates to many borrowers.

Loan Interest Rates   Interest rates on C&I loans are affected by the total quantity of loans demanded by firms relative to the bank's supply of loans. This supply is affected, in turn, by the cost and availability of the bank's liabilities. The interest rate on an individual loan is also affected by its risk and by the bargaining power of the borrower. In studying the role of bargaining power, it is useful to distinguish between small borrowers who do not have access to securities markets and large borrowers who do have access to securities markets. We shall start with an analysis of loans made to small borrowers who lack the national reputations that are essential for access to securities markets. Banks are able to exert some monopoly power over these borrowers. They pay a higher interest rate than borrowers who have access to securities markets.

Many business borrowers find it beneficial to have a long-standing relationship with a bank. In this relationship, a firm does its depository and other business at the same bank from which it obtains credit. With this arrangement, the bank is familiar with the financial condition of the firm, and it is able to evaluate the firm's credit worthiness at relatively low cost. There are good economic reasons why businesses establish long-standing relationships with banks. These relationships create an inertia on the part of borrowers, however, that tends to reduce competition among banks for business loans. A bank is aware that once a relationship is established with a firm, it is costly for that firm to shop around for banks providing cheaper credit. The firm is not known at other banks, and it is likely to encounter difficulty in finding a bank that is willing to extend credit unless that credit is the first in a sequence of loans under a long-standing relationship.

Borrower inertia allows a bank to charge a higher interest rate to its existing customers than would be the case if it were costless for businesses to switch banks. Furthermore, borrower inertia reduces the incentive of banks to use the loan interest rate as a means of competing for loan customers. A small reduction in the interest rate will not attract many customers away from other banks because of borrower inertia. A large reduction in the interest rate could overcome this inertia, but then other banks would reduce their interest rates in an effort to keep their customers. Similarly, a small rise in the interest rate may not drive many borrowers to other banks. A large increase in the interest rate would cause borrowers to switch banks provided other banks did not raise their loan interest rate. Banks set their loan interest rates as high as possible to exploit borrower inertia, and they resist using the interest rate as a means of competing for the customers at other banks.

In competing for borrowers who lack access to securities markets, banks engage in forms of nonprice competition that tend to cement long-standing customer relationships. The competition takes many forms, but it is common for banks to offer various services to their business customers at low cost in an effort to entice them into a long-term relationship. For example, banks offer convenient and low-cost transactions account services, they assist business with transactions in securities markets, and they often assist firms in monitoring and processing their business expenditures and receipts. This kind of competition helps establish long-term customers relationships in which businesses maintain deposit balances and borrow from the same bank.

Borrowers can at times turn the tie-in between loans and maintenance of account balances to their advantage. When shopping around for a bank with which to establish a long-standing relationship, firms attempt to obtain *loan commitments* where a bank promises to make credit available to a firm when it is needed. In return for doing its business with a bank, a firm gains the assurance that it can borrow in the future, provided, of course, that the firm can meet minimum credit standards. A loan commitment is valuable to many firms because it assures that a loan will be available in the event of a "liquidity squeeze" or other temporary problems. A bank that has the reputation of helping long-standing customers through transitory problems can expect to attract and retain a substantial amount of business.

The extent to which a bank can exploit borrower inertia by charging high interest rates for its loans depends upon the bargaining power of the business. If a firm is dissatisfied with its bank, it can threaten to take its business elsewhere. This threat limits the monopoly power of the bank. For the threat to be viable, however, the firm must find other banks offering more attractive credit terms than the current bank. This effort is not worthwhile unless the firm believes that its bank's loan terms are seriously out of line with those of other banks.

Small firms have difficulty in using the threat of switching banks as a method of achieving attractive loan terms. The banking business of a small firm is quantitatively not very important, so its existing bank has little incentive to treat it "right." Furthermore, other banks often will not go out of their way to attract the business that a small firm would bring with it. As a result, many banks do not compete actively for the business of small firms, and these firms tend to pay higher interest rates on their loans and receive fewer services than do larger firms.

In general, the larger the firm, the better the treatment it receives from its bank. Its threats to switch banks are heeded. There is competition for the business of larger firms. As long as a business does not have access to securities markets, however, its inertia allows banks to exercise some monopoly power. The degree of monopoly power that the bank can exercise depends upon the alternatives available to the firm to borrow from other banks.

Banks are not able to exercise any monopoly power over their major corporate customers because these corporations have access to securities markets. There is no inertia to exploit. If a bank attempted to increase the loan interest rate above the interest rate in securities markets, these firms would take their business elsewhere. The bank would not only lose these loan customers, but it would also lose the substantial account balances, securities transactions, pension fund administration, and other business of these corporations. This prospect prevents banks from exercising any important monopoly power over their large corporate customers.

Historically, large corporations depended upon banks for much of their short-term borrowing requirements and used securities markets for longer-term financing. Until the late 1960s, these corporations could be assured that competition among banks for their business would produce short-term credit from banks that was competitive with securities markets. Since that time, these corporations have come to rely more on securities markets and less on banks for their short-term credit needs. This development was part of a larger change in the banking environment that forced some fundamental alterations in bank lending to business.

In 1966 the Federal Reserve responded to accelerating inflation by restricting the growth of money and credit. The restrictive policy pushed market interest rates above the ceilings on bank accounts, and disintermediation occurred. Banks found it difficult to honor their loan commitments to their customers because their deposit accounts were shrinking. By selling securities and other assets, many banks were able to honor their commitments, but some banks were unable to meet all their commitments.

This turn of events significantly altered the behavior of banks and their customers. Informal loan commitments became less common and were replaced by formal commitments for which customers paid a fee. Banks have to honor these commitments, and they grant them more sparingly than the earlier informal commitments. Furthermore, banks developed CDs as a method of attracting funds when disintermediation occurs. CDs allowed banks to obtain funds, but their cost varies with market interest rates. As a result of this greater variability in interest costs, banks came to vary their loan interest rates more frequently.

In 1969 the Federal Reserve again restricted the growth of money and credit in the economy. The result was that the interest rates on CDs hit their ceilings, and banks were not able to replace their CDs as they matured. The banking system was not able to meet the demand for loans. This time, large corporate borrowers responded by borrowing directly in the securities markets. They replaced their bank borrowing with short-term debt called *commercial paper*, which is actively traded in an organized market. This market grew rapidly and became a major alternative to bank loans for major corporations.

In 1970 the interest rate ceiling on short-term, large CDs was suspended, and in 1973 the ceiling for the interest rates on all remaining large CDs was suspended. Since that time, large banks have been able to control their total liabilities through changes in their CDs and other managed liabilities. These banks are now able to meet loan demand. With the development of the commercial paper market, however, major corporations borrow from banks only when the interest rate on bank loans is competitive with the interest rate on commercial paper. In order to keep their loans competitive with the commercial paper market, banks now adjust the interest rate on loans to major corporations with the interest rate for commercial paper.

The greater flexibility of loan interest rates has received considerable public attention in recent years. This attention has been focused on the *prime interest rate*, which is an interest rate that is used by a bank as a guide in setting the interest rate on various loans. Historically, the prime rate was the interest rate that a bank typically charged its lowest risk (prime) borrowers for short-term loans. As explained later on, this is no longer the case, but the prime rate still serves as a base for setting the interest rates on loans to higher risk (nonprime) borrowers. The greater the risk of the loan or the smaller the bargaining power of the borrower, the greater the "markup" of the interest rate above the prime rate.

It is important to note that the prime rate and the markups over prime are determined by each bank in accordance with the degree of loan demand it is experiencing as well as the cost and availability of its liabilities. Prime rates differ to some extent among banks, but competitive pressures usually prevent the differences from being very large. The level of the prime rate moves roughly with market interest rates.

In recent years, the prime rate has become more flexible than it was in the past. This flexibility is in part the result of the development of liability management that increased the variability of bank costs and in part a result of increased variability in the commercial paper rate. The flexibility of the prime rate is also the result of banks making active use of *floating rate loans.* A floating rate loan does not have a fixed interest rate over its life, but, rather, the interest rate changes as the prime rate changes. For loans issued at the prime interest rate, the interest rate on the loan is changed to the new prime rate each time the prime rate is changed. For loans that are issued at a markup over prime, the interest rate is set at the new prime rate plus the markup.

Banks introduced floating rate loans as a method of protecting themselves against the risk of unexpected interest rate fluctuations. This risk occurs because banks often grant loans with maturities that exceed the maturity of the CDs used to support the loans. The expected return on a loan is determined primarily by the difference between the interest rate on the loan and the interest rate on the CDs used to support the loan. If the loan and the CD have the same maturity, a bank knows the interest rate for the loan and for the CD, so it "locks in" an expected rate of return equal to the difference between the two interest rates. If the maturity of the loan exceeds the maturity of the CD, it is necessary to replace the original CD with a new one when the original matures. For relatively long-term loans, it may be necessary to "roll over" CDs several times as they mature. The interest rate in the future at which maturing CD will be replaced cannot be known when the loan is granted. Thus, a bank must compare the interest rate on a loan against the current and expected future interest rates on CDs.

Uncertainty about future interest rates on CDs introduces an additional element of risk into lending. A bank has three methods of reducing this risk: it can issue longer-term CDs, it can grant shorter-term loans, or it can grant loans whose interest rate moves with market interest rates.[34] All three methods have been used

---

[34] A "futures" market for CDs has recently developed. A discussion of how banks can use this market to reduce or eliminate the risk associated with having a mismatch between the maturity of their loans and the maturity of their CDs is beyond the scope of this book.

to some degree, but banks often find it costly to issue longer-term CDs, and they frequently encounter borrower resistance to short-term loans. As a result, they have placed increasing reliance on floating rate loans. With these loans, when the interest rate on CDs or other managed liabilities rise, the bank increases the interest rate on its outstanding loans. This allows the bank to maintain a differential between the interest rate on its loans and the interest rate on its liabilities.

As we saw in the discussion of the term structure of interest rates in Chapter 6, a lender compares the expected rate of return on a long-term loan to the expected rate of return for a sequence of short-term loans. This comparison requires that the lender predict future short-term interest rates. Errors are made in these predictions, so the realized rate of return on a long-term loan may exceed or fall short of the realized rate of return on a sequence of short-term loans. It was argued in Chapter 6 that lenders prefer short-term loans to long-term loans because they fear that they will make errors in predicting the average level of future short-term interest rates. Banks are no exception to this rule, so they prefer to limit interest rate risk by holding short-term loans.

It is costly for both banks and borrowers to finance a long-term project by rolling over short-term loans. A floating rate loan eliminates these costs because the maturity of the loan can be long-term, but the interest rate is adjusted as though it were a short-term loan. This allows the bank to avoid the interest rate risk of a long-term loan while giving the borrower the guarantee of long-term credit. Floating rate loans are now used extensively by banks.[35] According to a recent Federal Reserve survey, over 25 percent of all shorter-term C&I loans and nearly 80 percent of longer-term loans have interest rates that float with the prime rate.

Heavy reliance on floating rate loans has produced a change in the meaning of the prime rate. It is no longer synonymous with the interest rate that is charged to largest corporate customers. These customers borrow from banks when bank loans are less costly than issuing securities. There are times when banks would like to raise the interest rate on their floating rate loans, but they do not want to raise the interest rate charged to large corporations. If the interest rate charged to large corporations rises above the interest rate in the commercial paper market, these firms will repay their bank loans and do their borrowing in the market. Other businesses lack access to securities markets and do not have this option. Under these circumstances, banks raise the "prime" rate and offer the major corporations a *discount from prime*. This allows the banks to continue to lend to major corporations at an interest rate that is competitive with the commercial paper market while raising the interest rate on loans to other borrowers. It should be noted that not only is the interest rate on new loans increased, but the interest rate on *existing* loans is also increased. By the offering of discounts from "prime," it is possible to increase the interest rate on both new and existing loans to

---

[35] As we shall see in Chapter 10, savings and loan associations and other mortgage lenders have also begun to use floating interest rates for their mortgage loans.

businesses that lack access to securities markets while keeping the interest rate charged to major corporations unchanged. Banks have discovered an effective means of practicing price discrimination!

The prime rate is no longer what its name suggests, but, rather, it is a base or index rate that is applied to new loans and to existing floating rate loans for borrowers who lack access to securities markets. Some borrowers pay prime, some pay a markup over prime, and major corporations receive a discount from prime.

The Liquidity of C&I Loans   Commercial and industrial loans are usually not sold prior to maturity because potential purchasers lack the information and monitoring capacity to assess and limit the risk on loans purchased from other banks. A lending bank has a great deal of information about the borrower that allows it to assess the risk of the loan. Furthermore, the lender has the expertise to advise, assist, and control the borrower should problems develop in making interest and principal payments. Most of this information and expertise is not available to a potential purchaser of the loan. As a result, no active market has developed in which existing loans are sold. Commercial and industrial loans provide liquidity only at maturity, so short-term loans are more liquid than longer-term loans.

There are two circumstances in which loans can be sold. First, a bank can sell a loan if it is willing to accept responsibility for payment of interest and principal in the event that the borrower fails to make payment. These loans are called *banker acceptances,* and they trade in an active market. Banks often do not want to issue acceptances because when they sell the loan, they lose the interest income, but they retain the risk. Banker acceptances usually involve loans to prime borrowers where the risks of delinquency or default are small.

The second method of selling loans is through the *participation market.* Frequently, several banks take part in a large loan. One bank, called the *lead bank,* negotiates with the borrower and draws up the loan agreement. The lead bank then sells parts of the loan to other lenders who participate in the loan. The lead bank typically retains a share of the loan and is responsible for collecting interest and principal from the borrower and for dispersing payments to the various participants.[36] If a bank that has participated in a loan wants to reduce its share, it occasionally can sell all or a part of its interest in the loan to the other participants or even to a new participant. This is possible because the lead bank has an interest in making the borrower honor the terms of the loan.

Aside from the liquidity that sales of loan participations offer, these loans have other benefits as well. They allow lenders to achieve increased diversification by investing a given amount of funds in a number of loans rather than in a single loan. Furthermore, they allow banks that have no direct contacts with large borrowers to get in on the "action." In the absence of participations, many banks are unable to lend to borrowers outside their localities. Loan participations open up new markets for these banks.[37]

---

[36] The lead bank receives fees for performing these services.

[37] These banks often use their correspondent banks as the source of loan participations.

Real Estate Loans

Table 8.8 summarizes the major types of bank loans that are secured by real estate. The first item, which accounts for 18 percent of the total, is loans for construction and land development. As mentioned before, these loans are for such activities as construction of shopping centers, apartment houses, and development of residential property. These loans are typically fairly short-term because they are repaid after the construction or development activities are completed. In practice, construction and development loans are little different from commercial and industrial loans except that they happen to be secured by real estate rather than by machinery or other assets. Banks use the same sort of monitoring and assessment procedures for these loans as they do for commercial and industrial loans. Loan interest rates are also determined in the same manner as for C&I loans.

The second category is loans secured by residential properties, which accounts for 55 percent of the total. These are primarily mortgage loans granted to households for the purpose of acquiring a home. Such loans are usually not subject to the restrictions and monitoring activities associated with loans to business. Rather, banks limit risk by securing the loan by the borrower's home, by insisting on down payments, and by determining that the borrower's income is sufficient to meet mortgage payments. The amount of default on mortgage loans is usually small. From time to time families may fall behind in their mortgage payments, but only in the most dire circumstances are they unable to come up with the necessary funds before losing their homes.

Mortgage loans typically have maturities of from twenty to thirty years, but most are repaid prior to maturity as households move from one location to another. On average, mortgage loans are repaid within eight to twelve years. Mortgage loans often can be sold prior to maturity, and organized markets have developed in recent years that have enhanced the liquidity of such loans. Historically, mortgage loans had a fixed interest rate over their life. Banks have started to grant mortgage loans with a floating interest rate, however.

The third type of real estate loans, which accounts for 27 percent of the total, is a catchall category that includes loans to business, farmers, and households that are secured by various types of real estate. This category highlights the difficulty in interpreting the significance of loans that are categorized by the assets that secure them. A loan secured by real estate is not necessarily used to purchase real estate. The property may already be owned by the borrower and used to secure a loan to finance expenditures that have little or nothing to do with real estate. For example, a business may use its land and buildings to secure a loan used to purchase machinery, or a farmer may use land to secure a loan for a new tractor. Even households frequently borrow against the net worth in their houses in order to finance various expenditures. Because of the difficulties in interpreting the significance of loans secured by real estate, it is probably best to think of loans that are made to business as business loans, loans made to farmers as farm loans, and loans made to households as consumer loans.

TABLE 8.8
HOLDINGS OF LOANS SECURED BY REAL ESTATE BY ALL INSURED COMMERCIAL BANKS (DECEMBER 31,1982)

	Billions of Dollars	Percentage of Total
Construction and development	$ 52	18
Residential properties	165	55
Other	81	27
Total	$298	100

Source: *Federal Reserve Bulletin*, April 1983, p. A74.

TABLE 8.9
HOLDINGS OF LOANS TO INDIVIDUALS BY ALL INSURED COMMERCIAL BANKS (DECEMBER 31,1982)

	Billions of Dollars	Percentage of Total
Automobiles and other durable goods	$105	55
Credit cards	37	19
All other	43	26
Total	$192	100

Source: *Federal Reserve Bulletin*, April 1983, p. A74.

Loans to Individuals

Over the last two decades, banks have expanded their loans to households and are currently one of the largest sources of credit to households. Mortgage loans have already been discussed, but many other types of credit are also offered. The three major categories of loans to individuals are shown in Table 8.9. The first are loans granted for the purpose of purchasing automobiles or other consumer durable goods, which account for 55 percent of total loans to individuals. These loans, which typically have maturities of from two to four years, are repaid in fixed installments covering both interest and principal and usually are secured by the durable good that is purchased. The second major form of loans to individuals is through bank credit cards, which account for 19 percent of the total. These loans are not secured by any asset, but banks establish credit limits based on the borrower's income as a method of limiting risk.

The third major category of loans to individuals is the catchall, "other" category. These loans cover a variety of different loans ranging from loans to repair and modernize houses to loans to finance college educations. In total, "all other" loans account for 24 percent of loans to individuals.

Because a loan to any individual is a small proportion of total loans in this category, banks get substantial benefits from diversification across borrowers. In general, consumer loans have maturities ranging from a few months to several years, and the interest rate is fixed over the life of the loan. There is no practical way for banks to sell consumer loans prior to maturity.

Long-standing customer relationships also play a role in lending to consumers. A household that has maintained an account with its bank for a number of years is more likely to be able to borrow from the bank than are other households. This is an effective device for encouraging households to be loyal customers.

Some Comments on the Relationship Between Liability Management and the Composition of Bank Asset Portfolios

Over the last three decades, the composition of bank asset portfolios has changed markedly. Figure 8.2 shows the holdings of cash assets, of securities, and of loans plus other assets for the banking industry as a percentage of total assets for 1952 through 1982. In 1952, nearly 25 percent of total assets was in cash assets, over 40 percent was in securities, and approximately 35 percent was held as loans and other assets. Thus, in 1952 approximately 65 percent of total assets were in cash assets and securities. Since 1952, cash assets as a percentage of total assets have fallen, and by the end of 1982 these assets constituted only about 11 percent of total assets. Relative holdings of securities experienced a more dramatic decline. In 1952 over 40 percent of total assets was securities, and by the end of 1982, 20 percent of total assets was in securities. The declining shares of cash assets and securities were offset in the rising share of loans and other assets. In 1952 only 35 percent of total assets were devoted to loans and other assets, but by the end of 1982, 69 percent of assets was in this form.

There are many reasons for the declining relative importance of cash assets and securities and for the concomitant increase in the relative importance of loans and other assets. Since World War II, the U.S. economy has achieved greater stability than existed prior to the war. This stability has reduced the riskiness of loans, and it has reduced the vulnerability of banks to large declines in their liabilities. As a result, banks do not require as large a safety margin of liquid assets as was the case in earlier times. At least equally important, however, is the ability of the banking industry to manage its liabilities, which has reduced its reliance on liquid assets, and this has allowed the industry to grow substantially. Banks can meet many of their liquidity needs by borrowing in the interbank market and by issuing other liabilities. As a result, it is not necessary to hold as large a percentage of total assets in liquid form. Furthermore, CDs and other managed liabilities have allowed banks to increase their role as financial intermediaries significantly. These liabilities have been invested primarily in loan and other assets. As a result, the percentage of total assets devoted to loans and other assets has risen.

FIGURE 8.2
PORTFOLIO SHARES:
ALL INSURED COMMERCIAL BANKS
(DECEMBER 31, 1952–1982).

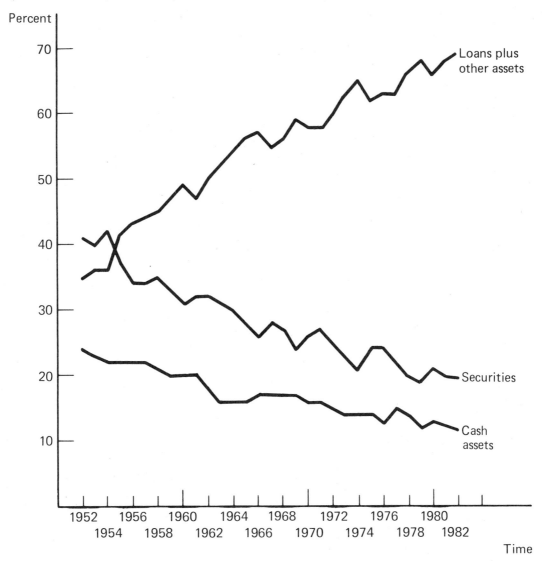

We conclude that liability management has increased the role of banks as financial intermediaries, and it has allowed banks to devote an increasing amount of their business to loans and other assets. The rising share of loans and other assets is largely caused by the increasing reliance that banks place on small denomination time accounts, CDs, and other liabilities to support their assets. The declining shares of cash assets and securities in total assets are largely the result of the declining importance of transactions accounts as the liabilities used to support assets.

OTHER ACTIVITIES OF BANKS

Banks are involved in a wide variety of activities that do not show up on their balance sheets as assets or liabilities. These activities generate substantial income for many banks, and they bring the banking industry into contact with a wide range of customers. The activities discussed in this section are often conducted by separate corporations affiliated with banks. The role of these affiliates is discussed in Chapter 9.

Many banks have *trust departments* that manage assets held in trust. Loosely speaking, a trust is wealth that is owned by an individual but controlled by someone else. For example, minor children may have inherited wealth. This wealth is placed in trust until the children reach legal age. It is common to commission a bank to manage the funds in the trust. The bank receives a fee for this service and is required to manage the trust in a manner that is specified in the trust agreement.

Trusts are created not only for minor children but also for many other purposes. Many trusts are established to avoid inheritance and other taxes. Furthermore, bank trust departments administer pension funds established by business customers and by individuals. In total, the banking system manages hundreds of billions of dollars of trusts and pension funds. These activities generate substantial income for banks, and they provide the banking system with substantial control over a vast amount of stocks, bonds, and real estate in the country.

Banks are also very heavily involved in the *leasing* business. Banks often purchase equipment such as computers, aircraft, railroad cars, or oil tankers and lease the equipment to businesses. By owning the equipment, a bank can take advantage of depreciation allowances and investment tax credits to lower its taxable income. The alternative to leasing is to lend the firm money to buy the equipment. If the business does not have sufficient taxable income to take full advantage of the depreciation allowance and the investment tax credit, the firm can benefit by leasing rather than borrowing. The business allows the bank to enjoy the tax benefits of owning the equipment in return for favorable lease payments. In many cases, the lease payments are substantially smaller than the interest payments for a loan. Bank leasing has grown rapidly in recent years, and banks own many of the airplanes used by major airlines as well as substantial amounts of equipment used by other businesses.

Banks earn substantial fees for providing various other services. For example, several major banks are *dealers* in securities markets, and many banks *underwrite* bonds issued by states and political subdivisions.[38] Several large banks are

---

[38] As explained in Chapter 9, banks are not allowed to underwrite securities issued by business, but they can "assist" a corporation in placing its securities.

affiliated with *finance companies* and *stock brokerage* firms, and they are also involved in *selling mortgage loans* in the secondary market.

When these many activities are combined with bank involvement in data processing, credit cards, travelers checks, and other functions, we see that banking covers a very wide range of activities. Banks today are the department stores of finance.

SUMMARY

Banks are important as financial intermediaries because of the size of the industry and because of the wide variety of means by which banks channel funds from surplus to deficit units in the economy. Banks are also important because they are depositories for transactions account balances and, therefore, are custodians for most of the nation's stock of money. This function represents a relatively small part of the banking business, however. Only about 25 percent of bank asset holdings are supported by transactions account liabilities. Well over half of all assets are supported by time account and other liabilities.

Many factors determine the kinds of liabilities that a bank issues and the kinds of assets that it holds. Transactions accounts, savings accounts, and small denomination time accounts fluctuate as the public makes deposits and withdrawals from these accounts. A bank reduces the size of these fluctuations by having a large number of accounts, but the fluctuations cannot be eliminated. The need to adjust to these fluctuations explains why a bank holds liquid assets and why it uses the market for interbank loans.

A bank does not adjust its transactions and savings account liabilities in response to short-term fluctuations in the supply of account balances or to fluctuations in loan demand. If a bank tried to meet an increase in loan demand or a decline in the supply of funds by increasing its transactions or savings account liabilities, it would have to raise the interest rate on both new and old accounts. This is usually more costly than increasing the interest rate on time accounts, where new and old accounts can be separated.

Small denomination time accounts are more flexible than transactions or savings accounts, but even they have drawbacks. The public does not adjust quickly or very predictably to changes in interest rates.

Large banks avoid these problems by issuing liabilities in organized markets to sophisticated buyers. Liability management has allowed large banks to grow rapidly over the last twenty years, and it has provided these banks with substantial flexibility in adjusting to shifts in loan demand and to shifts in the public's supply of funds. Managed liabilities include large denomination CDs, federal funds purchases and repurchase agreements, Eurodollars, and holding company debt. These instruments allow banks to issue liabilities in organized markets rather than wait passively for the public to come forward with new account balances.

The ability of banks to manage their liabilities has had significant consequences for the kinds of assets that they hold. In the 1950s, banks supported about 70 percent of their assets with transactions account liabilities. In order to contend with their inability to control these volatile liabilities, banks held about 65 percent of their assets in liquid form (cash assets and securities). With the growth of small-denomination time accounts and managed liabilities, banks today support only about 25 percent of their total assets with transactions account liabilities. Largely as a consequence of this shift in the composition of liabilities, banks today only hold about 30 percent of their assets as cash assets and securities.

Banks lend to business through commercial and industrial loans and through business loans secured by real estate. The banking industry holds a highly diversified portfolio of business loans with funds lent for virtually every kind of business activity. Business loans are complex agreements between lender and borrower in which the size of the loan, its maturity, and interest rate are negotiated. Banks limit risk by securing loans by various assets and by obtaining authority to intervene in the affairs of the firm should conditions merit. Risk of default or delinquency cannot be eliminated, however, and banks charge interest rates that are commensurate with loan risk.

Loan interest rates are also affected by the bargaining power of the borrower. Major firms have the most bargaining power. The threat of issuing securities or of shifting its business to another bank allows a major corporation to obtain the most favorable interest rate from banks. Other borrowers do not have the same amount of bargaining power, so banks can exert some monopoly power over them. The degree of monopoly power depends upon the importance of the customer's loan and other business to the bank and upon the ability of the borrower to switch banks. Small businesses have the least bargaining power, and they are most subject to monopolistic practices by banks. The loan, deposit account, and other activities of larger businesses that lack access to securities markets are often important to their bank. These firms are less subject to monopolistic practices by banks.

Historically, the interest rate that banks charge their business customers did not change frequently. Loan interest rates were sticky because of borrower inertia and because banks attempted to avoid using the interest rate in competing for loan customers. In recent years, loan interest rates have changed more frequently. This occurred because of increased volatility in the interest rates that banks pay for liabilities and because banks have made increasing use of floating rate loans. These loans can have a relatively long maturity, but their interest rate changes with a base interest rate established by the lending bank. Until recently, this base interest rate (prime rate) was the interest rate charged to a bank's lowest-risk customers. Today the prime rate is an index that moves up and down with market interest rates. Banks offer discounts from prime to low-risk borrowers with high bargaining power, and they offer markups over prime to higher-risk borrowers or to borrowers who have limited bargaining power or to both.

Over the last twenty years, banks have increased their lending to households and today are one of the most important sources of credit to this group. Loans to households range from long-term mortgage loans to short-term unsecured loans on credit cards. Interest rates on the various loans are rarely negotiated, and the interest rates are not changed frequently.

Banking is a very complex and exacting business. Space limitations have prevented a more complete account, but this chapter has summarized many of the key factors that affect bank behavior. These factors are important for understanding the role of banks as financial intermediaries, and they are crucial for understanding the role of banks in the monetary system. One factor that has not been covered in this chapter is the effect of regulation on bank behavior and on the safety of banks. This subject is the topic of the next chapter.

SELECTED REFERENCES

Ehrlich, Edna, "The Functions and Investment Policies of Personal Trust Departments," *Monthly Review*, New York: Federal Reserve Bank of New York, October 1972, pp. 255–270.

Havrilesky, Thomas and John Boorman, *Current Perspectives in Banking*, Arlington Heights, Ill.: AHM Publishing Corp., 1976.

Hester, Donald and James Pierce, *Bank Management and Portfolio Behavior*, New Haven: Yale University Press, 1975.

Hodgman, Donald, *Commercial Bank Loan and Investment Policy*, Urbana, Ill.: University of Illinois Press, 1963.

Mayer, Martin, *The Bankers*, New York: Balantine Books, 1976.

Silber, William, *Commercial Bank Liability Management*, Chicago: Association of Reserve City Bankers, 1978.

GOVERNMENT REGULATION OF COMMERCIAL BANKS

9

The primary objective of government regulation of commercial banks is to promote the stability of the banking system. Stability has been achieved. Although individual banks still fail from time to time, these failures have not triggered the financial panics and waves of bank failures that marked the economic history of the United States prior to the mid-1930s. Most of this success is attributable to having deposit insurance and an effective central bank, but regulation has played a part. This chapter describes the historical process through which the current regulatory structure evolved. The chapter also analyzes the economic consequences of regulations that limit competition among banks.

It is difficult to overstate the importance of historical factors in molding the current regulatory environment for banks. Furthermore, it is virtually impossible to understand the existing regulatory apparatus without reviewing the historical factors that produced it. Historical factors explain why there are so many government agencies, both federal and state, that regulate and supervise banks. Historical factors also explain the overlapping responsibilities of the various regulatory agencies. When one attempts to describe the current regulatory structure, it is rarely possible to complete the list of government agencies and their duties without evoking either laughter or tears from the audience. The reason for this response is that the current regulatory structure is mind boggling in its complexity.

SUMMARY OF THE STRUCTURE OF BANK REGULATION

The responsibility for regulating banks rests with both the federal government and with the fifty state governments. There is no simple division of authority between the federal government and state governments, however. Within the federal government there are three separate entities that regulate banks. Within the U.S. Treasury resides the office of the Comptroller of the Currency. The duties of the Comptroller no longer have anything to do with currency, but, rather, involve the regulation and supervision of *national banks*. These activities include issuing new charters (licenses to operate), approving mergers involving national banks, and regulating the activities of these banks. National banks are, by definition, banks that receive a federal charter. All national banks must have federal deposit insurance, and they all must be members of the Federal Reserve System (the Fed). These legal requirements bring the Federal Deposit Insurance Corporation (FDIC) and the Federal Reserve System into the picture. Thus, national banks are subjected to the supervision and rules of three federal agencies: the office of the Comptroller of the Currency, the FDIC, and the Federal Reserve.

Banks that are not national banks receive charters from the state in which they operate and are called *state-chartered banks*. Each of the fifty state governments establishes its own rules for granting charters and for regulating the activities of the banks that it charters. However, virtually every bank in the United States is covered by federal deposit insurance.[1] This insurance brings the federal government into the regulation of state-chartered banks through the FDIC. As a result, state-chartered banks must meet FDIC standards if they are to receive and retain deposit insurance.

Membership in the Federal Reserve System is optional for state-chartered banks. All banks that are members of the Federal Reserve System must have federal deposit insurance. Thus, those state-chartered banks that become members are subject to the rules and regulations of both the Federal Reserve System and the FDIC while remaining under jurisdiction of the state authorities. Insured state-chartered banks that are not members of the Federal Reserve System are regulated "only" by the states and by the FDIC.

The Federal Reserve's influence goes beyond national and state-chartered member banks. All depository institutions, including banks, that offer transactions accounts or nonpersonal time accounts are subject to reserve requirements administered by the Federal Reserve.[2] Thus, the Fed's regulations with respect to reserve requirements extend to nonmember state-chartered banks and to nonbank depository institutions. Other regulations of the Federal Reserve do not apply to nonmember banks, however, unless they are subsidiaries of a bank holding company.

The Federal Reserve has regulatory jurisdiction over the activities of bank holding companies and their nonbank affiliates. The Fed also regulates transactions between banks and nonbanking subsidiaries in holding companies. Despite the responsibilities of the Federal Reserve for regulating the activities of bank

---

[1] Some states require that banks receiving a state charter have federal deposit insurance; others do not. All states, however, allow their banks to have federal deposit insurance.

[2] Nonpersonal time accounts are accounts issued to any entity other than a natural person.

TABLE 9.1
JURISDICTION OF FEDERAL AND STATE BANK REGULATORS

Comptroller of the Currency	Federal Reserve	FDIC	States
National banks	National banks	National banks	All state-chartered banks
	State-chartered member banks	Insured state-chartered banks	
	Nonbank subsidiaries of holding companies		
	Bank holding companies		

holding companies, responsibility for regulating the activities of the bank or banks in a holding company is still divided among various regulators. Thus, banks in holding companies are regulated by the Comptroller of the Currency, the FDIC, and the Fed if they are national banks; by the state authorities, the FDIC, and the Fed if they are state-chartered members of the Federal Reserve; and by the state and the FDIC if they are not member banks.

An additional layer of complication is imposed by the supervision and regulation of the activities of banks and their holding company affiliates in international markets. In the interest of maintaining the sanity of the reader, these complications are not discussed. Even omitting international banking, this short summary suggests that one would have to work hard to produce a more complex and confusing regulatory structure. Table 9.1 summarizes the jurisdiction of the three federal agencies and of state regulatory authorities.

Rather remarkably, the system works better in practice than its complexity suggests. The various regulators have divided their responsibilities, and there is communication among them. The bulk of this chapter is devoted to explaining how the current crazy quilt of bank regulation evolved and how it operates.

A SHORT HISTORY OF BANKING AND OF BANK REGULATION IN THE UNITED STATES

Banking history in the United States has been marked by a struggle, which continues to this day, between those who favor a centralized federal system of banks and those who desire a decentralized system in which the individual states set the standards for banking. This struggle helps explain the evolution of the current regulatory structure. There are many reasons for the struggle, including such considerations as the appropriate role of the federal government relative to the states as well as the conflicting economic goals of farmers and consumers relative to the goals of industrial and financial firms.

The first commercial bank established in the country was the Bank of North America, established in Pennsylvania to assist in the financing of the Revolution. The Bank of New York and the Bank of Massachusetts were established in 1784. Until 1791 these were the only incorporated banks operating in the country.[3] The banks accepted deposits of specie (gold or silver coins) or bank notes and issued their own notes to depositors and borrowers. The bank notes were redeemable for specie. These notes were the banks' principle liabilities, but deposit accounts did exist.

In 1791 the First Bank of the United States (FBUS) was established by Congress. The bank was a joint venture between the federal government, which owned 20 percent of the bank's capital, and private individuals, who owned the remainder.[4] With dual ownership, the bank was both a profit-oriented firm and a government institution involved in efforts to improve the nation's monetary and banking systems. The FBUS issued notes, accepted deposits, and granted loans to private citizens. The federal government was also an important customer because it kept its account balances with the bank, and it borrowed from it. The bank had its head office in Philadelphia and was authorized to operate branches across state lines in several major cities. Through its branch system, the FBUS was able to transfer funds from one city to another. Its services were attractive to many customers.

The activities of the FBUS affected the activity of state-chartered banks. When the federal bank expanded its loans, the account balances and reserves of state banks rose because recipients of the expenditures from the loans often deposited the money in state banks. When the federal bank reduced loans, the reserves and account balances of state banks declined. Thus, the amount of lending by the FBUS affected the lending ability of other banks. Furthermore, customers often deposited notes issued by state-chartered banks with the First Bank of the United States. Holdings of these notes allowed the federal bank to flex its financial muscle against individual state banks. For example, if a state-chartered bank were deemed to be extending too much credit, the FBUS would demand redemption of the bank's notes for specie. In meeting the redemption, the state-chartered bank suffered a reduction in its reserves and was forced to reduce its extensions of notes and credit. By contrast, if a state-chartered bank was deemed to be behaving itself, its notes would be held by the federal bank rather than redeemed.

---

[3] Rather remarkably, in view of the virulent banking developments that followed, these three original banks survived and continue in operation today.

[4] The government obtained its contribution by borrowing from the bank. This dubious procedure meant that the government's investment did not contribute net worth to the bank. In later years private investors in state-chartered banks also learned to provide "net worth" by borrowing from the bank. These banks really had no net worth and were initiated in an unsound condition that often led to failure.

Thus, the economic power of the First Bank of the United States allowed it to affect the total quantity of credit in the economy as well as to punish banks that were in disfavor or to reward those that were in favor. To the extent that the FBUS encouraged expansion of money and credit in keeping with the needs of the economy and to the extent that its policies prevented state-chartered banks from expanding their lending activities beyond prudent limits, the policies had social benefit. To the extent that the policies stifled economic expansion and allowed the First Bank of the United States to monopolize lending, the policies were not socially beneficial.

The commercial banking and regulatory functions of the First Bank of the United States created a conflict of interest that helped to bring about its demise. There were situations in which the profit motive of the bank was in conflict with the exercise of its regulatory duties. It is difficult for a regulator to be a competitor with those institutions that it regulates. The regulatory activities of the FBUS were vulnerable to the criticism that they were exercised not to enhance the economic stability of the banking system but rather to line the pockets of the bank's stockholders.

Despite the presence of the FBUS, the number of state-chartered banks grew over the years, and by 1811 there were eighty-eight banks chartered by the states. Over these same years, criticism of the FBUS grew. State-chartered banks and state governments were vocal in their complaints as were economic groups that wanted greater money and credit expansion than was provided by the FBUS.[5] Congress bowed to the complaints and refused to renew the bank's charter. The charter lapsed in 1811, and the First Bank of the United States ceased to exist.

For the next five years only state-chartered banks functioned in the country. During this period, the number of banks expanded from 88 to 246, and the quantity of bank notes issued by these banks nearly tripled. The rapid growth of state-chartered banking was not without problems. The activities of state-chartered banks were unregulated, and several banks pursued imprudent policies. Loans with high risk were often granted, and fraud was not uncommon. The result was the failure of several banks.

It is useful at this point to examine the causes of bank failure. Failure occurs when the value of a bank's liabilities exceeds the value of its assets. This can occur as the result of bad loans or a liquidity crisis.

Unsound banking practices or plain bad luck can produce a situation where total note and deposit liabilities exceed the value of a bank's assets. For example, when borrowers default on loans, these loans become worthless, and the value of the bank's assets decline by the amount of the defaulted loans. The amount of liabilities that a bank has outstanding does not change when there are loan defaults, so assets decline relative to liabilities. As long as a bank has sufficient net worth, it can absorb loan defaults. After the defaults, net worth is lower, but a bank's assets

---

[5] The FBUS was also heavily owned by foreigners. The "evils" of this ownership were used as further evidence why the bank should be dissolved.

still exceed its liabilities. If loan defaults are larger than net worth, however, liabilities exceed assets, and the bank is *insolvent*. Net worth is negative. The bank does not have sufficient assets to cover its liabilities. When a bank fails, it liquidates its assets and pays off as much of its liabilities as possible. To the extent that liabilities exceed assets, holders of the bank's liabilities lose. The owners of the bank can lose their entire investment.[6]

A banking panic can also cause a bank to fail. Here it is useful to describe the effects of panics on bank solvency in an historical context where banks promised to redeem their notes for specie.[7] If a sufficient amount of notes and deposit liabilities were presented for conversion into specie, a bank would have insufficient reserves to meet the demand.[8] In this case, the bank had to sell assets for specie or borrow specie from another bank. Under ordinary circumstances, a sound bank could sell assets or borrow. It could withstand a "run" on its reserves. If demands for conversion of notes and deposit liabilities into specie were very large, however, even a sound bank could encounter difficulty in obtaining sufficient specie. It would exhaust any liquid assets and have to sell illiquid assets at depressed prices. It could avoid this problem by using its illiquid assets as collateral for loans from other banks rather than selling the assets. This might not be possible, however, if other banks were also experiencing losses of specie or if they questioned the quality of the bank's assets. In this situation, the bank faced a choice. It could continue to sell assets for specie at depressed prices in the hope that the run on its reserves would stop before asset prices declined to the point that the bank was insolvent. Alternatively, the bank could refuse to convert its notes and deposit liabilities into specie. Neither alternative was a good one. If the bank continued to convert its liabilities into specie, it was threatened with insolvency by its illiquidity. If it refused convertibility of its liabilities into specie, the bank avoided insolvency, but its notes and deposits lost acceptability to the public.

It did not take long for problems to develop for state-chartered banks following the demise of the First Bank of the United States in 1811. During the War of 1812, banks increased their issuance of notes dramatically at the same time that specie was flowing overseas. Thus, the fraction of notes backed by specie declined. The public lost faith and began to convert their holdings of notes into gold and silver. Liquidity problems developed, and many banks were unable to redeem their notes for specie. The notes issued by several banks became virtually worthless and ceased to circulate as media of exchange. The notes of other banks continued to circulate, but they were accepted in payment at a discount. For example, a 50 percent discount meant that $100 of notes were required to purchase

---

[6] Banks as corporations have limited liability. The owners of a bank can lose no more than their investment in the bank. Thus, their investment in the bank is wiped out, and the difference between liabilities and assets is absorbed by holders of the bank's liabilities.

[7] Insufficient liquidity can cause bank failures even when currency is not convertible into specie. The mechanics are different, however, and are described later in this chapter.

[8] Technically, only notes were redeemable for specie but a holder of deposit balances could make a withdrawal in the form of bank notes and then redeem the notes for specie.

$50 of goods and services. The extent of the discount depended upon the public's estimate of when (if ever) the issuing bank would restore convertibility of its notes for specie. Notes issued by banks that were able to maintain convertibility continued to circulate at full value. The various discounts on bank notes made the nation's monetary system chaotic.

The problems became particularly acute in 1814, when, following the British raids, banks in the District of Columbia, Baltimore, New York, and Philadelphia suspended convertibility of their notes. Only banks in New England were able to maintain convertibility. Widespread bank failures also occurred that injured not only note holders but also those who depended upon banks as a source of credit.

The instability of banks and the inconvertibility of bank notes induced the federal government in 1816 to try again to stabilize the banking system. In that year, Congress established the Second Bank of the United States (SBUS). The bank was given a twenty-year charter, and as in the case of its predecessor, ownership was divided between the federal government and private citizens although state governments were also allowed to participate.[9] The activities of the Second Bank of the United States were similar to those of its predecessor. Its activities in controlling state-chartered banks and limiting the growth of bank notes and credit in the country became equally unpopular.

The bank was attacked on every side. Proponents of hard money, that is, specie, were critical because notes issued by the SBUS were not fully backed by specie and, therefore, were considered inflationary. Proponents of easy money claimed that the bank was the captive of special interests who wanted high interest rates, restrictive credit, and deflation. State-chartered banks for reasons good and bad hated the institution. President Jackson vetoed legislation to extend the life of the bank, and in 1836 the charter for the Second Bank of the United States expired.

From 1836 to 1863 the nation entered another era in which only state-chartered banks existed. The number of state-chartered banks increased sharply, and there was rapid expansion of notes and credit in the economy. Bank failures were common despite efforts by several states to control their banks.

Until 1827 a bank could only receive a state charter if the application was approved by the state legislature. This situation enriched many politicians but failed to achieve stability in banking. In 1827 first Michigan and then other states became *free banking* states. Under free banking, any bank that met certain established criteria concerning amount of net worth and maintenance of reserves could receive a charter.

The move to free banking was a step in the right direction, but banking remained in a chaotic condition. Money and credit fluctuated widely, bank failures were common, and bank notes were often rendered valueless, or they traded at discounts as banks refused convertibility. There were as many different

[9] Some attempt was made to prevent the ownership in the SBUS from being concentrated in the hands of a few individuals.

kinds of money as there were different discounts of bank notes. The performance of banks in various states varied considerably. Massachusetts banks maintained their solid performance and were able to continue full convertibility of their notes, but banks in many other states were less successful.

Many states intensified the battle to control the activities of their banks, and several were successful. For example, in 1842, Louisiana passed the first law to require specific specie reserves against deposit accounts. Several other states did not enact legislation to control private banks but rather established their own state banks to issue notes and handle state transactions. The Bank of Indiana and the Bank of Missouri are two successful examples of such banks. All of these efforts helped reduce the instability of the banking system, but many problems remained.

The prospect of a Civil War added to the instability of the banking system, and the inconvertibility of notes became widespread. The federal government once again entered the picture.

In order to understand why the federal government re-established its presence in banking during the Civil War, we must briefly review the national monetary standard that was in effect prior to the war. From 1791 to 1861, the United States was on a metallic standard in which the U.S. government stood ready to mint gold or silver into coins, and the public was free to melt down coins to obtain bullion.[10] The country used a *bimetallic* standard of gold and silver in which gold was used for large denomination coins and silver was used for smaller denominations. These coins were *full bodied* money in that the value of gold or silver embodied in them was equal to the market price of gold or silver. It was these coins that were the specie into which bank notes and other paper currency could be converted.

With the outbreak of the Civil War, the federal government was faced with the prospect of financing large military expenditures. As with most other wars, the expenditures were not financed by increased taxation, but rather by borrowing and by money creation. War expenditures were initially financed by loans in specie extended by banks. The federal government immediately spent the specie, which quickly found its way back into banks to be lent again to the government. This procedure worked for a while until the worsening financial condition of the government became known to the public. This knowledge, coupled with general fears about note convertibility in a war situation, produced large conversions of bank notes into specie by the public. These conversions drained specie from banks and forced virtually all banks to suspend convertibility of their notes.

With the resources of the banking system drying up, the U.S. Treasury found it difficult to borrow. The Treasury then ceased to mint coins, and the United States abandoned a metallic standard for money. Specie was replaced by fiat money in the form of notes issued by the federal government. The notes were declared to be legal tender and came to be known as *greenbacks*. When the United States abandoned a monetary system where currency was convertible into specie, it was possible for the government to print greenbacks and use them to pay for war ex-

[10] Chapter 2 describes a commodity standard in detail.

penditures. Although greenbacks were legal tender, there was initial resistance by the public to accepting them. This resistance was reduced by offering the public the opportunity to convert greenbacks into interest-bearing debt of the government.

With the widening use of greenbacks, gold and silver were hoarded, and banks ceased to redeem their notes for specie. The nation had adopted a system of fiat money composed of greenbacks and nonconvertible notes issued by state-chartered banks. It was not illegal to use gold or silver for transactions or for backing bank notes, but there was no economic incentive to do so. Greenbacks were legal tender that had to be accepted for transactions. The nation experienced a classic case of Gresham's law, in which "bad money" (greenbacks) drove out "good money" (specie and convertible bank notes).

In 1863, Congress started the transition to a purely federal currency. The National Currency Act, which was subsequently retitled the National Banking Act, established within the U.S. Treasury the office of the Comptroller of the Currency. The Comptroller was authorized to charter *national banks,* which accepted greenbacks as deposits and were authorized to issue *national bank notes.*[11] National banks could issue $90 of these notes for every $100 of U.S. government securities that they purchased. The expansion of notes issued by a national bank was limited, however, to an amount equal to its net worth. National bank notes were not legal tender, but they were just as safe as greenbacks. If a national bank were to fail, the U.S. Treasury would convert its bank notes into greenbacks. Each national bank had to accept the notes issued by other national banks at par and the U.S. government also accepted national bank notes for payment of taxes and purchases of securities. Thus, for all intents and purposes, national bank notes and greenbacks were perfect substitutes.

The National Bank Act was an important step in the development of a more uniform currency in the United States. The National Bank Act also had profound implications for the structure of banking in the United States.

The National Banking Act followed the lead of the free banking states by establishing minimum net worth standards and other criteria for establishing national banks. The act also followed Louisiana by establishing reserves against notes and deposit accounts, and it gave the Comptroller of the Currency authority to regulate the safety and soundness of national banks.

Unlike the First and Second Banks of the United States, national banks did not involve joint ownership between the federal government and private parties. National banks were, and are, privately owned institutions whose goal is to make profits for their owners.

The federal government took an important step toward establishing a more uniform currency in 1866. In that year, notes issued by state-chartered banks were subjected to a 10 percent tax. This tax effectively made note issuance by state-chartered banks unprofitable, and these notes disappeared. The tax greatly in-

---

[11] Hence, the title Comptroller of the Currency.

creased the attractiveness of national bank charters, and many state-chartered banks converted to national bank status. Most banks that did not convert ceased operations. In 1860 there had been 1529 state-chartered banks; by 1868 there were 1640 national banks, and only 247 state-chartered banks remained.

By offering national bank charters and by taxing the note issues of state-chartered banks, the federal government accomplished two objectives. First, it largely replaced a banking system comprised of state-chartered banks with a system of national banks under federal jurisdiction. Second, it replaced the multitude of currencies issued by state-chartered banks with a more uniform currency composed of greenbacks and national bank notes. In the process, by tying the issuance of national bank notes to purchase of government securities, the government had a handy method of financing the Civil War.

In 1879 the United States returned to a metallic standard, and national bank notes became redeemable for specie. There no longer were thousands of different bank notes issued by state-chartered banks, but rather various forms of federal currency. The country remained on a metallic standard from 1879 to 1933, and a federal, convertible currency prevailed during this period.[12]

One might think that once deprived of their ability to issue notes in competition with national banks, all state-chartered banks would have disappeared. By 1870 this had almost occurred, but by the late 1870s the number of state-chartered banks began to increase. These banks were "born again" because there was nothing to prevent them from issuing liabilities in the form of transactions (demand deposit) accounts rather than bank notes. In fact, in the years leading up to the establishment of national banks, the use of notes was already declining relative to the use of transactions accounts as communication and speed of transport improved in the economy. The National Banking Act simply accelerated the process and led state-chartered banks to move aggressively into financing loans through transactions accounts rather than notes. The growing acceptance of checks as a medium of exchange made banking under a state charter increasingly attractive because of the generally milder regulatory standards imposed by the states.

Table 9.2 summarizes the number of banks in the United States from 1800 through 1910. The figures in the table show the rapid growth of state-chartered banks through 1860 and then the replacement of state-chartered banks by national banks in the 1860s. State-chartered banks started to rebound in the 1880s, and over the next two decades their numbers grew rapidly. From 1900 to 1910, the number of state-chartered banks expanded nearly fourfold, and by 1910 there were over twice as many state-chartered banks as national banks. As the twentieth century began, banking supervised by the states was once again an important element in the U.S. banking system.

The growth of transactions accounts was further encouraged by the relatively stringent requirements of the National Banking Act with respect to notes issued by national banks. Government debt, which backed national bank notes, did not

---

[12] Convertibility was abandoned for two years during World World I.

TABLE 9.2
NUMBER OF BANKS IN THE UNITED STATES
IN SELECTED YEARS: 1800–1910

	National	State	Total
1800		28	28
1830		329	329
1860		1,529	1,529
1865	1,294	349	1,643
1870	1,612	325	1,937
1880	2,076	650	2,726
1890	3,484	2,250	5,734
1900	5,007	3,731	8,738
1910	7,138	14,348	21,486

Source: *Statistical Abstract of the* United States, 1970.

grow. This inhibited the expansion of currency. To the extent that currency (bank notes) could not grow, there was an incentive for all banks to encourage the public to use transactions accounts instead.

The inflexibility in the supply of currency significantly increased the vulnerability of the banking system to financial panics. The degree of vulnerability was exemplified by the banking panics of 1893 and 1907. In those years, an increase in the number of bank failures weakened public confidence in banks. Runs on banks occurred in which many holders of deposit balances demanded payment in currency, that is, in national bank notes or in gold or silver certificates issued by the government. Several banks did not have sufficient currency and had to refuse conversion of deposit balances into currency. This produced panic among the public, further runs occurred, and inconvertibility became widespread. The suspension of convertibility allowed many banks to remain solvent because they avoided having to sell illiquid assets at depressed prices. This ultimately protected their depositors, but while the inconvertibility lasted, panic was widespread. Furthermore, depositors were injured while the inconvertibility was in effect because checks drawn on these accounts would be accepted in transactions only at a discount.

By placing stringent restrictions on the quantity of currency (bank notes) that could be issued by national banks, the National Bank Act limited the ability of banks to meet the demand for conversion of deposit balances into currency. Thus, the provisions of the act helped to produce banking panics.

Federal regulation and supervision of national banks probably enhanced their soundness, but failures were still common. Table 9.3 summarizes the bank failure experience in the United States over the period from 1865 to 1914.[13] These figures

---

[13] This time period is considered because no reliable data are available for periods prior to 1865 and 1914 was the year that the Federal Reserve System started operations.

TABLE 9.3
BANK FAILURES AND SUSPENSIONS (1865–1914)

	National Banks			State Banks		
	Number of Banks	Deposits (millions of dollars)	Percentage Total Deposits	Number of Banks	Deposits (millions of dollars)	Percentage Total Deposits
1865–69	16	$ 5.1	0.78	26	$ 1.8	0.58
1870–79	58	20.7	2.53	295	86.6	18.3
1880–89	50	28.2	1.94	195	37.7	3.68
1890–99	236	77.8	3.31	815	128.6	5.63
1900–09	145	127.2	2.43	685	439.1	7.19
1910–14	43	61.4	0.78	440	133.7	1.42

Source: C. D. Bremer, *American Banking Failures*, (New York: Columbia University Press, 1935).

show that both national and state-chartered banks were susceptible to failure. After 1870 a substantial number of bank failures occurred, and losses were particularly great in the 1890s and early 1900s. Although many more state-chartered banks failed than national banks, state-chartered banks were on average smaller. Figures for the dollar amount of deposits at failed banks indicate, however, that greater losses were sustained in total by state-chartered banks than by national banks. In order to allow for the different quantities of total deposit liabilities in the national and state-chartered banking systems, we have shown the amount of deposit liabilities at failed banks as a percentage of total deposit liabilities in the two banking systems. Failures of state-chartered banks were particularly great during the difficult period of 1870 to 1879, when the deposit liabilities at failed banks comprised 18.3 percent of the deposit liabilities of all state-chartered banks. During this period, the tax on the notes of state-chartered banks forced many of these banks to fail.

The experience summarized in Table 9.3 suggests that national banks were safer than state-chartered banks. This would seem to indicate that the federal government did a better job of supervising and regulating banks than did state governments. This may have been the case, but one must be cautious in reaching this conclusion. On average, state-chartered banks were smaller than national banks. Small banks were unable to diversify their asset holdings and their liabilities to the extent possible for large banks. As a result, small banks were often more risky than large banks. Many small banks were located in agricultural areas, where some local event, such as a crop failure or declining prices for the crops raised in the area, would depress the local economy and threaten the banks located in the region. It is not surprising, therefore, that the failure rate was greater for a system of small banks than for a system of large banks.

These considerations raise doubts concerning whether the federal government was, in fact, a better regulator than were state governments. It should also be noted that national charters did not make banks immune to failure. There was a substantial incidence of failure for both national and state-chartered banks over the period 1865 to 1914.

Following the panic of 1907, banking in the United States was extensively reviewed and investigated by Congress, various government agencies, and private citizens. These efforts culminated in the enactment of the Federal Reserve Act of 1913. In order to understand the initial design of the Federal Reserve System, we must look more closely at the features and shortcomings of the national banking system.

Notes issued by national banks were safe because they were backed by government securities and because the Comptroller of the Currency was authorized to make good on the notes should a national bank fail. Deposit accounts at national banks did not enjoy the guarantee accorded to bank notes. Deposit accounts were backed by reserve requirements in the form of vault cash plus deposit balances held with other banks. The extent and composition of required reserves depended upon the location of the bank. National banks in New York, Chicago, and St. Louis were called central reserve city banks, and they were required to hold 20 percent of their deposit account and note liabilities in the form of cash in their vaults. National banks in several other cities were designated as reserve city banks, and they also were required to hold 20 percent of their note and deposit account liabilities as reserves, but only one half (10 percent of notes and deposit balances) had to be vault cash. The other one half could be in the form of deposit balances that reserve city banks held at central reserve city banks. The remaining national banks were designated as country banks, and they were required to hold 15 percent of their note and deposit account liabilities as reserves with 40 percent (6 percent of notes and deposit balances) as vault cash and the remainder as deposit balances at reserve city or central reserve banks.

The rationale for this structure of reserve requirements was that central reserve, and to a lesser extent reserve city banks, were depositories for other banks. Larger banks, particularly those in major cities, provided various services, including check clearing, for other banks and were compensated for these services by receiving deposit balances from these banks. Furthermore, central reserve and reserve city banks competed for the deposit balances of other banks and paid interest on these accounts. The reserve requirement for central reserve city banks was solely in the form of vault cash because these banks were expected to be in a position to meet the currency needs of other banks that deposited funds with them. The lower vault cash requirements for reserve city and country banks mirrored their lesser role as depositories for other banks.

The National Banking Act promoted the liquidity and soundness of individual national banks. The requirement that banks hold reserves in the form of vault cash or deposit account balances with other banks, the existence of collateral requirements for notes, plus the presence of supervision and regulation did promote the safety of national banks.[14] Unfortunately, what was true for each bank considered individually was not necessarily true for the banking system as a whole.

---

[14] State regulators also imposed liquidity and other standards on their banks. The provisions of the National Bank Act were more stringent than were the standards applied in many states.

Banking crises occurred when the public lost faith in banks, and there were massive withdrawals of currency. These withdrawals far exceeded any normal seasonal declines and banks were unable to contend with the consequences. Central reserve and reserve city banks could not provide currency to other banks because their vault cash was depleted by currency withdrawals by their own customers. Despite the relatively high reserve requirements of vault cash, central reserve city banks could convert only 20 percent of their deposit liabilities into currency, and reserve city banks could convert only 10 percent. Under the fractional reserve system, there was not enough currency to go around when the public lost faith in banks. During these times, banks were forced to refuse convertibility of deposit account liabilities into currency.

THE ESTABLISHMENT OF CENTRAL BANKING IN THE UNITED STATES

From 1907 through 1913, there were heated debates concerning how to solve the nation's banking problems. The debates centered around the old issues of states rights, large versus small banks, and financial centers versus rural areas. The issues were finally settled by the Federal Reserve Act of 1913.[15]

The initial structure of the Federal Reserve indicates the compromises that were struck in order to get sufficient political support to obtain any reforms. The Federal Reserve Act was a step in the right direction, but as we shall see later in this chapter, it contained fatal flaws that prevented the Fed from preventing the greatest financial collapse in economic history that followed the crash of 1929.

There was great opposition to establishing a single central bank, such as existed in several other countries. Fears were expressed that a single central bank would be controlled by the interests of Wall Street or Washington, D.C., and there was general resistance to a substantial federal presence in the affairs of the central bank. Strenuous disagreement surfaced concerning whether the central bank should be a private bank for bankers or a government-operated institution. As a compromise, the central bank was formed as a *Federal Reserve System,* which was a loose confederation of twelve separate Federal Reserve banks. The affairs of the twelve banks were coordinated by a Federal Reserve Board in Washington, D.C.

Each Federal Reserve bank received a federal charter but was owned by its member banks. Reserve banks functioned as banks for banks. Each Federal Reserve bank issued its own currency called Federal Reserve notes. Reserve accounts were established at each Federal Reserve bank for the member banks in its district. Member banks could use their reserve balances to meet currency withdrawals or to clear checks. Member banks were also authorized to borrow from

---

[15] The Federal Reserve began operations in 1914.

their Federal Reserve bank. National banks were required to become member banks, but membership in the Federal Reserve System was made optional for state-chartered banks.

The Federal Reserve System covered the entire country, but the geographic division did not follow state boundaries. Instead, the country was divided into twelve Federal Reserve Districts of roughly equal "economic" size. The delineation of the twelve Federal Reserve districts and the location of each Federal Reserve bank within its district was determined by a combination of economic and political considerations. Economic factors explain the selection of New York and Chicago as cities for Federal Reserve banks, but only political considerations can explain why the state of Missouri received two Federal Reserve banks, one in St. Louis and the other in Kansas City.

Membership in the Federal Reserve System had several benefits to banks. Most important, member banks could use their Federal Reserve banks to obtain currency. A Federal Reserve bank was authorized to honor withdrawals from a member bank's reserve account by paying out currency. The Fed could meet the withdrawals because it was authorized to print notes. Furthermore, member banks could borrow from Federal Reserve banks. Thus, currency was to be available to banks even during periods of banking panics.[16] Federal Reserve banks also processed (cleared) the checks presented by member banks free of charge.[17]

There were also costs for being a member. Member banks had to hold a fraction of their deposit liabilities as required reserves in the form of funds deposited at their Federal Reserve bank or vault cash. These reserve balances earned no interest, unlike the interest that could be earned on reserves held with correspondent banks.[18] Member banks were also subjected to the regulation and supervision of the Federal Reserve. This regulation and supervision basically followed the provisions of the National Banking Act, so state-chartered member banks became subject to the same standards as national banks.

After weighing the benefits and costs of membership, relatively few state-chartered banks elected to become member banks. The Federal Reserve did

---

[16] As we shall see later, however, restrictions were placed on the ability of Federal Reserve banks to print notes or extend loans.

[17] Prior to the entry of the Federal Reserve into check processing, checks written on some banks were accepted for transactions only at a discount. The extent of the discount from par (i.e., the discount from the amount written on the check) depended upon the views of the public and of banks concerning the solvency of the bank upon which the check was written. Furthermore, substantial time was required to obtain payment on checks written on banks in distant locations. This time also produced discounts from par for checks written on these banks even if the banks were deemed able to make payment. Banks whose checks were accepted at discount were called nonpar banks. The Federal Reserve virtually eliminated nonpar banking by accepting all checks at par. This greatly facilitated the use of checks.

[18] A schedule of reserve requirements based on the old national bank division into central reserve city, reserve city, and country banks was adopted.

slowly gain state member banks, and by 1922 there were 1648 member banks with state charters. In that year there were 21,914 state-chartered banks, however, so less than 8 percent of these banks had elected to become members. Membership was not attractive to most small state-chartered banks because they obtained currency, loans, and check clearing services from large correspondent banks. In turn, most of these large banks were members, so they obtained currency, loans, and check clearing from the Federal Reserve. Thus, nonmember banks used the facilities of the Federal Reserve indirectly through their correspondent banks who were members.

Because many large state-chartered banks elected to be members, deposit liabilities at state member banks comprised 36 percent of deposit liabilities at all state-chartered banks. After 1922 the number of state member banks declined, and by 1929 only 6 percent of all state-chartered banks were members. Membership remained attractive to large banks, however, and state-chartered members accounted for nearly 40 percent of the total deposit liabilities at state-chartered banks. Thus, the Federal Reserve was not able to attract a sizable number of state-chartered banks, but the banks it did attract accounted for a sizable percentage of the total deposit liabilities at banks with state charters. It should be recalled that national banks were required to be members of the Federal Reserve System and that these banks were relatively large. As a result, in 1929 over 60 percent of the deposit balances in the banking system were held at member banks.

Superficially, Federal Reserve banks were similar to central reserve city banks under the old national banking system. Member banks held reserve balances at Federal Reserve banks just as country and reserve city banks held deposit balances at central reserve city banks. Federal Reserve banks extended credit to member banks just as large national banks lent to smaller banks. There was a crucial difference, however. Because of the restrictions on the issue of national bank notes, central reserve and reserve city banks were unable to dispense sufficient currency to other banks during a banking crisis. Federal Reserve banks, in contrast, were less restricted and were better able to make currency available.

The Federal Reserve Act provided for a fractional reserve system, so only a fraction of the currency withdrawn from a bank's deposit accounts could be met from its reserve account. For example, with reserve requirements of 20 percent, a $100 withdrawal from a transactions account reduced required reserves by $20. This allowed the bank to obtain $20 of currency from the Federal Reserve. As under the national banking system, the remaining $80 had to come from asset sales or from borrowing. Here again, the Federal Reserve was to provide a crucial service. If a member bank experienced difficulty in borrowing from other banks or if hasty asset sales were reducing asset prices, its Federal Reserve bank would serve as *lender of last resort*. In lending to a bank, the Federal Reserve bank simply added to the bank's reserve account, thus creating additional reserves in the banking system. The bank could withdraw the borrowed reserves in the form of currency.

The provisions of the Federal Reserve Act provided an "elastic currency" that was designed to expand when the public made currency withdrawals and contract when the public made deposits of currency. In principle, the elasticity of currency would allow the banking system to meet the public's demand for currency during panics. When public confidence returned, the quantity of currency would automatically decline as the public redeposited currency in banks and banks deposited the currency in their Federal Reserve banks.

Unfortunately, the mechanism for providing an elastic currency was flawed. Congress placed restrictions on the note issuance of Federal Reserve banks and required that their reserve account liabilities be secured by certain assets. Thus, these banks for bankers were regulated in much the same spirit as national banks had been regulated. The restrictions on Federal Reserve banks were simply less severe. Federal Reserve notes had to be backed by a gold reserve of 40 percent and also secured dollar-for-dollar by collateral in the form of eligible paper.[19] Member bank reserve balances had to be secured by an amount of gold equal to at least 35 percent of these balances. Finally, loans extended to member banks had to be secured either by U.S. government securities or by eligible paper.

Eligible paper consisted of short-term loans extended by banks to business for the purpose of financing trade, for example, for holding inventories. The idea was that these loans were backed by something "real," that is, actual commodities, and, hence, were safe. Federal Reserve banks were to act like commercial banks and to make only "good loans," that is, loans that were safe in accordance with accepted banking practices. To the extent that member banks lacked the government securities and eligible paper required as collateral, they could not borrow from Federal Reserve banks.

The reserve and collateral requirements for currency put an upper limit to the amount of Federal Reserve notes that could be put in circulation. Thus, the amount of currency that the Federal Reserve could provide during a banking panic was limited. Even if there had been no limits to currency issue, the gold reserve requirement for member bank reserve balances and the requirement that loans to member banks be secured by government securities or eligible paper limited the Federal Reserve's ability to avert banking crises.

The first real test of the Federal Reserve System came after the crash of 1929. Runs on banks developed, and member banks turned to the Federal Reserve for assistance. Reserve Banks issued additional currency and made loans available. The expansion in loans was not sufficient to cover the loss of reserves, however. With deteriorating economic conditions and the shrinking quantity of reserves in the banking system, bank loans declined. This meant that the quantity of commercial loans available to member banks as collateral for loans from the Federal Reserve was reduced. Because the quantity of deposit liabilities at member banks was declining and loans from Federal Reserve banks were scarce, member banks could not extend loans to nonmember banks. Nonmember banks found themselves little better off than under the old national banking system. Finally, the Federal Reserve apparently believed that its own supply of gold and eligible pa-

---

[19] Eligible paper is described later.

per would soon be insufficient to cover additional currency issues and reserve expansion, so it began to restrict extensions of credit to member banks.[20] The supply of currency and reserves was not sufficiently elastic to overcome the banking panic.

The Federal Reserve System did not stop the effects of massive currency withdrawals, and the worst banking collapse in United States history ensued. By any objective standard, the Federal Reserve System was a dismal failure. The very collapse that the System was created to avert occurred.

The waves of banking panic that befell the U.S. economy from 1930 to 1933 were unprecedented in magnitude and duration. Liquidity crises hit the banking system time and time again. In an effort to stay afloat, many banks suspended conversions of deposit liabilities into currency. Customers of many banks were able to write checks, but they could not withdraw currency. The inability to make currency withdrawals panicked customers at other banks, who then attempted to withdraw currency.

The number of banks that suspended convertibility of deposit accounts and the number of failures are staggering. Over 9000 banks suspended conversions during this period with 4000 suspensions occurring in 1933 alone. National banks, state-chartered member banks, and state-chartered nonmember banks were all affected. Suspension of currency payments was not sufficient to keep many banks solvent, and a large number failed. Over the period of 1930 to 1933 more than 9600 banks went out of operation. Closings occurred for all types of banks, but relatively small state-chartered banks in rural areas were hardest hit. All the efforts expended by the federal and state governments over the previous 100 years to make banks safe had failed to avert the calamity that hit the banking system.

THE FEDERAL DEPOSIT INSURANCE CORPORATION

In 1933 President Roosevelt declared what was euphemistically called a bank holiday. He closed the banks for an indefinite period but many were able to reopen after four days. The bank closings were designed to stop the panic and to give time to implement reforms that would bring order out of chaos.

The major reform was a very simple one. In 1933, the Federal Deposit Insurance Corporation (FDIC) was created to provide federal insurance for balances in bank accounts. With insurance, depositors were guaranteed by the government that they could get their money out of the bank. If a bank could not meet withdrawals, the government would provide the funds. This reform was remarkable in its simplicity and in its success. Since the founding of the FDIC, there have been no banking panics or any collapses of the banking system. The

---

[20] There is still disagreement as to whether or not reserve and collateral requirements prevented the Federal Reserve from acting more forcefully. Whatever the interpretation, the Federal Reserve System failed to avert the collapse of the banking system.

provision of deposit insurance was a simple and effective method of achieving banking stability.

The FDIC, like any insurance company, needs methods of controlling risk. This was accomplished by giving the FDIC authority for regulating and supervising insured banks. National banks and Federal Reserve member banks were (and are) required to have insurance. These banks were already regulated and supervised by the Comptroller of the Currency and the Federal Reserve. Deposit insurance was also made available to state-chartered banks that were not member banks. Those state-chartered banks that obtained insurance had to accept the regulation and supervision of the FDIC. Thus, the FDIC became the vehicle through which federal regulatory standards were applied to state-chartered nonmember banks. Because of the never-ending battle over states rights, federal law did not require state-chartered nonmember banks to obtain insurance.[21] There are obvious benefits of deposit insurance, however, and virtually all state-chartered nonmember banks obtained insurance. Almost all banks came under federal jurisdiction and federal regulatory standards. The FDIC was an effective vehicle for using a "voluntary" method of imposing federal standards.

In the drafting of the FDIC Act, there was considerable debate over the extent of insurance coverage and how the insurance fund should be financed. Finally, it was decided to provide total insurance protection to small depositors and partial protection to large depositors. Initially, the FDIC insured only the first $2500 of accounts held by each depositor at each bank. That limit was quickly raised to $5000 and has been increased over the years. Currently, deposit insurance covers the first $100,000 of accounts held by each depositor at each bank.

A simple formula was established that assessed each insured bank a flat annual fee based on its total deposit liabilities.[22] The fee was designed to allow the FDIC to build up an insurance fund sufficient to pay out claims to depositors when banks failed. As a safeguard, the FDIC was empowered to borrow through the U.S. Treasury should the size of the insurance fund be inadequate. The very existence of the FDIC stopped runs on banks and stopped the banking collapses that followed. The insurance fund has been more than adequate to meet the infrequent bank failures that have occurred since 1933.

OTHER FINANCIAL REFORMS OF THE 1930s

Deposit insurance was the most dramatic and direct reform of the 1930s but a number of important additional measures were adopted during the period that fostered stability in the banking system.

---

[21] To this day, FDIC insurance is not required for state-chartered, nonmember banks. Many states do require that state-chartered banks have FDIC insurance, however.

[22] Note that the fee is based on total deposit liabilities, not on insured deposit liabilities. This provision tends to overassess banks with large deposit accounts.

Reforms of the Federal Reserve System

The failure of the Federal Reserve System to prevent the collapse of the banking system brought forth a number of legislative reforms in the Banking Act of 1935 that made the Federal Reserve a more effective central bank. The Federal Reserve was given increased authority to lend to banks during emergencies. In particular, the Federal Reserve was authorized in any future emergency to make loans available to both member and nonmember banks. The loans could be secured by a variety of assets rather than narrowly defined eligible paper.[23] This reform authorized and indirectly encouraged the Federal Reserve to act as a true lender of last resort during any future banking crisis.

The Federal Reserve was also reorganized with major policymaking powers shifted from the individual Federal Reserve banks to a reconstituted Board of Governors in Washington, D.C. This reorganization gave the Fed a coherent national focus by reducing the autonomy of the twelve regional Federal Reserve banks. To provide a further increase in central power, a Federal Open Market Committee was established within the Federal Reserve. This committee was charged with the responsibility for conducting open market operations, that is, purchasing and selling market securities, with the objective of controlling the quantity of bank reserves in the economy. Beginning in the 1920s, the Federal Reserve had experimented informally with open-market operations but each Federal Reserve bank was free to pursue its own operations as it saw fit. The Banking Act of 1935 required the Federal Reserve banks to conduct only those open-market operations dictated by the Federal Open Market Committee. The committee itself was composed of the seven members of the Board of Governors and five of the twelve presidents of the Federal Reserve banks.[24] Thus, the Board of Governors in Washington, D.C. controlled a majority of the votes. As we shall see in Chapter 12, the Federal Open Market Committee has become the prime vehicle for the execution of monetary policy.

The constraint that the gold reserve requirement imposed on Federal Reserve notes and reserve liabilities was eased when the United States abandoned the gold standard in 1934. In that year, the government raised the price of gold by nearly 70 percent, that is, from $20.67 to $35 an ounce. The U.S. Treasury stood ready to purchase all the gold offered to it at the new price, but it ceased minting gold coins or issuing gold certificates. The Treasury paid for the gold with Federal Reserve notes or by checks drawn on the Fed.[25] Domestic monetary transactions

---

[23] This authority had been authorized initially in the Glass-Steagall Act of 1933, but it had not been fully used by the Federal Reserve.

[24] The twelve presidents of the Reserve Banks fill the five seats on a revolving basis that is described in Chapter 12.

[25] The mechanics of these transactions are discussed in Chapter 12.

in gold were forbidden. The Treasury would sell gold only for international transactions or for "legitimate" nonmonetary use such as gold teeth or jewelry. These steps produced a flood of gold into the U.S. Treasury, which in turn made gold available to the Fed to back currency and bank reserves. Gold backing for currency and reserves ceased to be a problem. Periodically since 1934, the gold reserve requirement did threaten to limit the Fed's activities. At those times the reserve requirements were reduced. Finally, in 1968 all gold reserve requirements were eliminated.

Reforms of the Banking System

There was general agreement in the 1930s that a major source of banking failures involved unsafe and unsound practices on the part of banks. Practices were discovered that involved unsavory, if not fraudulent, activity on the part of some bank officers and bank stockholders. These practices encompassed everything from large unsecured loans to bank officers to questionable loans granted to companies owned by bank officers or major stockholders. There were also instances where bank employees used funds obtained from bank loans to manipulate the prices of market securities. As a result, Congress placed severe restrictions on a bank's ability to lend to members of its boards of directors, bank officers, or other employees.

Prior to the 1930s, banks were allowed to underwrite securities and to act as brokers and dealers. Some banks bid up the prices of certain securities prior to selling them to the public or sold securities to the public when they had inside information that the firm involved was in financial trouble. In order to stop these and other practices, banks and their employees were forced to get out of the securities business.[26]

Legislation was also passed in 1935 to impose ceilings on the interest rates that banks could pay for their deposit liabilities. It was asserted that "destructive competition" among banks for deposit liabilities was a major cause of bank failures. According to this argument, competition among banks had pushed interest rates on deposit liabilities to unreasonable heights. Faced with these high interest costs, banks were forced to grant risky loans at high interest rates in order to earn profits. These risky loans fell into default in the early 1930s and many banks failed. It was concluded from this line of reasoning that if ceilings were imposed on the interest rates that banks paid for their liabilities, they would not be forced to acquire highly risky assets and, therefore, fewer banks would fail. Despite the

---

[26] Banks were allowed to continue some activities. For example, they could underwrite the general obligation bonds of state and local governments, they were allowed to serve as dealers for government securities, and they were not forced to give up their trust activities.

lack of evidence linking the interest rates paid on deposit liabilities to bank failures, Congress imposed interest rate ceilings. The Banking Act of 1935 prohibited any federally insured bank from paying interest on its demand deposit accounts. It also empowered the Comptroller of the Currency, the Board of Governors of the Federal Reserve, and the FDIC to impose interest rate ceilings on other bank liabilities.

The reforms of the 1930s were successful in eliminating banking panics and widespread bank failures. With the introduction of federal deposit insurance and with the reforms of the Federal Reserve System, stability of the banking system was finally achieved. The division of authority between federal and state regulators of banks and the division of regulatory authority among the three federal agencies have remained basically unchanged since the 1930s. The Monetary Reform Act of 1980 did extend reserve requirements to nonmember banks, however.

Over 150 years were required for the United States to settle on a division of authority between federal and state regulation of banks. The intrusion of the federal government into the regulatory process came slowly and grudgingly. The First and Second Banks of the United States were shortlived attempts to inject the federal government directly into banking and to use federal banks to regulate state-chartered banks. With the demise of the Second Bank of the United States, the federal government abandoned direct participation in the banking business in favor of enticement and coercion as methods of achieving regulatory control over private banks. National charters were offered to private banks, and federal control over national banks was achieved. Development of the national bank system was assured by imposing a tax on notes issued by state-chartered banks, which drove many out of business and induced others to convert to national charters. The growth of transactions accounts produced a resurgence of state-chartered banking. Thus, when the Federal Reserve was created, inducements were provided to encourage state-chartered banks to become members. Until the 1930s, however, most banks were still not regulated by the federal government. When federal deposit insurance was offered, virtually all remaining state-chartered banks came under federal jurisdiction.

Given the political resistance to a strong federal role in regulating banks, a slow and piecemeal approach was probably inevitable. History and politics explain why the process took so long and why there are three separate federal agencies involved in bank regulation. Together, the three agencies have regulatory power over virtually every bank in the country. This power was assumed, however, without depriving the states of authority to regulate the banks that they charter. The regulatory structure is messy but it does preserve states' rights while providing a strong federal presence. This division of responsibility between the federal government and the fifty state governments is called *dual banking*.

Space does not allow a discussion of the pros and cons of dual banking, and it does not allow a detailed account of the many regulations and supervisory standards that are currently applied to banks. Rather, the remainder of this chapter is devoted to a discussion of some economic consequences of bank regulation.

THE ECONOMIC CONSEQUENCES OF
BANK REGULATION

The primary objective of bank regulation is to achieve a safe and stable banking system in which panics and waves of bank failures are absent. Federal deposit insurance and an effective Federal Reserve are the ultimate sources of stability for the banking system. Bank regulation also plays a role, however. Federal and state regulators provide two types of safeguards against bank failures. The first type of safeguard involves supervising and regulating banks to make sure that they are not taking undue risks or engaging in other practices that endanger their depositors' money.[27] The regulators establish minimum net worth standards in order to limit leverage, require diversification of loans, limit the extent that banks can grant risky loans, establish minimum liquidity standards, and guard against fraudulent practices.

The second type of safeguard involves shielding banks from competition. When banks are restricted from competing actively for deposit balances or for loans, they are more profitable, and, hence, they are less likely to fail. Before we turn to the methods used to limit competition, it is useful to review the record of bank failures since the mid-1930s.

The regulatory reforms of the 1930s have been a resounding success in ensuring the safety and soundness of banks. Bank failures have been few and far between. The failures that have occurred are often the result of fraud or poor management. They usually involved small banks and, even in the very few cases where a large bank failed, the effects have not spread to other banks.

Table 9.4 summarizes failures of insured banks since the 1930s.[28] In the 46 years from 1934 through 1979, there were 566 bank failures, giving an annual failure rate of about 12 banks per year. Failures for 1934 through 1939 represent a final shakeout following the earlier economic collapse. Since 1940, the failure rate is approximately 6 banks per year. Over the period from 1940 to 1979, the aggregate quantity of deposit liabilities at failed banks was $5.76 billion. Thus, the average quantity of deposit liabilities at failed banks was approximately $144 million each year. Until the 1970s, the number was only about $21 million per year. In the 1970s, two large national banks failed. Their deposit liabilities comprised most of the deposit liabilities that were involved for the entire 46-year span.

The figures in Table 9.4 suggest that bank failures have ceased to be an important factor in the United States. Even these figures overstate the economic consequences of bank failure. In virtually every case, the FDIC was able to arrange either a merger or a takeover of the bank's major assets and liabilities so that service

[27] Because the FDIC insures the first $100,000 of each customer's deposit balances, the regulators are protecting the FDIC against losses as well as large depositors.
[28] From 1934 to 1979, 136 noninsured banks failed, with total deposit liabilities of $136 million.

TABLE 9.4
FAILURES OF INSURED BANKS (1934–1979)

Years	Number of Banks	Deposits (millions of dollars)
1934–39	315	$ 294
1940–49	100	236
1950–59	31	103
1960–69	44	287
1970–79	76	5,129
Total	566	$6,049

Source: Federal Deposit Insurance Corporation, *Annual Reports.*

to the community was not interrupted.[29] Even the two largest banking failures in U.S. history, San Diego National Bank in 1973 and Franklin National Bank in 1974, were handled without any interruption of services. The two banks were simply closed at the end of the business day, and the next day service was resumed under the name of another bank. It would not be stretching the point to say that, since 1933, bank failures have had no important consequences for the economy. There were, of course, consequences for stockholders who sustained losses and, very infrequently, for holders of large accounts that exceeded the FDIC insurance limit. These losses were important to these individuals, but they had no important implications for the banking system or for the economy.

Some observers assert that the low failure rate among banks has undesirable consequences. It is asserted that although government protection of banks limits failure, it stifles competition and innovation in banking. The merits of this assertion are discussed further on, but a few comments at this point might clarify the issues.

One effective way to assure the safety of banks is to limit the competition among them. Banks that do not have to contend with the rigors of competition for deposit liabilities and loans should, other things equal, find it much easier to survive. Government restrictions on bank competition have taken several forms. The entry of new competitors is restricted or blocked by the chartering policies of federal and state regulators. Limits on merger and branching activity can have the effect of protecting the profits of existing banks rather than enhancing competition. Finally, interest rate ceilings limit competition among banks, for deposit liabilities.

When government policies stifle competition among banks, the public can be the loser. Limitations on competition allow banks to charge higher interest rates on their loans, allow them to pay lower interest rates for deposit accounts, and

---

[29] Timely mergers reduce or eliminate the need for the FDIC to use its insurance reserves to protect depositors.

reduce the incentive for banks to provide a full range of services to their customers. The stated intent of federal and state regulations is not to produce high interest rates for loans, low interest rates for deposit accounts, or inadequate banking services. Rather, regulations are rationalized on the grounds that greater competion among banks would threaten the viability and soundness of many banks. Government regulatory policies favor competition so long as it is deemed compatible with a low rate of bank failure.

In order to appreciate the issues involved, we may find it useful to note that a trade-off between the benefits of vigorous bank competition and the benefits of having few bank failures is not a logical necessity. With the establishment of deposit insurance, the social and macroeconomic consequences of bank failures are greatly reduced. When an individual bank fails, all but the largest depositors are fully protected. As a result, deposit insurance removes the incentive of smaller depositors at sound banks to make withdrawals. Thus, banking panics are averted. Large depositors are only partially protected, however, so a bank failure could trigger panicked withdrawal by large depositors at sound banks. Under the current system, these withdrawals do not occur because large depositors know that it is unlikely their bank will be allowed to fail. If a bank encounters liquidity problems, the Federal Reserve will step in and provide loans. Even if a bank is no longer viable, it is likely to be merged into another bank before the accounts of large depositors are threatened. Thus, the current system provides total insurance protection to small depositors and regulatory assurances to large depositors that banks will not be allowed to fail.[30]

In principle, a great deal of regulatory interference could be eliminated if all deposit accounts were insured. With 100 percent insurance of deposit liabilities, banks could be allowed to compete to their hearts' content, and the failure of one bank would not result in panicked withdrawals of funds from other banks. Thus, the safety of the banking *system* would be independent of the solvency of each individual bank in the system. With total insurance, the economic benefits of increased competition could be achieved without endangering the stability of the banking system. These considerations have led some observers to advocate 100 percent deposit insurance coupled with deregulation of banks.

This proposal has some appeal, but it has some serious drawbacks. Without regulation, bank failures would probably increase significantly, resulting in inconvenience and costs to depositors and borrowers, who would have to find new banks. This problem could be alleviated by encouraging mergers between failing and healthy banks. Unfortunately, mergers often take substantial time unless expedited by the regulators. Furthermore, claims on the FDIC's insurance fund could increase significantly, requiring a substantial increase in assessments on banks. Finally, it is possible that if small banks were not protected, large banks would either take them over by merger or force them to fail.

---

[30] Or, in the rare instance when a bank fails, that large depositors will not be injured.

It is difficult to assess the degree to which deregulation of banks would increase the incidence of bank failures. There are some built-in safeguards in the absence of government regulation. Stockholders would not want to see their investments in banks wiped out, so they would insist that risk taking be limited.[31] Furthermore, bank managers want to keep their jobs and would strive to maintain bank soundness. Despite these stabilizing influences, bank failures would tend to rise in the absence of government regulation. The extent of the increase in bank failures could be controlled, however, by having the FDIC charge insurance premiums that are commensurate with bank risk. Highly leveraged banks, banks with concentrations of risky loans, or illiquid banks would pay a higher insurance premium than less risky banks. If the premiums were commensurate with the risk to the FDIC, banks would have an incentive to reduce their risk taking in order to pay a lower premium. This would reduce the incidence of failures.

Even if insurance premiums could be used to limit the incidence of bank failures, we are still left with the problem of small versus large banks. Preserving small banks has a long history in the United States. It should be noted, however, that it is by no means obvious that many small banks would be unable to compete successfully with large banks in the absence of many regulations. Small banks frequently offer more personalized services than their bureaucratic big brothers, and these services are attractive to many customers. Notwithstanding the possibility that many small banks could compete successfully against large banks in a deregulated environment, the fear that they would be unsuccessful has motivated much of bank regulation that limits competition.

Current regulatory procedures attempt to achieve stability of the banking system by maintaining the viability of each individual bank in the system. If one determines that the benefits of increased competition among banks are outweighed by undesirable side effects, then the current regulatory approach may be justified. If one believes that the benefits of increased competition outweigh the potential costs, then the current approach is questionable.

The remainder of this chapter discusses how existing laws and regulations limit competition among banks and how they produce the large number of banks that operate in the United States. It is also shown how many banks are able to compete vigorously despite the restrictions. This occurs, in part, because banks circumvent regulations designed to limit competition.

Chartering

The office of the Comptroller of the Currency approves charters for new national banks and the regulators of the fifty states approve charters for state-chartered banks. The FDIC and the Federal Reserve do not grant charters, and they are re-

---

[31] This assumes that bank stockholders are risk averse. If they are risk neutral or risk loving, they will not want to limit risk.

quired to accept national banks for insurance and for membership in the Federal Reserve System. The FDIC and Fed do have latitude when it comes to state-chartered banks, however. The FDIC determines whether a state-chartered institution meets its standards for federal insurance. It is possible for a new bank to be acceptable to its state regulator but unacceptable to the FDIC. In states that require FDIC insurance for banks, the FDIC can, in effect, veto state charters. In other states, the bank can be chartered but it is deprived of federal insurance. This prospect is sufficiently unattractive to founders of almost all new banks that they will not operate as an uninsured bank. Thus, the FDIC usually has the final word in the chartering of state-chartered banks. The Federal Reserve does not have this degree of power over new state-chartered banks. It can decline membership in the Federal Reserve System to the bank, but membership is rarely a major factor. Beginning in 1980, the Federal Reserve was required to make its services available to nonmember institutions, so membership is not a key issue to state-chartered banks.

Federal and state chartering laws establish requirements as to minimum net worth and the qualifications of banking management. Federal law requires that the federal agencies consider several additional factors when determining whether to grant a charter or to insure a new bank. Most important among these are the potential safety and soundness of a new bank, the needs of the community served by a new bank, and the implications for existing banks of having another competitor in the market. Standards vary among the states, but most are similar to those of the federal government. These standards provide the regulators with considerable latitude for granting or rejecting applications for new charters. The attitudes of regulators concerning new charters have varied over the years, but with the exception of the 1960s, when many new charters were issued, by and large, regulators have acted to restrict the number of new entrants into banking.

In most other industries, entry of new firms is not controlled by the government. Entry occurs when private individuals expect their investment in a new firm to earn them an attractive rate of return. The government does not concern itself with the potential profitability of the new firm or with the possible effects of entry on the profits of existing firms. The basic philosophy guiding the absence of government interference is that the marketplace should determine the profitability of new and existing firms. The philosophy is quite different when it comes to banks. The chartering laws assert, in essence, that the decisions of the market are not enough. It is presumed that investors want to take more risk than is socially desirable. Thus, regulators attempt to avoid the possibility that a new bank may fail by preventing it from ever going into business. Only if the new bank is highly likely to succeed will it be given a charter. There is also concern that the entry of a new bank will adversely affect the profitability of existing banks. The new entrant does not care what happens to the profitability of its competitors and, in fact, would be delighted to see the competitors become less profitable if it could become more profitable. Bank regulators are charged with the obligation of protecting both the new entrant and existing banks. If increased competition from entry reduces the profitability of existing banks, then the regulators can refuse to grant a charter. Thus, bank regulators protect the safety of new and existing banks by limiting entry into banking. This can have undesirable consequences. When existing banks do not fear the entry of new banks, they can monopolize their markets by paying low interest rates on their deposit accounts, charging high interest rates on their loans, and providing inferior services.

Merger Laws

The second major weapon in the regulators' arsenal for affecting competition among banks is control over bank mergers. Federal law empowered the Comptroller of the Currency, the Federal Reserve Board, and the FDIC to approve or reject mergers of banks falling under their jurisdictions. Thus, virtually all bank mergers fall under the jurisdiction of the federal government.[32] In acting upon a proposed merger, the regulators are required to consider the following factors for each bank involved: its financial history and condition, the adequacy of its net worth, its future earning prospects, the general conduct of its management, and the convenience and needs of the community to be served. The regulators are also required to take into consideration the effect of the merger on competition, including any tendencies towards monopoly. As a grand finale, they are empowered to approve only those mergers that are deemed to be in the public interest.

This list should convey some of the trials and tribulations of being a bank regulator. The regulators are to approve mergers that enhance safety and soundness, that avoid monopolizing behavior, and that are in the public interest. This is a tall order that involves weighing the possible benefits of merging a weak institution into a stronger one against the possible costs of an increase in monopoly power of the newly enlarged bank.

The problem is compounded because the term *tendency toward monopoly* is not well defined. For example, the merger of a number of small banks may create a large bank that is able to compete more effectively against large banks than could the small banks. In this case an increased concentration of deposit balances and assets in the newly merged bank does not represent an increase in monopoly power. In other cases, bank mergers can increase monopoly power.

Faced with the conflicting objectives of the merger law and the ambiguity of the term *tendency toward monopoly,* the banking authorities have tended to discourage mergers. Mergers are most likely to be approved if a bank shows signs that it might fail. Because mergers of healthy banks are often discouraged, many small banks continue to operate even though they are attractive candidates for mergers with other banks.

---

[32] State regulators are consulted concerning mergers involving state-chartered banks.

Branch Banking

Intrastate Branching

States' rights won over federal jurisdiction when it came to branching laws and regulations. In essence, each of the fifty states has its own branching laws and federal regulators are required to apply those laws to the banks under their jurisdiction.

The issue of branching has generated considerable acrimony and controversy throughout U.S. banking history. Fears concerning the power of a few large banks with vast branching systems have in many instances won out over efficiency and other considerations that argue for the existence of branching networks. The degree of concern over these issues varies greatly from state to state, however. In some states, such as Illinois, branching is severely restricted. At the opposite extreme are states like California that allow statewide branching. There are many different configurations among the fifty states. Some states allow only countywide branching, and others allow a bank to establish a branch only if the branch is not located in the vicinity of the head office of some other bank. It does not serve our purpose to give a detailed listing of all the configurations, although they do make enjoyable reading for someone with a perverse sense of humor.

In order to evaluate the branching question, we must discuss the economic issues involved. A branch of a bank is simply an office through which a bank transacts depository and other business. The head office of a bank typically provides a full range of services, and its branches perform the more specialized services required of the local community. There is no requirement or necessity for a branch to offer all services. For example, branches in suburban areas are primarily institutions that gather the deposit balances of suburban families and local merchants. These branches do relatively little lending and provide few special functions, such as foreign exchange transactions or trust account activities. Branches in commercial areas do a great deal of lending and engage in a number of specialized activities, but they receive relatively few deposit balances from households. There is no requirement that an individual branch balance its loans against its deposit balances or in any other way act as if it were a complete bank. Thus, a bank may have one branch with rapid growth in deposit balances but weak loan demand and another branch with strong loan demand and slow growth in deposit balances. This situation creates no problem because the head office can match the loan demand at one branch with the growth in deposit balances at another branch.

If a bank is prevented from establishing a branch in a particular locality, the alternative is for individuals to establish a *unit bank*. A unit bank is a bank with only one office. It is often much more difficult to establish a profitable unit bank in a community than it is to establish a branch. The costs of a unit bank tend to be higher and it must rely primarily upon the business of the local community for its profits. Given the greater profitability of branches, it is not surprising that many banks strongly favor laws and regulations that would allow them to establish branches freely. It is also not surprising that unit banks that already exist in a community are at least equally opposed to branching.

The branching laws of many states can be interpreted as protecting relatively small unit banks against the competition of branching networks.[33] It is often argued that if branching were less restricted, the giants would force small banks out of business. The community would suffer because the larger bank could then monopolize markets. Furthermore, because large institutions tend to be bureaucratic and impersonal, they cannot meet the specialized needs of the community. These same concerns have been voiced about a number of industries, including supermarkets, department stores, and drug store chains. The government does not prevent these businesses from operating out of many locations, but it does prevent banks from establishing branches.

If states that now prevent branch banking were to allow branching, the number of unit banks would decline. The cost of operating small unit banks is simply higher than the cost of maintaining an equal number of branches. It is less clear that the quality of banking services would diminish. Some of the most notorious cases of monopoly practices by banks can be found in areas with only one unit bank. Unit banks often do not fear entry of other banks into their market because of chartering and branching restrictions so they can exert a great deal of monopoly power.

It is erroneous to believe that statewide branching will necessarily lead to only a few banks. The state of California, for example, is dominated by four large banks, but there are over 250 banks operating in the state. There are nearly 1300 banks operating in Illinois and more than 1400 banks in Texas, but California has more offices per capita than do either Illinois or Texas.

These comparisons are not intended to extoll the virtues of large branching systems. There is legitimate reason for concern that, without some restrictions, deposit balances and loans could become highly concentrated in a few banks. This concern, however, is probably better handled by active use of the antitrust laws than through the patchwork quilt of state laws concerning branching.

One reason for making this assertion is to point out that if the goal of existing restrictions on new charters, mergers, and branching is to limit concentration of resources in banking, the efforts have not been very successful. Despite the multitude of small banks in the United States, most assets are concentrated in a small fraction of these banks. Table 9.5 shows the distribution of banking assets among banks of various size classes for 1979. In that year, 42 percent of all bank assets in the United States were held by the 33 banks with total assets in excess of $5 billion. Over 60 percent of all bank assets were held by the 186 banks with total assets in excess of $1 billion. These 186 banks constitute slightly over 1 percent of all the banks in the country. By contrast, 54 percent of all banks in the United

---

[33] Restrictions against branching can also make it difficult for the regulators to arrange a merger between a failing bank and a strong bank if, after the merger, the failing bank is prevented from operating as a branch.

TABLE 9.5
DISTRIBUTION OF TOTAL ASSETS BY SIZE OF BANK (1979)

Bank Asset Size (millions of dollars)	Number of Banks	Percent of Total	Total Assets (billions of dollars)	Percent of Total
Less than $5	1,104	7.5	$ 3,264	0.2
$ 5 –$ 9.9	2,147	14.6	16,248	0.9
$ 10 –$ 24.9	4,745	32.2	79,248	4.6
$ 25 –$ 49.9	3,378	22.9	119,503	6.9
$ 50 –$ 99.9	1,772	12.0	122,684	7.1
$100 –$299.9	1,071	7.3	171,569	10.0
$300 –$499.9	178	1.2	69,856	4.1
$500 –$999.9	157	1.1	105,607	6.1
$ 1.0–$ 4.9 billion	153	1.0	311,938	18.1
Over $5.0 billion	33	0.2	724,077	42.0
	14,738	100.0	$1,723,994	100.0

Source: 1979 FDIC *Annual Report*.

States have total assets of less than $25 million, yet these banks account for only 5.7 percent of all the bank assets in the country. One can hardly conclude from these data that the chartering, merger and branching laws have avoided concentration of resources in a relatively few banks.

Interstate Branching

Interstate branching is prohibited by federal and state law unless, through mutual agreement, individual states allow banks from other states to operate in their jurisdictions. Currently, a reciprocal agreement concerning interstate branching is in effect among the New England states; Maine has a reciprocal agreement with New York; and the states of Alaska and South Dakota allow banks from other states to operate within their borders. With the exception of these state-initiated cases of interstate branching, banks cannot cross state borders.

There is no other industry that is required by federal law to stop its activities at a stateline. Other depository institutions such as federally chartered savings and loan associations are not required by federal law to follow the branching laws of the states in which they reside. In fact, U.S. economic history has been marked by a breaking down of state barriers to allow nationwide markets for products and services. Banks have been unable to follow this trend.

In October 1982, Congress took a tiny step toward allowing interstate banking. If an insured bank with assets over $500 million fails and if no buyer can be found among banks in the state, an out-of-state bank or bank holding company can purchase it. The standards for acquisition by an out-of-state institution are stringent, and the law expires after three years. It remains to be seen whether this is a step toward interstate banking or the law is simply an expedient method of allowing the FDIC to dispose of some banks that are difficult to sell locally.

The criticism of interstate restrictions are essentially the same as for intrastate restrictions. The reason for treating interstate restrictions separately is to illustrate how easy it is for large banks to get around the restrictions. The ability to circumvent branching laws explains why such a high percentage of total assets in the banking system is concentrated in a relatively few large banks.

Many markets in which large banks operate are nationwide and even worldwide. For these markets, it is impossible to stop banking activities within a state or at state lines. For example, all large banks issue large denomination CDs that are sold on a national market and, in varying degrees, on regional markets. Information on the interest rates that a bank is paying on its CDs is readily available from the bank itself or from dealers. Anyone can buy these certificates irrespective of where the purchaser resides. For example, the large New York banks sell CDs to residents of New York, Illinois, Texas, and California and other parts of the country. Large banks in other states do the same thing. Thus, the market for CDs is nationwide, and banks are able to sell these liabilities any place they choose.[34] The major market for CDs is located in New York, but a purchaser need only make a telephone call to a dealer in order to make a purchase. Just as a California resident can buy stock on the New York Stock Exchange and a New York resident can buy stock on the Pacific Stock Exchange, these individuals can purchase CDs from any bank in the country.

Interstate and intrastate activities are not restricted to CDs. Large banks are often the lead bank for loans to major corporations. The lead bank sells participations in these loans to banks in various parts of the country. Loan participations allow banks all over the country to take part in loans originated in such cities as New York, San Francisco, or Chicago. Furthermore, large banks operate special offices in all major cities where they solicit loan business. Because these offices do not accept deposit balances, they are exempt from branching laws. Thus, a New York bank through its offices in San Francisco or Los Angeles can arrange a loan to a California airplane manufacturer or electronics firm while at the same time a California bank is arranging a loan to a major New York corporation. Finally, the federal funds market links together all the banks in the country. Small banks tend to be lenders in this market, and large banks tend to be borrowers. Thus, many small banks in Illinois or Texas lend funds to large banks in the nation's financial centers.

The implication of all this interstate activity is that when it comes to large banks and their corporate customers, there really are no effective restrictions to banking within a state or across state lines. Major corporations purchase bank liabilities or borrow from any location in the country. Large banks issue liabilities and lend

---

[34] Intrastate restrictions also do not affect sales of CDs. A Chicago or Houston bank can sell CDs to residents of Illinois or Texas even though these banks cannot establish branches in their states.

any place in the country. This has allowed large banks to expand whereas small banks have to rely on the deposit balances provided by local customers. It is not surprising that assets are concentrated in large banks.

The real restrictions on intrastate and interstate branching involve the activities of consumers and small businesses. They lack the resources to purchase CDs and other money market instruments, and they cannot borrow through the offices established by large banks for major corporations. It is small business and consumers who bear the brunt of restrictions on branching. If we weigh the benefits and costs of retaining restrictions on branching against removing the restrictions, the major consideration must be whether or not consumers and smaller businesses will benefit or suffer.

Limitations on the Payment of Interest on Deposit Liabilities

Not only are banks adept at circumventing branching laws, but they also learned to avoid restrictions concerning competition for deposit liabilities. As mentioned earlier, interest ceilings were imposed during the 1930s in an effort to eliminate so-called destructive competition as a cause of bank failure. Subsequent research indicates that banks that were paying relatively high rates of interest did not tend to be the banks that failed. The major sources of bank failures in the 1930s were liquidity crises and massive loan defaults. The payment of interest on deposits was not an important factor in these failures. Despite these findings, ceilings on interest rates for deposit liabilities have remained a part of bank regulation.

The experience with interest rate ceilings gives a valuable lesson in the futility of these devices. These restrictions were put in place because it was feared that banks could not "afford" interest rate competition. Competition was not eliminated, however; it simply squirted out in the relatively inefficient form of nonprice competition and in the development of new instruments. Nonprice competition increased the costs of deposit liabilities without increasing deposit balances commensurately. Competition from securities markets and money market mutual funds forced banks to develop competitive instruments. Efforts to protect bank profits by limiting their interest expense do not work. This lesson was finally learned and interest rate ceilings for most types of bank liabilities were eliminated in the early 1980s.

BANK HOLDING COMPANIES

Bank holding companies have become a major element in the American banking scene, and their activities have allowed many banks to circumvent regulations even further. Perhaps the best way to explain a holding company is to describe its historical roots. Prior to bank holding companies, organizations were formed called *banking chains*. A banking chain represented an early attempt to achieve the economies of branching without, in fact, establishing branches. An individual or group of individuals who owned stock in a number of banks would induce the various banks to coordinate activities. Coordination involved shifting loans from one bank to another, having one bank extend loans to another, and in other ways behaving like a branch system. Chain banking enhanced the profitability of the various banks, but each bank in the system was still required to be an ongoing, profitable institution on its own. Despite this restriction, some of the benefits of branching were achieved.

The next step was to coordinate the activities of a number of banks through a separate corporation that owned the stock of the individual banks. This corporation is known as a *holding company*.[35] Holding companies that control a number of banks can achieve some of the benefits of branch banking in states where actual branching is restricted.[36] Some states such as Texas do not restrict activities of multibank holding companies and other states such as Illinois simply prohibit their operation. Holding companies have become an effective means of circumventing branching restrictions in most states.

Some of the initial popularity of bank holding companies stemmed from their ability to operate banks in more than one state. Until 1956 a holding company could achieve some of the benefits of interstate branching by owning banks in more than one state. It could also engage in nonbanking activities through its nonbank subsidiaries. This included owning manufacturing and retail corporations.

By 1956 sufficient concern was expressed over the growing power of holding companies that Congress passed the Bank Holding Company Act. That act prevented any further acquisitions of banks across state lines, and it prohibited bank holding companies from owning companies that were not engaged in bank-related activities. Holding companies that already controlled banks in more than one state were allowed to continue to own shares in those banks. Holding companies that owned shares in companies engaged in nonbank-related activities were forced to divest their interests although exceptions were granted. With this act, further expansion into interstate banking through holding companies was stopped and banks could not be affiliated with nonbanking firms. Intrastate operations of holding companies continued.

Congress explicitly exempted *one-bank holding companies* from the provisions of the act. It was argued that in many small towns a bank would not be viable unless it could combine its activities with those of other enterprises, such as a local real estate or insurance agency. These activities were often controlled by a holding

---

[35] Holding companies are corporations and, therefore, have limited liability. Coordination of banks through chains did not have this advantage. Furthermore, a holding company can issue stocks and bonds to raise funds to acquire additional banks or to channel funds to existing banks in the holding company.

[36] It is not necessary for a holding company to own all the stock in a bank to control its activities. Often ownership of 25 percent or less of the stock is sufficient.

company. The exemption of one-bank holding companies from the 1956 law gained the support of a number of banks and entrepreneurs located in small towns.

One-bank holding companies did not gain national significance until 1966. Beginning in that year, the largest banks in the country began to convert into one-bank holding companies. Conversion was easy. The bank simply exchanged its stock for stock in the holding company. Private investors sent in their bank stock and were issued stock in the holding company. The holding company owned the bank's stock. This transfer was more than just legal hocus-pocus. A bank, through its holding company, could operate in a number of areas in which the bank itself was excluded. In 1966, there were interest rate ceilings on all liabilities of banks, including large CDs. Large banks hit on the clever idea of setting up one-bank holding companies that issued their own liabilities at market interest rates. The holding company then lent the funds to the bank. Bank holding companies are not banks and, hence, are not subject to interest rate ceilings on their liabilities. This allowed the banks to circumvent the interest rate ceilings. The ceiling for these liabilities became unenforceable, and the regulators subsequently suspended interest rate ceilings for large CDs.

Over a period of a few months, virtually every large bank in the United States formed a one-bank holding company. Thus, a loophole that was originally intended to apply only to small banks ended up being used by large banks. The only banks, in fact, that were precluded from becoming one-bank holding companies were those that were already members of multibank companies.

The loophole for one-bank holding companies also allowed large banks to operate in virtually any area they chose. For example, the historic division between banking and commerce that prevents banks from engaging in manufacturing or commercial activities was breached. This raised the specter that, in principle, a one-bank holding company could own both General Motors and Bank of America, so long as the stockholders of those two corporations agreed that it was in their interest to combine the firms. This possibility caused great concern, but it took Congress several years to determine how best to close the loophole. Perhaps in anticipation of congressional action, one-bank holding companies did not engage widely in nonfinancial activities.

In 1970, Congress finally closed the loophole with the One-Bank Holding Company Act. This act, in essence, subjected one-bank holding companies to the same restrictions as multibank holding companies. Thus, it was no longer possible for a single holding company to own both a manufacturing company and a bank.[37] Furthermore, for both multi-bank holding companies and the one-bank holding companies, Congress asserted certain guiding principles concerning the activities into which holding company subsidiaries could enter. The restrictions are some-

---

[37] A similar loophole was not closed for savings and loan associations. To this day, steel companies and insurance companies own S&Ls.

what complex but the essence of them is embedded in the principle that banks and their holding companies can engage only in "bank-related" activities.

Rather uncharacteristically, Congress appointed the Federal Reserve as the *single* agency to administer the holding company acts. The reader should not get too excited by this bit of consolidation of authority because the Federal Reserve has exclusive jurisdiction only over nonbank subsidiaries of the holding company and the holding company itself. The Fed also has authority to regulate the financial transactions that occur between a bank and other elements of the holding company. A bank or banks in the holding company are regulated as always; that is, the Federal Reserve has jurisdiction over state member banks whereas the Comptroller of the Currency and the FDIC have jurisdiction over the national and state-nonmember banks that are members of holding companies.

The Federal Reserve was given the duty of determining specifically what are bank-related activities. The Fed did not simply supply a list of allowable activities, but rather often waited for holding companies to ask for authority to engage in some activity or for some party to challenge the right of a holding company to engage in an activity. The Federal Reserve then determined whether the activity was allowable or not. Those activities that have been judged neither allowable nor nonallowable are, of course, in limbo. The list of allowable and unallowable activities is enumerated in Table 9.6.

Inspection of the contents of the table indicates that virtually all the activities that are allowed for holding companies are also permitted for a bank itself. One might wonder, then, why banks have chosen to engage in certain activities through a nonbank subsidiary of a holding company rather than through the bank itself. The primary reason is to avoid regulation.

For example, banks are allowed to execute orders placed by their customers for acquisitions of stocks, bonds and other securities, but they cannot offer investment advice or actively solicit business. These restrictions are the result of the Glass-Steagall Act of 1933, which barred banks from being in the securities business. The restrictions were not too onerous until the mid- and late 1970s, when brokerage firms, insurance companies, and money market mutual funds combined forces to offer a highly attractive array of financial services to the public. This put banks at a competitive disadvantage, and they lost many customers. The banks retaliated in 1982 by acquiring discount stock brokerage firms through their holding companies. These firms do not offer investment advice, so their acquisition is not in direct violation of the Glass-Steagall Act. They do actively solicit business. These acquisitions were approved by the Federal Reserve Board, and banks were able to compete more aggressively with nonbank financial intermediaries.

As another example, bank holding companies are allowed to engage in the consumer finance business, and, of course, banks also lend to consumers. Banks, however, are restricted in their ability to open offices to serve consumers. In a unit banking state, the only office available is the main office, and even in states without branching restrictions, the offices must stop at state lines. By operating a finance company as a subsidiary of a holding company, rather than lending to

TABLE 9.6
APPROVED AND DISAPPROVED ACTIVITIES FOR BANK
HOLDING COMPANIES

Activities Approved	Activities Denied
Extensions of credit	Insurance premuim funding
Mortgage banking	(combined sales of mutual
Finance companies: consumer, sales, and	funds and insurance)
commercial	Underwriting life insurance not
Credit cards	related to credit extension
Factoring	Real estate brokerage
Industrial bank, Morris Plan bank, industrial	Land development
loan company	Real estate syndication
Servicing loans and other extensions of credit	General management consulting
Trust company	Property management
Investment or financial advising	Computer output microfilm
Full-payout leasing of personal and real	services
property	Underwriting mortgage guaranty
Investments in community welfare projects	insurance
Providing bookkeeping or data-processing	Operating a travel agency
services	
Acting as insurance agent or broker, primarily	
in connection with credit extensions	
Underwriting credit life, accident, and health	
insurance	
Providing courier services	
Management consulting for unaffiliated banks	
Issuance and sale of traveler's checks	
Buying and selling gold and silver bullion and	
service coin	
Issuing money orders and general-purpose,	
variable, denominated payment instruments	
Futures commission merchant to cover gold	
and silver bullion and coins	
Underwriting certain federal, state, and	
municipal securities	

consumers through a banking office, the holding company can open offices anywhere it chooses.[38] This is allowable under current law because a finance company does not accept deposit accounts and, therefore, is not considered to be a bank or a branch. Similar stories of how a bank holding company can circumvent

[38] The Federal Reserve has, at times, limited the locations in which a finance company subsidiary of a holding company can operate. These limitations are imposed in order to stop potential monopoly practices and have nothing to do with branching laws.

restrictions on branching can be told about leasing companies, credit credit operations, and other activities.[39]

Many more examples could be given, but the point is that the holding company movement represents a response to the restrictions on the activities of banks. Some observers want to curtail or eliminate bank holding companies because they believe their activities erode the effects of bank regulation. Other observers believe that holding companies are beneficial because they provide banks a means of circumventing laws that have little or no social value. There can be little doubt that the activities of bank holding companies have helped erode the significance of the laws and regulations. It is also probably true that it is impossible to control the activities of banks to the extent that some critics would desire. If additional restrictions are put on banks and their holding companies, these institutions are likely to develop new methods of circumventing the regulations.

SUMMARY

This chapter has described the historical process that established regulatory control over banks and achieved stability for the banking system. This historical process explains the complex division of authority among the several regulatory agencies, and it helps explain why banks are subject to so many regulatory restrictions.

Prior to the establishment of greenbacks and national bank notes in the 1860s, there was no national currency in the United States. Notes issued by individual banks circulated along with specie as media of exchange. Specie and notes were often not physically held by the public but deposited in banks. Thus, much of the money in the economy was either issued by banks as notes or held by banks. This meant that the safety of notes and deposit balances was no greater than the safety of the individual banks that issued the notes or accepted deposits. When a bank failed or when it refused convertibility of its notes and deposit account liabilities into specie, the public saw its money rendered worthless. It was natural, therefore, to associate the safety of money with the safety of the individual banks issuing money. This explains the efforts of the states and of the federal government to regulate and control banks. It also explains why the federal government established national bank notes and a national system of banks.

When the federal government stopped issuing greenbacks after the Civil War, the nation's money was composed primarily of gold and silver certificates plus national bank notes. State-chartered banks no longer issued notes because of the tax that the federal government imposed. It appeared that money was finally safe be-

---

[39] In 1982, the Federal Reserve Board allowed Citicorp, the holding company for Citibank of New York, to acquire Fidelity Savings and Loan of California, which had failed. This may open the door for further acquisitions of S&Ls across state lines.

cause the Comptroller of the Currency guaranteed the safety of national bank notes should a national bank fail. Furthermore, failures were considered unlikely because the activities of national banks were heavily regulated.

The national bank system did not succeed in making money safe because the safety of bank account balances was not assured. State-chartered banks expanded rapidly using the vehicle of transactions account liabilities, and national banks also increased their account liabilities. This meant that when a bank failed or encountered liquidity problems, it could not honor currency withdrawals from its accounts. Once again the public was faced with worthless money (bank accounts), and panics developed. Solutions were sought in further restrictions on the activities of individual banks. As before, it was argued that with increased restrictions, banks would be less likely to fail and, therefore, depositors were less likely to be injured. These efforts did not succeed because banking panics were the result of insufficient liquidity, not irresponsible bankers.

The banking panic of 1907 led to the establishment of the Federal Reserve in 1914. The Federal Reserve issued currency and was instructed to provide currency to liquidity-starved banks during panics. Through loans to banks and convertibility of bank reserve accounts into currency, the Fed was to eliminate bank instability. There were fatal flaws in the original design of the Federal Reserve System, however. Since the Federal Reserve was a bank for bankers, it was required to operate on a "safe and sound" basis. It had collateral and reserve requirements for the issuance of currency and for its reserve account liabilities. Furthermore, only national banks were required to be members of the Federal Reserve System. Membership was optional for state-chartered banks. Most of these banks did not become members and were not directly touched by the central bank.

The great crash of 1929 and the banking collapse that followed revealed that the efforts at banking reform were ineffectual. The massive number of bank failures in the early 1930s demonstrated once and for all that in a liquidity crisis no bank is necessarily sound. Furthermore, in a liquidity crisis the Federal Reserve cannot act like a private bank, prudently dispensing loans and cautiously limiting the amount currency it issues.

These lessons were finally learned, and two fundamental reforms occurred in the 1930s. First, bank accounts were insured by the federal government so that bank failures would not hurt small depositors. As a result, runs on solvent banks were avoided. Second, the Federal Reserve was converted into an effective central bank responsible for providing currency and bank reserves during a panic.

With the reforms of the 1930s, a regulatory structure was established that remains to this day. The federal government has regulatory control over virtually every bank in the country. The office of the Comptroller of the Currency has jurisdiction over national banks, the Federal Reserve has jurisdiction over member banks, and the FDIC has jurisdiction over all federally insured banks. State regulators have jurisdiction over all banks that are not national banks. Thus, there is substantial overlapping of authority. The various regulatory agencies attempt to coordinate their activities in order to avoid conflicts and duplication of effort.

With these reforms, the safety and soundness of the banking system do not require the safety and soundness of each bank in the system. The safety of the banking system is assured by the FDIC and the Fed. These assurances are available even if individual banks fail. Bank regulation continues to stress the need to protect individual banks from failure, however. Old ideas die hard, and it is natural for regulators to feel responsible for protecting "their" banks from failure. This attitude persists despite the fact that deposit insurance eliminates most of the undesirable consequences of bank failure. The FDIC protects its insurance fund by limiting claims on the fund.

Bank regulation today is still concerned with ensuring the safety and soundness of individual banks. The bank regulators are highly successful in preventing bank failures. Some regulations, such as requirements for minimum net worth, liquidity, and asset diversification, involve limiting risk taking by banks. This form of regulation is probably necessary in order to limit claims on the FDIC's insurance fund. Short of imposing insurance premiums that are commensurate with the riskiness of each bank, the FDIC and other regulators probably have to limit risk taking by banks. Claims on the insurance fund have been small because of these regulations and because weak banks are merged with stronger banks before failure occurs.

Many regulations are not designed to limit risk taking, however. Rather, they are designed to protect banks and bank profits by limiting competition. These controversial restrictions have reduced bank failures. Bank regulation restricts entry of new banks into the industry by limiting the number of new charters that are granted. Regulation further limits competition by restricting intrastate branching in many states as well as interstate branching. Regulation also limits competition by prohibiting the payment of interest on demand deposit accounts and limiting the interest rate that can be paid on certain other kinds of accounts.

These restrictions on competition are motivated by the desire to avoid bank failures and to protect small banks from large banks. There is considerable disagreement about the need to protect banks from failure to the degree that has been accomplished since the 1930s. There is also disagreement about the desirability of protecting small banks from large banks. Irrespective of how one feels about these matters, many regulations do limit competition in banking.

One reason that bank deregulation has not received the attention that one might expect is that large banks have succeeded in circumventing many of the anticompetitive regulations. Through sales of liabilities in national markets and through operation of loan offices, large banks have the near equivalent of nationwide branching for their large corporate customers. Through liability management and through the activities of affiliates of holding companies, large banks have also avoided restrictions on interest rates for many types of liabilities. Restrictions on bank mergers often do not stand in the way of expansion of large banks, they expand by other means. Large banks control most of the banking resources in the United States, but small banks still flourish. Some small banks prosper because of restrictions on competition; others prosper because they offer a competitive product to the public.

It appears that households and small business have been the primary losers from anticompetitive bank regulation. Considerable pressure has been exerted on Congress and state legislatures in recent years to eliminate these regulations. The efforts have succeeded for interest rate ceilings on bank accounts; they have not succeeded for chartering, branching, or merger policy.

Despite the many successes of large banks in circumventing regulations, banking remains a highly regulated industry. Rather remarkably, banks compete despite the regulations, and they are often among the most innovative of American enterprises. Competition and innovation are often concentrated in providing services for large corporate customers, however. There has been less competition and innovation when it comes to providing services for households and small business.

SELECTED REFERENCES

Alhadeff, David, *Monopoly and Competition in Banking*, Berkeley: University of California Press, 1954.

Cagan, Phillip, "The First Fifty Years of the National Banking System—An Appraisal," in Dean Carson (ed.), *Banking and Monetary Studies*, Homewood, Ill.: Irwin, 1963, pp. 15–42.

Chase, Samuel and John Mingo, "The Regulation of Bank Holding Companies," *Journal of Finance*, May 1975, pp. 281–92.

Friedman, Milton and Anna Schwartz, *A Monetary History of the United States 1867–1960*, Princeton, N.J.: Princeton University Press, 1963.

Hammond, Bray, "Banking before the Civil War," in Dean Carson (ed.), *Banking and Monetary Studies*, Homewood, Ill.: Irwin, 1963, pp. 1–14.

Klebaner, Benjamin, *Commercial Banking in the United States: A History*, Hinsdale, Ill.: Dryden Press, 1974.

Rhoades, Stephen, "The Competitive Effects of Interstate Banking," *Federal Reserve Bulletin*, January 1980, pp. 1–8.

Scott, Kenneth and Thomas Mayer, "Risk and Regulation in Banking: Some Proposals for Federal Deposit Insurance Reform," *Stanford Law Review*, May 1971, pp. 857–902.

Studenski, Paul and Herman Kross, *Financial History of the United States* (2nd ed.), New York: McGraw-Hill, 1963.

Varvel, Walter, "FDIC Policy Toward Bank Failures," *Economic Review*, Federal Reserve Bank of Richmond, September–October 1976, pp. 3–12.

THRIFT INSTITUTIONS

10

Savings and loan associations, mutual savings banks, and credit unions are depository institutions that deal primarily with households. Because these institutions specialize in offering savings and time accounts to households, they are often called "thrift institutions," or just "thrifts." Savings and loan associations (S&Ls) specialize in real estate finance, with the bulk of their business devoted to providing mortgage loans to households. S&Ls do engage in a limited amount of short-term lending to consumers and businesses, however. Mutual savings banks (MSBs) are also involved in real estate finance, but a substantial portion of their assets are in the form of loans of various maturities to business, and they hold a limited amount of corporate stock. Credit unions (CUs) specialize in providing short-term consumer loans to their members.

Historically, S&Ls, MSBs and CUs offered the only opportunity for ordinary households to earn an interest income on their savings or to obtain credit on reasonable terms. Today most households have many alternatives for earning interest on their savings, and they have a variety of sources of credit. These alternatives developed only after thrift institutions demonstrated to commercial banks and other institutions that it was profitable to serve the financial needs of households.

Despite the development of alternative investment outlets and sources of credit to households, S&Ls, MSBs and CUs continue to specialize. This specialization is, in part, a natural development in which certain types of institutions serve a particular segment of the economy. Continued specialization is encouraged and often required, however, by governmental policy. Thus, S&Ls and MSBs have the expertise that naturally leads them to specialize in providing mortgage loans to households. This natural propensity to specialize is reinforced by laws and regulations ensuring that these institutions hold most of their assets in the form of mortgage loans. Credit unions specialize in providing relatively short-term loans to their members. This natural specialization is also reinforced by laws and regulations that prevent these institutions from directing much of their activities toward other types of loans.

Continued specialization of savings and loan associations and mutual savings banks has posed serious problems for public policy in recent years.[1] Because these institutions lack highly diversified asset portfolios and because they finance long-term assets with short-term liabilities, they have difficulty in coping with the spiraling interest rates that have beset the economy since the mid-1960s.

The government first tried to ease the problems of S&Ls and MSBs by developing programs designed to aid these institutions while still requiring that they retain their specialization. When these efforts failed, the government embarked on a program to loosen the regulations that bind their activities. Despite these efforts, S&Ls and MSBs are still highly specialized, and they continue to confront significant problems. The difficulties that these institutions face provide some valuable lessons concerning governmental efforts to force specialization when economic conditions require flexibility.

This chapter begins with a brief overview and history of thrift institutions. We then turn to a discussion of the performance of these institutions since the mid-1960s. It is shown that increased competition with banks and other financial intermediaries, as well as competition with securities markets, has created serious difficulties for the thrifts. Government efforts to solve their problems by imposing interest rate ceilings on the liabilities of these institutions and by developing various support programs are described. We then discuss why these efforts failed and why the government has begun the process of decontrolling the thrift institutions. The chapter concludes with an analysis of the current condition of these institutions.

AN OVERVIEW OF THE THRIFT INSTITUTIONS

Balance sheets showing the major assets and liabilities of thrift institutions, along with their net worth, are shown in Table 10.1. Of the three types of institutions, S&Ls are the largest. As of December 1982, S&Ls held $706 billion of assets, which accounted for 73 percent of the total assets held by all types of thrift institutions. Mortgage loans are the dominant kind of asset held by S&Ls, accounting in the aggregate for 68 percent of all their assets. Cash plus other liquid assets account for 12 percent of total S&L assets. Other assets, which include construction

---

[1] For reasons given later in this chapter, the problems for credit unions have not been so severe.

TABLE 10.1
BALANCE SHEETS FOR THRIFT INSTITUTIONS (DECEMBER 1982)

	Amount (billions)	Percentage of Total Assets	Percentage of Total Assets in All Specialized Institutions
Savings and Loan Associations			
Assets			
Mortgage loans	$482	68	
Liquid assets	85	12	
Other assets	139	20	
Total assets	$706	100	73
Liabilities and Net Worth			
Savings and time accounts	$566	80	
Other liabilities	114	16	
Net worth	26	4	
Total	$706	100	
Mutual Saving Banks			
Assets			
Mortgage loans	$ 94	54	
Corporate securities	36	21	
Other assets	44	25	
Total assets	$174	100	18
Liabilities and net worth			
Savings and time accounts	$155	89	
Other liabilities	10	6	
Net worth	9	5	
Total	$174	100	
Credit Unions			
Assets			
Loans	$51	57	
Other assets	38	43	
Total assets	$89	100	9
Liabilities			
Deposit accounts	$80	90	
Net worth	9	10	
Total	$89	100	

Total assets all thrifts: $969

Source: *Federal Reserve Bulletin*, April 1983, p. A27.

loans and other loans to business plus a small amount of consumer loans, make up the remaining 20 percent of total assets. These figures clearly document the high degree of specialization by S&Ls in the financing of homes and other real estate activities. S&Ls support these assets primarily by savings and time accounts.[2] Like banks, S&Ls support only a small percentage, 4 percent, of their total assets by net worth. High leverage is an important characteristic of thrift institutions.

Mutual savings banks held $174 billion of assets which accounted for 18 percent of the assets held by all thrift institutions combined. As is true of S&Ls, mortgage loans are the most important kind of asset held by MSBs. These loans account for 54 percent of total assets, so they are not as dominant a factor as for S&Ls. Corporate securities account for 21 percent of all assets held by MSBs. These securities, which include commercial paper as well as corporate stocks and bonds, provide MSBs with substantially greater portfolio diversification than is available to S&Ls. Other assets held by MSBs include highly liquid assets such as cash and short-term government securities, as well as longer-term securities, construction loans, and consumer loans. In total, these other assets represent 25 percent of all assets. They again illustrate the greater asset diversification achieved by MSBs relative to S&Ls. On the liability side of the balance sheet, we see that savings and time accounts support 89 percent of all assets. Other liabilities support only 6 percent of asset holdings for MSBs. This is a substantially smaller percentage than for S&Ls and represents, in large part, the fact that most MSBs do not have access to government loans, whereas S&Ls do. Leverage for MSBs is high, with net worth accounting for 5 percent of all asset holdings.

The balance sheet for credit unions indicates that the $89 billion of assets held by these institutions at the end of 1982 accounted for only 9 percent of all assets held by thrift institutions. Because of their small size and their minor participation in mortgage lending, these institutions will receive less attention in this chapter than S&Ls and MSBs. Their role is discussed, however, because they were instrumental in developing consumer credit in the United States. The $51 billion of loans held by credit unions consists almost exclusively of consumer installment loans. Some of the loans are secured by automobiles or other consumer durable goods, and others are unsecured loans. Although credit unions now have limited authority to grant mortgage loans, their participation in this activity is small. Consumer loans account for 57 percent of all assets held by CUs. The remaining 43 percent is held in government securities and other liquid assets. Credit unions support 90 percent of their asset holdings by savings and time accounts. Their leverage is relatively low with 10 percent of total assets supported by net worth.

---

[2] Accounts at S&Ls and CUs are often called share accounts. We shall call them savings and time accounts because for our purposes they are indistinguishable from savings and time accounts at commercial banks or mutual savings banks. The thrift institutions offer transactions accounts. These accounts, which are included under saving and time accounts in Table 10.1, are discussed later.

The corporate structure of mutual savings banks, of many savings and loan associations, and of credit unions is different from that of banks. Mutual savings banks have no external stockholders; rather, they are owned by their depositors. This means that profits of MSBs are either paid out to depositors in the form of interest payments on accounts or are added to net worth. Most S&Ls are also mutual associations, and they also are owned by their depositors. However, over 25 percent of the assets of the S&L industry are held by institutions that are owned by stockholders. These stock associations can distribute profits through dividends, and they can add to their net worth by retaining profits or by issuing additional shares.

Credit unions are cooperative institutions that are owned by their members. These institutions accept deposits from their members and lend to their members. They can purchase government securities or other market instruments, however. Membership in a credit union is restricted to individuals with a "common bond" established by a common place of employment or residence or by a common age group, religion, and so on. Most credit unions are located in factories or other business locations that are convenient to members. Space is often donated by employers, and credit union employees often serve without compensation.

Credit unions are truly cooperative ventures because they deal only with their members. All mutual savings banks and many S&Ls are owned by their depositors, but these institutions are not required to lend to their depositors. They can grant mortgage and other loans to anyone they choose. Credit unions can lend only to their members. Cooperation among members is not always easy because some members tend primarily to be depositors and other members tend primarily to be borrowers. Depositors want high interest income on their accounts and tend to favor high interest charges on loans, whereas borrowers want low interest on loans. It is impressive that credit unions have been successful in reconciling these conflicting objectives. Most credit unions are able to achieve basic agreement about what is a "fair" return to depositors and a "fair" interest charge on loans.

Credit unions are able to charge relatively low interest rates on their loans because they are able to achieve low loan delinquencies and defaults. Very few borrowers are delinquent or default on their loans because most credit unions can obtain loan payments through payroll deductions. Loan payments are deducted from a member's pay check by the employer and paid to the credit union. Other lenders do not have this opportunity. This device is particularly valuable because it allows credit union members to obtain unsecured credit at low cost.

The regulatory structure for thrift institutions is similar to the structure for banks in the sense that both the federal and state governments grant charters and regulate institutions under their jurisdictions. Unlike the situation for banks, however, each type of institution has only a single federal regulator.

One important rationale for regulating thrift institutions is to ensure their safety and soundness. This activity is little different from that for commercial banks and it involves roughly the same procedures, including limiting competition, that were discussed in Chapter 9.

Savings and loan associations are chartered and regulated by the Federal Home Loan Bank Board for federal institutions and by state authorities for state-chartered S&Ls. Mutual savings banks are regulated almost exclusively by state authorities. Federal charters only became available to MSBs in 1978 and are administered by the Federal Home Loan Bank Board. Since 1978, few MSBs have availed themselves of federal charters. Credit unions are chartered and regulated by the National Credit Union Administration for federal credit unions and by state authorities for state-chartered CUs. Until 1970, credit unions were treated as the poor stepchildren of depository institutions by the federal government. No fancy regulatory agency was established to regulate these institutions. Instead, regulatory authority was passed from one existing agency to another. The Farm Credit Administration was initially given jurisdiction over federal credit unions in 1934. In 1942 the duties were shifted to the FDIC, which, in turn, passed the buck to the Social Security Administration in 1948. Finally, in 1970 federal credit unions got their own federal agency when the National Credit Union Administration was established as an independent agency. This agency now has sole authority for chartering and regulating federal credit unions. Federal insurance for the liabilities of CUs also became available in 1970.

The regulatory approach for thrift institutions departs from the approach for banks when it comes to the scope of allowed activities. Government regulation ensures that the thrift institutions remain specialized. For example, the regulatory environment for S&Ls is much more restrictive than for banks. A large body of law and regulation has developed that is designed to delineate the kinds of activities in which S&Ls can engage. These laws and regulations are far too complex to describe here, but their main thrust has been to limit S&Ls to mortgage lending. Until recently, S&Ls were expected to hold certain assets for liquidity purposes and to place all remaining funds in mortgage loans. This was accomplished by a combination of regulatory requirements and tax incentives that prevented S&Ls from achieving meaningful diversification of their asset portfolios. The situation was changed somewhat in 1980 and 1982, when Congress authorized S&Ls to increase their holdings of business and consumer loans relative to mortgage loans. Despite this change, S&Ls are still expected to hold much of their assets in mortgage loans.

The laws and regulations for S&Ls are fundamentally different from these for commercial banks. In essence, S&Ls are not allowed to engage in any activity unless allowed by law. In contrast, banks are allowed to engage in any activity unless it is prohibited by law. This means that banks are free to innovate and adjust their activities in response to changing economic conditions. Savings and loan associations find innovation more difficult, and they are restricted in their ability to adjust to changing economic conditions because new activities are usually not specifically allowed by existing laws and regulations.

The same kinds of restrictions are placed on the activities of mutual savings banks except that these institutions are allowed to invest in corporate securities and other assets to a much greater extent than are S&Ls. For credit unions there are restrictions on the investments that can be made outside the area of consumer installment loans. They are also restricted by the necessity of accepting deposits and granting loans only to their members.

Much of the regulation of thrift institutions involves an effort by the government to allocate credit to certain segments of the economy. S&Ls and MSBs are expected to channel funds into housing, and credit unions are expected to channel funds into consumer loans. The effort to allocate credit through thrift institutions has been increasingly difficult in recent years and has often failed. One of the important lessons of this chapter is that credit allocation, no matter how desirable in principle, is extremely difficult to accomplish in a market economy.

The reasons why S&Ls, MSBs, and CUs were selected as the government's vehicles for credit allocation become apparent when we review the history of these institutions. The great contributions of these institutions to serving the financial needs of households made it natural for the government to attempt to retain their historical specialization. There is a fundamental difference, however, between specialization that is the result of natural economic forces and specialization that is the result of government regulations. Forced specialization can threaten the viability of thrift institutions when the economic environment changes. Government policy over the last two decades has been concerned with attempting to keep S&Ls, MSBs, and CUs viable while still requiring that they retain their specialization. These efforts have been increasingly unsuccessful and have recently led to attempts to ease the regulatory constraints that are placed upon them.

A BRIEF HISTORY OF THRIFT INSTITUTIONS TO 1966

During the early economic history of the United States, the financial system did not serve the needs of households. Commercial banks were primarily concerned with issuing notes and with providing loans and depository services to businesses and to wealthy individuals. There were no safe financial assets available to ordinary households, and loans were often available only from family and friends or from lenders who charged exceedingly high rates of interest.

An attractive financial asset first became available to ordinary households in 1816 when mutual savings banks were established in Philadelphia, Boston, and New York. These institutions were established by groups of wealthy individuals who sought to promote social harmony by encouraging thrift and ownership of property by the "working class." The wealthy individuals provided the initial capital (net worth) for the savings banks and served as trustees to manage the institutions.

Savings banks offered deposit accounts to households and used the funds to purchase market securities and other assets. Though controlled by their boards of trustees, the institutions were mutually owned by their depositors. All earnings less operating expenses were either paid out to depositors as interest income or added to the net worth of the institutions to support additional expansion of assets.

Mutual savings banks were primarily concerned with providing an attractive investment opportunity for ordinary households. Thus, MSBs purchased stocks, bonds, and other assets consistent with profitable and safe investment of their depositors' funds. Though MSBs did grant loans to their depositors, their primary function was to make profitable and safe investments in market securities.

Because of the orientation of mutual savings banks toward investment in market securities, the borrowing needs of most households were still unmet. This deficiency was partially remedied in 1836, when households began to form cooperative building and loan associations in which they pooled their savings and lent to each other for the purpose of purchasing a home. Members made monthly deposits until sufficient funds were accumulated to entitle them to purchase ownership shares in the association. Once a share was acquired, a member could borrow from the association to purchase a house. Receipt of interest on these loans allowed the association to pay interest on its members' shares.

The popularity of these associations spread rapidly. As S&Ls developed and grew they lost their cooperative identity in the sense that they lent to borrowers who were not depositors. Savings and loan associations were also formed that were corporations owned by external stockholders. Stock associations did not enjoy rapid growth until after World War II, however.

The development and growth of MSBs and S&Ls benefited many households. Not only could households earn an attractive return on their savings, but funds were also made available to finance the purchases of houses. Many borrowing needs of the public were still unmet, however. For example, most households could not borrow to establish a business, and loans were rarely available during emergencies such as illness or temporary unemployment. These needs began to be met in 1909, when the first credit unions were established. Credit unions were cooperative ventures in which individuals banded together in order to pool their savings and to dispense loans to their members. Cooperation and trust were important because, unlike MSBs and S&Ls, credit unions granted loans that typically were not secured by homes or by account balances. Loans by credit unions were often secured only by the promise of the borrower to repay. For the early credit unions, membership was often limited to persons who were known and trusted by other members. This usually involved some common bond such as a common place of employment or a common neighborhood or religious affiliation.

Mutual savings banks, saving and loan associations, and credit unions met different needs of households, and they all expanded in number and size. As the institutions grew in importance, various states adopted laws and regulations concerning the chartering and operation of these depository institutions. The federal government stayed out of the picture and left regulation to the states.

The federal government finally became involved following the economic and financial collapse of the early 1930s. Although thrift institutions were much less affected by the collapse than banks, they did encounter difficulties, and some failed. Households withdrew funds from their accounts because they needed their savings to support expenditures during rising unemployment and because they were fearful for the safety of their savings. At the same time, loan defaults at the thrifts rose. Many institutions responded by temporarily refusing to honor withdrawals and by refusing to renew maturing loans. These actions saved most institutions from insolvency, but they inflicted damage on the households who were depositors or borrowers.

In 1933, Congress passed legislation giving S&Ls insurance coverage and offering them a regulatory structure similar to that for banks. Federal chartering became available for savings and loan associations as an alternative to state charters. The Federal Home Loan Bank System (FHLBS) was established for S&Ls, modeled in many respects after the Federal Reserve System. Twelve district banks were established that made loans available to S&Ls in order to meet their liquidity problems.[3] The Federal Home Loan Bank Board (FHLBB) was established in Washington, D.C., to supervise and coordinate the activities of the twelve district banks. Membership in the Federal Home Loan Bank System was made mandatory for federally chartered S&Ls and optional for state-chartered institutions.

Deposit insurance was provided for S&Ls through the Federal Savings and Loan Insurance Corporation (FSLIC). Insurance was made mandatory for federal S&Ls and optional for state-chartered S&Ls. Most state-chartered S&Ls chose to be insured and, as a result, fell under the regulatory jurisdiction of the FSLIC. The FSLIC is a subsidiary of the Federal Home Loan Bank System, unlike the FDIC, which is an independent banking agency.

National charters were not made available for mutual savings banks at that time, but they could obtain federal deposit insurance through the FDIC. They could also become members of the Federal Reserve System, but few did. Federal charters were made available for credit unions, but deposit insurance was not made available to either federal or state-chartered credit unions. This treatment of mutual savings banks and credit unions was the result of the politics of the time. Federal insurance became available to credit unions in 1970, and federal charters became available for mutual savings banks in 1978.

The federal government also introduced a program in the 1930s to aid mortgage borrowers and lenders. This program had long-term implications for housing finance in the United States and for the future development of S&Ls and MSBs. Most mortgage loans had maturities of only three to five years. Interest was paid periodically, but loan payments usually did not cover repayment of all the principal. In normal times, lenders would issue a new mortgage loan at maturity if the borrower had not accumulated sufficient funds to repay the loan. In the 1930s, S&Ls and MSBs often did not renew maturing mortgage loans but rather demanded repayment of principal. Many borrowers were unable to repay their loans, and they lost their homes.

---

[3] The Federal Home Loan Bank System is not a central bank because it cannot create reserves or issue currency. The FHLBS borrows funds in the market and lends the funds to S&Ls. It is a financial intermediary, not a central bank.

The government provided direct relief to mitigate the plight of mortgage borrowers and lenders by establishing the Home Owners Loan Corporation (HOLC). The corporation, which was administered by the Federal Home Loan Bank System, purchased delinquent home mortgages from S&Ls and other mortgage lenders. The HOLC was a godsend to homeowners because it provided a means of avoiding default on their mortgage debt. The corporation converted short-term mortgage loans into long-term loans and reduced the interest rates on the loans. Homeowners could spread their mortgage payments over twenty years or more rather than over three to five years. This lengthening of maturities and reduction of interest rates allowed most households to meet their payments and retain their homes.[4] Purchases of mortgage loans by the HOLC also greatly eased the burden on private mortgage lenders by taking mortgage loans off their hands. Elimination of these loans from the portfolios of S&Ls, MSBs, and other lenders prevented substantial losses to these lenders and provided them with liquidity.[5]

The activities of the Home Owners Loan Corporation improved the situation for lenders and homeowners and, at the same time, introduced a type of mortgage loan that became the dominant method of financing homes in the United States. The corporation demonstrated that households can meet their mortgage payments if the payments can be kept relatively small by spreading (amortizing) payments of principal over a substantial period of time. The Home Owners Loan Act required that new mortgage loans granted by federally chartered S&Ls be long-term, fully amortized loans. These loans were so popular with the public that state-chartered S&Ls also started to use them almost exclusively. The long-term, fully amortized mortgage loan became virtually the only way that houses were financed in the U.S.[6]

Following the reforms of the early 1930s, thrift institutions began to expand again. They came into their own during the rising prosperity following the end of World War II. Table 10.2 shows the total assets held by the thrift institutions in 1946, 1956, and 1965. For comparative purposes, the total assets of commercial banks (CBs) are also shown. In 1946, thrifts held $29.3 billion of assets. Of this total, 35 percent was held by S&Ls; 64 percent, by MSBs; and 1 percent, by credit unions. Thus, mutual savings banks were the dominant type of thrift institution. In 1946, commercial banks held $132.8 billion of assets. The total asset holdings of thrift institutions were 22 percent of the assets held by banks.

---

[4] As we shall see below, federal insurance of mortgage loans was also provided under certain circumstances.

[5] Many lenders had extended and liberalized the terms of their mortgage loans in order to help their customers avoid foreclosures, which would further depress house prices and increase losses to lenders. However, the need for liquidity and the fear of insolvency prevented lenders from achieving the wholesale conversion of mortgage loans into long-term instruments that was achieved by the HOLC.

[6] As we shall see in this chapter, this mortgage instrument has caused problems in recent years and is no longer popular with many lenders.

TABLE 10.2
ASSET HOLDINGS FOR THRIFT INSTITUTIONS (1946–1965)

	1946			1956			1965		
	Assets (billions)	Percentage of Total		Assets (billions)	Percentage of Total	Average Annual Growth 1946–1956 (%)	Assets (billions)	Percentage of Total	Average Annual Growth 1956–1965 (%)
S&Ls	$ 10.2	35		$ 37.7	52	13.9	$129.6	65	14.7
MSBs	18.7	64		31.7	44	5.4	59.1	30	7.2
CUs	.4	1		2.9	4	21.9	11.0	5	16.0
Total	$ 29.3	100		$ 72.3	100	9.4	$199.7	100	12.0
CBs	$132.8			$190.6		3.7	$336.4		6.5
Thrifts as percentage of CBs	22.1			37.0			59.4		

Source: Board of Governors of the Federal Reserve System, *Flow of Funds Accounts 1946–1975*, December 1976.

By 1956, the picture had changed significantly. All types of thrift institutions had grown, but the expansion of S&Ls was remarkable. These institutions accounted for 52 percent of all assets held by thrift institutions. Mutual savings banks grew less rapidly, and their share of the assets held by thrifts fell from 64 percent in 1946 to 44 percent in 1956.[7] Credit unions grew rapidly, and by 1956 they accounted for 4 percent of all assets held by thrift institutions. The expansion of the thrifts was more rapid than for banks. By 1956 the total assets held by S&Ls, MSBs, and CUs combined were 38 percent of the assets held by banks.

The growth of thrift institutions was even more rapid for the period 1956 through 1965. S&Ls continued to grow most rapidly and by 1965 accounted for 65 percent of all assets held by thrift institutions. Though MSBs continued to grow, their relative share continued to shrink, and by 1965 they accounted for only 30 percent of all thrift assets. Credit unions also grew rapidly, but their relative share only rose from 4 to 5 percent. By 1965 thrift institutions had grown to the point where their total asset holdings were nearly 60 percent of the assets held by banks. Thrifts had become a major factor in the financial system.

Over the period from 1946 through 1965, there was increasing competition between the thrift institutions and commercial banks. The spectacular growth of the thrifts induced banks to start to emulate them. Banks began actively to solicit savings and time deposit accounts from households, and they also devoted an increasing share of their business to mortgage and other consumer lending. In 1946 banks had only 7 percent of their total assets invested in mortgage and other types of loans to households. By 1956 the percentage had risen to 20 percent, and by 1965, 37 percent of all bank assets were in loans to households. Thrift institutions had led the way in lending to households, but banks were quick to respond when the profitability of this type of lending was demonstrated. Commercial banks had come to hold more mortgage loans than mutual savings banks, and they granted more loans to consumers than credit unions.

Commercial banks were limited in their ability to expand their total assets because their deposit accounts had interest rate ceilings whereas the accounts of S&Ls, MSBs, and CUs did not. The Banking Act of 1933 explicitly prohibited payment of interest on demand deposit accounts and gave the federal banking regulators authority to impose ceilings on the interest rates paid on time and savings accounts of banks.

Interest rate ceilings for savings and time accounts were unimportant throughout the 1930s and during World War II because the ceilings were well above competing interest rates. The situation changed after the war. Savings and loan associations, mutual savings banks, and credit unions were not subject to interest rate ceilings. They were able to offer more attractive terms on their accounts than banks. In the decade that followed, thrift institutions grew nearly

---

[7] Only seventeen states issue charters to mutual savings banks. This restricted the growth of MSBs. Despite the geographic restrictions, MSBs managed to grow more rapidly than commercial banks.

three times as rapidly as banks. By 1957 it became clear that banks were at a competitive disadvantage, and their interest rate ceilings were raised for the first time in twenty-one years. The new ceilings rates quickly proved to be too low, however, and rapid growth of thrift institutions continued.

In 1963, President Johnson established an Interagency Coordinating Committee composed of the heads of the Federal Reserve Board, the FDIC, and the Federal Home Loan Bank Board. The Secretary of the Treasury also participated.[8] Only accounts at commercial banks were subject to interest rate ceilings at that time, but the Coordinating Committee was empowered to discuss issues relating to the effects of interest rate ceilings on the institutions under their jurisdiction. In 1964 the ceiling interest rates for bank savings and time accounts were raised to levels more competitive with the interest rates offered by thrift institutions.

THRIFT INSTITUTIONS 1966 THROUGH 1979

The Interagency Coordinating Committee received its first real test in 1966. In that year, rising expenditures on the Vietnam War, coupled with an economy that was already operating at high levels of capacity utilization, produced inflationary pressures. The Federal Reserve responded by tightening monetary policy, which raised market interest rates. Thrift institutions did not raise the interest rates on their accounts and, as a result, some S&Ls and MSBs experienced sizable outflows of funds. There was a commensurate reduction in the growth of mortgage lending.

In an effort to reduce bank competition for savings and time accounts, the federal banking regulators actually *lowered* the interest rate ceilings for commercial bank savings and time accounts. This action was designed to allow S&Ls and MSBs to attract funds relative to commercial banks in order to expand their mortgage lending. Congress also responded by passing the Interest Rate Adjustment Act of 1966, which gave the Federal Home Loan Bank Board (FHLBB) authority to set interest rate ceilings for S&L accounts and the FDIC authority to set interest rate ceilings for mutual savings banks.[9] The act also required the various regulators to consult with each other before establishing their respective ceilings.

The FHLBB and the FDIC quickly established interest rate ceilings for S&Ls and MSBs that were higher than those for commercial banks. The *differential* between interest rate ceilings for S&Ls and MSBs relative to banks ranged from three quarters of a percentage point for savings accounts to one quarter of a percentage point for long-term time accounts.

---

[8] In 1977 the administrator of the National Credit Union Administration became a member of the committee.

[9] There was no authority to establish interest rate ceilings for credit unions.

Interest rate ceilings were imposed because many S&Ls and MSBs argued that they could not "afford" to pay higher interest rates on their accounts. At that time, most of the liabilities of these institutions were in the form of savings accounts. S&Ls and MSBs did not believe it would be profitable to raise the interest rate on savings accounts as a method of attracting increases in these accounts, but they feared that competition among themselves might lead to an increase.[10] They called upon the federal government to prevent "destructive competition" by imposing interest rate ceilings. The problem of competition with commercial banks was addressed by allowing S&Ls and MSBs to pay a higher interest rate on their liabilities than commercial banks could pay.[11] The differential was achieved by fixing the interest rates paid by S&Ls and MSBs at prevailing levels and reducing the ceiling rates paid by commercial banks.

It was also argued that commercial banks have a competitive advantage during periods of rising interest rates. Because banks hold short-term assets, these assets mature relatively quickly and can be replaced with new assets earning a higher interest income. Thus, banks can afford to pay higher interest rates for their liabilities. This allows them to "outcompete" S&Ls and MSBs, which are stuck with long-term assets with fixed interest rates. Furthermore, commercial banks enjoyed a competitive advantage because they could offer transactions accounts as well as savings and time accounts. S&Ls and MSBs could not offer transactions accounts. It was asserted that the public preferred the convenience of one-stop banking and would take its savings and time account business to banks if banks were allowed to pay the same interest rates as were paid by S&Ls and MSBs. It was concluded, therefore, that not only should commercial banks and other depository institutions be subjected to interest rate ceilings but also that the interest rate ceilings applied to commercial banks should be lower than for other depository institutions.[12]

The imposition of interest rate ceilings and of interest rate differentials was rationalized as necessary tools for supporting S&Ls and MSBs and, therefore, for supporting housing finance. These ceilings became a centerpiece for government policies designed to channel funds into housing finance. Despite the importance placed on ceiling interest rates by thrift institutions and their regulators, the ceilings did not achieve a steady flow of funds into savings and loan associations and mutual savings banks. When interest rates on alternative assets rose above ceiling

---

[10] It was explained in Chapter 7 why it is often not profitable to raise the interest rate on savings accounts.

[11] The regulation under which the Federal Reserve sets interest rate ceilings for member banks is called Regulation Q. It became common practice to refer to interest rate ceilings applied to the liabilities of all types of depository institutions as Regulation Q ceilings and to say that S&Ls and MSBs enjoy a differential above the Regulation Q ceilings.

[12] Lest the reader conclude that commercial bankers were the good guys in this interest-rate-fixing scheme, it should be noted that the banking industry was in favor of interest rate ceilings. It only opposed the interest rate differential accorded to the liabilities of the thrift institutions.

interest rates, the public withdrew funds from accounts in depository institutions and invested them in alternative instruments. The flow of funds into savings and loan associations, mutual savings banks, *and* commercial banks was reduced when market interest rates exceeded the interest rates paid on accounts at those institutions. In every episode in which market interest rates rose appreciably above ceiling interest rates, there was disintermediation, and the availability of mortgage loans was reduced.

Figure 10.1 compares the interest rate ceilings for savings accounts, and for time accounts with maturities of two and a half to four years, to the interest rate on three-month Treasury bills for the period of 1965 through 1979.[13] In 1966 the interest rate on Treasury bills rose above the interest rate ceiling for savings accounts, and many customers at S&Ls and MSBs withdrew their funds from these accounts for investment in market instruments. In 1967 the Treasury bill rate fell below the interest rate ceiling for savings accounts, and the public shifted funds back into S&Ls and MSBs. In 1968 the Treasury bill rate again rose above the interest rate ceiling for savings accounts and many institutions experienced a loss of funds in these accounts. Until mid-1968, the interest rate ceiling for two-and-a-half to four-year time accounts was above the interest rate on Treasury bills, and the public increased its holdings of these accounts. In 1969 market interest rates exceeded the interest rate ceilings on all liabilities of the S&Ls and MSBs. Many institutions experienced substantial reductions in their account liabilities, At the begining of 1970, interest rate ceilings for the liabilities of S&Ls and MSBs were increased, but market interest rates remained above the ceilings during most of the year. As a result, disintermediation continued. Toward the end of 1970, market interest rates fell below the interest rate ceilings, and thrift institutions experienced substantial inflows of funds from the public. These institutions grew rapidly until 1973, when market interest rates again rose above ceiling rates. The ceilings were increased in 1973, but market interest rates rose above the new ceilings. In 1973 and 1974 there was disintermediation. During the period of 1975 to 1977, market interest rates fell. S&Ls and MSBs were able to expand their time account liabilities rapidly, and even savings accounts were attractive to the public during 1976 and 1977. In 1978 and 1979, market interest rates were far in excess of the interest rate ceilings.[14]

During the period 1966 through 1979, the growth of liabilities at S&Ls and MSBs declined when market interest rates rose above interest rate ceilings. Growth accelerated when market interest rates fell below the ceilings. Interest rate ceilings insulated thrift institutions from competition among themselves, and

[13] Interest rate ceilings for short-term time accounts were below the ceilings for two-and-a-half to four-year accounts but above the ceiling for savings accounts. The interest rate on three-month Treasury bills should be viewed as a proxy for short-term market interest rates in general.
[14] In 1978 S&Ls and MSBs were authorized to issue six-month time accounts with interest rate ceilings tied to the interest rate on Treasury bills. These are discussed later.

FIGURE 10.1
INTEREST RATE ON THREE-MONTH
TREASURY BILLS VERSUS INTEREST
RATE CEILINGS ON SAVINGS AND
TIME ACCOUNTS AT S&Ls AND MSBs (1966–1980).

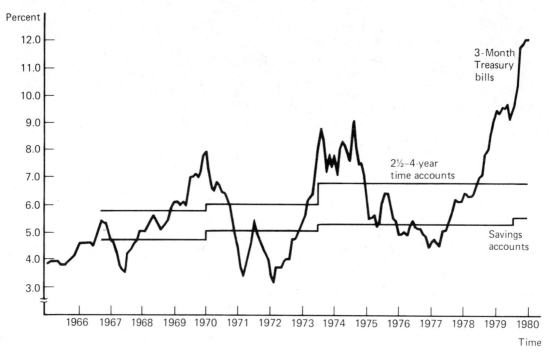

from competition from commercial banks, but the ceilings could not insulate the institutions from competition from securities market instruments.

When the growth of liabilities at S&Ls and MSBs slowed, the quantity of funds available for mortgage lending also grew less rapidly. The demand for mortgage loans exceeded the supply, and the interest rate on mortgage loans rose. In many instances, borrowers could obtain loans if they were willing to pay a sufficiently high interest rate. In other cases, they were informed by lenders that loans were not available. In this latter situation, lenders engaged in *credit rationing*. A rise in the interest rate on mortgage loans increases the cost of acquiring a house and reduces the demand for houses. Credit rationing directly reduces the demand for houses because households cannot borrow needed funds.

Historically, residential construction expenditures have accounted for 20 to 30 percent of total gross investment expenditures in the United States. Changes in the cost and availability of mortgage loans have substantial effects on residential housing expenditures and upon aggregate economic activity in general.

FIGURE 10.2
NET ACQUISITIONS OF MORTGAGE
LOANS BY S&Ls AND MSBs.

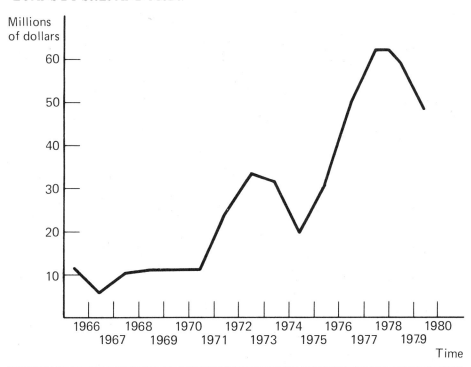

Figure 10.2 shows the net acquisition of mortgage loans by S&Ls and MSBs for the years 1965 through 1979.[15] The figure indicates that when market interest rates exceeded interest rate ceilings on the liabilities of S&Ls and MSBs, that is, in 1966, 1969–1970, 1973–1975 and 1978–1979, the acquisitions of mortgage loans declined.[16] During 1971–1972 and 1975–1977 market interest rates were below the ceilings, and the acquisition of mortgage loans by S&Ls and MSBs was high.

Figures 10.1 and 10.2 show in graphical terms that as market interest rates fluctuated above and below the interest rate ceilings, there were waves of disintermediation and reintermediation that affected the ability of S&Ls and MSBs to extend mortgage credit. Fluctuations in the availability of credit from these institutions led the government to institute programs to stabilize the mortgage market.

[15] Net acquisitions are new extensions of credit less repayments of existing loans.
[16] In 1969–1970, net acquisitions of mortgage loans remained flat rather than declining. Time accounts were still attractive to households during part of the period and S&Ls were also able to borrow from Home Loan Banks. These sources of funds prevented net mortgage acquisitions from falling.

PROGRAMS TO SUPPORT THE MORTGAGE MARKET

The federal government actually began a policy of stabilizing the mortgage market in the 1930s. The programs increased in number and scope over the years and came to full fruition after 1965. The number of programs and agencies involved is large. This book is not the place to provide an exhaustive list, but some of the basic types of programs are outlined.

In 1934 the Federal Housing Administration (FHA) was established to provide federal insurance for residential mortgage loans. FHA insurance encouraged private lenders to grant new mortgage loans because the federal government promised to make good on the loans should the borrower default. Various restrictions were placed on these loans in terms of minimum down payment and size of the loan, but they became widely used. The Veterans Administration (VA) later provided similar guarantees for mortgage loans extended to veterans.

Over the years, the government pursued policies to enhance the liquidity of mortgage loans and to stabilize the mortgage market. It was often difficult for a lender to sell mortgage loans because the financial condition of the borrower and the nature of the property securing the loan were not known to potential buyers. As a result, these loans were not liquid. In 1937 the Federal National Mortgage Association (FNMA) was established, which "made a market" in federally insured mortgage loans (i.e., it bought and sold mortgage loans). It acted as a dealer in mortgage loans and greatly improved the liquidity of these loans. It was also authorized to hold mortgage loans for investment purposes. This allowed lenders to originate mortgage loans and sell them to FNMA when they were unable or unwilling to hold the loans in their own portfolios. FNMA obtained its funds to purchase mortgage loans by borrowing in the securities market as a federal agency. Thus, FNMA was a financial intermediary. This institution was originally authorized to buy or sell only the mortgage loans insured by the FHA or the VA. In 1966, FNMA was converted into a quasi-private institution with government regulation but private ownership. In 1970 its activities were expanded to include purchases and sales of conventional mortgage loans.

In 1968 the Government National Mortgage Association (GNMA) was established in order to purchase federally subsidized mortgage loans extended to lower income families by S&Ls, MSBs and other lenders. Over the years its activities have been expanded, and it now is allowed to purchase FHA and VA insured mortgages as well as conventional mortgage loans. GNMA differs from the other agencies because it is allowed to pay a subsidy to sellers of mortgages. When interest rates on new mortgage loans rise, the value of old loans with lower interest rates declines. Loans with lower interest rates must be sold at a discount to compensate the purchaser for the lower interest rate relative to the interest rate on new loans. GNMA is authorized to purchase mortgage loans from various depository institutions at par, that is, full value, and then sell them at a discount. The loss is absorbed by the government, that is, by taxpayers. This institution allows mortgage lenders to avoid capital losses on their mortgage loans by shifting the loss to the government.

In 1970 the government established the Federal Home Loan Mortgage Corporation (FHLMC) to help enhance the marketability of conventional mortgages. The Mortgage Corporation, which is affiliated with the Federal Home Loan Bank System, purchases conventional mortgage loans and resells them to various market participants. The activities of the FNMA and the FHLMC are similar, but the latter institution deals primarily with S&Ls. Both the FHLMC and FNMA help make a market in mortgage loans. It is not necessary for individual S&Ls or other lenders to find purchasers of their mortgages. They can sell them to the FHLMC or FNMA, and these institutions in turn locate the ultimate purchasers. These market makers can also hold mortgages in their own portfolios if they choose.

The activities of the FNMA, GNMA, and FHLMC also allow lenders to sell new mortgage loans. Thus, during periods of disintermediation, depository institutions can originate mortgage loans and quickly sell them to these agencies. The mortgage originator receives a fee for its services, but does not have to hold the mortgage loans in its portfolio. This allows depository institutions to continue to grant mortgage loans and to earn fee income from new mortgages even when they are experiencing disintermediation. The agencies either resell the loans to pension funds and other investors or hold the loans in their own portfolios.

Along with the efforts to provide depository institutions with the ability to rid themselves of unwanted mortgage loans, the government, through the Federal Home Loan Bank System, has at times been an important source of funds to S&Ls. During periods of disintermediation, Federal Home Loan Banks borrow funds in the market and lend the proceeds to S&Ls. These loans allow S&Ls to hold more mortgage loans than would otherwise be the case. Savings and loan associations have to pay market interest rates for these loans, but the interest rate at which the Federal Home Loan Bank System borrows and lends is often less than the costs to S&Ls of alternative forms of credit.

This brief description of the government's support programs for mortgage loans gives an indication of the importance that is placed in the United States on providing funds to finance the acquisition of housing. During periods of high market interest rates and disintermediation, the agencies of the federal government provide much of the financing of housing. For example, over 50 percent of the funds for home mortgage loans in 1974 came from the government's mortgage loan support programs. In 1979 nearly 45 percent came from the government. Home ownership and the ability to purchase and sell houses easily have remained important elements of the government's economic and social policy. One may agree or disagree with the emphasis placed on the financing and ownership of homes, but the emphasis placed on housing has resulted in an impressive array of federal programs designed to support mortgage lenders, most notably S&Ls and MSBs.

THE DECLINING ROLE OF SAVINGS ACCOUNTS

From 1965 through 1977, interest rate ceilings on time accounts were usually above short-term market interest rates. The ceiling for savings accounts was often below market interest rates. Not surprisingly, for most of this time interval, the growth in the liabilities of S&Ls and MSBs was in the form of time accounts rather than savings accounts. The change in the composition of liabilities issued by S&Ls and MSBs during this period was remarkable. For example, in 1966 over 88 percent of all S&L liabilities were savings accounts. By 1977 only 38 percent of total liabilities were savings accounts. Savings accounts were often not attractive, so the public either switched from savings accounts to time accounts or invested in market instruments.[17] In an effort to reduce its competition with S&Ls and MSBs, the U.S. Treasury raised the minimum denomination of Treasury bills to $10,000. This effectively prevented small savers from investing in Treasury bills and left many savers with few alternatives but to hold savings accounts at depository institutions.

Because the interest rate on time accounts was usually above market interest rates and because many small savers could not invest in market instruments, S&Ls and MSBs were able to expand their liabilities and holdings of mortgage loans, on average, from 1965 through 1977. Liability growth and mortgage acquisitions fluctuated widely, however, as market interest rates moved above and below the interest rate ceilings on savings and time accounts. Beginning in 1978, the interest rate on Treasury bills rose above the ceiling rates on all types of S&L and MSB liabilities and remained at high levels. This meant that these depository institutions had difficulty in marketing their time accounts to large investors. Most small savers appeared to be stuck because of the minimum denomination for Treasury bills. The plight of small savers gave impetus to money market mutual funds, which began to compete with depository institutions for the savings of the public. These mutual funds frequently had minimum initial investments of $2500-$5000 and, therefore, were accessible to both large and smaller investors.[18]

Faced with the increased competition from securities markets and from money market mutual funds, depository institutions turned to their regulators for assistance. Relief came in the form of authorization to issue *money market certificates.* These certificates had a maturity of six months and an interest rate ceiling that moved with the interest rate on six-month Treasury bills. In an effort to avoid paying market interest rates to small savers, the minimum denomination for money market certificates was set at $10,000. In order to neutralize competition from commercial banks, S&Ls and MSBs were allowed to pay one quarter of one percent more on their certificates than commercial banks.[19]

The introduction of money market certificates allowed depository institutions to compete against securities markets for the funds of larger investors. By keeping

---

[17] Large S&Ls and MSBs also began to issue large denomination certificates of deposit. These liabilities are similar to CDs offered by large banks, and they are not subject to interest rate ceilings.

[18] Money market mutual funds were discussed in Chapter 4, and they are covered in detail later in this chapter.

[19] In 1979 the differential was eliminated when the interest rate on six-month Treasury bills exceeded nine percent.

the interest rate on their certificates in line with market interest rates, depository institutions ceased losing funds to the securities markets. Disintermediation appeared to be a thing of the past.

The solution was only partially successful, however, because money market certificates had several drawbacks. Because they had a single maturity, money market certificates are most attractive to the portion of the public that wanted a six-month instrument. This consideration was particularly important because penalties were imposed for early withdrawals from these accounts. Furthermore, money market certificates induced S&Ls and MSBs to shorten the average maturity of their liabilities. These institutions began to finance long-term, fixed interest rate mortgage loans with six-month certificates instead of issuing longer-term liabilities. This meant that when determining the profitability of a mortgage loan, institutions had to compare the fixed interest income from a loan of up to thirty years' maturity against the uncertain cost of six-month certificates that would be rolled over for the next twenty-five to thirty years. This was playing the term structure of interest rates with a vengeance.[20] Finally, money market certificates were often not as attractive to the public as money market mutual funds. Small savers, in particular, continued to be attracted by these mutual funds because of their relatively small denominations. Despite these drawbacks, money market certificates became the most important source of funds for most S&Ls and MSBs.

TRANSACTIONS ACCOUNTS FOR THRIFT INSTITUTIONS

Until recently, transactions accounts were exclusively the domain of commercial banks. The monopoly over transactions accounts gave commercial banks an advantage over S&Ls, MSBs, and CUs. Bank customers could do all their business in one location if they held their transactions, savings, and time accounts at a bank. If they held savings or time accounts at other kinds of institutions, they still had to use a bank for transactions accounts.

The Consumers Savings Bank of Worcester, Massachusetts, broke the transactions accounts monopoly of commercial banks in 1972. This mutual savings bank initially had attempted to offer demand deposit accounts but was stopped by the courts, who ruled that the law allowed only commercial banks to offer these accounts. This ruling induced the mutual savings bank to invent a new kind of transactions account that technically was not a demand deposit account. Consumers Savings began to offer a savings account that featured the ability to write "negotiable orders of withdrawal" from the account. It issued to each customer a book of withdrawal orders that looked exactly like any other book of checks. When the

---

[20] This problem helped spawn mortgage loans with floating interest rates. These are discussed later in this chapter.

customer wrote a check, it was accepted in payment like any other check and deposited in a bank or other depository institution. The recipient presented the check to Consumers Savings, which transferred funds out of its customer's savings account.

Consumers Savings Bank had established a negotiable order of withdrawal or *NOW* account that for all intents and purposes was a demand deposit account, but in the eyes of the law was not a demand deposit account. This invention had three effects. First, it broke the commercial bank monopoly over transactions accounts. Second, it evaded the prohibition of paying interest on demand deposit accounts because a NOW account was technically a savings account. Third, it incurred the wrath of the commercial bank industry, which did not like the idea of losing its monopoly and did not welcome the prospect of paying interest on transactions accounts.

Consumers Savings Bank was able to offer NOW accounts because it was not under federal regulation. It was chartered by the State of Massachusetts, and it was insured by a state-administered insurance fund. NOW accounts were legal under Massachusetts law. If the savings bank had been under federal jurisdiction, it would have been prevented from offering NOW accounts. This is an excellent example of the benefits of dual "banking." If Consumers Savings had been under federal jurisdiction, the NOW account would not have been invented, and perhaps to this day we would not earn interest on our transactions accounts.

Other state-insured mutual savings banks in Massachusetts and New Hampshire quickly followed Consumer Savings' lead. This placed depository institutions in those states that were under federal jurisdiction at a competitive disadvantage. Congress entered the picture in 1974 and declared that all federally insured depository institutions could offer NOW accounts in the New England states as an "experiment." Federally insured depository institutions in other states could not offer them.[21] The federal regulators imposed a single interest rate ceiling for NOW accounts issued by all types of federally insured depository institutions. Thus, there was no interest rate differential for NOW accounts issued by S&Ls and MSBs over the interest rate paid by commercial banks.

Over time, depository institutions in adjoining states began to lobby for the power to offer NOW accounts in order to avoid losing business to institutions in New England. Congress widened the experiment to cover New York and Pennsylvania. With this move, most of the mutual savings banks in the United States were able to issue NOW accounts.

Most of the savings and loan associations are not located in these states, and they continued to be prevented from issuing transactions accounts. Savings and loan associations in states where NOW accounts were not authorized began to market savings accounts from which customers could make preauthorized payments. With these accounts, customers would instruct their S&L to pay their utili-

---

[21] Commercial banks outside of New England did not have to face the competition from NOW accounts and successfully blocked their authorization in other areas.

ty bills, make their mortgage payments, and conduct other expenditures, using funds in their savings accounts. Authorization for payment was often accomplished by telephone calls from customers to their S&Ls. The S&L withdrew the funds from the customers' accounts and sent checks to the businesses designated by the customer. Some banks also offered these telephone transfer accounts, but S&Ls had the advantage of paying one quarter of one percent more on their savings accounts than banks were allowed to pay.

At roughly the same time, a few S&Ls experimented with offering electronic funds transfer (EFT) services to their customers. With these systems, customers could make cash withdrawals and execute expenditures by using a card that was inserted into computer terminals at grocery stores and other remote locations. Expenditures for groceries and other purposes were executed electronically by reducing the customer's savings account balance and increasing the merchant's account by the amount of the expenditure. These EFT accounts offered the S&Ls' customers an interest-bearing transactions account.

The Federal Reserve entered the picture in 1976 by authorizing member banks throughout the country to offer automatic transfer systems (ATS). These accounts are similar in substance to NOW accounts but are technically not the same and, therefore, appeared not to be covered by legislation concerning NOW accounts. Technically, with an automatic transfer system the depositor has a demand deposit account from which checks are written. If the demand deposit account has insufficient funds, the bank is authorized to transfer funds automatically from a savings account to the demand deposit account. Because a demand deposit account pays no interest, it never pays to keep any balances in that account. Rather, customers arrange to have funds transferred automatically from their savings account to their demand deposit accounts when each check is presented for payment. This procedure seems complicated, but operationally the transfers are done automatically by computers. All that customers have to know is that they have accounts that earn interest against which checks can be written.

The use of automatic transfer systems gave banks outside the NOW account states a significant competitive advantage over other types of depository institutions. Only banks could offer the demand deposit accounts that are a necessary component of the transfer system.[22]

In 1977 the administrator of the National Credit Union Administration authorized nationwide share draft accounts (SDs) for credit unions that are similar to NOW accounts. These accounts allowed credit unions to compete against commercial banks for the transactions account business of their members.

The authorization of ATS accounts and of SD accounts put S&Ls that were outside the NOW account states at a serious competitive disadvantage. They

[22] Telephone transfer accounts and EFT accounts offered by S&Ls could not be used for all transactions. An ATS account is as flexible as a demand deposit account, and it earns interest. Some S&Ls attempted to offer ATS accounts by maintaining demand deposit accounts for their customers at banks tied to the customers' savings accounts at the S&Ls. Administration of these accounts was costly and cumbersome.

sued, claiming that the Federal Reserve and the National Credit Union Administration lacked authority to authorize ATS and SD accounts. An organization of small banks also sued because it did not like any of this costly stuff. Both groups won their law suits. The courts ruled that automatic transfer systems and share draft accounts were simply transparent methods of evading federal law. However, the "damage" had already been done. The use of ATS and SD had spread sufficiently to make dismantling difficult. Furthermore, if ATS and SDs were eliminated, households would lose the benefits of receiving interest on their transactions accounts. The courts understood the situation and allowed the use of ATS and SD accounts to continue temporarily until Congress could act. In 1980, Congress finally authorized depository institutions throughout the country to offer interest-bearing transactions accounts.

MONEY MARKET MUTUAL FUNDS

Money market mutual funds are a relatively recent development in the financial system, and their growth until 1983 was phenomenal. Money market mutual funds ceased their rapid growth in 1983 after depository institutions were authorized to offer transactions and savings accounts that have no interest rate ceilings. The introduction of these accounts was largely a consequence of the success of the "money funds" in luring away the customers of depository institutions. This earned the funds a niche in American financial history and makes it worthwhile to review their success story.

Money market mutual funds thrived because they are not subject to the interest rate ceilings and other regulations that were applied to depository institutions. Their success is an excellent example of how a market economy finds means of circumventing arbitrary regulations.

A money market mutual fund issues shares to the public and uses the funds to purchase short-term (money market) instruments. The interest income on the investments, less operating costs, is passed on to shareholders. Along with paying market rates of interest, money funds offered several additional advantages to the public over the liabilities issued by depository institutions. Unlike money market certificates, which had a minimum denomination of $10,000, the minimum initial investment in a money market mutual fund was often $2500 or less. Furthermore, additional shares could be purchased at any time in minimum denominations of $100. Unlike any time account, there is no maturity for the mutual funds shares, so investors can liquidate their shares on demand. Withdrawals are easy. Shareholders notify a fund by telephone or in writing of the desire to make a withdrawal. The money fund either sends the customer a check or arranges to have the funds transferred to the customer's account in a depository institution. Alternatively, customers can make withdrawals by check. The check writing feature is similar to the automatic transfer systems used by banks. A customer establishes a demand deposit account in the bank used by the money market mutual fund. No funds are transferred into this account until the customer writes a check and the check is presented to the bank for payment. At that time, the bank notifies the money market mutual fund to transfer the amount written on the check from the customer's share account to his or her demand deposit account. The bank then uses these funds to make payment on the check. Until 1983, most money market mutual funds set a minimum denomination of from $250 to $500 per check. With the competition from depository institutions, this practice is disappearing.

The income earned on money market mutual fund shares varies with market interest rates. The mutual funds invest in a variety of short-term assets ranging from large denomination CDs to commercial paper. The mutual funds hold highly diversified portfolios containing the debt instruments of a number of large banks and a variety of large corporations. The mutual funds also diversify their assets by holding instruments of different maturities. Some instruments mature in a few days, and other instruments mature in several months. All the assets are short-term, however, with an average maturity that is typically from twenty to thirty days. Some money market mutual funds invest only in short-term securities issued by the U.S. government. These mutual funds diversify their asset holdings by maturity.

This brief description gives an indication of why money market mutual funds became popular with the public. They offer highly liquid assets paying a market rate of return that have low transactions costs and small denominations. In many respects they were superior to deposit accounts at banks, S&Ls, and MSBs. They offered a market rate of return on accounts that are the near equivalent of transactions accounts. Although the minimum denomination for checks prevents them from being used completely as transactions accounts, this complication was outweighed by the interest rate advantage over the 5.5 percent return available on NOW or ATS accounts. Shares in money market mutual funds are not insured, however. The lack of insurance makes these funds too risky for some households. The degree of risk in these funds is discussed later.

Money market mutual funds grew slowly until 1978. As market interest rates rose above the interest rate ceilings for accounts at depository institutions, the growth of money market mutual funds accelerated. The funds nearly tripled in size in 1978, and they had a fourfold expansion in 1979.

Large investors have always been able to earn a market rate of return on their assets.[23] When market interest rates rise above the interest rate ceilings on deposit accounts, they withdraw their money from depository institutions and invest in market instruments. Smaller investors cannot purchase many types of market instruments because of the large denominations and because costs are relatively high for small transactions in securities. This situation allowed depository institutions to practice price discrimination by paying market interest rates to large depositors and lower interest rates to small depositors. The government aided and

---

[23] Because of their flexibility and convenience, many business and institutional investors (e.g., pension funds) use money market mutual funds.

abetted this price discrimination by maintaining interest rate ceilings for all accounts except large denomination CDs and by setting the minimum denomination of Treasury bills and of money market certificates at $10,000. These government actions were rationalized as necessary in order to protect the earnings of the thrift institutions and, therefore, to ensure an adequate flow of funds into housing finance. In effect, the government assigned to small savers the burden of supporting housing.

Money market mutual funds allowed small savers to have the last laugh. When they withdrew their funds from accounts at depository institutions for investment in shares of money market mutual funds, small savers indirectly purchased the Treasury bills and CDs that were not available to them directly. Money market mutual funds effectively eliminated the price discrimination that had been practiced by depository institutions.

Although the growth of money market mutual funds from 1977 through 1979 was remarkable, expansion of the funds was retarded by two factors. First, they were prevented by regulations of the Securities and Exchange Commission (SEC) from advertising their service aggressively. Only cautious advertisements in the financial section of newspapers were allowed. As a result, most public awareness of the availability of money market mutual funds came as the result of word of mouth. Second, money market mutual funds were not well understood by the public. Many households were fearful that investment in money market mutual funds would be risky. It is true that these mutual fund shares are not insured, but their risk is low. There are money market mutual funds that purchase only short-term debt issued by the U.S. government. There is no risk of default on these securities. The only risk is from fluctuations in interest rates that affect the value of shares. Other money market mutual funds purchase short-term debt issued by private firms, so there is some risk. This risk is small, however, because only the CDs of the largest banks and the commercial paper of the largest corporations are purchased. Furthermore, the debt of a large number of firms is purchased by a money market mutual fund, so diversification reduces risk even further.

Despite the low risk of investing in money market mutual funds, many depositors at banks, S&Ls, MSBs, and CUs remained wary and refused to participate in the stampede to money market mutual funds. As knowledge of these funds spread, however, an increasing number of households switched from accounts at depository institutions to share accounts at money market mutual funds. In 1980 the SEC relaxed its restrictions on advertising, and the money funds started to compete actively against depository institutions. At that time, there was a further acceleration in the growth of these mutual funds.

Despite the problems that thrifts encountered in competing with money funds, they managed to grow rapidly, on average, from 1965 through 1979. Their growth was not steady because of disintermediation and reintermediation, but these institutions expanded impressively over the period. Table 10.3 shows the total assets of S&Ls, MSBs, and CUs in 1965 and in 1979. The assets of commercial banks are also shown for comparative purposes. From 1965 through 1979, the average growth of S&L assets was 11.3 percent per year. This rapid growth allowed S&Ls

TABLE 10.3
ASSET HOLDINGS FOR DEPOSITORY INSTITUTIONS (1965 and 1979)

	1965			1979		
	Assets (billions)	Percentage of Total	Average Annual Growth 1956–1965 (%)	Assets (billions)	Percentage of Total	Average Annual Growth 1965–1979 (%)
S&Ls	$129.6	65	14.7	$ 579.1	72	11.3
MSBs	59.1	30	7.2	165.0	20	7.6
CUs	11.0	5	16.0	62.3	8	13.2
Total	$199.7	100	12.0	$806.4	100	10.5
CBs	$336.4		6.5	$1,162.7		9.3
Thrifts as percentage of CBs		59.4			69.4	

Source: Board of Governors of the Federal Reserve System, *Flow of Funds Accounts*, December 1976 and February 1980.

to increase their share of the total assets in thrift institutions from 65 percent in 1965 to 72 percent in 1979. Mutual savings banks continued to grow more slowly than other types of institutions, and their share of total assets fell from 30 percent in 1965 to 20 percent in 1979. Credit unions experienced the most rapid growth (13.2 average percent per year), and their share of the total assets of thrifts rose from 5 percent in 1965 to 8 percent in 1979. Thrift institutions in total had an average growth of 10.5 percent per year. This was greater than the 9.3 percent growth of banks. As a result, the ratio of assets held by thrift institutions to assets held by banks rose from 59.4 percent in 1965 to 69.4 percent in 1979.

The information reported in Table 10.3 suggests that the problem faced by thrift institutions over the period 1965 through 1979 lay not with their ability to grow. The problem was primarily that their growth was erratic. This led to sharp fluctuations in the cost and availability of mortgage loans. Furthermore, the rapid growth of money market mutual funds indicated that the fluctuations in mortgage credit were apt to increase in the future. It was primarily these considerations that led Congress to pass financial legislation in 1980 that reduced the constraints on thrifts.

THE DEPOSITORY INSTITUTIONS DEREGULATION AND MONETARY CONTROL ACT OF 1980

In 1980 Congress passed the most important financial reform legislation since the 1930s. The Depository Institutions Deregulation and Monetary Control Act (DIDMCA) authorized NOW, ATS, and SD accounts nationwide; it required that interest rate ceilings on all deposit accounts except demand deposits be gradually eliminated; it increased the powers of savings and loan associations and mutual savings banks; and it imposed universal reserve requirements for the liabilities of all depository institutions.[24]

Over the years, a virtual unanimity developed among economists that thrift institutions should be granted broader investment powers, that they should be allowed to offer transactions accounts, and that interest rate ceilings for the liabilities of depository institutions should be eliminated. Many studies and recommendations appeared over the years to deregulate depository institutions, but Congress did not act. Calls for deregulation began with the Commission on Money and Credit and the Heller Commission in the 1960s. The Hunt Commission and the FINE study added their voices in the 1970s. Efforts to pass legislation in 1973 and 1975 failed.

Legislation was not passed because of fears that deregulation of depository institutions would have a deleterious effect on the financing and construction of housing. It was argued by the opponents of deregulation that an adequate supply of credit for the construction and purchase of housing was possible only if S&Ls and MSBs were required to direct their activities to real estate finance. Furthermore, if these institutions were to compete for funds in a free market, the costs of their liabilities would rise, and, therefore, mortgage interest rates would rise. It was concluded by the opponents of reform that continued specialization of S&Ls and MSBs and maintenance of interest rate ceilings on the liabilities of depository institutions were necessary to meet the nation's housing objectives.

Forcing S&Ls and MSBs to specialize in mortgage lending and imposing ceilings on interest rates for deposit accounts had not succeeded in stabilizing the cost and availability of mortgage credit. Furthermore, efforts to stabilize the mortgage market through government support programs were not successful. Despite these facts, representatives of labor unions, realtors, builders, thrift institutions, and small banks feared that deregulation would make the situation worse for them, and they successfully opposed reform legislation.

By 1980 events had evolved to the point that reform legislation was virtually inevitable. Automatic transfer systems and share draft accounts had expanded to the point that Congress could not turn back the clock by eliminating them. Yet the courts had determined that ATS and SD accounts were not permissible under existing law. Congress had little choice but to allow interest-bearing transactions accounts nationwide. Furthermore, banks, S&Ls, and MSBs were already issuing most of their liabilities in the form of money market certificates and large denomination CDs, which were paying a market rate of return. Despite the use of these instruments, many depository institutions were losing out to money market mutual funds.[25] It had become obvious that interest rate ceilings were not a viable

---

[24] The act exempted interest rates on various types of loans granted by depository institutions from state usury ceilings, it modified the Truth in Lending Act, and it had other features that are not discussed here.

[25] To a small extent, money market mutual funds purchased CDs from thrift institutions. In these instances, there was no net loss of funds by thrifts.

method of protecting depository institutions and that they must be eliminated for all savings and time accounts. It was also clear that S&Ls had to be given greater flexibility in selecting their asset portfolios if they were to survive in a world in which they offered transactions accounts and in which interest rate ceilings were eliminated for all their liabilities. Finally, with thrift institutions authorized to offer transactions accounts, the distinction between these institutions and banks was blurred. It did not make much sense to allow the Federal Reserve to impose reserve requirements on the liabilities of member banks and not on the same liabilities of other depository institutions.

These considerations led to the Depository Institutions Deregulation and Monetary Control Act (DIDMCA), which was signed into law by President Carter on March 1, 1980. The act eliminated interest rate ceilings for the savings and time accounts of all depository institutions. In order to ease the burden on these institutions, Congress allowed for a transition period, during which interest rate ceilings were to be gradually increased and then eliminated. For the transition period, authority over setting interest rate ceilings for the liabilities of depository institutions was transferred from the various regulatory agencies to a Depository Institutions Deregulation Committee (DIDC). This committee is comprised of the Secretary of the Treasury and the Chairmen of the Federal Reserve Board, the FDIC, Federal Home Loan Bank Board, and the National Credit Union Board. Congress directed the committee to phase out interest rate ceilings as rapidly as economic conditions warranted but no later than March 31, 1986. After that date the committee will cease to exist.

The act granted authority to offer interest-bearing transactions accounts to all insured depository institutions in the country. Thus, Congress allowed banks to continue to offer ATS accounts and credit unions to continue to offer SD accounts. All S&Ls, MSBs, and banks were authorized to offer NOW accounts. Households throughout the country became able to obtain interest-bearing transactions accounts from any type of depository institution. Interest-bearing transactions accounts were available only to households and to charitable organizations. All other economic agents, including business and governments, were still stuck with demand deposit accounts that paid no interest.

The act also significantly increased the flexibility of S&Ls. Congress authorized federally chartered S&Ls to hold up to 20 percent of their assets in consumer loans, commercial paper, and other corporate debt securities. Federal S&Ls were also authorized to offer credit card services and to engage in trust activities. Finally, Congress allowed all federal S&Ls to operate remote service units (computer terminals) for purpose of receiving deposits, granting withdrawals, and receiving payments on loans.[26] These various reforms reduced but did not eliminate the specialization of S&Ls. Congress determined that these institutions should continue to be primarily concerned with housing finance. It was recognized, howev-

---

[26] These units can be located at grocery or department stores or at other separate locations. They serve many of the functions of branches without being subject to branching restrictions.

er, that S&Ls must have greater flexibility in offering services to households and businesses if they were to remain viable. Congress also granted greater powers to federally chartered MSBs by allowing them to accept demand deposit accounts from business.

The act imposed universal reserve requirements for all federally insured banks, S&Ls, MSBs, and CUs, and it required the Federal Reserve to charge for its services. These provisions of the act are discussed in Chapter 12. For purposes of this chapter, it is sufficient to observe that these provisions provided greater competitive equity among depository institutions by subjecting them all to reserve requirements and by preventing the Federal Reserve from offering free services to member banks.

THRIFT INSTITUTIONS 1980 THROUGH 1982

By allowing thrift institutions to offer transactions accounts and by liberalizing the investment powers of S&Ls, Congress increased the ability of thrifts to compete within the financial system. Interest rate ceilings were still in effect, however. As a result, these institutions were still unable to compete effectively with money market mutual funds for the savings of many households. Furthermore, the investment powers of S&Ls and MSBs were still restricted primarily to real estate finance, and they encountered great difficulty in the environment of the high and volatile interest rates of 1980 through 1982. This section reviews the experiences of S&Ls and MSBs over that period.

Thrift institutions were not very successful in attracting transactions accounts away from banks. S&Ls and MSBs are not allowed to pay a higher interest rate than banks for these accounts, and despite vigorous advertising campaigns they did not attract much of the transactions account business. Credit unions were allowed to pay a higher interest rate on their transactions accounts, but their limited memberships have prevented them from being much of a factor.

Furthermore, market interest rates rose to record highs in 1980 and 1981. As a result, there was an acceleration in the public's withdrawals of funds from savings and time accounts in favor of investment in money market mutual funds and market securities. The Depository Institutions Deregulation Committee provided some relief by eliminating the fixed interest rate ceiling on time accounts with maturities of two and a half years or more. The interest rate ceiling was tied to the interest rate on two-and-a-half-year Treasury securities.[27] Thus, six-month certificates and two-and-a-half-year certificates paid interest rates that were com-

---

[27] S&Ls and MSBs were allowed to pay one quarter of one percent more on these time accounts than were commercial banks. The Garn-St Germain Depository Institutions Act of 1982, described later, eliminated all interest rate differentials no later than January 1, 1984 and they were actually eliminated on October 1, 1983.

petitive with market securities. Savings accounts and all time accounts other than the six-month and two-and-a-half-year certificates still had fixed interest rate ceilings that were completely out of touch with market interest rates.

Money market mutual funds grew at a phenomenal rate from 1980 through 1982. These mutual funds had total assets of about $45 billion at the end of 1979. By late 1982, their total assets had grown to over $250 billion! Much of this growth occurred at the expense of thrift institutions. Because of interest rate ceilings, these institutions were not able to compete with mutual funds for the savings of many households. Savings accounts at S&Ls and MSBs continued to pay 5.5 percent interest, and households shifted their funds from these accounts to money market mutual funds, which were paying as much as 17 percent. Even the time accounts whose interest rates were tied to the interest rates on Treasury securities were not as attractive as money market mutual funds or market securities for many households. As a result, the growth of these time accounts was limited.

In response to a depressed housing industry and to rising fears of insolvency for several large S&Ls and MSBs, Congress provided additional relief. As part of President Reagan's 1981 tax reduction package, Congress authorized depository institutions to offer special *all saver certificates* between October 1, 1981 and December 31, 1982, for which the first $1000 of interest income ($2000 for a joint return) was exempt from federal income tax. The certificates had a maturity of one year, and there was no minimum denomination requirement. There was an interest rate ceiling for these accounts equal to 70 percent of the interest rate on one-year Treasury securities. Because the interest income on these accounts was exempt from tax, their rate of return was competitive with alternative investments for many households with marginal tax brackets above 30 percent.

The tax-exempt feature of the all saver certificates allowed S&Ls and MSBs to pay an interest rate on these certificates that was below prevailing market interest rates.[28] Since the income from money market mutual funds is taxable, all saver certificates allowed thrift institutions to compete with these funds without having to pay the interest rates that these funds offered. Thus, Congress authorized an instrument that limited the interest costs for S&Ls and MSBs while allowing them to compete against money market mutual funds and market securities.[29]

The federal regulators helped reduce further the interest cost of depository institutions by allowing holders of the taxable six-month certificates to withdraw their funds prior to maturity without penalty provided that the funds were invested in the tax exempt all saver certificates.[30]

---

[28] Any depository institution could offer these accounts, but Congress required that institutions use the funds to support housing finance or loans to farmers.

[29] There are few, if any, free lunches in the world. The tax exempt feature of the all saver certificate amounted to a subsidy to depository institutions. Government revenues were reduced with all saver certificates.

[30] Congress also helped depository institutions by increasing the maximum contributions that households could make to retirement accounts.

Despite these developments, S&Ls and MSBs continued to rely heavily on six-month money market certificates as their source of funds to support their mortgage lending. The interest rates on these short-term liabilities rose dramatically over the period 1980 through 1982. The mortgage loans that were supported by these liabilities continued to earn a fixed interest income whereas the interest rates paid on the liabilities increased. As a result, S&Ls and MSBs saw their profits replaced by losses in 1980, and the trend worsened in 1981 and 1982.

It has been argued that long-term, fixed interest rate mortgage loans are no longer appropriate investments for thrift institutions. The cost of liabilities issued by S&Ls and MSBs fluctuate widely, but the income from their existing mortgage loans remains fixed. Before we discuss the merits of this argument, it is useful to review what the problem is.

One function of a financial intermediary is to borrow short term and to lend long term. When a financial intermediary extends a long-term loan and finances the loan with short-term liabilities, it must predict the future cost of its short-term liabilities. A long-term loan is profitable only if it can be financed by rolling over short-term liabilities that, on average, have lower interest cost than the interest income on the loan. In determining the expected rate of return on a mortgage loan, a depository institution must compare the interest rate on this long-term loan to the current and expected future interest rates for the liabilities that will support the loan. We know from the discussion of the term structure of interest rates presented in Chapter 6, that the loan is profitable only if the (geometric) average of current and future interest rates on the short-term liabilities is less than the interest rate on the long-term loan. In a world with volatile interest rates, it is difficult for the lender to predict the future cost of its liabilities. This makes it risky to grant long-term loans supported by short-term liabilities. The greater the risk, the greater the risk premium that the lender will demand. One of the activities of a financial intermediary is to earn the risk premium and to bridge the gap between short-term and long-term interest rates.

Until the mid-1960s, the risk premium was low. Market interest rates were stable and had proved to be quite predictable. Since the mid-1960s, interest rates have fluctuated widely about a rising trend. Both the fluctuations and the general rise in interest rates have been difficult, if not impossible, to predict. The inability to predict future interest rates has caused serious problems for mortgage lenders. For example, a mortgage loan extended in the 1960s at 6 percent interest might have looked like a good investment at the time, but by the 1970s it had proved to be a terrible investment indeed.

Fluctuations in interest rates and their rising trend have been caused mainly by variations in the rate of inflation and by various attempts by the government to control inflation. Time and time again lenders have found that their forecasts of future short-term interest rates have been wrong and the cost of their liabilities have exceeded expectations. This is precisely the problem that S&L and MSBs faced from 1980 through 1982.

Figure 10.3 compares the interest rate on new mortgage loans to the interest rates that S&Ls and MSBs paid on their liabilities from 1967 through 1982. Until

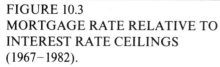

FIGURE 10.3
MORTGAGE RATE RELATIVE TO
INTEREST RATE CEILINGS
(1967–1982).

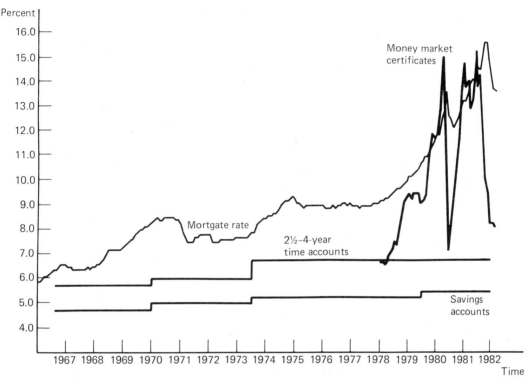

1978, when money market certificates became available, the interest rate paid on the liabilities of the thrift institutions was determined by the interest rate ceilings for various types of accounts. During the 1960s, most of the liabilities were in the form of savings accounts although the share of time accounts was increasing. The interest rate ceilings for both savings and time accounts were always below the interest rate on mortgage loans. Both S&Ls and MSBs earned substantial profits. Profitability continued into the 1970s as mortgage interest rates rose far above the interest rate ceilings on savings and time accounts. When market interest rates rose above the ceiling interest rates, disintermediation occurred, and the thrift institutions were not able to expand their lending substantially. They attempted to expand their lending by issuing large denomination CDs and by borrowing from Home Loan Banks or other sources. These sources of funds were more costly because it was necessary to pay market interest rates for these liabilities. As a result, profitability of the thrift institutions was reduced during periods of disintermediation.

In 1978, S&Ls and MSBs began to issue six-month money market certificates with an interest rate tied to the interest rate on six-month Treasury bills. As indicated earlier, the use of the certificates by S&Ls and MSBs expanded rapidly, and they soon became a major source of funds for these institutions. After 1978, the interest rate on these liabilities rose far above the interest rate ceilings for savings accounts and other types of time accounts. When the money market certificates became available, S&Ls and MSBs had no way of knowing that their interest costs would rise so substantially in future years. This led them to grant mortgage loans that were to prove to be highly unprofitable.

Consider the case of an S&L in mid-1978 that granted a thirty-year mortgage loan at a fixed interest rate of 9.5 percent. It supported the loan by money market certificates that had an interest rate of 7.5 percent when the mortgage loan was granted. The 2.0 percentage point spread between the 9.5 percent loan and the 7.5 percent certificates made the loan profitable when it was granted. Money market certificates have a maturity of six months. When they mature, new certificates must be issued that pay an interest rate that is tied to the prevailing interest rate on six-month Treasury bills. After mid-1978, the interest rate on Treasury bills rose sharply and remained high except for a few months in 1980. This meant that the 9.5 percent mortgage loan did not earn sufficient interest income to cover the interest cost of the six-month certificates used to support the loan. As a result, a loan that appeared to be profitable when it was granted proved to be unprofitable. If the S&L had known that the interest rates on six-month certificates were going to rise as they did, it would not have granted the mortgage loan at 9.5 percent interest. It would have charged an interest rate sufficiently high to compensate it for the future costs of its liabilities. The S&L did not predict the increase in Treasury bill rates and, as a result, granted a loan that proved to be unprofitable.

As Figure 10.3 indicates, the interest rate on mortgage loans increased after mid-1978. This increase was attributable in part to the rising interest rate on current money market certificates. The mortgage interest rate also rose as thrift institutions and other lenders attempted to protect themselves against future increases in the interest rate on six-month certificates. The interest rates on Treasury bills and on mortgage loans rose to record highs. Many of the mortgage loans held by depository institutions were granted in the 1970s at interest rates of 9 to 10 percent or less. These loans came to be supported by six-month certificates and other liabilities costing 15 percent or more. Even the mortgage loans of 12 to 13 percent granted in 1980 were not profitable at the interest rates for liabilities of 1981. This situation produced record losses for S&Ls and MSBs in 1981 and 1982. Many institutions failed, and there was a flurry of mergers to avoid further failures.

Events from 1978 through 1982 illustrate the problems that can arise for institutions that support long-term, fixed interest rate mortgage loans with short-term liabilities. Errors in forecasting future short-term rates can produce substantial loss for mortgage lenders. It is possible that short-term interest rates will fall in the future and that the mortgage loans currently held by depository institutions will become profitable. There is no assurance that this will occur, however.[31] It is clear that mortgage lending is more risky for thrift institutions than it was in the past. In a world of volatile short-term interest rates, it is risky to support long-term loans with short-term liabilities. As a result, a substantial risk premium has been built into mortgage interest rates.

There are two direct methods of reducing this risk. Mortgage lenders can lengthen the maturity of their liabilities, or they can shorten the maturity of their mortgage loans. From 1978 through late 1981, thrift institutions actually short-ened the maturity of their liabilities. This occurred because they placed in-creased reliance on six-month certificates. The shortening of the maturity of lia-bilities increased interest rate risk.

Beginning in late 1981, the regulators began to relax the interest rate ceilings for all small denomination time accounts. In August 1981 the ceiling for time ac-counts with maturities of two and a half to three and a half years was tied to the interest rate on two-and-a-half-year Treasury securities. In December of 1981, the interest rate ceiling was eliminated for time accounts held in retirement plans. Both of these actions allowed thrifts to compete more effectively for longer-term accounts. In May of 1982, the ceiling for time accounts with maturities of over three and a half years were totally eliminated. This further increased the ability of thrifts to lengthen the maturity of their liabilities. Also in May 1982 depository in-stitutions were allowed to offer ninety-one-day time accounts whose interest ceil-ing was tied to the interest rate on ninety-one-day Treasury bills. This was fol-lowed in September 1982 by authority to issue time accounts with maturities of seven to thirty-one days whose ceiling was also tied to the interest rate on ninety-one-day Treasury bills. These last two actions obviously did not encourage lengthening of the maturity of thrift liabilities, but they did allow them to compete more effectively with money market mutual funds.

Thrift institutions also moved to reduce interest rate risk by issuing mortgage loans with a floating interest rate. With these loans, the interest rate is not fixed over the life of the mortgage, but rather it moves with market interest rates. There are various forms of these loans but two types that have gained popularity. The first type is the *variable rate mortgage,* which is a mortgage loan with a fixed matu-rity whose interest rate varies periodically with market interest rates.[32] In an effort to protect borrowers from large increases in their interest payments, state law and federal regulation initially restricted the extent that interest rates could increase over the life of the loan. These restrictions were subsequently reduced or eliminated and interest rates on these loans are now free to fluctuate with market interest rates. The second type of variable interest loans involves a *rollover mort-gage* in which a mortgage loan is granted for a fixed maturity of twenty-five to

---

[31] Furthermore, if the mortgage interest rate falls substantially, many holders of high-interest loans will refinance.
[32] To a limited extent, borrowers are allowed to extend the maturity of their loans in a manner that leaves the monthly payments unaffected.

thirty years, but the interest rate on the loan is renegotiated every three to five years. Over each three-to-five-year interval, the interest rate is fixed, and, therefore, the monthly payments are also fixed. These mortgage instruments and others like them all involve, in one way or another, an attempt on the part of mortgage lenders to reduce their interest rate risk. These instruments allow thrift institutions to vary the interest rate charged on a mortgage loan in a manner that accords with prevailing interest rates for their liabilities.

Mortgage loans with floating interest rates shift the interest rate risk from the lender to the borrower. Borrowers must make the calculations concerning what they expect short-term interest rates to be in the future in order to evaluate the current and future costs of their mortgage debt. Mortgage lenders have had only limited success in inducing households to bear this risk.

Despite the increased powers granted to thrift institutions by the Depository Institutions Deregulation Act of 1980 and despite the significant progress in relaxing interest rate ceilings, the 1979-1982 period was a terrible one for S&Ls and MSBs. The high level of interest rates during this period drove the costs of liabilities above the returns on their asset portfolios. Mortgage interest rates reached record levels, and as a result the demand for mortgage credit was low. This meant that virtually all of the mortgage loan income of S&Ls and MSBs was provided by old loans with relatively low interest rates. Thrift institutions experienced record losses, and some went out of business.

In October 1982, Congress acted to deregulate further depository institutions and to improve their competitive position in the financial system. The new law was nearly as revolutionary as the 1980 Act.

The Garn-St Germain Depository Institutions Act of 1982[33]

The Garn-St Germain Act accelerated the deregulation of thrift institutions, and it granted regulators extraordinary powers to handle the many failures of thrift institutions that were occurring. In essence, the 1982 act gave regulators authority to pick up the pieces from the disastrous experiences of the last several years. It then went about deregulating depository institutions in an effort to avoid similar problems in the future. Space does not allow a description of the powers granted to regulators to expedite mergers and to use other methods of handling failed thrift institutions. Rather, we shall devote the discussion to the deregulation aspect of the law.

The Garn-St Germain Act took another substantial step in liberalizing the powers of thrift institutions. Federally chartered thrifts (S&Ls and savings banks) are authorized to engage in commercial lending. By 1984 these institutions can devote up to 10 percent of their assets to commercial lending. Furthermore, thrifts are allowed to accept demand deposits from customers who have established a

---

[33] This act is named after the chairmen of the Senate and House Banking Committees, respectively.

loan relationship with them. These powers mean that thrift institutions can, to a substantial extent, act like commercial banks. Furthermore, the maximum amount of consumer lending by these institutions was raised from 20 to 30 percent of total assets. Their powers to purchase state and local securities was increased, and lending for nonresidential real estate was also liberalized. Thrift institutions now have substantial authority to hold diversified asset portfolios.

The Garn-St Germain Act also authorized depository institutions to offer an account with no interest rate ceiling that is competitive with money market mutual funds. This new *money market account* is a mixture of a transactions account and a savings account. Depositors are allowed to make six transactions per month with these accounts; a maximum of three can be by check; and the remainder, by preauthorization. Money market accounts have a minimum balance requirement of $2500, and are available to individuals, nonprofit organizations, governmental units, *and* business.

The money market account allowed depository institutions to compete effectively with money market mutual funds. Because there is no interest rate ceiling, the accounts can pay an interest rate that is competitive with money funds. Furthermore, the accounts are insured. This gives them a distinct advantage over money market mutual funds. The only disadvantage of the new account is the limitation on the number of transactions allowed. This has not proved to be a major disadvantage. The public shifted substantial sums from money funds to the new accounts.

Following passage of the Garn-St Germain Act, the Depository Institutions Deregulation Committee (DIDC) authorized depository institutions to offer transactions accounts to individuals, nonprofit organizations, and governments that have no interest rate ceiling. These *super NOW accounts* have a minimum balance requirement of $2500 and no limitation on the number of transactions that can be conducted. There is a reserve requirement for super NOW accounts that prevents depository institutions from paying as high an interest rate on them as for money :market accounts. With the introduction of insured money market and super NOW accounts, depository institutions have achieved a competitive advantage over money market mutual funds.

Finally, the Garn-St Germain Act required that all interest rate differentials for the liabilities of thrifts over those of commercial banks be eliminated by January 1, 1984. The DDIC responded by eliminating all the interest rate differentials on October 1, 1983. At the same time, it eliminated interest rate ceilings and minimum balance requirements for all time accounts with maturities greater than 31 days. Now banks and thrifts are free to compete for time accounts. Accounts with maturities of 7–31 days and denominations of at least $2500 also had their interest rate ceiling eliminated. The only accounts with interest rate ceilings are those with maturities of 7–31 days and denominations of $2500, ordinary passbook accounts, and NOW accounts with balances below $2500. All of these types of accounts have an interest rate ceiling of 5 1/4 percent.

The reforms of the 1980 and 1982 laws substantially increased the flexibility of thrift institutions. This flexibility greatly reduced the forced specialization of depository institutions. With greater flexibility to issue liabilities and to acquire various assets, these institutions are in a better position to weather future storms. As an indication of the liberating force of the 1980 and 1982 laws, the share of total assets devoted to mortgage loans by S&Ls fell from 80 percent in 1980 to 68 percent in 1982. This downward trend is likely to continue for years to come. The extent to which the thrifts continue to specialize in housing finance will be determined more by economic choice and less by government control.

SUMMARY

This chapter has described the role of savings and loan associations, mutual savings banks, and credit unions in the financial system. These thrift institutions in total hold over $900 billion of assets, so their sheer size assures them an important role as financial intermediaries. The importance of these depository institutions has been disproportionate to their size, however, because of their special role in serving the financial needs of households. Historically, they were the only institutions that offered households a safe and renumerative place to invest their savings, and they were usually the only source of loans to households. Today, thanks in part to the pioneering efforts of the thrifts, households have many alternatives available for their savings and for their borrowing.

Because the government viewed S&Ls and MSBs as vehicle for allocating credit to housing, laws and regulations were developed limiting their activities primarily to housing finance. The constraints placed on S&Ls and MSBs had little significance until the mid-1960s. At that time, market interest rates began to fluctuate sharply about a rising trend. This behavior of interest rates had adverse effects on the thrifts. In an effort to assist S&Ls and MSBs while maintaining their specialization in housing finance, the government imposed interest rate ceilings on their liabilities and developed massive programs to purchase their mortgage loans during periods of disintermediation. Interest rate ceilings proved to be increasingly ineffective and increasingly discriminatory with each episode of disintermediation. Wealthy customers simply withdrew their funds from saving and time accounts and invested in securities when market interest rates rose above the interest rate ceilings on the liabilities of depository institutions. Less wealthy customers could not invest in market securities because of the large denominations of these instruments. Small savers were stuck with the returns available on savings and time accounts.

Since 1978, market interest rates have remained above the interest rates on ordinary savings and time accounts. The government allowed depository institutions to compete against market securities by offering six-month time accounts with an interest rate ceiling tied to the interest rate on six-month Treasury bills. By imposing a $10,000 minimum denomination for these accounts, depository institutions could offer an instrument that was attractive to relatively wealthy customers while continuing to pay low interest rates on the accounts of smaller savers.

Money market mutual funds developed that offered market interest rates and high liquidity to both small and large investors. These mutual funds were very successful in attracting funds away from depository institutions. These funds grew to the point that Congress finally voted to eliminate interest rate ceilings. Because of fear that S&Ls and MSBs could not afford to pay market interest rates immediately, interest rate ceilings were only allowed to be eliminated gradually. Major progress has been made, however. Super NOW accounts, money market savings accounts, and virtually all time accounts have no ceilings. All other ceilings will disappear by 1986.

Rapid growth of money market mutual funds from 1978 through 1982 led Congress and DIDC to authorize transactions accounts without interest rate ceilings. These accounts have made thrift institutions competitive within the financial system.

Forcing thrift institutions to specialize in housing finance did not insulate the housing industry from the effects of interest rate fluctuations. Mortgage interest rates rose, and the availability of housing loans declined when market interest rates rose. When interest rates declined, mortgage interest rates fell, and the availability of credit increased.

Market forces induced the government to eliminate interest rate ceilings and to enhance the powers of S&Ls and MSBs. The thrift institutions responded by reducing the share of total assets devoted to mortgage loans and increasing the share devoted to business and consumer loans. These changes are an inevitable consequence of the need to diversify asset portfolios in the environment of high and variable interest rates that have prevailed over the past two decades.

SELECTED REFERENCES

Federal Reserve Bank of Boston, *Housing and Monetary Policy*, Conference Series No. 4, Boston, 1970.

_____, *Policies for a More Competitive Financial System*, Conference Series No. 8, Boston, 1972.

_____, *The Future of the Thrift Industry*, Conference Series No. 24, 1981.

U.S. Congress, House Committee on Banking Currency and Housing, *Financial Institutions and the Nation's Economy, Compendium of Papers Prepared for the FINE Study*, James Pierce (ed.), 94th Congress, 2nd session, 1976.

THE ROLE OF DEPOSITORY INSTITUTIONS IN DETERMINING THE QUANTITY OF MONEY

11

Depository institutions play a key role in determining the quantity of money in the economy. We will see in later chapters that changes in the quantity of money affect interest rates, real output, and the price level. It is important, therefore, that the forces determining the quantity of money be understood. The role of depository institutions is stressed, and considerable attention is paid to the mechanics of how money is created. The primary goal of the chapter, however, is to demonstrate that the quantity of money is determined not only by depository institutions but also by the portfolio decisions of the public and by the policy actions of the Federal Reserve.

We define the quantity of money to be the sum of all coin and currency held by the public plus all the transactions account balances held by the public in depository institutions.[1] As indicated in Chapter 1, this is called M1. Until recently, only commercial banks were allowed to offer transactions accounts, so discussions of the money supply dealt with the behavior of banks. As we saw in Chapter 10, commercial banks have lost their monopoly over transactions accounts, and now savings and loan associations, mutual savings banks, and credit unions also handle these accounts. As a result, we must include these institutions in our discussion.

SOME IMPORTANT INSTITUTIONAL DETAIL

Before we turn to the discussion of the money supply, it is necessary to describe the structure of reserve requirements for depository institutions and to discuss the

---

[1] That is to say, coin and currency plus transactions accounts held outside of bank vaults, the Federal Reserve, and the U.S. Treasury.

mechanics of how funds are transferred from one institution to another. Knowledge of these details is crucial for understanding how the quantity of money is determined.

The Structure of Reserve Requirements

The Monetary Control Act of 1980 authorizes the Federal Reserve to assess reserve requirements against certain liabilities issued by depository institutions. The Federal Reserve requires federally insured depository institutions to hold a percentage of these liabilities in the form of reserves. The actual percentage, for example, 10 percent, is called the *reserve requirement*. The reserve requirement is multiplied by the amount of "reservable" liabilities for an institution to determine the quantity of its *required reserves*. The essential feature of required reserves is that they are held idle. They are funds that cannot be used by a depository institution to grant loans or purchase securities. Required reserves may be held either in a reserve account at the Federal Reserve or in the form of vault cash. Depository institutions that are not members of the Federal Reserve System are allowed to hold their required reserves in the form of vault cash plus account balances with other institutions. These institutions then deposit the funds with the Federal Reserve.

The Monetary Control Act specifies two types of liabilities that are subject to reserve requirements: transactions accounts and nonpersonal time accounts. The law requires the Federal Reserve to impose a reserve requirement of 3 percent for the first $25 million of transactions account liabilities of each depository institution. The Fed is authorized to impose a reserve requirement of between 8 and 14 percent for transactions account liabilities at each institution in excess of $25 million. This reserve requirement is presently 12 percent. The Federal Reserve is also authorized to impose reserve requirements against some of the time account liabilities of depository institutions. Here a distinction is made between liabilities issued to persons and liabilities issued to businesses, governments, and other "nonpersons." The Federal Reserve is not allowed to impose reserve requirements against time account liabilities issued to persons. The law does authorize the Fed to impose a reserve requirement of between 0 and 3 percent for the nonpersonal time account liabilities of depository institutions.[2] The present reserve requirement is 3 percent for nonpersonal time account liabilities with maturities of less than four years and zero for liabilities with maturities of four years or more. As a final complication, the Garn-St Germain Depository Institutions Act of 1982 exempts the first $2 million of "reservable liabilities" (e.g., transactions and nonpersonal time accounts) from reserve requirements.

Transfers of Funds Between Depository Institutions

Knowledge of how funds are transferred from one depository institution to another is crucial for understanding how the quantity of money is determined. Funds

---

[2] A reserve requirement is also imposed on certain Eurodollar and holding company liabilities. These complications are discussed later in the chapter.

are transferred by use of reserve accounts at the Federal Reserve.[3] Depository institutions maintain reserve balances at the Fed for two reasons. First, they are required by law to hold a fraction of their transactions and nonpersonal time account liabilities as required reserves. Second, institutions use their reserve accounts to conduct transactions. The Federal Reserve is a bank for depository institutions, and reserve accounts are the equivalent of transactions accounts for these institutions. When a depository institution issues additional liabilities or sells assets, it initially puts the funds received into its reserve account. When the quantity of liabilities declines or when an institution purchases assets, it pays the funds out of its reserve account. Thus, the balances in reserve accounts fluctuate from day to day as depository institutions conduct their transactions.[4] A reserve balance must not fall below the minimum required by law, however. Reserve requirements can also be met by holdings of vault cash. We omit a discussion of vault cash because it complicates the story without adding any substance. Reserve requirements do not have to be met day by day. Rather, a depository institution must maintain an average reserve balance for a week that is a fraction of its average account liabilities.[5] Reserve deficiencies are allowed under certain circumstances. When an institution has a reserve balance greater than the minimum required by law, it is holding *excess reserves*.

Now consider two depository institutions, cleverly called Bank A and S&L B. Simplified balance sheets for the two institutions are given as follows.

Bank A

Assets		Liabilities and Net Worth	
Reserves at Fed	$ 1,000	Transactions accounts	$10,000
Loans and securities	9,750	Net worth	750
Total	$10,750	Total	$10,750

S&L B

Assets		Liabilities and Net Worth	
Reserves at Fed	$ 5,000	Transactions accounts	$50,000
Loans and securities	48,750	Net worth	3,750
Total	$53,750	Total	$53,750

[3] Funds can also be transferred directly from one institution to another. For simplicity, these transactions are not considered.

[4] Many institutions also maintain accounts at private depository institutions for much the same purposes.

[5] Under current regulations, required reserves in a week are determined by average liabilities two weeks earlier. The complications produced by this lagged reserve accounting are not considered here. This subject is discussed in Chapter 18.

The depository institutions hold only two kinds of assets: reserve balances at the Federal Reserve and loans plus securities. For simplicity, we do not let them hold vault cash. Transactions accounts are the institutions' only liabilities, and the difference between their assets and their liabilities is net worth. The Federal Reserve is assumed to have a reserve requirement of 10 percent, so each institution holds 10 percent of its transactions account liabilities in a reserve account as required reserves. Neither institution has a reserve balance in excess of 10 percent of its liabilities, so there are no excess reserves. Bank A has total assets of $10,750 composed of $1000 of reserves and $9750 of loans and securities. These loans and securities represent the total credit extended by the institution. The bank supports its asset holdings with $10,000 of transactions accounts and $750 of net worth. S&L B has $53,750 of total assets, of which $5000 is at the Fed and $48,750 is invested in loans and securities. These assets are supported by $50,000 of transactions accounts, and $3750 of net worth.

Assume that a depositor at Bank A writes a $1000 check to a merchant who deposits the money in S&L B. The bank must honor the check on demand. When the S&L presents the check to the Federal Reserve for payment, the Fed transfers $1000 from the reserve account of Bank A to the reserve account of S&L B. The balance sheet of Bank A after the transfer of reserves is shown as follows.

	Bank A		
Assets		Liabilities and Net Worth	
Reserves at Fed	$ 0	Transactions accounts	$9,000
Loans and securities	9,750	Net worth	750
Total	$9,750	Total	$9,750

With the transfer, the assets and liabilities of Bank A fall by $1000. The bank still has transactions account liabilities of $9000 and it is legally required to hold 10 percent, or $900, as required reserves with the Fed against these liabilities. With the transfer of $1000 of reserves to S&L B, the bank has a reserve deficiency of $900, which must be eliminated.[6] Assume that Bank A cannot borrow or in any other way manage its liabilities, so its only option is to sell $900 of assets. Because of their high liquidity and low transactions costs, the bank sells securities. For simplicity, assume that the securities are purchased by S&L B. This assumption is not crucial, but it allows us to study the transfer of funds between institutions with a minimum of complexity. After the sale of securities, the balance sheet of Bank A appears as $900 of reserves at the Fed, $8850 of loans and securities, $9000 in

---

[6] If the check had been for more than $1000, the bank would not have sufficient funds in its reserve account to cover the check. In this case, the Fed would still increase the reserve account of S&L B by the amount of the check, and it would require Bank A to cover its entire reserve deficiency.

transactions account liabilities, and $750 in net worth. The bank's assets decline by $1000: $100 comes from the reduction of required reserves, which results from the $1000 decline in transactions account liabilities, and $900 comes from a reduction in securities.

Bank A			
Assets		Liabilities and Net Worth	
Reserves at Fed	$ 900	Transactions accounts	$9,000
Loans and securities	8,850	Net worth	750
Total	$9,750	Total	$9,750

The adjustments for S&L B are the reverse of those of Bank A. When the S&L receives the $1000 deposit, its assets and liabilities rise by $1000. Initially, the entire increase in assets is in the form of balances at the Federal Reserve, which rise by $1000 from $5000 to $6000. Its balance sheet appears as follows:

S&L B			
Assets		Liabilities and Net Worth	
Reserves at Fed	$ 6,000	Transactions accounts	$51,000
Loans and securities	48,750	Net worth	3,750
Total	$54,750	Total	$54,750

Because reserve balances at the Fed earn no interest, S&L B has an incentive to extend additional credit, that is, to purchase securities or grant loans. The S&L cannot use the entire $1000, however, because 10 percent, or $100, must be held as required reserves against the $1000 addition to its transactions account liabilities. It does have $900 of excess reserves, however, which it uses to purchase the securities sold by Bank A. After the securities are purchased, the balance sheet shows that the S&L still has $1000 more assets, of which $100 is in additional required reserves and $900 is in additional loans and securities.

S&L B			
Assets		Liabilities and Net Worth	
Reserves at Fed	$ 5,100	Transactions accounts	$51,000
Loans and securities	49,650	Net worth	3,750
Total	$54,750	Total	$54,750

After all the smoke has cleared, Bank A has $1000 less assets, and S&L B has $1000 more assets. The total assets held by the two institutions combined have not changed. Furthermore, the bank has $100 less reserves at the Fed, and the S&L has $100 more, so the combined reserve balance of the two institutions has not changed. Finally, Bank A reduced its loans and securities by $900, and S&L B increased its loans and securities by the same amount. The total quantity of credit extended by the two institutions combined has not changed.

When there is a transfer of funds from the bank to the S&L, the total quantity of transactions accounts and credit is unchanged. This story could be told for any pair of institutions. Thus, transfers of transactions account balances from one depository institution to another do not affect the total quantity of transactions accounts in the economy or the total quantity of loans and securities held by depository institutions.

There is an exception, however, to this conclusion. It was assumed that neither institution wants to hold any excess reserves. If this assumption is relaxed, transfers of funds can affect the total quantity of loans and securities held by depository institutions. If Bank A, for example, held reserve balances at the Fed in excess of the $1000 needed to meet its reserve requirements for the original $10,000 of transactions account liabilities, it could use these excess reserves to help cover the loss of funds. Consider the alternative balance sheet for Bank A shown below.

Bank A

Assets		Liabilities and Net Worth	
Reserves at Fed	$ 2,000	Transactions accounts	$10,000
Loans and securities	8,750	Net worth	750
Total	$10,750	Total	$10,750

In this case, the bank has $10,000 of transactions account liabilities but it holds $2000, rather than $1000, as reserves at the Fed. Its required reserves are $1000, so its excess reserves are also $1000. Because of these excess reserves, the bank has extended only $8750 of credit rather than the $9750 of loans and securities held in the case where it has no excess reserves. Now when Bank A loses $1000 of transactions accounts, it can meet the entire loss from its excess reserves. The $1000 is transferred from its reserve account to the account of S&L B. After the transfer, the bank's balance sheet shows reserves at the Fed of $1000, of which $900 is required to cover the $9000 of remaining transactions account liabilities, and $100 is excess reserves. Bank A still holds $8750 of loans and securities.

Bank A

Assets		Liabilities and Net Worth	
Reserves at Fed	$1,000	Transactions accounts	$9,000
Loans and securities	8,750	Net worth	750
Total	$9,750	Total	$9,750

If S&L B takes the $1000 increase in transactions accounts, sets aside $100 as required reserves, and uses the remaining $900 to acquire loans and securities, there is an expansion of credit for the two institutions combined. Bank A does not reduce its loans and securities, and S&L B raises its loans and securities by $900, so total credit extended by the two institutions rises by $900. When there is a transfer of funds from one institution to another and the institution that loses funds covers all or part of the loss from excess reserves and when the receiving institution does not add a like amount to its excess reserves, the loans and securities for the two institutions combined expand. This occurs even though the quantity of transactions account liabilities in the two institutions combined has not changed.

In general, the decisions of depository institutions concerning their holdings of excess reserves affect the degree to which the quantity of credit changes when there are transfers of funds from one institution to another. If neither institution holds any excess reserves or if both hold the same percentage of their liabilities as excess reserves, a transfer of funds does not affect the quantity of credit (loans and securities). If the institutions differ in the percentage of their liabilities held as excess reserves, there is a change in the total quantity of loans and securities when transactions account balances move from one institution to another. If the losing institution withdraws a larger amount of excess reserves than the gaining institution adds to excess reserves, credit expands. If the losing institution withdraws a smaller amount from excess reserves than the gaining institution adds to excess reserves, total credit declines. If the two institution have different percentage reserve requirements, the quantity of credit is also affected by transfers of funds. In all cases, however, the quantity of total transactions account liabilities in the two institutions combined is unchanged when funds shift from one institution to another.[7] In order to determine how the total quantity of liabilities changes, we must turn to transactions that do not involve a simple transfer of funds between institutions.

THE MULTIPLE EXPANSION AND CONTRACTION OF MONEY

We will start the discussion by making some simplifying assumptions that allow us to focus on the mechanics of the multiple expansion and contraction of money. These assumptions are subsequently relaxed or modified to provide a more realistic account of how the portfolio choices of depository institutions and of the

---

[7] We will see later that if depository institutions hold different proportions of their liabilities as excess reserves, a transfer of funds produces a multiple expansion or contraction in the quantity of transactions accounts and credit.

public affect the quantity of money in the economy. The assumptions are as follows:

1. Transactions accounts are the only liability issued by depository institutions.
2. The interest rate on transactions accounts is fixed.
3. All institutions have the same percentage reserve requirement against their transactions accounts.
4. Depository institutions do not want to hold any excess reserves.
5. The public does not change its holdings of currency.
6. Banks do not change their holdings of vault cash.

It is shown later that, given these assumptions, the only way that the total quantity of money can change is for the total quantity of reserves held by depository institutions to change.

Under the preceding assumptions, the policies of the Federal Reserve determine the quantity of reserves held by depository institutions.[8] When the Fed increases its lending to depository institutions or when it purchases securities, the total quantity of reserves increase. When the Fed reduces its loans or when it sells securities, the total quantity of reserves declines.

The relationship between Federal Reserve loans and the total quantity of reserves is straightforward. When the Fed extends credit to a depository institution, it simply increases the institution's reserve balance by the amount of the loan. This increases the total quantity of reserves in the depository system because the borrowing institution increases its reserves and no other institution experiences a loss of reserves. When a depository institution repays a loan, the Fed reduces its reserve balance without increasing the reserve balances of any other institution. In this case, the total reserves in the system decline. As a central bank, the Federal Reserve has the authority to create or destroy reserves with the stroke of a pen (computer).

The Fed also affects the quantity of reserves when it purchases or sells securities. The Federal Reserve pays for securities by writing a check on itself. The seller deposits the check with a depository institution and that institution presents the check to the Fed for payment. Payment is made by increasing the institution's reserve balance by the amount of the check. The Fed simply creates this addition to the institution's reserve account. The ability of the central bank to create or destroy reserves is a basic feature of a fiat monetary system. The reserves of all other institutions are unaffected, so when the Federal Reserve purchases securities, it increases total reserves. When the Federal Reserve sells a security, the purchaser writes a check to the Fed. The Federal Reserve, in turn,

---

[8] The determination of total reserves is discussed in detail in Chapter 12.

reduces the reserve balance of the depository institution upon which the check is written. Thus, when the Federal Reserve sells securities it reduces total reserves.[9]

With these preliminaries out of the way, we can now determine how a change in the quantity of reserves affects the quantity of transactions accounts and money in the economy. Assume that the Federal Reserve purchases $1000 of securities from a dealer.[10] The dealer deposits the Fed's check with Bank A. That bank presents the check to the Fed and has its reserve balance increased by $1,000. Because the money came from the Fed, the dealer's deposit is not offset by a reduction of the quantity of transactions accounts or reserves at any other depository institution. The total quantity of transactions accounts money and reserves in the economy rise by $1000.

The balance sheets for Bank A before and after the $1000 purchase of securities by the Fed are shown as follows.

Bank A: Before Security Purchase

Assets			Liabilities and Net Worth	
Reserves at Fed			Transactions accounts	$10,000
Required	$1,000			
Excess	0	$ 1,000		
Loans and securities		9,750	Net worth	750
Total		$10,750	Total	$10,750

Bank A: After Security Purchase

Assets			Liabilities and Net Worth	
Reserves at Fed			Transactions accounts	$11,000
Required	$1,100			
Excess	900	$ 2,000		
Loans and securities		9,750	Net worth	750
Total		$11,750	Total	$11,750

Before the Federal Reserve's purchase of securities, the bank has transactions account liabilities of $10,000. It has $1000 in its reserve account, which, with a 10 percent reserve requirement, is just sufficient to meet its required reserves. It had no excess reserves. When the Federal Reserve purchases the securities, the dealer

---

[9] In practice, checks are rarely written. The Fed purchases and sells securities through dealers. It directly increases or decreases the reserve account of a dealer's depository institution.

[10] See Chapter 4 for a description of securities dealers.

that sold them deposits the Fed's $1000 check with Bank A. The Federal Reserve covers its check by increasing the reserve account of Bank A by $1000. Thus, the transactions account liabilities of Bank A rise by $1000, and its reserve balances at the Fed rise by $1000. The $1000 rise in transactions account liabilities increases required reserves by $100 from $1000 to $1100. Total reserve balances rose by $1000, so excess reserves are now $900.

By assumption, the bank does not want to hold excess reserves; it uses the entire $900 to expand its loans.[11] Assume that Bank A grants the loan by issuing a check for $900 to the borrower.[12] The borrower uses the $900 to buy new textbooks. The bookstore deposits the $900 check in S&L B.[13] The S&L presents the check to the Fed, which transfers $900 from the reserve account of Bank A to the reserve account of S&L B. Thus, there is a transfer of funds from Bank A to S&L B. This transfer is different from the transfers of funds discussed earlier, however, because it does not involve a shift of transactions account balances from nme institution to another. It is the $900 of excess reserves at Bank A that are transferred to S&L B. The dealer's initial $1000 deposit remains with Bank A. These balances support $100 of additional required reserves and $900 of additional loans at Bank A. The quantity of transactions accounts and of reserves at S&L B rises by $900 without a reduction in the quantity of transactions account balances at Bank A.

The balance sheet for Bank A after it lends $900 and after the Fed has transferred the $900 from its reserve account to the account of S&L B is shown as follows.

Bank A

Assets			Liabilities and Net Worth	
Reserves at Fed			Transactions accounts	$11,000
Required	$1,100			
Excess	0	$ 1,100		
Loans and securities		10,650	Net worth	750
Total		$11,750	Total	$11,750

[11] The important factor for the expansion of money and credit is that the bank uses the $900 to extend additional credit rather than holding the $900 as excess reserves. Whether the bank grants loans or purchases securities is immaterial.

[12] There are three ways a depository institution can pay for assets: it can pay out currency, it can write a check on itself, or it can increase the account balance of the borrower. For reasons that are explained later, the form in which payment is made is immaterial to the expansion of money and credit that ensues. The story is most easily told, however, by assuming that depository institutions grant loans or purchase securities by writing checks on themselves.

[13] As long as reserve requirements are the same for all depository institutions, the identity of the institution is immaterial, that is, it could be Bank A, S&L B or Bank Z. If reserve requirements differ among institutions or if institutions differ in their propensity to hold excess reserves, the identity of the institution is material. These complications are discussed later.

The change in the balance sheet of S&L B is shown as follows. The transactions account liabilities and the reserves of S&L B rise by $900. It needs to hold 10 percent of the increased liabilities as required reserves, so required reserves rise by $90, and excess reserves rise by $810.

S&L B

Change in Assets			Change in Liabilities and Net Worth	
Reserves at Fed			Transactions accounts	$900
Required	$ 90			
Excess	810	$900		
Loans and securities		0	Net worth	0
Total		$900	Total	$900

Because S&L B does not want to hold any additional excess reserves, it uses the $810 to grant a new loan. The S&L grants the loan by issuing a check to the borrower, who makes an expenditure. The recipient of the expenditure, in turn, deposits the $810 in MSB C. The check is presented to S&L B for payment, which honors the check by transferring its $810 of excess reserves into the reserve account of MSB C. The reserve balance of S&L B declines by $810 whereas the transactions account liabilities and reserve balance of MSB C rise by $810. The required reserves at MSB C increase by $81, and MSB C uses the remaining $729 of excess reserves to grant new loans.

A pattern of expansion for transactions accounts and loans emerges. Each time a depository institution receives new deposits, it sets aside 10 percent as required reserves and uses the remaining excess reserves to extend additional credit. As institutions receive new deposits and acquire additional earning assets, the total quantity of transactions accounts and assets rise in the system. The increases in transactions account liabilities that occur at each institution in the chain remain with that institution.[14] It is excess reserves that get passed from one institution to the next as each institution spends its excess reserves to acquire additional earning assets. Each institution can only lend 90 percent of its increased liabilities, so the rise in transactions accounts and excess reserves at the next institution are 10 percent smaller than at the previous one. This absorption of funds into required reserves limits the total expansion of transactions accounts for the system as a whole.

The process of expansion of transactions account liabilities and credit can be viewed as a series of steps as shown in Table 11.1 The first and crucial step involves an injection of reserves into the depository system in the form of a $1000 security purchase by the Federal Reserve, which is deposited in Bank A. This

---

[14] We will see later that even if depositors withdraw funds from their newly expanded accounts, the expansion of transactions accounts and assets in the depository system is not affected so long as the funds are transferred from one institution to another.

TABLE 11.1
INSTITUTION-BY-INSTITUTION EXPANSION OF TRANSACTIONS ACCOUNTS,
REQUIRED RESERVES, AND CREDIT FOLLOWING AN INITIAL INCREASE IN
RESERVES OF $1000

Step	Δ Transactions Accounts	Δ Required Reserves	Δ Credit (loans and securities): Equals Expenditure of Excess Reserves
1. Bank A	$1,000.00	$100.00	$900.00
2. S&L B	900.00	90.00	810.00
3. MSB C	810.00	81.00	729.00
4. CU D	729.00	72.90	656.10
5. Bank E	656.10	65.61	590.49
6. Bank F	590.49	59.05	531.44
7. S&L G	531.44	53.14	478.30
8. Bank H	478.30	47.83	430.47
9. MSB I	430.47	43.05	387.42
10. Bank J	387.42	38.74	348.70
.	.	.	.
.	.	.	.
.	.	.	.
20. CU T	135.08	13.51	121.57
.	.	.	.
.	.	.	.
.	.	.	.
	0.0	0.0	0.0

increases the quantity of transactions accounts and of reserves in the system by
$1000. Under the assumption that Bank A does not want to hold excess reserves,
it uses $100 for required reserves and spends the $900 of excess reserves by
granting a new loan. Thus, the bank's expansion of credit is equal to its
expenditure of excess reserves. The expansion of transactions accounts, required
reserves, and credit (expenditure of excess reserves) are shown as step 1 in Table
11.1. In the second step, the $900 lent by Bank A is deposited in S&L B, which
sets aside $90 and has the remaining $810 as excess reserves.[15] These excess
reserves are spent by granting a new loan. The borrower of the $810 lent by S&L
B makes expenditures, and the funds are deposited in MSB C. That institution
sets aside 10 percent, or $81, and uses the remainder to expand credit. This is
shown as step 3. Because of the rising quantity of transactions accounts in the
system, required reserves rise, and the amount of excess reserves that is passed
from one institution to the next is reduced with every step. The process continues
until there are no excess reserves to lend. At this point, required reserves in the

---

[15] Recall that the excess reserves of Bank A are spent when it transfers $900 to the reserve
account of S&L B.

TABLE 11.2
CUMULATIVE EXPANSION OF TRANSACTIONS ACCOUNTS, REQUIRED
RESERVES AND CREDIT FOR THE DEPOSITORY SYSTEM FOLLOWING AN
INITIAL INCREASE IN RESERVES OF $1000

Step	Transactions Accounts	Required Reserves	Excess Reserves	Total Reserves	Credit: Loans and Securities
1. Bank A	$ 1,000.00	$ 100.00	$900.00	$1,000.00	$ 900.00
2. S&L B	1,900.00	190.00	810.00	1,000.00	1,710.00
3. MSB C	2,710.00	271.00	729.00	1,000.00	2,439.00
4. CU D	3,439.00	343.90	656.10	1,000.00	3,095.10
5. Bank E	4,095.10	409.51	590.49	1,000.00	3,685.59
6. Bank F	4,685.59	468.56	531.44	1,000.00	4,217.03
7. S&L G	5,217.03	521.70	478.30	1,000.00	4,695.33
8. Bank H	5,695.33	569.53	430.47	1,000.00	5,125.80
9. MSB I	6,125.80	612.58	387.42	1,000.00	5,513.22
10. Bank J	6,513.22	651.32	348.68	1,000.00	5,861.90
.	.	.	.	.	.
.	.	.	.	.	.
20. CU T	8,784.23	878.42	121.58	1,000.00	7,905.81
.	.	.	.	.	.
.	.	.	.	.	.
.	.	.	.	.	.
	10,000.00	1,000.00	0.0	1,000.00	9,000.00

system rise by the cumulative total of $1000, that is, by the amount of the initial
security purchase that got the process going. At this point, there are no excess
reserves in the depository system, and the process stops.

The reason that the process comes to end is illustrated in Table 11.2. This table
shows the cumulative expansion of transactions accounts, required reserves, and
credit for the system of depository institutions as a whole. The table also shows
the shrinking amounts of excess reserves in the system. For step 1 the numbers in
Tables 11.1 and 11.2 are the same except that Table 11.2 has columns showing the
quantity of excess reserves and of total reserves in the system that result from the
Fed's $1000 security purchase. The initial deposit at Bank A causes the quantity
of total reserves (required plus excess) to rise by $1000. Step 1 of Table 11.2
shows the situation for Bank A at the instant that it grants the $900 loan, but
before its check is deposited in S&L B. Thus, at the end of step 1, Bank A has
$100 of required reserves and $900 of excess reserves. The $1000 of total reserves
injected into the system is still held by Bank A.

When the borrower spends the proceeds of the loan and the recipient of the
expenditure deposits the check, the quantity of transactions accounts at S&L B
rises by $900 and the excess reserves of Bank A fall by $900 as it transfers the
funds into the S&L's reserve account. It should be stressed that the initial $1000

deposit remains at Bank A. It is the $900 of excess reserves lent by Bank A that is deposited in S&L B.[16] With this deposit, S&L B has $90 of additional required reserves and $810 of additional excess reserves. The total increase of reserves in the system is still $1000. Required reserves are $100 higher at Bank A and $90 higher at S&L B for a total cumulative increase in required reserves of $190. Bank A has eliminated its excess reserves, but S&L B now has $810 of additional excess reserves. Thus, the increase in total reserves (required plus excess) in the system is still $1000, that is, $190 + $810 = $1000.

As long as Bank A has excess reserves, its portfolio is not in balance because it wants to eliminate the excess reserves to expand its holdings of loans. When Bank A adjusts its portfolio by spending the $900 of excess reserves, that expenditure throws S&L B out of portfolio balance because the S&L now has $810 of excess reserves that it does not want. S&L B adjusts its portfolio by granting a loan for $810. Until the check that S&L B writes for the loan is presented for payment by MSB C, the S&L continues to hold excess reserves. This situation is shown as step 2.

Each time a depository institution spends its excess reserves, that is, acquires loans or securities, it produces excess reserves for another institution. The system as a whole can get rid of excess reserves only by expanding credit and, therefore, expanding transactions accounts. With each step, there are more transactions accounts in the system and, hence, more required reserves. More and more of the initial $1000 injection of reserves is absorbed by required reserves, and, therefore, the quantity of excess reserves in the system declines. With the shrinking quantity of excess reserves, the additions to loans and securities (credit) and the additions to transactions accounts decrease with each step as shown in Table 11.1. Eventually, the total quantity of transactions accounts rises sufficiently in the depository system to absorb the entire $1000 reserve injection into required reserves.[17] At this limiting point, there are no more excess reserves, and all depository institutions are in portfolio balance.

As shown in Table 11.2, with a 10 percent reserve requirement, the initial increase in reserves of $1000 is multiplied into a $10,000 increase of transactions accounts in the system as a whole. This $10,000 expansion of transactions accounts supports $1000 of additional required reserves and $9000 of additional holdings of loans and securities for depository institutions.

There are two behavioral assumptions that allow us to predict the expansion of transactions accounts and credit that results from the initial injection of reserves into the system. First, we assumed that depository institutions do not want to hold any excess reserves. This implies that when an institution receives an increase in its liabilities, it sets aside 10 percent of the increase to satisfy the reserve requirement and always lends the remaining 90 percent. The recipients of the

---

[16] The customer deposits a $900 check with S&L B. That S&L receives payment on the check from Bank A.

[17] As we will see later, if institutions want to hold excess reserves, the quantity of transaction accounts expands only to the point that the reserve injection is absorbed by required reserves and *desired* excess reserves.

expenditures made by borrowers must decide what to do with the money. Here we have the second assumption. It is assumed that the money is always redeposited in a depository institution. The behavior of both depository institutions and the public is crucial to the story. Depository institutions get rid of unwanted excess reserves by granting loans. The public receives the money from the loans and puts it right back into depository institutions. Each time the funds are deposited by the public, depository institutions must set 10 percent aside as required reserves. Thus, each institution in the chain is able to lend 10 percent less than the preceding institution. When transactions accounts expand by $10,000, the initial $1000 reserve injection is absorbed into required reserves. There are no more excess reserves, and the process stops.

Given our assumptions about the behavior of depository institutions and the public, the expansion of transactions accounts and credit is determined by the reserve requirement. It determines the fraction of an increase in transactions accounts that must be used for additional required reserves. The higher this fraction, the smaller the amount of funds to support additional lending and, therefore, the smaller the expansion of transactions accounts in the system. The lower the reserve requirements, the greater the expansion in transactions accounts.

For a $1000 reserve injection, transactions accounts expand by $20,000 if the reserve requirement is 5 percent, but they only expand by $5000 if the reserve requirement is 20 percent. Transactions accounts rise by $1000 if the reserve requirement is 100 percent. Given our assumptions about the behavior of banks and the public, if the reserve requirement is zero, transactions accounts and credit expand without limit. We will discuss the case of a zero reserve requirement after more realistic assumptions are adopted.

Before we turn to the general expression that shows the relationship between changes in reserves and changes in the quantity of transactions accounts in the system, it is useful to discuss some issues within the context of the specific example summarized in Tables 11.1 and 11.2.

It should be noted that the amount of expansion of transactions accounts does not depend on how depository institutions spend their excess reserves. For ease of exposition, it is assumed that they grant loans, but the excess reserves could be used to purchase securities. The sellers of securities receive checks from the purchasing institution. They deposit the checks in their depository institutions, and the expansion of transactions accounts proceeds as before. In fact, it is not even necessary for depository institutions to purchase assets for the expansion process to continue. Bank A could take the $900 of excess reserves from the original $1000 deposit and blow the whole thing on a three-martini lunch for its employees.[18] Alternatively, it could take the $900 and increase its own deposit

[18] If the bank uses its excess reserves to purchase goods or services rather than to extend credit, this expenditure has a direct effect on aggregate demand in the economy. Thus, the total economic effect of the three-martini lunch may be different from the effect of extending additional credit. The effect on the quantity of transactions accounts in the economy is the same, however, at least for the simple world described in the text.

account at a correspondent bank.[19] In either case, the bank has spent its excess reserves, and the expenditure is deposited back in a depository institution.

It may seem to the reader that the story summarized in the tables is artificial. At each step in the process, it is assumed that the deposits that flow into a depository institution remain with it. Thus, the $1000 deposited with Bank A stay at that bank, the $900 deposited in S&L B stay there, and so on. This assumption must appear to be highly unrealistic. After all, the initial depositor of the $1000 may decide to make an expenditure and to write a check for the purchase. Similarly, the recipient of the $900 expenditure made by the borrower from Bank A, who deposits the money in S&L B, may not hold the funds idle. It is likely that the various depositors will use their newly expanded accounts to finance expenditures.

Superficially, it appears that the story of the multiple expansion of the quantity of transactions accounts does not hold up because depositors do not cooperate by holding their account balances idle. When they make expenditures, their depository institutions must sell assets (reduce credit) in order to meet withdrawals. We will show, however, that the story does hold up even when account balances do not remain idle.

We need only return to the discussion of transfers of funds from one institution to another to demonstrate that the story is not altered. Consider Bank A, which was the recipient of the initial $1000 deposit. It set aside $100 of required reserves and lent the remaining $900. If the depositor later writes a check for $1000, Bank A must reduce its assets by $1000. It accomplishes this by reducing its loans and securities by $900 and by reducing its reserve balance by the $100 of formerly required reserves freed by losing $1000 of transactions accounts. The liabilities and assets of Bank A do shrink. The $1000 check written by the customer will be deposited in some institution, however. If the check is deposited in Bank A, that bank does not have to shrink after all. If the check is deposited in some other institution, Bank A does contract, but the liabilities and assets of the other institution expand. The contraction of transactions accounts and credit at Bank A are offset by the expansion of transactions accounts and credit at the other depository institution.

We conclude, therefore, that the expansion of transactions accounts and credit summarized in Tables 11.1 and 11.2 does not hinge on the assumption that once a deposit is made in an institution, that account remains dormant. In the real world, transactions account balances shift from one institution to another. These shifts of funds affect individual institutions, but they do not affect the quantity of

[19] Depository institutions are allowed to deduct the account balances they hold at other private institutions from their own liabilities when calculating required reserves. For example, if Bank A deposits funds in Bank Z, the required reserves of Bank A decline, and the required reserves of Bank Z rise. Thus, an increase in correspondent balances does not raise required reserves in the system as a whole, and the expansion process for transactions accounts is unaffected.

transactions accounts and credit in the economy. The only exceptions to this conclusion arise when institutions differ in their propensities to hold excess reserves or when institutions differ in their reserve requirements. These exceptions are discussed later.

For simplicity, the discussion has assumed that depository institutions grant loans by issuing checks to borrowers. Loans are granted in this manner, but other methods are used as well. The expansion in the quantity of money and credit in the economy is not affected by the method used by depository institutions to make payment for loans. Consider the case where institutions grant loans by paying out currency to borrowers. Bank A grants its loan of $900 by paying the borrower with currency rather than with a check. The bank obtains the money by withdrawing $900 of currency from its reserve account at the Fed. The borrower takes the $900 and makes an expenditure. The recipient of the currency deposits it in S&L B. That institution now has an increase in its transactions account liabilities of $900. It lends $810 of currency and deposits $90 of currency into its account at the Fed as required reserves. The $810 of currency lent by S&L B is deposited in MSB C, and the process continues. As long as each recipient of the cash expenditures deposits the currency in a depository institution, the expansion of money and credit is exactly the same as when institutions grant loan by writing checks on themselves. The only difference is that reserves are temporarily reduced when the currency is in the hands of either the borrower or the recipient of the borrower's expenditure. This complication makes the story about total reserves and their allocation between required and excess reserves more complicated, but it does not affect the conclusion concerning the expansion of money and credit.

Depository institutions can also finance loans by increasing the accounts of their borrowers. In this case, which is the most common, the borrowers withdraw the money to make expenditures by writing checks on their own accounts. The recipients of the payments deposit the checks in their own depository institutions. These institutions obtain payment from the institutions upon which the checks are written by having funds transferred into their reserve accounts. As long as the withdrawals by borrowers are matched by deposits of recipients, the reserves stay within the system, and the multiple expansion of money and credit continues.

Many accounts of the multiple expansion of money and credit consider only the case where loans are granted by increasing borrowers' accounts. There is nothing wrong with considering only this case because loans made by currency and bank checks produce the same multiple expansion of money and credit as do loans granted by increasing borrowers' accounts. The problem with focusing on increases in depositors' accounts, however, is that it can give the impression that depository institutions do something magical when they "create" increases in these accounts. It is easy for the unwary reader to conclude that depository institutions make "something out of nothing" when they expand the accounts of borrowers. When a loan is granted by increasing a borrower's account, the depository institution has, in a sense, increased its own liabilities. These liabilities do not remain with the institution, however, because the borrower must start paying interest on the loan as soon as it is granted. It makes no sense for a borrower to pay interest on a loan and to keep the funds idle in a transactions account. Borrowers arrange for their loans to be granted at a time when they can quickly make expenditures. Thus, borrowers withdraw the borrowed funds from their accounts. A depository institution cannot in any meaningful sense create its own liabilities because borrowers withdraw the funds and the liabilities disappear. When institutions lend, they transfer their excess reserves to borrowers. The same transfer occurs whether a loan is granted in the form of currency, a check written on a depository institution, or an increase in the borrower's account balance.

The *system* of depository institutions, in conjunction with the public which redeposits funds, creates money in the sense that an increase in the quantity of total reserves produces a multiple expansion of transactions account liabilities. An individual depository institution lends (spends) its excess reserves. The money that is lent is deposited in other depository institutions. These deposits support additional extensions of credit and additional subsequent deposits. An injection of reserves gets the process started, and fractional reserve requirements produce the multiple expansion of money and credit.

Contractions in Money and Credit

We can now turn to contractions in money and credit. The story can be told quickly because contractions involve the same process as expansions but in reverse. To show this, we will again go through a numerical example, but the reader is spared much of the gory detail.

Assume that depository institutions are in portfolio equilibrium in the sense that the levels of reserves, of transactions accounts, and of credit in the system are not changing and that there are no excess reserves. Transfers of funds among institutions are occurring, but they do not affect the total quantity of money and credit in the depository system.

Now assume that the Federal Reserve sells a $1000 security to a dealer with an account at Bank A. The Fed reduces the reserve balance of Bank A by $1000, and the bank reduces the dealer's transactions account balance by $1000. The Fed's security sale reduces Bank A's liabilities by $1000 and, with a reserve requirement of 10 percent, also reduces Bank A's required reserves by $100. This $100 is used to help meet the withdrawal from the dealer's account. The bank is still $900 short, however. It had no excess reserves, so it incurs a $900 reserve deficiency at the Fed. The bank removes this deficiency by selling $900 of its assets. For simplicity, assume that the bank sells $900 of securities. The purchaser of the securities pays for them by writing a check on S&L B. This results in the transfer of $900 from the reserve account of S&L B to the account of Bank A. Bank A now has sufficient funds to meet the $1000 withdrawal by the dealer: $100 of reduced required reserves and $900 from the sale of securities.

S&L B has lost $900 of funds, however, and it must cover this loss. It obtains $90 from the reduction of required reserves and makes up the remaining $810 reserve deficiency from the sale of securities. The securities are purchased by someone with an account in MSB C, so that institution's liabilities fall by $810. MSB C responds by selling securities, and the process continues.

The Federal Reserve's sale of securities produces a $1000 decline in the quantity of reserves in the depository system. This loss of reserves produces a multiple contraction in the quantity of transactions accounts and credit. As each depository institution sells assets to meet withdrawals from its transactions accounts, it forces some other institution out of equilibrium. Because part of the loss is met from reduced required reserves, each succeeding institution in the chain experiences a smaller reduction in transaction account liabilities than does the preceding institution. The process continues until the quantity of transactions accounts in the system falls sufficiently to reduce required reserves in the system by $1000. At this point, no institution has a reserve deficiency. With a reserve requirement of 10 percent, the quantity of transactions accounts must decline by $10,000. A $1000 reduction in reserves leads to an aggregate decline in transactions accounts of $10,000, just as a $1000 increase in reserves produced an expansion of $10,000.

The story about the contraction of transactions accounts and credit was told, assuming that depository institutions always sell securities in order to meet reductions in their transactions account liabilities. This assumption simplifies the story, but it is not essential. If institutions sell loans rather than securities, the purchasers of the loans reduce their transactions account balances to pay for the loans, and the process is exactly the same as for sales of securities.[20] The story is slightly more complicated if an institution reduces its loan portfolio by not reinvesting the proceeds from maturing loans. Consider the case where Bank A has a $900 loan maturing the same day that the dealer purchases the $1000 security from the Fed. In this case, the bank can meet the withdrawal from the dealer's transactions account without selling assets. The system as a whole is still affected, however, because the borrower had to obtain the $900 from somewhere. If the borrower draws down an account balance at another depository institution or sells an asset to obtain the $900, other institutions are affected. If the borrower reduces his or her account balances at Bank A, that bank experiences an additional $900 loss of account liabilities and still must sell assets. We conclude, therefore, that the method by which depository institutions reduce their assets does not affect the relationship between the initial reduction in reserves and the ensuing decline in the quantity of transactions accounts.

---

[20] One depository institution might sell securities or loans to another institution. Assuming there are no excess reserves, the purchasing institution must sell some other asset in order to make the purchase. This reduces the quantity of transactions accounts in other depository institutions.

THE GENERAL EXPRESSIONS FOR THE MULTIPLE EXPANSION OR CONTRACTION OF MONEY

Now that the basic issues in the multiple expansion and contraction process have been discussed, we can develop the general algebraic expressions for the relationships between reserves and transactions accounts. The first step is to define some symbols:

> TR is the quantity of total reserves in the system
>
> RR is the quantity of required reserves in the system
>
> ER is the quantity of excess reserves in the system
>
> T is the quantity of transactions accounts in the system
>
> r_T is the reserve requirement for transactions accounts.

Total reserves in the system are the sum of required reserves and excess reserves: $TR = RR + ER$. Required reserves are equal to the reserve requirement times the quantity of transactions accounts: $RR = r_T T$. Therefore, we have $TR = r_T T + ER$. Because it is assumed that depository institutions do not want to hold any excess reserves, the depository system achieves equilibrium when $ER = 0$, so

$$TR = r_T T .$$

Excess reserves are zero when all reserves are required reserves. Rearranging this expression for total reserves, we see that the quantity of transactions accounts depends upon the reserve requirement and the quantity of reserves:

$$T = \frac{TR}{r_T} .$$

Thus, the quantity of transactions accounts in the system is a multiple of the quantity of total reserves in the system, where the *multiplier, m,* is given by

$$m = \frac{1}{r_T} .$$

For example, if $r_T = .10$, then $m = 10$. Every \$1 of reserves in the system is multiplied into \$10 of transactions accounts.

Because we have assumed that the public does not change its holdings of currency, the change in the quantity of money, ΔM, is equal to the change in the quantity of transactions account liabilities, that is, $\Delta M = \Delta T$. Thus, the expression for the change in money is the same as for transactions accounts,

$$\Delta M = \frac{\Delta TR}{r_T} .$$

The multiplier for transactions accounts and for money, m, is the reciprocal of the reserve requirement, that is,

$$\Delta T = m \, \Delta TR$$

where $m = 1/r_T$. The lower the reserve requirement, the higher the multiplier. For example, if the reserve requirement is 5 percent rather than the 10 percent assumed earlier, we have $\Delta T = \$1000/.05 = \$20,000$; thus, halving the reserve requirement doubles the multiplier. Conversely, the higher the reserve requirement, the lower the multiplier. In the limiting case of a 100 percent reserve requirement, we have $m = 1$, so $\Delta T = \Delta TR$, and there is no multiple expansion of transactions accounts. The multiplier is one. The other limiting case of a zero reserve requirement is more troublesome because $m = 1.0/0.0$, which is not defined. It is an implication of the assumptions we have made so far that the multiplier is not defined when the reserve requirement is zero. With a zero reserve requirement, none of the injection of reserves is absorbed into required reserves. In this case, the quantity of transactions accounts apparently expands without limit. We will show later, however, when more realistic cases are considered, that a zero reserve requirement does not give an infinite expansion of transactions accounts.

It is remarkable that a complex system of depository institutions could produce such a simple expression for the relationship between the quantity of reserves and the quantity of transactions accounts in the economy. This simplicity occurs because of the assumptions that we have made. These assumptions are examined in the remainder of the chapter, and it is shown that their elimination or modification affects the multipliers between total reserves and the quantity of transactions accounts and money in the economy.

MORE REALISTIC CASES

An injection of reserves into the system produces a multiple expansion of the quantity of transactions accounts because (1) depository institutions are willing to use these reserves to extend additional credit and (2) the public is willing to deposit funds in depository institutions. The reserve injection is recycled by these two groups. Depository institutions spend excess reserves on loans and securities, and the public then deposits the funds at various depository institutions. In the simple case considered so far, the reserve requirement is the only factor that limits the expansion of transactions accounts.

In the cases to be considered later, several factors are considered that affect the degree to which depository institutions and the public recycle funds. These factors affect the multiplier relationships between reserves and the quantity of transactions accounts and of money in the economy.

The Role of Excess Reserves

In the discussion of the relationship between changes in reserves and changes in the quantity of transactions accounts, it was assumed that depository institutions do not want to hold excess reserves. We will now determine the effect that the demand for excess reserves has on the multiplier.

In order to analyze the role of excess reserves, we make the simplifying assumption that depository institutions want to hold a constant fraction of their transactions accounts liabilities as excess reserves. The rationale for this assumption is that the greater the quantity of transactions accounts at a depository institution, the greater is the need for excess reserves to protect it against costly asset sales when unexpected declines in transactions accounts occur. This assumption is fairly plausible, and it simplifies the analysis.[21] Denoting excess reserves as ER and the fraction of transactions accounts held as excess reserves by e, we have $e = ER/T$ and $ER = eT$. Furthermore, for changes, we have $\Delta ER = e\Delta T$. Thus, for every \$1 increase or decrease in the quantity of transactions accounts, depository institutions change their holdings of excess reserves by the amount, e.

The demand for excess reserves reduces the multiplier for transactions accounts and money. Now when a depository institution receives additional transactions account liabilities, it increases its holdings of both required reserves and excess reserves. As a result, a larger quantity of reserves is held idle at each step of the recycling process, and the expansion of transactions accounts and credit is reduced. Expansion stops when all reserves are absorbed into required reserves *and* desired excess reserves.

When depository institutions want to hold excess reserves, we get a new expression for the multiplier. Total reserves, TR, are composed of required reserves, RR, and excess reserves, ER, that is, $TR = RR + ER$. When the multiplier process has run its course, no depository institution is holding more excess reserves than it wants to hold. We have assumed that institutions want to hold the fraction, e, of their transactions account liabilities as excess reserves, so $ER = eT$. We know that required reserves are $r_T T$, so $TR = r_T T + eT$, or collecting terms $TR = (r_T + e)T$. Solving for the total level of transactions accounts, we have

$$T = \frac{TR}{(r_T + e)}.$$

The multiplier, m, is now given by

$$m = \frac{1}{(r_T + e)}.$$

The demand for excess reserves leads depository institutions to add funds to their reserve accounts, and the multiplier is reduced. Clearly, the larger the fraction e,

---

[21] We will examine later the more realistic case where the fraction of transactions accounts held as excess reserves varies with the economic factors.

the smaller the multiplier. The limiting case occurs when banks place all their transactions account liabilities in their reserve accounts. In this situation, $r_T + e = 1$, or $e = 1 - r_T$, and $m = 1$. This is the equivalent of 100 percent reserve banking. In this case, there is no multiple expansion of transactions accounts.

For changes in the quantity of transactions account liabilities, we have

$$\Delta T = \frac{\Delta TR}{(r_T + e)}.$$

Because we continue to assume that the public does not change its currency holdings, $\Delta M = \Delta T$, so

$$\Delta M = \frac{\Delta TR}{(r_T + e)}.$$

The discussion of the demand for excess reserves highlights the fact that it is the acquisitions of loans and securities by depository institutions that keeps the expansion of transactions accounts and credit going. Whenever depository institutions place funds in their reserve accounts, they reduce the amount of credit expansion and, therefore, reduce the amount that is passed on to the next institution. Both required reserves and excess reserves reduce credit expansion. As far as the multiplier is concerned, it makes no difference whether depository institutions add to their required reserves or to their excess reserves. Additions to either have the effect of reducing the multiplier.

Depository institutions not only hold excess reserves at the Fed and in their vaults, but they also have accounts at private depository institutions. These funds serve the same function as excess reserves for the depositing institution. However, the multiplier is not reduced when funds are deposited in these accounts because the institution into which the funds are deposited can expand credit. Only deposits into a reserve account at the Fed or into vault cash represent a leakage for the system because the funds are held idle.

While required and excess reserves have the same effect on the multiplier, there is an economic difference between them. Required reserves are set by the Federal Reserve and remain fixed until the Fed decides to change them. The demand for excess reserves by depository institutions is based on economic decisions concerning the profitability of holding excess reserves as opposed to extending credit. This demand is affected by the variability and predictability of transactions accounts at individual depository institutions, by the interest rates that can be earned on loans and securities, and by the transactions costs of asset purchases and sales. As these factors change, the percentage of transactions accounts held as excess reserves also changes. Thus, e is not a constant but, rather, varies with economic conditions. For example, when interest rates on loans and securities rise, the demand for excess reserves declines, and the multiplier increases. When the variability of transactions accounts increases, the demand for excess reserves increases, and the multiplier falls.

Now we have left the realm of mechanical multiplier relationships and can allow for economic behavior. The portfolio choices of depository institutions concerning the allocation of assets between excess reserves and holdings of loans and securities affect the quantity of transactions accounts and money in the economy.

The multiplier is also affected by where the public holds its transactions balances. For reasons explained in Chapter 8, small depository institutions hold more excess reserves than large institutions. If the public shifts its account balances from large institutions to small ones, the demand for excess reserves in the system as a whole increases. As a result, the multiplier declines. If the public shifts its account balances to large institutions, the total demand for excess reserves declines, and the multiplier rises.

As explained in Chapter 8, the federal funds market allows depository institutions to hold a minimum amount of excess reserves. When a depository institution has a reserve deficiency, that is, when its required reserves exceed the amount in its reserve account, it can borrow from institutions with excess reserves. This transaction allows the borrowing institution to cover its reserve deficiency, and it allows the lender to earn an interest income rather than hold noninterest-bearing excess reserves. Depository institutions use the federal funds market actively, and typically less than 4 percent of all reserves in the system is excess reserves. The ratio of excess reserves to transactions accounts is less than 0.3 percent. The percentage fluctuates somewhat, but it does not achieve sufficient size to make the ratio of excess reserves to transactions accounts, e, a significant factor in the multiplier relationships between total reserves and the quantity of money in the economy.

Because this is the case, why make a big deal out of excess reserves? The reason is historical. Prior to the monetary reforms of the 1930s, fluctuations in the quantity of excess reserves were important. When banks feared a financial panic, which usually entailed massive withdrawals of currency from transactions accounts, they significantly increased their holdings of excess reserves. This conservative action by banks raised the ratio of excess reserves to transactions accounts, e, which reduced the quantity of money and credit in the economy. The decline in the quantity of money and credit weakened the economy, and banking panics often followed. The very attempt by banks to protect themselves and their depositors against banking panics by increasing excess reserves helped to bring the panics about. During periods of economic expansion and prosperity, the danger of banking panics was small and banks significantly reduced their demand for excess reserves. Thus, e declined and the multiplier rose. Fluctuations in e helped to produce economic instability.

As we saw in the Chapter 9, deposit insurance and the Federal Reserve System have effectively eliminated the threat of banking panics. As a result, banks and other depository institutions no longer vary their demand for excess reserves in a destabilizing fashion. Furthermore, the Federal funds market has almost eliminated excess reserves.

The Role of Currency

Excess reserves are not the only factor that affects the multiplier relationship between total reserves and the quantity of money in the economy. Quantitatively much more important than excess reserves is the public's demand for currency. Up to this point, in describing how changes in reserves produce changes in the quantity of transactions accounts and money, we assumed that the public does not change its holdings of currency. The public does, in fact, vary the amount of currency that it holds, and these variations affect the multiplier relationships for transactions accounts and for money.

The expansion of money and credit is reduced to the extent that the public decides to hold currency rather than transactions accounts.[22] To see that this is the case, let us return to the earlier discussion where depository institutions grant loans by paying out currency to borrowers. It was assumed that each time a loan is granted, the borrower makes an expenditure, and the recipient deposits the currency in a depository institution. If the currency is held by the public rather than deposited in a depository institution, the transactions accounts at the next institution in the process do not rise. Because the quantity of transactions accounts does not rise, that institution cannot expand its loans.

An important reason that the public holds both transactions accounts and currency is to conduct transactions. The choice between currency and transactions account balances depends upon a variety of factors, but probably the most important is the composition of transactions in the economy. Currency is primarily used to purchase items where the use of transactions accounts is inconvenient or impossible. For example, many retail transactions such as movie tickets and dry cleaning require cash. In contrast, transactions between firms are typically conducted using transactions accounts, and households make many large transactions, as for rent or mortgage payments, with these accounts. If we assume as a first approximation that the mix of transactions using currency and those using transactions account balances remains relatively fixed in the economy, then it is plausible to assert that the public maintains a constant mix between its holdings of currency and its holdings of transactions account balances. This implies that the ratio of currency, C, to transactions account balances is constant. Denoting this ratio or fraction as c, we can write $c = C/T$.

The ratio of currency to transactions accounts in the United States in recent years has been somewhat in excess of .35. Assuming this ratio is constant, the public adds $35 to its currency holdings for every $100 it adds to its transactions account balances. Conversely, if transactions accounts fall by $100, currency holdings decline by $35. In reality, the relationship between currency and transactions accounts is not so mechanical, and the ratio, c, is not a constant. But let us initially assume that it is.

To see the role of the public's demand for currency, we compare a situation in which the public does not change its currency holdings when transactions account balances change to one in which currency holdings are changed when account balances change. In both cases, it is assumed that the Federal Reserve purchases

---

[22] We will show in the next section that the public's decision to hold savings and time accounts, rather than either currency or transactions accounts can also affect the multiplier.

$1000 of securities, that all depository institutions have a reserve requirement, r_T, of 10 percent, and that all institutions have a ratio of desired excess reserves to transactions account liabilities, e, of 5 percent.

Table 11.3 shows the step-by-step expansion of transactions accounts following the $1000 purchase of securities by the Fed. In Panel I, it is assumed that the public does *not* add to its currency holdings as account balances rise, that is, $c = \Delta C / \Delta T = 0.0$. Panel II shows the step-by-step expansion of transactions accounts, but now it is assumed that for every $1.00 increase in account balances, the public adds $0.35 to its holdings of currency, that is, $c = \Delta C / \Delta T = 0.35$.

The expansion of transactions accounts indicated in Panel I is similar to the expansion shown in Table 11.1 except that, in Panel I, depository institutions add to their desired excess reserves as their liabilities rise. Bank A receives a $1000 deposit from the dealer who sold securities to the Fed. The bank adds $100 to its required reserves and $50 to its desired excess reserves. It has $850 of unwanted excess reserves remaining, which it uses to expand its loans. The recipient of the expenditure from the loan deposits the $850 in S&L B. Of the $850, $85 goes to required reserves, $42.50 to desired excess reserves, and the remaining $722.50 of unwanted excess reserves is recycled by S&L B as new loans. The process continues until there are no unwanted excess reserves. This occurs when total transactions account liabilities in the depository system have risen to the point that required reserves plus *desired excess reserves* in the system have increased by $1000. Recall that it is assumed that, during the process of expanding transactions accounts, the public does not change its holdings of currency.

Panel II repeats the process, but this time the public adds to its currency holdings as transactions account balances rise. In this case, when the Fed purchases $1000 of securities, Bank A does not receive $1000 but only $740. The dealer deposits the Fed's $1000 check and immediately makes a cash withdrawal of $260, leaving a net increase of $740 in the transactions account. This allocation results in the desired ratio of currency to transactions account balances of .35. The seller of the securities holds 26 percent of the proceeds of the sale or $260 as currency and 74 percent or $740 as account balances. An allocation of 26 percent of the total receipt to currency and 74 percent to the transactions account balance gives a ratio of currency to transactions account balances of $.26/.74 = .35$. As a result of the currency drain, Bank A has $740 to work with rather than $1000. It uses $74 as required reserves, $37 as desired excess reserves, and recycles the remaining $629 of unwanted excess reserves as new loans. The recipient of the expenditure from the loan deposits the $629 in S&L B but immediately withdraws 26 percent or $163.54 as currency and retains the remaining $465.46 in the S&L. Note that whereas Bank A lends $629.00, S&L B receives only $465.46 because the S&L's customer makes a currency withdrawal. In the absence of currency drains, Panel I shows that the transactions account liabilities of S&L B rise by $850. With the currency drains that occur at Bank A and S&L B, transactions accounts rise only by $465.46 at the S&L.

At every step in the process, currency drains occur as each recipient of the expenditures from loans adds to his or her currency holdings. Each depository

TABLE 11.3
INSTITUTION-BY-INSTITUTION EXPANSION OF TRANSACTIONS ACCOUNTS,
REQUIRED RESERVES, DESIRED EXCESS RESERVES, AND CREDIT, FOLLOWING
A $1000 SECURITY PURCHASE BY THE FED[a]

Step	Δ Transactions Accounts	Δ Required Reserves $r_T = .10$	Δ Desired Excess Reserves $e = .05$	Δ Credit: Equals Unwanted Excess Reserves	Currency
		Panel I: c = 0.0			
1. Bank A	$1,000.00	$100.00	$50.00	$850.00	$ 0.0
2. S&L B	850.00	85.00	42.50	722.50	0.0
3. MSB C	722.50	72.25	36.12	614.13	0.0
4. CU D	614.13	61.41	30.71	522.01	0.0
5. Bank E	522.01	52.20	26.10	443.71	0.0
.	.	.	.	.	.
.	.	.	.	.	.
.	.	.	.	.	.
10. Bank J	231.62	23.16	11.58	196.88	0.0
.	.	.	.	.	.
.	.	.	.	.	.
.	0.0	0.0	0.0	0.0	0.0
		Panel II: c = .35			
1. Bank A	$740.00	$74.00	$37.00	$629.00	$260.00
2. S&L B	465.46	46.55	23.27	395.64	163.54
3. MSB C	292.77	29.28	14.64	248.85	102.87
4. CU D	184.15	18.42	9.21	156.52	64.70
5. Bank E	115.82	11.58	5.79	98.45	40.70
.	.	.	.	.	.
.	.	.	.	.	.
.	.	.	.	.	.
10. Bank E	11.40	1.14	.57	9.69	4.01
.	.	.	.	.	.
.	.	.	.	.	.
.	0.0	0.0	0.0	0.0	0.0

[a] For both panels, $r_T = .10$ and $e = .05$.

institution receives a smaller increase in transactions account liabilities and, therefore, recycles a smaller amount as new loans in Panel II than in Panel I. For
example, Bank J receives only $11.40 of new transactions account liabilities when
there are currency drains, but it receives $231.62 when there are no drains.

The effect of currency drains on the total expansion of transactions account balances in the economy can be seen by comparing Panels I and II of Table 11.4.
Panel I shows the cumulative expansion of transactions account balances in the
system when there are no currency drains. Panel II shows the cumulative expan-

TABLE 11.4
CUMULATIVE EXPANSION OF TRANSACTIONS ACCOUNTS, REQUIRED RESERVES, DESIRED EXCESS RESERVES, AND CREDIT FOLLOWING A $1000 SECURITY PURCHASE BY THE FED[a]

Step	Transactions Accounts	Required Reserves	Desired Excess Reserves	ΔCredit Equals: Unwanted Excess Reserves	Total Reserves	Currency	Total Reserves Plus Currency
			Panel I: $c = 0.0$				
1. Bank A	$1,000.00	$100.00	$ 50.00	$850.00	$1,000.00	$ 0.0	$1,000.00
2. S&L B	1,850.00	185.00	92.00	722.50	1,000.00	0.0	1,000.00
3. MSB C	2,572.50	257.25	128.63	614.12	1,000.00	0.0	1,000.00
4. CU D	3,186.63	318.66	159.33	522.01	1,000.00	0.0	1,000.00
5. Bank E	3,708.64	370.86	185.43	443.71	1,000.00	0.0	1,000.00
.	.	.	.	.	.	.	.
.	.	.	.	.	.	.	.
All	$6,666.67	$666.67	$333.33	0.0	$1,000.00	0.0	$1,000.00
			Panel II[b]: $c = .35$				
1. Bank A	$ 740.00	$ 74.00	$ 37.00	$629.00	$740.00	$260.00	$1,000.00
2. S&L B	1,205.46	120.55	60.27	395.64	576.46	423.54	1,000.00
3. MSB C	1,498.23	149.82	74.91	248.85	473.58	526.41	1,000.00
4. CU D	1,682.38	168.24	84.12	156.53	408.89	591.11	1,000.00
5. Bank E	1,798.21	179.83	89.91	98.45	368.18	631.81	1,000.00
.	.	.	.	.	.	.	.
.	.	.	.	.	.	.	.
All	$2,000.00	$200.00	$100.00	$ 0.0	$300.00	$700.00	$1,000.00

[a] For both panels, $r_T = .10$ and $e = .05$.
[b] Some numbers are adjusted slightly to remove the effect of rounding errors.

sion of transactions account balances when the public maintains a currency-transactions account ratio of .35.

Panel I shows that the quantity of transaction account balances in the system grows as funds are recycled. It is assumed that the public does not add to its currency holdings, so the quantity of total reserves in the system is permanently increased by $1000 as a result of the Fed's purchase of securities. Each depository institution achieves portfolio equilibrium following an increase in its liabilities by adding to its required reserves and its desired excess reserves and by spending the remaining excess reserves on new loans. This recycling of unwanted excess reserves produces additional transactions account liabilities for the next depository institution in the system. The system achieves equilibrium when the entire $1000 increase in reserves is absorbed into required and desired excess reserves. This occurs when the total increase in the quantity of transactions accounts is $6,666.67.

Panel II shows that when there are currency drains, the quantity of reserves in the depository system does not permanently increase by $1000. Total reserves in the system rise by $1000 only until the seller of the securities makes a cash withdrawal. Step 1 shows the situation after the withdrawal has occurred. Total reserves rise by $740 rather than $1000 because the remaining $260 is held as currency. At each step, the quantity of reserves in the system is less than in the previous step because the public increases its currency holdings. The sum of total reserves and currency is always $1000, but as the process continues, more and more of the total is currency.

The initial injection of reserves does not stay within the system but continues to drain out as currency. The currency drain reduces total reserves in the system and reduces the ability of depository institutions to recycle funds and expand the quantity of transactions accounts. When the process comes to an end, the initial $1000 increase in total reserves is reduced to $300. Because of currency drains, total transactions accounts in the system rise by only $2000 in response to the *initial* increase in total reserves of $1000. This occurs because the initial increase in total reserves ends up being only a $300 permanent increase in reserves. The $300 permanent increase in total reserves is fully absorbed into required reserves and desired excess reserves when total transactions accounts rise by $2000. Comparison of Panels I and II indicates that when the public maintains a ratio of currency to transactions account balances of .35, there is a powerful dampening effect on the expansion of transactions accounts in the economy.

The effect of currency drains on the multiplier can be shown algebraically. When the expansion process is completed, total reserves must be allocated between required and desired excess reserves. Thus,

$$\Delta TR = r_T \Delta T + e \Delta T = (r_T + e)\Delta T .$$

Now, however, total reserves in the system vary with changes in currency holdings. The *initial* injection of reserves, ΔTR_0 (the $1000 in the example), is partially offset by the loss of reserves into currency as the quantity of transactions account balances rises. Thus, part of the $1000 of reserves that the Fed injects into the system is drained out as the public increases its currency holdings. The actual net change in reserves after the expansion is completed, ΔTR, is $\Delta TR = \Delta TR_0 - c\Delta T$. Rearranging terms, we have $\Delta TR_0 = \Delta TR + c\Delta T$. The initial injection of reserves, ΔTR_0, is allocated between the reserves that remain in the system, ΔTR, and additional currency holdings, $c\Delta T$. Thus, $\Delta TR_0 = r_T\Delta T + e\Delta T + c\Delta T = (r_T + e + c)\Delta T$. Solving for ΔT we obtain

$$\Delta T = \frac{\Delta TR_0}{(r_T + e + c)}$$

or $\Delta T = m_T\Delta TR_0$, where the multiplier for the change in the quantity of transactions accounts, m_T, is

$$m_T = \frac{1}{(r_T + e + c)} .$$

The variable ΔTR_0 is used to indicate that we have the multiplier for the *initial* injection of reserves, not for the final *net* change in reserves after currency drains occur.[23]

When we discussed the roles of required and excess reserves earlier, it was not necessary to distinguish between initial and net reserve injections because all the reserves stayed in the system. Now with changes in currency holdings that vary positively with changes in transactions accounts, reserves do not stay constant as transactions accounts change. In fact, it is the drain of currency that reduces the multiplier effect of the initial reserves injection. The initial injection has a reduced effect precisely because part of the increase in reserves is only temporary.

When there are no currency drains, we have $\Delta TR_0 = \$1000$, $r_T = .10$, $e = .05$, and $c = 0.0$. In this case $m_T = 1/(r_T + e) = 1/.15 = 6.66667$, so $\Delta T = 6.66667(\$1000) = \$6,666.67$. Note that the change of total reserves in the depository system is $\$1000$ at the beginning and at the end of the expansion process. When $c = .35$, $m_T = 1/(r_T + e + c) = 1/(.10 + .05 + .35) = 1/.5 = 2.0$, so $\Delta T = 2.0(\$1000) = \$2000$. The reason for the reduction in the multiplier and, therefore, for the smaller increase in total transactions accounts is that the expansion of total reserves by the end of the process is less than at the beginning. We know that when the process is completed, $\Delta TR = \Delta TR_0 - c\Delta T$. At that point, $\Delta T = \$2000$, and because $\Delta TR_0 = \$1000$, we have $\Delta TR = \$1000 - .35(\$2000) = \$300$. Thus, the net change in reserves is only $\$300$, not the initial $\$1000$. Observe that when $\Delta TR = \$300$, we have $\Delta T = \$300/(r_T + e) = \$300/(.15) = \$2000$. This is the value for ΔT we obtained from the multiplier for ΔTR. The currency drains took away all but $\$300$ of the initial $\$1000$ reserve increase, so it is not surprising that the expansion in transactions accounts is reduced.

---

[23] As we shall see in Chapter 15, the initial change in reserves equals the change in the monetary base. Because the net change in the monetary base is the change in reserves plus the change in currency, it is unaffected by currency movements. Thus, the initial change in the monetary base equals the net change. Multipliers for the monetary base are given in Chapter 15.

Currency drains also affect the multiplier for the quantity of money. In fact, with currency drains, the multipliers for transactions accounts and for money are no longer the same. It is convenient to postpone the discussion of the money multiplier until we have introduced time accounts into the analysis.

The Role of Saving and Time Account Liabilities

We have assumed that transactions accounts are the only liability issued by depository institutions. This assumption allowed us to focus on some of the basic factors involved in the multiplier relationship between total reserves and the quantity of transactions accounts in the economy. In this section, we examine the role of time accounts in determining the quantity of transactions accounts in the economy.

As mentioned in the introduction to this chapter, time account liabilities issued by depository institutions to natural persons are not subject to reserve requirements whereas nonpersonal time accounts are subject to reserve requirements. This means that these two categories of time accounts have different effects on the quantity of transactions accounts in the economy. We will begin by analyzing the role of nonpersonal time accounts and then turn to personal time accounts.

Nonpersonal Time Accounts

Any time account issued by a depository institution to an entity other than a "natural person" is called a nonpersonal time account and is subject to reserve requirements. These liabilities include savings and time accounts issued to businesses and to governments. Nonpersonal time accounts also include time accounts issued to natural persons that are transferable. These accounts are included to prevent reserve requirements from being circumvented. Otherwise, depository institutions could avoid reserve requirements by issuing CDs to persons and have them transfer title to nonpersons.

Nonpersonal time accounts are composed primarily of large denomination certificates of deposit (CDs). Large depository institutions use these CDs to manage their liabilities. This means that the quantity of nonpersonal time accounts is large and that this quantity fluctuates in response to fluctuations in both loan demand and market interest rates. Changes in the quantity of nonpersonal time accounts can have a significant affect on the quantity of transactions accounts in the economy and on the amount of credit extended by depository institutions.[24] Nonpersonal time accounts are almost exclusively the liabilities of commercial banks. A few large S&Ls and MSBs issue large denomination CDs, but most thrift institutions issue personal rather than nonpersonal time accounts.

---

[24] Nonpersonal time accounts with initial maturities of four years or more have a zero reserve requirement. Their effect is the same as for personal time accounts.

Denoting the quantity of nonpersonal time accounts issued by depository institutions as N and the reserve requirements as r_N, required reserves against these accounts are $r_N N$. Total required reserves in the system are required reserves against transactions accounts plus required reserves against nonpersonal time accounts: $RR = r_T T + r_N N$. Total reserves, TR, are required reserves plus excess reserves, ER, so $TR = r_T T + r_N N + ER$. Assuming that depository institutions do not hold any excess reserves against nonpersonal time accounts and that they maintain a constant ratio of excess reserves to transactions accounts, we have $ER = eT$. Now we can write $TR = r_T T + r_N N + eT$ and collecting terms, $TR = (r_T + e)T + r_N N$. Neglecting currency drains for the moment, for changes in total reserves we have, $\Delta TR = r_T \Delta T + r_N \Delta N + e \Delta T = (r_T + e)\Delta T + r_N \Delta N$. Solving for ΔT, we obtain

$$\Delta T = \frac{\Delta TR}{(r_T + e)} - r_N \frac{\Delta N}{(r_T + e)}.$$

This expression indicates that the response of transactions accounts to a change in total reserves depends upon what is happening to nonpersonal time accounts. Consider the case of an increase in total reserves. If nonpersonal time accounts rise at the same time that transactions accounts increase, required reserves for nonpersonal time accounts increase, and the expansion of transactions accounts is reduced. Conversely, if N falls, required reserves against these accounts decline, and the expansion of transactions accounts is increased.

In order to see what is going on, let us assume that the ratio of nonpersonal time accounts to transactions accounts is constant. Denoting the ratio as n, we have $n = N/T$. Observing that $\Delta N = n \Delta T$, we can write the expression for the change in total reserves as $\Delta TR = \Delta RR + \Delta ER = r_T \Delta T + r_N \Delta N + e \Delta T = r_T \Delta T + r_N n \Delta T + e \Delta T = (r_T + r_N n + e)\Delta T$. Solving for ΔT, we obtain

$$\Delta T = \frac{\Delta TR}{(r_T + r_N n + e)}.$$

As we saw earlier, part of an initial injection of reserves into the system might drain out in the form of increased currency holdings by the public. Assuming that the public maintains a constant ratio, c, of currency to transactions accounts, we can write the expression for the change in transactions accounts in terms of the initial change in total reserves, ΔTR_0:

$$\Delta T = \frac{\Delta TR_0}{(r_T + r_N \cdot n + e + c)}.$$

This expression shows that the effect of an initial change in reserves, ΔTR_0, on the change in transactions accounts, ΔT, varies inversely with the reserve requirement on transactions accounts, r_T, inversely with the fraction of transactions accounts that depository institutions hold as excess reserves, e, and inversely with the fraction of the expansion of transactions accounts that ends up as a currency drain, c. The expression also contains a term, $r_N \cdot n$, which is the product of the reserve requirement on nonpersonal time accounts, r_N, and the ratio of these accounts to transactions accounts, n. The reserve requirement r_N indicates the increase in required reserves that occurs per dollar of increase in N. The ratio n is the increase in N that occurs per dollar of increase in T. Thus, if $n = .50$, when transactions accounts rise by \$100, nonpersonal time accounts rise by \$50.[25] This \$50 increase in N raises required reserves by $r_N(\$50)$. So if the reserve requirement against nonpersonal time accounts, r_N, is 5 percent, the rise in required reserves is $.05(\$50) = \$2.50$. If the reserve requirement against transactions accounts, r_T, is 10 percent, for every \$100 rise in transactions accounts, there is a \$10 increase in required reserves against these accounts plus a \$2.50 increase in required reserves coming from the expansion of nonpersonal time accounts. This additional rise in required reserves reduces the expansion of transactions accounts that can occur.

The role that nonpersonal time accounts play in affecting the relationship between reserves and the quantity of transactions accounts can be seen most clearly by returning to the simple world where depository institutions do not hold any excess reserves and the public does not hold any currency, that is, e and c are zero. We have already analyzed this world when the public deposits all the proceeds from credit expansion by depository institutions into transactions accounts.

Panel I of Table 11.5 shows the institution-by-institution expansion of transactions accounts when the public uses only transactions accounts. As before, it is assumed that there is a \$1000 purchase of securities by the Fed and that the reserve requirement on transactions accounts, r_T, is 10 percent. The figures in Panel I are exactly the same as in Table 11.1. The only factor that limits the expansion of transactions accounts in this world is the increase in required reserves against these accounts. When all of the initial injection of reserves is used as required reserves against transactions accounts, the expansion of transactions accounts stops.

Panel II also assumes a reserve injection of \$1000 and that r_T is 10 percent. Here, however, we do not require that the public uses only transactions accounts. Rather, it assumed that the public maintains a constant relationship between its holdings of nonpersonal time accounts and its holdings of transactions accounts. In Panel II it is assumed that for every additional \$1 of transactions accounts, the public holds an additional \$.50 of nonpersonal time accounts, that is, $n = \Delta N / \Delta T = .50$. It is also assumed that the reserve requirement for nonpersonal time accounts, r_N, is 5 percent.

Step 1 in Panel II shows the situation at Bank A following a \$1000 purchase of securities by the Fed from a business.[26] The business deposits the Fed's check in its transactions account at Bank A. That bank receives payment from the Fed, and its reserve balance rises by \$1000. The business does not want to hold the en-

---

[25] The ratio of nonpersonal time accounts to transactions accounts is currently about .90. A figure of .50 is used in the text to simplify the arithmetic.

[26] Throughout the discussion we will assume that only businesses sell securities and receive loans. If individuals (persons) sell securities and borrow, they cannot deposit funds in nonpersonal time accounts. Personal time accounts are discussed later.

TABLE 11.5
INSTITUTION-BY-INSTITUTION EXPANSION OF TRANSACTIONS ACCOUNTS, NONPERSONAL TIME ACCOUNTS, TOTAL LIABILITIES, REQUIRED RESERVES, AND CREDIT FOLLOWING A $1000 SECURITY PURCHASE BY THE FED[a]

Step	ΔTransactions Accounts	ΔNonpersonal Time Accounts	ΔTotal Liabilities	ΔRequired Reserves Against Transactions Accounts	ΔRequired Reserves Against Nonpersonal Time Accounts	ΔTotal Required Reserves	ΔCredit Equals: Unwanted Excess Reserves
			Panel I: n = 0.0				
1. Bank A	$1,000.00	$ 0.0	$1,000.00	$100.00	$ 0.0	$100.00	$900.00
2. S&L B	900.00	0.0	900.00	90.00	0.0	90.00	810.00
3. MSB C	810.00	0.0	810.00	81.00	0.0	81.00	729.00
4. CU D	729.00	0.0	729.00	72.90	0.0	72.90	656.10
5. Bank E	656.10	0.0	656.10	65.10	0.0	65.61	590.49
.	.	.	.	.	.	.	.
10. Bank J	387.42	0.0	387.42	38.74	0.0	38.74	348.70
.	.	.	.	.	.	.	.
	0.0	0.0	0.0	0.0	0.0	0.0	0.0
			Panel II: n = .5				
1. Bank A	$ 666.67	$333.33	$1,000.00	$ 66.67	$16.67	$ 83.34	$916.66
2. S&L B	611.11	305.55	916.66	61.11	15.28	76.39	840.27
3. MSB C	560.18	280.09	840.27	56.02	14.00	70.02	770.25
4. CU D	513.50	256.75	770.25	51.35	12.84	64.19	706.06
5. Bank E	470.71	235.35	706.06	47.07	11.77	58.84	647.22
.	.	.	.	.	.	.	.
10. Bank J	304.65	152.33	456.98	30.47	7.62	38.09	418.89
.	.	.	.	.	.	.	.
	0.0	0.0	0.0	0.0	0.0	0.0	0.0

[a] For both panels, $r_T = .10$, $r_N = .05$, $e = 0.0$, and $c = 0.0$.

tire amount in a transactions account, however. It calculates that in order to maintain the ratio N/T at .50, it must transfer one third of the $1000 or $333.33, into a nonpersonal time account and retain two thirds, or $666.67, into its transactions account.[27] As shown in step 1 of Panel II, total liabilities at Bank A rise by $1000. Total liabilities also rose by $1000 in step 1 of Panel I, but now the entire increase is no longer in transactions accounts. In Panel II, transactions accounts rise by $666.67, and nonpersonal time accounts rise by $333.33. The reserve requirement for transactions accounts is .10, so required reserves against these accounts rise by $66.67. The reserve requirements against nonpersonal time accounts is .05, so required reserves against these accounts rise by $16.67. Total required reserves rise by $83.34. It is assumed that the bank does not want to hold any excess reserves, so unwanted excess reserves are $1000 − $83.34 = $916.66. The bank spends these excess reserves by expanding its holdings of loans by $916.66. Note that in Panel I, the entire $1000 increase in liabilities is in the form of transactions accounts. These accounts have a higher reserve requirement than nonpersonal time accounts, so the increase in required reserves at Bank A in Panel I is $100, as compared to $83.34 in Panel II. In Panel II, Bank A has a larger quantity of excess reserves than in Panel I, so it can expand its loans by more, that is, $916.66 versus $900.

When Bank A expands its loans in Panel II, the funds are deposited in S&L B, so its total liabilities rise by $916.66. Of this total, two thirds, or $611.11, goes into increased transactions accounts, and one third, or $305.55, goes into a nonpersonal time account. Required reserves for transactions accounts rise by $61.11, and they rise by $15.28 for nonpersonal time accounts, so total required reserves increase by $76.39. The S&L does not want to hold additional excess reserves, so it has $840.27 of unwanted excess reserves that it uses to expand its holdings of loans. This $840.27 is deposited in MSB C, with two thirds going into transactions accounts and one third into nonpersonal time accounts.

At each step in the process, the increase in the quantity of transactions accounts and of nonpersonal time accounts produces an increase in required reserves. Because the reserve requirement for nonpersonal time accounts is less than for transactions accounts, each institution in Panel II has more funds to lend than in Panel I. As a result, the increase in total liabilities at each institution (after Bank A) is greater in Panel II than I. The increase in transactions accounts is smaller at each institution in Panel II than in Panel I, however, because the public deposits part of the funds into nonpersonal time accounts rather than exclusively into transactions accounts. Both transactions and nonpersonal time accounts continue to rise until required reserves in the system have increased by $1000. At this point there are no excess reserves for depository institutions to lend, and the process stops.

---

[27] By depositing one third of the proceeds of the security sale in a nonpersonal time account and two thirds in a transactions account the business maintains the ratio $n = \Delta N/\Delta T = .50$, that is, $333.33/$666.67 = .50.

The cumulative expansion process is shown in Table 11.6. Panel I shows the cumulative expansion when all funds are deposited in transactions accounts. As shown earlier for Table 11.2, the expansion process comes to an end when total transactions accounts in the economy rise by $10,000. At this point the expansion of required reserves is $1000, which equals the initial increase in reserves. Panel II shows the situation when there are nonpersonal time accounts. After the initial deposit of funds at Bank A, the cumulative expansion of total liabilities $(T + N)$ is greater in Panel II than in Panel I, but the expansion of transactions accounts is less. In both panels, the expansion process comes to an end when required reserves have increased by $1000. When there are nonpersonal time accounts (Panel II), total liabilities expand by $12,000 as compared to $10,000 when there are only transactions accounts (Panel I). In Panel II, transactions accounts grow by only $8000 as opposed to $10,000 in Panel I. Nonpersonal time accounts expand by $4000 in Panel II, so total liabilities expand by a greater amount in Panel II than I. As a result, total credit extended by depository institutions also expands by a greater amount.

We will turn to the implications of this greater credit expansion later. The important conclusion at this point is that a given change in total reserves produces a smaller increase in the quantity of transactions accounts the greater is the preference of the public for nonpersonal time accounts relative to transactions accounts and the greater is the reserve requirement on nonpersonal time accounts.

In constructing Tables 11.5 and 11.6, we assumed that e and c are zero. The relationship between the change in reserves and the change in transactions accounts is given by $\Delta T = \Delta TR /(r_T + n \cdot r_N)$. Allowing for excess reserves and currency drains would not have changed the basic conclusion.[28] So long as the reserve requirement for nonpersonal time accounts is greater than zero, the greater the preference of the public for nonpersonal time accounts relative to transactions accounts, n, the smaller is the expansion of the quantity of transactions accounts that results from an initial increase in reserves. Similarly, for a given value of n, the higher the reserve requirement on nonpersonal time accounts, r_N, the smaller is the expansion of transactions accounts. Only if n or r_N is zero do nonpersonal time accounts play no role in determining the expansion of transactions accounts following an initial injection of reserves into the system.

The existence of nonpersonal time accounts affects the degree to which the quantity of transactions accounts responds to changes in total reserves. The extent of the effect depends upon the size of the reserve requirement, r_N, and upon the relationship between changes in transactions accounts and changes in nonpersonal time accounts, n. The reserve requirement is set by the Federal Reserve. The value of n is determined by the portfolio choice of the public concerning the desired holdings of nonpersonal time accounts relative to transactions accounts. Depository institutions themselves can affect this choice by changing the interest rate that they pay on nonpersonal time accounts.

---

[28] It is left to the reader to determine the expansion in transactions accounts when $e = .05$ and $c = .35$.

TABLE 11.6
CUMULATIVE EXPANSION OF TRANSACTIONS ACCOUNTS, NONPERSONAL TIME ACCOUNTS, TOTAL LIABILITIES, REQUIRED RESERVES, AND CREDIT FOLLOWING A $1000 SECURITY PURCHASE BY THE FED[a]

Step	Transactions Accounts	Nonpersonal Time Accounts	Total Liabilities	Required Reserves Against Transactions Accounts	Required Reserves Against Nonpersonal Time Accounts	Total Required Reserves	Total Credit
			Panel I: n = 0.0				
1. Bank A	$ 1,000.00	$ 0.0	$ 1,000.00	$100.00	$ 0.0	$ 100.00	$ 900.00
2. S&L B	1,900.00	0.0	1,900.00	190.00	0.0	190.00	1,710.00
3. MSB C	2,710.00	0.0	2,710.00	271.00	0.0	271.00	2,439.00
4. CU D	3,439.00	0.0	3,439.00	343.90	0.0	343.90	3,095.10
5. Bank E	4,095.10	0.0	4,095.10	409.51	0.0	409.51	3,685.59
.	.	.	.	.	.	.	.
10. Bank J	6,513.22	0.0	6,513.22	651.32	0.0	651.32	5,861.90
.	.	.	.	.	.	.	.
All	10,000.00	0.0	10,000.00	1,000.00	0.0	1,000.00	9,000.00
			Panel II:[b] n = .50				
1. Bank A	$ 666.67	$ 333.33	$ 1,000.00	$ 66.67	$ 16.67	$ 83.34	$ 916.66
2. S&L B	1,277.77	638.88	1,916.66	127.78	31.94	159.72	1,756.94
3. MSB C	1,837.95	918.98	2,756.93	183.80	45.95	229.75	2,527.18
4. CU D	2,351.45	1,175.73	3,527.18	235.15	58.79	293.94	3,233.24
5. Bank E	2,822.16	1,411.08	4,233.24	282.22	70.55	352.77	3,880.47
.	.	.	.	.	.	.	.
10. Bank J	4,648.71	2,324.36	6,973.07	464.87	116.22	581.09	6,391.98
.	.	.	.	.	.	.	.
All	8,000.00	4,000.00	12,000.00	800.00	200.00	1,000.00	11,000.00

[a] For both panels, $r_T = .10$, $r_N = .05$, $e = 0.0$, and $c = 0.0$.
[b] Some numbers are adjusted slightly to remove the effect of rounding errors.

Personal Time Accounts

Personal time accounts are not subject to reserve requirements. These liabilities constitute about 40 percent of the total liabilities of commercial banks and over 90 percent of the liabilities of S&Ls, MSBs and CUs. When funds are deposited into personal time accounts, depository institutions' total liabilities are increased, but their required reserves do not increase. Thus, all the funds in these accounts are available to support lending and holdings of securities.

When there is no reserve requirement on a particular type of account, the public's decision to hold balances in that account rather than in transactions or nonpersonal time accounts does not affect the multiplier relationship between reserves and the quantity of transactions accounts in the economy. This is easily illustrated by considering the simplified world in which depository institutions do not want to hold any excess reserves and the public does not want to hold any currency, that is, e and c are zero.

Panel I of Table 11.7 shows the institution-by-institution expansion of transactions accounts and of nonpersonal time accounts when the public does not hold personal time accounts. The figures in Panel I are the same as in Panel II of Table 11.5. Panel II of Table 11.7 shows the institution-by-institution expansion of transactions accounts and of personal time accounts when the public holds transactions accounts and personal time accounts, but no nonpersonal time accounts. In Panel II it is assumed that the public maintains a constant ratio of its holdings of personal time accounts to transactions accounts. It is assumed that for every $100 increase in the quantity of transactions accounts, the public wants to hold $50 in personal time accounts.[29] Denoting the quantity of personal time accounts as P and the ratio of personal time accounts to transactions accounts as p, we have $p = P/T$, or in change form, $p = \Delta P / \Delta T = .50$.

In Panel II, the Federal Reserve buys $1000 of securities, and the seller deposits $666.67 into a transactions account at Bank A and $333.33 into a personal time account. In both Panels I and II, total liabilities and reserves at Bank A rise by $1000. In Panel I, required reserves rise by $83.34 because there is a reserve requirement against both transactions accounts and nonpersonal time accounts. In Panel II, required reserves rise by only $66.67 because there is no reserve requirement for personal time accounts. In both panels it is assumed that depository institutions do not want to hold any excess reserves, so the expansion of credit (unwanted excess reserves) at Bank A is the difference between the rise in its total liabilities and the rise in its required reserves. In Panel I the credit expansion is $916.64, and in Panel II it is $933.33. Thus, when there are personal time accounts rather than nonpersonal time accounts, Bank A can expand its credit by a

---

[29] In reality, the ratio of personal time accounts to transactions accounts is almost 4.0. There are nearly $4 of personal time accounts in the economy for every $1 of transactions accounts. The ratio of .5 is used in the text to simplify the arithmetic and to allow easy comparison with the case for nonpersonal time accounts.

TABLE 11.7

INSTITUTION-BY-INSTITUTION EXPANSION OF TRANSACTIONS ACCOUNTS, TIME ACCOUNTS, TOTAL LIABILITIES, REQUIRED RESERVES, AND CREDIT FOLLOWING A $1000 SECURITY PURCHASE BY THE FED[a]

Step	ΔTransactions Accounts	ΔTime Accounts	ΔTotal Liabilities	ΔRequired Reserves Against Transactions Accounts	ΔRequired Reserves Against Time Accounts	ΔTotal Required Reserves	ΔCredit Equals: Unwanted Excess Reserves
		Panel I: n = .5, p = 0.0					
		Nonpersonal Time Accounts					
1. Bank A	$666.67	$333.33	$1,000.00	$66.67	$16.67	$83.34	$916.66
2. S&L B	611.11	305.55	916.66	61.11	15.28	76.39	840.27
3. MSB C	560.18	280.09	840.27	56.02	14.00	70.02	770.25
4. CU D	513.50	256.75	770.25	51.35	12.84	64.19	706.06
5. Bank E	470.71	235.35	706.06	47.07	11.77	58.84	647.22
.	.	.	.	.	.	.	.
10. Bank J	304.65	152.33	456.98	30.47	7.62	38.09	418.89
.	.	.	.	.	.	.	.
	0.0	0.0	0.0	0.0	0.0	0.0	0.0
		Panel II: p = .5, n = 0.0					
		Personal Time Accounts					
1. Bank A	$666.67	$333.33	$1,000.00	$66.67	$ 0.0	$66.67	$933.33
2. S&L B	622.22	311.11	933.33	62.22	0.0	62.22	871.11
3. MSB C	580.74	290.37	871.11	58.07	0.0	55.07	813.04
4. CU D	542.03	271.01	813.04	54.20	0.0	54.20	758.84
5. Bank E	505.89	252.95	758.84	50.59	0.0	50.59	708.25
.	.	.	.	.	.	.	.
10. Bank J	358.29	179.15	537.44	35.83	0.0	35.83	501.61
.	.	.	.	.	.	.	.
	0.0	0.0	0.0	0.0	0.0	0.0	0.0

[a] For both panels, $r_T = .10$, $r_N = .05$, $e = 0.0$, and $c = 0.0$.

larger amount. These funds expended by Bank A are deposited in S&L B, and the process continues.

A comparison of Panels I and II indicates that, at every step in the process, depository institutions lend a greater quantity of funds and total liabilities (after Bank A) rise by a larger amount when depositors use personal time accounts rather than nonpersonal time accounts. The absence of a reserve requirement for personal time accounts allows depository institutions to recycle all the funds deposited to these accounts. When funds are deposited in transactions or nonpersonal time accounts, depository institutions must set aside required reserves against these accounts and, they cannot, therefore, expand their holdings of securities and loans (i.e., recycle funds) by as much.

Table 11.8 shows the cumulative expansion of liabilities and credit. Panel I gives the expansion when the public uses nonpersonal time accounts, and Panel II gives the expansion when personal time accounts are used. Because there is no reserve requirement for personal time accounts, the expansion of liabilities and of credit in the system is larger in Panel II than Panel I. When customers use nonpersonal time accounts, total liabilities in the system rise by $12,000 (Panel I); but when they use personal time accounts, these rise by $15,000 (Panel II). In Panel I, transactions accounts rise by $8000, but in Panel II they rise by $10,000. The $10,000 rise in the quantity of transactions accounts in Panel II is the same increase that occurs when the only type of account used by the public is transactions accounts. This can be seen by examining Panel I of Table 11.6, where the increase in transactions accounts is also $10,000. Thus, when the public wants to hold balances in personal time accounts rather than transactions accounts, the multiplier for transactions accounts is unaffected.

We conclude that the availability of personal time accounts does not inhibit the expansion of the quantity of transactions accounts. Depository institutions lend all of the funds deposited in personal time accounts. These loans produce further deposits into transactions accounts and personal time accounts. Only increases in the quantity of transactions account liabilities produce increases in required reserves. We know that the expansion process comes to an end when all of the initial $1000 injection of reserves is absorbed into required reserves. Because only the expansion in transactions accounts increases required reserves, the quantity of transactions accounts rises until the $1000 injection of reserves is absorbed by required reserves against transactions accounts. With a reserve requirement of 10 percent, this occurs when the quantity of transactions accounts rises by $10,000.

Because the public is assumed to maintain a ratio of personal time accounts to transactions accounts of .5, the quantity of personal time accounts rises by $5000. Thus, the quantity of total liabilities in the system rises by $15,000. Because we have assumed that depository institutions hold no excess reserves, the increase in the total amount of credit (loans and securities) extended by depository institutions equals the rise in total liabilities less the rise in required reserves, that is, $15,000 − $1000 = $14,000.

Looking at Panel I, we see that when nonpersonal time accounts are used, transactions accounts rise by $8000 and nonpersonal time accounts rise by $4000 so

TABLE 11.8
CUMULATIVE EXPANSION OF TRANSACTIONS ACCOUNTS, TIME ACCOUNTS, TOTAL LIABILITIES, REQUIRED RESERVES, AND CREDIT FOLLOWING A $1000 SECURITY PURCHASE BY THE FED[a]

Step	Transactions Accounts	Time Accounts	Total Liabilities	Required Reserves Against Transactions Accounts	Required Reserves Against Nonpersonal Time Accounts	Total Required Reserves	Total Credit
			Panel I:[b] $n = .50, p = 0.0$				
		Nonpersonal Time Accounts					
1. Bank A	$ 666.67	$ 333.33	$ 1,000.00	$ 66.67	$ 16.67	$ 83.34	$ 916.66
2. S&L B	1,277.77	638.88	1,916.66	127.78	31.94	159.72	1,756.94
3. MSB C	1,837.95	918.98	2,756.93	183.80	45.95	229.75	2,527.18
4. CU D	2,351.45	1,176.73	3,527.18	235.15	58.79	293.94	3,233.24
5. Bank E	2,822.16	1,411.08	4,233.24	282.22	70.15	352.77	3,880.47
.	.	.	.	.	.	.	.
10. Bank J	4,648.71	2,324.36	6,973.07	464.87	116.22	581.09	6,391.98
.	.	.	.	.	.	.	.
All	8,000.00	4,000.00	12,000.00	800.00	200.00	1,000.00	11,000.00
			Panel II:[b] $n = .5, n = 0.0$				
		Personal Time Accounts					
1. Bank A	$ 666.67	$ 333.33	$ 1,000.00	$ 66.67	$ 0.0	$ 66.67	$ 933.33
2. S&L B	1,288.89	644.44	1,933.33	128.89	0.0	128.89	1,804.44
3. MSB C	1,869.63	934.81	2,804.44	186.96	0.0	186.96	2,617.48
4. CU D	2,411.66	1,205.82	3,617.48	241.17	0.0	241.17	3,376.31
5. Bank E	2,917.55	1,458.77	4,376.32	291.76	0.0	291.76	4,084.56
.	.	.	.	.	.	.	.
10. Bank J	4,983.90	2,491.95	7,475.85	498.39	0.0	498.39	6,977.46
.	.	.	.	.	.	.	.
All	10,000.00	5,000.00	15,000.00	1,000.00	0.0	1,000.00	14,000.00

[a] For both panels, $r_T = .10$, $r_N = .05$, $e = 0.0$, and $c = 0.0$.
[b] Some numbers are adjusted slightly to remove the effect of rounding errors.

total liabilities rise by \$12,000. The increase in total liabilities in Panel II is \$15,000. The smaller rise in Panel I occurs because increases in both transactions and nonpersonal time accounts raises required reserves. The initial \$1000 injection of reserves into the system is absorbed into required reserves for a smaller increase in total liabilities. Because total liabilities rise by a smaller amount in Panel I, total credit in the system expands by \$11,000 when there are only nonpersonal time accounts as opposed to \$14,000 when there are only personal time accounts.

The Money and Credit Multipliers

The various cases just studied can now be integrated to give expressions for the multipliers for the quantity of money in the economy and for the total quantity of credit extended by depository institutions. The quantity of money and of credit in the economy depend upon the reserve requirements for various types of liabilities issued by depository institutions and upon the public's choices concerning the kinds of accounts that they use.

In order to obtain the multiplier for the quantity of money in the economy, we must start with the multiplier for transactions accounts. When depository institutions hold no excess reserves and the public holds no currency, the multiplier relation between an initial change in total reserves, ΔTR_0, and the expansion of transactions accounts in the economy is given by the expression

$$\Delta T = \frac{\Delta TR_0}{(r_T + n \cdot r_N)} ,$$

so the multiplier for transactions accounts, m_T, is $1/(r_T + n \cdot r_N)$ and $\Delta T = m_T \cdot \Delta TR_0$. The multiplier depends upon the reserve requirement on transactions accounts, the ratio of nonpersonal time accounts to transactions accounts, and the reserve requirement for nonpersonal time accounts. Holdings of personal time accounts by the public do not affect the multiplier and, therefore, do not affect the change in the quantity of transactions accounts.

The multiplier relation for transactions accounts can be modified to allow for the demand for excess reserves by depository institutions and to allow for the public's demand for currency. When depository institutions increase their holdings of excess reserves as transactions accounts increase, reserves drain into excess reserves and the multiplier for transactions accounts is reduced. When the public increases its currency holdings as transactions accounts rise, reserves drain out of the system, and the expansion of transactions accounts is reduced. Assuming that depository institutions maintain a constant ratio of excess reserves to transactions accounts, e, and that the public maintains a constant ratio of currency to transactions accounts, c, the relationship between an initial change in reserves and the change in transactions accounts is

$$\Delta T = \frac{\Delta TR_0}{(r_T + n \cdot r_N + e + c)} .$$

The multiplier for transactions accounts is

$$m_T = \frac{1}{(r_T + n \cdot r_N + e + c)} \; .$$

The quantity of money in the economy is composed of the quantity of currency, C, and of transactions accounts, T, held by the public. Using M to denote money, we have $M = C + T$. For changes in the quantity of money, we have $\Delta M = \Delta C + \Delta T$. Assuming that the public maintains a constant ratio of currency to transactions accounts, we have $c = \Delta C / \Delta T$. It follows, then, that $\Delta C = c\Delta T$, and because $\Delta M = \Delta C + \Delta T$, $\Delta M = c\Delta T + \Delta T$, or

$$\Delta M = (1 + c)\Delta T \; .$$

Thus, so long as the public maintains a constant ratio of currency to transactions accounts, c, changes in the quantity of money are proportionate to changes in the quantity of transactions accounts. The relationship between an initial change in reserves and a change in the quantity of transactions accounts is $\Delta T = m_T \Delta TR_0$, so $\Delta M = (1 + c)m_T \Delta TR_0$. Recalling that $m_T = 1/(r_T + n \cdot r_N + e + c)$, we have:

$$\Delta M = \frac{1 + c}{(r_T + n \cdot r_N + e + c)} \cdot \Delta TR_0 \; .$$

This expression indicates that there is a multiplier relationship between an initial change in the quantity of total reserves, ΔTR_0, and the change in the quantity of money, ΔM. The *money multiplier, m_M*, is

$$m_M = \frac{1 + c}{(r_T + n \cdot r_N + e + c)}$$

and $\Delta M = m_M \Delta TR_0$. The money multiplier is determined by the reserve requirements for transactions accounts and nonpersonal time accounts as well as by the portfolio decisions of the public and of depository institutions. The public determines the amount of currency, transactions accounts, and nonpersonal time accounts that it wants to hold. The public's demands for currency, transactions accounts, and nonpersonal time accounts are affected by transactions needs and the expected rates of return and risk on these assets relative to other assets. Depository institutions affect these demands by varying the interest rates on nonpersonal time accounts and for those transactions accounts that do not have an interest rate ceiling. The interest rates that depository institutions are willing to pay for these accounts are affected, in turn, by the expected rates of return and risks for the assets that they hold. We conclude that the interaction of the portfolio decisions of the public and of depository institutions jointly determine c and n. Finally, depository institutions determine the amount of excess reserves that they want to hold, and this decision determines e.

The money multiplier is the same as the multiplier for transactions accounts except that m_M has the term $(1 + c)$ in the numerator. This additional term appears because the public's holdings of currency is a component of money. Perhaps the easiest way to see the effects of currency demand on the money multiplier is through an example. Assume that $r_T = .10$, $r_N = .05$, $e = .05$, $c = .35$, and $n =$

.50. Now consider the effect of a $1000 purchase of securities by the Federal Reserve. The change in the quantity of transactions accounts is given by $\Delta T = \Delta TR_0/(r_T + n \cdot r_N + e + c)$, so $\Delta T = 1000/[.10 + .50(.05) + .05 + .35] = \$1000/.525 = \$1904.76$. A $1000 increase in the initial quantity of reserves produces a $1904.76 increase in the quantity of transactions accounts in the economy. This increase is smaller than any of the increases we have obtained from earlier examples. This is because we have included for the first time all the factors that determine the transactions account multiplier. After we allow for reserve requirements against both transactions and nonpersonal time accounts, for desired excess reserves, and for the drain of reserves into currency holdings, the expansion of transactions accounts is only $1904.76. The expansion of the quantity of money is larger than this, however, because although currency drains reduce the expansion of transactions account balances, the increased currency holdings are part of the quantity of money.

We know that $\Delta TR = \Delta TR_0 - c\Delta T$, that is, the net expansion of reserves in the system is the initial increase, ΔTR_0, less the currency drains that occur. Because we have assumed that the public maintains a constant ratio between its holdings of currency and transactions accounts, the currency drain is $c\Delta T$. In our example, the net increase in reserves is $\Delta TR = \$1000 - .35(\$1904.76) = \$1000.00 - \$666.67 = \$333.33$. Thus, the public added $666.67 to its currency holdings. Since currency is money, we have a total increase in the quantity of money of $\Delta M = \Delta C + \Delta T = \$666.67 + \$1904.76 = \$2571.43$. The initial $1000 increase in total reserves produces a $1904.76 increase in the quantity of transactions accounts and a $666.67 increase in currency holdings for a $2571.43 increase in the quantity of money. This figure can be obtained directly from the expression for the money multiplier: $\Delta M = \Delta TR_0(1 + c)/(r_T + n \cdot r_N + e + c) = \$1000(1.35)/[.10 + .50(.05) + .05 + .35] = \$1350/.525 = \$2571.43$. Put another way, the money multiplier is proportionate to the transactions account multiplier where the factor of proportionality is $(1 + c)$, so $m_M = (1 + c)m_T$. In our example, $m_T = 1/.525 = 1.90476$, and $m_M = (1.35)(1.90476) = 2.57143$, so $\Delta M = m_M\Delta TR_0$, and $\Delta M = (2.57143)\$1000 = \$2571.43$.

Controlling the Quantity of Money in the Economy

In recent years, the Federal Reserve has placed considerable emphasis on controlling the quantity of money in the economy, and it is often criticized when the quantity of money deviates from the targets that the Fed establishes. Although the topic of controlling money occupies considerable space in Chapters 18 and 19, we can see from the expression for the money multiplier that many determinants of the quantity of money are outside the direct control of the Federal Reserve. The Fed does control reserve requirements, and it can affect the quantity of reserves in the economy. Thus, the Fed can increase the multiplier by reducing required reserves, and it can decrease the multiplier by raising required reserves. The Federal Reserve can also determine the initial change in reserves. Thus, the Fed has two methods of affecting the change in the quantity of money. It can leave reserve requirements unchanged and change the quantity of reserves, or it can leave the quantity of reserves unchanged and change reserve requirements. It can, of course, change both reserves and reserve requirements at the same time. The choices involved are discussed in Chapter 12.

There are several determinants of the money multiplier that are not directly determined by the Federal Reserve. The ratio of nonpersonal time accounts to transactions accounts is determined by the portfolio choices of the public. These choices are affected by changes in wealth and income, as well as by the interest rates that depository institutions pay on transactions and nonpersonal time accounts relative to interest rates on other assets available to the public. As we saw in Chapter 7, the interest rates that depository institutions pay for liabilities that are not subject to binding interest rate ceilings depend upon the public's demand for loans. None of these factors is under the direct control of the Federal Reserve. Similarly, the demand for excess reserves by depository institutions depends upon the interest rates that can be earned on alternative uses of funds, upon transactions costs, and upon the variability and predictability of their liabilities. These factors are also beyond the direct control of the Fed. Furthermore, the public's demand for currency depends upon the portfolio choices of the public. The decision to hold currency is affected by the level of transactions in the economy, by interest rates, and by the mix of transactions between those requiring currency and those using transactions account balances. As before, these factors cannot be controlled directly by the Fed.[30]

Finally, the actual structure of reserve requirements is complex. Small depository institutions have lower reserve requirements than large institutions, and nonpersonal time accounts with maturities of four years or more have no reserve requirement. As the public shifts funds between large and small institutions or between short-term and long-term nonpersonal time accounts, required reserves in the system change. These shifts affect the multipliers for transactions accounts and for money.

If the public and depository institutions cooperate by maintaining constant values for n, e, and c and if there are no switches among size of institution or among maturity of accounts, the Federal Reserve can directly control the quantity of money in the economy by changing reserves or by changing reserve requirements. History has proved that n, e, and c are not constant. Unexpected changes in these ratios produce unexpected changes in the money multiplier. Furthermore, there are unexpected shifts among institutions of different size and among time accounts of different maturities. These changes limit the ability of the Fed to control the quantity of money in the economy.

---

[30] During the panicked conditions of the early 1930s, the public increased its demand for currency, and banks increased their demand for excess reserves. This increased c and e, which produced a substantial decline in the money and credit multipliers. The fall in the multipliers accounted for much of the decline in money and bank credit that occurred during the period.

The Quantity of Nonpersonal Time and Personal Time Accounts

Time accounts are not media of exchange and, therefore, are not included in our definition of money. These accounts are important, however, because they are significant components of the asset portfolios held by the public. Time accounts are also important because depository institutions use these accounts to support most of their lending. It is important for us, therefore, to determine how the quantity of nonpersonal time accounts and of personal time accounts respond to a change in the quantity of reserves.

Let us begin with nonpersonal time accounts. Assuming that the public maintains a constant ratio of nonpersonal time accounts to transactions accounts, n, $\Delta N = n \Delta T$. Because $\Delta T = m_T \Delta TR_0$, we have $\Delta N = n \cdot m_T \Delta TR_0$. Thus, there is a multiplier relationship between an initial change in reserves and the change in the quantity of nonpersonal time accounts. We have $\Delta N = m_N \cdot \Delta TR_0$, where the nonpersonal time account multiplier, m_N, is $m_N = n \cdot m_T$. The multiplier for nonpersonal time accounts, m_N, is proportional to the transactions account multiplier, m_T, where n is the factor of proportionality, that is, $m_N = n \cdot m_T$. Recalling that $m_T = 1/(r_T + n \cdot r_N + e + c)$, we have:

$$m_N = \left[\frac{n}{r_T + n \cdot r_N + e + c} \right]$$

and

$$\Delta N = \left[\frac{n}{r_T + n \cdot r_N + e + c} \right] \Delta TR_0 .$$

Thus, an initial increase in the quantity of reserves produces an expansion in the quantity of nonpersonal time accounts. In terms of our standard example, we have $\Delta TR_0 = \$1000$, $n = .50$, $r_T = .10$, $r_N = .50$, $e = .05$, and $c = .35$. So

$$\Delta N = \left[\frac{.50}{.10 + .50(.05) + .05 + .35} \right] \cdot \$1000 = \$952.38$$

and

$$m_N = .95238 .$$

We conclude that the initial $1000 increase in total reserves produces a $952.38 increase in the quantity of nonpersonal time accounts.

There is also a multiplier for the quantity of personal time accounts. Assuming the public maintains a constant ratio of personal time accounts to transactions accounts, we have $p = \Delta P / \Delta T$ and $\Delta P = p \Delta T$. Because $\Delta T = m_T \Delta TR_0$, $\Delta P = p \cdot m_T \Delta TR_0$. The multiplier for personal time accounts, m_P, is $m_P = p \cdot m_T$. Thus, $\Delta P = m_P \Delta TR_0$, or

$$\Delta P = \left[\frac{p}{r_T + n \cdot r_N + e + c} \right] \Delta TR_0 .$$

From our standard example, $p = .50$, m_N is .95288, and the expansion of personal time accounts is $952.38.

Total Liabilities and Credit in the System

Now that we have discussed the multipliers for transactions accounts, nonpersonal time accounts and personal time accounts, we can obtain multipliers for the total liabilities of all depository institutions. Total liabilities, TL, are the sum of the three types of accounts, so $TL = T + N + P$, or in changes, $\Delta TL = \Delta T + \Delta N + \Delta P$. We want to determine the change in the total liabilities of the depository system that results from an initial change in the quantity of reserves, ΔTR_0. We have shown that $\Delta T = m_T \Delta TR_0$, $\Delta N = m_N \Delta TR_0$, and $\Delta P = m_P \Delta TR_0$, so $\Delta TL = m_T \Delta TR_0 + m_N \Delta TR_0 + m_P \Delta TR_0$. Under the assumption that the public maintains constant ratios of nonpersonal time accounts and of personal time accounts to transactions account balances, the multiplier for total liabilities is easily obtained. In this situation $m_N = n \cdot m_T$, and $m_P = p \cdot m_T$, so

$$\Delta TL = m_T \Delta TR_0 + n \cdot m_T \Delta TR_0 + p \cdot m_T \Delta TR_0$$
$$= (m_T + n \cdot m_T + p \cdot m_T)\Delta TR_0$$

and

$$\Delta TL = (1 + n + p)m_T \Delta TR_0 .$$

Thus, the multiplier for the total liabilities of all depository institutions, m_{TL}, is proportionate to the transactions account multiplier, where the factor of proportionality is $(1 + n + p)$, that is, $m_{TL} = (1 + n + p)m_T$. Thus, $\Delta TL = m_{TL}\Delta TR_0$, or

$$\Delta TL = \left[\frac{1 + n + p}{r_T + n \cdot r_N + e + c} \right] \Delta TR_0 .$$

Total credit extended by depository institutions, TC, is the difference between their total assets, TA, and their total reserves, TR. Thus, $TC = TA - TR$. Total assets are supported by the liabilities that depository institutions issue plus their net worth, NW. Thus, $TA = TL + NW = T + N + P + NW$. Because $TC = TA - TR$, we have $TC = TL + NW - TR = T + N + P + NW - TR$. Depository institutions take their liabilities and net worth, deposit their required reserves and any desired excess reserves at the Fed, and use the remaining funds to extend credit, that is, acquire loans and securities. Thus, total credit is total liabilities and net worth less total reserves.

We can use the expression for total liabilities to obtain the multiplier relation between a change in total reserves and the change in total credit. For changes in total credit, we have $\Delta TC = \Delta TA - \Delta TR = \Delta TL + \Delta NW - \Delta TR$. Assume that there is no change in net worth, that is, $\Delta NW = 0$, so $\Delta TC = \Delta TL - \Delta TR$. The change in total liabilities is $\Delta TL = \Delta T + \Delta N + \Delta P$. The change in total reserves is the change in required reserves plus the change in desired excess reserves,

$\Delta TR = r_T \Delta T + r_N \Delta N + \Delta ER$. Thus, $\Delta TC = \Delta T + \Delta N + \Delta P - r_T \cdot \Delta T - r_N \Delta N - \Delta ER$. Collecting terms we have:

$$\Delta TC = (1 - r_T)\Delta T + (1 - r_N)\Delta N + \Delta P - \Delta ER .$$

This expression indicates that only the proportion of transactions accounts that does not have to be invested in required reserves $(1 - r_T)$ is used to support the expansion of credit. If $r_T = .10$, then $(1 - .10) = .9$, so 90 percent of the increase in transactions accounts supports additional credit. Similarly, only the proportion of the increase in nonpersonal time accounts that is not invested in required reserves $(1 - r_N)$ is used to support additional credit. Because there is no reserve requirement against personal time accounts, all the increase in these accounts supports additional credit. The final term indicates that given ΔT, ΔN, and ΔP, when depository institutions add to their excess reserves, total credit is reduced. Letting $\Delta N = n \cdot \Delta T$, $\Delta P = p \cdot \Delta T$, and $\Delta ER = e \cdot \Delta T$ we have $\Delta TC = (1 - r_T)\Delta T + (1 - r_N)n \cdot \Delta T + p\Delta T \quad e\Delta T$, so

$$\Delta TC = [(1 - r_T) + (1 - r_N)n + p - e]\Delta T .$$

The change in total credit is proportional to the change in transactions accounts, where the factor of proportionality is $[(1 - r_T) + (1 + r_N)n + p - e]$. Because $\Delta T = m_T \Delta TR_0$, we have $\Delta TC = [(1 - r_T) + (1 - r_N)n + p - e]m_T \Delta TR_0$. Recalling that $m_T = 1/(r_T + n \cdot r_N + e + c)$, we have

$$\Delta TC = \left[\frac{(1 - r_T) + (1 - r_N)n + p - e}{r_T + n \cdot r_N + e + c} \right] \Delta TR_0 .$$

Thus, the total credit multiplier, m_{TC}, is

$$m_{TC} = \frac{(1 - r_T) + (1 - r_N)n + p - e}{r_T + n \cdot r_N + e + c}$$

and $\Delta TC = m_{TC} \Delta TR_0$.

A reduction in the reserve requirement for either transactions accounts or for nonpersonal time accounts increases all multipliers. With lower reserve requirements, less reserves are absorbed into required reserves at each step in the process, and the expansion of credit and liabilities is greater. The behavior of the public and of depository institutions also affects the multiplier. As long as r_N is less than r_T, a rise in nonpersonal time accounts does not cause as large an absorption of reserves into required reserves as a rise in transactions accounts. This implies that the greater the amount of nonpersonal time accounts that the public wants to hold relative to transactions accounts, the greater the multiplier for total credit. When the public increases its holdings of personal time accounts relative to transactions accounts, required reserves do not rise at all. Thus, the greater is p, the greater is the total credit multiplier. Furthermore, the lower the demand for excess reserves by depository institutions, the greater the multiplier because each round of credit and liability expansion produces a smaller absorption of reserves into desired excess reserves. Finally, the lower the public's demand for currency, the greater the multiplier because less of the initial increase in reserves, ΔTR_0, drains out of the system as currency.

Variability of the Multipliers

Throughout the discussion of the various multipliers, we assumed that the public maintains constant ratios of currency, nonpersonal time accounts, and personal time accounts to transactions accounts and also that depository institutions maintain a constant ratio of excess reserves to transactions accounts. These assumptions were useful for simplifying the discussion, but they are not realistic. The assumption of constant ratios suggests mechanical relationships between reserves and the quantity of money and credit in the economy. In reality, the relationships are far from mechanical because they are affected by the economic decisions of the public and of depository institutions. These decisions affect c, n, p and e, which cause the multipliers to change. Thus, the economic decisions of the public and of depository institutions affect the quantity of money and credit in the economy. At every point in time there are money and credit multipliers, but the multipliers change over time with economic conditions.

Summary of the Multipliers

It might be helpful at this point to summarize the several multiplier relationships that we have derived. Table 11.9 shows the multipliers for changes in the quantity of transactions accounts, money, nonpersonal time accounts, personal time accounts, total liabilities of depository institutions, and total credit extended by these institutions. We can see that all the multipliers are affected by reserve requirements for transactions accounts and for nonpersonal time accounts. Thus, by changing reserve requirements, the Federal Reserve can affect the relationship between an initial change in total reserves, ΔTR_0, and changes in T, M, N, P, TL, and TC. All the multipliers are also affected by the ratios of nonpersonal time accounts, currency, and excess reserves to transactions accounts. Thus, the portfolio decisions of the public and the portfolio decisions of depository institutions affect all the multipliers through their effects on n, c, and e. Because there is no reserve requirement for personal time accounts, the ratio of these accounts to transactions accounts does not affect the multipliers for transactions accounts, money, or nonpersonal time accounts. This ratio, p, does affect the multipliers for personal time accounts, total liabilities of depository institutions, and total credit extended by these institutions. Thus, the portfolio decisions of the public and of depository institutions affect P, TL, and TC.

The effects of r_T, r_N, e, c, n and p on the several multipliers can be illustrated by numerical examples. The first row of Table 11.10 shows the effects of an initial increase in total reserves of $1000 for the standard example of $r_T = .10$, $r_N = .05$, $e = .05$, $c = .35$, $n = .50$, and $p = .50$. In the remainder of the table, each of the ratios (r_T, r_N, e, c, n, and p) is changed to determine its effects on the multipliers. In row 2, the reserve requirement on transactions accounts, r_T, is reduced from .10 to .075 whereas all of the other factors (i.e., r_N, e, c, n, and p) are kept the same as in the standard example. By comparing the figures in row 2 with the figures for the standard example (row 1), we see that a reduction in r_T increases the multi-

TABLE 11.9
SUMMARY OF THE MULTIPLIERS

1. Transactions accounts:

$$m_T = \frac{1}{r_T + n \cdot r_N + e + c}.$$

2. Money:

$$m_M = \frac{(1+c)}{r_T + n \cdot r_N + e + c} = (1+c)m_T.$$

3. Nonpersonal time accounts:

$$m_N = \frac{n}{r_T + n \cdot r_N + e + c} = n \cdot m_T.$$

4. Personal time accounts:

$$m_p = \frac{p}{r_T + n \cdot r_N + e + c} = p \cdot m_T.$$

5. Total liabilities:

$$m_{TL} = \frac{(1+n+p)}{r_T + n \cdot r_N + e + c} = (1+n+p)m_T.$$

6. Total credit:

$$m_{TC} = \frac{(1-r_T)+(1-r_N)\cdot n + p - e}{r_T + n \cdot r_N + e + c} = [(1-r_T)+(1-r_N)\cdot n + p - e]m_T.$$

TABLE 11.10
EFFECTS OF CHANGES IN r_T, r_N, e, c, n, and p ON THE EXPANSION OF TRANSACTIONS ACCOUNTS, MONEY, NONPERSONAL AND PERSONAL TIME ACCOUNTS, TOTAL LIABILITIES, AND TOTAL CREDIT[a]

Case	Transactions Accounts ΔT	Money ΔM	Nonpersonal Time Accounts ΔN	Personal Time Accounts ΔP	Total Liabilities ΔTL	Total Credit ΔTC
1. Standard example[b]	$1,904.76	$2,571.43	$ 952.38	$ 952.38	$3,809.52	$3,476.19
2. r_T= .075	2,000.00	2,700.00	1,000.00	1,000.00	4,000.00	3,700.00
3. r_N= 0.0	2,000.00	2,700.00	1,000.00	1,000.00	4,000.00	3,700.00
4. e = .025	2,000.00	2,700.00	1,000.00	1,000.00	4,000.00	3,700.00
5. c = .325	2,000.00	2,650.00	1,000.00	1,000.00	4,000.00	3,700.00
6. n = 0.0	2,000.00	2,700.00	0.0	1,000.00	3,000.00	2,700.00
7. p = 0.0	1,904.76	2,571.43	952.38	0.0	2,857.14	2,523.81

[a] All cases assume a $1000 security purchase by the Fed.
[b] Assumes $r_T = .10$, $r_N = .05$, $c = .35$, $n = .50$, and $p = .50$.

pliers. For example, an initial increase in reserves of $1000 increases the quantity of money by $2541.43 when the reserve requirement on transactions accounts is 10 percent (row 1), but money expands by $2,700.00 when the reserve requirement is 7.5 percent (row 2). By comparing the two rows of the table we see that there is a greater expansion in all the quantities when r_T is reduced from .10 to .075. Thus, all of the multipliers are increased.

In row 3, r_T is returned to .10, and the reserve requirement on nonpersonal time accounts, r_N, is reduced from 5.0 to 0.0. We see that if r_N is reduced by 5 percentage points, that is, from 5.0 percent to 0.0 percent, we have the same effect on the multipliers as we did by reducing r_T from 10 to 7.5 percent. The reserve requirement on nonpersonal time accounts has to be reduced by twice as much because r_N is multiplied by n. The ratio of nonpersonal time accounts to transactions accounts is set at .50, so a reduction in r_N has only half the effect of a reduction in r_T. Even though a larger change in r_N is required, we see that the Federal Reserve can use either r_T or r_N as methods of changing the multipliers.

In row 4, the reserve requirement for nonpersonal time accounts is returned to .05, as in the standard example, and the ratio of excess reserves to transactions accounts, e, is reduced from .05 to .025. Here we see that the effect of reducing e by 2.5 percentage points, that is, from 5 to 2.5 percent, is the same as reducing r_T by 2.5 percentage points or r_N by 5 percentage points. Thus, the portfolio decisions of depository institutions concerning the amount of excess reserves that they hold can have a significant effect on the multipliers.

Row 5 illustrates that a change in c does not have the same effect on all the multipliers. In row 5, e is returned to a value of .05, and the ratio of currency to transactions accounts, c, is reduced by 2.5 percentage points from 35 percent to 32.5 percent. Except for the money multiplier, this reduction in c has the same effect on the multipliers as the reductions in r_T, r_N and e. The expansion of money in row 5 is greater than in row 1. This illustrates that when the public reduces its holdings of currency relative to transactions accounts, the money multiplier increases. When $c = .35$ (row 1), the quantity of money expands by $2571.43 in response to an initial reserve injection of $1000. When $c = .325$ (row 5), money expands by $2650. The increase in the money multiplier is not as large for a reduction in c as it is for reductions in r_T, r_N, or e, however. The increase in the quantity of transactions accounts is $2000 in rows 2 through 5. When c falls, the public is holding less currency relative to transactions accounts. Because both currency and transactions accounts are money, the increase in the quantity of money is smaller in row 5 than in rows 2, 3, and 4. We conclude from this case that a reduction in c increases all the multipliers but that there is a smaller effect on the money multiplier.

Row 6 shows the effects of a change in the ratio of nonpersonal time accounts to transactions accounts. Here several of the multipliers are affected differently. In row 6, c is returned to .35, and n is reduced from .50 to 0.0. In the standard example of row 1, it is assumed that the public adds $.50 to nonpersonal time accounts for every $1.00 added to transactions accounts. In row 6, it is assumed that nonpersonal time account balances do not change as transactions accounts rise. Here we see that the initial $1000 injection of reserves produces a $2000 increase in transactions accounts and a $2700 increase in money. When $n = .50$ (row 1), the figures are $1904.76 and $2571.43 for the expansions in transactions accounts and money. We conclude that a reduction in n increases the multipliers for ΔT and ΔM. In fact, the reduction in n from .5 to 0.0 has the same effect on ΔT and ΔM as the reductions in r_T, r_N, and e as shown in rows 2 through 4. The reduction in n increases the multipliers for ΔT and ΔM because there is a reserve requirement for nonpersonal time accounts. In the standard example (row 1), when $n = .5$, these accounts rise as transactions accounts rise. The rise in N increases required reserves, which limits the expansion in transactions balances and money that can occur. When $n = 0.0$, there is no increase in nonpersonal time accounts, and the expansion of T and M is greater.

Because the ratio of personal time accounts to transactions accounts, p, is still .50 in row 6, the $2000 increase in transactions accounts is associated with a $1000 increase in personal time accounts. Because nonpersonal time accounts do not rise, the increase in total liabilities for the depository system is only $3000 in row 6. This is a smaller expansion for TL than in row 1, where $n = .50$. Furthermore, the increase in total credit extended by depository institutions is $2700. This is also smaller than the expansion of TC shown in row 1. We conclude that a reduction in n increases the multipliers for transactions accounts and money, but *decreases* the multipliers for total liabilities and total credit. Thus, the portfolio decisions of the public concerning the amount of nonpersonal time accounts to hold relative to transactions accounts have opposite effects on the expansion of money and credit. For a given initial increase in total reserves, ΔTR_0, a decline in n produces greater growth of money but lower growth of credit extended by depository institutions.

Row 7 gives another example of how the relationship between the expansion of money and credit can be disturbed. Here the ratio of nonpersonal time accounts to transactions accounts, n, is returned to .50, and the ratio of personal time accounts to transactions accounts, p, is reduced from .50 to 0.0. By comparing rows 7 and 1, we see that a reduction in p from .50 to 0.0 has no effect on the multipliers for transactions accounts, money, or nonpersonal time accounts. When total reserves increase, there is the same increase in these quantities when $p = .50$ (row 1) as when $p = 0.0$ (row 7). The expansion of transaction accounts, money, and nonpersonal time accounts is unaffected by p because there is no reserve requirement on personal time accounts. Thus, the portfolio decisions of the public concerning the amount of personal time accounts to hold have no effect on the quantity of money, transactions accounts or nonpersonal time accounts.[31] The decisions do affect the expansion in total liabilities and total credit, however. When $p = .5$ (row 1), the total liabilities of the depository system expand by $3809.52, and total credit expands by $3476.19. When $p = 0.0$, total liabilities only increase by

---

[31] Assuming that e, c, and n do not change when p changes.

$2857.14 and total credit increases by $2523.81. We conclude that a reduction in the ratio of personal time accounts to transactions accounts reduces the multipliers for total liabilities and total credit while having no effect on the multipliers for money, transactions accounts, or nonpersonal time accounts. The growth of money is not affected when the public reduces its demand for personal time accounts, but the growth of credit extended by depository institutions is reduced. As in the previous case, the portfolio decisions of the public concerning the demand for time accounts disturbs the relationship between the expansion of money and the expansion of credit in the economy.

THE RELATIONSHIP BETWEEN THE QUANTITY OF MONEY AND THE QUANTITY OF CREDIT IN THE ECONOMY

As the discussion surrounding Table 11.10 summarized the multiplier relationships developed in this chapter, the usual summary section is omitted. Rather, we shall conclude with some remarks on the relationship between the quantity of money and the quantity of credit in the economy. Because both money and credit affect economic activity and inflation, it is important to determine the relationship between these two quantities.

Up to this point we have discussed only the quantity of credit extended by depository institutions. These institutions are an important source of credit to the economy, but there are many other sources. As was indicated in Chapter 4, mutual funds, insurance companies, pension funds, and finance companies are important sources of credit in the economy. Furthermore, households and businesses extend credit directly through securities markets. The total supply of credit in the economy is the sum of the supplies from all these sources.

The effects of the public's demand for the liabilities of financial intermediaries other than depository institutions and the effects of the public's demand for securities are similar to the effects of its demand for personal time accounts. Consider the case of a loan granted by Bank A. The borrower spends the money, and the recipients of the expenditures deposit the funds in transactions accounts. These recipients then allocate the money among various assets. Assume the public writes checks on its newly expanded transactions accounts to purchase shares in mutual funds. Because there is no reserve requirements for the mutual funds, they can extend additional credit by the amount that their liabilities to the public have risen. This is the same increase in credit that would occur if the public had deposited the same amount in personal time accounts rather than invested in mutual fund shares.

When the public invests part of its assets in mutual fund shares, the total quantity of credit in the economy rises, but required reserves do not increase. Thus, the total quantity of transactions accounts and of money that can be supported by the total reserves in the depository system is unaffected. This means that the greater the public's use of mutual funds, the greater the amount of credit that gets extended in the economy for a given quantity of total reserves, transactions accounts, and money.

We have used mutual funds as an example, but it should be noted that when the public places funds with any financial intermediary other than a depository institution and when the public purchases securities directly in the market, the quantity of credit rises, but required reserves do not rise. The same phenomenon occurs when the public places funds in personal time accounts. In all these situations, funds are recycled, and credit expands without any additional reserves being absorbed into required reserves. This means that the more the public uses these investment outlets and the less it uses transactions accounts or nonpersonal time accounts, the greater is the total quantity of credit in the economy for a given quantity of total reserves and money.

There are many factors involved in determining the quantity of money and the quantity of credit in the economy. The Federal Reserve plays an important role in determining these quantities, but so do depository institutions, other financial intermediaries, securities markets, and the general public. We have devoted significant space in this text to the portfolio decisions of the public, to the behavior of depository institutions and other financial intermediaries, as well as to securities markets. We have not yet fully discussed the Federal Reserve. That institution is the topic of the next chapter.

SELECTED REFERENCES

Burger, Allen, *The Money Supply Process*, Belmont, Cal.: Wadsworth, 1971.

Tobin, James, "Commercial Banks as Creators of 'Money,'" Dean Carson (ed.), *Banking and Monetary Studies*, Homewood, Ill.: Irwin, 1963.

THE FEDERAL RESERVE SYSTEM

12

The Federal Reserve as the nation's central bank is an important and powerful institution. It is the ultimate source of liquidity for the economy, and it is responsible for controlling the quantity of money and credit in the economy. The Fed's activities crucially affect real output and employment, interest rates, the rate of inflation, and economic growth.

Liquidity crises that marred our earlier economic history can be stopped by a central bank that is willing and able to grant loans and purchase assets in sufficient quantity. In a system of fiat money there is no external constraint, such as gold, that limits movements in the quantity of money and credit in the economy. The Federal Reserve System (the Fed) provides the constraint by limiting the quantity of reserves in the depository system. This responsibility is crucial to the nation's economic well-being because if the growth of money and credit is too slow, economic recession and stagnation occur. If the growth of money and credit is too rapid, inflation results.

This chapter describes the methods that the Fed uses to ward off liquidity crises and the methods it uses to affect the quantity of money and credit, as well as the level of interest rates, in the economy.[1] These two activities comprise *monetary policy*. The theory and actual practice of monetary policy are discussed in detail in the chapters that follow this one. The current chapter lays the foundation for that discussion by describing the structure and basic functions of the Fed.

---

[1] This chapter is concerned only with domestic economic factors. The Federal Reserve's activities in the international sphere are discussed in Chapter 17.

THE STRUCTURE OF THE FEDERAL RESERVE SYSTEM

The Federal Reserve System is comprised of the Board of Governors located in Washington, D.C., the twelve regional Federal Reserve banks, and the private banks that are members of the system. This section describes the functions of the Board of Governors and the Federal Reserve banks, and it describes their relationship to member banks.

The Board of Governors of the Federal Reserve System

The Board of Governors of the Federal Reserve System is composed of seven members who are appointed by the President of the United States subject to the consent of the Senate. The full term of a governor is fourteen years, and a governor can serve only one full term.[2] The President also appoints, subject to Senate confirmation, one of the seven Board members to be chairman and one member to be vice-chairman. The appointments of chairman and vice-chairman are for four years and can be renewed provided that the fourteen-year terms have not expired. The appointment of the chairman is important because that individual is more powerful than the other governors.[3] The chairman represents and speaks for the Board of Governors and for the Federal Reserve System in relations with the President, the Congress, and foreign governments. The chairman of the Board also serves as chairman of the Federal Open Market Committee (FOMC), which, as we will see, is the most important policymaking body within the Federal Reserve System. Finally, the chairman determines the assignments given to other governors in overseeing and guiding the operations of the Federal Reserve System. This gives the chairman the opportunity to use carrots or sticks, or both, in achieving his goals when dealing with other members of the Board.

The Board of Governors has most of the power within the Federal Reserve System. The Board is located in Washington, D.C., and does not engage in the actual "nuts and bolts" of central banking. Rather, it is concerned with setting general policies for the Federal Reserve System. In that capacity, the Board oversees the operations of the Federal Reserve banks and exercises a major voice in the execution of monetary policy. Monetary policy decisions are shared with the Federal Reserve banks. Both the members of the Board and representatives of the Federal Reserve banks are members of the Federal Open Market Committee.

---

[2] The fourteen-year term is designed to insulate Board members from political pressures. Several other factors also tend to promote the independence of the Fed from politics. The significance of this independence is discussed later.

[3] The office of vice-chairman carries considerably less power than that of chairman.

The Board of Governors has a dominant voice on that committee, however, because it controls a majority of the votes. The Board has sole responsibility for setting reserve requirements within allowable ranges established by Congress.

A major function of the Board is to coordinate the activities of the Federal Reserve banks in order to achieve a national monetary policy. The Board exerts its influence over the Federal Reserve banks by having final authority over their budgets and by approving the appointments of the president and senior vice-president of each Reserve Bank.

In addition to its functions in determining monetary policy and in overseeing the activities of the Federal Reserve banks, the Board of Governors has many other duties. Regulatory responsibilities actually claim most of the Board's time. These duties include (1) regulation and supervision of member banks, (2) administration of the Bank Merger Act, (3) administration of the Bank Holding Company Act, (4) regulation of the foreign activities of U.S. banks, (5) setting and administering margin requirements for loans extended to finance the acquisition of corporate securities, and (6) administration of the Truth in Lending Act. The first four duties are described elsewhere in this book and are not discussed here. Margin requirements and administration of the Truth in Lending Act are described in the appendix to this chapter.

An important additional function of the Board of Governors is to collect and publish data on the financial condition of the economy. Data on reserves and interest rates, various measures of the quantity of money, as well as data on the assets and liabilities of depository institutions and a host of other factors are published periodically by the Board. These publications provide official data used by scholars, business, other government agencies, and the general public to analyze monetary policy and the general financial condition of the economy. The staff of the Board of Governors also conducts research on a variety of monetary and regulatory issues.

The Federal Reserve Banks

Figure 12.1 provides a map showing the boundaries of each Federal Reserve district and the location of the Reserve Bank within the district. Each Federal Reserve Bank is named after the city in which it is located.

Federal Reserve banks have many duties. Their presidents are members of the FOMC, and they grant loans to depository institutions, maintain reserve accounts, administer reserve requirements for depository institutions, and they also do the field work for the Board of Governors in the administration of its many regulatory responsibilities. Federal Reserve banks perform a variety of services for depository institutions and for the federal government such as distributing currency and coins, clearing checks, and transferring funds from one reserve account to another. Federal Reserve banks are also responsible for recommending changes in the discount rate, which is the interest rate charged to depository institutions for loans. Finally, Federal Reserve banks collect and publish regional data on finan-

FIGURE 12.1
THE FEDERAL RESERVE SYSTEM.

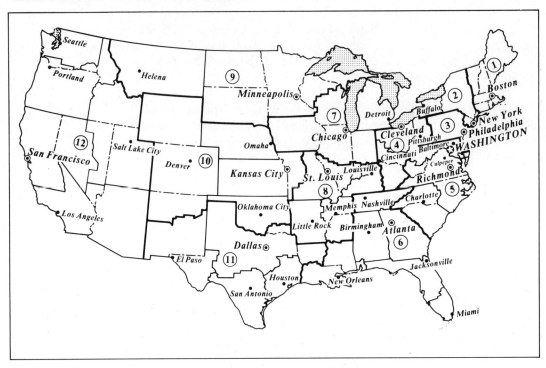

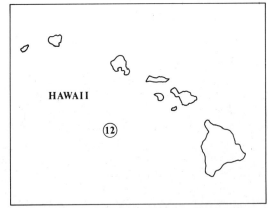

cial and other economic conditions, and they conduct economic research on various regional and national issues. The Federal Reserve Bank of New York has the additional responsibility of purchasing and selling market securities on the instructions of the FOMC.

The organizational structure of the Federal Reserve banks is an anachronism whose logic can be found in the compromises that were made when the Federal Reserve System was established. These compromises produced a blend of private and governmental representation. Each Federal Reserve bank is a separate corporation whose stock is owned by its member banks. Although member banks in each district technically own their Federal Reserve bank, this ownership is not very meaningful. When a bank joins the Federal Reserve System, it is required to purchase stock in its Federal Reserve bank. The stock offers a return of up to 6 percent per year.

A Federal Reserve bank has a nine-person board of directors, the members of which serve three-year renewable terms. Six directors are elected by the member banks in the district and three are appointed by the Board of Governors. Of the six directors elected by member banks, three are class A directors, who are bankers, and three are class B directors, who are selected with consideration to the "interest of agriculture, commerce, industry, services, labor and consumers." This is a tall order for the selection of the three class B directors. The remaining three directors (class C) are selected by the Board of Governors to represent the public. These directors cannot be officers or stockholders of banks. The Board of Governors also appoints one of the class C directors as the chairman of the board of directors.

The board of directors of a Federal Reserve bank has several important functions. One function is to appoint the president and senior vice-president of the Federal Reserve bank. The five-year renewable appointments of these officials are subject to the approval of the Board of Governors in Washington, D.C. Each board of directors also helps guide the operation of its Federal Reserve bank and is involved to a very limited degree in monetary policy. This involvement arises from the requirement of the Federal Reserve Act that directors of Federal Reserve banks propose changes in the discount rate. The board of directors also sets the salary of the president and senior vice-president of the Federal Reserve bank, subject to the approval of the Board of Governors.

The president and senior vice-president of a Federal Reserve bank operate much like the chief executive officers of any corporation and are responsible for the operations of the bank. As we will see later, the president is also involved in the execution of monetary policy through participation in the Federal Open Market Committee. The senior vice-president represents the Federal Reserve bank at FOMC meetings when the president does not attend.

The present structure of the Federal Reserve System causes fewer problems for public policy than one might suppose. In practice, member bank ownership of Federal Reserve banks and the activities of the boards of directors of Federal Reserve banks have little significance for the execution of monetary policy or for other central banking activities. The only active role played by member banks is in the election of two thirds of the directors of each Federal Reserve bank. The boards of directors have little actual influence on activities of the central bank because their actions are subject to the veto of the Board of Governors.

The Relationship of the Federal Reserve to Depository Institutions

The Depository Institutions Deregulation and Monetary Control Act of 1980 subjected all federally insured depository institutions to reserve requirements, and it required the Federal Reserve to make its services available to all insured depository institutions. This law fundamentally altered the relationship between the Federal Reserve and depository institutions.

From 1914 to 1980, the Federal Reserve had direct contact only with member banks. As explained in Chapter 9, when the Federal Reserve was founded, it was viewed as a bank for bankers. The federal government required national banks to be members of the Federal Reserve System, but membership was optional for state-chartered banks. State-chartered banks that did not want to be subjected to reserve requirements and federal regulation could be nonmember banks. They did not have direct access to Federal Reserve loans and other services.

Although the Federal Reserve evolved from a bank for bankers into a modern central bank with general monetary policy obligations, until 1980 its relationship with depository institutions did not change. Membership was still limited to national banks and to those state-chartered banks that volunteered to join the System. This meant that during liquidity crises, the Fed had to invoke special emergency powers in order to lend to nonmember institutions. Furthermore, the presence of nonmember institutions meant that the multiplier relationships between the quantity of reserves and the quantity of money and credit in the economy were affected by the distribution of the public's account balances between member and nonmember institutions. When account balances moved from member to nonmember institutions, the required reserves of members fell, but there was no offsetting increase in required reserves for nonmembers. If the total quantity of reserves in the depository system remained unchanged, there was an expansion of money and credit. Conversely, when the public shifted account balances from nonmember to member institutions, required reserves rose, and the quantity of money and credit fell. The presence of nonmember depository institutions made it more difficult for the Fed to control the quantity of money and credit.

The problem posed by nonmember institutions was not crucial as long as most of the deposit accounts in the economy were held at member banks. For many years this was the case. Over time, however, an increasing proportion of the total liabilities of depository institutions was issued by nonmember institutions. Many state member banks canceled their membership because the benefits of membership in terms of check clearing, access to loans, and other services no longer outweighed the costs of reserve requirements and regulation by the Federal Reserve.[4] Many new banks were state-chartered and decided not to become member banks. Furthermore, specialized depository institutions grew rapidly, and their liabilities were not subject to reserve requirements. By 1980 over 30 per-

---

[4] Recall that required reserves earn no interest.

cent of all transactions account balances in the country were located at non-member institutions, and most of the saving and time account liabilities in the country were at nonmember institutions.

The problem took on a new dimension in 1980 because nonbank depository institutions throughout the country were to be given authority to issue transactions accounts. This authority meant that not only would the transactions accounts of nonmember banks be exempt from reserve requirements, but so also would the transactions accounts of savings and loan associations, mutual savings banks and credit unions. Thus, as the transactions accounts at these institutions grew, an increasing proportion of total transactions accounts in the country would be exempt from reserve requirements.

Over the years, the Fed had proposed legislation to make membership in the Federal Reserve System compulsory for all insured commercial banks. Opposition by nonmember banks always defeated the legislation. Finally, the Federal Reserve conceded that universal membership was not needed for controlling money and credit, only universal reserve requirements. With this concession, Congress authorized the Fed to impose reserve requirements against the transactions accounts and nonpersonal time accounts of all depository institutions.

The Depository Institutions Deregulation and Monetary Control Act of 1980 did not require nonmembers to become members of the Federal Reserve System, so it did not subject them to any of the Federal Reserve's other regulatory authority. The legislation empowered the Fed to impose reserve requirements on nonmember depository institutions. Congress instructed the Federal Reserve to make loans available to nonmember institutions and to provide services, such as check clearing, on the same basis as for member banks.

The act radically altered the relationship between the Fed and depository institutions by forcing the Federal Reserve to divorce its regulatory duties from its functions as a central bank. In the past, the Federal Reserve had direct control over only member banks. This control involved not only reserve requirements and access to Federal Reserve loans and services, but also the authority to supervise and regulate member banks. The new law broke the link between central banking and regulatory functions. Now the Fed can affect all depository institutions through reserve requirements and access to borrowing even though it does not necessarily regulate those institutions.[5] For purposes of monetary policy, the distinction between member and nonmember institutions is no longer relevant.

---

[5] The Federal Reserve's regulatory duties were described in Chapter 9. Depository institutions that are not member banks are allowed to use a third party in dealing with the Fed. For example, an S&L can hold its reserve balance at a Federal Home Loan bank, which transfers the funds to a Federal Reserve bank. Nonmember banks can hold their reserves at a correspondent bank, and credit unions can use the National Credit Union Administration's Central Liquidity Fund for the same purposes. In all cases, the third party transfers the reserves to its reserve account at a Federal Reserve bank. This arrangement allows the Fed to impose reserve requirements on nonmembers, and it allows nonmember institutions to avoid direct contact with the Fed.

THE INSTRUMENTS OF MONETARY POLICY

With the structural characteristics of the Federal Reserve in mind, we can now turn to the instruments of monetary policy. The Federal Reserve has three primary methods of implementing monetary policy: open market operations, reserve requirements, and loans to depository institutions. These three methods or *instruments* have basically the same effect on the quantity of money and credit in the economy. Open market operations are the most frequently used instrument because of their convenience and flexibility. Changes in reserve requirements and extensions of loans to depository institutions also play a role, however.

Open Market Operations

Open market operations involve purchase and sales of market securities by the Federal Reserve. As we saw in Chapter 11, when the Fed purchases securities, reserves in the depository system increase. When the Federal Reserve sells securities, reserves decline. Open market operations are the primary instrument of monetary policy because of their flexibility. These operations are so flexible that it is perfectly possible for the Federal Reserve to be buying securities in the morning and selling them in the afternoon. Thus, the Fed can quickly change the quantity of reserves in the depository system, using open market operations.

In practice, open market operations are almost exclusively conducted by using U.S. government securities. The Fed buys and sells these securities through dealers. These dealers receive payment from the Fed or make payments to the Fed through direct transfers between their banks and the Federal Reserve.

Even though the Federal Reserve uses government securities as the vehicle for open market operations, in principle it could buy or sell any asset and still have the same effect on the quantity of reserves. For example, the Fed could do open market operations in used cars.[6] If open market operations were conducted with used cars or with some other commodity, the price of the commodity would be affected. Political pressure might be exerted to have the Federal Reserve manipulate the price of the commodity. Even if the Fed did not yield to the pressure, it could be accused of making purchases and sales with the objective of enriching or impoverishing holders of the commodity rather than with the objective of affecting the quantity of reserves. The same sort of problem would arise if the Fed conducted open market purchases by using the securities issued by private firms. The problem is reduced by operating almost exclusively with securities is-

---

[6] The law does not allow the Fed to execute open market operations in commodities, and it is unlikely that it would get into the commodity business even if the transactions were allowed. Purchases and sales of commodities and services constitute fiscal policy and are the responsibility of the executive and legislative branch of government. Fiscal policy is not under the jurisdiction of the Federal Reserve.

sued by the U.S. government.[7] Federal Reserve purchases and sales of government securities can have a direct effect on their price but at least the Fed avoids pressure to manipulate the prices of securities issued by private parties.

There have been times when the U.S. Treasury has been displeased by the effect that Fed policy has on the prices and interest rates for its securities. As a result, conflicts have arisen between the central bank and the Treasury. The relationship between the Fed and the Treasury is discussed later. At this point it suffices to say that one reason the Fed is independent of the Treasury is to insulate it from pressure to manipulate the prices of government securities.

The Federal Open Market Committee

Decisions concerning open market operations are made by the Federal Open Market Committee (FOMC). This committee is composed of the seven members of the Board of Governors and representatives of five of the Federal Reserve banks. Reserve Banks serve on the FOMC on a rotating basis. By tradition, the chairman of the Federal Reserve Board serves as chairman of the FOMC, and the president of the Federal Reserve Bank of New York is vice-chairman of the committee. Representatives of all twelve Federal Reserve banks participate in the discussions at each meeting, but only five of the twelve can vote.[8]

Voting participation of the Federal Reserve banks is complex and is the result of political compromises concerning centralized versus decentralized control within the Federal Reserve System. In 1935, when the FOMC was established by Congress, a degree of centralization was achieved by giving the Board of Governors most of the votes. Because there are twelve Federal Reserve banks, they cannot all be represented at once if the Board of Governors is to have most of the votes. It was determined that only five of the twelve Federal Reserve banks could vote at any meeting. The task became, therefore, to allocate five votes among the twelve Federal Reserve banks. This was determined by a combination of economic and political factors.

Owing to its prominence and its central role in the purchase and sale of securities, the Federal Reserve Bank of New York always votes on the FOMC. This leaves four votes to divide up among the remaining eleven Federal Reserve banks. The Federal Reserve Banks of Chicago and Cleveland are allowed to vote during alternate years. The special treatment of these two Federal Reserve banks mirrors the economic and political power enjoyed by the Chicago and Cleveland districts in 1935. The remaining three votes rotate among the remaining nine Federal Reserve banks. In other words, the remaining Federal Reserve banks vote during every third year.

[7] The Fed does have limited authority to purchase banker acceptances and municipal securities. The authority is rarely used.
[8] The president of each Federal Reserve bank is the primary representative. The senior vice-president sits on the committee when the president does not attend.

The FOMC meets in Washington, D.C., and meetings are held frequently, typically every six weeks. In its deliberations, the FOMC determines the growth of reserves, money, and credit that it wants to achieve for the economy. These decisions are expressed in the form of a *directive* to the Federal Reserve Bank of New York. The FOMC also establishes a range over which the interest rate on federal funds can fluctuate from month to month. The FOMC's decision process and the actual form of the directive are discussed in Chapter 18.

The Federal Reserve bank of New York acts as an agent for the FOMC in the purchase and sales of securities. Responsibility for following the instructions in the directive rests with the *manager of the open market account,* who is an officer of the Federal Reserve Bank of New York. Actual open market operations are conducted through what is called the *trading desk.* The trading desk is not a desk at all, but that term is applied to a room full of people who actually execute purchases and sales of securities in accordance with the instructions from the account manager. The manager is in daily communication with FOMC members and their staffs concerning the actual execution of open market operations.

Adherence to the FOMC's directive is more difficult than it might appear. Purchases and sales of government securities by the Fed are not the only influence on the quantity of reserves in the depository system. For example, as described in Chapter 11, withdrawals and deposits of currency by the public affect the quantity of reserves in the system and, therefore, affect the quantity of money and credit in the economy. In order to achieve targets for reserves, money, and credit, the manager must take into account changes in currency holdings by the public. Consider the case where pursuit of the directive indicates that reserves should rise by $1 billion in a week from their value in the previous week. This does not necessarily imply that the desk should purchase $1 billion of securities. It is possible that the public will deposit $1 billion in currency in depository institutions during the week. If this occurs, the desk does nothing. Alternately, if the public does not change its currency holdings, the desk must purchase $1 billion of securities. Finally, if the public were to withdraw $1 billion of currency, reserves would fall by $1 billion in the absence of open market operations. In this case, it is necessary for the desk to actually purchase $2 billion of securities.

There are several factors other than currency movements that affect the quantity of reserves. These include withdrawals or deposits to the Treasury's account at the Federal Reserve and changes in the quantity of borrowing by depository institutions from the Federal Reserve. The trading desk must take all these factors into account when engaging in open market operations in order to achieve the desired objective for reserves. Substantial purchases and sales of securities are often required just to offset the effect of these factors and to leave the quantity of reserves unchanged. The gruesome details of the many factors that affect reserves are given at the end of this chapter. For purposes of the present discussion, suffice it to say that the FOMC sets objectives for the quantity of reserves that it believes to be consistent with its objectives for money, credit, and economic activity. It is the job of the account manager to achieve the specified quantity of reserves through open market operations.

Reserve Requirements

Reserve requirements also affect the quantity of money and credit in the economy. For a given quantity of reserves, an increase in reserve requirements reduces the quantity of money and credit in the economy; a reduction in reserve requirements increases the quantity of money and credit. The Federal Reserve Board has sole responsibility for setting reserve requirements, subject to upper and lower limits established by Congress.

In principle, changes in reserve requirements could be used rather than open market operations for controlling the quantity of money and credit in the economy. In practice, reserve requirements are a cumbersome instrument. When reserve requirements are changed, each depository institutions covered by reserve requirements must be notified. This is a difficult proposition in light of the large number of institutions involved and the complex schedule of reserve requirements that has been developed. Reserve requirements vary for depository institutions of different sizes, and they vary for different types of liabilities. Frequent changes in reserve requirements would probably drive depository institutions and the Fed crazy trying to keep track of what was going on. It is far easier to keep reserve requirements fixed and to vary the quantity of reserves through open market operations.

Another complicating factor is that reserve requirements directly affect the profitability of depository institutions. Required reserves earn no interest, so when reserve requirements are increased, institutions must hold an increased proportion of their assets in noninterest bearing form. Raising reserve requirements is highly unpopular with depository institutions because it hits them in their pocketbooks. Reductions in reserve requirements are, of course, always welcomed by these institutions. The Fed can avoid these effects on the profitability of depository institutions by keeping reserve requirements constant and using open market operations instead.

The Federal Reserve Board does change reserve requirements from time to time. The changes are infrequent, however, and are primarily used either to dramatize a shift in policy or to have a selective effect on the depository system. For example, if the Federal Reserve Board determines that a significant tightening of policy is required, it might make its point by raising reserve requirements. Changes in reserve requirements have also been used in an effort to have a selective impact on the depository system. For example, special reserve requirements have been imposed on large CDs and other liabilities of major depository institutions in an effort to curtail their activities without affecting smaller institutions.

The Depository Institutions Deregulation and Monetary Control Act of 1980 dramatically altered the level and coverage of reserve requirements. All depository institutions offering transactions accounts or nonpersonal time accounts, or both, are now subject to reserve requirements. The structure of reserve requirements is complex. For depository institutions with total transactions accounts of $25 million or less, the reserve requirement is a flat 3 percent of these accounts. There is no authority to vary this reserve requirement. For depository institutions with to-tal transactions accounts in excess of $25 million, the reserve requirement is 3 per-cent for the first $25 million of these accounts and 12 percent of the amount in ex-cess of $25 million. The Federal Reserve Board has authority to vary the reserve requirement between 8 and 14 percent for total transactions accounts in excess of $25 million. The $25 million cutoff is indexed. As the transactions accounts at all institutions grow over time, the cutoff is raised proportionately. Finally, the Garn-St Germain Depository Institutions Act of 1982 exempted the first $2 mil-lion of "reservable liabilities" from reserve requirements. This exemption figure is also indexed to grow with the size of reservable liabilities in the depository system.

The reserve requirement for nonpersonal time accounts is 3 percent for all depository institutions irrespective of their size. The Board has authority to vary the reserve requirement on these accounts between 0 and 9 percent.

Congress also gave the Board authority to impose special supplemental reserve requirements of up to 4 percent for transactions accounts at every depository insti-tution. The imposition of supplemental reserve requirements must be affirmed by at least five Board members. With supplemental reserve requirements, required reserves can be as high as 7 percent for the first $25 million of transactions ac-counts at each institution and as high as 16 percent for total accounts in excess of $25 million.

Finally, Congress gave the Federal Reserve special "extraordinary" powers for imposing reserve requirements. "Upon a finding of at least 5 members of the Board that extraordinary circumstances require such action," the Board may, after consulting with the appropriate committees of Congress, impose any reserve re-quirement that it wants on any liability of any class of depository institution. These extraordinary reserve requirements can be imposed for only 180 days, but they may be extended indefinitely, 180 days at a time, by a vote of at least five Board members.

The reserve requirement situation is, in fact, much more complicated than indi-cated in the text. The 1980 law revolutionized the coverage of reserve require-ments. Nonmember banks, savings and loan associations, mutual savings banks, and credit unions were subjected to reserve requirements for the first time. Furth-ermore, reserve requirements for member banks were reduced. The law provided for an eight-year phase-in of reserve requirements for nonmember depository in-stitutions. For member banks there is a four-year phase-in of the new structure of reserve requirements.

The fairly detailed, but simplified, description of the current structure of reserve requirements has probably destroyed any interest that the reader has in the sub-ject. The reason for describing the structure of reserve requirements is to demon-strate that it is a mess! It will remain so for years to come. The complicated struc-ture of reserve requirements, with an eight-year phase-in for nonmembers and a four-year phase-in for members and no phase-in for interest bearing checking ac-counts offered for the first time, means that the multiplier relationships between reserves and the quantity of money and credit will be difficult to predict. It will be many years before the relationships settle down.[9] In this environment, it is unlikely that the Federal Reserve Board will make active use of changes in reserve requirements as an instrument of monetary policy.

Loans to Depository Institutions

Loans by the Federal Reserve to depository institutions constitute the third major tool of monetary policy.[10] The role of these loans is probably the least understood of the three instruments of policy and receives the most confused coverage in the media. It might be helpful to begin our discussion by defining some terms. In the early days of the Federal Reserve, the major method of providing reserves was through loans to member banks. Short-term loans granted by member banks to their customers were typically used as collateral for the loan from the Fed. Interest on the Federal Reserve's loans was typically paid in advance. For example, a member bank borrowing $100 for a year would actually receive only $95 at the beginning of the year and would repay $100 at the end of the year. Because a $100 loan granted by the member bank to a customer served as collateral for the loan from the Fed, it was said that the Federal Reserve discounted the collateral, that is, lent $95 for $100 of collateral.[11] The interest rate charged by the Federal Reserve to a member bank was called the discount rate.[12] In modern times, institutions no longer discount the loans used as collateral, but the term *discount rate* persists as the name given the interest rate that the Federal Reserve charges for its loans. Furthermore, in conducting their lending operations, Federal Reserve banks once had windows, like tellers' windows, at which loans were arranged. These windows have long since fallen from use, but it is still said that institutions borrow from the *discount window.*

In principle, the Federal Reserve can vary the discount rate in a manner designed to achieve any quantity of borrowing by depository institutions that it desires. This implies that the Fed can change the quantity of reserves in the depository system by changing the discount rate. For example, if the Federal Reserve wants increased reserve growth, it can lower the discount rate, encourage in-

[9] We will also see in Chapter 18 that errors in predicting the money and credit multipliers reduce the efficacy of using reserves as the instrument for controlling the growth of money and credit.

[10] The Depository Institutions Deregulation and Monetary Control Act of 1980 made Federal Reserve loans available to nonmember depository institutions that offer transactions or nonpersonal time accounts.

[11] In essence, the Fed bought the $100 loan at a discount ($95) and sold the loan back to the member bank at par ($100) at the end of the year.

[12] Banks typically lent to their customers by charging interest in advance, that is, by discounting the loan. The loan was then rediscounted at the Fed. The interest rate charged by the Fed was often called the rediscount rate.

creased borrowing at the discount window, and expand the quantity of reserves. If it wants to reduce the quantity of reserves, it can raise the discount rate and discourage borrowing at the discount window. This exercise requires knowledge of the degree of response of borrowing at the discount window by depository institutions to changes in the discount rate. By frequent changes in the discount rate, however, relatively close control over the quantity of reserves could probably be achieved. This method of controlling the quantity of reserves is used in some other countries but not in the United States. Since the establishment of the FOMC and the active use of open market operations, the discount window has ceased to function as a primary source of reserves.

Figure 12.2 shows the relationship of the discount rate to the interest rate on federal funds from 1965 through mid-1983. Recall that the federal funds rate is the interest rate that a depository institution must pay when it borrows from another depository institution rather than the Federal Reserve. Figure 12.2 clearly shows that the discount rate is typically below the federal funds rate and that the discount rate does not change as frequently as the federal funds rate. Both the discount rate and the federal funds rate have changed somewhat more frequently in recent years.[13]

It might appear that keeping the discount rate below the federal funds rate is a great boon to borrowers. When the discount rate is less than the federal funds rate or other market interest rates, a depository institution can increase its profits by borrowing from the Fed and lending the funds in the market. So long as the discount rate remains below market interest rates, this could produce an insatiable demand for borrowing from the Fed, and the growth of reserves would be virtually unlimited.[14] Because the Federal Reserve does not change the discount rate very often, and the discount rate is typically below market interest rates, it must find some way to ration or restrict credit through the discount window. This is accomplished by *administration* of the discount window. Depository institutions cannot borrow all that they would like at the discount window when the discount rate is less than market interest rates.

Administration of the discount window is a subtle affair in which the rules of the game are never completely specified but are understood by both the Fed and borrowing institutions. In essence, depository institutions should borrow only if they have no other viable alternative. It is not appropriate for a depository institution to borrow and then lend the proceeds of the loan in the market. Institutions that are lenders in the federal funds market are not supposed to borrow from the discount window. The discount window is primarily available for emergencies

---

[13] The importance of the relationship between the discount rate and the federal funds rate for the Fed's ability to control the quantity of money and credit is discussed in Chapter 19.
[14] As we saw in Chapter 7, expected profits are raised by borrowing from the Fed and lending in the market, but risk is also increased because leverage rises. If depository institutions are risk averse, there is a limit to the amount they will borrow from the Fed when the discount rate is less than market interest rates.

FIGURE 12.2
DISCOUNT RATE VERSUS
FEDERAL FUNDS RATE 1965–MID-1983.

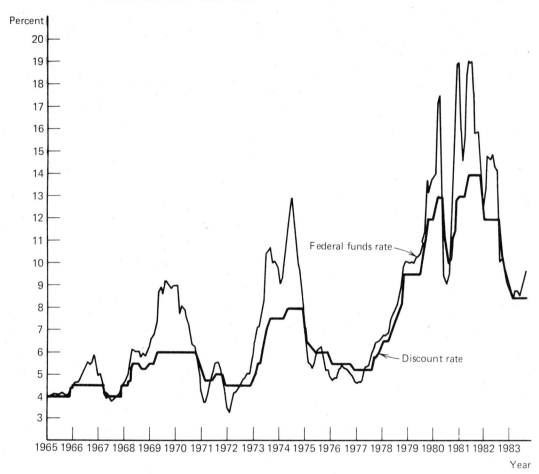

and for cushioning the shock of unexpected fluctuations in liabilities. If a depository institution experiences a reduction in its liabilities, it can use the discount window, but it is expected to quickly repay its debt. Furthermore, each institution is monitored to determine the frequency of its borrowing. Frequent borrowing is frowned upon. Small depository institutions that cannot borrow in the federal funds market or lack other ways of managing their liabilities have easier access to the discount window than do large institutions.

It is often said that institutions are reluctant to borrow from the discount window. This reluctance is understandable considering the hassle involved. Furthermore, because a borrower knows that frequent borrowing is not tolerated, that borrower has to weigh the benefits of borrowing today against the costs of not being able to borrow tomorrow. There probably is some reluctance on the part of many depository institutions to borrow because heavy use of the discount window could be taken as evidence by large depositors of illiquidity and other problems. These depositors might withdraw their funds if the institution is a heavy user of the discount window.

Another use of the discount window is to assist a depository institution with serious liquidity problems. For example, if depositors are making large withdrawals, the Fed will open up the discount window to that institution. This occurs relatively infrequently, but it is essential to providing stability for the financial system. The most famous example of this use of the discount window is provided by the now defunct Franklin National Bank, which borrowed over $1 billion in 1974 from the discount window because it could not roll over its maturing CDs.

The Federal Reserve also has authority to make loans to virtually anyone during periods of emergency. The existence of an emergency must be affirmed by a vote of at least five members of the Federal Reserve Board. Once this is affirmed, virtually anyone can come to the discount window for credit. This emergency feature gives the Fed full authority and flexibility to meet a financial crisis. This authority has not been used, but it is available. It is more frequently the case that the Fed encourages indirect loans to businesses and individuals. The Fed makes it known that depository institutions granting loans to these parties can turn around and use the loans as collateral for borrowing at the discount window. This method was used, for example, when financial markets became unsettled following the failure of the Penn Central Railroad in 1970. The Fed opened up the discount window, and panic was averted.

The final use of the discount window involves what is called the *seasonal borrowing privilege*. Institutions that have a decided seasonal pattern to their liabilities are allowed, under certain circumstances, to borrow during seasonal lows and to repay their loans during seasonal highs. These loans are used primarily to help smaller institutions, usually located in agricultural areas, that are not able to practice liability management. Large institutions are convinced by the Fed that they have no seasonal problems.

In summary, the discount window is the vehicle through which the Fed acts as a lender of last resort to the financial system. Quantitatively, loans by the Federal Reserve to depository institutions are not an important source of reserves for the system. The discount window is important to individual institutions because it allows them to cushion the effects of fluctuations in liabilities and to avoid adverse effects of large withdrawals from customer's accounts.

The Discount Rate

The role of the discount rate is probably the least understood of the Federal Reserve's tools. According to the conventional accounts in the media, the discount rate is important because changes in the cost of borrowing from the Fed lead to changes in the interest rates that depository institutions charge for loans. This story seems plausible but is incorrect. Borrowing by depository institutions at the discount window is such a small part of their total liabilities that changes in the discount rate have no practical effects on their costs and, therefore, have no effect on the interest rate they charge for loans. An example should make the point. In June of 1980, total liabilities of all commercial banks in the United States were roughly $1.5 trillion. Their borrowing from the Federal Reserve in that month was $2.6 billion, which is less than two tenths of 1 percent of total liabilities.[15] A change in the discount rate, almost no matter how large, could have no significant effect on the total cost of bank liabilities.

In countries where loans by the central bank are a quantitatively important source of reserves, a change in the interest rate on those loans can have an important effect on the interest rates in the economy in general. In the United States, administration of the discount window prevents borrowing from being quantitatively important, and it also prevents changes in the discount rate from having any significant direct effect on other interest rates in the economy. As we will see later, changes in the discount rate are sometimes used by the Federal Reserve to signal a change in policy that does have implications for interest rates in the economy. A change in the discount rate, however, has no discernible effect, except as a signal.

Administration of the discount window allows the Federal Reserve to control the quantity of borrowing without frequent changes in the discount rate. Administration of the discount window does become more difficult, however, the greater the amount that market interest rates exceed the discount rate. The more that market interest rates exceed the discount rate, the more profitable it is for depository institutions to borrow from the Fed. As a result, the tales that these institutions tell about why their borrowing is justified become increasingly inventive. Thus, as market interest rates rise above the discount rate, total borrowing by depository institutions rises. When borrowing becomes difficult to control, the Fed responds by raising the discount rate.

A look back at Figure 12.2 verifies that the gap between market interest rates and the discount rate can sometimes be quite large. For example, in March 1980 the interest on federal funds (interbank loans) was in excess of 17 percent, and the discount rate was 13 percent. This 4 percentage point spread offered a great profit potential to borrowers, and an increasing number of institutions turned to the discount window. It is remarkable, however, that the Fed controlled the surge of loan demand in this environment and kept the aggregate level of borrowing at the discount window under $3 billion. In March 1980 total reserves in the system were over $43 billion, so borrowing constituted only about 7 percent of total reserves. This percentage is high by historical standards. The discount rate was changed in the following month to take the pressure off the discount window, and the quantity of borrowing declined.

---

[15] June 1980 was selected because borrowing of $2.6 billion is a large figure by historical standards.

It is often a mystery to many observers why the discount rate is usually kept below market interest rates and why the Federal Reserve changes the discount rate infrequently. After all, life would be much easier for the Fed if the discount rate were simply set above market interest rates or if the discount rate were moved continuously with market interest rates.[16]

There are two reasons why the Fed does not move the discount rate with market interest rates and why it usually keeps the discount rate below market interest rates. The first reason goes back to the use of the discount window as a safety valve. It could be counterproductive to extend credit at high rates of interest to depository institutions with serious liquidity problems. If the discount rate were sufficiently high, these institutions could suffer a significant erosion in earnings because of the increased expense. These institutions can generally least afford a decline in earnings.

The second reason for infrequent changes in the discount rate involves the so-called *announcement effect*. At times the Federal Reserve changes the discount rate to signal a shift in policy. For example, if the Fed has decided to fight inflation by aggressively slowing the growth of reserves, it changes the discount rate to dramatize the policy shift. Similarly, if the economy is moving toward a recession and the Fed wants to expand the quantity of reserves, it might underscore the policy shift by reducing the discount rate.

The reader might wonder why the Federal Reserve does not announce its policy rather than use a change in the discount rate as a signal. There is no obvious answer to this question except to point out that the Fed rarely makes clear announcements and that it views changes in the discount rate as a useful method of communicating with the public. It is true that about the only time that the Federal Reserve makes the national TV news is when the discount rate is changed. The news stories usually overstate the significance of the discount rate, but at least they convey the message that the Fed has changed policy.

Because the Federal Reserve has used the discount rate to signal shifts in policy, it is often reluctant to change the discount rate for fear that the change will be misinterpreted. There are times when the Fed has not changed policy and market interest rates are moving in a manner consistent with previous policy decisions. The change in market interest rates may call for a change in the discount rate in order to keep it vaguely in line with the market. There is a danger that this change in the discount rate might be taken by the public as a signal of a shift in policy when, in fact, there has been no change in policy. The Fed attempts to avoid this problem by changing the discount rate infrequently.

Problems in interpreting changes in the discount rate could be avoided if the Federal Reserve explained its policy actions in clear English. It could then explain when a change in the discount rate signals a shift in policy rather than a technical adjustment of the discount rate to market interest rates. As long as the

---

[16] It is said that there is a *penalty rate* when the discount rate exceeds market interest rates. A penalty rate is used in some countries but not in the United States.

discount rate is changed infrequently, however, market participants are likely to view any change as a shift in policy irrespective of whether the Fed has changed policy or not.

The Relationship Among the Three Instruments of Monetary Policy

Open market operations, reserve requirements, and loans to depository institutions are all methods by which the Federal Reserve affects the quantity of money and credit in the economy. Because these three instruments can produce roughly the same effect on the quantity of money and credit, only one of them needs to be used for conventional monetary policy. The Federal Reserve has elected for practical reasons to use open market operations as the primary instrument. Although changes in the discount rate and even changes in reserve requirements receive more attention in the media, open market operations are the real workhorse of monetary policy.

The purpose of this section is to demonstrate that all three instruments can produce roughly the same effect on the quantity of money and credit in the economy. We shall use the simplest version of the multiplier relationship between reserves and money described in Chapter 11.[17] There it was shown that the relationship is given by $M = m_M TR = (1/r_T)TR$, where M is the quantity of money, m_M is the money multiplier, r_T, is the reserve requirement for transactions accounts, and TR is the quantity of total reserves.

Let us begin by comparing open market operations to changes in reserve requirements as instruments of monetary policy. Open market operations affect the quantity of total reserves in the system. Assume the FOMC instructs the manager of the open market account to increase the quantity of reserves by the amount ΔTR. The Board of Governors is aware of the intentions of the FOMC and keeps the reserve requirement unchanged. From the simple multiplier relation we have $\Delta M = m_M \Delta TR = (1/r_T)\Delta TR$. Thus, given the reserve requirement r_T, the increase in the quantity of money is a multiple $(1/r_T)$ of the change in total reserves produced by open market operations.

Now consider the case where the Board of Governors decides to increase the quantity of money by reducing the reserve requirement on transactions accounts. The FOMC is aware of the decision to reduce the reserve requirement and instructs the manager of the open market account to keep the quantity of total reserves unchanged. In this case, we have $\Delta M = \Delta m_M TR$ or $\Delta M = [\Delta(1/r_T)]TR$. Thus, given total reserves, TR, the change in the quantity of money is a multiple of the change in the multiplier.

---

[17] Using a more complex multiplier that allows for currency drains and other factors would not change the conclusions. The analysis considers only a change in the quantity of money, but a similar story could be told for a change in the quantity of credit.

The Federal Reserve can achieve a given increase in the quantity of money either by increasing total reserves or by reducing the reserve requirement. Perhaps a numerical example will make the point. Assume the initial level of reserves is $50, the reserve requirement is 10 percent, and the quantity of money is $500. This implies that $M = 1/.10(\$50) = 10(\$50) = \$500$. Now the FOMC wants to increase the quantity of money by $10. If the reserve requirement is kept constant, we have $\Delta M^* = (1/r_T)\Delta TR$, where ΔM^* is the desired change in the quantity of money. We need only to solve for ΔTR to determine the necessary change in reserves: $\Delta TR = r_T \Delta M^*$. For $\Delta M^* = \$10$, we have $.10(\$10) = \$1$. Total reserves must be increased by $1 to achieve a $10 increase in the quantity of money.

The same $10 increase in the quantity of money can be achieved by reducing the reserve requirement while keeping total reserves unchanged. Here we have $\Delta M^* = \Delta m_M TR = [\Delta(1/r_T)]TR$ or $\Delta(1/r_T) = \Delta M^*/TR$, so $\Delta(1/r_T) = \$10/\$50 = .20$. Thus, the money multiplier (the reciprocal of the reserve requirement) must rise by .20 percentage points. The original multiplier was $1/.10 = 10$, so the new multiplier is 10.20. This implies a new reserve requirement of $1/10.20 = .098$ or 9.8 percent. We can check this result by solving for the new quantity of money. This gives $M = (1/.098)\$50 = 10.2(\$50) = \$510$. A reduction of the reserve requirement by .2 percentage points from 10 percent to 9.8 percent produces a $10 increase in the quantity of money from $500 to $510.

The same kind of argument can be applied to a desired decline in the quantity of money. Only the signs are reversed. We can conclude, therefore, that the Federal Reserve can achieve a desired change in the quantity of money either through open market operations or through a change in reserve requirements.

We can now show that a desired change in quantity of money can also be achieved by varying the quantity of loans from the discount window. In this case, we have to distinguish between two sources of reserves. Reserves are supplied through open market operations and through loans by the Federal Reserve. Let us call the first source nonborrowed reserves and the second source borrowed reserves. Symbolically, we have $TR = NBR + BR$ where NBR and BR are nonborrowed and borrowed reserves, respectively. Now we see that the Fed has two methods of changing the level of total reserves. It can either change NBR through open market operations or it can change BR by changing the discount rate. In terms of the earlier numerical example, a $1 increase in total reserves produces a desired increase in the quantity of money of $10. The increase in total reserves can be achieved either by increasing nonborrowed reserves by $1 through open market operations or by increasing borrowed reserves by $1.

We conclude that open market operations, changes in reserve requirements, or changes in the quantity of loans granted by the Fed to depository institutions can be used to achieve a desired change in the quantity of money or credit. Because only one instrument is needed to achieve the change, the Fed primarily uses open market operations because of their greater flexibility and convenience. As we saw in Chapter 9, however, the money multiplier is affected by the portfolio choices of the public and of depository institutions. This means that the Federal Reserve is not assured of achieving its objectives for money or credit, no matter what instrument is used.

Credit Controls

During its history, the Federal Reserve has from time to time attempted to control certain kinds of credit. For example, in 1929, the Federal Reserve attempted to curb "speculative" loans that were granted for the purpose of buying stocks and bonds. Its only tool was the use of "moral suasion," that is, arm-twisting, and the Fed's efforts were not successful.[18] During World War II, the Federal Reserve had legal authority to set minimum down payments and maturities for consumer loans. This authority was granted in order to restrict the quantity of consumer borrowing in an effort to reduce the demand for consumer goods. Similarly, during the Korean War, the Fed was authorized to restrict the quantity of consumer loans, and it also had authority to determine the minimum down payments and maximum maturities of certain kinds of real estate loans. After the end of each war, the Fed lost its authority to impose restrictions on these types of loans. More recently, the Federal Reserve has occasionally used moral suasion to discourage banks from granting "unproductive" loans such as lending for corporate takeovers or for construction of gambling casinos. These efforts have had very little effect.

In 1969, Congress passed the Credit Control Act. This little noticed but remarkable law gave the Board of Governors authority to regulate and control *any and all* forms of credit once the President of the United States determined that credit controls were needed to combat inflation. The law, in principle, granted to the Federal Reserve total control over all forms of credit in the United States. This authority was unprecedented in the United States and had few, if any, counterparts in other developed countries.

In early 1980, President Carter introduced a number of measures designed to reduce the high inflation rate that existed at the time.[19] In March of that year, he called for the imposition of credit controls. A reluctant Federal Reserve responded by producing a set of credit controls that extended far beyond the Fed's normal area of influence. In addition to imposing special reserve requirements on depository institutions and on money market mutual funds, the Board placed restrictions on the expansion of consumer credit and upon "nonessential" extensions of credit by various kinds of lenders. The control program did slow credit expansion in large part because it created considerable confusion and apprehension in financial markets. The result was a sharp decline in real output, and the program was discontinued in the summer of 1980. The Credit Control Act expired in June of 1982.

[18] As described in the appendix, in 1934 the Fed was given authority to vary margin requirements to control this lending.
[19] These policies are discussed in Chapter 19.

THE ROLE OF THE FEDERAL RESERVE WITHIN GOVERNMENT

When Congress created the Federal Reserve System in 1913, it attempted to insulate the central bank from transient political considerations. This was achieved by sheltering the Federal Reserve from the variable political winds that blow in Washington, D.C. Although it has been eroded to some extent in recent years, the independence of the Fed remains to this day.

Independence of the central bank was achieved by excluding the Federal Reserve from the normal political process. Congress did not make the Fed an agency of the executive branch of government, so its decisions and activities are not under the control the President. The President of the United States does appoint the seven members of the Board of Governors and appoints the chairman and vice chairman of the Board. Once these appointments are made, however, the President has no further role in Federal Reserve affairs. Neither the President nor Congress has any control over Federal Reserve bank presidents or other officers.

Congress also excluded the Federal Reserve from the budgetary process. The Federal Reserve is self-financing through the interest income it earns on government securities and on loans to depository institutions. Most of the Fed's income comes from its portfolio of government securities. The U.S. Treasury pays interest on these securities just as it would to a private holder.[20] In fact, the Fed's income far exceeds its expenditures, and it "voluntarily" returns the surplus to the Treasury.

There are other agencies such as the Office of the Comptroller of the Currency and the FDIC that are self-financing, but their budgets are set by Congress. The budget of the Federal Reserve System is not reviewed or approved by Congress. The Federal Reserve Act allows the Federal Reserve System to expend funds and engage in activities as it sees fit. The Board of Governors is required to provide an annual report to Congress, specifying how it expended funds in the previous year, but it is not required to report its budgetary plans. Congress can use its budgetary authority to induce conventional government agencies to heed its wishes. Because Congress cannot affect the Fed's budget, it is unable to use this potent weapon to affect Federal Reserve policies. Congress can, of course, amend the Federal Reserve Act to bring the Fed under budgetary control. It has been unwilling to do so.

The fourteen-year term of office for Board members provides a third means of assuring the independence of the Federal Reserve. Long-term appointments insulate Board members from political pressures that could be exerted if they were appointed for shorter, renewable terms of office. Furthermore, the fourteen-year

---

[20] The relationship between the Treasury and the Fed is discussed later.

terms of Governors are staggered so that a single term expires every two years. Thus, during a four-year term, the President of the United States can be guaranteed only two appointments.

By establishing fourteen-year terms and by staggering Board appointments, Congress appears to have achieved a high degree of insulation of the Board of Governors from politics. In practice there is less insulation than one might think because deaths and resignations produce a more rapid turnover in Board membership than the long-term appointments and the scheme of staggered terms suggest. When death or resignation creates a vacancy on the Board, an individual is appointed by the President, with Senate confirmation, to fill the balance of the unexpired term. Individuals who are appointed to fill an unexpired term are eligible for reappointment to a full term.

The four-year term for the chairman and vice-chairman of the Board of Governors suggests that these individuals are not as insulated as the other five Governors from political pressures. Each chairman and vice-chairman owes the appointment to the President and tends to have some allegiance to the President's policies and a concern for the President's political welfare. This situation tends to reduce somewhat the political independence of the Fed and allows the President of the United States to engage in economic policies that are likely to be supported by the chairman and vice-chairman of the Federal Reserve Board.

The importance of the four-year term for the chairman and vice chairman is muddied somewhat by the fact that their terms of office need not be coterminous with that of the President. If the previous chairman and vice chairman resign when a new President takes office, the terms will be coterminous. If they do not resign, a new chairman and vice chairman can be appointed only after the four-year terms of their predecessors expire. A rather extreme example is illustrated by the situation for President Reagan. He took office in January of 1981, but the term of appointment for Paul Volcker, then the chairman of the Board, extended until August 1983. This occurred because the previous chairman, William Miller, resigned in August 1979 to become Secretary of the Treasury and Volcker was appointed to serve a four-year term. Volcker's tenure as chairman apparently did not cause a problem for President Reagan. He appointed Volcker to a second term as Chairman in 1983.

Despite the oddity of a noncoterminous appointment, any President has the opportunity sometime during his term to appoint a chairman and vice-chairman. This gives the President the opportunity to have some direct effect on Federal Reserve policies.

The Federal Reserve is fond of saying that it is not independent of the federal government, but rather "independent within the government." It is not totally clear what this term means, but it suggests that though the Fed is not a "team player," at least it is on the team. The relationship is something like a field goal kicker on a professional football team. The kicker does not engage in most team activities and is something of a loner, but the kicker is often responsible for winning or losing the game.

COORDINATION OF FEDERAL RESERVE
POLICIES WITH THE POLICIES
OF THE PRESIDENT AND CONGRESS

There are several ways that the Federal Reserve coordinates its activities with other elements of the government. The chairman of the Board of Governors represents the Federal Reserve in various policy discussions. In particular, the chairman meets with the President, the Secretary of Treasury, and other members of the executive branch to discuss economic policies. Other Board members and various staff representatives also have lines of communications with their counterparts within the executive branch. It is important to observe, however, that the frequency and quality of the communication between the Federal Reserve and the executive branch depend crucially on the voluntary cooperation of the parties involved. They are not required to coordinate policies or even to divulge their policy intentions to each other.

The Federal Reserve's contact with Congress is more formal. The chairman of the Federal Reserve Board testifies periodically before the Congress on the state of the economy and on monetary policy. Other governors also testify from time to time. The Federal Reserve is required by law to submit to Congress an annual report describing and explaining its monetary policy decisions during the previous year. Until the 1970s, the Fed was not required to inform Congress of its policy intentions and rarely volunteered such information.

Even a brief inspection of the Fed's annual reports and its testimony reveals a tendency for the Federal Reserve to be less than forthright in its descriptions of policy decisions. Central bankers are by nature rather secretive creatures who do not welcome public discussions of their policies. Beginning in the 1970s, as waves of inflation and unemployment hit the economy, many members of Congress became increasingly interested in and concerned about monetary policy. This interest and concern produced a movement within Congress to make the Fed more accountable for its actions.

Congress moved to bring monetary policy decisions more into the public domain. In 1975, Congress passed House Concurrent Resolution 133 which called for the Fed to announce its objectives over the coming year with respect to growth in various measures of money and credit. In 1978, Congress passed the Full Employment and Balanced Growth Act (popularly called the Humphrey-Hawkins Act). This act requires the Federal Reserve to announce its plans concerning the growth of money and credit in the economy *and* to explain the relationship between these plans and the economic goals enumerated by the President of the United States. Though the Federal Reserve meets the letter of this law, its policy announcements are made in such general and equivocal terms that to many observers it does not meet the spirit of the law. Congressional control over the Fed remains weak. A more detailed discussion of the coordination of Federal Reserve policies with the rest of the government appears in later chapters, where specific policy issues are addressed.

RELATIONSHIP WITH THE U.S. TREASURY

The Federal Reserve has a special relationship with the Treasury and acts in many respects as the government's banker. The Treasury has accounts with Federal Reserve banks, which it uses to deposit tax receipts and to make expenditures.[21] The Federal Reserve also assists the Treasury in managing the national debt. Reserve Banks make interest payments on the debt by reducing the Treasury's account balances, they accept bids by the public for purchases of new government securities, they deliver the securities for the Treasury, and they assist in the transfer of government securities from one holder to another.

In all these activities, the Fed operates as agent for the Treasury, that is, it simply executes transactions that are ordered or authorized by the Treasury. There is no monetary policy involved in these activities; the Fed is simply operating as the government's bank.

It is important to distinguish these activities from monetary policy actions. When it comes to monetary policy, the Fed is independent of the Treasury. There is an "arm's length" relationship between monetary and fiscal policy in the United States. Consider the case where the government's expenditures exceed its receipts, that is, there is a budget deficit that must be financed. In the United States, there is only one way that the deficit can be financed; the Treasury must borrow by issuing additional securities.[22] The Treasury is not authorized to issue money as a method of financing the deficit; only the Federal Reserve can issue money. Furthermore, with minor exceptions, the Federal Reserve is prevented by law from lending directly to the Treasury.

If the Fed could make direct loans to the Treasury, the Treasury would, in effect, be "printing" money to finance the deficit. In that case, the Fed would pay for the securities by simply increasing the Treasury's account balances at the Federal Reserve. The Treasury would then use these balances to finance the excess of its expenditures over its receipts. The recipients of the checks written by the Treasury would deposit the funds in depository institutions, and the quantity of reserves in the system would rise. The increase in reserves would produce a multiple expansion of money and credit in the economy. In this situation, the deficit would be financed by the creation of reserves. These additional reserves would produce a multiple expansion of money and credit.

Because the Fed is prevented from lending directly to the Treasury, the government must issue the debt to the general public. The issuance of this debt does not

---

[21] The Treasury also has accounts at commercial banks. The relationship between the accounts at commercial banks and accounts at the Fed is discussed at the end of this chapter.

[22] To a limited extent the government could draw down its account balances or sell assets to cover the deficit. The government's holdings of account balances or other assets are rarely large enough for this to be a viable alternative.

affect the quantity of reserves in the system. When the Treasury sells debt to the public, purchasers write checks to the Treasury. If these checks are deposited by the Treasury in Federal Reserve banks, there is a reduction of reserves in the system. The reduction is only momentary, however, because the Treasury immediately spends the funds to cover its deficit. The recipients of the expenditures then deposit the checks in depository institutions, and the reserves are returned to the system. If the Treasury deposits the checks in depository institutions, there is not even a momentary loss of reserves. In that case, balances are simply transferred from accounts held by the public to accounts held by the Treasury, and the funds never leave the depository system.

When the Treasury sells additional debt to the public, the quantity of reserves in the depository system is unaffected, but the stock of debt held by the public increases. The interest rate on government debt must rise relative to other interest rates in order to induce the public to hold more government securities.[23] At this point, the Federal Reserve enters the picture. If the Fed finds the increase in interest rates consistent with its objectives for monetary policy, it will not respond. If, however, it believes that the increase in interest rates will dampen aggregate demand in the economy to the point that its policy objectives cannot be met or if it succumbs to pressure from the Treasury, it will respond. The response takes the form of eliminating, or at least reducing, the rise in interest rates. This is accomplished by open market operations; the Fed purchases government securities from the public. These purchases have two effects. First, they limit the initial rise in interest rates on government securities because there is now an increase in demand for these securities. Second, the purchase of securities by the Fed increases total reserves and produces a multiple expansion of money and credit in the economy. Part of the expansion of credit takes the form of increased purchases of government securities by depository institutions and by the public. These purchases also limit the rise in the interest rates on government debt. If the Fed is willing to inject sufficient reserves into the system, the interest rates on government securities need not rise.[24]

Even though the Federal Reserve is independent of the Treasury and is not allowed to make direct loans to it, the Fed can accomplish the equivalent of providing direct loans by engaging in open market operations. The potential is there, but the decision concerning whether or not to engage in open market operations rests with the FOMC. Having the Fed independent of the Treasury does not guarantee that the Fed will refuse to finance the deficit through open market operations, but it makes refusal easier.

The Treasury does not like to pay higher interest rates on its debt because the increased interest payments increase the budget deficit. The Treasury has a tend-

---

[23] The effect of deficits and of government debt on interest rates is discussed in detail in Chapter 15.

[24] We shall see in Chapter 16 that attempts by the Fed to keep interest rates from rising can produce inflation in the longer run. If inflation does occur, nominal interest rates do rise.

ency, therefore, to want deficits to be financed indirectly by the Fed. By making the Federal Reserve independent of the Treasury, Congress made it more difficult for the executive branch to pressure the Fed into financing deficits through expansion of reserves, money, and credit in the economy.

There have been several times when the pressure on the Fed to finance deficits has been effective. For example, during World War II, the Federal Reserve did provide reserves by purchasing government bonds issued to finance the war. This limited growth in the government's interest costs. The Treasury liked the arrangement so much that it continued until 1952. At that time, an accord was achieved between the Treasury and the Federal Reserve absolving the central bank from the responsibility for purchasing government securities to keep the Treasury's interest costs at low levels. Since that time, the Fed has operated independently of the Treasury, but on occasion, as during the Vietnam War, the Federal Reserve has provided a substantial growth of reserves to mitigate the rise in interest rates. Similar activities also occurred periodically during the 1970s.

In summary, Congress made the Fed independent of the executive branch and independent of transient political forces. This independence helped the Fed to pursue monetary policies that were not dictated by the need to limit increases in interest rates during periods of high government expenditures and large deficits. There have been times, however, that the Federal Reserve did not act very independently and it did help finance the deficits.

In recent years, Congress has taken a more active interest in monetary policy. The Federal Reserve remains a policy agency with considerable autonomy, but it now must disclose and defend its policy decisions and plans before Congress. Increased disclosure will probably make it somewhat more difficult for the Federal Reserve to "go its own way" with policy. This development is viewed with dismay by some observers and with delight by others. Whatever one's views concerning the value of independence of the Federal Reserve from the political process, there is little doubt that some of the independence of the central bank has been eroded in recent years. A thorough review of the pros and cons of independence must await the analysis of the role of monetary policy in the economy, which comprises the next several chapters.

Before we turn to the analysis of monetary policy it is instructive to end this chapter with a discussion of the nuts and bolts of central banking. Knowledge of the arcane subjects in this final section is helpful for understanding how monetary policy is actually put into practice.

THE NUTS AND BOLTS OF CENTRAL BANKING

This section describes the check clearing, currency dispensing, and other activities that constitute the nuts and bolts of central banking. These activities are of some interest in their own right, and their description helps motivate an analysis of the various factors, other than open market operations, that affect the quantity of reserves in the depository system.

Check Clearing

A major activity of Reserve Banks is to clear checks. Until 1980 this service was performed almost exclusively for member banks. Since 1980, check clearing has been available to any type of depository institution.

When the Federal Reserve System began operations in 1914, it provided check-clearing services without charge to member banks. The service was provided for two reasons. First, the prospect of receiving the service was an inducement for membership for state-chartered banks. These banks could view their required reserves as a sort of compensating balance that "paid" for the service. This was a natural way to look at the situation because many banks held balances with banks in financial centers as compensation for handling their customers' checks. Banks in financial centers would accept checks drawn on banks in other locations, reduce the account balances by the amount of the checks, and arrange to ship the checks to the bank upon which they were written. The Federal Reserve banks often offered superior services and many state-chartered banks became members.

The second reason for providing check clearing involved a desire by the central bank to improve the nation's payment system. In the days prior to the establishment of the Federal Reserve, communication among banks at distant locations was slow. This meant that often a significant period of time was required before a check written on a particular bank finally arrived for collection. As a result, the bank into which the check was deposited often had to wait a substantial period of time before it could collect the funds. Usually, the bank reacted to this situation by requiring the distant bank to maintain balances with it. If no balances were held, it would not accept the check at face value. The latter response meant that an individual depositing a check from a distant bank would not receive full credit. Rather the bank would accept the check at a discount from its face value, that is, a discount from par.

The need for distant banks to hold compensating balances reduced the profitability of these banks and retarded the expansion of banking across the country. Discounts from par meant that checks of equal face value written on different banks had different values. Thus, transactions accounts, which had become a major type of money in the country, were not homogeneous because checks written against them had different values depending upon the location of the bank. This situation retarded the use of transactions accounts as a form of money.

The Federal Reserve solved the problem by agreeing to make payment on checks given to it for collection within a proscribed period of time. This practice continues to this day. A Federal Reserve bank guarantees that if a depository institution gives it a check for collection, within two days the institution will receive the funds. The Reserve bank cannot always deliver the check to the depository institution upon which it is written in two days. In those cases, the Reserve Bank increases the reserve balance of the institution that has given it the check for collection by the amount of the check. This means, in essence, that the Fed extends the depository institution a loan. Like any loan from the Federal Reserve, these loans increase the quantity of reserves in the system. The depository institution upon which the check is written does not have its reserves decline because it has not received the check. The institution into which the check is deposited receives an increase in its reserves, so the reserves in the system rise. When the check is finally presented to the depository institution upon which it is written, its reserves are reduced.

Most checks do clear, that is, end up at the depository institution upon which they are written, in two days. These checks do not provide any net provision of reserves. There are many checks that do not clear in two days, however, and these checks lead to a temporary addition to reserves by the Fed. This provision of reserves is called *Federal Reserve float*. Because there are always checks in the collection process that do not clear in two days, there are always reserves provided by Federal Reserve float. The quantity of reserves provided by Federal Reserve float is variable. It depends upon the location of the depository institutions upon which checks are written, and upon the state of the transportation system. Breakdowns of transportation or bad weather can lead to sharp increases in this source of reserves.

Most checks in the United States are not cleared by Federal Reserve banks. The private depository system clears most of the checks itself. Depository institutions arrange to have checks delivered to institutions upon which they are written. Private institutions do their own check clearing when the costs are lower or when they can obtain payment in less than two days, or both. Depository institutions in large cities have highly automated "clearinghouses" that process checks and obtain settlement among institutions in one day. Furthermore, large institutions maintain courier services that deliver checks for payment in distant cities. In the jet age, it is often possible to obtain payment for checks in less than two days.

As a part of correspondent relationships, large depository institutions provide check-clearing services for smaller institutions. Depository institutions pay for the service by maintaining account balances with the clearing institution or by paying fees. Prior to 1980, correspondent relations were usually necessary for institutions that were not members of the Federal Reserve System. Banks providing check-clearing services were typically member banks, and they would process the checks either through the Fed or via private means depending upon the speed and cost of the two alternatives.

In 1980, when reserve requirements were imposed on nonmember depository institutions, the Fed was required to make its check-clearing facilities available to nonmember institutions. One might think that access to Federal Reserve banks by nonmember institutions would sharply reduce the amount of correspondent banking. This did not occur for two reasons. First, there are many instances in which private check clearing can be accomplished more rapidly than clearing through the Fed. In those instances, correspondent banking is often still attractive. Second, Congress required the Federal Reserve to start charging for its check-clearing services. Federal Reserve banks charge fees for the actual processing of checks, and they assess an interest charge for Federal Reserve float. The imposition of charges and fees by the Fed often makes private correspondent relationships less expensive than use of Federal Reserve facilities.

Immediately Available Funds

Many transactions in the United States are conducted by having Federal Reserve banks directly transfer funds from the reserve account of one depository institution to the reserve account of another. These direct transfers avoid the need to process checks, and they allow payment to be received immediately rather than waiting until the checks have cleared. One important source of same-day money is the market for federal funds. When depository institutions borrow and lend in this market, they do not use checks. Rather, they instruct Federal Reserve banks to transfer funds from the reserve account of the lending institution to the account of the borrowing institution. These transfers occur during the day in which the loan is made, so the borrowing institution has immediate access to the funds. In fact, the term *federal funds market* means the market in Federal Reserve funds, that is, the market for reserve account balances.

Loans among depository institutions are not the only transactions that involve immediate transfer of funds from one reserve account to another. Many large transactions by business and wealthy individuals are also conducted with "same-day" money. It is often the case that customers of depository institutions are not allowed to have access to funds deposited by check until the check has cleared.[25] After all, the depository institution does not receive payment until the check clears. This problem is avoided when the customer is paid in the form of funds that are directly transferred from the reserve account of one depository institution to another. A customer's depository institution receives the funds immediately, so it is willing to give the customer immediate access to the funds.

Payments through transfers from one reserve account to another are somewhat cumbersome. They require notification of the depository institution from which funds are transferred, notification of the institution receiving the funds, and, of course, notification of Federal Reserve banks involved in the transfer. If the transfer occurs between two depository institutions in the same Federal Reserve district, only one Federal Reserve bank is involved. If the transfer occurs between institutions in two districts, it is necessary to involve two Federal Reserve banks.

Direct payment from one reserve account to another occurs primarily for large transactions. Depository institutions typically charge for this service, and Federal Reserve banks are now required to assess charges. Despite the cost, it is often

---

[25] "Clearing" occurs when the Fed increases the reserve balance of the institution into which the check is deposited.

worthwhile in large transactions for the recipient of a payment to gain immediate access to the funds rather than wait for a check to clear. While the check is clearing, the recipient loses interest income that could be earned by investing the funds. As methods of automating transactions are improved, the costs of immediate transfers of funds will decline, and their use should increase. In principle, when there is full electronic "banking," most transactions will involve electronic transfers of funds, and the use of checks will diminish substantially.

Currency and Coin Services

Federal Reserve banks are the ultimate source of currency and coin in the United States. The Fed is completely passive in the provision of currency and coin, however. The quantity of currency and coin in the hands of the public is determined by the public's demand for this kind of money.

Depository institutions keep currency and coin in their vaults in order to meet withdrawals by their customers. These holdings are called vault cash. Depository institutions are also passive in meeting the public's demand for currency and coin. They meet cash withdrawals by the public by drawing down the currency and coin in their vaults. When vault cash reaches a low level, they obtain additional currency and coin from the Fed. Many institutions obtain the cash directly by making cash withdrawals from their accounts at a Federal Reserve bank. Other institutions obtain the cash from correspondent institutions which, in turn, obtain their currency and coin from a Federal Reserve bank.

When the public reduces its holdings of currency and coin, the process is reversed. Customers deposit cash in their accounts. These deposits add to the vault cash of depository institutions. When the quantity of vault cash exceeds what is deemed necessary for meeting withdrawals, depository institutions take the surplus currency and coin and deposit the money to their own accounts at the Fed or at correspondent institutions. Correspondents deposit their excess vault cash with a Federal Reserve bank.

Federal Reserve banks themselves hold currency and coin in their vaults. When these holdings fall below minimum levels, more currency is printed, and additional coins are minted. When coin and currency are deposited at Federal Reserve banks, the notes and coins are examined for wear and tear. Old currency and coins that have deteriorated are destroyed and replaced with new ones.

As we saw in Chapter 11, changes in the public's demand for currency and coin affect the quantity of reserves in the depository system. Legal reserves of depository institutions, that is, reserves that legally satisfy reserve requirements, are composed of reserve balances at Federal Reserve banks and vault cash. When the public makes cash withdrawals, vault cash is reduced, so legal reserves are reduced. If depository institutions replenish their vault cash they make cash withdrawals from their reserve accounts at the Fed. These withdrawals do not reduce total reserves because both reserve accounts and vault cash are legal reserves for purposes of reserve requirements. Thus, it is the public's increased holdings of currency and coin that affects total reserves in the system, not the policies of institutions concerning their vault cash.

When the public makes deposits of currency and coin, total reserves are increased. It makes no difference whether depository institutions increase their vault cash or deposit the cash at the Fed. In both cases, the quantity of reserves is increased.

The only active agents in this process are members of the public. The public decides how much currency and coin it wants to hold, and that quantity is passively provided by depository institutions and the Federal Reserve. The public cannot be forced to hold either more or less currency and coin than it desires. If, for example, the Fed attempted to increase the public's holdings of currency by using currency to purchase securities in the market, the public would simply deposit any unwanted currency in depository institutions. Furthermore, because currency and coin are legal tender, neither the Fed nor depository institutions can refuse to honor withdrawals of cash by the public. Thus, the quantity of currency and coin held by the public is completely determined by the public's demand for it. It is the job of the Federal Reserve to provide the quantity demanded.

Until 1980, the Federal Reserve provided currency and coin to member banks without charge. In that year, the Fed was required to provide currency services for all depository institutions. In 1981 it was required to charge members and nonmembers alike for the costs of handling currency transactions.[26]

Maintenance of Accounts for the Treasury

The U.S. Treasury holds accounts at Federal Reserve banks. These accounts are used for tax receipts and to finance various government expenditures. The Treasury uses its accounts at Federal Reserve banks much as the public uses its accounts at depository institutions.

Changes in the Treasury's account balance at the Fed affect the quantity of reserves in the depository system. The Treasury adds to its balance by receiving tax payments or by selling debt. The public pays taxes or buys securities from the Treasury by writing checks.

When there is a transfer of funds from the public to the Treasury's account at the Federal Reserve, the quantity of reserves in the depository system declines. Reserves of depository institutions are reduced, and the Treasury's balance at the Fed increases. When the Treasury expends funds from its account at the Federal Reserve, the recipients of the expenditures deposit the checks in depository institutions. These deposits increase total reserves. Thus, when the Treasury adds to its account at the Fed, reserves are reduced; when it withdraws from that account, reserves are increased.

---

[26] The charges for currency transactions should induce depository institutions to hold more of their reserves in the form of vault cash and less in the form of reserve balances.

The Treasury also maintains *tax and loan accounts* with private depository institutions. These accounts are used to reduce the effects of Treasury activities on total reserves in the system. If the Treasury deposits its receipts in an account at a depository institution, the quantity of reserves in the system is unaffected. When taxpayers or purchasers of debt write checks to the Treasury, the reserves and transactions account liabilities of their depository institutions are reduced. If the Treasury deposits these checks in its accounts with depository institutions, their reserves and liabilities increase. There is simply an interinstitution transfer of reserves and the total quantity of reserves in the system is unaffected. Similarly, when the Treasury draws down its accounts at depository institutions to finance expenditures, there is also an interinstitution transfer of reserves and the total quantity of reserves in the system is unaffected.

The only time that changes in the Treasury's tax and loan accounts with depository institutions affect the quantity of reserves is when there are transfers between these accounts and the Treasury's account at the Fed. As before, when the Treasury adds to its Fed account, depository institutions lose reserves, and when it reduces that account, they gain reserves.

The Treasury's decisions concerning use of its Fed account relative to its accounts with private depository institutions affect the total quantity of reserves in the system. The Treasury attempts to coordinate its uses of these two kinds of accounts with the general reserve policies of the Federal Reserve.

Other Transactions of the Treasury that Affect Reserves

The Federal Reserve assists the Treasury in purchasing and selling gold or other assets. These transactions also affect the quantity of reserves in the system.

Before the United States totally abandoned the gold standard in 1971, the Treasury bought and sold gold for international purposes. Even though gold was not used for domestic transactions, the purchases and sales of gold still affected the quantity of reserves in the depository system. The Treasury purchased gold by first selling a gold certificate to the Federal Reserve. The Fed paid for the gold certificate by increasing the Treasury's account balance. The Treasury used these funds to purchase the gold. The seller of gold deposited the funds in a depository institution. When all the smoke had cleared, the Treasury had the gold, the Fed had a gold certificate, and the reserves in the depository system had risen by the amount of the purchase of the gold. This transaction was the functional equivalent of an open market operation in gold. In the United States, the Treasury rather than the central bank owns the gold, so gold certificates were sold to the Fed rather than the gold itself.

When the Treasury sold gold, the process was reversed. The public paid for the gold by writing checks on depository institutions. The Treasury deposited the funds in its account at the Fed. It then used these funds to retire (buy back) gold certificates held by the Federal Reserve. The Fed returned the gold certificates and reduced the Treasury's reserve account by the amount of the gold purchase. When the gold sale was completed, the Treasury held less gold, the Fed held fewer gold certificates, and the reserves in the depository system were reduced by the amount of the gold sale.

Today the Treasury no longer engages in such gold transactions. There are, however, billions of dollars of gold certificates that are still held by the Federal Reserve that represent gold that had previously been purchased by the Treasury. The Treasury still sells gold from time to time. Now, however, the gold is sold at auction rather than at the official gold price. The Treasury is not required to retire outstanding gold certificates with the proceeds of these sales. Rather, it can use the funds to finance expenditures. When the Treasury sells gold and makes expenditures, there is no effect on the quantity of reserves. Reserves leave the depository system when the public purchases the gold, but the reserves are returned to the system when the Treasury makes its expenditures.

Although gold certificates are no longer issued and retired, the Treasury does engage in transactions with the International Monetary Fund using certificates that affect reserves in the depository system much as gold certificates had affected reserves. The International Monetary Fund (IMF) issues Special Drawing Rights (SDRs) for member countries. These SDRs are sold in the form of certificates. The role of the IMF is discussed in Chapter 17, but for purposes of this chapter, SDRs can be viewed as international assets held by the Treasury. The Treasury issues SDR certificates to the Fed in return for an increase in its account balance. It uses the funds to purchase SDRs. The IMF deposits the funds in depository institutions. This purchase by the Treasury is the functional equivalent of an open market purchase, and it increases the quantity of reserves in the system.

The Federal Reserve also assists the Treasury in foreign exchange transactions. The Fed purchases and sells foreign "exchange," that is, foreign money and foreign denominated assets. When the Fed purchases foreign exchange, it pays for the assets by writing a check on itself. The sellers of foreign exchange deposit the funds in depository institutions, and the quantity of reserves in the system rises. When the Fed sells foreign exchange, it accepts payment in the form of checks written on depository institutions. The Fed reduces the account balances of these institutions, so the quantity of reserves in the system declines. Changes in the Fed's holdings of foreign exchange have the same effect on the quantity of reserves in the depository system as open market operations. When its holdings of foreign exchange increase, reserves rise; when its holdings of foreign exchange decline, reserves are reduced.

Agent for Foreign Central Banks

The Federal Reserve provides various services for foreign central banks. These central banks hold account balances with the Fed that are used primarily for financial transactions. Foreign central banks hold dollar denominated assets in the United States just as the Federal Reserve holds foreign-denominated assets in other countries. Most of the assets are held in the form of securities and other market instruments. When securities are purchased by foreign central banks using their accounts at the Fed, there is an increase in reserves in the system. When they sell securities and add to their accounts at the Fed, reserves are reduced.

The Federal Reserve also conducts various transactions for foreign central banks. Most important of these is the purchases and sales of U.S. government securities. Thus, some of the open market operations of the Federal Reserve are not for its own account but for the accounts of foreign central banks.

THE FEDERAL RESERVE'S BALANCE SHEET AND ITS RELATION TO TOTAL RESERVES IN THE DEPOSITORY SYSTEM

All the major items that comprise the Federal Reserve's balance sheet have now been described. In this section, the balance sheet is related to the quantity of reserves in the depository system.

The Federal Reserve's balance sheet is important because it lists all the factors by which the Fed affects the quantity of reserves in the depository system. When the Fed acquires assets, it simultaneously issues liabilities, and these liabilities contribute to the quantity of reserves in the depository system. Table 12.1 shows the balance sheet for the Federal Reserve on December 31, 1982. The various items in the balance sheet give an indication of the relative importance of the several assets that the Fed holds and of the liabilities that it issues.

Assets

By far the largest asset held by the Federal Reserve is its portfolio of government securities. These securities were purchased as a result of open market operations. The $148.8 billion of these securities dwarf the $1.48 million of acceptances, which are also part of open market operations. Loans granted by the Fed to depository institutions total only $717 million. This figure indicates the quantitative unimportance of the discount window as compared to open market operations. Holdings of gold certificates amount to about $11 billion. This figure is relatively large, but it has not risen for a number of years. Holdings of SDRs are $4.6 billion. Holdings of foreign denominated assets are relatively small and amount to only about $5.8 billion. The category "cash items in process of collection" represents the total value of all checks the Reserve Banks have received from depository institutions but for which the Fed has not yet received payment. These amount to over $9.8 billion. This asset item is a factor in determining Federal Reserve float. All other assets amount to about $4.6 billion and are comprised of buildings, equipment, and other assets.

TABLE 12.1
CONSOLIDATED BALANCE SHEET OF THE FEDERAL RESERVE
DECEMBER 31, 1982 (MILLIONS OF DOLLARS)

Assets

U.S. Treasury and agency securities	$148,837
Acceptances	1,480
Loans to depository institutions	717
Gold certificates	11,148
SDR certificates	4,618
Foreign denominated	5,764
Cash items in process of collection	9,807
All other	4,564
Total assets	$186,935

Liabilities and Net Worth

Federal Reserve notes	$141,990
Deposit accounts:	
Reserve accounts of depository institutions	27,489
U.S. Treasury account	5,033
Foreign official and other accounts	1,361
Deferred availability cash items	7,072
Other liabilities	2,272
Net worth	2,718
Total liabilities and net worth	$186,935

Source: Federal Reserve *Bulletin*, February 1983, p. A12.

Liabilities

The largest single liability of the Federal Reserve is for the Federal Reserve notes (currency) that it has issued. This amounts to nearly $142 billion. The second largest liability is the deposit accounts of the Fed's customers. Most of these liabilities are reserve accounts of depository institutions, which amount to over $27 billion. The remainder is comprised of the $5 billion account balance of the U.S. Treasury, and $1.4 billion of balances of foreign central banks and other official institutions.

The item "deferred availability cash items" refers to the value of checks that the Federal Reserve has received for collection from depository institutions but has not yet paid to those institutions. If the Federal Reserve always waited to pay depository institutions until it received payment from the institutions upon which checks are written, the liability item called "deferred availability cash items" would always equal the asset category cash items in the process of collection. As explained earlier, if the Fed has not presented the checks and reduced the reserve account of institutions upon which checks are written by the end of two days, it goes ahead and increases the reserve accounts of institutions that submitted checks for collection. Thus, on December 31, 1982, the Fed had $9.807 billion of uncollected cash items as an asset but only $7.072 billion of deferred availability cash items, that is, of items for which it has not yet increased reserve accounts. The difference between cash items and deferred availability is the amount by which the Fed has increased reserve accounts of depository institutions prior to reducing the reserve accounts of institutions upon which checks are written. Thus, it is Federal Reserve float and amounts to $9.807 billion − $7.072 billion = $2.735 billion in this case. As explained earlier, Federal Reserve float increases bank reserves.

Other liabilities of the Fed are bookkeeping items representing obligations to purchase assets and earnings that have not yet been paid as dividends or added to net worth. The net worth of the Federal Reserve represents the acquisition of stock by member banks and the additions to net worth that occur when the Fed retains a portion of its profits rather than returning all profits to the Treasury.

When the Federal Reserve's balance sheet is combined with the monetary accounts of the Treasury, we can list all the factors that determine the quantity of reserves in the depository system. Table 12.2 gives the accounting for total reserves for December 31, 1982. The table is divided into factors that supply funds for reserves and factors that absorb funds from reserves. By taking the difference between the factors supplying funds for reserves and the factors absorbing funds, we obtain the total quantity of reserves for the depository system.

The first component in factors supplying funds for reserves is total Federal Reserve credit. Whenever the Federal Reserve extends additional credit, there is an increase in the quantity of funds that is potentially available for additional reserves. The total quantity of Federal Reserve credit is primarily in the form of government securities, held by the Fed, but loans to depository institutions, Federal Reserve float and other assets acquired by the Fed are also components.

The second component in factors supplying reserves is the monetary operations of the Treasury. Whenever the Treasury acquires additional gold or SDRs, there is an increase in the supply of funds that are potentially available for reserves.[27] The next item is Treasury coin and currency outstanding. When the Treasury issues additional coin and currency, there is an increase in the supply of funds that are potentially available for the reserves of depository institutions.[28] The total quantity of funds that is potentially available for reserves is determined by adding the total credit of the Federal Reserve to the monetary accounts for the Treasury. On December 31, 1982, this gave a total of $193.211 billion.

[27] For purposes of describing the factors supplying reserves, we use the actual gold and SDR holdings of the Treasury rather than the gold and SDR certificates held by the Fed. The difference between these magnitudes is the quantity of "nonmonetized" gold and SDRs.
[28] The Treasury no longer issues new currency, but it has old currency outstanding. Technically, the Treasury still issues all coins. The quantity of Federal Reserve notes outstanding is not included because it has already been counted in total Federal Reserve credit. When the Fed extends credit, it either dispenses currency (Federal Reserve notes) or it increases its deposit account liabilities. The mix between the two is determined by the currency demand of the public and depository institutions.

TABLE 12.2
DETERMINANTS OF TOTAL RESERVES IN THE DEPOSITORY SYSTEM
DECEMBER 31, 1982 (MILLIONS OF DOLLARS)

Factors Supplying Funds for Reserves

Federal Reserve credit		
U.S. Treasury and agency securities	$148,837	
Loans to depository institutions	717	
Float	2,735	
Other Federal Reserve assets	11,370	
Total		$163,659
Treasury		
Gold stock	$ 11,148	
SDRs	4,618	
Treasury currency outstanding	13,786	
Total		29,552
Total factors supplying funds		$193,211

Factors Absorbing Funds from Reserves

Currency in the hands of the public		$138,242
Treasury cash holdings		429
Treasury balances at the Fed		5,033
Foreign and other official balances at the Fed		1,361
Other Federal Reserve liabilities and net worth		4,990
Total factors absorbing funds		$150,055
Total Reserves (total supplying less total absorbing)		$43,156
Reserve balances at Reserve banks	$ 26,489	
Vault cash	16,667	
		$ 43,156

Source: *1982 Annual Report*, Board of Governors of the Federal Reserve System, pp. 236–237.

The funds are absorbed by a number of factors other than the reserves of depository institutions. The holdings of coin and currency by the public are the largest factor absorbing funds. When the public adds to its holdings of coin and currency, there is a reduction in the quantity of funds available for reserves of depository institutions. The cash holdings of the Treasury are only a minor factor absorbing funds. These cash holdings are composed of gold, for which certificates have not been issued, and of the Treasury's own holdings of coin and currency that it needs for transactions purposes. The role of the remaining items was explained when we discussed the Fed's balance sheet. When the Treasury adds to its balance at the Fed or when foreign central banks and other official institutions add to their account balances, funds are absorbed, and less of the supply of funds is available for reserves of depository institutions. Similarly, when the Fed increases its other liabilities or net worth, funds are absorbed. In total, $150.055 billion were absorbed by factors other than reserves of depository institutions. Because $193.211 billion was potentially available for reserves and $150.055 billion was absorbed by other uses, reserves of depository institutions were $43.156 billion on December 31, 1982.[29] These reserves are comprised of $26.489 billion in reserve balances at the Federal Reserve and $16.667 billion of vault cash.

The discussion of the factors determining the quantity of reserves in the depository system gives an indication of the practical problems that confront the manager of the Fed's open market account. When the FOMC desires to achieve a particular quantity of reserves in the depository system, the manager must take into account all the factors other than open market operations that affect reserves. Consider the case where the FOMC instructs the manager of the open market account to maintain the quantity of reserves at their present level. In order to achieve this objective, the manager has to offset movements in any of the other factors affecting reserves. For example, if there is a substantial snow storm, it will take a longer than normal time for the Fed to collect on the checks it is processing. Because the institutions that left the checks for collection will have their reserve accounts increased after two days, this means that Federal Reserve float will rise. When float increases, reserves increase. The manager has to offset this effect by selling securities on the open markets. Similarly, if borrowing at the Fed increases or if Treasury holdings of SDRs increase, the manager has to sell securities to offset the effect on reserves. On the other side of the ledger, if the public increases its holdings of coin and currency or if the Treasury adds to its account balance at the Fed, reserves in the depository system decline. If the quantity of reserves is to remain unchanged, the manager has to purchase a sufficient quantity of securities to offset the decline in reserves that would otherwise occur.

The role of the many factors affecting reserves demonstrates the importance of having flexible open market operations. The Federal Reserve engages in open market operations every day in order to offset the effects on total reserves of changes in float, borrowing, the public's currency demand, the Treasury's balance, and other factors. These factors can change quickly and sharply. Open market operations are excellent instruments for offsetting undesired changes in reserves.

This section concludes with a brief description of the composition of total reserves. Table 12.3 shows for December 31, 1982, the distribution of total reserves between vault cash and reserve balances at the Fed, between required and excess reserves, and between nonborrowed and borrowed reserves. Both

---

[29] Total reserves (reserve account balances and vault cash) plus currency and coin held by the public are the total monetary liability of the government to the private sector. This total is called the monetary base. Its role is discussed in Chapter 15.

TABLE 12.3
DISTRIBUTION OF TOTAL RESERVES
DECEMBER 31, 1982

	Quantity	Percent of Total		Quantity	Percent of Total		Quantity	Percent of Total
Vault cash	$16,667	39	Required	$41,391	96	Nonborrowed	$42,439	98
Reserve balances	26,489	61	Excess	1,765	4	Borrowed	717	2
Total	$43,156	100	Total	$43,156	100	Total	$43,156	100

vault cash and reserve balances can be used to satisfy reserve requirements. The decision concerning the form in which reserves are held is left up to depository institutions. In December 1982, they held 39 percent of total reserves in the form of vault cash and 61 percent as reserve balances at Federal Reserve banks. This mix varies according to the needs of depository institutions for vault cash.

The amount of reserves that are held in excess of required reserves is also determined by depository institutions. The figures for December 1982, illustrate how the existence of the federal funds market has almost eliminated excess reserves. Only 4 percent of total reserves of depository institutions is excess reserves; the remaining 96 percent are required reserves.

Similarly, the discount window is not a sizable source of reserves for depository institutions. Only 2 percent of the total reserves of depository institutions is borrowed reserves. Although the mix between borrowed and nonborrowed reserves does change in response to changes in the spread between market interest rates and the discount rate and other factors, borrowed reserves are never a sizable fraction of total reserves. The discount window is heavily administered. This simply demonstrates that the Federal Reserve uses open market operations rather than the discount window as its primary method for determining the quantity of reserves in the depository system.

SUMMARY

The Federal Reserve System is the nation's central bank. It is responsible for regulating the quantity of money and credit in the economy, for affecting interest rates, and for preventing liquidity crises. The Fed also provides a number of services to the U.S. Treasury and to depository institutions that help make the financial system perform smoothly.

The Federal Reserve System is comprised of the Board of Governors in Washington, D.C., and twelve Federal Reserve Banks located throughout the country. The Board of Governors is responsible for setting reserve requirements, and it approves changes in the discount rate. The Federal Open Market Committee (FOMC) is composed of the seven members of the Board of Governors plus five of the twelve Presidents of Federal Reserve banks serving on a rotating basis.

Reserve requirements, the discount rate, and open market operations are the three primary instruments of monetary policy. They all can be used to achieve roughly the same objectives concerning the quantity of money and credit and also the level of short-term interest rates. Furthermore, they all can be used to avert liquidity crises. Open market operations are the most flexible of the three instruments and, therefore, are the primary instrument of monetary policy. This means that the FOMC is the major policymaking body within the Federal Reserve System. The discount window is an important instrument for averting liquidity crises.

The Federal Reserve has a substantial amount of freedom within the government to pursue the monetary policies that it wants. Although the Fed must report to Congress concerning its past policies and it must announce its plans for policy in the future, there is no congressional control over the actual policies that the Fed pursues. The President of the United States influences the Federal Reserve to the extent of appointing new Board members when vacancies arise. Board members have fourteen-year terms of office, however, so a President has limited ability to affect monetary policy through appointments of Board members. Greater influence is achieved through appointing the Chairman of the Board, who serves a four-year term. Once the appointment is made, however, the President cannot control the Chairman.

Congress and the President have only limited means of exerting their wills on the Federal Reserve. The central bank in the United States has a great deal of autonomy in determining national monetary policy. As we shall see in the remaining chapters of this book, monetary policy has a profound effect on output, employment, and inflation.

APPENDIX
FEDERAL RESERVE RESPONSIBILITIES CONCERNING MARGIN REQUIREMENTS AND THE TRUTH IN LENDING ACT

The regulatory duties of the Federal Reserve are primarily concerned with banks and bank holding companies. Margin requirements and the Truth In Lending Act represent two cases where Congress expanded the Fed's regulatory powers beyond banking.

MARGIN REQUIREMENTS

The Securities and Exchange Act of 1934 authorized the Board of Governors to regulate the use of credit for purchasing or holding securities. This authority was a part of the sweeping reforms of the securities industry that were achieved in the 1930s. These reforms were largely a response to the stock market crash of 1929 and to the collapse of other securities markets that followed.

During the 1920s, loans were readily available to finance purchases of securities. This credit allowed people to purchase large amounts of securities relative to the amount of their own wealth that was invested; that is, they were highly leveraged. The prices of stocks were rising in the 1920s, and leverage allowed the public to increase the rate of return earned from investing in the stock market. The availability of credit fueled a stock market boom. When the stock market fell in 1929, lenders feared that the value of stocks used to secure their loans might not be sufficient to cover the loans. At that point lenders "called" their loans, informing borrowers that they either had to come up with more collateral to secure the loans or that their stocks would be sold. Many borrowers could not supply additional collateral and were forced to sell their stocks. These sales produced further declines in stock prices and further loan calls. There is little doubt that the heavy use of credit contributed to the stock market boom of the 1920s and to the market crash of 1929. The behavior of the stock market was a sad example of the risks involved in using leverage.

The Securities and Exchange Act of 1934 allowed the Federal Reserve to limit leverage. This was accomplished by authorizing the Board of Governors to establish the minimum percentage of the value of a security that an investor must put up for himself or herself. For example, if the margin requirement is 70 percent, the public has to invest at least $70 of its own money for every $100 of securities purchased. This implies that no more than 30 percent of the value of securities can be supported by loans.

The Board of Governors has authority to change the percentage margin for securities loans. Since 1934, the margin requirement has ranged from 40 percent, that is, 40 percent investor's money and 60 percent loan, to 100 percent, that is, 100 percent investor's money and zero percent loan. The margin requirement is currently 50 percent.

The margin requirements set by the Board apply to all lenders including brokers, dealers, and banks. Not all securities are covered, however. Most noticeably, securities issued by the federal government and by state or local governments are not covered by margin requirements.

In practice, margin requirements have limited effect in reducing leverage and risk taking in securities markets. Margin requirements cover only credit extended by brokers, dealers, and banks for the purpose of purchasing or holding securities. There is nothing to prevent investors from borrowing against other assets, such as houses, and using the money to purchase securities. With high margin requirements, investors have incentive to use other assets to secure loans used to purchase or hold securities.

THE TRUTH IN LENDING ACT

In 1968, Congress passed the Truth in Lending Act requiring that lenders disclose credit terms to borrowers on a uniform and consistent basis. Prior to passage of the act, confusing and often deceptive claims were made by lenders concerning the interest rates they charged. For example, some lenders would advertise that they charged only 2 percent interest, neglecting to mention that the charge was 2 percent per *month* rather than per year. Other lenders would quote an annual interest rate but neglect to mention that the loan was discounted, that is, the interest was deducted in advance. Thus, a borrower would take out a loan of $1000 at 10 percent interest per year, but obtain only $900. At the end of the year, the borrower was required to repay the $1000 of principal. The actual interest rate on this loan is $(\$1000-\$900)/\$900 = .111$, or 11.1 percent. These and other practices made it difficult for borrowers to determine the true interest rate and to compare interest rates offered by various lenders.

The Truth in Lending Act made comparison easier by requiring uniform calculation and disclosure of interest rates. The act has other provisions that afford borrowers protection against unsavory practices by lenders. For example, borrowers are allowed a three-day "cooling off" period, during which time they can cancel a loan agreement. This is called the right of rescission. It provides protection against "hard sell" practices of some lenders.

The Board of Governors has sole responsibility for issuing regulations concerning uniform disclosure of interest charges and other provisions of the Truth in Lending Act. Enforcement of the regulations is spread among various government agencies, however. The Board enforces the regulations only with respect to state-chartered member banks. As new methods of extending credit are constantly being developed, the Board must continue to develop new regulations and interpret its existing regulations. As a result, administration of the Truth in Lending Act is an ongoing activity.

SELECTED REFERENCES

Board of Governors of the Federal Reserve System, *The Federal Reserve System, Purposes and Functions* (6th ed.), Washington, D.C., 1974.

Maisel, Sherman, *Managing the Dollar*, New York: Norton, 1973.

Pierce, James, "The Myth of Congressional Supervision of Monetary Policy," *Journal of Monetary Economics*, 1978:4, pp.363–370.

AGGREGATE EXPENDITURES AND INCOME

13

This and the next four chapters build a theoretical structure that allows us to analyze the role of monetary and financial variables in the macroeconomy. With this structure, it is possible to study the effects of monetary and financial variables on aggregate output, employment, and the price level. The present chapter is concerned with some basic determinants of aggregate expenditures on goods and services and of aggregate income. The analysis of this chapter is incomplete because it holds wages and prices constant, allows no independent role for aggregate supply, and excludes both the government and international factors. These important complications are introduced in later chapters. This chapter is kept as simple as possible to lay a foundation for the richer theoretical structure of later chapters. Despite its relative simplicity, the chapter does offer some important lessons concerning the role of monetary and financial variables in the macroeconomy.

Before we start the analysis, a word of explanation may be useful concerning the theoretical approach taken in Chapters 13 through 17. The present chapter is "Keynesian" in the sense that it stresses the determinants of aggregate expenditures and income without regard for the effects of aggregate supply and the price level. The Keynesian approach is used because it is a convenient starting point. In later chapters, when government, wealth, aggregate supply, the price level, and international factors are introduced, we end up with a theoretical structure that is far removed from the conventional Keynesian model of most textbooks. It is also far removed from the "monetarist" approach of other texts. The model developed in Chapters 13 through 17 summarizes the richer and more general approach of modern monetary and financial macroeconomics. That approach has elements of Keynesianism and of monetarism, but it avoids the extreme assumptions of either approach.

THE FLOW OF OUTPUT, INCOME, AND EXPENDITURES

The relationships among the flows of aggregate output, income, and expenditures in the economy can be described in terms of a simple diagram. In Figure 13.1, the economy is divided into firms and households. For simplicity, it is assumed that there is no saving or investment. Thus, the economy produces only consumption goods. Households provide firms with the factor services (labor, capital, land, and management) needed to produce the output. In the top half of the diagram, households provide factor services and receive income payments from firms. In the bottom half of the diagram, firms sell goods and services to households.

Note that the physical flow of factor services from households to firms is matched by the flow of money income payments from firms to households. Similarly, the physical flow of goods and services from firms to households is matched by the flow of money expenditures from households to firms. By definition, the value of aggregate output produced by firms equals the total income earned by households. The value of output is the sum of all the payments, including profits, made to produce the output. Thus, the value of output equals income. Similarly, by definition, the sales of goods and services by firms equals the expenditures on goods and services by households. Thus, sales equal expenditures.

In Figure 13.1, the output of firms equals household expenditures on goods and services. Households exactly spend an amount equal to their incomes--no more, no less--on the output produced by firms. In this situation, the flows are in equilibrium (balance). Firms purchase factor services from households, which produce the income that allows households to purchase all of the output produced by firms. Output, Q, equals income, Y, which equals household expenditures for consumption goods, C, or $Q = Y = C$.

As we saw in Chapter 3, households typically do not spend all their income on consumption because they want to save. Similarly, firms do not produce only consumption goods; they also produce investment goods. These investment goods are sold to other firms, and they add to the economy's capital stock. In this situation, household income exceeds expenditures on consumption goods by the amount of saving, S, so $Y = C + S$, or $S = Y - C$.[1] Firms produce output not only for sale to households, but also for sale to other firms in the form of investment goods. Thus, total output is $Q = Q_C + Q_I$ where Q_C is output of consumption goods and Q_I is output of investment goods. Total expenditures in the economy, E, are the sum of expenditures by households on consumption goods, C, and expenditures by firms on investment goods, I, so $E = C + I$.

The economy is in equilibrium when total output equals total expenditures, that is, when $Q = E$, or $Q_C + Q_I = C + I$. We know that total income is equal to total output, so $Y = Q$, and, therefore, $Y = Q_C + Q_I = C + I$. Because $Y = C + S$, we have $Q = Q_C + Q_I = C + I = C + S$.

---

[1] Here we adopt the more familiar national income definition of income and saving rather than the definitions in Chapter 3, which allowed for capital gains and losses on existing assets. We shall introduce capital gains and losses in Chapter 15.

FIGURE 13.1
THE FLOW OF INCOME, OUTPUT,
AND EXPENDITURES.

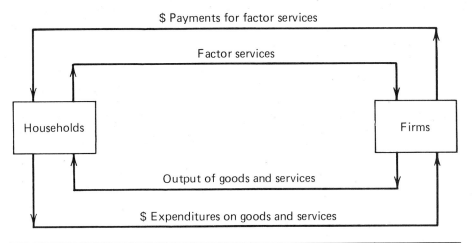

Figure 13.2 shows the situation when there are saving and investment. House-hold saving is not directly and automatically transferred to investing firms. Rather, households typically place their savings in financial assets such as stocks, bonds, shares of nondepository financial intermediaries and in accounts of depository institutions. These elements of the financial system channel saving to firms for investment in physical capital.

In Figure 13.2, firms produce output of consumption and investment goods, which creates income for households. Part of the income is used for consumption expenditures, and part is saved. The saving is channeled, via the financial system, to firms that use the resources to acquire the investment goods produced by firms. The circular flow is in balance because the output of consumption and investment goods is equal to the expenditures that households and firms make on consumption and investment goods.

It is not necessarily true that the output firms want to produce equals the amount of goods and services that households and firms want to purchase. We must appeal to theory to describe how the consumption and saving decisions of households are brought into balance with the production and investment decisions of firms.[2]

---

[2] Because wages and prices are assumed to be constant, it is implicitly assumed that total output adjusts passively to changes in aggregate expenditures. We use the term *aggregate expenditures* rather than *aggregate demand* because the price level is being held constant. The assumption of a fixed price level implies a horizontal aggregate supply schedule. With horizontal supply, output is determined solely by aggregate demand (expenditures). Chapter 16 discusses the more realistic case where aggregate supply interacts with aggregate demand.

FIGURE 13.2
THE FLOW OF INCOME, OUTPUT,
AND EXPENDITURES WITH
SAVING AND INVESTMENT.

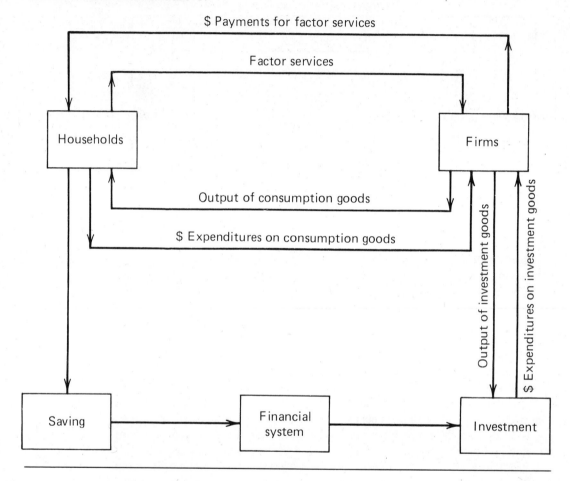

THE THEORY OF AGGREGATE
EXPENDITURES AND INCOME

We start the discussion by neglecting the financial sector of the economy. This allows the analysis to be kept as simple as possible while illustrating the importance of having desired saving equal desired investment. The financial sector is brought in at a later point.

The economy is in equilibrium when firms want to produce an output of consumption goods that equals the expenditures on consumption goods that consumers want to make. Equilibrium in the economy also requires that the desired output of investment goods equals desired expenditures on the investment goods. Both of these balances are achieved when the desired saving of households equals the desired investment of firms. The relationship can be summarized symbolically. In equilibrium, $Q = Q_C + Q_I$, $Y = C + S$, $E = C + I$, and $Q = Y = E$. This balance is achieved when $Q_C = C$ and $Q_I = I$. Because $Q - Q_C = Q_I = Y - C = S$, we have $I = S$.

Desired consumption and saving are affected by the income that households earn. We saw in Chapter 3 that consumption and saving are influenced by previous, current, and expected future income because households strive to smooth consumption over their life cycles. The wealth that households currently hold also affects their consumption, as do their expectations of future interest rates. In this chapter, we abstract from these life-cycle considerations and assume that consumption and saving vary only with the income that households currently earn from providing the factors of production to firms. Thus, the concept of net income stressed in Chapter 3 and, therefore, the role of capital gains and losses are not considered at this point. This is also true of the roles of wealth and of the interest rate.

Assume that desired aggregate consumption and saving are determined by simple linear functions of the form

$$C = c_0 + c_1 Y$$
$$S = s_0 + s_1 Y.$$

The parameter c_1 is the *marginal propensity to consume* and indicates the change in consumption that is produced by a change in income. The parameter s_1 is the *marginal propensity to save,* and it is the change in saving that occurs when income changes. The intercept terms c_0 and s_0 in the consumption and saving functions are discussed later.

By definition, income is consumption plus saving; income that is not consumed must be saved. Thus, $Y = C + S$, $S = Y - C$, and $C = Y - S$.[3] The decision of how much to consume is also the decision of how much to save. Thus, the consumption and saving functions are not independent of each other. They are two ways of looking at the same thing:

$$C = c_0 + c_1 Y,$$

but

$$C = Y - S$$

---

[3] Recall that the government is not considered in this chapter. As a result, there are no government expenditures, transfer payments, and taxes. In this situation, aggregate income equals consumption plus saving.

so

$$Y - S = c_0 + c_1 Y$$

and

$$S = -c_0 + (1 - c_1) Y .$$

If income is zero, $C = c_0$ and $S = -c_0$. Households are consuming $C = c_0$ even though they have no income. This can be accomplished only if they are dissaving by the same amount; that is, $S = s_0 = -c_0$. If there is no income, consumption plus saving must equal zero, so $c_0 + s_0 = 0$.

The part of an increase in income that is not consumed must be saved. The part of a reduction in income that does not reduce consumption must reduce saving. This implies that the marginal propensity to save, s_1, is $(1 - c_1)$, that is, one minus the marginal propensity to consume. Thus, $c_1 + s_1 = 1$.

The relationship between the consumption and saving functions is shown in Figure 13.3. The intercept of the consumption function, c_0, indicates that there is positive consumption even though income is zero. This consumption is possible because households dissave, that is, have negative saving, when income is zero. Thus, $c_0 = -s_0$.[4] As income rises, consumption rises, and dissaving is reduced. At the income Y_C, consumption equals income and saving is zero. At incomes greater than Y_C, both consumption and saving are positive. The slope of the consumption function is the marginal propensity to consume, $\Delta C / \Delta Y = c_1$, and the slope of the saving function is the marginal propensity to save, $\Delta S / \Delta Y = s_1$. By definition, $s_1 = 1 - \Delta C / \Delta Y = (1 - c_1)$. Both the consumption and saving functions have an upward slope indicating that an increase in income produces an increase in both consumption and saving; a decrease in income produces a decrease in consumption and saving. This implies that the marginal propensity to consume is less than one. For $s_1 = (1 - c_1)$ to be positive, c_1 must be less than one.

In order to complete the story about the determination of aggregate expenditures, we must specify investment behavior. We assume for simplicity that capital goods do not wear out. This allows us to avoid the distinction between gross and net investment. We again appeal to Chapter 3 and assume that desired investment of the aggregate of all firms is negatively related to the interest rate on bonds, R:

$$I = i_0 - i_1 R .$$

The relationship between the interest rate and desired investment is shown in Figure 13.4. At a sufficiently high interest rate, R_m, there is no investment because there are no projects for which the discounted present value of the net income

[4] Households can maintain consumption in excess of income only if they have wealth or can borrow against future income. With dissaving, wealth is reduced, and eventually wealth runs out. Thus, the consumption and saving functions of Figure 13.3 apply to relatively short periods of time. These short-run relationships are used in this chapter to illustrate the effects of shifts of the consumption and saving functions on aggregate income.

FIGURE 13.3
THE RELATIONSHIP BETWEEN THE
CONSUMPTION AND SAVING FUNCTIONS.

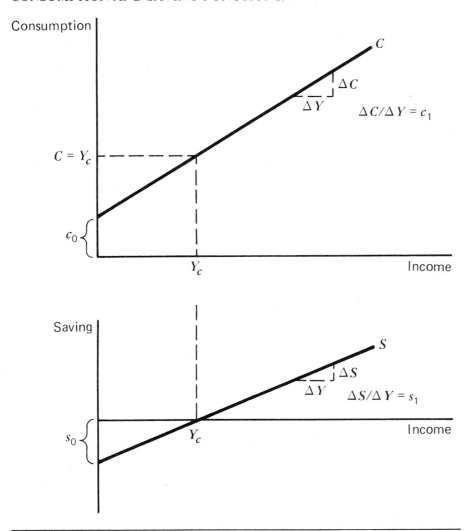

from the project exceeds the purchase price of the equipment. As the interest rate declines, more and more projects become profitable. Thus, investment rises as the interest rate falls. The slope of the function, $\Delta I / \Delta R = -i_1$, shows the responsiveness of investment to a change in the interest rate. When the interest rate is zero, $I = i_0$. This indicates that there is a limited number of profitable projects even at a zero interest rate. The intercept i_0 can also be interpreted as measuring

FIGURE 13.4
DESIRED INVESTMENT.

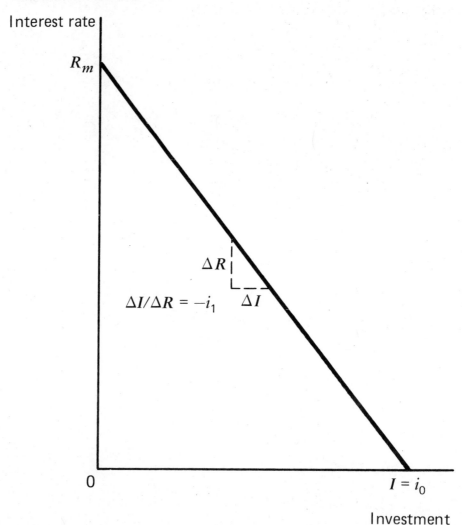

the effect on investment of the expected net income flows from investment projects. If these expected flows increase, i_0 increases, and the investment function shifts to the right. Firms invest more at each interest rate. If expected income flows are reduced, i_0 declines, and the investment function shifts to the left. Firms invest less at each interest rate.

With the specification of consumption, saving, and investment behavior, the pieces can be put together to determine the level of aggregate expenditures and income. Initially, it is assumed the interest rate is constant.

FIGURE 13.5
DETERMINATION OF
EQUILIBRIUM AGGREGATE
EXPENDITURES AND INCOME.

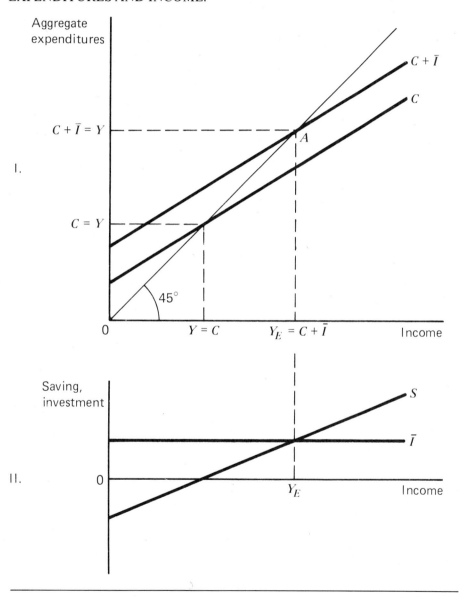

Consider the economy when it is at an initial equilibrium. Panel I of Figure 13.5 shows the equilibrium in terms of the relationship between desired expenditures and income. We know that, in equilibrium, desired expenditures must equal income.[5] This is indicated by the 45° line going through the origin. At every point on this line, expenditures equal income. The problem is to determine the value of income, Y, at which consumption plus investment expenditures equal income. We start to solve the problem by plotting the consumption function $C = c_0 + c_1 Y$, which gives the relationship between desired consumption expenditures and income. If there were no investment, equilibrium would occur at the point where the consumption function intersects the 45° line. At this point, we have $Y = C$, which is the equilibrium of the circular flow of Figure 13.1. We are considering a world where there is investment, however, so equilibrium cannot occur at this point. It is necessary to add investment expenditures to consumption expenditures to get total expenditures. Because the interest rate is assumed constant, desired investment is also a constant. Using a bar to indicate that it is constant, investment is $\bar{I}$. The relationship between total expenditures $(C + \bar{I})$ and income is a line parallel to the consumption function, which exceeds consumption expenditures at every value of income by the fixed amount of investment $\bar{I}$. Equilibrium is achieved at point A, where total desired expenditures, $C + \bar{I}$, equal income, Y_E.

The equilibrium can also be shown by considering the relationship between saving and investment. In panel II, saving and investment are plotted on the vertical axis; and income, on the horizontal axis. As explained earlier, the saving function is $S = s_0 + s_1 Y = -c_0 + (1 - c_1)Y$. Because we have assumed the interest rate is fixed, investment expenditures are given by the horizontal line $\bar{I}$. Equilibrium is achieved when desired saving equals desired investment. This must occur at the same income as when desired consumption plus investment equals income. Thus, in equilibrium $S = I$, and $Y_E = C + I$.

The economy will remain at the equilibrium income, Y_E, as long as aggregate expenditures remain constant. In order to show how income changes, we must change aggregate expenditures. Recall that wages and prices are held constant. Aggregate output is assumed to adjust to aggregate expenditures.[6] Assume that households decide that they want to save a larger proportion of their incomes. This change can be shown as an upward shift in the saving function from S to S' in Panel II of Figure 13.6. The old saving function is $S = s_0 + s_1 Y$; the new function is $S = s'_0 + s_1 Y$ where $s'_0 > s_0$. Recall that $s_0 = -c_0$, so $s'_0 = -c'_0$. An upward shift in the saving function implies a downward shift in the consumption function of the same absolute magnitude. This downward shift in the consumption function from C to C' and in the total expenditure function from $C + \bar{I}$ to $C' + \bar{I}$ (recall $I = \bar{I}$) is shown in Panel I.

Now we have a situation at the initial equilibrium income, Y_E, in which desired saving is greater than desired investment (Panel II) and in which desired expenditure is less than income (Panel I). When households decide to save more out of their incomes, they have simultaneously decided to consume less out of their in-

---

[5] Recall that output and income are defined to be always equal to each other.
[6] Chapter 16 introduces wage and price changes, so changes in aggregate supply can affect aggregate demand and equilibrium income.

FIGURE 13.6
THE EFFECT OF A SHIFT IN THE
CONSUMPTION AND SAVING FUNCTIONS.

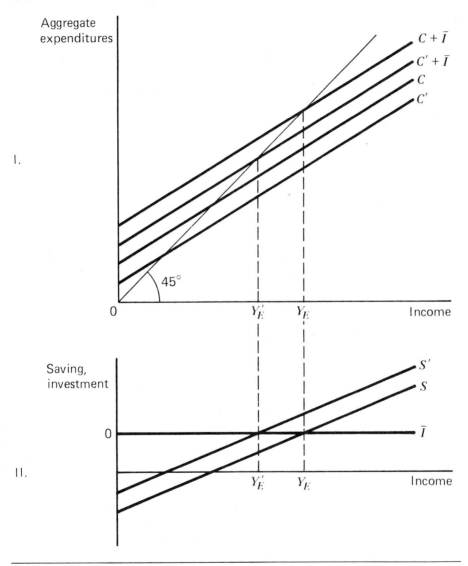

comes. This means that at the old equilibrium Y_E, desired expenditures, $C' + \bar{I}$, are now less than income and output. The initial and temporary effect of having output and income exceed desired expenditures is for firms to accumulate unwanted inventories of consumption goods. Firms do not want to retain these inventories, however, so they cut production and, therefore, reduce payments to the factors of production. The reduction in income leads to a further reduction in consumption expenditures and to further reductions in income.

For every dollar reduction in income, consumption is reduced by less than a dollar because the marginal propensity to consume, c_1, is assumed to be less than one. The reduction of consumption produces an additional decline in income, however. This produces a further decline in consumption of c_1 times the decline in income. The interaction of income and consumption produces a contraction in income and consumption that is a multiple of the initial downward shift in the consumption function. For example, if the marginal propensity to consume is .90, an initial $1 decline in income produces a $.90 decline in consumption. This reduces income by $.90, which leads to a further decline in consumption of $.9(\$.90) = \$.81$. With lower consumption, income is reduced, which leads to even lower consumption. At each step in the process, the reduction in consumption is less than the reduction in income. This occurs because households also reduce saving when income falls. The reductions in income and consumption become smaller and smaller at each step in the process. This allows the economy to achieve a new equilibrium where income and consumption have stopped falling. This new equilibrium is shown in Panel I as Y'_E.

The same story can be told in Panel II. Here, the initial upward shift in the saving function produces an excess of desired saving over desired investment at the initial equilibrium Y_E. This means that households want to withdraw more from the expenditure stream at Y_E through saving than firms want to add to expenditures through investment. With this new higher rate of saving, firms cannot sell all their output, so production and income decline. The decline in income reduces desired saving by the marginal propensity to save times the decline in income.[7] Because investment is assumed fixed at $\bar{I}$, income must decline until, at the new lower level of income, saving is reduced back to equality with investment. Because the marginal propensity to save is less than one, a multiple contraction of income is required to reduce saving back to equality with investment.

Because investment is assumed to be fixed at $\bar{I}$, when there is an upward shift in the saving function, income must fall. Households want to save a higher fraction of their incomes. If income were to remain at Y_E, this would produce a larger amount of saving. Income must fall, however, because the desired increase in saving reduces aggregate expenditures and income. As long as investment remains at $\bar{I}$, income must fall until, at the new lower level of income, Y'_E, households are saving the same amount as at Y_E. This is called the *paradox of thrift* because attempts to raise desired saving simply reduces income and keeps the level of saving in the economy unchanged. We shall see later that this paradox need not occur when the interest rate is allowed to change.

The reader can easily verify that a decline in income also occurs when the saving and consumption functions are kept at their initial positions but investment shifts down instead. Alternatively, an increase in income occurs when the con-

---

[7] Recall that $s_1 = (1 - c_1)$.

sumption function shifts upward (saving function shifts down) or when the invest-ment function shifts up. Instead of going through a graphical exposition of the effects of various shifts, a general algebraic expression shows the effects. The ex-pression for equilibrium income can be obtained from the model we have specified:

$$C = c_0 + c_1 Y$$

$$S = s_0 + s_1 Y = -c_0 + (1 - c_1) Y$$

$$I = \bar{I}$$

$$Y = C + I$$

$$Y = C + S .$$

Using the expression for aggregate expenditures,

$$Y = C + \bar{I} = c_0 + c_1 Y + \bar{I}$$

so

$$(1 - c_1) Y = c_0 + \bar{I}$$

and

$$Y = \frac{c_0}{(1 - c_1)} + \frac{\bar{I}}{(1 - c_1)} .$$

Recalling that c_1 is the marginal propensity to consume, $(1 - c_1)$ is the marginal propensity to save, s_1. Thus,

$$Y = \frac{c_0}{s_1} + \frac{\bar{I}}{s_1} .$$

For a change in income, we have

$$\Delta Y = \frac{\Delta c_0}{s_1} + \frac{\Delta \bar{I}}{s_1} .$$

This expression says that if the consumption function shifts upward from c_0 to c'_0, that is, $\Delta c_0 = (c'_0 - c_0)$, then the rise in income is $\Delta Y = \Delta c_0 / s_1$. Similarly a shift in investment from $\bar{I}$ to $\bar{I}'$, that is, $\Delta \bar{I} = (\bar{I}' - \bar{I})$, results in a change in income of $\Delta \bar{I} / s_1$.

Now we see an analogy with the money and credit multipliers of Chapter 11. In those multipliers, reserve requirements played a key role because they pro-duced a leakage from the expansion (contraction) process. Here the leakage is provided by saving. A rise in income, ΔY, produces an increase in saving equal to $s_1 \Delta Y$. This saving is a leakage from aggregate demand. Income that is saved is income that is not used for consumption and, therefore, does not contribute to a further expansion in income. There is a multiplier relationship between a shift in the consumption or investment functions and changes in income. In the simple model considered so far, the multiplier is $1/s_1$. As we shall see later, when we al-low for changes in the interest rate and for changes in investment, this multiplier becomes more complicated.

The first step in allowing for these factors is relatively straightforward. Initially, we wrote the expression for desired investment as $I = i_0 - i_1 R$. This indicates that desired expenditures by firms for investment goods varies negatively with the interest rate, R. As long as the interest rate does not change or as long as a firm's expectations concerning the flow of net income from investment projects does not change, that is, i_0 is fixed, investment remains constant. We have already analyzed the effect of a change in i_0. This shifts the level of investment up or down and produces a multiple change in aggregate expenditures and income. Now we want to analyze the relationship among the interest rate, investment, and aggregate expenditures. At this point, there is no mechanism in the model for determining the interest rate, but we can still discuss how investment, total expenditures, and income behave when the interest rate changes.

Panel I of Figure 13.7 shows the relationship between the demand for investment goods by firms and the interest rate. The lower the interest rate, the greater the amount of investment goods demanded by firms. Panel II shows saving and investment relative to income. As before, saving varies positively with income. Investment is shown as a horizontal line indicating that the level of income is assumed not to affect investment. Now, however, there is a different investment line in Panel II for each interest rate. In particular, I_0 is the investment that is demanded in Panel I at interest rate R_0. As the interest rate is reduced from R_0 to R_1 to R_2, firms increase their investment expenditures, and the horizontal investment line in Panel II shifts up from I_0 to I_1 to I_2.

At the interest rate R_0, investment is I_0, and saving equals investment at the income level Y_0. Thus, if the interest rate is R_0, equilibrium income must be Y_0. This is confirmed in Panel III by showing that aggregate expenditures $(C + I_0)$ equal income at Y_0. If the interest rate falls to R_1, investment rises to I_1. At the initial level of income, Y_0, desired investment exceeds desired saving (see Panel II). This means that firms are adding more to expenditures than savers are withdrawing and there is a multiple expansion of income to Y_1. When income rises, desired saving increases. Income must rise until saving has increased to the point that it has matched the increase in investment. The rise in income is $Y_1 - Y_0 = (I_1 - I_0)/s_1$. We note in Panel III that at the new equilibrium income Y_1, desired expenditures equal income. If the interest rate is reduced to R_2, investment rises to I_2, and again desired investment exceeds desired saving. Income must rise to Y_2 where $Y_2 - Y_1 = (I_2 - I_1)/s_1$.

We conclude that when the interest rate is low, desired investment is high. With high desired investment, there is a greater equilibrium income. Thus, when the interest rate is low, aggregate expenditures and income are high.[8]

The relationship between the interest rate and income is plotted in Figure 13.8. This relationship summarizes the information obtained from the three panels of Figure 13.7. Thus, the interest rate R_0 and income Y_0 correspond to R_0 and Y_0 in

---

[8] In Chapter 15 we examine the effects of having consumption increase when the interest rate declines.

FIGURE 13.7
THE EFFECT OF THE INTEREST
RATE ON AGGREGATE
EXPENDITURES AND INCOME.

I.

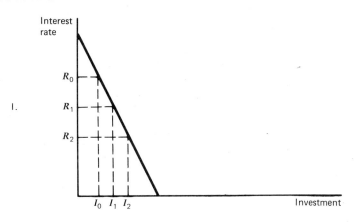

II.

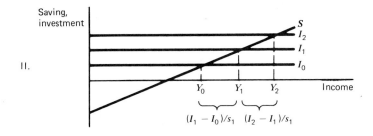

III.

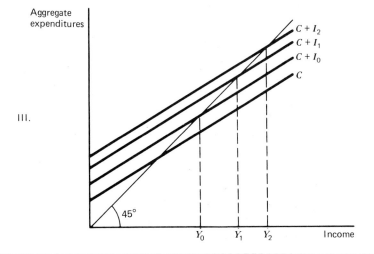

Figure 13.7 and so on. The relationship in Figure 13.8 is called the *IS* curve because it indicates the values for the interest rate and income at which desired investment and saving are equal. The *IS* curve is downward sloping because lower interest rates produce higher investment and higher income. We will use the *IS* curve extensively in this and the next several chapters because it is a convenient way to summarize the relationship between the interest rate and aggregate expenditures.

The *IS* curve can be derived from the consumption, saving, and investment functions:

$$C = c_0 + c_1 Y$$

$$S = s_0 + s_1 Y = -c_0 + (1 - c_1) Y$$

$$I = i_0 - i_1 R$$

$$Y = C + I$$

$$Y = C + S .$$

Because $Y = C + I$, $Y = c_0 + c_1 Y + i_0 - i_1 R = (c_0 + i_0) + c_1 Y - i_1 R$, so $(1 - c_1) Y = (c_0 + i_0) - i_1 R$. Because $(1 - c_1) = s_1$,

$$Y = \frac{c_0 + i_0}{s_1} - \frac{i_1}{s_1} R .$$

This algebraic expression is convenient for analyzing the determinants of shifts in the *IS* curve, the extent of the shifts, and the steepness of the curve's slope. We shall see in later chapters that these factors have important implications for economic stability and for the efficacy of monetary and fiscal policy. For the *IS* curve, it is convenient to solve for income in terms of the interest rate, that is, Y is on the left-hand side of the equation. This allows us to discuss shifts in the *IS* curve, given the interest rate, in terms of changes in c_0 or i_0 times the multiplier, $1/s_1$.

The relationship between a change in the interest rate and a change in income is $\Delta Y / \Delta R = -i_1/s_1$. A rise in the interest rate requires a decline in income of i_1/s_1 to retain equality of desired saving and investment. A unit rise in the interest rate produces a decline of i_1 in investment. This fall in investment produces a multiple decline in income where the multiplier is $1/s_1$. Income falls until desired saving equals desired investment.

The intercept term $(c_0 + i_0)/s_1$ indicates the determinants of income, given the interest rate. The *IS* curve shifts when there is a shift in aggregate expenditures. This can come from either a shift in the consumption function or a shift in the investment function. For example, if the consumption function shifts up, its intercept rises from c_0 to c'_0. Given the interest rate, income must rise by $\Delta Y = (c'_0 - c_0)/s_1 = \Delta c_0/s_1$, that is, by the multiplier times the shift in the consumption function. Similarly, if the investment function shifts up its intercept rises from i_0 to i'_0. Given the interest rate, the rise in income must be

FIGURE 13.8
THE *IS* CURVE.

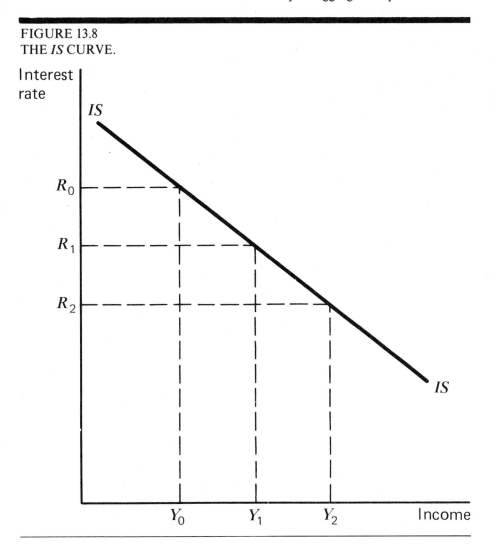

$\Delta Y = (i'_0 - i_0)/s_1 = \Delta i_0/s_1$. Upward shifts in the consumption or investment functions mean that at each interest rate there must be a higher income than before to maintain equality of desired saving and investment. Thus, the *IS* curve shifts to the right. The curve shifts to the left when the consumption or investment functions shift down. In this case, there must be a lower level of income at each interest rate.

Panel I of Figure 13.9 compares two *IS* curves. The curve on the left is relatively steep, and the curve on the right is relatively flat. The convention in graphing the *IS* curve is to put R on the vertical axis and Y on the horizontal axis. This gives a slope of the *IS* curve of $\Delta R/\Delta Y$, which is the inverse of the slope derived

FIGURE 13.9
THE SLOPE AND SHIFTS IN THE *IS* CURVE.

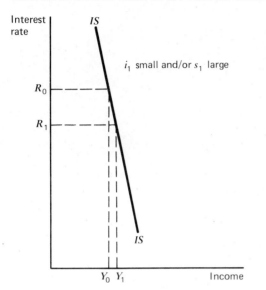

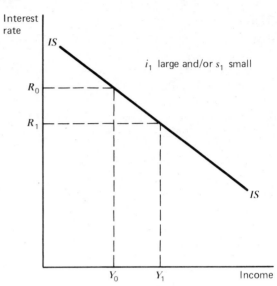

I.

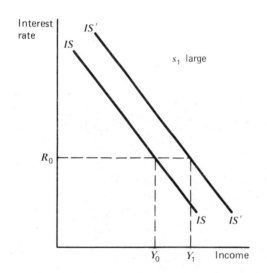

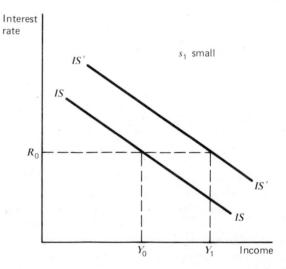

II.

above, that is, the inverse of $\Delta Y / \Delta R$.[9] Because $\Delta Y / \Delta R = i_1 / s_1$, the slope of the *IS* curve in the graph is $\Delta R / \Delta Y = s_1 / i_1$. The *IS* curve is steep when $\Delta R / \Delta Y = s_1 / i_1$ is large. This occurs when the interest sensitivity of investment demand, i_1, is small or when the marginal propensity to save, s_1, is large, or both. When i_1 is low, only a small increase in investment occurs when the interest rate declines. For a given value of the marginal propensity to save, s_1, the smaller is the increase in investment, the smaller is the increase in income that occurs when the interest rate declines. Thus, when i_1 is small, the *IS* curve is steep. Alternatively, for a given value of i_1, the larger the marginal propensity to save, s_1, the larger the leakage of income into saving and, therefore, the smaller the increase in income that occurs when investment rises. Thus, when s_1 is large, the *IS* curve is steep. The *IS* curve is relatively flat when $\Delta R / \Delta Y = -s_1 / i_1$ is small. This occurs when the interest sensitivity of investment, i_1, is large or when the marginal propensity to save is small, or both. In this case, a decline in the interest rate produces a relatively large increase in income. This is shown in the *IS* curve on the right in Panel I.

Panel II shows the effect of the marginal propensity to save on the extent of the shift in the *IS* curve. The *IS* curve shifts when either the consumption function or the investment function shifts. Given the interest rate, R_0, the effect on income of a shift in the consumption function, Δc_0, or in the investment function, Δi_0, depends upon the size of the marginal propensity to save, s_1. For the *IS* curve on the left, s_1, is large. This means that a shift in the consumption or investment function produces a relatively small change in income. The shift in the *IS* curve is small. For the *IS* curve on the right, s_1, is small. In this case, a shift in the consumption or investment function has a relatively large effect on income. The shift in the *IS* curve is relatively large.

Though *IS* curves describe the relationship between income and the interest rate, they do not allow us to determine the equilibrium values of either income or the interest rate. The lesson of the *IS* curve is that in order to determine equilibrium aggregate expenditures and income we must know the interest rate. We can determine the interest rate only after we have introduced the financial sector of the economy.

THE FINANCIAL SECTOR

The financial sector of the economy has important effects on both interest rates and aggregate expenditures. The portfolio decisions of the public concerning the forms in which existing wealth and additions to wealth (saving) are held are crucial elements in determining equilibrium income and interest rates.

---

[9] The graph has implicitly put R on the left-hand side of the equation for the *IS* curve and Y on the right-hand side, that is, $R = (c_0 + i_0)/i_1 - (s_1/i_1)Y$.

We saw in Chapter 4 that the public holds its wealth in many forms. For purposes of this chapter, the complexities of the financial system are neglected in order to focus on some basic elements of financial decisions. In particular, it is assumed that the public holds its wealth only in the form of money and corporate bonds. Furthermore, it is assumed that all money is currency. This latter assumption allows us to abstract from the complexity of the depository system. It is also assumed that firms finance all their investment projects by issuing bonds. Firms issue new bonds when old bonds mature and capital goods never wear out. Under these assumptions, the stock of capital used by firms equals the quantity of bonds held by the public. The assumption that all investment is bond financed allows us to abstract from complications created by permitting firms to finance investment from retained earnings or from sales of stock (ownership shares). The analysis can be expanded to consider more realistic cases, but the conclusions would not be substantially altered.

The portfolio decisions of the public concerning the allocation of wealth between money and bonds is an important element in determining the interest rate on bonds. For simplicity, assume that the expected nominal rate of return on corporate bonds equals the current interest rate on these bonds. Thus, there are no expected capital gains or losses. The nominal rate of return on money (currency) is zero. Also assume that the price level is not expected to change, so the real expected rates of return on bonds and money equal their nominal expected returns.

As explained in Chapter 5, the public wants to hold a diversified portfolio composed of both bonds and money.[10] The proportion of wealth that the public wants to devote to money and the proportion that it wants to devote to bonds depend upon the rate of return on bonds and upon the degree of risk aversion by the public. If the interest rate on bonds rises, the public wants to hold more of its wealth in bonds and less in money. When wealth is fixed, any increase in the holdings of bonds must be offset by an equal reduction in the holdings of money. This implies that an increase in the interest rate on bonds produces an increase in the quantity of bonds demanded and an equal decrease in the quantity of money demanded. Furthermore, given the interest rate, the public divides an increase in wealth between money and bonds in order to maintain a diversified portfolio. These considerations involve the *portfolio demand* for money and bonds. This demand describes the desire of the public to hold money and bonds as stores of value.

Though money is a store of value, it is also the medium of exchange. This characteristic provides an additional reason for the public to demand money. The demand for money that stems from its use as the medium of exchange is called the *transactions demand* for money. This demand exists even if the portfolio demand for money is zero.

---

[10] With the price level fixed, the portfolio allocation problem reduces to the simple case discussed in the appendix to Chapter 5.

FIGURE 13.10
MONEY HOLDINGS OF A
HOUSEHOLD.

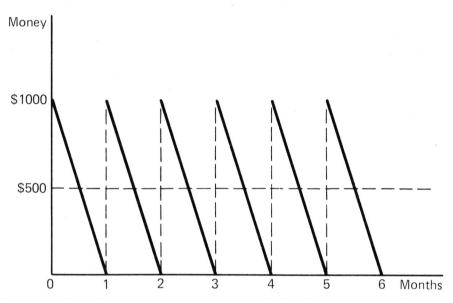

In order to see how the transactions demand for money works, let us return to a diagram presented in Chapter 3 (Figure 3.7). This diagram is reproduced here as Figure 13.10. In constructing the diagram, we assumed that a household receives $1000 of income at the beginning of each month and spends the entire income on consumption during the month. It is further assumed that consumption is spread evenly during the month. The household begins each month with money holdings of $1000 (its income) and ends each month with no money. Note that except at the end of the month, the household is holding some money. Furthermore, the average amount of money held during each month is $500. This is true in each and every month, so the household has an average money balance during the year of $500. Money balances are held during the month simply because money received earlier has not yet been spent.

When households spend money on consumption, this produces sales receipts and increased money balances for firms. Firms are accumulating money balances as households are reducing their balances. Figure 13.11 shows how the quantity of money is allocated between households and firms during each month. Here it is assumed that firms make all their expenditures for factor services at the end of each month. We can see from the diagram that money flows back and forth between households and firms. Because their receipts and expenditures are not synchronized, both households and firms hold money during the month.

FIGURE 13.11
MONEY HOLDINGS OF
HOUSEHOLDS AND FIRMS.

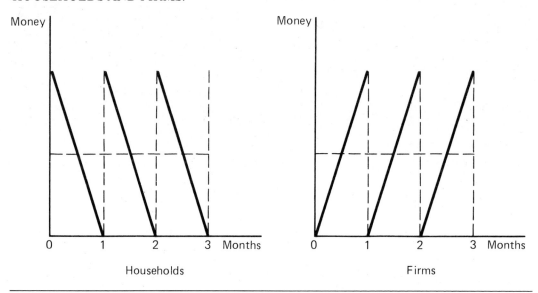

The example in Figure 13.11 can be used to show that the amount of money held by the households and firms depends upon (1) the frequency with which income payments are received (paid), (2) the amount of income payments (receipts), and (3) the pattern of expenditures during the month. First, consider the behavior of households. Panel I of Figure 13.12 shows the effect on average money holdings for a household if it is paid $500 twice a month rather than $1000 at the beginning of each month. If the frequency of income receipts is increased from once to twice a month, the average money balance falls from $500 to $250. Increasing the frequency of income receipts reduces the quantity of money demanded. Panel II shows the effect of halving the income of the household, assuming it is paid once a month. If monthly income falls from $1000 to $500, average money balances fall from $500 to $250. Thus, the demand for money decreases when income decreases, and it increases when income increases. Panel III shows the effect of changing the pattern of expenditures during the month. If most of the expenditures occur at the beginning of the month rather than being spread evenly, average money balances fall from $500 to $250. If consumption expenditures had been bunched at the end of the month rather than the beginning, average money balances would increase. We conclude from these diagrams that the amount of money that is held by a household is affected by the frequency of its income receipts, by the size of these receipts, and by the timing of expenditures.

FIGURE 13.12
FACTORS AFFECTING MONEY DEMAND OF A HOUSEHOLD.

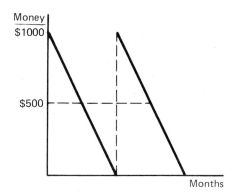

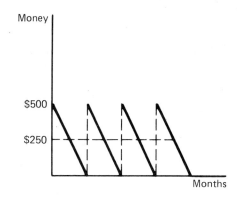

I.

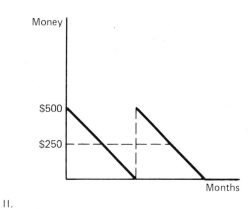

II.

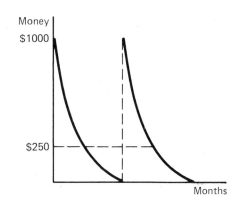

III.

The money demand of firms is also affected by the frequency, magnitude, and timing of receipts and expenditures. If a business makes payments for its factors of production twice a month rather than once a month, it accumulates only half as much money balances before expenditures are made. Similarly, if the firm's receipts and expenditures are increased, it accumulates larger money balances prior to making expenditures. Finally, changes in the timing of expenditures and receipts also affect the average money balances held by firms.[11]

Note that the circulation of money between households and firms generates income. The ratio of the flow of income, Y, to the stock of money, M, is called the *income velocity of money, V*,

$$V = \frac{Y}{M}.$$

Because money changes hands several times during a year in income-generating transactions, annual aggregate income is several times as large as the stock of money. For example, aggregate income (GNP) in the United States in 1982 was approximately, $3000 billion and the quantity of money was approximately $400 billion. This gives an income velocity of money of 6.0. On average, the quantity of money changed hands 6 times during 1982 in income-generating transactions. Many transactions are for asset purchases and other nonincome-generating activities. The velocity of money for all types of transactions is in excess of 115. Money changes hands many times to support all the transactions that occur in a highly developed economy.

It was noted above that changes in the frequency of payments and receipts affect the demand for money. These changes affect the average amount of money that is required to conduct a given level of income-generating transactions. That is to say, changes in the frequency of payments and receipts affect the income velocity of money. When the frequency of payments and receipts increases, velocity rises; when the frequency decreases, velocity falls.

Money demand and income velocity are also affected by interest rates. The discussion that follows, and indeed the remainder of this text, looks at money demand rather than at money's income velocity. This is done in order not to complicate the analysis unnecessarily. The reader should bear in mind, however, that when interest rates rise and the quantity of money demanded declines, velocity rises. The public economizes on money balances when interest rates are high. In order to accomplish the same income-generating transactions, money's income velocity rises. When interest rates are low, the public demands a relatively large amount of money balances. In this case, income-generating transactions are accomplished with a lower income velocity of money.

---

[11] When households spend most of their money receipts early in the month, they reduce their average money balance, but this increases the average money balances of firms. At any time, the balances held by households and firms must equal the amount of money in the economy. The implications of having money demand equal money supply are discussed later.

With these comments in mind, let us now turn to the discussion of the effects of interest rates on money demand. Up to this point it has been assumed that past income receipts that have not yet been spent are held in the form of money. This need not be the case. Because money earns no interest in our model, the opportunity cost of holding money is the interest income that can be earned by holding bonds rather than money.[12] In principle, households and firms can buy bonds almost as soon as they receive income payments, and they can sell bonds as money is needed for expenditures. This strategy allows households and firms to earn an interest income rather than hold money, which earns no interest. If bonds were perfectly divisible and if there were no transaction costs in buying and selling bonds, no one would want to hold money for transactions purposes.

Bonds are not perfectly divisible, however, and there are transactions costs in buying and selling them. As a result, the best strategy is often to hold money rather than bonds. If we leave indivisibilities aside for a moment, it is profitable to hold a bond rather than money only if the interest income (more generally, the rate of return) over the period that the bond is held exceeds the transactions costs of first buying the bond and then selling it.

Recall that a household or firm needs money later on in the month to finance transactions. If income receipts are held in the form of money until expenditures are made, there are no transactions costs of buying and selling bonds, but there is also no interest income. If bonds are held until the expenditures are made, an interest income is earned, but transactions costs are also incurred.

In deciding whether to hold money or bonds as temporary stores of value, a household or firm must compare the interest income from the bond to the transactions costs of first buying and then selling the bond. The interest income depends upon how long the bond is held. For example, the interest income from holding a bond for one day is 1/365 of the annual interest income. The annual income from a $1000 bond at 10 percent interest is $100. This translates into a daily interest income of $0.27. If the transactions costs of buying a bond the first day and selling it the next exceed $0.27, a negative rate of return would be earned by holding a bond for a day. It is more profitable to earn the zero rate of return on money. Thus, transactions costs do not have to be very large before holding a bond for a day is unprofitable. The longer that a bond is held, the greater is its rate of return net of transactions costs. For example, a bond that is held for thirty days earns 30/365 of the annual return. The interest income from a $1000 bond held for thirty days is $8.22 at 10 percent interest. It may be profitable to hold a bond for a month rather than an equal amount of money.

Consider the case of a household. It is usually not profitable to convert the entire monthly income receipts into bonds and then sell the bonds as the funds are needed for consumption. If this were done, it would be necessary to sell some bonds virtually as soon as they are purchased in order to finance consumption expenditures for the first day of the month. Expenditures for the second day would require selling bonds that day and so on. This implies that for expenditures made during the early days of the month, it is likely that transactions costs exceed the small amount of interest income from holding bonds for such a short period of time. It is usually only profitable to convert part of the initial income receipt into bonds. For example, half of the $1000 monthly income receipt ($500) can be used to buy bonds. The remaining $500 finances consumption during the first half of the month. The $500 of bonds are sold at midmonth to finance the remaining consumption during the month. In this case, the household has a maximum of $500 in money and holds an average of $250 for the month. This simple investment strategy allows the household to cut its money holdings in half and to earn an interest income, less transactions costs, on $500 held for half a month.

Whether or not this investment strategy is profitable depends upon transactions costs relative to the interest rate on bonds. Given transactions costs, the higher the interest rate on bonds, the more profitable it becomes to hold bonds instead of money. Furthermore, at a sufficiently high interest rate, it is profitable for the household to place two thirds of the $1000 monthly income ($666.67) into bonds while using the remaining third ($333.33) to pay for consumption for the first third of the month. When this money is exhausted, the household sells $333.33 of bonds to finance another third of consumption expenditures. When two thirds of the month is over, this money is exhausted, requiring the remaining $333.33 of bonds to be sold. This strategy allows the household to earn interest on the first $333.33 of bonds for one third of a month and to earn interest on the remaining $333.33 for two thirds of a month.

We conclude that the higher the interest rate on bonds, the smaller the amount of money that a household or firm wants the hold. We also conclude that the higher the transactions costs, the larger the quantity of money that is demanded. These conclusions give the money demand schedule, M^D, for a household or firm in Figure 13.13. The lower the interest rate on bonds, R, the greater the quantity of money demanded. Conversely, the higher the interest rate on bonds, the smaller the quantity of money demanded. If transactions costs rise, the curve shifts to the right to $M^D{}'$ indicating that a larger quantity of money is demanded at each interest rate on bonds. This occurs because at each interest rate the profitability of holding bonds rather than money is reduced when transactions costs are higher. Thus, a household or firm wants more money and less bonds than before. The money demand schedules becomes horizontal at the interest rates R_0 and R_1, indicating that, at these interest rates, transactions costs equal the interest income on bonds that are held until the last day of the month. Thus, it is never profitable to hold bonds rather than money as a temporary store of value.

Although the principles of the transactions demand for money can be applied to any household or firm, transactions costs per dollar of bond are lower for households and firms with high incomes than for those with small incomes. Some transactions costs are fixed such as the cost of contacting a dealer or broker. When larger quantities of bonds are purchased or sold, these fixed costs are spread over the entire transaction. Thus, the larger the bond transaction, the lower the costs per dollar of transaction. Furthermore, quantity discounts on fees charged

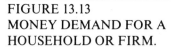

FIGURE 13.13
MONEY DEMAND FOR A
HOUSEHOLD OR FIRM.

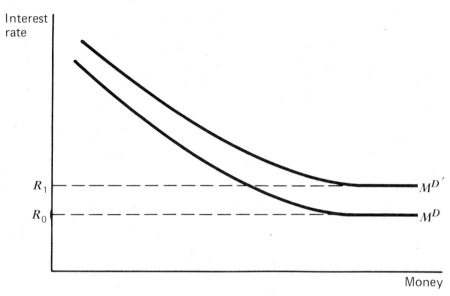

by brokers and dealers are available for larger transactions. As a consequence, the transactions costs per dollar are smaller for large transactions than for small. This means that it may be profitable for a high-income firm or individual to purchase bonds for a short period of time whereas it is unprofitable for those with lower incomes. Furthermore, minimum denominations for bonds preclude many households and small firms from using bonds as actively as do participants for whom minimum denominations are unimportant.[13]

Despite these complications, we shall assume that it is possible to aggregate the transactions demand for money for all households and firms in the economy. This total transactions demand for money has the property that when the interest rate on bonds is high, the transactions demand for money in the economy is low. Furthermore, when transactions costs are high, the aggregate transactions demand for money is high. Finally, when the level of income in the economy is high, the transactions demand for money is high.

The discussion of the transactions demand for money has assumed that households and firms know the patterns of their income receipts and expenditures with certainty. This is almost never the case. Unexpected fluctuations in the levels and

[13] Transactions costs and indivisibilities prevent lower income households or firms from purchasing bonds. They simply hold money until the funds are needed for expenditures.

timing of both receipts and expenditures do occur. This means that households and firms can find themselves holding more money than they expected when there are unanticipated increases in income or decreases in expenditures. They will have smaller money holdings than expected when income receipts are less than expected or when expenditures are greater than expected. These considerations mean that money holdings of individual households and firms fluctuate with unanticipated movements in income and expenditures.

When income receipts are larger than expected or when expenditures are less than anticipated, households and firms will be holding more money than they planned. Whether or not they want to get rid of these money balances (buy bonds) depends upon whether the increase is perceived as temporary or more permanent. If the increase is believed to be shortlived, it may be most profitable simply to hold the money rather than buy bonds. Income could fall the next day, or expenditures could rise, requiring the household or firm to come up with the money. If bonds had been purchased, the transactions costs would exceed the interest income, and it would have been more profitable to have held money.

Similarly, households and firms know that they can encounter situations where there are unexpected declines in income receipts or unexpected increases in expenditures. When these events occur, the households or firms must come up with the money to cover the imbalance between expenditure and receipts. If sufficient money balances are on hand, there is no problem. If money holdings do not cover the expenditures, it is necessary to sell bonds. This raises three problems. First, the bonds may be sold before they have earned enough interest income to cover transactions costs. In this case, the household or firm that expected to earn a positive rate of return on the bonds will end up earning a negative return. Second, if the interest rate has risen unexpectedly, the price of bonds may be lower than expected. This means that the rate of return from holding the bonds is lower because a capital loss is incurred when the bonds are sold. Third, for large firms and wealthy households, it may not be possible to sell large quantities of bonds quickly without depressing their price. This potential illiquidity of bonds will induce these economic units to hold more money and fewer bonds to avoid problems of illiquidity.

Uncertainty about future income and expenditures, as well as uncertainty about future bond prices, induces the public to demand more money than would be the case in a world of certainty. Households and firms hold larger money balances to avoid unprofitable bond sales when there is an unanticipated need for money. Furthermore, an unanticipated increase in money balances is not converted into bonds if the increase is viewed as transitory. Uncertainty about income and expenditures and uncertainty about future bond prices add to the transactions demand for money.

We saw earlier that money is demanded as a store of value in addition to its use for transactions purposes. The portfolio demand for money depends upon the expected rate of return and risk for bonds and upon the preferences of the public. The lower the expected return on bonds or the higher their risk, or both, the greater the portfolio demand for money and, therefore, the greater the desired share of money in portfolios. The portfolio demand for money combined with the transactions demand explain why households and firms hold money even when it earns a zero rate of return.

When the transactions and portfolio demands are combined, we have the total demand schedule for money in the economy. This money demand schedule is shown as M^D in Panel I of Figure 13.14.[14] The money demand schedule represents both the transactions demand for money and any portfolio demand that comes from longer-term considerations of asset diversification. It should be noted that this demand schedule is different from schedules used for other assets. In conventional demand schedules, the own price or own rate of return is on the vertical axis. With the money demand schedule, the interest rate on the competing asset (bonds) is shown rather than the interest rate for money. This is done because the interest rate on money is assumed to be fixed at zero. In this situation, we are interested in the response of the quantity of money demanded to changes in the interest rate on bonds. Panel II shows the demand schedule for bonds, B^D. This is a conventional asset demand schedule; the higher the interest rate on bonds, the larger the quantity demanded.

In the two-asset world that we are considering, the money demand and bond demand schedules bear a simple relationship to each other. Consider what happens when there is an increase in the interest rate on bonds from R_0 to R_1. The bond demand schedule, B^D, in Panel II indicates that the public increases the quantity of bonds demanded from B_0 to B_1. The money demand schedule, M^D, in Panel I indicates that the public reduces the quantity of money demanded from M_0 to M_1. In the two-asset world of bonds and money, the increase in the quantity of bonds demanded must be matched by a reduction of equal size in the quantity of money demanded. Thus $(B_1 - B_0) = -(M_1 - M_0)$. Given total wealth $(W = M + B)$, an increase in the interest rate induces the public to reshuffle its wealth by wanting to put a larger share of wealth in bonds and a smaller share in money. Because wealth is assumed to be fixed, it must be true that the slope of the money demand schedule is the negative of the slope of the bond demand schedule. Thus, $\Delta M^D/\Delta R = -\Delta B^D/\Delta R$. Given wealth, a rise in the interest rate reduces the quantity of money demanded by the amount that it increases the quantity of bonds demanded.

Figure 13.14 also shows the relationship between the money and bond demand schedules when there is an increase in income (transactions). When income rises, the public wants a larger quantity of money to conduct the higher level of transactions. This means that when income increases, the money demand schedule shifts right to $M^{D\prime}$. For a given value of the interest rate, the public demands a larger quantity of money than before. Given wealth, this implies that the public reduces its demand for bonds by the same amount. Thus, the bond demand schedule shifts left to $B^{D\prime}$.

---

[14] For simplicity, the money demand schedule is taken to be linear. The implications of having a nonlinear schedule, as in Figure 13.13, are discussed in Chapter 16.

FIGURE 13.14
DEMAND SCHEDULES FOR MONEY
AND BONDS.

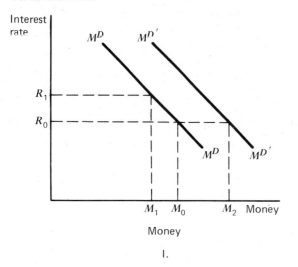

I.

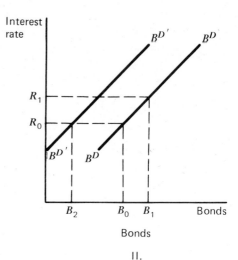

II.

At the interest rate R_0 the public initially demands the quantity of money M_0 and the quantity of bonds B_0. When income rises, the money demand schedule shifts right from M^D to $M^{D'}$. The public now wants to hold a larger quantity of money $(M_2 - M_0)$ at the interest rate R_0. Where does it plan to get the money? We see the answer in the bond demand schedule. The bond demand schedule shifts left to $B^{D'}$. The public plans to get the additional money by selling bonds. For every \$1 increase in desired money holdings, there must be a \$1 decrease in desired bond holdings. The bond demand schedule shifts to the left by the same amount that the money demand schedule shifted to the right. Thus $(M_2 - M_0) = -(B_2 - B_0)$.

If there is a decline in income, there is a reduction in the transactions demand for money. The public wants to hold a smaller quantity of money than before, and the money demand schedule shifts to the left. Given wealth, this must mean that the public wants to hold a larger quantity of bonds. Thus, the bond demand schedule shifts to the right by an equal amount. We conclude that the change in money demand with respect to a change in income is the negative of the change in bond demand with respect to a change in income: $\Delta M^D / \Delta Y = -\Delta B^D / \Delta Y$.

The effects of changes in wealth on money and bond demand are discussed in Chapter 15. Here we assume wealth is constant and for simplicity do not include it in the specification of the money and bond demand functions. With this simplification in mind, the relationship between money demand and bond demand can be summarized algebraically. Assuming the demand functions are linear, we have:

$$M^D = m_0 - m_1 R + m_2 Y$$
$$B^D = b_0 + b_1 R - b_2 Y.$$

The intercepts m_0 and b_0 allow us to account for shifts in the money and bond demand functions. If the public wants to hold more money given the interest rate, income, and wealth, then m_0 increases. Because wealth is fixed, this must mean that the public wants to hold fewer bonds. An increase in m_0 implies a decrease in b_0 of equal size. Thus, $m_0 = -b_0$, so $m_0 + b_0 = 0.0$.

Given income and wealth, a rise in the interest rate reduces the quantity of money demanded and increases the quantity of bonds demanded. The reduction in money demand must equal the rise in bond demand. Thus, $m_1 = -b_1$, so $b_1 + m_1 = 0.0$. Given the interest rate and given wealth, a rise in income increases the quantity of money demanded and reduces the quantity of bonds demanded by an equal amount: $m_2 = -b_2$, so $m_2 + b_2 = 0.0$. Because $b_0 = -m_0$, $b_1 = -m_1$, and $b_2 = -m_2$, the bond demand function can be written as

$$B^D = -m_0 + m_1 R - m_2 Y.$$

The bond demand function is implied by the money demand function.

We can now turn to an analysis of how the demands for money and bonds are brought into equality with the supplies of these two assets. Assume that the supply of money and the supply of bonds are fixed. This means that the actual quantities of money and bonds are constant and, therefore, do not vary with the interest rate or income. Given income and wealth and given the fixed quantities of money and bonds, we can analyze how the interest rate on bonds is determined.

Figure 13.15 shows the relationship between money demand and supply, and between bond demand and supply. The money and bond demand schedules are drawn for a given value of income, Y_0. Thus, the notation $M^D(Y_0)$ and $B^D(Y_0)$ means money and bond demand *given* Y_0. Note that the interest rate on bonds, R_0, at which bond demand equals bond supply, is also the interest rate at which money demand equals money supply. This must be true because money and bonds are substitutes and money plus bonds equal wealth. Consider the interest rate R_1, which is higher than R_0. The money demand schedule is downward sloping, indicating that the higher the interest rate, the smaller the quantity demanded (given Y_0). At the high interest rate, R_1, the quantity of money demanded, M_1, is less than the fixed quantity of money $\overline{M}$. This occurs because at R_1 the public wants to hold more bonds and less money than at R_0. The quantity of bonds that the public wants to hold at the interest, R_1, is B_1. Thus, the quantity of bonds demanded, B_1, exceeds the quantity of bonds available, $\overline{B}$. In our two-asset world, the excess demand for bonds, that is, the amount by which the quantity of bonds demanded exceeds the supply, $(B_1 - \overline{B})$, must equal the excess supply of money, that is, the amount by which the quantity of money exceeds the quantity demanded, $(\overline{M} - M_1)$. At the interest rate, R_1, the public attempts to

FIGURE 13.15
DETERMINING THE INTEREST RATE.

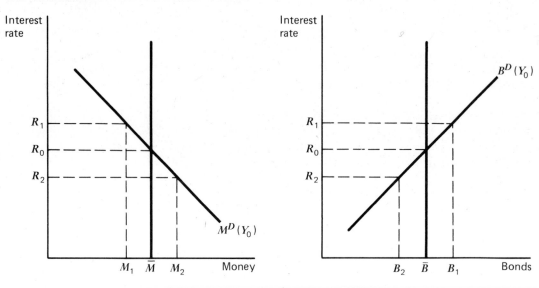

reduce its money holdings by purchasing bonds. Because there are no more bonds available, the price of bonds rises, and the interest rate falls. As the interest rate declines, the quantity of money demanded increases along the money demand schedule, and the quantity of bonds demanded declines along the bond demand schedule. The interest rate declines until the quantity of money demanded equals the fixed supply, and the quantity of bonds demanded equals the fixed supply of bonds. This occurs at the interest rate R_0.

It might occur to the reader that when the price of bonds rises and the interest rate falls, the value of the public's wealth rises. Conversely, when the interest rate rises, bond prices fall, and the value of wealth declines. The effects of changes in interest rates on the value of wealth are considered in Chapter 15.

If the interest rate is R_2, the quantity of money demanded exceeds the fixed supply. The public attempts to increase its money holdings by selling bonds. Thus, the excess demand for money, $(M_2 - \overline{M})$ equals the excess supply of bonds, $(\overline{B} - B_2)$. As the public sells bonds in an effort to obtain more money, the interest rate rises. Because there is no more money to be had, the interest rate must rise until the quantity of money equals the fixed supply. This occurs at the interest rate R_0.

Now let us see how changes in income affect the interest rate. The higher income, the more money is needed for transactions purposes. This implies that, given the interest rate, the higher the income, the greater the quantity of money demanded and the lower is the quantity of bonds demanded. Thus, when income

FIGURE 13.16
THE EFFECT OF INCOME ON THE
INTEREST RATE.

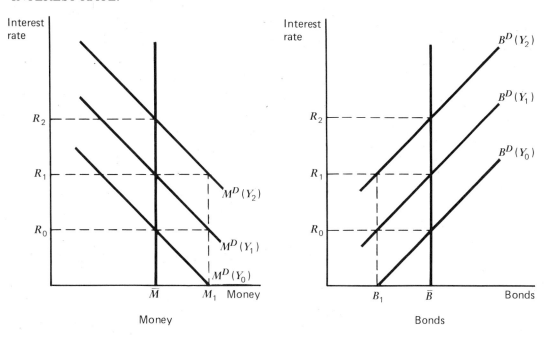

rises, the public wants to hold more money for transactions purposes, and it attempts to get this money by selling bonds. Figure 13.16 shows the diagrams for money and bonds at different levels of income. There is a different money demand schedule for each level of income. For any given value of the interest rate, when income is high, the quantity of money demanded is high. Similarly, at any given interest rate, when income is high, the quantity of bonds demanded is low. Because wealth is assumed to be fixed, when money demand shifts to the right, bond demand shifts to the left by the same amount.

Consider what happens to the interest rate when income rises from Y_0 to Y_1. The money demand schedule shifts to the right from $M^D(Y_0)$ to $M^D(Y_1)$, and the bond demand schedule shifts left from $B^D(Y_0)$ to $B^D(Y_1)$. At the initial interest rate R_0, the quantity of money demanded now exceeds the supply by $(M_1 - \overline{M})$ and the quantity of bonds exceeds the amount demanded by $(\overline{B} - B_1)$. Thus $(M_1 - \overline{M}) = -(B_1 - \overline{B})$. The public wants to increase its money balances because the transactions demand for money has increased. It does this by selling bonds. The sale of bonds reduces their price and increases the interest rate. The interest rate rises until money demand again equals money supply and bond demand equals bond supply. This occurs at the interest rate R_1.

Note that because the quantities of money and bonds are fixed, the interest rate must rise sufficiently to offset the effects of the increased transactions demand for money. At the interest rate R_0, when income rises to Y_1, the public wants to hold the quantity of money M_1. The actual quantity of money in the economy is fixed at $\overline{M}$. There is no more money available. As the public attempts to get more money, it sells bonds. This increases the interest rate on bonds. The interest rate continues to rise until the demands for money and for bonds are brought back into balance with their fixed supplies. This occurs at the interest rate R_1.

Figure 13.16 shows that as income rises from Y_0 to Y_1 to Y_2, the interest rate rises from R_0 to R_1 to R_2. The higher the income, the higher the transactions demand for money. Because the quantities of money and bonds are fixed, the interest rate must rise to offset the effect of income on the quantity of money demanded.

Figure 13.17 shows the relationship between the interest rate and income. The higher the income, the higher the interest rate required to equate money and bond demand to their fixed supplies. Thus, the higher the income, the higher the interest rate. The upward-sloping line in Figure 13.17 summarizes the information that is in Figure 13.16. Thus, the interest rate, R_0, and the income, Y_0, in Figure 13.17 correspond to R_0 and Y_0 in Figure 13.16, and so on. This relationship between income and the interest rate is called the *LM* curve. It represents points of equilibrium for money demanded and supply.[15]

We have shown why the *LM* curve is upward sloping, but we have not indicated why the slope might be relatively steep or flat. The slope of the *LM* curve is determined by the sensitivity of money demand to changes in income and by the sensitivity of money demand to changes in the interest rate.[16]

The role of the sensitivity of money demand to changes in income is illustrated in Figure 13.18. In Panel I, a rise in income produces a relatively small increase in money demand. In Panel II, the same increase in income produces a large increase in money demand. Thus, the income sensitivity of money demand, m_2, is larger in Panel II than in Panel I. Note that the rise in income produces a larger increase in the interest rate in Panel II than in Panel I. This is not surprising. It is assumed that the interest sensitivity of money demand (the slope of the money demand schedule) is the same in both panels. In Panel II the increase in income from Y_0 to Y_1 produces a larger increase in the quantity of money demanded at interest rate R_0 than in Panel I. Thus, a larger increase in the interest rate is required in Panel II to reduce the quantity of money demanded back to the fixed

---

[15] Following Keynes, the money demand function is often called the liquidity preference function and is denoted by the letter *L*. We have not used that terminology or notation, but we do follow tradition by labeling the curve *LM* to denote equality between money demand (*L*) and money supply (*M*). It should be noted that points on the *LM* curve also denote equality between bond demand and bond supply.

[16] Because of the interdependency of money and bond demand, one could just as easily say that the slope of the *LM* curve is determined by the income and interest sensitivity of bond demand.

FIGURE 13.17
THE *LM* CURVE.

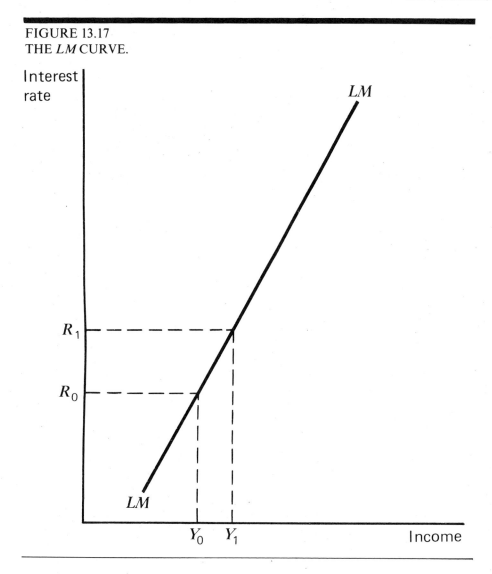

supply. We conclude that the greater the sensitivity of money demand to changes in income, m_2 (i.e., the greater the the shift in the money schedule demand when income changes), the greater the increase in the interest rate. Thus, the greater m_2, the steeper the *LM* curve.

The role of the interest sensitivity of money demand, m_1, is illustrated in Figure 13.19. In Panel I the money demand schedules are relatively flat. Thus, a change in the interest rate produces a relatively large change in the quantity of money demand. This means that m_1 is relatively large. In Panel II, money demand is less sensitive to changes in the interest rate. A change in the interest rate produces

FIGURE 13.18
THE EFFECT OF THE INCOME
SENSITIVITY OF MONEY DEMAND
ON THE RELATIONSHIP BETWEEN
INCOME AND THE INTEREST RATE.

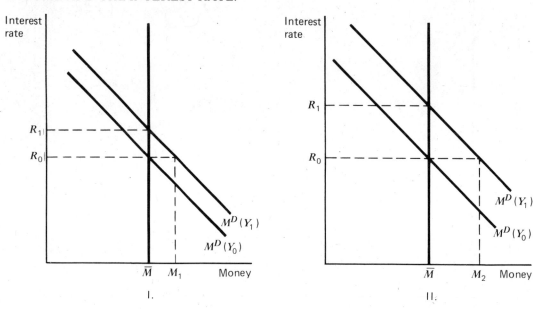

a relatively small change in the quantity of money demanded. This means that m_1 is relatively small. The less sensitive money demand is to changes in the interest rate, that is, the smaller m_1, the steeper the money demand schedule.

In both Panels I and II the response of money demand to an increase in income is assumed to be the same. Thus, in both cases, a rise in income from Y_0 to Y_1 produces an increase in the quantity of money demanded from M_0 to M_1. The interest rate must rise because at the interest rate R_0 the quantity of money demanded exceeds the supply in both panels by $(M_1 - \overline{M})$. The rise in the interest rate in Panel I is less than in Panel II, however. In Panel I, a rise in the interest rate produces a relatively large reduction in the quantity of money demanded. As a result, the interest rate does not have to rise by as much in Panel I to produce equality of money demand with the fixed supply as it does in Panel II. Thus, in Panel I demand equals supply at the interest rate R_1. At this interest rate, demand still exceeds supply in Panel II, so the interest rate has to rise further to R_2 to produce equilibrium. We conclude that the steeper the money demand schedule, that is, the smaller m_1, the greater the increase in the interest rate that is required to equate money demand with supply when income increases. Thus, the smaller m_1, the steeper the LM curve.

FIGURE 13.19
THE EFFECT OF THE INTEREST
SENSITIVITY OF MONEY DEMAND
ON THE RELATIONSHIP BETWEEN
INCOME AND THE INTEREST RATE.

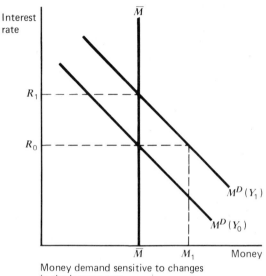

Money demand sensitive to changes
in the interest rate

I.

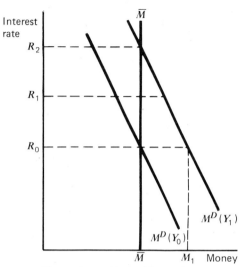

Money demand insensitive to changes
in the interest rate

II.

The determinants of the slope of the *LM* curve can be expressed algebraically. The *LM* curve shows the combinations of income levels and interest rates for which money demand equals money supply.[17] In our model,

$$M^D = m_0 - m_1 R + m_2 Y$$

$$M^D = \overline{M}.$$

Thus

$$\overline{M} = m_0 - m_1 R + m_2 Y$$

and

$$R = \frac{(m_0 - \overline{M})}{m_1} + \frac{m_2}{m_1} Y. \quad [18]$$

[17] The bond demand function is implied by the money demand schedule. Furthermore, bond demand equals bond supply when money demand equals money supply. It is not necessary, therefore, to take the bond market explicitly into account when deriving the *LM* curve.

[18] For the *LM* curve, it is convenient to solve for the interest rate in terms of income. This allows us to discuss shifts in the *LM* curve for a given value of income.

The slope of the LM curve, $\Delta R / \Delta Y$, is m_2/m_1. Thus, the slope is the response of money demand to a change in income, m_2, relative to the response of money demand to a change in the interest rate, m_1. It was shown in Figure 13.18 that the greater m_2, the greater the change in the interest rate required to equate money demand to the fixed supply when income changes. Furthermore, it was shown in Figure 13.19 that the smaller the response of money demand to a change in the interest rate, m_1, the greater the change in the interest rate required to equate money demand to the fixed supply when income changes. We conclude, therefore, that the greater m_2 is or the smaller m_1 is, or both, the steeper the LM curve is. The steeper the LM curve, the greater the increase in the interest rate required to equate money demand and supply when income rises.

The term $(m_0 - \overline{M})/m_1$ in the LM curve describes the factors that make the curve shift when income is unchanged. The first term in the parentheses is the intercept for the money demand schedule, m_0. If m_0 increases, the public wants to hold a larger amount of money given the interest rate and income.[19] As shown in Panel I of Figure 13.20, the interest rate rises from R_0 to R_1 when the money demand schedule shifts to the right. The extent of the shift in the money demand schedule is $m_0' - m_0 = \Delta m_0$. Given this shift, the extent of the rise in the interest rate is determined by the interest sensitivity of money demand, m_1. Note that the interest rate has risen, *given* income Y_0. This implies that the shift in the money demand schedule from $M^D(Y_0)$ to $M^{D\prime}(Y_0)$ makes the LM curve shift up. With the higher money demand schedule $M_D{}'$, the interest rate rises from R_0 to R_1 when income is Y_0. Thus, we move from point A on the LM curve in Panel II to point A' on the curve LM'. A' is only one point on the new curve LM'. Other points are obtained by considering the interest rates that must prevail to equate money demand to money supply at different levels of income. When income rises above Y_0, there is an increase in the transactions demand for money, and the interest rate must rise. The higher income, the higher the interest rate required to equate money demand with money supply. At each income level, the public demands a larger quantity of money when the intercept of the money demand schedule is m'_0 rather than on m_0. As a consequence, there is a higher interest rate at each income level than before. When the intercept of the money demand schedule increases, the LM shifts to up to LM'. At each income, there is a higher interest rate on LM' than LM. The extent of the upward shift of LM to LM' is $\Delta m_0/m_1$.

Another factor that shifts the LM curve is a change in the quantity of money $\Delta \overline{M}$. It is necessary to be careful at this point because we want to leave wealth unchanged. Because $\overline{W} = \overline{M} + \overline{B}$, this can be accomplished only if the quantity of bonds is reduced by the amount that the quantity of money increases: $\Delta \overline{M} = -\Delta \overline{B}$ or $(\overline{M}_1 - \overline{M}_0) = -(\overline{B}_1 - B_0)$. This feat can be achieved with an open market operation by the Federal Reserve. Recall that in our simplified world, all money is currency. For the quantity of money to increase, the Fed must purchase

---

[19] This implies that the public wants to reduce its bond holdings by the same amount.

FIGURE 13.20
SHIFTS IN MONEY DEMAND
PRODUCE SHIFTS IN THE *LM*
CURVE.

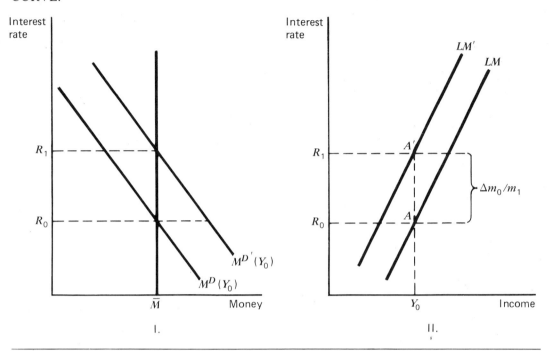

bonds with currency. Because there is no depository system, there is no multiple expansion of money and credit. The increase in money is simply the currency that the Fed issues to purchase bonds. Thus, the quantity of money (currency) increases, and the quantity of bonds decreases by an equal amount.[20] The Fed's open market operation leaves wealth unchanged but it has changed the quantities of money and bonds in the economy.[21]

Figure 13.21 shows the effect of an increase in the quantity of money, assuming that wealth is unchanged. In Panel I(a) the quantity of money increases from $\overline{M}_0$ to $\overline{M}_1$. The quantity of money demanded is now less than the quantity of money in the economy at the interest rate R_0. The public attempts to get rid of the

---

[20] The quantity of bonds, $\overline{B}$, includes only bonds held by the public. Thus, when the Fed purchases bonds, $\overline{B}$ declines and $\overline{M}$ rises.

[21] We are cheating a little bit here because the purchase of bonds raises their price and reduces the interest rate. The increase in the price of bonds increases their value which raises wealth. Complications of this sort are discussed in Chapter 15.

FIGURE 13.21
A CHANGE IN THE QUANTITY OF
MONEY (GIVEN WEALTH) SHIFTS
THE *LM* CURVE.

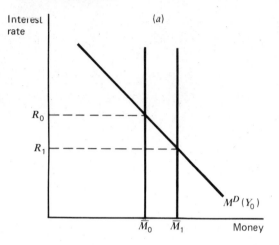

(a)

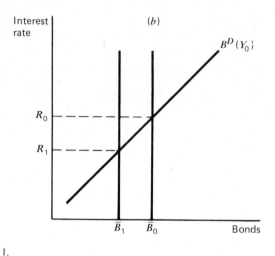

(b)

I.

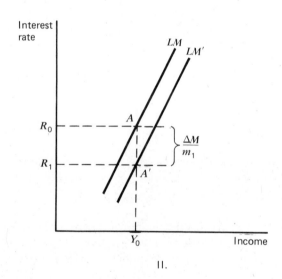

II.

unwanted money by purchasing bonds. This increases the price of bonds and reduces the interest rate. The interest rate must fall to R_1, where the public is willing to hold the larger quantity of money.

Panel I(*b*) shows the bond market. The quantity of bonds is reduced to $\bar{B}_1$, when the Fed purchases bonds and increases the quantity of money to $\bar{M}_1$. At the initial interest rate R_0, the public still wants to hold the quantity $\bar{B}_0$ of bonds. The public attempts to obtain bonds by reducing its money holdings. Thus, there is an excess of money supply over money demand equal to the excess of bond demand over bond supply. As the public attempts to purchase bonds, the price of bonds rises and the interest rate falls. The interest rate must fall to R_1 where the public is willing to hold the smaller quantity of bonds $\bar{B}_1$.

In the description of the movement to the lower interest rate R_1, income is held constant at Y_0. Thus, there is a lower interest rate at income Y_0. This means that the increase in the quantity of money (and decrease in the quantity of bonds) produces a downward shift in the LM curve. There is a movement from point A on the LM curve of Panel II to point A' on LM'. The extent of the shift depends upon the size of the increase in the quantity of money and upon the interest sensitivity of money demand. The steeper the money demand schedule, the larger the decline in the interest rate that occurs for a given increase in the quantity of money (purchase of bonds by the Fed). Thus, the smaller is m_1, that is, the smaller the interest sensitivity of money demand, the greater the shift in the LM curve.

The increase in the quantity of money gives only one point on LM' because we have assumed that income is Y_0. If income rises above Y_0 (not shown in Figure 13.21), there is an increase in the transactions demand for money, and the money demand schedule shifts to the right. This produces an increase in the interest rate. Thus, the higher the income, the higher the interest rate at which money demand equals money supply. Because the quantity of money is greater as a result of the Fed's open market operation, the interest rate required to equate money demand and supply is lower at every income level. Thus, the LM curve shifts from LM to LM' as shown in Panel II of Figure 13.21. The extent of the downward shift is $(\bar{M}_1 - \bar{M}_0)/m_1 = \Delta \bar{M}/m_1$.

PUTTING THE PIECES TOGETHER: DETERMINING INCOME AND THE INTEREST RATE

In this section, the IS and LM curves are combined to determine the equilibrium values of income and the interest rate. It is shown that there is an interaction between aggregate expenditures, as summarized by the IS curve, and the financial sector, as summarized by the LM curve. This interaction determines the interest rate and income.

The IS curve indicates the combinations of income and the interest rate at which desired saving is equal to desired investment. The higher income, the greater saving. In order for this higher saving to equal desired investment, the interest rate must be lower to induce greater investment. Thus, the IS curve is downward sloping. In principle, the economy can be at any point on the IS curve. If income is high, the interest rate must be low in order to equate desired saving and investment. If income is low, the interest rate must be high. The IS curve indicates the combinations of income and the interest rate that equate desired savings and investment. It cannot tell us what the actual interest rate and income will be in the economy.

The *LM* curve indicates the combinations of income and the interest rate at which money demand equals the fixed quantity of money. The higher the income, the higher the transactions demand for money and, therefore, the higher the interest rate that equates money demand with money supply. Thus, the *LM* curve is upward sloping. In principle, the economy can be at any point on the *LM* curve. Thus, income and the interest rate may be high, or income and interest rate may be low. All we know from the *LM* curve is that when income rises, the interest rate must also rise to maintain equality of money demand and money supply. The *LM* curve cannot tell us what the actual value of the interest rate and of income will be.

Income and the interest rate are determined simultaneously by the interaction between the financial (*LM*) and the real (*IS*) sectors of the economy. This interaction is summarized by the intersection of the *IS* and *LM* curves. Panel I of Figure 13.22 shows the intersection of an *IS* and an *LM* curve. The economy is at equilibrium at Y_E and R_E because desired saving equals desired investment and the demand for money equals the supply of money. Panel II shows aggregate expenditures, saving and investment, money demand and supply, and bond demand and supply. When income is Y_E and the interest rate is R_E, everything is in balance. Aggregate expenditures equal income, saving equals investment, money demand equals money supply, and bond demand equals bond supply.

The economy moves from one equilibrium to another when there are shifts in the *IS* and *LM* curves. In discussing these shifts, we recall that the *IS* curve is a summary of the behavioral relations specifying investment demand, saving, and consumption. Thus, the *IS* curve shifts because there are shifts in the consumption and saving functions or in the investment function. Similarly, the *LM* curve summarizes the behavioral relations in the money and bond markets under the assumption of a fixed quantity of money and bonds. The *LM* curve shifts because the demand schedules for money and bonds shift or the quantities of money and bonds change.

Because there are so many factors that can shift the *IS* and *LM* curves, the discussion can be made more orderly by looking at the situation algebraically. The aggregate expenditure (*IS*) sector is given by

$$Y = C + I$$
$$Y = C + S$$
$$C = c_0 + c_1 Y$$
$$S = s_0 + s_1 Y = -c_0 + (1 - c_1) Y$$
$$I = i_0 - i_1 R .$$

FIGURE 13.22
DETERMINING THE EQUILIBRIUM
INCOME AND INTEREST RATE.

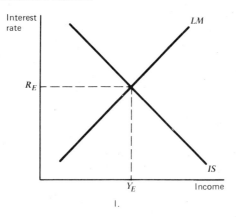

I.

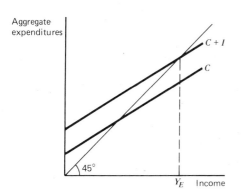

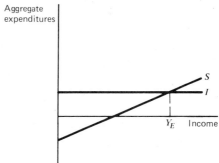

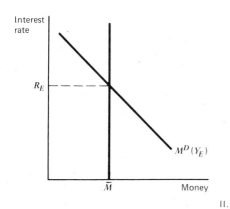

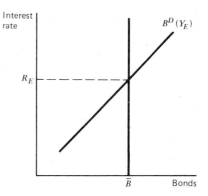

II.

The financial (LM) sector is given by

$$M^D = m_0 - m_1 R + m_2 Y$$

$$B^D = b_0 + b_1 R - b_2 Y = -m_0 + m_1 R - m_2 Y$$

$$M^D = \overline{M}$$

$$B^D = \overline{B} .$$

Solutions for the IS and LM sectors give the following IS and LM curves:

IS:

$$Y = \frac{c_0 + i_0}{s_1} - \frac{i_1}{s_1} R ,$$

LM:

$$R = \frac{m_0 - \overline{M}}{m_1} + \frac{m_2}{m_1} Y .$$

The IS curve shifts with shifts in the consumption and investment functions, that is, with c_0 and i_0. The extent of the shift in the IS curve for given shifts in the consumption or investment function depends upon the marginal propensity to save, s_1. The LM curve shifts with shifts in the money demand function, m_0, and with changes in the quantity of money, $\overline{M}$. The extent of the shift depends upon the interest sensitivity of money demand, m_1.

For the IS curve, shifts in the consumption and investment functions produce a change in the income that goes with a *given* value of the interest rate. When the real and financial sectors interact, a shift in the IS curve is combined with a fixed LM curve. There is a change in the interest rate when income changes, and this, in turn, affects the amount by which income changes. Thus, income and the interest rate interact as the economy moves from one equilibrium to another. Similarly, for the LM curve, shifts in the money demand function or changes in the quantity of money produce a change in the interest rate that goes with a *given* value of income. When a shift in the LM curve is combined with a fixed IS curve, the level of income changes when the interest rate changes. This, in turn, affects the changes in the interest rate. Again, the interest rate and income interact as the economy moves from on equilibrium to another.

Figure 13.23 shows the effect on the interest rate and income when the IS curve shifts to the right. Assume the shift occurs as the result of an upward shift in the consumption function from c_0 to c'_0. Thus, $\Delta c_0 = c'_0 - c_0$. Given the initial value of the interest rate, R_E, aggregate expenditures and income rise by $\Delta Y = \Delta c_0 / s_1$. Thus, if the interest rate were to remain constant, the decision of households to devote a higher proportion of income to consumption (and, therefore, a lower proportion of income to saving) produces a multiple expansion in aggregate expenditures and income to Y_H. The size of the multiplier is determined by the marginal propensity to save, s_1. We know, however, that the interest rate cannot

FIGURE 13.23
THE EFFECTS OF A SHIFT IN THE
IS CURVE.

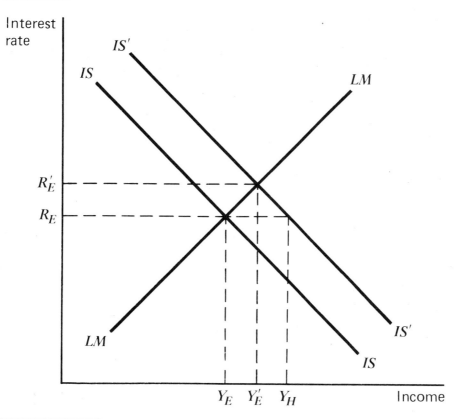

remain constant when income increases. The rise in income increases the transactions demand for money. Thus, at the initial interest rate, R_E, the public wants
to hold more money and less bonds when income increases. This produces an increase in the interest rate. The increase in the interest rate reduces investment.
This response of investment limits the expansion of income.

The new equilibrium occurs at the intersection of *IS'* with *LM*. Income is
higher at Y'_E than at Y_E, but the expansion of income is smaller than indicated by
the multiplier relation $(Y_H - Y_E) = \Delta Y = \Delta c_0/s_1$. When income rises, the interest rate also rises because of the increased transactions demand for money.
Thus, we move up the *LM* curve. This rise in the interest rate reduces investment
demand. As the interest rate increases, we move up *IS'*. The rise in the interest
rate also encourages the public to economize on its money balances. This reduces

the excess demand for money. The excess demand is also reduced because income does not rise by the full amount ($Y_H - Y_E$). In the new equilibrium, income and the interest rate rise to Y'_E and R'_E, respectively.[22]

The amount by which income increases and the extent of the rise in the interest rate depend upon a variety of factors. The role of the various factors can be summarized algebraically by solving the *IS* and *LM* sectors simultaneously for income and the interest rate. The expression for income is

$$Y = \frac{c_0 + i_0 - (i_1/m_1)m_0 + (i_1/m_1)\overline{M}}{s_1 + (m_2/m_1)i_1}.$$

This rather formidable expression is useful for evaluating the effects of shifts in the *IS* and *LM* curves on the equilibrium level of income.[23]

Let us return to a shift in the *IS* curve caused by an upward shift in the consumption function. The expression for income indicates the change in income that results for a change in the intercept of the consumption function. Thus,

$$\Delta Y = \frac{\Delta c_0}{s_1 + (m_2/m_1)i_1}.$$

The extent of the rise in income following an upward shift in the consumption function depends, in part, upon the multiplier for aggregate income given the interest rate, that is, upon s_1. The smaller the marginal propensity to save, s_1, the greater the increase in income.

The extent of the rise in income following a shift in the *IS* curve also depends upon the slope of the *LM* curve, m_2/m_1. If the increase in income did not produce an increase in the transactions demand for money, then $m_2 = 0.0$, and the rise in income would be the full amount $\Delta c_0/s_1$. In this case, the *LM* curve is horizontal, and income rises by the full amount of the shift in the *IS* curve. When the transactions demand for money is not zero, the multiplier is reduced (larger denominator). The effect of the transactions demand for money, m_2, on the change in income depends upon the ratio of m_2 to the interest sensitivity of money demand, m_1. Note that the ratio m_2/m_1 is the slope of the *LM* curve. For a given value of m_1, the greater the increase in money demand in response to a rise in income, m_2, the greater the increase in the interest rate required to equate money demand to money supply. Thus, the greater m_2 is, the steeper the *LM* curve is. The greater the rise in the interest rate required to maintain equilibrium between money demand and money supply when income rises, the smaller the rise in income. This is true because when the interest rate rises, investment demand is reduced (i_1). Furthermore, the smaller m_1 is, the less sensitive money

---

[22] We have used the expository device of separating the movement from one equilibrium to another into a series of steps. In reality, all variables are adjusting at once.

[23] An expression can also be derived for the interest rate. As it is sufficient for our purposes to analyze algebraically the effects of *IS* and *LM* shifts on income, the reader is spared from wrestling with the expression for the interest rate.

demand is to a change in the interest rate. Thus, the smaller m_1 is, the greater the increase in the interest rate required to equate money demand to money supply when there is an increase in the transactions demand for money. The smaller m_1, the greater the rise in the interest rate and, therefore, the greater the negative effect on investment. Thus, a low value of m_1 reduces the multiplier. Conversely, if money demand is highly sensitive to the interest rate, that is, if m_1 is large, the multiplier is not reduced very much.

Finally, the size of the multiplier is affected by the sensitivity of investment to a change in the interest rate. The higher the sensitivity of investment demand to a change in the interest rate, i_1, the greater the reduction in investment that occurs when the interest rate rises. This decline in investment reduces the expansion of income that occurs when the consumption function shifts up. Thus, the greater i_1 is, the smaller the multiplier is.

Figure 13.24 shows the effect on the rise of income of having LM curves with different slopes. This involves different values for the ratio m_2/m_1. The LM curve is relatively flat when the transactions demand for money is not very responsive to a change in income, (small m_1), or when money demand is highly sensitive to a change in the interest rate (large m_2), or both. If $m_1/m_2 = 0.0$, the LM curve is horizontal (LM_1), and there is a full multiplier effect, $\Delta c_0/s_1$, from an upward shift in the consumption function. In this case, income rises from Y_0 to Y_1, and there is no increase in the interest rate. The higher m_1/m_2, the steeper the LM curve and the smaller the increase in income. Thus, for LM_2, income rises only from Y_0 to Y_2, and the interest rate rises from R_0 to R_2. In the limiting case, m_1/m_2 is infinite, and the LM curve is vertical (LM_3). In this situation, the interest rate rises to R_3, and there is no rise in income. When the LM curve is vertical, the interest rate must rise until investment is reduced sufficiently to offset the effects of the upward shift in the consumption function. Only then is money demand brought back into equality with money supply.

Figure 13.24 illustrates the importance of the financial sector in determining equilibrium income in the economy. Because a rise in income increases the transactions demand for money, the interest rate must rise to bring money demand into equality with the fixed quantity of money. The increase in the interest rate reduces investment. This, in turn, reduces the expansion of income.

With an upward-sloping LM curve, the paradox of thrift is less of a paradox. A decrease in desired saving produces a downward shift in the saving function and an upward shift in the consumption function. This does produce a rise in income and saving, but it is no longer true that saving has to return to its value prior to the shift. Because the interest rate rises, investment is reduced and the expansion of income is retarded. The steeper the LM curve, the smaller the rise in income and, therefore, the smaller the induced rise in saving.

This discussion illustrates the importance of an upward-sloping LM curve, but it also illustrates that the interest sensitivity of investment is important in determining the change in income that occurs when the IS curve shifts. Figure 13.25 shows the effects on the change in income of different values of the interest sensitivity of investment demand, i_1. When $i_1 = 0.0$, investment is totally unresponsive

FIGURE 13.24
THE EFFECT ON INCOME AND THE
INTEREST RATE OF AN UPWARD
SHIFT IN THE CONSUMPTION
FUNCTION FOR *LM* CURVES OF
DIFFERENT SLOPES.

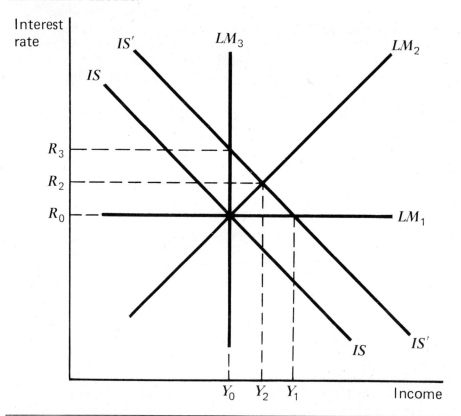

to a change in the interest rate. In this case, the rise in the interest rate that results
from the rise in income does not reduce investment. The *IS* curve is vertical. This
situation is shown in Panel I. When the *IS* curve is vertical, there is a full multiplier effect, $\Delta c_0/s_1$, of an upward shift in the consumption function. The *IS* curve
shifts from *IS* to *IS'*. The rise in income increases the interest rate, but investment
is not reduced. The interest rate has to rise to R_1, where money demand equals
the fixed supply when income is Y_1.

When the interest sensitivity of investment demand is not zero, the *IS* curve is
downward sloping. The larger i_1, the flatter the curve. Panel II shows the situation where a rise in the interest rate chokes off a large amount of investment. The

FIGURE 13.25
THE EFFECT ON INCOME AND THE
INTEREST RATE OF AN UPWARD
SHIFT IN THE CONSUMPTION
FUNCTION FOR *IS* CURVES WITH
DIFFERENT SLOPES.

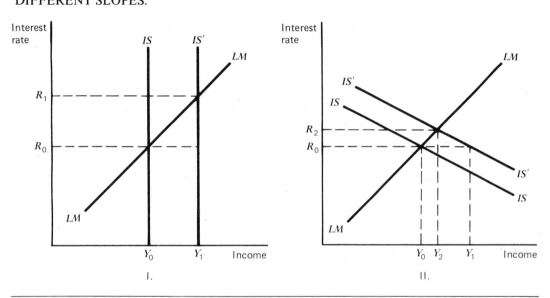

I.

II.

rise in income is reduced from $(Y_1 - Y_0)$ to $(Y_2 - Y_0)$. Thus, as the *IS* curve becomes flatter, the rise in income is reduced.[24]

It should be noted that the relationship between the extent of the rise in the interest rate and the extent of the rise in income depends upon the slopes of both the
IS and the *LM* curves. In Figure 13.24, when the *LM* curve is flat, there is no rise
in the interest rate, and, therefore, there is no reduction in investment demand.
Thus, there is the full multiplier effect, $\Delta c_0/s_1$. The diagram illustrates that the
steeper the *LM* curve, the larger the increase in the interest rate, and the smaller
the rise in income. In Figure 13.25, the flatter the *IS* curve, the smaller the rise in
income, and the smaller the rise in the interest rate. In this situation, an increase in
the interest rate produces a large reduction in investment demand. This limits the
rise in income, and it also limits the increase in the transactions demand for money. Thus, neither income nor the interest rate rise very much. If the *IS* curve is
relatively steep, a rise in the interest rate does not produce a substantial reduction

[24] In the limiting case, i_1 is infinite, the *IS* curve is horizontal, and income does not rise at
all.

in investment demand. In this case, there is a relatively large rise in both income and the interest rate.

We now turn to the effects of a shift in the *LM* curve. The curve shifts as a result of either a shift in the money demand function or a change in the quantity of money. When the money demand schedule shifts, the change in income is

$$\Delta Y = -\Delta m_0 \cdot \frac{i_1/m_1}{s_1 + (m_2/m_1)i_1}.$$

When the money demand schedule shifts up, that is, Δm_0 is positive, the interest rate rises, and income falls. When the demand schedule shifts down, that is, when Δm_0 is negative, the interest rate falls, and income rises. We get the same multiplier expression for change in the quantity of money.[25]

$$\Delta Y = \Delta \overline{M} \cdot \frac{i_1/m_1}{s_1 + (m_2/m_1)i_1}.$$

An increase in the quantity of money, given the money demand function, has the same effect as a downward shift in money demand, given the quantity of money. In both cases, the quantity of money exceeds the demand at the initial values of the interest rate and income. This leads to a reduction in the interest rate and a rise in income. A decrease in the quantity of money or an upward shift in money demand causes money demand to exceed money supply at the initial values of the interest rate and income. This raises the interest rate and reduces income.

Now let us examine the multiplier in more detail. An increase in the quantity of money shifts the *LM* curve down by the amount $\Delta \overline{M}/m_1$.[26] Given income, the smaller the interest sensitivity of money demand, the greater the decline in the interest rate required to equate the quantity of money demanded to the increased supply. Thus, the smaller m_1, the larger the downward shift in the *LM* curve. The effect that this shift has on income depends upon the slopes of the *IS* and *LM* curves.

For the *IS* curve, $\Delta Y/\Delta R = -i_1/s_1$. This indicates the rise in aggregate income that results from a decline in the interest rate. The greater the interest rate sensitivity of investment demand, i_1, the greater the increase in investment that results from a decline in the interest rate. The extent of the effect of the increase in investment on aggregate expenditures depends upon the marginal propensity to save, s_1. Thus, the greater i_1 or the smaller s_1, or both, the flatter the *IS* curve.

Panel I of Figure 13.26 shows that if the *IS* curve is relatively flat (IS_1), there is a relatively large expansion of income ($Y_1 - Y_0$) as a result of a downward shift in the *LM* curve from *LM* to *LM'*. Conversely, if the *IS* curve is steep (IS_2), there is a relatively small rise in income ($Y_2 - Y_0$). Note that with a flat *IS* curve, the de-

---

[25] Recall that this means that there is an open market operation that changes the quantity of bonds dollar for dollar with a change in money.
[26] The discussion is restricted to the effects of an increase in the quantity of money but the same effects occur when there is a downward shift in the money demand function.

FIGURE 13.26
THE EFFECTS ON INCOME AND THE
INTEREST RATE OF AN INCREASE
IN THE QUANTITY OF MONEY.

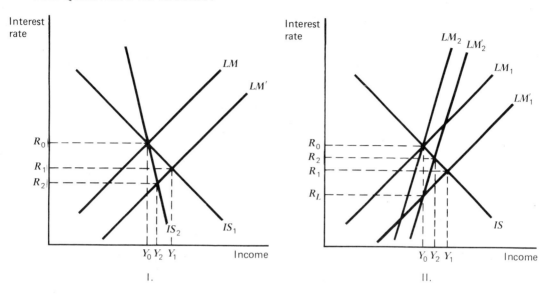

I.   II.

cline in the equilibrium interest rate is less than for a steep *IS* curve. With a flat
IS curve, the rise in income is greater, and this produces a larger increase in the
transactions demand for money than occurs for a smaller rise in income. The
higher transactions demand for money produces a relatively large upward shift in
the money demand schedule. This offsets some of the decline in the interest rate
that occurs when the quantity of money increases.

Panel II shows the effects on the equilibrium income and interest rate of
different assumptions concerning the slope of the *LM* curve. Consider the case of
a relatively flat *LM* curve. An increase in the quantity of money shifts LM_1 to
LM'_1. Given income Y_0, this would reduce the interest rate to R_L. At this low interest rate, desired investment exceeds desired saving, so income rises. The rise in
income increases the transactions demand for money. Thus, the money demand
function shifts up and the interest rate rises relative to R_L. Income continues to
rise, and the interest rate continues to increase relative to R_L until a new equilibrium is reached at Y_1 and R_1. Income is higher and the interest rate is lower relative to the initial equilibrium Y_0 and R_0. Now consider a downward shift in the
LM curve of the same magnitude but with steeper *LM* curves. The shift from
LM_2 to LM'_2 would also produce a decline in the interest rate to R_L if income
remained at Y_0. As before, the decline in the interest rate increases investment

expenditures. Now, however, with a steeper LM curve, a rise in income produces a larger increase in the interest rate relative to R_L. This occurs because the income sensitivity of money demand, m_2, is greater for LM_2 and LM'_2 than for LM_1 and LM'_1.[27] With the steeper curve, LM'_2, the new equilibrium is at Y_2 and R_2. Thus, the steeper the LM curve, the smaller the increase in income, and the smaller the decline in the interest rate that occurs when the quantity of money increases.

SUMMARY

In this chapter we looked at the interaction of the financial (LM) and real (IS) sectors of the economy. In order to keep the story as simple as possible, we held the price level constant, the government sector was absent, there were no depository institutions, and international considerations were excluded. Even in this simple world, monetary and financial variables affect interest rates and aggregate income.

Aggregate expenditures (consumption and investment) are affected by aggregate income and interest rates. Money and bond demand are also affected by aggregate income and interest rates. The economy is in equilibrium when the quantity of money demanded equals the supply of money and when desired saving equals desired investment. Equality of money demand and supply implies equality of bond demand and supply. Equality of desired saving and investment implies that aggregate income equals desired aggregate expenditures. Equilibrium is achieved through interaction of the financial and real sectors of the economy. This determines both aggregate income and the interest rate. Shifts in consumption or investment demand and shifts in money demand or supply affect aggregate income and the interest rate.

The response of income and interest rates to these shifts depends upon the marginal propensity to save, the interest sensitivity of investment demand, the income sensitivity of money demand, and the interest rate sensitivity of money demand. As we shall see in the next chapter, these factors have important implications for monetary and fiscal policy.

---

[27] The size of the downward shift in the LM curve depends upon the size of m_1. The lower the interest sensitivity of money demand, m_1, the greater the reduction in the interest rate that equates money demand to the increased supply at the income, Y_0 (see Figure 13.19). Thus, the smaller m_1, the larger the downward shift in LM. Panel II of Figure 13.26 shows the effect of different values of the income sensitivity of money demand, m_2, given m_1.

SELECTED REFERENCES

Dornbusch, Rudiger and Stanley Fischer, *Macroeconomics*, 2nd ed., New York: McGraw-Hill, 1981.

Gordon, Robert, *Macroeconomics*, 2nd ed., Boston: Little, Brown and Company, 1981.

THE ROLE OF GOVERNMENT AND OF DEPOSITORY INSTITUTIONS

14

This chapter expands the *IS-LM* model of Chapter 13 to include the government and depository institutions. These additions allow us to identify some of the effects of fiscal and monetary policy on aggregate expenditures, income and interest rates. Various mixes of monetary and fiscal policy designed to achieve high levels of output and rapid capital formation are studied. The price level is still held constant and international considerations are excluded in this chapter, however. This limits our ability to analyze the effects of monetary and fiscal policy fully.

THE GOVERNMENT

Government purchases of goods and services are a component of aggregate expenditures.[1] When the government purchases defense goods; when it pays military and civilian wages; and when it purchases supplies, computers, and other equipment, it is contributing to aggregate expenditures. Thus, government purchases of goods and services contribute directly to the income of the factors of production. Total output in the economy, Q, equals total income, Y, which equals total expenditures: $Q = Y = C + I + G$, where G is government purchases of goods and services.

---

[1] The government sector includes the federal government as well as state and local governments. Since we are concerned with fiscal policy, only the role of the federal government is considered explicitly.

Other activities of government affect aggregate expenditures indirectly. In Chapter 13 it was shown that total income is allocated between consumption and saving: $Y = C + S$. This is no longer true when we allow for the government sector. Part of the income earned by the factors of production goes to the government as taxes. This means that income available for consumption and saving is reduced by the amount of taxes paid. Furthermore, much of government spending is not for goods and services, but rather for social security payments, welfare, unemployment compensation, and interest on government debt. These expenditures are called *transfer payments*. They are not payments for currently produced goods and services and, therefore, are not payments for factor services. Transfer payments do add to the income of households, however.

Taxes and government transfers affect the income that is available to households for consumption and saving. This income is called *disposable income* and is defined as $Y_d = Y - T + TP$, where Y_d is disposable income, Y is aggregate income (output), T is taxes, and TP is transfer payments. Thus, given total income, tax payments reduce disposable income, and transfer payments increase disposable income. It is disposable income that the public allocates between consumption and saving: $Y_d = C + S$. Consumption plus saving does not equal total income in the economy; it equals disposable income. The relationship between aggregate expenditures and aggregate income is given by

$$C + I + G = Y = C + S + (T - TP).$$

Aggregate expenditures equal aggregate income, but they exceed consumption plus private saving by the excess of the public's tax payments over receipts of transfer payments.

With the introduction of the government sector, the consumption and saving functions of Chapter 13 must be modified. Consumption and saving do not depend on total income, they depend upon disposable income. Consider the consumption and saving functions used in Chapter 13. In those functions, it was assumed that only income affects consumption and saving behavior. They must be rewritten as

$$C = c_0 + c_1 Y_d$$
$$S = s_0 + s_1 Y_d \, .$$

Because $Y_d = C + S$, it is still true that the saving function is implied by the consumption function; that is, $s_0 = -c_0$, and $s_1 = (1 - c_1)$.

In order to see how taxes and transfer payments affect consumption and saving, we must specify the determinants of tax payments and of transfer payments. Assume that all taxes are income taxes imposed on the income from factor services and that there is a single tax rate, t, for all factor income.[2] Given these sim-

___

[2] It is implicitly assumed that taxes are not imposed on transfer payments. This is a valid assumption for many types of transfer payments but not for interest on government debt. It is possible to allow for taxation of these transfer payments, but the analysis would be complicated and the basic conclusions in the text would not be affected.

plifying assumptions, the tax receipts of the government (tax payments of the public) are

$$T = tY \ .$$

Thus, if $t = .20$, taxes rise by \$.20 for every \$1 increase in aggregate income.

Now let us turn to transfer payments. Some government transfer payments are unrelated to economic conditions whereas others vary with income and interest rates. For example, there are base levels of social security, welfare, and other payments that do not vary with aggregate income or interest rates. Some transfer payments do vary with economic conditions, however. For example, when aggregate income is high, fewer people receive welfare and unemployment benefits than when income is low. Furthermore, when interest rates are high, interest payments on government debt are higher than when interest rates are low. These considerations suggest an expression for transfer payments of the form

$$TP = tp_0 - tp_1 Y + tp_2 R \ .$$

The parameter, tp_0, indicates the base level of transfer payments that is independent of income and the interest rate. The parameter tp_1 enters with a negative sign indicating that when income rises, transfer payments decline, and that when income falls, the payments increase. The parameter tp_2 gets a positive sign indicating that transfer payments (interest payments) rise when the interest rate increases, and they fall when the interest rate declines. Changes in the interest rate only affect government interest payments for existing debt as old securities mature and new ones are issued. Because a substantial proportion of government securities matures during any year, the effects of interest rate changes are quickly translated into changes in government interest payments.

Recalling that the consumption function is

$$C = c_0 + c_1 Y_d$$

and

$$Y_d = Y - T + TP$$

we have

$$C = c_0 + c_1 (Y - T + TP) \ .$$

Because

$$T = tY$$

and

$$TP = tp_0 - tp_1 Y + tp_2 R$$

we have

$$C = c_0 + c_1 (Y - tY + tp_0 - tp_1 Y + tp_2 R)$$

so

$$C = c_0 + c_1 tp_0 + c_1 (1 - t - tp_1) Y + c_1 tp_2 R \ .$$

Thus, consumption varies with aggregate income, Y, but the relationship depends not only upon the marginal propensity to consume, c_1, but also upon the tax rate, t, and upon the responsiveness of transfer payments to changes in income, tp_1. An example makes the point. Assume the marginal propensity to consume is 0.8, the tax rate is 0.3, and transfer payments fall by \$0.05 when income rises by \$1, that is, $tp_1 = 0.05$. Given the interest rate, R, and given the base level of transfer payments, tp_0, a rise in total income of \$100 increases tax payments by \$20, and it reduces transfer payments by \$5. Thus, when aggregate income increases by \$100, disposable income rises by \$75. Consumption rises by the marginal propensity to consume times the increase in disposable income, or .8(\$75) = \$60.00. Even though the marginal propensity to consume is 0.8, a \$100 rise to aggregate income only produces a \$60 increase in consumption.

The expression derived for the consumption function allows us to calculate the rise in consumption directly. The change in consumption is

$$\Delta C = c_1(1 - t - tp_1)\Delta Y$$

$$\Delta C = .8(1.0 - 0.2 - 0.05)\$100 = 0.8(0.75)\$100 = \$60.$$

Note that without a government sector, aggregate income and disposable income are the same, so $\Delta Y = \Delta T_d = \$100$. Thus, $\Delta C = 0.8(\$100) = \$80$. There is a larger increase in consumption than is the case when taxes rise and transfer payments decline in response to a rise in aggregate income. Thus, the effect of tax payments that vary positively with income and of transfer payments that vary negatively with income is to reduce the sensitivity to consumption to changes in aggregate income. We shall see later that the tax and transfer systems act as "built-in stabilizers" that reduce economic fluctuations.

Now consider the situation where aggregate income remains unchanged, but the interest rate rises. This increases interest payments on government debt. These transfer payments rise by $tp_2\Delta R$. Thus, with aggregate income unchanged, disposable income rises by $tp_2\Delta R$. This increase in disposable income raises consumption by the marginal propensity to consume times the change in disposable income, or $\Delta C = c_1 tp_2 \Delta R$. Thus, with aggregate income unchanged, a rise in the interest rate increases consumption.

The *IS* Curve

The role of the government sector in affecting aggregate expenditures and income can be seen by deriving a new *IS* curve for the model of Chapter 13. When that model is modified to include the government sector, we have

$$Y = C + I + \overline{G}\ ^3$$

---

[3] A bar over government expenditures on goods and services indicates that this element of aggregate expenditures is assumed to be fixed.

$$Y_d = Y - T + TP$$

$$T = tY$$

$$TP = tp_0 - tp_1 Y + tp_2 R$$

$$C = c_0 + c_1 Y_d$$

$$I = i_0 - i_1 R .$$

The solution to these equations gives the following expression for the *IS* curve:

$$Y = \frac{c_0 + i_0 + \overline{G} + c_1 tp_0}{1 - c_1(1 - t - tp_1)} - \frac{(i_1 - c_1 tp_2)}{1 - c_1(1 - t - tp_1)} R .$$

Note that if there were no government sector, $\overline{G}$, tp_0, tp_1, and t would all be zero and the expression reduces to

$$Y = \frac{c_0 + i_0}{1 - c_1} - \frac{i_1}{1 - c_1} R .$$

Because $1 - c_1 = s_1$,

$$Y = \frac{c_0 + i_0}{s_1} - \frac{i_1}{s_1} R$$

which is the expression for the *IS* curve obtained in Chapter 13.

It is instructive to compare the *IS* curves with and without a government sector. When there is a government, the intercept of the *IS* curve is

$$\frac{c_0 + i_0 + \overline{G} + c_1 tp_0}{1 - c_1(1 - t - tp_1)} .$$

This indicates that if there is a shift in the consumption function, the change in income, given the interest rate, is

$$\Delta Y = \frac{\Delta c_0}{1 - c_1(1 - t - tp_1)} .$$

This is a smaller change in income (smaller shift in *IS*) than occurs when there is no government, that is, when t and tp_1 are zero

$$\Delta Y = \frac{\Delta c_0}{1 - c_1} .$$

The change in income is smaller when there is government because changes in aggregate expenditures coming from the shift in the consumption function change disposable income by less than they change aggregate income. As a result, the induced change in consumption is less, and, therefore, the total change in income is reduced. The higher the tax rate, t, and the greater the negative response of transfers to a change in income, tp_1, the smaller the change in disposable income for a given change in aggregate income. Thus, the larger t and tp_1 are, the smaller the shift in the *IS* curve is.

Sources of shifts in the *IS* curve can be summarized in terms of the income multiplier, given the interest rate. Expressing this multiplier as $m_Y(R)$,

$$\Delta Y = \Delta c_0 \cdot m_Y(R) \quad ^4$$

$$\Delta Y = \Delta i_0 \cdot m_Y(R)$$

$$\Delta Y = \Delta \bar{G} \cdot m_Y(R)$$

$$\Delta Y = c_1 \Delta tp_0 \cdot m_Y(R)$$

where

$$m_Y(R) = \frac{1}{1 - c_1(1 - t - tp_1)}.$$

Note that a change in government expenditures on goods and services, $\Delta \bar{G}$, has the same effect on income as a change in c_0 or i_0. All three factors represent shifts in aggregate expenditures, which produce the same multiple change in income. Taxes and transfer payments act as built-in stabilizers that reduce the responsiveness of aggregate expenditures and income to shifts in the consumption and investment functions or to changes in government spending.

A change in government expenditures has a larger effect on equilibrium income than does a change in the base level of transfer payments, Δtp_0. When government expenditures on goods and services rise, there is a direct increase in aggregate expenditures and income. Once aggregate income increases, disposable income rises, and, therefore, consumption increases. When transfer payments increase, that is, $\Delta tp_0 > 0$, there is no direct increase in aggregate expenditures on currently produced output. Disposable income does increase, however, and there is an induced increase in consumption. An increase in transfer payments misses the "first-round" of the increase in aggregate income and, therefore, produces a smaller increase in equilibrium income. Thus, the initial increase in aggregate expenditures is only the initial increase in consumption that occurs when transfer payments increase. This increase in consumption is $c_1 \Delta tp_0$. It is this magnitude that produces a multiple expansion of income. For example, if the marginal propensity to consume, c_1, is 0.8, a rise in transfer payments has only eight tenths of the effect of a rise of equal size in government expenditures on goods and services.

The slope of the *IS* curve is also affected when government is introduced. In the absence of government,

$$\Delta Y / \Delta R = -i_1 / s_1.$$

With government,

$$\Delta Y / \Delta R = -(i_1 - c_1 tp_2) / [1 - c_1(1 - t - tp_1)].$$

---

[4] The interest rate, R, is shown in parentheses to indicate that the multipliers are for a given value of R.

Thus, the numerator is reduced, and the denominator is increased when the government sector is introduced. With a government sector, a rise in the interest rate is associated with a smaller reduction in aggregate expenditures. When the interest rate rises, there is a reduction in investment as shown by the parameter i_1 in the numerator. This fall in aggregate demand is offset to the extent that the rise in the interest rate produces increases in interest payments on government bonds. This increase in transfer payments raises disposable income, and consumption rises by $c_1 tp_2$ for every \$1 increase in disposable income. Thus, a rise in interest payments on government debt (transfer payments) offsets some of the decline in investment that occurs when the interest rate rises. Conversely, if the interest rate declines, investment increases. This raises aggregate expenditures and income. The rise is offset to some degree by a decline in transfer payments and disposable income that occurs when interest payments on government bonds decline.

The denominator of the slope of the *IS* curve is the multiplier expression discussed earlier. It was already shown that the income tax and transfer payments increase the denominator. Thus, the greater t and tp_1, the smaller the multiplier. We conclude that the tax and transfer payment systems produce a smaller change in income in response to a change in the interest rate than would exist in the absence of government.

Figure 14.1 compares the shifts in the *IS* curve and the slopes of IS curve for a world with government to one without government. We see that the rightward shift in the *IS* curve that occurs when the consumption or investment function shifts up is smaller when there are government taxes and transfer payments. The *IS* curve is also steeper when there is a government sector.[5] The shifts in the *IS* curve are smaller, and the *IS* curve is steeper, the higher is the tax rate, t, and the greater is the negative response of transfer payments to a change in income, tp_1. The size of the response of interest payments on government debt (transfer payments) to a change in the interest rate, tp_2, affects the slope of the *IS* curve, but not the size of the shifts. The larger is tp_2, the steeper is the slope of the *IS* curve.

Fiscal Policy: Step I

With the introduction of the government sector, it is possible to examine the effects of changes in government spending and taxes on aggregate expenditures and equilibrium income. The government has four instruments for affecting aggregate expenditures and income. It can change expenditures on goods and services, $\bar{G}$; it can change the base level of transfer payments, tp_0; it can change

---

[5] In discussing the slope of the *IS* curve in the text, we concluded that the government sector reduces $\Delta Y / \Delta R$. Recall that the convention in graphing the *IS* curve is to put R on the vertical axis and Y on the horizontal axis. Thus, the slope of the *IS* curve in Figure 14.1 is $\Delta R / \Delta Y$. Government reduces $\Delta Y / \Delta R$, so it raises $\Delta R / \Delta Y$.

FIGURE 14.1
EFFECT OF THE GOVERNMENT
SECTOR ON THE *IS* CURVE.

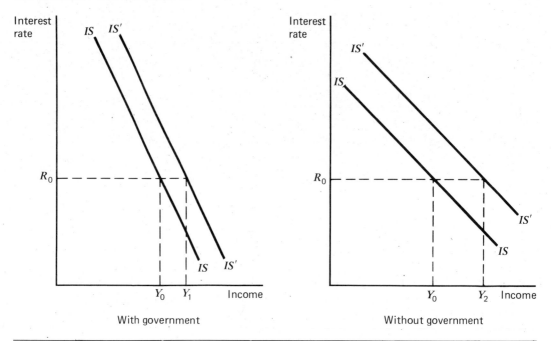

the tax rate, t; and it can change the responsiveness of transfer payments to changes in income, tp_1. The government has no direct control over interest payments on its debt, however, so tp_2 cannot be treated as a policy variable.[6]

Panel I of Figure 14.2 shows the equilibrium income, Y_0, and interest rate, R_0, for given values of $\bar{G}$, tp_0, t, and tp_1. Assume that there is unemployed labor and productive capacity at Y_0. Policymakers want income to rise to Y^* because at that point the economy is producing up to its potential. At Y^* there is "full employment" of the nation's resources.[7] By changing its policy instruments, the government can shift the *IS* curve to the right until it intersects the *LM* curve at Y^*. Panel II shows the situation where the government has raised its expenditures on goods and services, $\Delta \bar{G}$, sufficiently to produce the desired shift in the *IS* curve. The extent of the required change in $\bar{G}$ depends upon the multiplier for

---

[6] It is shown in Chapter 15 that the method by which the government finances a deficit that is, by issuing additional money or by issuing additional bonds, affects the interest rate. This is not the same as being able to change tp_2, however.

[7] Y^* is called long-run aggregate supply. It is discussed in Chapter 16 along with the reasons why actual output can deviate from Y^*.

FIGURE 14.2
ACHIEVING DESIRED INCOME BY
AN INCREASE IN GOVERNMENT
SPENDING.

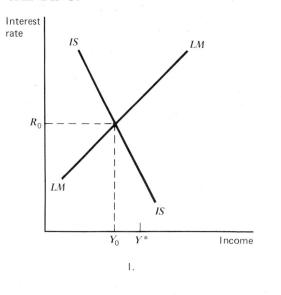

I.

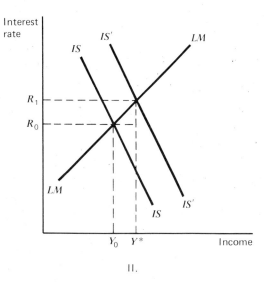

II.

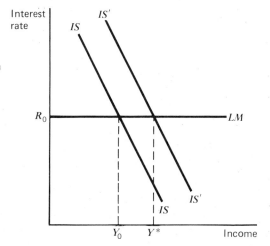

III.

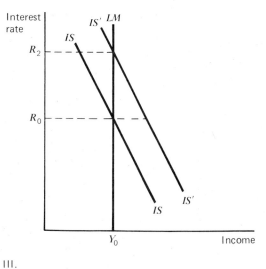

$\Delta \bar{G}$, given the interest rate, and upon the slopes of the *IS* and *LM* curves. The smaller the multiplier, $m_Y(R)$, the greater the required change in $\bar{G}$. Furthermore, the steeper the *LM* curve or the flatter the *IS* curve, or both, the greater the required change in $\bar{G}$.

The desired level of aggregate income, Y^*, can also be achieved by increasing the base level of transfer payments, tp_0, rather than $\bar{G}$. The rise in tp_0 must be larger than the increase in $\bar{G}$, however, because some of the increase in transfer payments is saved. As result, the initial effect of a rise in base level transfers is $c_1 \Delta tp_0$. To have the same effect as a rise in $\bar{G}$, it is necessary that the increase in transfer payments be sufficiently large to offset the initial increase in saving. Thus, $c_1 \Delta tp_0 = \Delta \bar{G}$ or $\Delta tp_0 = \Delta \bar{G}/c_1$. For example, if the marginal propensity to consume is 0.8, the rise in tp_0 must be $1.0/0.8 = 1.25$ times as large as the increase in $\bar{G}$ to have the same effect.

Note that at the new higher equilibrium level of income, Y^*, the interest rate rises to R_1. This occurs because the LM curve is upward sloping. The IS curve is downward sloping, however. A rise in the interest rate reduces investment relative to what it would be if the interest rate did not rise.[8] This reduction in interest sensitive spending (investment) is often called *crowding out*. The idea is that the rise in government spending ($\Delta \bar{G}$ or $\Delta tp_0/c_1$) raises income. The larger transactions demand for money at this higher income raises the interest rate. The rise in the interest rate crowds out interest sensitive private spending relative to what would exist if the interest rate did not rise. The steeper the LM curve, the larger the increase in the interest rate and the larger the amount of crowding out.

The rise in income increases the transactions demand for money. When the quantity of money remains fixed, this leads to an increase in the interest rate. The degree of crowding out depends upon the slopes of the IS and LM curves. The role of the financial sector of the economy can be seen in Panel III of Figure 14.2. In the left-hand diagram, the LM curve is horizontal. In this case the interest rate does not rise, and there is no crowding out. Because there is no reduction in interest sensitive spending, the increase in $\bar{G}$ or tp_0 required to achieve Y^* is not as large as when the interest rate rises. The right-hand diagram shows the opposite extreme when the LM curve is vertical. In this case, the rise in the interest rate is so great that the expansionary effect of a rise in government spending is offset by the decline in interest sensitive spending. The rise in government spending totally crowds out private spending, and income does not rise. In this case, a change in fiscal policy cannot produce a change in income. Thus, Y^* is unattainable through changes in fiscal policy. No matter how large the increase in government spending, there is an offsetting decline in interest sensitive spending. When $\bar{G}$ or tp_0 rise, the interest rate increases, and the additional government spending replaces private spending. A vertical LM curve is an extreme case, but we see that the steeper the LM curve, given the slope of the IS curve, the greater the increase in the interest rate, and the greater the degree of crowding out of private spending.

Assuming that the LM curve is not vertical, a rise in income from Y_0 to Y^* is possible. It is not necessary that this be accomplished through an increase in

---

[8] Recall that the increase in transfer payments that results from an increase in the interest rate is already built into the slope of the IS curve.

government spending, however. The government can cut the tax rate instead.[9] A reduction in the tax rate, t, increases disposable income and produces a rise in consumption relative to aggregate income. Thus, given income, Y_0, the consumption function shifts up. This produces a multiple expansion in income.

Panel I of Figure 14.3 shows the rise in income from Y_0 to Y^* that results from a reduction in the income tax rate. Note that the reduction in the tax rate not only shifts the IS curve to the right, but it also makes the curve more flat.

Panel II compares the effects of expansionary fiscal policy produced by an increase in $\bar{G}$ versus a reduction in t. The curve $IS(\Delta \bar{G})$ shows the shift in the IS curve that occurs when $\bar{G}$ increases. Note that the slope of $IS(\Delta \bar{G})$ is the same as for the initial curve, IS_0. When $\bar{G}$ increases, aggregate income would rise to Y_2 if the interest rate remained unchanged at R_0. The interest rate rises, however, and equilibrium income is Y^*. The curve $IS(\Delta t)$ shows the shift in the IS curve that occurs when t is reduced. Note that if the interest rate remained unchanged at R_0, the reduction in t would raise aggregate income to Y_3. The curve $IS(\Delta t)$ is flatter than $IS(\Delta G)$. This implies that as the interest rate rises, there is a larger reduction in aggregate income when we move along $IS(\Delta t)$ rather than $IS(\Delta \bar{G})$. In order to achieve Y^*, the tax cut has to be sufficiently large to offset the negative effect of the flatter IS curve.

Despite the complication of a flatter IS curve, a reduction in the tax rate can produce a rise in income from Y_0 to Y^*. There is also crowding out of interest-sensitive spending when the tax rate is reduced. Now, however, it is increased consumption expenditures produced by the tax cut that does the crowding out. We see, then, that any rightward shift in the IS curve produces crowding out of interest-sensitive spending so long as the LM curve is upward sloping. Thus, upward shifts in the consumption or investment functions, tax cuts, and increases in government spending all produce crowding out. This point is stressed because some observers seem to believe that it is only increases in government spending that crowd out interest-sensitive spending. This is not true.

We conclude that fiscal policy can be used to achieve a goal for aggregate income as long as the LM curve is not vertical. The examples considered involved raising income from Y_0 to Y^*, but the same argument applies for reducing income. Aggregate expenditures might be too high. In this case, expenditures exceed "full employment" output, and inflation will ultimately result.[10] The excess aggregate expenditures can be eliminated by cutting government spending or by increasing the tax rate. Either of these changes shifts the IS curve to the left and reduces equilibrium income. The reduction in the interest rate that occurs depends upon the slopes of the IS and LM curves. The fall in the interest rate

---

[9] The government can also affect aggregate expenditures by changing the sensitivity of transfer payments to changes in income. The effects of the policy variable, tp_1, are not discussed because they are similar to the tax rate.

[10] Inflation is discussed in Chapter 16.

FIGURE 14.3
ACHIEVING DESIRED INCOME BY
A TAX CUT.

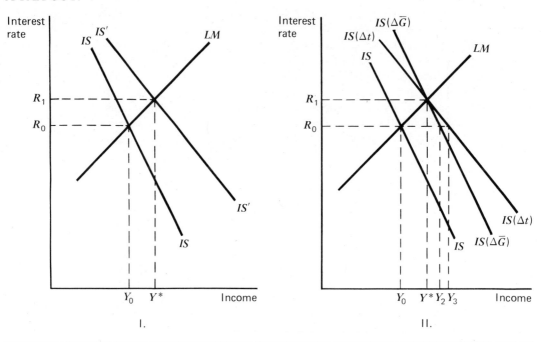

I.   II.

produces an increase in interest sensitive spending. Thus, there is "crowding in" rather than crowding out of interest sensitive spending.

Monetary Policy: Step I

The government can affect aggregate demand and income by using monetary policy rather than fiscal policy. Figure 14.4 shows the situation where initial equilibrium income, Y_0, is less than "full employment" income Y^*. The government can purchase bonds through its central bank. This increases the quantity of money, shifts the LM curve down to LM', and produces a rise in income. Government expenditures on goods and services, the tax rate, and the relationship for transfer payments are assumed to be unchanged. This means that the IS curve remains unchanged. The government (Federal Reserve) increases the quantity of money sufficiently to shift the LM curve to the point that it intersects the IS curve at Y^*.

Because the IS curve is fixed, the interest rate must decline to the point that aggregate expenditures rise to Y^*. The extent of the required increase in the quantity of money and the extent of the decline in the interest rate depend upon the slopes of the IS and LM curves. As pointed out earlier, the higher the tax rate and the greater the reduction in transfer payments that accompanies an increase

FIGURE 14.4
ACHIEVING DESIRED INCOME BY
MONETARY POLICY.

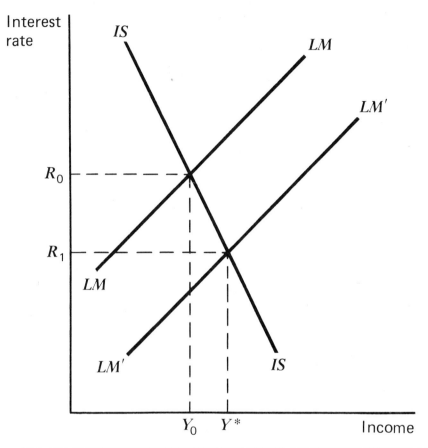

in income, the steeper the *IS* curve. Thus, the higher t and tp_1, the greater the increase in the quantity of money and the greater the reduction in the interest rate required to move the economy from Y to Y^*. Thus, taxes and transfer payments reduce the effect of a given change in the quantity of money on equilibrium income. This means that when t and tp_1 are high, larger changes in the quantity of money are required to move from Y to Y^* than when t and tp_1 are low. There is also a larger decline in the interest rate for a given increase in the quantity of money when t and tp_1 are high.

The relationship between the required change in the quantity of money and the fiscal policy instruments t and tp_1 illustrates that fiscal and monetary policy are interconnected. The extent of the interconnection is discussed in detail later, but some comments are appropriate at this point. When discussing fiscal policy, we assumed that monetary policy remained unchanged. This meant that shifts in the

IS curve produced by changes in fiscal policy caused movements along a fixed *LM* curve. Similarly, it was assumed that shifts in the *LM* curve produced by changes in monetary policy caused movements along a fixed *IS* curve.

A middle course is possible where fiscal and monetary policy are used together. In Panel I of Figure 14.5 the economy is moved from Y_0 to Y^* by expansionary monetary and fiscal policy. The *IS* curve shifts to the right from IS_0 to IS_1 because of an increase in government spending.[11] The *LM* curve shifts down from LM_0 to LM_1 because of an increase in the quantity of money. The combined effect is to raise income from Y to Y^* while having no change in the interest rate.

A combination of monetary and fiscal policy has two consequences that are different from those of using either policy to the exclusion of the other. First, smaller changes in the quantity of money and smaller changes in fiscal policy are required when there is a combination policy. The second effect of using a combination of monetary and fiscal policy is that crowding out can be eliminated. Consider the case where an increase in government expenditures on goods and services and an increase in the quantity of money are used to raise aggregate demand and income. The increase in $\overline{G}$ does not lead to a rise in the interest rate and a reduction of interest sensitive spending because the quantity of money is also increased. Thus, an increase in government spending does not crowd out private spending when there is also an appropriate increase in the quantity of money.

Panel II of Figure 14.5 shows how a combination policy reduces excessive aggregate expenditures and reduces income from Y_0 to Y^*. In this case there is a reduction in government expenditures that shifts the *IS* curve left from IS_0 to IS_1 and a reduction in the quantity of money that shifts the *LM* curve up from LM_0 to LM_1. Aggregate expenditures decline to Y^*, but the interest rate does not change. If fiscal policy is used by itself, a larger reduction in spending is required, and the interest rate declines. Thus, interest sensitive spending is stimulated. If monetary policy is used by itself, a larger reduction in the quantity of money is required, and the interest rate rises. Thus, interest sensitive spending is discouraged. When a combination policy is used, smaller changes in $\overline{G}$ and $\overline{M}$ are required and interest sensitive spending is unaffected.

The examples in Figure 14.5 involved combining monetary and fiscal policy in order to have no effect on the equilibrium interest rate. This is only one combination among many. Many combinations of monetary and fiscal policy can achieve Y^*. This implies that the choice of the mix is determined by considerations other than wanting to achieve Y^*. Consider the case where it is a national goal to increase the growth of the capital stock in order to have a higher level of Y^* in the future. This can be accomplished by encouraging investment spending relative to consumption and government spending. Thus, policymakers want a high ratio of

---

[11] We shall usually discuss fiscal policy in terms of changes in government spending. This is done to simplify the analysis by avoiding the complications caused by changes in the slope of the *IS* curve when t or tp_1 change. The reader should be aware, however, that fiscal policy can be conducted by varying t and tp_1.

FIGURE 14.5
USING A COMBINATION OF
MONETARY AND FISCAL POLICIES
TO ACHIEVE DESIRED INCOME.

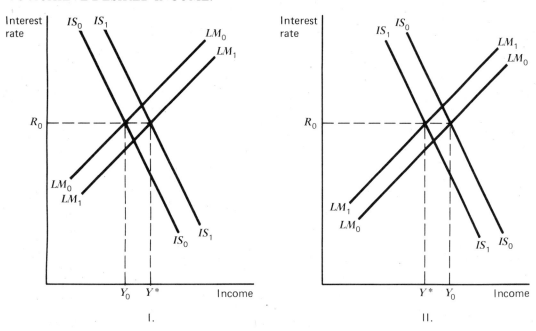

I.

II.

investment to aggregate income. In this situation, it is better to stimulate aggregate expenditures through an increase in the quantity of money rather than by fiscal policy. An increase in the quantity of money reduces the interest rate and encourages investment. An increase in government spending or a tax cut tends to crowd out investment.

The opposite argument applies to a policy designed to reduce aggregate expenditures. If heavy reliance is placed on monetary policy, there is a relatively large reduction in the quantity of money and a relatively large upward shift in the *LM* curve. This increases the interest rate and reduces aggregate expenditures. The increase in the interest rate discourages investment. This effect can be reduced by putting primary reliance on fiscal policy. A cut in government spending shifts the *IS* curve to the left. An increase in the tax rate shifts the *IS* curve to the left and makes it flatter. Either policy reduces aggregate expenditures and produces a decline in the interest rate. Thus, when national goals are to reduce aggregate expenditures and to encourage investment, fiscal policy should be used.

In fact, a policy combination that involves a large reduction in government spending or a large tax increase plus an *increase* in the quantity of money can reduce aggregate expenditures and encourage investment. It might appear that monetary and fiscal policies are working at cross-purposes in this situation, but they are not. The purpose of the increase in the quantity of money is not to offset the effect of the restrictive fiscal policy on aggregate expenditures. Rather, the purpose of the increase in the quantity of money is to encourage investment expenditures and capital formation while fiscal policy is reducing other components of aggregate expenditures. This policy combination is appropriate if the nation places heavy emphasis on economic growth and, therefore, wants to achieve a high value of investment relative to full employment output, Y^*. If monetary and fiscal policy are coordinated properly, aggregate expenditures and income are reduced from Y to Y^*, but investment expenditures are high relative to consumption and government spending. This is an excellent example of why it can be important to coordinate monetary and fiscal policy.

THE ROLE OF DEPOSITORY INSTITUTIONS

Up to this point we have studied the determinants of aggregate expenditures, income, and the interest rate for a world without depository institutions. This allowed us to simplify the discussion because all money is currency. The Federal Reserve's open market operations change the quantity of money dollar for dollar with changes in its holdings of bonds. Furthermore, when there are no depository institutions, the public (households and firms) is the only source of credit.

Most money is not currency. Approximately two thirds of all money (M1) balances are in the form of transactions account liabilities of depository institutions. Furthermore, depository institutions also offer time accounts. The remainder of this chapter is concerned with how depository institutions affect aggregate expenditures, income, and the interest rate.

We saw in Chapter 11 that the quantity of money is determined jointly by the Federal Reserve, the public, and depository institutions. The Federal Reserve sets reserve requirements and it determines the quantity of reserves in the depository system, but it cannot directly determine the quantity of money. That quantity is affected by the portfolio choices of the public and of depository institutions.

In Chapter 11, it was shown that the quantity of money can be expressed as a multiple of total reserves

$$M = m_M TR$$

where

$$m_M = \frac{(1+c)}{r_T + n \cdot r_M + e} \quad ^{12}$$

---

[12] Note that the currency ratio, c, does not appear in the denominator. Here we are talking about the quantity of reserves that remains in the system after currency flows have occurred. A discussion of this issue is given in Chapter 11.

and

c is the ratio of currency to transactions accounts

r_T is the reserve requirement for transactions accounts

n is the ratio of nonpersonal time accounts to transactions accounts

r_N is the reserve requirement for nonpersonal time accounts .

e is the ratio of excess reserves to transactions accounts.

This expression indicates that an open market operation, which changes the quantity of reserves in the depository system, produces a multiple change in the quantity of money. For example, a $1 purchase of bonds by the Fed reduces the value of bonds in the hands of the public by $1, and it increases the quantity of reserves by $1. This produces an increase in the quantity of money of $m_M \cdot \$1$. Because the decrease in the quantity of bonds no longer equals the increase in the quantity of money, the *LM* curve derived in Chapter 13 must be modified.

The *LM* Curve

It is possible to derive an *LM* curve when there are depository institutions, but the algebra is messy. The quantity of money is currency plus transactions accounts. Currency earns no interest, but some transactions accounts pay a market interest rate. This complicates derivation of the *LM* curve. In addition, time accounts are not part of the quantity of money, but they are a source of credit extended by depository institutions. Variations in the quantity of time accounts affect the supply of money and credit in the economy and, therefore, affect interest rates.

It is beyond the scope of this text to show a full-fledged *LM* sector when there are all these complications. Rather, a simplified *LM* relationship is shown, and then the role of interest bearing transactions accounts is discussed informally. The *LM* curve that is derived shows some of the effects of the depository system, and it serves as a convenient vehicle for the informal analysis of several complicating factors.

The money demand schedule is assumed to have the same form as in Chapter 13,

$$M^D = m_0 - m_1 R + m_2 Y .$$

In Chapter 13, the quantity of money was assumed to be fixed. This assumption was appropriate because all money was currency and the quantity of currency was exactly determined by the Federal Reserve. The quantity of money (currency) changed dollar for dollar with the Fed's open market operations. When there are depository institutions, this assumption is no longer appropriate. The Fed cannot set the quantity of money because this quantity is determined endogenously by the public and depository institutions. The quantity of bonds changes dollar for dollar with open market operations, but the quantity of money does not.

When the Fed purchases bonds, total reserves rise by the amount of the purchase. When the Fed sells bonds, total reserves fall by the amount of the sale. Thus, there is a one-to-one relationship between changes in the quantity of bonds and changes in total reserves. There is, however, a multiplier relationship between total reserves and the quantity of money.

The multiplier relationship $M = m_M TR$ is often viewed as a money supply function. This is not technically correct because the multiplier is affected by the public's demand for money relative to other assets. The determination of the quantity of money can be handled adequately only by specifying demand functions for currency, transactions accounts, and nonpersonal time accounts. These are then combined with the supply functions of depository institutions for transactions accounts and nonpersonal time accounts. The interaction of the demand and supply functions jointly determines the quantity of currency, transactions, and nonpersonal time accounts as well as the interest rates on bonds and on the liabilities of depository institutions. Such models are beyond the scope of this book.

The approach here is to assume that transactions accounts are the only liability of depository institutions and that these accounts earn no interest. Under this assumption the money-multiplier relationship is $M = m_M TR$ where

$$m_M = (1 + c)/(r_T + e).$$

In the formal derivation of the LM curve, the multiplier, m_M, is assumed to be fixed. The effects of changes in the multiplier are discussed later.

When money supply is allowed to interact with money demand, an LM curve can be derived that shows the combinations of the interest rate and income for which money demand equals money supply. The model underlying the LM curve is

$$M^D = m_0 - m_1 R + m_2 Y$$
$$M^S = m_M \overline{TR}$$
$$M^D = M^S.$$

Setting demand equal to supply and solving for the interest rate, we obtain the LM relationship

$$R = \frac{[m_0 - m_M \overline{TR}]}{m_1} + \frac{m_2}{m_1} Y.$$

The LM curve derived in Chapter 13, where all money was currency and money was exogenously determined, was

$$R = \frac{[m_0 - \overline{M}]}{m_1} + \frac{m_2}{m_1} Y.$$

These two LM curves differ only in that the exogenous $\overline{M}$ of Chapter 13 is replaced by $m_M \overline{TR}$ in this chapter. If the quantity of reserves and the money multiplier are constant, the quantity of money is also constant. Thus, $\overline{M} = m_M \overline{TR}$, and the LM curves are the same. Because there are depository institutions, the Fed cannot control the quantity of money directly. It can control the quantity of reserves, however. If the money multiplier is constant, when the Fed sets total reserves, it implicitly is setting the quantity of money. We saw in Chapter 11 that the money multiplier is not constant because it varies with portfolio shifts by the public and depository institutions. This complication is discussed later in this chapter. For the time being, we assume that the multiplier is constant.

A comparison of the two LM curves indicates that a given change in the quantity of total reserves in a world with depository institutions produces a larger change in the interest rate than occurs when the quantity of money changes by the same amount in a world without depository institutions. When there are depository institutions, $\Delta R / \Delta \overline{TR} = m_M / m_1$; when there are no depository institutions, $\Delta R / \Delta \overline{M} = 1/m_1$. Thus, $\Delta R / \Delta \overline{TR}$ is m_M times larger than $\Delta R / \Delta \overline{M}_1$. This larger change in the interest rate occurs because with depository institutions, a change in the quantity of reserves produces a multiple change in the quantity of transactions accounts. Depository institutions use transactions accounts to purchase bonds. Thus, a change in the quantity of reserves produces a multiple change in the quantity of transactions accounts *and* in the demand for bonds by depository institutions. This multiple change in the demand for bonds affects the interest rate. In a world without depository institutions, this cannot occur.

In order to see what is going on, let us look at the market for bonds. For simplicity, it is assumed that the quantity (supply) of bonds is fixed. The demand for bonds is composed of two parts. First, there is the demand for bonds by the public (households and firms). This demand is the one studied in Chapter 13, where the public chooses between bonds and money. In addition, there is the demand for bonds by depository institutions. The demand for bonds by depository institutions is equal to the total credit that they extend. Total credit (bond holdings), TC, equals total liabilities of depository institutions less required reserves, RR, and excess reserves, ER. Because all liabilities are assumed to be transactions accounts, T, we have $TC = T - RR - ER$. Required reserves are the reserve requirement ratio, r_T, times transactions account liabilities, or $RR = r_T T$. Excess reserves are assumed to be a constant fraction, e, of transactions accounts, so $ER = eT$. Combining terms, $TC = T - r_T T - eT = [(1 - r_T) - e]T$. Because all credit is assumed to be in the form of bonds, the demand for bonds by depository institutions, B_{DI}^D, is $B_{DI}^D = [(1 - r_T) - e]T$. Thus, when transactions accounts rise, the demand for bonds by depository institutions also rises. If, for example, the reserve requirement is 20 percent and depository institutions want to hold 5 percent of their transactions account liabilities as excess reserves, $B_{DI}^D = (1 - 0.20 - 0.05)T = 0.75T$. In this case, a $1 rise in transactions accounts produces a $.75 rise in the demand for bonds by depository institutions.

The total demand for bonds in the economy, B^D, is composed of the demand for bonds by the public, B_P^D plus the demand for bonds by depository institutions, B_{DI}^D, or $B^D = B_P^D + B_{DI}^D$, Using the bond demand function developed in Chapter 13 to describe the public, we have:

$$B_P^D = b_0 + b_1 R - b_2 Y .$$

The total demand for bonds is

$$B^D = b_0 + b_1 R + b_2 Y + [(1 - r_T) - e]T .$$

Consider the effect of a change in the public's tastes that increases the quantity of money demanded and decreases the quantity of bonds demanded, that is, $\Delta b_0 < 0$. Assume that income, wealth, and total reserves are given.[13] Because total reserves are fixed, the quantity of money is constant. The public sells bonds in an effort to get more money. The supplies of money and bonds are constant. This implies that the interest rate on bonds has to rise sufficiently to induce the public to hold the same quantity of money as before. At the given level of income, the interest rate rises. Thus, the LM curve shifts up. The LM curve for a world with depository institutions indicates that the change in the interest rate that is, the shift in the LM curve, is $\Delta R = \Delta m_0 / m_1$. This is the same shift as occurs when there are no depository institutions. With total reserves fixed, shifts in money and bond demand represent the behavior of the public, and we get the same change in the interest rate in worlds with and without depository institutions.

Changes in income also shifts the public's money and bond demand. Inspection of the expressions for the LM curves in worlds with and without depository institutions indicates that the slope is $\Delta R / \Delta Y = m_2 / m_1$ in both cases. Thus, depository institutions do not affect the slope of the LM curve.

Now consider the case of an increase in reserves produced by a purchase of bonds by the Federal Reserve. When reserves rise, the quantity of bonds falls by an equal amount. The rise in the quantity of reserves produces a multiple expansion in the quantity of transactions accounts and money. Panel I of Figure 14.6 shows the relationship between money and bonds. At the initial equilibrium the public holds the quantity of money $M_0 = m_M \overline{TR}_0$ at the interest rate R_0. The initial quantity of bonds is $\overline{B}_0$, and this equals the total demand for bonds, $B_P^D + B_{DI}^D = B^D$, at the interest rate R_0. The purchase of bonds by the Fed increases total reserves from $\overline{TR}_0$ to $\overline{TR}_1$ and decreases the quantity of bonds from $\overline{B}_0$ to $\overline{B}_1$. The quantity of money rises from M_0 to M_1, which is a multiple of the increase in reserves. Thus, the quantity of money rises by more than the quantity of bonds falls. The excess supply of money is $M_1 - M_0$; the excess demand for bonds is $B_1 - B_0$. According to the money demand schedule, the interest rate falls to R_1. Looking at the bond market, with the initial bond demand schedule, B^D, the interest rate only falls to R_2. This apparent inconsistency between the interest rate that equates money demand to supply and the interest rate that equates bond demand to supply disappears when we allow for the increase in the demand for bonds by depository institutions.

The quantity of money rises because depository institutions extend credit; that is, they purchase bonds. When transactions accounts rise, depository institutions set aside a fraction as required reserves, they add to their desired excess reserves, and they use the remainder to purchase bonds. Thus, there is an increase in the demand for bonds by depository institutions equal to $[(1 - r_T) - e]\Delta T$. This is shown by a rightward shift of the bond demand schedule from B^D to $B^{D'}$. With

[13] Here we neglect the effect of interest rate changes on the value of existing bonds. This complication is discussed in the next chapter.

FIGURE 14.6
THE EFFECTS OF A PURCHASE OF
BONDS BY THE FED WHEN THERE
ARE DEPOSITORY INSTITUTIONS.

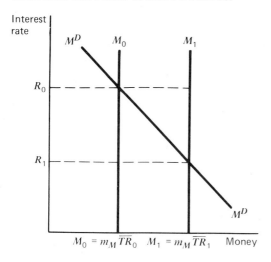
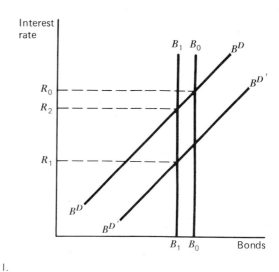

I.

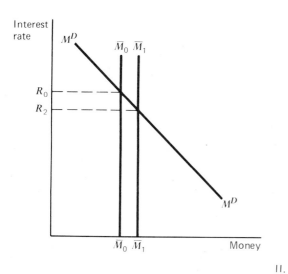
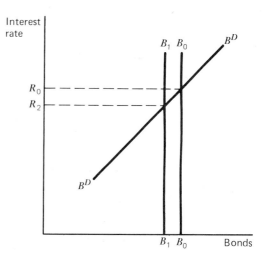

II.

the greater demand for bonds produced by the increase in transactions accounts, the interest rate on bonds falls to R_1. The interest rate that equates money demand to the increased supply is also the interest rate that equates the decreased supply of bonds to the increased demand.

Panel II shows why the interest rate does not fall so much in a world without depository institutions. Here the purchase of bonds by the Fed increases the quantity of money by the same amount as it decreases the quantity of bonds. There are no depository institutions, so there is no multiple expansion of money and no rightward shift of bond demand. The excess supply of money equals the excess demand for bonds, and the interest rate only falls to R_2.

We conclude that open market operations by the Fed produce larger changes in the interest rate when there are depository institutions. This means that open market operations produce larger shifts in the LM curve. The slope of the LM curve is not affected by depository institutions, however.

The larger shift in the LM curve in a world of depository institutions demonstrates the role of these institutions as financial intermediaries. When the public holds its money balances with depository institutions rather than as currency, these institutions lend the funds. This produces a larger demand for bonds. A purchase of securities by the Fed produces a multiple expansion of transactions accounts and bond demand. This multiple expansion does not occur when the public holds money in the form of currency.

Transactions Accounts that Pay a Market Interest Rate

In the derivation of the LM curve, it was assumed that noninterest-bearing transactions accounts were the only liability of depository institutions. In this section, we examine the effects of transactions accounts that pay a market interest rate.

In 1983 depository institutions were allowed to offer transactions accounts to nonbusiness customers that have no interest rate ceiling. This development requires us to modify our specification of money demand and of the LM curve. A full analysis of the issue is beyond the scope of this book, but we can offer some comments concerning the possible effects of this regulatory reform.

For simplicity, assume that all money is interest-bearing transactions accounts. As before, the demand for money varies negatively with the interest rate on bonds and positively with income. Now, however, the demand for money also varies positively with the interest rate on transactions accounts. Given the interest rate on bonds and income, the higher the interest rate on transactions accounts, the greater the quantity of money demanded.

Money demand can be approximated by the following linear relationship:

$$M^D = m_0 - m_1 R_B + m_1 R_M + m_2 Y$$

where R_B is the interest rate on bonds and R_M is the interest rate on money (transactions accounts). Note that the interest sensitivity of money demand with respect to the bond interest rate, m_1, is the negative of the interest sensitivity of money demand with respect to the interest rate on money. This indicates that money and bonds are substitutes. We can write the expression for money demand as

$$M^D = m_0 - m_1 (R_B - R_M) + m_2 Y.$$

Thus, it is the differential between the interest rates on bonds and money,

$(R_B - R_M)$, that affects money demand.[14] An increase in the bond interest rate relative to the interest rate on money decreases the quantity of money demanded. An increase in the interest rate on money relative to the interest rate on bonds increases the quantity of money demanded.

We saw in Chapter 7 that depository institutions issue transactions account liabilities in order to acquire loans. In the absence of an interest rate ceiling, when the expected return on loans is high, these institutions pay a higher interest rate for transactions accounts. In terms of our simple macromodel, this means that the interest rate on transactions accounts is high when the bond interest rate is high, and it is low when bonds have a low interest rate. We also saw in Chapter 7 that the interest rate on transactions accounts is less than the interest rate on loans to cover operating costs and to provide a positive rate of return to the owners of depository institutions. We conclude that depository institutions move the interest rate on money (transactions accounts) with the interest rate on bonds, but the money interest rate is below the bond interest rate.

The relationship between the interest rates on money and bonds can be shown symbolically

$$R_M = gR_B$$

where g is greater than zero but less than one, that is, $(0 < g < 1)$. Substituting, this relationship into the money demand function, we get:

$$M^D = m_0 - m_1(R_B - R_M) + m_2 Y = m_0 - m_1(R_B - gR_B) + m_2 Y$$
$$= m_0 - m_1(1 - g)R_B + m_2 Y .$$

The effect of having interest-bearing money is to reduce the sensitivity of money demand to the bond interest rate from m_1 to $m_1(1 - g)$. The higher the value of g, the lower the interest sensitivity of money demand [recall that $(0 < g < 1)$].

The new expression for money demand indicates that when money pays interest, a given change in the bond interest rate produces a smaller change in the quantity of money demanded. Thus, the money demand schedule and, therefore, the *LM* curve become steeper. This occurs because the money interest rate moves with the bond interest rate. Consider the case where the quantities of money and bonds are fixed and there is an increase in income. This raises the transactions demand for money. At the initial interest rates for money and bonds, there is an excess demand for money and an excess supply of bonds. The sale of bonds lowers their price and increases the bond interest rate. Other things being equal, this reduces the quantity of money demanded. The rise in R_B produces an increase in R_M, however. With a higher return on bonds, depository institutions want to attract additional transactions account balances. The rise in R_M reduces the negative effect on money demand from the rise in R_B. This implies that when

---

[14] Note that the differential $(R_B - R_M)$ is smaller today than it was when there were interest ceilings for transactions accounts. The removal of the ceilings on many accounts reduces the differential and increased the quantity of money demand.

income rises, a relatively large increase in R_B is required to induce money holders to reduce money demand back to the fixed supply.

We conclude that when money pays interest, a rise in income produces a larger increase in the bond interest rate. By a similar argument, a decline in income produces a larger decline in R_B when money pays interest. The large response of the bond interest rate to changes in income implies that the *LM* curve is steeper when money pays interest. The slope of the *LM* curve when money pays interest is $\Delta R / \Delta Y = m_2 / [m_1(1 - g)]$. When money does not pay interest, the slope is smaller, that is, $\Delta R / \Delta Y = m_2 / m_1$. With a steeper *LM* curve, shifts in the *IS* curve have a smaller effect on income, and shifts in the *LM* curve have a larger effect. Fiscal policy is less potent, and monetary policy is more potent when money pays a market rate of interest.

In the real world, money is comprised of currency, demand deposit accounts, and interest-bearing transactions accounts. Currency and demand deposit accounts earn no interest. This means that only transactions accounts that pay a market interest rate have a lower sensitivity of demand to changes in the bond interest rate. The presence of currency and demand deposit accounts limits the extent to which the *LM* curve is steeper. As transactions accounts paying market interest grow as a percent of total money, the *LM* curve becomes increasingly steep.

There are other factors that also limit the possible increase in the slope of the *LM* curve. The preceding analysis assumed that the sensitivity of money demand to the interest rates on money and bonds, m_1, is unaffected by the introduction of money that pays a market rate of return. In reality, it is unlikely that this is the case. When money earns no interest, it is held primarily because the transactions costs of acquiring interest-bearing assets exceed the expected return on these assets. There may be some portfolio demand for money, but it is likely to be relatively small. When money earns a market rate of return, the portfolio demand for money increases. Not only does this shift the money demand schedule to the right, but it also tends to increase the sensitivity of money and bond demand to changes in the interest rate differential for the two assets, $(R_B - R_M)$. This occurs because the public is making portfolio switches between money and bonds that have nothing to do with the use of money as a medium of exchange. When it comes to portfolio demand, the public treats money like any other asset and makes relatively large shifts between the two assets when $(R_B - R_M)$ changes. This suggests that the parameter, m_1, is higher when money pays a market interest rate. To the extent to which m_1 is higher, the slope of the *LM* curve is not increased so much when money pays interest. Actually, it is possible that the slope is not increased at all, or that the slope decreases.

The issue cannot be resolved on theoretical grounds. It is an empirical question involving the extent of the increase in m_1 that occurs when money pays interest and the size of the parameter g in $R_M = gR_B$. The greater the increase in m_1, the smaller the increase (or the larger the decrease) in the slope of the *LM* curve. The greater g is, the larger the increase in the slope of the *LM* curve is. Because there is such limited experience with transactions accounts that pay a market interest rate, there is no empirical evidence available to determine m_1 or g. The issues cannot be resolved until experience is gained with the new transactions accounts. The public's behavior concerning money market mutual funds suggests, however, that the increase in m_1 might be large. There have been substantial shifts between money funds and other assets when relative rates of return changed. This experience suggests that the slope of the *LM* curve might not increase very much. It is possible that the curve will be flatter when money pays a market interest rate.

SUMMARY

This chapter expanded on the model of Chapter 11 to include the government sector and depository institutions. It was shown that tax receipts automatically rise, and transfers automatically fall when aggregate income rises. Tax receipts fall, and transfers rise when income falls. This makes the government sector act as a built-in stabilizer that reduces fluctuations in aggregate income. The built-in stabilizer effect does not require any change in policy instruments. The movements in tax receipts and transfers are automatic.

The question of the mix of monetary and fiscal policy arises when the nation has goals concerning stimulating capital formation. The objective of a high rate of capital formation calls for a monetary policy that keeps interest rates relatively low and a fiscal policy that restrains aggregate demand.

The chapter then turned to the role of depository institutions. These institutions make monetary policy more potent by increasing the response of interest rates to changes in the quantity of reserves. For example, depository institutions, as financial intermediaries, produce a multiple expansion in money and credit when there is an increase in reserves. This causes a larger decline in the interest rate than would occur in the absence of depository institutions.

The chapter concluded with an analysis of the possible effects of transactions accounts that pay a market interest rate. These accounts will make monetary policy more potent and fiscal policy less potent if the interest sensitivity of money demand does not increase. If the interest sensitivity does rise, the effect is reduced. It is conceivable that the portfolio demand for these transactions accounts will be sufficiently sensitive to relative interest rates that monetary policy could be less potent and fiscal policy more potent. There is no direct empirical evidence on this issue. This is a new source of uncertainty for monetary policy.

SELECTED REFERENCES

Dornbusch, Rudiger and Stanley Fischer, *Macroeconomics*, (2nd ed.), New York: McGraw-Hill, 1981.
Gordon, Robert, *Macroeconomics*, (2nd ed.), Boston: Little, Brown and Company, 1981.

AN EXPANDED MACROMODEL

15

This chapter expands the model of Chapter 14 to allow for greater interaction between the real and the financial sectors of the economy. This is accomplished by letting consumption and saving be affected by interest rates, by letting investment be affected by income, and by allowing for the effects of changes in wealth on both the real and financial sectors of the economy. Although these additional linkages between the real and financial sectors complicate the model considerably, they allow us to study the effects of monetary and fiscal policy in greater depth than was possible with the simple model. This greater depth is particularly important in analyzing the effects of government budget deficits and surpluses.

THE EXPANDED MODEL

The *IS* Curve

So far we have considered a model in which consumption and saving are not affected by wealth or by the interest rate. This allowed a relatively simple explanation of the relationship between aggregate income and the interest rate. In order to describe more fully the role of financial factors, we must now examine a somewhat more complicated world.

It was argued in Chapter 3 that consumption and saving are affected not only by current income but also by the wealth that households have accumulated. Recall that wealth allows households to smooth consumption relative to income. They accumulate wealth (save) so that they can maintain consumption in the future when income falls owing to retirement or other factors. The greater the amount of wealth that has been accumulated, the smaller the desire to accumulate additional wealth.

It is not possible to embody these intrinsically dynamic considerations fully in the static models of this book. It is possible to approximate the implications of the life-cycle hypothesis, however, by assuming that the amount of wealth in the economy affects consumption and saving. In particular, it is assumed that the greater wealth, given income, the higher consumption. As shown in Figure 15.1, increases in wealth from W_0 to W_1 to W_2 shift the consumption function up. Thus, given disposable income, $(Y_d)_0$, consumption rises from C_0 to C_1 to C_2 as wealth rises. Because income equals consumption plus saving, the saving function shifts down by the amount that the consumption function shifts up. Thus, given disposable income, $(Y_d)_0$, saving falls from S_0 to S_1 to S_2.

It was also argued in Chapter 3 that the interest rate can affect consumption and saving. The direction of the effect cannot be established theoretically, however. A rise in the interest rate can in principle lead to either a rise or a fall in saving. Given current and expected future disposable income, a rise in the interest rate induces households to postpone consumption, that is, to save more today and consume more in the future. The rise in the interest rate increases current and expected future disposable income, however, and this increase leads households to increase their current consumption. There is both a substitution and an income effect from the increase in the interest rate. The substitution effect induces households to reduce current consumption when the interest rate rises, but the income effect induces them to increase current consumption. It is not possible to establish theoretically which effect is larger. We shall assume, however, that the substitution effect exceeds the income effect and, therefore, that a rise in the interest rate reduces consumption and increases saving.[1] As shown in Figure 15.2, where consumption and saving are graphed against disposable income, increases in the interest rate from R_0 to R_1 to R_2 shift the consumption function down and the saving function up.

The effect of wealth and the interest rate on consumption and saving can be shown as follows:

$$C = c_0 + c_1 Y_d + c_2 \overline{W} - c_3 R$$
$$S = s_0 + s_1 Y_d - s_2 \overline{W} + s_3 R .\ [2]$$

Because disposable income must still be divided between consumption and saving, that is, $Y_d = C + S$

$$S = -c_0 + (1 - c_1) Y_d - c_2 \overline{W} + c_3 R .$$

---

[1] At this point we are neglecting the effects on consumption and saving of capital gains and losses on existing assets produced by changes in the interest rate.

[2] A bar is placed over wealth to indicate that wealth is assumed to be fixed.

FIGURE 15.1
THE RESPONSE OF CONSUMPTION
AND SAVING TO INCREASES IN WEALTH.

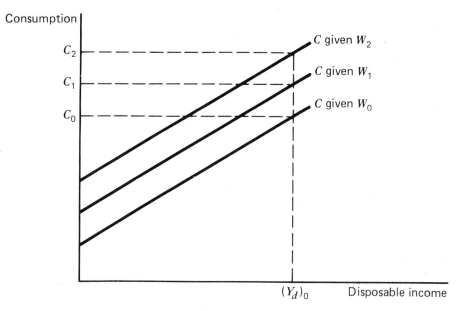

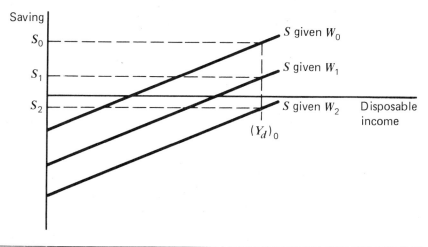

Thus, a rise in wealth, given disposable income and the interest rate, increases consumption and reduces saving by the same amount. Similarly, an increase in the interest rate, given disposable income and wealth, reduces consumption and increases saving by the same amount.

FIGURE 15.2
THE RESPONSE OF CONSUMPTION
AND SAVING TO INCREASES IN
THE INTEREST RATE.

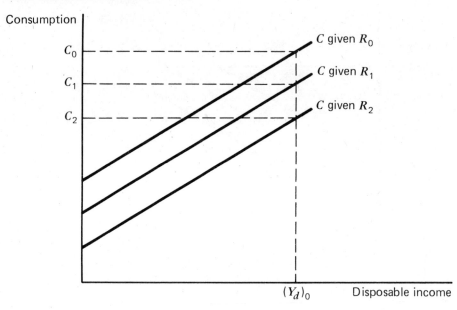

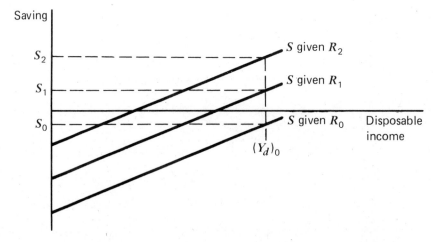

The next step in expanding the model is to look more closely at investment. So far, we have assumed that investment depends only on the interest rate. The dependence of investment on the interest rate follows from the discussion of discounted present value presented in Chapter 3. The expression for discounted present value indicates, however, that investment is not only affected by the interest rate but also by the stream of net income that firms expect to earn from investment projects. This suggests that a rise in aggregate expenditures and income increases the flow of expected future income and, therefore, increases investment expenditures. Investment occurs because firms want to increase their capital stocks. Thus, investment is an intrinsically dynamic phenomenon. Dynamic factors do not fit easily into our static model, but we shall approximate the effect by assuming that investment varies positively with aggregate income, Y. Thus, given the interest rate, when income is high, investment demand is high.

The dependence of investment on income can be shown as

$$I = i_0 - i_1 R + i_2 Y.$$

Given income, when the interest rate is high, investment demand is low. Given the interest rate, however, when income is high investment demand is high. Figure 15.3 shows that given the interest rate, R_0, the investment function shifts to the right when aggregate income rises from Y_0 to Y_1 to Y_2. Thus, investment rises from I_0 to I_1 to I_2.

With the new expressions for consumption, saving, and investment, there is a new IS curve. The expanded model is

$$Y = C + I + \overline{G}$$

$$Y_d = Y - T + TP$$

$$T = tY$$

$$TP = tp_0 - tp_1 Y + tp_2 R$$

$$C = c_0 + c_1 Y_d + c_2 \overline{W} - c_3 R$$

$$I = i_0 - i_1 R + i_2 Y.$$

The solution to these equations gives the following expression for the IS curve.

$$Y = \frac{c_0 + i_0 + c_2 \overline{W} + \overline{G} + c_1 tp_0}{1 - c_1(1 - t - tp_1) - i_2} - \frac{(i_1 + c_3 - c_1 tp_2)}{1 - c_1(1 - t - tp_1) - i_2} R.$$

It is instructive to compare this expression for the IS curve to the more simple one obtained in Chapter 14, where consumption and saving depended only on income and when investment depended only on the interest rate

$$Y = \frac{c_0 + i_0 + \overline{G} + c_1 tp_0}{1 - c_1(1 - t - tp_1)} - \frac{i_1 - c_1 tp_2}{1 - c_1(1 - t - tp_1)} R.$$

The income multiplier for the expanded model is

$$m_{Y(R)} = \frac{1}{1 - c_1(1 - t - tp_1) - i_2}$$

and for the simpler model, it is

$$m_{Y(R)} = \frac{1}{1 - c_1(1 - t - tp_1)}$$

where $m_Y(R)$ is the income multiplier given the interest rate.

FIGURE 15.3
THE RESPONSE OF INVESTMENT
TO INCREASES IN INCOME.

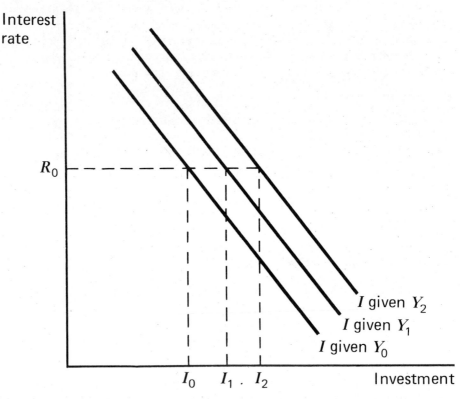

The multiplier is larger (smaller denominator) when investment varies positively with income. Consider the response of aggregate expenditures and income in the expanded model when the consumption function shifts up.[3] The increase in aggregate expenditures increases income. This produces additional consumption *and* additional investment. Saving is a leakage from aggregate expenditures that limits the multiple expansion of income. However, the rise in investment increases aggregate expenditures, which increases the multiple expansion of income. The increase in investment that results from the rise in income tends to offset some of the leakage of income into saving. The greater the sensitivity of investment demand to a change in income, i_2, the larger the multiplier. This

---

[3] We have the same multiplier for an upward shift in the investment function and for an increase in government purchases of goods and services.

FIGURE 15.4
EQUILIBRIUM INCOME WHEN
INVESTMENT VARIES POSITIVELY
WITH INCOME.

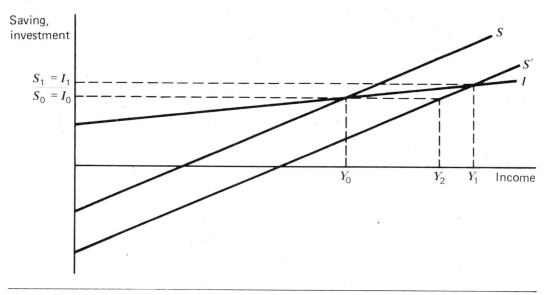

means that the larger i_2 is, the greater is the rightward shift of the IS curve that results from an upward shift in the consumption function.

Figure 15.4 shows the relationship between saving and investment when investment varies positively with income. The investment function is upward sloping, indicating that when income is high, desired investment is high. The initial equilibrium is shown at Y_0, where saving equals investment. If the consumption function shifts up, the saving function shifts down to S'. Thus, at Y_0, desired investment exceeds desired saving. The increase in consumption at Y_0 increases aggregate expenditures and income. The new equilibrium is at Y_1, where saving again equals investment. Because investment increases with income, there is more investment and saving at Y_1 than at Y_0.

In the simple model, investment is constant, given the interest rate. Thus, given investment, I_0, income only rises to Y_2. At Y_2, income rises to return saving to the same level as at Y_0. This is sufficient to return saving to equality with a constant level of investment. Thus, the rise in income is less when investment does not increase with income.

Note that in the expanded model a decrease in desired saving (i.e., a downward shift in the saving function) actually produces an *increase* in saving. The rise in income is so large that saving is greater at Y_1 than at Y_0. Thus, when investment varies positively with income, the paradox of thrift is reinforced.

With the introduction of wealth as a factor affecting consumption and saving, there is an additional source of shifts in the *IS* curve. A rise in wealth increases consumption, given income, by the amount $c_2 \Delta \overline{W}$. Given the interest rate, the rise in income is $\Delta Y = c_2 \Delta \overline{W} / [1 - c_1(1 - t - tp_1) - i_2]$. Thus, the *IS* curve shifts to the right when there is an increase in wealth.

The slope of the *IS* curve is also changed when we move to the expanded model. In the simpler model, $\Delta Y / \Delta R = -(i_1 - c_1 tp_2)/[1 - c_1(1 - t - tp_1)]$. In the expanded model, $\Delta Y / \Delta R = -(i_1 + c_3 - c_1 tp_2)/ [1 - c_1(1 - t - tp_1) - i_2]$. For the expanded model, when the interest rate falls, there is an increase in investment *and* a rise in consumption (decline in saving). The rise in consumption in response to a decline in the interest rate is an additional source of aggregate expenditures. This produces a larger increase in income in response to a decline in the interest rate than for the simple model. Thus, when consumption varies negatively with the interest rate (the expanded model), the *IS* curve becomes flatter. The greater the sensitivity of consumption (and saving) to a change in the interest rate, that is, the greater c_3, the flatter the *IS* curve.[4]

The *IS* curve also becomes flatter when investment is responsive to income. In this situation, a fall in the interest rate increases investment and consumption directly, but the rise in aggregate income produces additional increases in consumption *and* investment. The greater the sensitivity of investment demand to income, that is, the greater i_2, the greater the rise in income. Thus, the *IS* curve becomes flatter with increases in i_2.

Figure 15.5 compares the *IS* curves for the simple and expanded models. We see that when the interest rate affects consumption and saving and when income affects investment, the relationship between the interest rate and income in the economy can be quite different from what it is for the simpler model. When the consumption or investment functions shift or when government spending changes, the shift in the *IS* curve is larger in the expanded model (Panel II) than in the simpler model (Panel I). Furthermore, changes in wealth shift the *IS* curve in the expanded model. Finally, the *IS* curve for the expanded model (Panel II) is flatter than for the simple model (Panel I).

The larger multiplier in the expanded model makes fiscal policy more potent, but it also increases the size of fluctuations in income when there are consumption or investment expenditures fluctuations or when there are fluctuations in wealth. We saw in Chapter 14 that monetary policy (*LM* shift) has a larger effect when the *IS* curve is relatively flat than when it is steeply sloped. Thus, when consumption varies negatively with the interest rate and when investment varies positively with income, the potency of monetary policy is increased. The vulnerability of the economy to *LM* shifts coming from shifts in money demand or from the money multiplier is increased, however. These issues are discussed in detail in Chapter 18.

---

[4] Recall that the slope of the *IS* curve is $\Delta R / \Delta Y$, so a large value of c_3 reduces $\Delta R / \Delta Y$.

FIGURE 15.5
IS CURVES FOR THE SIMPLE AND
EXPANDED MODELS.

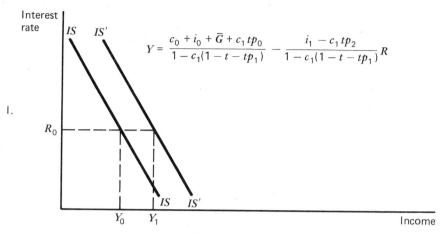

Simple model

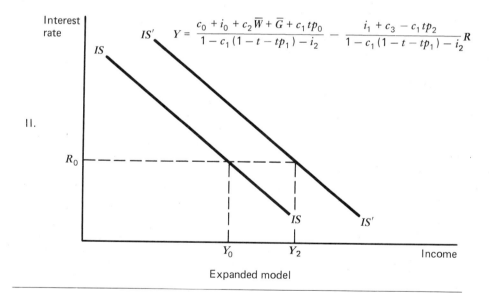

Expanded model

The *LM* Curve

In this section we examine the effects of wealth on the demand for money and bonds. The analysis of the effects of the public's portfolio choices are sufficiently complex that we study the issues involved initially for the simplified world of Chapter 13. Thus, it is assumed that there are no depository institutions and that all money is currency. Furthermore, we omit the government budget at this point so there are no government bonds. All bonds are issued by private firms to finance investment expenditures. In later sections, we shall allow for government bonds and depository institutions.

Given our assumptions, total wealth, W, must be allocated between money, M, and corporate bonds, B, that is, $W = M + B$. Furthermore, any change in the public's wealth must be mirrored in changes in holdings of money and bonds: $\Delta W = \Delta M + \Delta B$. Wealth changes when there is saving, and saving is disposable income less consumption, so

$$Y_d - C = S = \Delta W = \Delta M + \Delta B .\,{}^5$$

When the public saves, it does not spend all its income on current consumption. The increase in wealth that this saving provides is placed in additional holdings of money and corporate bonds. These stores of value can be used to support consumption expenditures in the future. The total quantity of wealth (money and bonds) that the public holds is the summation of past saving. The relationship between saving and changes in wealth gives a direct link between the financial and real sectors of the economy.

Consider the effect on money and bond demand of a change in wealth. Because wealth is money plus bonds, if there is an increase in wealth, the public must allocate the increase between money and bonds. If wealth declines, the public must reduce its holdings of money plus bonds. This implies that $\Delta W = \Delta M^D + \Delta B^D$. When wealth increases, the demand schedules for both bonds and money shift to the right. When wealth declines, both demand schedules shift to the left. Thus, $\Delta M^D/\Delta W > 0$ and $\Delta B^D/\Delta W > 0$. Because the change in wealth must be allocated between the changes in bonds and money, $\Delta M^D/\Delta W + \Delta B^D/\Delta W = 1.\,{}^6$

The relationship between money demand and bond demand can be summarized algebraically. Assuming the demand functions are linear, we have:

$$M^D = m_0 - m_1 R + m_2 Y + m_3 \overline{W}$$
$$B^D = b_0 + b_1 R - b_2 Y + b_3 \overline{W} .$$

Given the interest rate and given income, an increase in wealth produces an increase in the demands for money and for bonds that equals the increase in wealth, so $m_3 + b_3 = 1.0$. This implies that $b_3 = (1 - m_3)$. The proportion of an increase in wealth that does not increase money demand must increase bond demand.

---

[5] We allow later for changes in wealth coming from capital gains and losses.
[6] This must be true because $\Delta M^D/\Delta W + \Delta B^D/\Delta W = (\Delta M^D + \Delta B^D)/\Delta W$ and $\Delta M^D + \Delta B^D = \Delta W$, so $\Delta W/\Delta W = 1$.

We shall now show that a change in wealth can shift the LM curve. When wealth increases, there is an increase in the quantity of money without an offsetting decline in the quantity of bonds or an increase in the quantity of bonds without an offsetting decline in the quantity of money. Consider the case of an increase in the quantity of money that is not offset by a decrease in the quantity of bonds. This increase in wealth cannot be accomplished by open market operations, which change the mix of wealth between money and bonds, but not the total amount of wealth. The government can increase the quantity of money without reducing the quantity of bonds by printing additional money (currency) to finance an increase in government spending.[7] This transaction increases the quantity of money, but it does not reduce the quantity of bonds. Thus, there is an increase in wealth held by the public.

Figure 15.6 shows the diagram for money and bonds when there is an increase in wealth in the form of money. In the diagram for money, the quantity of money increases from $\overline{M}_0$ to $\overline{M}_1$. If the money demand schedule remains fixed, the interest rate must fall. In the diagram for the bond market, the quantity of bonds has not changed. If the bond demand schedule remains fixed, the interest rate does not change. Thus, in terms of money, the quantity of money exceeds the demand at the interest rate R_0, and the interest rate must fall. In terms of bonds, demand equals supply, and the interest rate does not fall. There is an inconsistency between the two diagrams. In Chapter 13, when we discussed the effects of an increase in the quantity of money (open market operations), the quantity of bonds declined to leave wealth unchanged. In that case (Figure 13.21), there is no inconsistency. Money supply exceeds money demand, and bond demand exceeds bond supply, so the interest rate falls. Now there is an inconsistency because money supply exceeds money demand but bond supply equals bond demand.

The inconsistency is eliminated when we allow for the effect of wealth on money demand and bond demand. Given the interest rate R_0 and income Y_0, the public allocates the increased wealth between money and bonds. Panel I of Figure 15.7 shows the situation where wealth is increased by the increase in money, $\Delta W = \Delta M = \overline{M}_1 - \overline{M}_0$, and the public wants to hold the *entire* increase in wealth in the form of money, (i.e., $m_3 = 1.0$). In this case, given R_0 and Y_0, the money demand schedule shifts right by the full amount of the increase in wealth. There is no change in the interest rate. The supply of money increases from $\overline{M}_0$ to $\overline{M}_1$, which would reduce the interest rate if money demand did not shift. But, money demand does shift because the public has more wealth and, given R_0 and Y_0, it wants to hold the entire increase in wealth as money. This implies that the bond demand schedule does not shift. The demand for bonds continues to equal the fixed supply at R_0. Given income, the interest rate does not change even though money and wealth have increased. Thus, there is no shift in the LM curve. We conclude that when there is an increase in the quantity of money that increases

---

[7] The increase in government spending also raises aggregate expenditures and income. This effect is discussed later.

FIGURE 15.6
AN APPARENT INCONSISTENCY
BETWEEN THE MONEY AND BOND MARKETS.

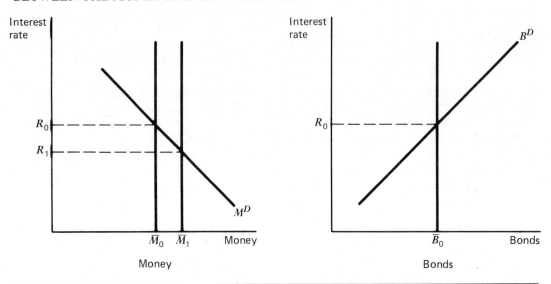

wealth and when the public wants to hold *all* of this additional wealth as money, the *LM* curve does not shift.

This conclusion appears to contradict the earlier discussion where we showed that an increase in the quantity of money shifts the *LM* curve down. In that discussion, however, the quantity of money increased as a result of an open market purchase of bonds by the Fed. Wealth did not change because the quantity of bonds declined dollar for dollar with the increase in the quantity of money. Now we are analyzing the effects of an increase in the quantity of money that also increases wealth. The wealth effect on money demand changes the conclusion. It is not necessary for the interest rate to decline when the quantity of money increases *if* there is also an increase in wealth and *if* the public wants to hold the entire increase in wealth as money.

This can be shown by considering the expression for the *LM* curve. In the simplified world we are considering at this point, there are no depository institutions so the quantity of money is exogenously determined and equals $\overline{M}$. Thus we have:

$$M^D = m_0 - m_1 R + m_2 Y + m_3 \overline{W}$$
$$M = \overline{M}.$$

FIGURE 15.7
THE EFFECT OF CHANGES IN
WEALTH THAT ARE IN THE FORM
OF MONEY.

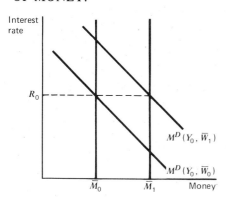
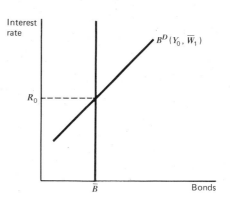

I.

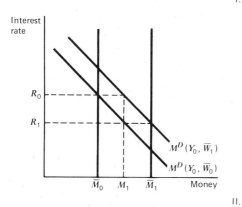
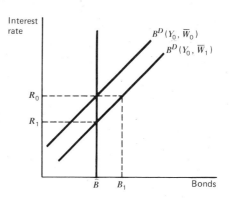

II.

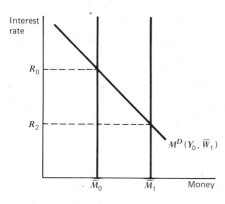
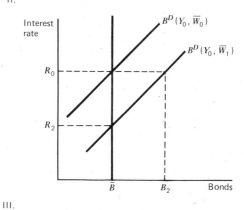

III.

Setting money demand equal to the exogenous supply and solving for the interest rate, we obtain

$$R = \frac{m_0 - \overline{M} + m_3 \overline{W}}{m_1} + \frac{m_2}{m_1} Y .$$

When the quantity of money increases but there is no change in wealth, the interest rate declines by $\Delta \overline{M}/m_1$, given income. The LM curve shifts down. When the increase in the quantity of money involves an increase in wealth, $\Delta W = \Delta M$ and the change in the interest rate is $\Delta R = (-\Delta \overline{M} + m_3 \Delta \overline{M})/m_1$. If the public wants to allocate the entire increase in wealth to money, $m_3 = 1.0$, so $\Delta R = (-\Delta \overline{M} + \Delta \overline{M})/m_1 = 0.0$. The LM curve does not shift.

Now let us consider a less extreme case where the public wants to divide the increase in its wealth between money and bonds. In this situation, $m_3 < 1.0$ and $\Delta R = (-\Delta \overline{M} + m_3 \Delta \overline{W})/m_1$. But the increase in wealth is in the form of money, so $\Delta \overline{M} = \Delta \overline{W}$ and $\Delta R = (-\Delta \overline{M} + m_3 \Delta \overline{M})/m_1 = -(1 - m_3)\Delta \overline{M}/m_1 = -(1 - m_3) \Delta \overline{W}/m_1$. The term $(1 - m_3)$ is the share of the increase in wealth (money) that the public wants to allocate to bonds.[8] The larger this share, the larger the downward shift in the LM curve.

Panel II of Figure 15.7 shows what happens to the interest rate at income Y_0 when the public wants to split the increase in wealth, which is in the form of money, equally between money and bonds, that is, $m_3 = .5 = (1 - m_3)$. In this situation, both the money demand and the bond demand schedules shift to the right. Now, however, the shift in the money demand schedule is less than the change in the supply of money. Thus, at the interest rate R_0, the actual quantity of money in the economy, $\overline{M}_1$ exceeds the quantity demanded, M_1. Furthermore, the bond demand schedule also shifts to the right. At the interest rate R_0, the quantity of bonds demanded, B_1, exceeds supply, $\overline{B}$. The public uses the excess supply of money to purchase bonds. This reduces the interest rate to R_1. At the lower interest rate, the public is willing to hold the increased quantity of money and the fixed supply of bonds, $\overline{B}$.

To summarize, at the initial interest rate, R_0, the public wants to hold half of its increased wealth as money and half as bonds. The actual increase in wealth is all in the form of money. The interest rate must fall sufficiently to induce the public to hold all of the increase in its wealth as money and none as bonds. This occurs at the interest rate R_1.

We conclude that when the increase in wealth is in the form of money, but the public wants to divide the increase in wealth between money and bonds, the interest rate must decline, given income, Y_0. Thus, the LM curve shifts down. The extent of the shift depends upon how the public wants to divide its increased

---

[8] Recall that m_3 is the proportion of an increase in wealth that the public wants to allocate to money and b_3 is the proportion it wants to allocate to bonds. Because $m_3 + b_3 = 1$, $(1 - m_3) = b_3$.

wealth between money and bonds at the interest rate R_0, that is, upon m_3.[9] The smaller m_3 is, the smaller is the increase in wealth that the public wants to hold as money and the greater is the increase in wealth that the public wants to hold as bonds, $(1 - m_3)$. When the increase in wealth is in the form of money, the lower m_3 is, the greater the decline in the interest rate is and, therefore, the greater the shift in the *LM* curve.

Panel III shows the situation when the increase in wealth is in the form of money, but the public does not want to hold any more money at the interest rate R_0 and income Y_0. In this situation, $m_3 = 0.0$ and $(1 - m_3) = 1.0$; the public wants to hold the entire increase in wealth in the form of bonds. Thus, the money demand schedule does not shift, and the bond demand schedule shifts to the right by the full amount of the increase in wealth. At the interest rate R_0, the public now wants to hold the quantity B_2 of bonds, where $(B_2 - B_1) = \Delta W$. There are no more bonds to hold, so the interest rate must fall sufficiently to induce the public to hold the increased quantity of money and to be satisfied with holding no more bonds. In this limiting case of $m_3 = 0.0$, the interest rate must fall to R_2, which produces the largest downward shift in the *LM* curve.

Now let us consider the opposite case, where the increase in wealth takes the form of an increase in the quantity of bonds. It is convenient to postpone the analysis of the effects of increasing government bonds until later in the chapter. Here we increase the quantity of corporate bonds, which are assumed to finance investment expenditures. Unless m_3 is zero, an increase in wealth in the form of bonds shifts the *LM* curve up. The greater the increase in wealth that the public wants to hold as money, m_3, given the interest rate and income, the larger the upward shift in the *LM* curve. When a change in wealth is in the form of bonds, the expression for the change in the interest rate is $\Delta R = m_3 \Delta \overline{W}/m_1$.

Figure 15.8 shows the effect on the interest rate of an increase in wealth that is in the form of bonds. Panel I shows the situation when $m_3 = 0.0$ and $(1 - m_3) = 1.0$; that is, the public wants to hold all the increased wealth in the form of bonds. In this case, the money demand schedule does not shift, and the increase in the supply of bonds from $\overline{B}_0$ to $\overline{B}_1$ is exactly matched by a shift in the demand for bonds. The interest rate does not change. We conclude that when the increase in wealth is in the form of bonds, the *LM* curve does not shift if the public wants to hold the *entire* increase in wealth as bonds at the interest rate R_0 and income Y_0. Thus, if $m_3 = 0.0$ and, therefore, $(1 - m_3) = 1.0$, there is no shift in the *LM* curve.

Panel II shows the change in the interest rate that occurs when the increase in wealth is in the form of bonds, but $m_3 = .5 = (1 - m_3)$. In this case, the public wants to split the increased wealth equally between money and bonds, but there is no additional money to hold. At the interest rate R_0, both the money demand and the bond demand curves shift to the right. Because the public wants to allocate

---

[9] The extent of the shift also depends upon the sensitivity of money demand to a change in the interest rate, m_1. The lower m_1, the greater the shift in the *LM* curve.

FIGURE 15.8
THE EFFECT OF A CHANGE IN
WEALTH THAT IS IN THE FORM OF BONDS.

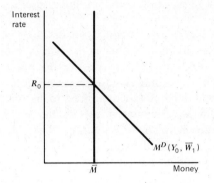
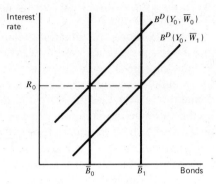

I.

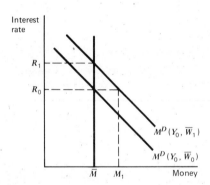
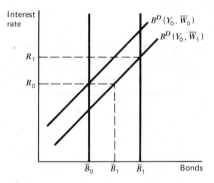

II.

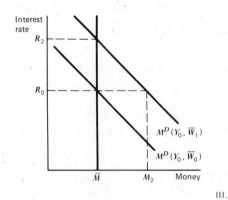
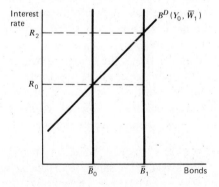

III.

half of its increased wealth to money, the rightward shift in the bond demand schedule is not sufficiently large for the public to hold the increased supply of bonds willingly at the interest rate R_0. At that interest rate, there is an excess demand for money of $(M_1 - \overline{M})$ and an excess supply of bonds equal to $(\overline{B}_1 - B_1)$. The public sells bonds in an attempt to increase its money balances. There is no more money available, so the interest rate must rise sufficiently to induce the public to hold all its increased wealth in the form of bonds. This occurs when the interest rate rises to R_1. Thus, at income Y_0, the interest rate rises from R_0 to R_1; the *LM* curve shifts up.

Panel III shows the situation when $m_3 = 1.0$ and $(1 - m_3) = 0.0$. This means that the public wants to hold the entire increase in wealth as money. The actual increase in wealth is in bonds. In this situation, the interest rate must rise sufficiently to induce the public to reverse its portfolio decision totally. In equilibrium, the entire increase in wealth must be in bonds and none in money. When $m_3 = 1.0$, the money demand schedule shifts by the full increase in wealth, and the bond demand schedule does not shift at all. There is an excess demand for money $(M_2 - \overline{M})$, which equals the increase in wealth. Because the increase in wealth is in the form of bonds, there is an excess supply of bonds of $(\overline{B}_1 - \overline{B}_0)$. The public attempts to sell bonds in order to increase its money holdings. This reduces bond prices and increases the interest rate. The interest rate must rise to equate money demand with money supply and bond demand with bond supply. This occurs at the interest rate R_2, which is higher than R_1 in Panel II. Thus, the upward shift in the *LM* curve is larger in Panel III than Panel II.

We conclude that when an increase in wealth takes the form of bonds, the *LM* curve shifts up. The extent of the shift depends upon m_3, the public's preferences for money versus bonds when wealth increases. The larger the share of the increased wealth that the public wants to allocate to bonds, the smaller the shift in the *LM* curve. When the public wants to allocate the entire increase in wealth to bonds, that is, $m_3 = 0.0$, bond demand shifts by the increase in bond supply, and the *LM* curve does not shift. Conversely, the larger m_3 is, the smaller is the proportion of the increased wealth that the public wants to allocate to bonds and, therefore, the greater the excess supply of bonds. Thus, the greater m_3, the greater the upward shift in the *LM* curve. The limiting case occurs when $m_3 = 1.0$. In this situation $(1 - m_3) = 0.0$, so the public does not want to hold any more bonds, given R_0 and Y_0. In this situation, there is the largest shift in the *LM* curve.

We can now summarize the effects of changes in wealth on the *LM* curve. When an increase in wealth is in the form of money, the *LM* shifts down. The extent of the shift depends upon the public's portfolio demand for money versus bonds. If the public wants to put the entire increase in wealth into bonds, that is, $m_3 = 0.0$, we get the largest shift in the *LM* curve. The larger the share of the increase in wealth that the public wants to allocate to money, given the interest rate and given income, the smaller the shift in the *LM* curve. When the public wants to place the entire increase in wealth in money, that is, $m_3 = 1.0$, there is no shift in the *LM* curve.

An increase in the quantity of money need not lead to a shift in the *LM* curve, but almost certainly will. When the increase occurs as a result of an open market operation, the *LM* does shift down. In this situation, wealth does not change; the quantity of money increases, but the quantity of bonds decreases by the same amount. When the increase in the quantity of money occurs as the result of an increase in wealth, however, the quantity of bonds is not reduced. In this situation, there is an increase in both the quantity of money and the amount of wealth held by the public. To the extent that the public wants to hold the additional wealth in the form of money, the reduction in the interest rate is reduced at the given income level, Y_0, and, therefore, the downward shift in the *LM* curve is reduced. In the extreme case where the public wants to hold the entire increase in wealth in the form of money, the increase in the quantity of money is matched by an equal increase in money demand, and the interest rate does not decline. Thus, the *LM* curve does not shift at all.

The effects on the *LM* curve of an increase in the quantity of bonds is the opposite of the case of an increase in the quantity of money. If the quantity of bonds increases with wealth unchanged, there has been an open market sale of bonds by the Fed. The quantity of bonds increases, and the quantity of money decreases. Thus, there is a decline in the quantity of money, given wealth. This produces an upward shift in the *LM* curve. When the increase in the quantity of bonds occurs at the result of an increase in wealth, however, the quantity of money is not reduced. This increase in the quantity of bonds need not produce an upward shift in the *LM* curve, but almost certainly will. The greater the share of increased wealth that the public wants to devote to bonds, that is, the larger $(1 - m_3)$ is, and, therefore, the smaller m_3 is, then the smaller is the shift in the *LM* curve. In the limiting case where the public wants to hold the entire increase in wealth in the form of bonds, the demand for bonds increases by the same amount as the supply, and the interest rate does not have to rise, given income. In this case, an increase in the quantity of bonds does not shift the *LM* curve. Conversely, the larger m_3, the smaller the increase in wealth that the public wants to allocate to bonds, given R_0 and Y_0. The larger m_3, the greater the upward shift in the *LM* curve when an increase in wealth is in the form of bonds. The largest shift occurs when $m_3 = 1.0$.

DETERMINING INCOME AND THE INTEREST RATE

In this section we show that when the interest rate and wealth affect consumption, when income affects investment, and when wealth affects money (and bond) demand, the interaction between the real and financial sectors is increased. The real and financial sectors are highly interdependent.

The *IS* curve developed in this chapter is

$$Y = \frac{c_0 + i_0 + c_2 \overline{W} + \overline{G} + c_1 t p_0}{1 - c_1(1 - t - t p_1) - i_2} - \frac{i_1 + c_3 - c_1 t p_2}{1 - c_1(1 - t - t p_1) - i_2} R$$

and the *LM* curve, assuming no depository institutions, is

$$R = \frac{m_0 - \overline{M} + m_2 \overline{W}}{m_1} + \frac{m_2}{m_1} \, Y \, .$$

The expressions for the *IS* and *LM* curves can be combined to solve for the equilibrium income and interest rate. We shall not do that here because the expressions are a mess! Rather, we shall analyze the interaction between the real and financial sectors more informally.

Earlier in this chapter it was shown that when investment is sensitive to changes in income (i.e., $i_2 > 0.0$), there are relatively large shifts in the *IS* curve when the consumption or investment functions shift, when wealth changes, or when there is a change in fiscal policy (government expenditures, transfers, or tax rates). The degree to which these shifts affect equilibrium aggregate income depends upon the slope of the *LM* curve. If the *LM* curve is steep, that is, a high ratio of the income sensitivity of money demand to the interest rate sensitivity (m_2/m_1), the large shifts in the *IS* curve do not produce large changes in equilibrium income. There is a substantial change in the interest rate that affects interest sensitive expenditures (investment and consumption).[10] If the *LM* curve is not very steep, however, shifts in the *IS* curve produce relatively large changes in equilibrium income. There is a relatively small change in the interest rate, so there is little offsetting crowding out or crowding in of interest sensitive spending.

When investment is sensitive to changes in income, the *IS* curve also becomes flatter, that is, $\Delta R / \Delta Y$ is reduced. The slope is further reduced when consumption varies negatively with the interest rate. When these effects are taken into account, shifts in the *LM* curve produce relatively large changes in equilibrium income. Thus, monetary policy becomes more potent, and shifts in money demand or changes in the money multiplier also have a greater effect on equilibrium income.

Changes in wealth shift both the *IS* and the *LM* curves and, therefore, affect the equilibrium income and interest rate. An increase in wealth raises consumption at the initial income and interest rate. Thus, the *IS* curve shifts to the right, and equilibrium income rises. If the increase in wealth is in the form of money, the *LM* curve shifts down. This produces a further increase in aggregate expenditures and income. The extent of the downward shift in *LM* depends upon the sensitivity of money demand to an increase in wealth, m_3, and upon the interest sensitivity of money demand, m_1. If both m_3 and m_1 are small, there is a large downward shift in money demand, and it is possible that the equilibrium interest rate is reduced when wealth increases.

If the increase in wealth is in the form of bonds, there is the same rightward shift in the *IS* curve, but now the *LM* curve shifts up. This limits the rise in aggregate expenditures and income because there is a relatively large rise in the interest rate that crowds out interest sensitive spending.

---

[10] The change in the interest rate also affects wealth. This is discussed later.

Up to this point, we have taken wealth to be exogenous to the model. This might appear to be an innocuous assumption, but it is not. Wealth is affected by investment and by interest rates.[11]

The capital stock in the economy is the sum of all previous investment that has occurred.[12] Investment is a flow. It is the expenditures, per unit of time, that firms make to add to their capital. Thus, investment increases the capital stock. Constant net investment expenditures imply a constant *increase* in the capital stock and in wealth. The effects of the increases in the capital stock and wealth can be handled only with a dynamic model, which is beyond the scope of this book.

Interest rates also affect wealth. When the interest rate rises, the price of bonds (and the value of the capital stock) declines. When the interest rate falls, the price of bonds (and the value of the capital stock) rises. In our simple model, the value of bonds and the value of the capital stock are the same.[13] For simplicity, we shall talk about the value of bonds rather than about the value of the capital stock when referring to wealth. The reader should note, however, that bonds are simply a claim on the capital stock. Thus, we could just as easily define wealth to be the sum of money and the capital stock rather than money plus bonds.

Because the price of bonds varies inversely with the interest rate, open market operations by the Federal Reserve do not leave wealth unchanged. For example, an open market purchase of bonds by the Fed increases the quantity of money and decreases the quantity of bonds. The public will sell the bonds only if their price rises, that is, if the interest rate falls. The increase in the price of bonds produces a capital gain for bondholders. Thus, an open market purchase of bonds increases the quantity of money, and it also increases the price of bonds that are still held by the public. Thus, wealth increases. Similarly, an open market sale of bonds reduces their price and increases the interest rate. Bondholders experience a capital loss. Thus, the quantity of money and the value of bonds held by the public both decline; wealth falls.

We conclude that open market operations not only affect the composition of wealth between money and bonds, but they also affect the amount of wealth. Thus, an increase in the quantity of money is more expansionary than previously indicated. It not only reduces the interest rate; it also encourages additional consumption spending because households are wealthier. A decrease in the quantity of money is more contractionary than indicated earlier. Not only does the interest rate rise, but consumption demand is also reduced because of the capital losses to bondholders. Though it is beyond the scope of this book, it can be shown that this wealth effect, which depends upon the interest rate, makes the *IS* curve flatter.

---

[11] We shall see in Chapter 16 that the real value of wealth is also affected by the price level.

[12] Strictly speaking, some investment replaces capital that has worn out. For simplicity, it is assumed that capital does not wear out. The basic conclusions about the effects of changes in wealth are not affected when replacement investment is included in the analysis.

[13] Recall that we are holding the price level constant.

Changes in wealth also affect the *LM* curve. When the interest rate rises, the value of bonds and, therefore, of wealth declines. Unless wealth holders want to reduce the quantity of bonds demanded by the full extent of the capital loss (i.e., $m_3 = 0.0$), they reduce the quantity of money demanded. It can be shown that this implies a flatter *LM* curve. A rise in income requires a smaller increase in the interest rate to equate money demand to supply because the wealth effect limits the increase in the quantity demanded. It can also be shown that the wealth effect reduces the size of the shifts in the *LM* curve that occur when open market operations change the quantity of money.

We conclude that because the value of wealth varies inversely with the interest rate, both the *IS* and the *LM* curve becomes flatter. Thus, the potency of both monetary and fiscal policies are increased. This also means, however, that nonpolicy-induced shifts in the *IS* and *LM* curves have a greater effect on aggregate expenditures and income.

THE FINANCIAL EFFECTS OF FISCAL POLICY

Up to this point it has been assumed that fiscal policy has no direct effect on the financial sector of the economy. It was shown in Chapter 14 that fiscal policy affects the financial sector indirectly because policy-induced changes in income affect the transactions demand for money. In fact, it is the transactions demand for money that produces an increase in the interest rate when there is a stimulative fiscal policy and that produces a decline in the interest rate when there is a restrictive fiscal policy. Thus, the transactions demand for money is responsible for the crowding out and crowding in from changes in fiscal policy.

It is shown in this section that there is more to crowding out and crowding in than the transactions demand for money. In particular, the behavior of the interest rate in response to a change in fiscal policy depends upon how the government finances budget deficits and how it disposes of budget surpluses. Budgetary considerations have direct consequences for the financial sector of the economy that affect aggregate income, interest rates, and the share of interest-sensitivity spending in total spending. For example, it is shown that when a deficit is financed by issuing government bonds, the interest rate on these bonds rises in order to induce the public to hold them. This interest rate increase produces crowding out of interest-sensitive spending in addition to the crowding out that occurs as a result of the stimulative effect of a rise in government spending or a cut in taxes.

Let us begin by showing how budget deficits or surpluses affect the relationships between saving and investment. Aggregate expenditures are $C + I + \bar{G}$, and aggregate income is $Y = C + S + (T - TP)$. Thus

$$Y = C + I + \bar{G} = C + S + (T - TP)$$

so

$$I + \bar{G} = S + (T - TP)$$

and

$$I = S + (T - TP - \bar{G}).$$

When government tax receipts exceed transfer payments and expenditures on goods and services, the government's income, T, exceeds its spending, $(TP + \bar{G})$. This saving is the government's budget surplus. When tax receipts are less than government spending, $(T - TP - \bar{G})$ is negative, and the government is dissaving. This dissaving is the government's budget deficit. Using the symbol S_G to denote government saving, we have $S_G = (T - TP - \bar{G})$. As $I = S + (T - TP - \bar{G})$, we see that

$$I = S + S_G.$$

Thus, investment equals private saving, S, plus government saving S_G.

When there is a government sector, investment is not necessarily equal to private saving. Net saving in the economy, S_N, is private saving, S, plus government saving S_G, that is, $S_N = S + S_G$. When there is a budget surplus, government saving is positive, so equilibrium investment exceeds private saving by the amount of the surplus. When there is a budget deficit, spending $(\bar{G} + TP)$ exceeds tax receipts, T. Government saving is negative, that is, $S_G = (T - TP - \bar{G}) < 0$. In this case, net saving is less than private saving, and investment is less than private saving by the amount of government dissaving (deficit). Only when the government's budget is exactly balanced does investment equal private saving.[14]

When government spending exceeds tax receipts, the deficit must be financed. This is done by either selling bonds to the public or by issuing money.[15] Now we see the direct link between the government's budget and the financial sector. When the government runs a budget deficit, the quantity of bonds or money, or both, must increase. It is important to note that a budget deficit is a flow. It is the difference between the flow of spending and the flow of tax receipts. A constant deficit implies a continuing *increase* in the quantity of bonds or money, or both, in the economy.

When government spending is less than tax receipts, something must be done with the accumulating savings. The savings are used to decrease the quantity of bonds or the quantity of money, or both. A constant budget surplus implies a constant reduction in the quantity of government bonds or money, or both.

---

[14] The relationship between saving and investment becomes even more complex when we introduce the foreign sector in Chapter 17.

[15] The government could sell assets, that is, sell oil leases, and so on. These activities occur, but they are usually small relative to the size of deficits. We assume for simplicity that deficits are always financed by selling bonds or issuing money.

Because budget deficits and surpluses affect the quantity of bonds or money, or both, in the economy, it is necessary to specify how changes in the quantities are held. This is done by including government bonds in the wealth held by the public. Thus, total wealth is money (currency), M, plus government bonds, GB, and corporate bonds, CB, that is, $W = M + GB + CB$.[16] When the public saves, it is adding to its holdings of wealth (net worth). This can take the form of increases in the holdings of money, government bonds, or corporate bonds.

Now consider a budget deficit. Because a budget deficit is financed by issuing additional bonds or money, or both, $(\bar{G} + TP - T) = \Delta M + \Delta GB$. Saving equals the change in wealth (net worth), so $S = \Delta W = \Delta M + \Delta GB + \Delta CB$. We continue to assume that all investment is financed by issuing corporate bonds, so $\Delta CB = I = S - (G + TP - T)$. The public has to save enough not only to purchase the increased quantity of corporate bonds that is issued to finance investment expenditures, but also to acquire the increased quantity of money or government bonds issued to finance the deficit.

Let us consider the implications of having a deficit financed by issuing additional government bonds versus a deficit financed by issuing additional money. We shall assume that the public treats corporate bonds and government bonds as perfect substitutes. This means that the public views corporate and government bonds as equivalent assets just as money holders view two $5 bills to be the equivalent of one $10 bill. Given this assumption, the public is unconcerned whether an increase in the quantity of bonds is the result of an increase in corporate bonds or an increase in government bonds. This assumption provides a significant simplification in the discussion that follows and is made in most macromodels. We relax this unrealistic assumption in the appendix to this chapter. It is shown in the appendix that the conclusions reached in the body of this chapter concerning the effects of a bond-financed deficit are not as clear-cut as they might appear.

The Effects of a Bond-Financed Deficit

With the assumption that government and corporate bonds are perfect substitutes, the total quantity of government and corporate bonds can be combined to obtain total bonds, B; that is, $B = GB + CB$. By combining government and corporate bonds into a single total, B, we can use the LM sector developed earlier in the chapter to analyze the financial effects of government deficits.

Let us first examine the financial effects of an increase in government spending that produces a deficit that is financed by issuing bonds. In this case, $S = \Delta W = \Delta CB + \Delta GB = \Delta B$. Thus, the public's saving and, therefore, its additional wealth must be devoted to increased holdings of corporate and government

---

[16] Recall that in our simple world, the value of corporate bonds equals the value of the capital stock.

bonds. When corporate and government bonds are perfect substitutes, we can use a result obtained earlier. An increase in wealth that is in the form of bonds produces an upward shift in the *LM* curve. The public wants to devote part of the increased wealth to money. It can be induced to hold the entire increase in wealth as bonds only if the interest rate is higher at each level of income. The extent of the upward shift in the *LM* curve depends upon the proportion of the increase in wealth that the public wants to allocate to increased money holdings, given the interest rate on bonds.[17]

The *LM* curve does not shift up only in the extreme case where the public wants to allocate all its increased wealth to bonds and, therefore, none to money [i.e., $m_3 = 0$ and $b_3 = (1 - m_3) = 1.0$]. The demand for bonds shifts to the right by the same amount as the quantity of bonds increases.[18] In this situation, the effects of a bond-financed deficit produced by an increase in government spending is described in Panel I of Figure 15.9. The *IS* curve shifts to the right to *IS'*, and the *LM* does not shift. The equilibrium is at Y_1 and R_1. The only financial affect of the deficit comes from the increased transactions demand for money at the higher level of income. The interest rate must rise to the point that the public is willing to hold the same quantity of money at income Y_1 as it was at Y_0. This rise in the interest rate crowds out interest sensitive spending. As was explained earlier, however, this is the same crowding out that occurs when the *IS* curve shifts to the right as a consequence of any increase in aggregate expenditures. An upward shift in the consumption or investment function produces the same crowding out of interest-sensitive spending as results from the increase in government spending. Thus, the increase in the quantity of bonds that results from the government's budget deficit has no effect on the economy when the public is willing to hold the entire increase in government bonds at the initial interest rate.

In all other cases, the increase in government bonds does have an independent effect on the economy. Panel II of Figure 15.9 shows such a situation. Here it is assumed that at the interest rate R_0, the public wants to devote part of its saving (increased wealth) to money; that is, $m_3 > 0.0$. In this situation, the *LM* curve shifts up to *LM'*. This upward shift in the *LM* curve produces a new equilibrium in which the rise in the interest rate is larger and the rise in income is smaller than for Panel I. Now the deficit has an effect on the interest rate over and above that produced by an increase in the transactions demand for money. The larger rise in the interest rate crowds out additional interest sensitive spending and limits the rise in income.

The bond-financed deficit also affects the *IS* curve. The increase in wealth represented by the increased quantity of government bonds increases consump-

---

[17] Note that the same argument holds when corporate bonds are issued rather than government bonds.

[18] This extreme case was shown in Figure 15.8.

FIGURE 15.9
EFFECTS OF A BOND-FINANCED
INCREASE IN GOVERNMENT SPENDING.

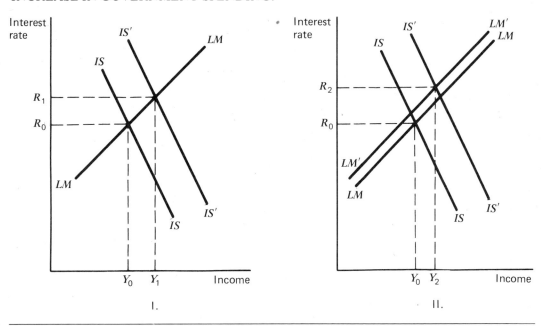

I.

II.

tion expenditures given income and the interest rate.[19] Thus, the increase in wealth shifts the *IS* curve to the right. This increase in aggregate demand raises income, but it also raises the interest rate. Thus, there is further crowding out of interest-sensitive spending.

There are so many forces at work when there is a change in fiscal policy that it is instructive to go step-by-step through the movement from one equilibrium to another. For simplicity, assume that the government's budget is exactly in balance at the initial equilibrium (R_0, Y_0) of Figure 15.10. Because government saving is zero at this equilibrium, private saving equals investment. Now let government expenditures on goods and services increase. This shifts the *IS* curve to the right to *IS'* and produces a series of financial and real effects as the economy moves to a new equilibrium.

[19] To the extent that the public anticipates higher taxes in the future to cover the interest and principal payments for the government debt, it will not feel wealthier and, therefore, will not raise consumption. See Robert J. Barro, "Are Government Bonds Net Worth?" *Journal of Political Economy*, December 1974.

FIGURE 15.10
STEP-BY-STEP ANALYSIS OF A
BOND-FINANCED INCREASE IN
GOVERNMENT SPENDING.

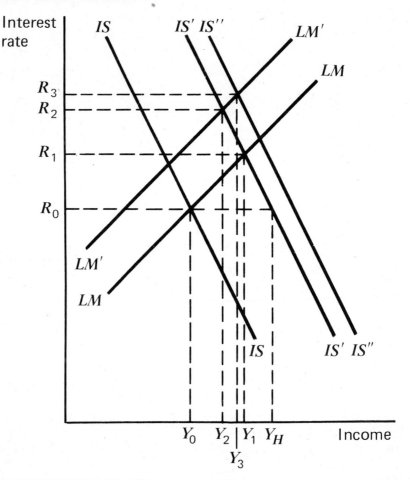

At the initial interest rate, R_0, the IS curve shifts to the right by the amount $\Delta Y = \Delta \overline{G} \cdot m_{Y(R_0)}$. If this were the end of the story, income would rise to Y_H. When the interest rate remains at R_0 there is, of course, no crowding out. At Y_H, investment equals private saving less the budget deficit. Private saving is higher at Y_H that at Y_0. In fact, saving increases sufficiently to match both the higher level of investment at Y_H and to offset the government's dissaving. The size of the deficit at Y_H depends not only upon the increase in $\overline{G}$ but also upon the increase in tax receipts and the reduction in transfer payments that occur when the economy moves from Y_0 to Y_H. The larger the multiplier, $m_{Y(R_0)}$, the greater the increase in income and, therefore, the greater the rise in tax receipts and the decline in transfer payments. The response of tax receipts and transfer payments reduces the size of the deficit. In fact, for a sufficiently larger multiplier, there could be a balanced budget, or even a surplus at Y_H.[20]

Equilibrium does not occur at Y_H, however, because the interest rate rises. The increase in the interest rate reduces interest-sensitive spending, so income rises only to Y_1. Thus, there is a smaller increase in tax receipts and a smaller decline in transfer payments when income rises to Y_1 rather than to Y_H. The steeper the LM curve and the flatter the IS curve, the smaller the rise in income is. These slopes determine how much Y_1 falls short of Y_H and, therefore, how much larger the deficit is at Y_1 than at Y_H.

In the limiting case where the LM curve is vertical, income does not rise at all when there is an increase in $\overline{G}$. In this case, the deficit equals the increase in government spending plus the increased interest payments on government bonds. The interest rate rises sufficiently to choke of an amount of interest-sensitive spending that is equal to the increase in government spending. Private saving equals the lower level of investment plus the deficit.

We assume that the LM curve is not vertical, so the equilibrium occurs at Y_1. Thus, income rises, but there is a deficit. Because we are assuming that the deficit is bond financed, the quantity of government bonds rises by the amount of the deficit. Note that we have not yet allowed for any financial effects of the increase in the quantity of government bonds. The interest rate rises from R_0 to R_1 solely as a consequence of the transactions demand for money. Assuming that the public does not want to put all its saving into bonds, the interest rate must rise further. This is shown as an upward shift in the LM curve to LM'. This financial effect of the deficit raises the interest rate to R_2 and decreases the rise in income to Y_2. The deficit is larger at Y_2 and R_2 than at Y_1 and R_1. Tax receipts are lower, and transfer payments are higher because of the lower income and higher interest rate.

When wealth increases, consumption rises. The upward shift in the consumption function produces a further rightward shift in the IS curve. To the extent that the IS curve shifts up with the larger quantity of government bonds, the negative effects on income are reduced. Thus, if the IS curve shifts to IS″, income is Y_3.[21] At this income, however, the interest rate is even higher. This crowds out additional interest sensitive spending, and it increases interest payments on government bonds. The increased interest payments tend to offset the higher tax receipts and the lower income-related transfer payments that occur at Y_3. For the sake of

---

[20] It can be shown that the budget remains in balance if $m_{Y(R_0)} = 1/(t + tp_1)$. If $m_{Y(R_0)}$ is less than $1/(t + tp_1)$, there is a budget deficit. If $m_{Y(R_0)}$ is greater than $1/(t + tp_1)$, there is a surplus.

[21] In the diagram, Y_3 is between Y_2 and Y_1. This is not the only possibility. For example, if the increased quantity of bonds produces a rightward shift in the IS curve that is large relative to the upward shift in LM, Y_3 could be higher than Y_2. Although this produces a higher income, it also produces a higher interest rate and additional crowding out.

argument, assume that these two effects just offset each other at Y_3 and R_3, so the deficit remains constant. This, then, is the equilibrium.

We cannot end the story with equilibrium shown in Figure 15.10. Note that the deficit, $(\bar{G} + TP - T)$, is a flow. As long as the government is spending more than its receipts, the quantity of government bonds continues to rise. The LM and IS curves continue to shift up, and the interest rate continues to rise. Thus, the amount of crowding out of interest-sensitive spending continues to increase. More and more investment spending is choked off. The fall in investment spending reduces the amount of new corporate bonds that is issued and reduces the growth of wealth. This limits the shifts in the IS and LM curves. As long as the government continues to run a deficit that is bond financed, however, the quantity of government bonds increases, and this puts additional upward pressure on interest rates.

We see that a complex dynamic adjustment is unleashed once government spending increases and a budget deficit develops that is financed by issuing bonds. This does not mean that the economy gets out of control, but it does mean that the government has to adjust spending and taxes over time to offset undesirable movements in income and interest rates.

The Effects of a Money-Financed Deficit

Now let us consider the effects of an increase in government spending that is financed by issuing money. Recall that the depository system has not been introduced yet, so all money is currency.

The initial rightward shift in the IS curve that is produced by an increase in government expenditures is the same no matter whether the deficit is financed by issuing more money or by issuing more bonds. The shift in the LM curve is different, however. Now the increase in wealth is all in the form of money. Except in the extreme case where the public wants to hold the entire increase in wealth in the form of money, the LM curve shifts down. The public can be induced to hold the larger quantity of money only if the interest rate is lower at every level of income.

The responses of the equilibrium income and interest rate are shown in Figure 15.11. Because the IS curve shifts right and the LM curve shifts down, the rise in income from a money-financed increase in government spending is larger then for a bond-financed increase (compare Figures 15.10 and 15.11). The rise in the transactions demand for money is accompanied by an increase in the supply of money, so the LM curve shifts down. The downward shift in the LM curve is limited, however, to the extent that the public wants to hold its increased wealth in the form of money. Thus, in Figure 15.11, the interest rate does rise to R_1. Furthermore, the increase in wealth shifts the IS curve to the right to IS''. This produces an additional rise in income and in the interest rate. The rise in the interest rate is far smaller, however, than the increase that occurs when the rise in government spending is financed by issuing bonds rather than money.

FIGURE 15.11
EFFECTS OF A MONEY-FINANCED
INCREASE IN GOVERNMENT SPENDING.

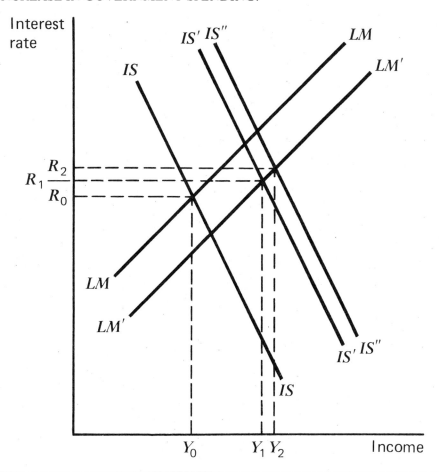

We conclude that a rise in government spending (or a tax cut) that is financed by issuing additional money is more expansionary than when it is financed by issuing bonds. This occurs because the interest rate does not have to rise or at least not rise very much when the deficit is money financed. As a consequence, there is less crowding out of interest-sensitive spending. Thus, the decision concerning how to finance the deficit has significant implications for the equilibrium income and interest rate.

The dynamic response of the economy to a continuing deficit is also affected by the financing decision. Note that income rises appreciably when the deficit is money financed, but the rise in the interest rate is small. Thus, the increase in tax receipts and the reduction in income-related transfer payments are sizable. Furthermore, transfer payments that are interest payments on the government debt do not rise very much. There is no increase in the quantity of government bonds, and maturing bonds are replaced by new ones at an interest rate that is not much higher than R_0. Thus, tax receipts increase and total transfer payments decline. This reduces the size of the deficit. Furthermore, as long as there is a deficit, the quantity of money continues to increase. This increases the wealth of the public, which shifts the *IS* curve to the right and the *LM* curve down. As income continues to rise, income-sensitive transfer payments continue to decline and income tax receipts continue to rise. Eventually, the rising tax receipts and falling transfer payments eliminate the deficit. At that point there is no further dynamic adjustment. This is a far different story from that for a bond-financed deficit where the *IS* and *LM* curves continue to shift.

How Should a Deficit be Financed?

The choice between a bond and a money-financed deficit has significant implications for income, the interest rate and for the extent of crowding out. It is natural to ask, then, just how should a deficit be financed? There is no simple answer to this question. The answer depends crucially upon the reasons for the deficit and upon the status of the economy. While a full analysis cannot be given because we have not introduced the price level, a few examples make the point.[22]

Consider a deficit that is caused by a downward shift in the consumption or investment function. Assume that this produces a recession, that is, a significant amount of unemployed resources. Further assume that the government does not change fiscal policy. Government expenditures on goods and services remain constant, the tax rate is not changed, and the base level of transfer payments is constant. In this situation, the fall in aggregate expenditures and income reduces tax receipts and raises income-related transfer payments. With government expenditures on goods and services held constant, the fall in tax receipts and rise in transfer payments create a deficit. By keeping fiscal policy unchanged, the government moderates the decline in aggregate demand and income. Falling tax receipts and rising transfer payments prevent disposable income from declining by as much as does aggregate income. This limits the decline in consumption and reduces the size of the multiplier. Thus, when fiscal policy remains unchanged, the government sector acts as a built-in stabilizer, which limits the decline in income and aggregate demand.

---

[22] It is also shown in the appendix that the results are less clear-cut than indicated here when we drop the assumption that government and corporate bonds are perfect substitutes.

Implicit in the government's role as a built-in stabilizer is a budget deficit. Note that this deficit results from the effects of the recession and not from a shift in fiscal policy. If the government finances the deficit by issuing bonds, the *LM* curve shifts up, and the interest rate rises. This further retards aggregate demand by choking off interest sensitive spending. This is a pure case of crowding out caused by a budget deficit. The initial leftward shift in the *IS* curve reduces income and reduces the transactions demand for money. If this were the end of the story, there would be crowding in because the reduction in the interest rate increases interest-sensitive spending. The government budget goes into deficit, however, at the lower level of income. When the deficit is bond financed, the *LM* curve shifts up. This upward shift produces crowding out. Thus, if the government keeps the quantity of money constant and increases the quantity of bonds, it pushes up interest rates, worsens the recession, and makes the deficit even larger. This tends to offset the stabilizing effects of the unchanged fiscal policy.

Alternatively, the government can finance its deficit by expanding the quantity of money. In this case, the *LM* curve shifts down. This reduces the interest rate, stimulates spending, and helps eliminate the recession. The decline in the interest rate, and the rise in income reduce the deficit.[23]

The Federal Reserve determines the extent to which a deficit is financed by bonds or by money. The U.S. Treasury always issues bonds to the public in order to cover a deficit. If the Federal Reserve stays out of the picture, this means that the quantity of bonds in the hands of the public increases, and the *LM* curve shifts up. Alternatively, if the Fed engages in an open market purchase of securities, the quantity of money rises, and the quantity of bonds in the hands of the public does not rise. In this case, the *LM* curve shifts down. When the Federal Reserve buys the bonds, it "*monetizes*" the new debt. This simply means that it holds the additional bonds, and the public holds additional money rather than bonds.

Unless fiscal and monetary policies are coordinated, the built-in stabilizer role of the government could disappear. If the Fed refuses to monetize the newly issued government debt, the *LM* curve shifts up, and the rise in interest rates intensifies the recession.[24] In this case, monetary and fiscal policy are working at cross-purposes.

The second example of a deficit also involves a recession, but this time the government responds by cutting taxes or raising spending. This raises the deficit above what would occur in the passive case discussed earlier. If the deficit produced by the active policy is bond financed, part of the stimulus is lost because the *LM* curve shifts up. This case provides an example of the need to coordinate fiscal and money policy. If monetary policy refuses to monetize the new debt, that

---

[23] Should the *IS* curve shift back to the right, however, the Federal Reserve must take the money out of the economy through open market operations if excess aggregate expenditures are to be avoided. This and related issues are discussed in Chapter 18.

[24] To the extent that the increase in wealth shifts the *IS* curve up, the recession is not intensified.

is, increase the quantity of money, interest rates will be higher, and interest sensitive spending will be lower than if the deficit is monetized. Fiscal policy can still work against the recession, but if monetary policy refuses to go along, the two policies will be at cross-purposes. A larger fiscal stimulus is required if monetary policy refuses to increase the quantity of money. This and the preceding case are examples of why it may not be beneficial to have an independent Federal Reserve.

Now consider a deficit at the opposite extreme. Assume that the economy is operating at a high level of activity and that the government creates a deficit by either raising expenditures or cutting taxes. This policy shifts the *IS* curve to the right and creates excess demand in the economy.[25] Although the best policy is to avoid this fiscal stimulus in the first place, assume that the stimulus does occur. In this case, it is better to finance the deficit by issuing bonds rather than by issuing money. The increase in the quantity of bonds shifts the *LM* curve up, which raises the interest rate and crowds out interest-sensitive spending. This serves to offset some of the expansionary effects of the fiscal policy. If the deficit is financed by issuing money rather than bonds, the *LM* curve shifts down, and excess demand in the economy is increased. By refusing to increase the quantity of money, the Federal Reserve can at least reduce the excess demand created by the fiscal stimulus. This case is an example of how bad fiscal policy can be offset to some degree by good monetary policy. It is also an example of why it can be beneficial to have an independent Federal Reserve.

GOVERNMENT BUDGET DEFICITS AND SURPLUSES WHEN THERE ARE DEPOSITORY INSTITUTIONS

In order to keep a complicated story as simple as possible, we analyzed the effects of government budget deficits and surpluses, assuming that there are no depository institutions. This meant that money was currency and we did not have to worry about transactions accounts. We saw in Chapter 14 that the presence of depository institutions amplifies the effects of monetary policy, and it also amplifies the effects of money demand shifts. The purpose of this section is to determine the role of depository institutions when there are government budget surpluses and deficits. In the process of explaining that role, we introduce the important concepts of the monetary base.

The analysis is complicated by the fact that transactions account balances are part of the quantity of money, but they are not part of the wealth of the private sector of the economy. This can be seen from Table 15.1, which shows simplified

---

[25] Recall that we are holding the price level constant. In reality, excess aggregate demand produces inflation and deficient aggregate demand produces deflation. The relationship between aggregate demand and the price level is analyzed in Chapter 16.

TABLE 15.1
CONSOLIDATING THE BALANCE SHEET FOR THE PUBLIC WITH THE BALANCE SHEET OF DEPOSITORY INSTITUTIONS

The Public
(households and firms)

Assets	Liabilities
Currency (C^P)	
Transactions accounts (T)	
Nonpersonal time accounts (N)	
Personal time accounts (P)	
Government bonds (GB^P)	
Corporate bonds (CB^P)	Corporate bonds (CB)
Physical capital (K)	

Depository Institutions

Assets	Liabilities
Currency (C^{DI})	Transactions accounts (T)
Reserve accounts (TR)	Nonpersonal time accounts (N)
Corporate bonds (CB^{DI})	Personal time accounts (P)
Government bonds (GB^{DI})	

The Private Sector
(the public plus depository institutions)

Assets
Currency ($C^P + C^{DI}$)
Reserve accounts (TR)
Government bonds ($GB^P + GB^{DI}$)
Physical capital (K)

balance sheets for the public and for depository institutions. The table also shows the consolidated balance sheet for the entire private sector. The public (households and firms) holds as assets currency, transactions accounts, nonpersonal accounts, personal time accounts, government bonds, corporate bonds, and physical capital. For simplicity, loans granted by depository institutions to the public are treated as bonds. Thus, it is assumed that bonds are the only liability issued by the public. These bonds are held by both the public and depository institutions. The net worth of the public equals total assets less corporate bonds. The assets of depository institutions are currency (vault cash), reserve balances at the Fed, government bonds, and corporate bonds. These assets are supported by the transactions, nonpersonal time, and personal time account liabilities issued by depository institutions. Depository institutions are assumed for simplicity to have no net worth, so their total assets equal their total liabilities.

When the public and depository institutions are combined to form the private sector, many of the assets and liabilities cancel out. Thus, for the private sector as a whole, the transactions accounts, nonpersonal time accounts, and personal time accounts held as assets by households and firms are offset by an equal amount of liabilities of depository institutions. Thus, T, N, and P make no contribution to the wealth of the private sector. Similarly, the bonds (liabilities) issued by corporations to depository institutions are offset by the corporate bonds that are assets of depository institutions.[26] For the private sector as a whole, wealth (net worth) equals total assets, which are comprised of currency, reserves, government bonds, and physical capital. Transactions accounts and other liabilities issued by depository institutions are not part of the wealth of the private sector. Only currency is part of wealth.

There are two means by which the total wealth of the private sector changes. The capital stock (measured by corporate bonds) increases as a result of investment by firms in plant and equipment. This investment increases the capital stock, and it increases the wealth of the private sector. We continue to assume that all investment is financed by corporate bonds, that capital never wears out, and that any maturing bonds are replaced by new ones. These assumptions allow us to measure the value of the capital stock by the value of bonds. Under the assumption of a fixed price level, the value of corporate bonds moves one-for-one with the value of capital stock. Thus, the demand for corporate bonds is really the demand for the capital stock. Thus, when we talk about corporate bonds, we are really talking about the capital stock.[27]

The remaining elements of wealth: currency, total reserves, and government bonds are the liabilities of the government sector to the private sector. The total size of these liabilities changes as a result of budget deficits and surpluses. When the government runs a budget deficit, its total liabilities rise. A deficit is financed by issuing additional currency, by increasing reserves of depository institutions, or by issuing government bonds. Thus, $(\overline{G} + TP - T) = \Delta C + \Delta TR + \Delta GB$. When the government runs a budget surplus, its liabilities fall.

In the United States, deficits are initially financed by the sale of bonds. The public buys the bonds and the Treasury uses the funds to finance government spending. As explained in Chapter 12, these transactions do not change the quantity of reserves in the depository system. Thus, initially, wealth rises by the increase in government bonds when there is a deficit. The Federal Reserve determines whether or not to purchase any of the bonds from the public. If it decides to purchase some of them, the Fed pays for the securities by increasing the reserve balances of depository institutions. The quantity of bonds held by the public declines, and the amount of reserves in the depository system rises by the amount of the open market operation. The decline in the quantity of bonds held by the pub-

---

[26] Depository institutions are owned by the public, so their net worth is a component of the public's wealth (net worth). It is possible to allow for the net worth of depository institutions, but that complicates the analysis without adding any substance. In the interest of simplicity, we assume that depository institutions have no net worth.

[27] If the reader is uncomfortable about measuring the asset capital by the liability corporate bonds, then substitute the expression capital stock for corporate bonds in the analysis that follows. No conclusions are affected.

lic equals the increase in the quantity of reserves. When the Fed purchases the bonds issued by the Treasury, it replaces bonds with reserves as the source of the increase in wealth.

The demand for currency also plays a role in determining how a deficit is financed. To see how this works, we have to return to the discussion of the relationship between reserves and currency provided in Chapter 12. The total quantity of currency held by the private sector of the economy is comprised of currency held by the public (households and firms) plus the vault cash of depository institutions. When members of the public increase their currency holdings, they reduce their account balances at depository institutions in exchange for the currency. This depletes the vault cash of depository institutions. These institutions replenish their vault cash by reducing their reserve balances at the Federal Reserve in exchange for new currency issued by the Fed. Thus, an increase in currency demand by the public leads to an increase in the quantity of currency that is issued by the government (Fed) and to a decrease in the quantity of reserves in the depository system.

Now let us consider the case where there is a deficit and the Federal Reserve purchases all the bonds issued by the Treasury. This means that the entire deficit is financed by an increase in the reserves of depository institutions. Suppose, however, that the public happens to increase its demand for currency. This decreases total reserves and increases the quantity of currency. Total reserves rise by the Fed's bond purchase less the increase in currency. In this situation, the deficit equals the increase in total reserves plus the increase in currency. Finally, consider the case where the public does not change its demand for currency, but depository institutions want to increase their holdings of vault cash. Depository institutions obtain the additional currency (vault cash) from the Federal Reserve, which reduces their reserve accounts by the amount of the transaction. In this case, the deficit still equals the increase in total reserves plus the increase in currency. This time, however, the additional currency is held by depository institutions rather than by the public. In the interest of simplicity, we shall assume in the remainder of the chapter that changes in currency holdings are the result of changes in the public's demand for currency. The reader should note, however, that currency can also change as a result of changes in the demand for vault cash.

The manner in which a deficit is financed is not determined by the Treasury. It issues government bonds. If the Fed decides to purchase the bonds, the deficit ends up being financed by an increase in total reserves. If the public decides to hold more currency, however, the increase in total reserves is reduced by the amount that currency increases. In this case, the deficit ends up being financed by the net increase in reserves plus the increase in currency. Thus, the Federal Reserve and the public ultimately determine how the deficit is financed.

Fiscal policy determines expenditures on goods and services, it sets programs for transfer payments, and it sets tax rates. Thus, fiscal policy affects the size of the deficit. The U.S. Treasury finances the deficit by issuing government bonds. If the Fed does not engage in open market operations and if the public does not change its currency holdings, then $(\bar{G} + TP - T) = \Delta GB$. If the Fed purchases some of the bonds, the increase in the quantity of bonds in the hands of the public is reduced, and total reserves rise. In this case $(\overline{G} + TP - T) = \Delta GB + \Delta TR$. Furthermore, for every dollar increase in the public's currency holdings, total reserves decline by a dollar. Thus, to the extent that the public increases its holdings of currency, the increase in total reserves is reduced, so $(\overline{G} + TP - T) = \Delta GB + \Delta TR + \Delta C$.

Monetary policy determines the amount of the deficit that is financed by an increase in government bonds. This is true even when we allow for changes in currency demand. Consider the case where the Fed wants the entire deficit to be financed by bonds. Assume that the public increases its holdings of currency. It might appear that the Fed's plans have been thwarted because currency rises. This is not the case, however, because total reserves fall by the amount that currency rises, so $\Delta C = -\Delta TR$. The deficit is still financed by bonds. Alternatively, consider the case when the Fed wants to purchase all the government bonds arising from a deficit, but the public increases its currency holdings. In this situation, the Fed buys the bonds, but the rise in total reserves is offset to the extent that currency holdings increase. The deficit in this case equals $\Delta TR + \Delta C$.

These examples illustrate that the deficit is initially financed by the Treasury's issuing government bonds, but the Fed determines the amount of the deficit that ultimately is financed by ΔGB. It is this ultimate change in government bonds that must be held by the public. The mix between ΔTR and ΔC is determined by the public. It is the total, $\Delta TR + \Delta C$, however, that determines the extent to which the deficit is financed by ΔGB. The sum of total reserves and currency is called the *monetary base*, *MB*. Thus, $MB = TR + C$. The public determines C, but the Fed can adjust TR through open market operations to achieve any desired value of *MB*. Thus, the Federal Reserve can determine the monetary base and, therefore, determine the extent to which a deficit is financed by a change in government bonds versus a change in the monetary base. The deficit is $(\overline{G} + TP - T) = \Delta GB + \Delta TR + \Delta C = \Delta GB + \Delta MB$. By controlling ΔMB, the Fed controls the size of ΔGB. If the Federal Reserve holds the monetary base constant, that is, $\Delta MB = 0.0$, the entire deficit is financed by government bonds. If the monetary base rises, the amount of the deficit that is financed by government bonds is reduced by the amount that the monetary base increases.

THE RELATIONSHIP BETWEEN THE MONETARY BASE AND THE *LM* CURVE

It is instructive to see how changes in the monetary base are related to the *LM* curve and how changes in the mix between currency and reserves affect the curve. Here we allow for the effects of nonpersonal time accounts on interest rates and income.

Let us start by deriving a money multiplier for the monetary base. The monetary base is total reserves plus currency, $MB = TR + C$. Total reserves are required reserves plus excess reserves, $TR = RR + ER$. Required reserves are $RR = r_T T + r_N N$. Assuming that the ratio of nonpersonal time accounts to transactions accounts (n), the ratio of excess reserves to transactions accounts (e), and the ratio of currency to transactions accounts (c), are constant, we have $N = nT$, $ER = eT$, and $C = cT$. Thus, $MB = TR + C = r_T T + r_N nT + eT + cT$, and $MB = (r_T + r_N n + e + c)T$. Solving for transactions accounts, we get:

$$T = 1/(r_T + r_N n + e + c)MB .$$

This gives us the multiplier relationship between the monetary base and transactions accounts.

Because $M = C + T$ and $C = cT$, $M = cT + T = (1 + c)T$. Substituting the expression for T, we get,

$$M = [(1 + c)/(r_T + r_N n + e + c)]MB$$

which is the multiplier relationship between the monetary base and the quantity of money.[28]

This expression indicates that the quantity of money is a multiple of the monetary base. Though we will not show the algebra, the total credit extended by depository institutions is also a multiple of the monetary base.[29] This suggests that the Federal Reserve does not have to purchase all the government bonds initially issued to finance the deficit in order for the deficit to be "monetized." Leaving wealth effects aside for the moment, when the monetary base increases, there is a multiple expansion in transactions accounts, personal time accounts, and nonpersonal time accounts. This implies that there is also a multiple expansion in the demand for bonds (supply of credit) by depository institutions. Part of this credit expansion goes for purchase of government bonds. In particular, assume that $\Delta GB_{DI}^D = m_{GB} \cdot \Delta MB$, where ΔGB_{DI}^D is the demand for government bonds by depository institutions and m_{GB} is the multiplier relation between the change in the monetary base and this demand for government bonds.

We know that the deficit is $(\overline{G} + TP - T) = \Delta GB + \Delta MB$. The trick is to determine the increase in the monetary base that generates an increased demand for government bonds by depository institutions that equals the net increase in government bonds, ΔGB, that occurs after the monetary base increases. We want the net increase in government bonds to equal the increase in the demand for

---

[28] Vault cash is not included in the definition of money (M1), but it is included in the money base. For simplicity, this complication is not taken into account. It can be shown that allowing for the inclusion of vault cash in the monetary base does not alter the conclusions in the text.

[29] The derivation is analogous to that shown in Chapter 11 for the relationship between total credit and total reserves.

government bonds by depository institutions, that is, $\Delta GB = \Delta GB_{DI}^{D}$. Because $\Delta GB_{DI}^{D} = m_{GB} \Delta MB$, we have $(\overline{G} + TP - T) = \Delta GB + \Delta MB = m_{GB} \Delta MB + \Delta MB$, and $(\overline{G} + TP - T) = (1 + m_{GB})\Delta MB$. The required change in the monetary base is $\Delta MB = (\overline{G} + TP - T)/(1 + m_{GB})$.

An example makes the point. Assume $m_{GB} = 3.0$, and the deficit is $1 billion. In this case $\Delta MB = \$1$ billion$/4.0 = \$250$ million. If the government has a deficit of $1 billion and the Fed purchases $250 million of the bonds that the Treasury issues, the net increase in the quantity of bonds is $750 million. The $250 million increase in the monetary base produces an increase in the demand for government bonds by depository institutions of $\Delta GB_{DI}^{D} = m_{GB} \Delta MB = 3.0(\$250$ million$) = \$750$ million. This equals the net increase in the quantity of bonds.

In the simple example we considered, the net increase in the quantity of government bonds equals the increase in the demand for the bonds, so there is no tendency for the interest rate to rise, given income. Thus, the *LM* curve does not shift even though the Fed purchases only 25 percent of the bonds issued to finance the deficit. If it purchases a smaller percentage than this, the *LM* curve shifts up; if it purchases more than 25 percent, the *LM* curve shifts down.

We saw earlier in this chapter that the public's demand for bonds depends upon wealth. A deficit increases the net worth of the public, $\Delta W = \Delta GB + \Delta MB$, and increases the public's demand for bonds. We shall not go through the analysis when wealth is considered because the conclusions reached earlier are qualitatively unchanged. When the government has a budget deficit that is totally bond financed, that is, $\Delta MB = 0$, the *LM* curve shifts up. To the extent that the monetary base increases, the amount of upward shift is reduced. For a sufficiently large increase in the monetary base, the *LM* curve shifts down. Thus, the Federal Reserve determines both the direction and the extent of the shift in the *LM* curve that accompanies a budget deficit.

In determining its policy response to a deficit, the Federal Reserve must determine not only the amount to finance by an increase in the monetary base, but also how to react to currency flows once the monetary base is increased. Assume that there is a budget deficit and the Fed buys some of the bonds issued by the Treasury. This means that $(\overline{G} + TP - T) = \Delta GB + \Delta TR$. Further, assume that initially the public does not change its currency holdings, so $\Delta C = 0.0$ and $\Delta MB = \Delta TR$. Thus, the change in the monetary base equals the change in total reserves. Now depository institutions and the public interact to produce a multiple expansion of money and credit. The expansion that occurs depends upon whether the Federal Reserve decides to maintain the increase in total reserves or the increase in the monetary base. If there are currency drains during the money expansion process, the Fed cannot maintain the initial increase in both reserves and the monetary base.

Consider the case where the Fed maintains the increase in the monetary base. This involves engaging in no further open market operations following the initial one that purchased some of the bonds from the deficit and increased total reserves. As the quantity of transactions accounts rises, the public increases its holdings of currency.[30] The increase in currency reduces total reserves relative to the initial increase from the Fed's purchase of bonds. The monetary base is unaffected by the increase in currency because $MB = TR + C$, and every dollar increase in currency is offset by a dollar decrease in total reserves. Thus, the currency drain that occurs when transactions accounts increase does not affect the monetary base, but it does reduce total reserves. When the Fed maintains the initial increase in the monetary base, it allows currency drains to affect total reserves. As shown in Chapter 11, when this policy is pursued, the expansion in money and credit is smaller than when the effect of currency drains on reserves is offset by further open market operations.

If the Fed pursues a policy that maintains the initial increase in total reserves, the monetary base increases by more than the initial increase from financing the deficit. In this case, the initial increase in total reserves remains in the system because the Fed purchases additional bonds to offset the effect of the expansion of currency. This means that the total increase in the monetary base is the initial increase coming from purchasing some of the bonds from the deficit plus the increase in currency. Thus, there is a larger expansion in money and credit than occurs when the Fed maintains the initial increase in the money base.

Which of these two policies the Fed should pursue depends upon what it is trying to accomplish. If it wants to maximize the expansionary effect of monetizing the deficit, it should pursue the total reserves policy. If it wants to limit the expansionary effect, it should pursue the monetary base approach.

SUMMARY

This chapter expanded on the model developed in Chapters 13 and 14 to study several additional linkages between the financial and real sectors of the economy. It was shown that when consumption and saving depend upon the interest rate and wealth, when investment depends upon income, and when money and bond demand depend upon wealth, the financial and real sectors of the economy are highly interdependent. This interdependence is heightened by the fact that the value of wealth is affected by the interest rate.

It was also shown that the sensitivity of the economy to policy changes and to exogenous shifts in aggregate expenditures or in money demand is increased in the expanded model. Both the *IS* and the *LM* curves are flatter, and income multipliers are increased relative to the simpler model of Chapter 14.

Most of this chapter was devoted to discussing how government budget deficits affect economic activity and interest rates. It was shown that when deficits are

---

[30] As explained in Chapter 11, there is no simple, mechanical relationship between ΔT and ΔC that keeps c constant. For simplicity, we assume that c is constant, however.

bond financed, the public's portfolio allocation of the increased financial wealth between money and bonds causes the *LM* curve to shift up. This crowds out interest-sensitive spending. This crowding out occurs in addition to any crowding out that occurs as the result of an increase in the interest rate coming from an increase in the transactions demand for money. A bond-financed deficit produces portfolio crowding out, as opposed to transactions demand crowding out, even during a recession when the *IS* curve shifts to the left. When a deficit is financed by an increase in the monetary base and by the resulting increase in the credit extended by depository institutions, portfolio crowding out does not occur.

The issue of coordinating monetary and fiscal policy arises when determining how to finance a deficit. If the Federal Reserve refuses to monetize a deficit (increase the monetary base), interest rates rise. This is counterproductive when there is unemployment and fiscal policy is attempting to stimulate the economy. Monetizing a deficit at high levels of employment adds to the stimulus to aggregate expenditures and creates inflationary pressures. In this case, the Fed should refuse to monetize the deficit.

The chapter concluded with a discussion of the monetary base. It was shown that the monetary base is a component of the public's financial wealth and that changes in the monetary base determine the extent to which the Federal Reserve allows a deficit to be bond financed.

APPENDIX

CROWDING OUT ONCE AGAIN: THE CASE OF THREE ASSETS

Up to this point, it has been assumed that corporate and government bonds are perfect substitutes. This assumption is inconsistent with the facts. Government bonds do not have default risk; corporate bonds do have this risk. This is why the yields on government bonds are less than the yields on corporate bonds. If the risk on corporate bonds were constant, the yield on corporate bonds would be the yield on government bonds plus a constant risk premium. Corporate and government bonds could still be perfect substitutes. In reality, the risk on corporate bonds fluctuates with economic conditions. This prevents corporate and government bonds from being perfect substitutes.

In this appendix, the assumption of perfect substitutes is abandoned, and the financial sector is expanded to include money, corporate bonds, and government bonds as three distinct assets. It is shown that the issue of crowding out is less clear-cut when there are more than two assets available to the public.

With three distinct assets available to the public, it is necessary to modify the *LM* curve. The public allocates its wealth among money, government bonds, and corporate bonds: $W = M + GB + CB$. There are now two interest rates in the economy: the interest rate on government bonds, R_{GB}, and the interest rate on corporate bonds, R_{CB}. This means that it is no longer possible to talk about "the" interest rate.

The demand for money is still composed of a transactions demand and a portfolio demand. Now, however, when the public increases the quantity of money demanded as income increases, it can sell either government bonds or corporate bonds. Furthermore, the demand for money is sensitive to both the interest rate on government bonds and on corporate bonds. These considerations can be summarized in the following money demand function

$$M^D = m_0 - m_1 R_{GB} - m_2 R_{CB} + m_3 Y + m_4 \overline{W} .$$

Given income, wealth, and the interest rate on corporate bonds, a rise in the interest rate on government bonds reduces the quantity of money demanded. Given income, wealth, and the interest rate on government bonds, a rise in the interest rate on corporate bonds reduces the quantity of money demanded. The parameter m_3 has a positive sign indicating that when income rises, given R_{GB}, R_{CB}, and $\overline{W}$, there is an increase in the transactions demand for money. The parameter for wealth, m_4, indicates the proportion of an increase in wealth that the public wants to hold as additional money balances, given R_{GB}, R_{CB}, and Y.

The demand for government bonds is

$$GB^D = gb_0 + gb_1 R_{GB} - gb_2 R_{CB} - gb_3 Y + gb_4 \overline{W} .$$

Given income, wealth, and the interest rate on corporate bonds, a rise in R_{GB} increases the quantity of government bonds demanded. Given income, wealth, and the interest rate on government bonds, a rise in the interest rate on corporate bonds, R_{CB}, reduces the quantity of government bonds demanded. Thus, government and corporate bonds are assumed to be substitutes in the portfolios of the public. Note, however, they are not perfect substitutes.[31] The income parameter, gb_3, has a negative sign indicating that a rise in income, given R_{GB}, R_{CB}, and $\overline{W}$, reduces the quantity of government bonds demanded. This indicates that an increase in the transactions demand for money is met, in part, by a desire to sell government bonds. Finally, gb_4 indicates the proportion of an increase in wealth that the public wants to allocate to government bonds when R_{GB}, R_{CB}, and Y are held constant.

The demand for corporate bonds is

$$CB^D = cb_0 - cb_1 R_{GB} + cb_2 R_{CB} - cb_3 Y + cb_4 \overline{W} .$$

Given R_{CB}, Y, and $\overline{W}$, a rise in R_{GB} reduces the quantity of corporate bonds demanded. This indicates that corporate and government bonds are substitutes, but again not perfect substitutes. The parameter cb_2 has a positive sign indicating that given R_{GB}, Y, and $\overline{W}$, a rise in R_{CB} increases the quantity of corporate bonds

---

[31] If government and corporate bonds are close substitutes, gb_2 is large. If they are not close substitutes, gb_2 is small. If they are perfect substitutes, gb_2 is infinite.

demanded. When income rises, given R_{GB}, R_{CB}, and $\overline{W}$, the increase in the transactions demand for money is met in part by a desire to sell corporate bonds. Thus, cb_3 has a negative sign. Finally, cb_4 indicates the share of an increase in wealth that the public wants to allocate to an increase in corporate bonds when R_{GB}, R_{CB}, and Y are constant.

It is apparent from the description of the demand for money, government bonds, and corporate bonds, that the relationships are interconnected. The relationship among the demands for the three assets can be seen by looking at the demand functions together

$$M^D = m_0 - m_1 R_{GB} - m_2 R_{CB} + m_3 Y + m_4 \overline{W}$$

$$GB^D = gb_0 + gb_1 R_{GB} - gb_2 R_{CB} - gb_3 Y + gb_4 \overline{W}$$

$$CB^D = cb_0 - cb_1 R_{GB} + cb_2 R_{CB} - cb_3 Y + cb_4 \overline{W}.$$

As long as wealth is held constant, a change in interest rates or in income can produce only a reshuffling of the public's desired holdings of the three assets. Thus, if R_{GB} rises, the public wants to hold more government bonds. Given wealth, this can be accomplished only by reducing money holdings and selling corporate bonds. This implies that $m_1 + gb_1 + cb_1 = 0.0$. By the same argument, if R_{CB} rises, the public wants to hold more corporate bonds. Given wealth, this implies that the public wants to hold less money and less government bonds. Thus, $m_2 + gb_2 + cb_2 = 0.0$. The parameters of income must also sum to zero. A rise in income increases the demand for money. The public attempts to obtain the additional money by selling both government and corporate bonds. Thus, $m_3 + gb_3 + cb_3 = 0.0$. The sum of the parameters for wealth must be one. An increase in wealth must be allocated among the three assets. Thus, $m_4 + cb_4 + gb_4 = 1.0$. Finally, a shift in the intercept of one of the demand functions must be offset by shifts in the opposite direction for the other two assets. For example, if m_0 increases, the public wants to hold more money given R_{GB}, R_{CB}, Y and $\overline{W}$. This implies that the public wants to hold less government and corporate bonds. Thus, gb_0 and cb_0 decrease. Given wealth, $m_0 + gb_0 + cb_0 = 0.0$.

A full analysis of the three-asset model is beyond the scope of this book. A few comments are in order, however, to throw some additional light on the issue of crowding out. Recall that when government and corporate bonds were assumed to be perfect substitutes, crowding out occurred for two reasons. First, an expansionary fiscal policy causes a rightward shift in the IS curve, which increases income. This raises the transactions demand for money and raises the interest rate. Second, if the deficit is bond financed, the increase in the quantity of government bonds shifts the LM curve up and produces a further increase in the interest rate. These two factors produce a rise in the interest rate that crowds out interest-sensitive spending.

When we allow for the fact that government and corporate bonds are not perfect substitutes, the same basic forces are at work, but now we have to be concerned about the effects on the interest rate for government bonds versus the effects on the interest rate for corporate bonds. The interest rate on corporate bonds is the most relevant interest rate when determining the effect of a deficit on investment spending. It is the interest rate that firms pay when they borrow to finance investment projects, and it is the interest rate that a firm can earn when it lends to another firm.

The interest rate on government bonds is also relevant, however, because the public holds a diversified portfolio composed of corporate bonds, government bonds, and money. If the interest rate on government bonds rises, the public wants to increase the share of wealth devoted to government bonds and to reduce the shares allocated to corporate bonds and money. Thus, when R_{GB} rises, the public attempts to sell corporate bonds and to reduce money balances in order to buy government bonds. This increases the interest rate on corporate bonds. Thus, the interest rate on government bonds affects the interest rate on corporate bonds and, therefore, indirectly affects investment.

With the interrelationships among corporate bonds, government bonds, and money in mind, let us consider the effect of a budget deficit that is financed by issuing government bonds. Assume that government expenditures on goods and services, $\overline{G}$, increases and that this produces a budget deficit. Aggregate expenditures increase, which raises income and the transactions demand for money. The public attempts to obtain additional money balances by selling both government and corporate bonds. This raises both R_{GB} and R_{CB}. Because the quantity of money is fixed, these interest rates must rise until the public is willing to hold the same quantity of money as before. Thus, the effect of the rise in the transactions demand for money is basically the same as in the two-asset case. The rise in income pushes up interest rates, and the higher interest rates reduce interest sensitive spending.

The deficit also increases the quantity of government bonds in the economy. The effects of this increase are not so straightforward. Unless the public wants to hold the entire increase in wealth in the form of government bonds, R_{GB} must rise. Equilibrium occurs when R_{GB} rises sufficiently relative to R_{CB} to induce the public to hold the larger quantity of government bonds. This does not necessarily mean that R_{CB} rises, however. Consider the case where the public wants to hold most of its increased wealth in the form of corporate bonds (i.e., cb_4 is close to one). R_{CB} could actually fall. The public sells government bonds in an effort to purchase more corporate bonds. This pushes R_{GB} up and R_{CB} down. The rise in the interest rate on government bonds reduces the quantity of corporate bonds demanded, however, and this reduces the downward pressure on R_{CB}.

If corporate and government bonds are close substitutes, the parameter cb_1 in the corporate bond demand equation is large. If this parameter is sufficiently large, the rise in R_{GB} reduces the demand for corporate bonds so much that R_{CB} rises. Thus, if corporate and government bonds are very close substitutes, an increase in the quantity of government bonds increases both R_{GB} and R_{CB}. This occurs even though, at the initial interest rates and income, the public wants to put a substantial share of increased wealth from the deficit into corporate bonds. In this case, the portfolio effect of the increase in the quantity of government bonds produces crowding out of interest-sensitive spending. If corporate and government bonds are not very close substitutes, however, the rise in R_{GB} is not sufficient to keep R_{CB} from falling when the public attempts to put a substantial share of its increased wealth into corporate bonds. A fall in R_{CB} stimulates interest-sensitive spending. In this case, there is crowding in rather than crowding out produced by the portfolio effects of the larger quantity of government bonds.

Consider the case where the public wants to hold the entire increase in wealth in the form of money. There are still sales of government bonds, but now the public wants to hold money rather than corporate bonds. In this case, there are no purchases of corporate bonds, so there is no pressure for R_{CB} to fall. Because corporate and government bonds are substitutes, a rise in R_{GB} induces the public to sell corporate bonds and to buy government bonds. This raises the interest rate on corporate bonds. In this situation R_{GB} and R_{CB} must rise sufficiently to induce the public to hold the same quantity of money and the larger quantity of government bonds. Because both interest rates rise, there is portfolio crowding out of interest sensitive spending.

It is impossible to predict on theoretical grounds whether a deficit that increases the quantity of government bonds raises or lowers the interest rate on corporate bonds at the initial income level, Y_0. Thus, it is impossible to predict whether there is portfolio crowding out or portfolio crowding in. The response of R_{CB} depends upon the share of the increase in wealth that the public wants to devote to corporate bonds at the initial interest rates and income, upon how responsive the demand for government bonds is to a rise in R_{GB}, and upon the degree to which corporate and government bonds are substitutes.

The greater the share of the increase in wealth that the public wants to place in money and government bonds at the initial income and interest rates, the smaller the share it wants to devote to corporate bonds. When wealth increases as a result of a deficit and the public wants to devote a relatively small share to corporate bonds, there is not much downward pressure on R_{CB}. Alternatively, if the share of increased wealth devoted to corporate bonds is large, there is substantial downward pressure on R_{CB}. Because the deficit is financial by an increase in the quantity of government bonds, R_{GB} rises. The extent of this increase is affected by the degree of responsiveness of the demand for these bonds to a change in R_{GB}, that is, by gb_1. The smaller gb_1 is, the greater is the increase in R_{GB} required to equate the quantity of government bonds demanded to the increased supply caused by the deficit. Conversely, the larger gb_1, the smaller the increase in R_{GB}. Finally, the demand for corporate bonds is affected by R_{GB}. If corporate and government bonds are not very close substitutes, cb_1 is relatively small, so a rise in R_{GB} does not reduce the demand for corporate bonds very much. In this case, the rise in R_{GB} does not put much upward pressure on R_{GB}. Conversely, if cb_1 is large, a rise in R_{GB} produces substantial upward pressure on R_{CB}.

We conclude from all this that, given the initial level of aggregate demand and income, a rise in the quantity of government bonds caused by a deficit increases the interest rate on corporate bonds and causes portfolio crowding out if cb_4 and gb_1 are small and cb_1 is large. Thus, the greater the rise in R_{CB} and the greater the portfolio crowding out, (1) the smaller is the portion of the increase in wealth that is devoted to corporate bonds at the initial interest rates and income, (2) the smaller is the sensitivity of the demand for government bonds to the increase in R_{GB}, and (3) the greater is the degree to which corporate and government bonds are substitutes. Conversely, the larger are cb_4 and gb_1, and the smaller is cb_1, the smaller is the rise in R_{CB} and the smaller is the amount of crowding out. Indeed, it is possible for R_{CB} to fall when there is a deficit even though R_{GB} rises. In this case, there is portfolio crowding in rather than crowding out.

This analysis of portfolio crowding out is an excellent example of why it can be deceptive to work with a two-asset model. In a two-asset model, government, and corporate bonds are assumed to be perfect substitutes, so portfolio crowding out occurs. In the more realistic case where the two types of bonds are not assumed to be perfect substitutes and, therefore, a three-asset model is required, portfolio crowding out need not occur.

The significance of this conclusion is that it is impossible to predict whether a rise in aggregate demand coming from a bond-financed increase in government spending is less or more expansionary than a rise in aggregate demand coming from a shift in the consumption function. In the two-asset case the rise in $\bar{G}$ is less expansionary because there is portfolio crowding out as well as transactions crowding out. In the three-asset case, transactions crowding out could be offset to some degree by portfolio crowding in. If this occurs, a rise in $\bar{G}$ is more expansionary than an upward shift in the consumption or investment functions. In this case, the government's deficit does not retard interest sensitive spending; it actually encourages the spending by reducing the upward pressure on R_{CB}.

It turns out, then, that the portfolio effect of a bond-financed deficit is an empirical issue. The empirical evidence is scant and unreliable concerning the effect of wealth on the demand for corporate bonds, on the interest sensitivity of the demand for government bonds, and on the degree to which government and corporate bonds are substitutes. At this writing, the issue is an open one. In the remainder of this text, we shall assume that government and corporate bonds are close substitutes. This allows us to use the two-asset model that is a foundation of the *IS-LM* apparatus. In the two-asset model of money and bonds, portfolio crowding out does occur. The reader is warned, however, against drawing any strong conclusions concerning the degree to which a bond-financed budget deficit crowds out interest sensitive spending.

SELECTED REFERENCES

Dornbusch, Rudiger and Stanley Fischer, *Macroeconomics* (2nd ed.), New York: McGraw-Hill, 1981.

Friedman, Benjamin, "Crowding Out or Crowding In? Economic Consequences of Financing Government Deficits," *Brookings Papers on Economic Activity*, 3:1978, pp. 593–641.

Gordon, Robert, *Macroeconomics* (2nd ed.), Boston: Little, Brown and Company, 1981.

Tobin, James, "Money and Finance in the Macroeconomic Process," *Journal of Money, Credit and Banking*, May 1982, pp. 171–204.

DETERMINING REAL OUTPUT, THE PRICE LEVEL, AND INFLATION

16

In this chapter, we study aggregate supply and show how the interaction of aggregate demand and aggregate supply determines real output, the price level, and the inflation or deflation rate. It is shown that aggregate supply determines real income and output in the long run, but that aggregate demand has a powerful effect on real output and income in the shorter run. Furthermore, investment expenditures increase the capital stock, which increases long-run aggregate supply. Much of the chapter is concerned with explaining how economic policy can control inflation. It is shown that, in the short run, policymakers often face a trade-off between inflation and unemployment. This trade-off creates a dilemma for policy because it is not possible to achieve both full employment and price stability in the short run. Within this context, the special problems of stagflation, where unemployment and inflation occur at the same time, are considered. The chapter concludes with a discussion of the long-run determinants of inflation. It is shown that expansionary monetary policy is a necessary ingredient for chronic inflation.

AGGREGATE SUPPLY

In Chapters 13 through 15, prices were held constant. This simplified the analysis, but it prevented us from seeing the powerful constraint that aggregate supply imposes on the economy, and it prevented us from studying the determinants of the price level. When holding prices constant, it was implicitly assumed that the output of goods and services passively adjusts to changes in aggregate demand. In reality, output is not determined in this passive manner. Rather, it is determined by a combination of technological and economic factors that are summarized in an aggregate supply function. This function determines the total amount of goods and services that firms want to produce.

It is useful to start the discussion with an analysis of the determinants of aggregate supply in the long run. By the long run, we mean a period of time long enough that wages and prices adjust to their equilibrium values. The analysis of aggregate supply in the shorter run, where wages and prices have not fully adjusted, is outlined later.

Long-run Aggregate Supply

The theory of long-run aggregate supply is a straightforward application of the microeconomic theory of the firm to the economy as a whole. Production decisions are affected by technological and economic considerations. Technology determines how the inputs of the factors of production are transformed into output of goods and services. Economic decisions determine the mix of the factors of production that is selected to produce a particular output, and they determine the total output that is produced.

Let us start the discussion by looking at technological factors. The total output that the economy can produce is described by the aggregate production function. For simplicity, it is assumed that there are only two factors of production: labor and capital. The aggregate production function is

$$Q = f(L, K)$$

where Q is total output, L is labor, and K is capital. The function, f, describes how inputs of labor and capital are transformed into output.[1] Thus, total output is determined by the amount of labor and capital employed and by the technical relationship, f, describing the transformation of inputs into output.

The demand for factor services, that is, L and K, is derived from the desire to produce output, which, in turn, is derived from the demand for output. The demand for labor services is isolated most easily by assuming that the amount of capital is fixed. Panel I of Figure 16.1 shows the production function relationship, PF, between labor input and aggregate output when K is fixed.

When labor input is zero, output is zero because both labor and capital are necessary for production. When labor input is small, the curve is steep, indicating that an increase in labor produces a relatively large increase in output. This occurs because these few workers are highly productive when there is a fixed capital stock in place. As additional labor is employed, the slope of the curve becomes less steep, and eventually it becomes flat. This is the principle of the declining marginal product of labor. When more and more labor is employed to

---

[1] More precisely, the production function describes the minimum amounts of labor and capital required to produce a given level of output.

FIGURE 16.1
THE AGGREGATE PRODUCTION
FUNCTION AND THE MARGINAL
PRODUCT OF LABOR.

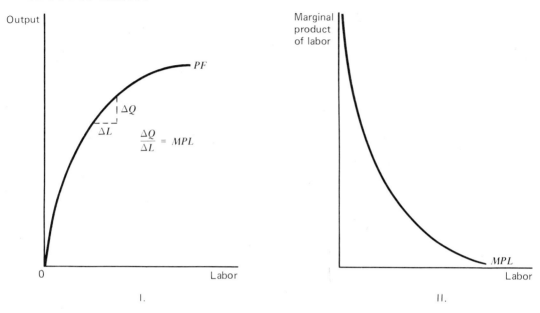

work with the fixed stock of capital, the additional output obtained from increasing labor by one more unit declines. The slope of the curve, $\Delta Q / \Delta L$, is the marginal product of labor. The relationship between the marginal product of labor and the amount of labor employed is shown in Panel II of Figure 16.1. The marginal product of labor, *MPL*, is initially high, and it falls as the amount of labor employed to work with the fixed capital stock increases.

Panel I of Figure 16.1 describes the relationship between the amount of labor employed and the output produced in the economy. It cannot tell us how much output is produced or how much labor is employed. To determine the amount of output that firms want to produce and the amount of labor they want to employ, we must introduce some economic considerations.

The relationship between economic and technological factors can be shown most easily by considering the behavior of an individual firm. A firm wants to produce an output that maximizes its profits. This is accomplished by producing at the output where marginal cost equal marginal revenue. It can be shown that if the firm cannot affect the price of its product or the prices of the factors of production, profit maximization occurs when the value of the marginal product of each factor of production equals the price of that factor. This means that the firm maximizes profits when the value of the marginal product of labor equals the wage rate. The value of the marginal product is output price times the amount of output produced with the addition of another unit of labor. There is profit maximization when

$$P_i MPL_i = W_i$$

where P_i is the price of the output produced by the ith firm, MPL_i is the marginal product of labor for that firm, and W_i is the wage rate that it pays.

In determining aggregate output and the aggregate demand for labor, we are assuming that the economy operates like a gigantic firm. Thus, firms produce an aggregate output at which the value of the marginal product of labor equals the wage rate. For the economy as a whole

$$P \cdot MPL = W$$

where P is a price index measuring the price of aggregate output, MPL is the marginal product of labor from the aggregate production function, and W is an index measuring the wage rate in the economy. Dividing both sides of this expression by P we obtain

$$MPL = W/P .$$

The price index, P, is the price level. The ratio of the wage rate to the price level, W/P, is the real wage rate. It measures the purchasing power of the wage rate. Thus, we have the result that firms produce an aggregate output at which the marginal product of labor equals the real wage rate.

This result allows us to derive a demand schedule for labor and to determine the level of output that firms want to produce. Panel II of Figure 16.1 has shown that the marginal product of labor declines as the amount of labor increases. Because firms equate the marginal product to the real wage rate, $MPL = W/P$, we can convert the MPL curve in Panel II of Figure 16.1 into the labor demand schedule, LD, in Panel I of Figure 16.2. The labor demand schedule is also downward sloping. If the real wage rate is $(W/P)_0$, firms demand the quantity of labor L_0. At L_0, $MPL = (W/P)_0$, and profits are maximized. If the real wage rate falls to $(W/P)_1$, the marginal product of the quantity of labor L_0 exceeds the real wage rate. Firms increase their demand for labor. As the quantity of labor utilized by firms increases, the MPL falls. The marginal product of labor is brought into equality with the lower real wage rate when the quantity of labor rises to L_1. Conversely, if the real wage rate rises from $(W/P)_0$ to $(W/P)_2$, the marginal product of the quantity of labor L_0 is less than the real wage rate. Firms cut back on labor to L_2, where the MPL rises to equality with the higher real wage rate.

Panel II of Figure 16.2 shows that the real wage rate also determines the quantity of output produced. When the real wage rate is $(W/P)_0$, firms demand the quantity of labor L_0 (Panel I), and this quantity of labor produces the output Q_0. When the real wage rate is $(W/P)_1$, firms demand the quantity of labor L_1 and produce the output Q_1. Conversely, when real wage rate is $(W/P)_2$, firms hire L_2 of labor and produce Q_2 of total output.

When there is a change in technology, both the production function and the labor demand schedule shift. Consider the case where a technological advance

FIGURE 16.2
THE DEMAND FOR LABOR AND
THE DETERMINATION OF REAL OUTPUT.

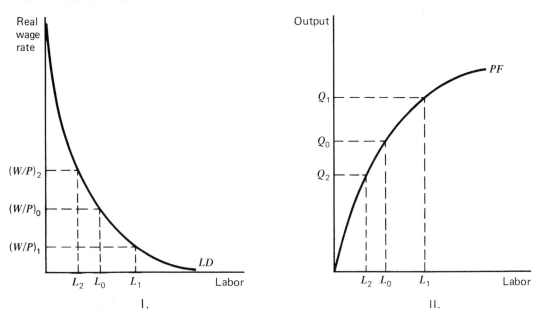

allows firms to produce more output for a given input of labor. Panel I of Figure 16.3 shows that the production function shifts up from PF to PF'. Thus, at L_0 firms can now produce Q'_0 rather than Q_0, and at L_1, they can produce Q'_1 rather than Q_1. Note that the production function must still go through the origin. When labor input is zero, there is no output. This implies that when labor is L_0, the slope of PF' is greater than the slope of PF. Similarly, the slope of PF' for L_1 is greater than the slope of PF. Recall that the slope of the production function is the marginal product of labor. Thus, with the change in technology, the marginal product of labor for a given quantity of labor is higher than it used to be. This means that at any given real wage rate, firms demand more labor than they did before. This is shown in Panel II of Figure 16.3 where the technological advance shifts the labor demand schedule to the right from LD to LD'. When the real wage rate is $(W/P)_0$, firms demand L'_0 of labor rather than L_0, or at $(W/P)_1$ they demand L'_1 rather than L_1. This means that firms want to produce more than Q'_0 or Q'_1 (not shown). As we shall see later, however, the actual increase in output is constrained by the available supply of labor at each real wage rate.

Changes in the stock of capital also produce shifts in the production function and in the demand for labor. When there is investment, the stock of capital increases. The economy can produce more output than it did before. This means that the production function shifts up as from PF to PF' in Panel I of Figure 16.3.

FIGURE 16.3
THE EFFECT OF TECHNICAL
CHANGE ON REAL OUTPUT AND
THE DEMAND FOR LABOR.

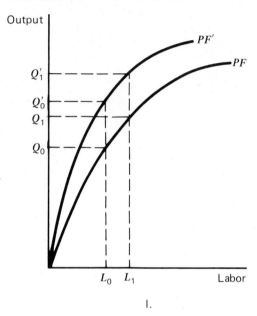

I.

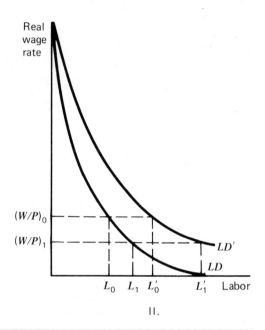

II.

The larger stock of capital also increases the marginal product of labor, so the demand for labor schedule shifts to the right as in Panel II of Figure 16.3.[2]

The Supply of Labor and the Determination of the Real Wage Rate in the Long Run

Up to this point, we have taken the real wage rate as given. This was useful for developing the labor demand schedule, but it is now necessary to describe how the real wage rate is determined. This is accomplished by introducing the supply of labor. The interaction of the demand and supply of labor determines the real wage rate and the quantity of labor employed in the long run.

The shape of the aggregate supply of labor is not obvious. The conventional assumption is that the supply curve, *LS*, is upward sloping, as shown in Panel I of Figure 16.4. This schedule indicates that the higher the real wage rate, the greater

---

[2] We shall see later in this chapter that labor and capital are not the only factors of production. In particular, raw materials and energy sources are important factors. Changes in the availability of these factors of production also shift the production function.

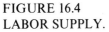

FIGURE 16.4
LABOR SUPPLY.

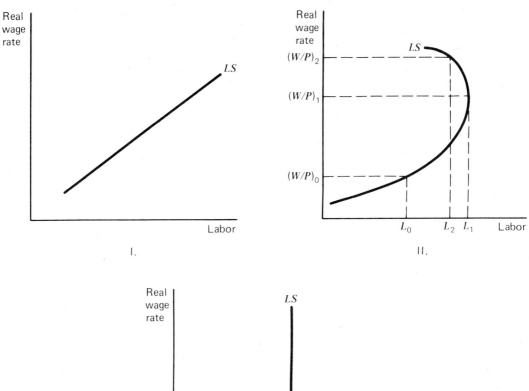

the amount of labor services that the public wants to provide. The idea is that the
public can be induced to enjoy less leisure and to provide more labor services if
rewarded by a higher real wage rate. The higher real wage rate allows the public
to earn a higher income, and there is an incentive to substitute work for leisure.

Whether or not a higher real wage rate brings forth more labor supplied
depends upon how the public wants to use its higher income. If the public wants
to consume more goods and services, then the quantity of labor supplied increases

when the real wage rate increases.[3] It is necessary to earn a higher wage income in order to consume more goods and services. This is accomplished by working more. Alternatively, if the public wants to consume its higher "income" by enjoying more leisure, then a rise in the real wage rate may not increase the quantity of labor supplied. With a higher real wage rate, it is possible to work less and still earn the same money income, that is, to consume the same quantity of goods and services. In this case, the higher real wage rate leads to a reduction in the quantity of labor supplied. The public ends up consuming its increased real income in the form of leisure.

The response of the quantity of labor supplied to a rise in the real wage rate depends upon the public's preferences for money income versus leisure. It is possible that the public comes to favor leisure over money income as income rises. This can lead to a situation where, at a sufficiently high real wage rate, the labor supply curve becomes backward bending. This is shown in Panel II of Figure 16.4. As the real wage rate rises from $(W/P)_0$ to $(W/P)_1$, the quantity of labor supplied rises from L_0 to L_1; we have a standard upward-sloping labor supply schedule. At the real wage rate $(W/P)_1$, the curve becomes vertical, and for values of real wage rate that are greater than $(W/P)_1$, the supply schedule is downward sloping. A rise in the real wage rate from $(W/P)_1$ to $(W/P)_2$ actually reduces the quantity of labor supply from L_1 to L_2.

There is no way to predict on theoretical grounds whether the labor supply schedule becomes backward bending or not. Empirical studies do not show any important effect of the real wage rate on the quantity of labor supplied.[4] Thus, the quantity of labor services that the public offers appears to be independent of the real wage rate. This implies the labor supply schedule shown in Panel III of Figure 16.4. In the light of the empirical evidence and in the absence of any theoretical basis for assuming the contrary, we assume that the labor supply schedule is vertical.

The assumption of a vertical labor supply schedule does not mean that the quantity of labor is always fixed. Population growth, changes in preferences concerning leisure versus money income, and changes in social customs affect the quantity of labor supplied. For example, population growth shifts the labor supply schedule to the right as workers enter the labor force. A change in social attitudes that increases the participation of women in the labor force also shifts the labor supply schedule to the right.

Panel I of Figure 16.5 shows that the intersection of the labor demand and supply schedules determines the real wage rate and the quantity of labor. Thus, for

---

[3] Workers may save part of the higher income and use the savings to consume in the future.

[4] Here we are talking about the labor supply schedule for a given generation of workers. There is evidence that over longer time periods the labor supply schedule becomes backward bending. This explains the substantial reduction in the length of the workday and workweek that has occurred over the last 100 years.

FIGURE 16.5
DETERMINING THE REAL WAGE
RATE AND AGGREGATE OUTPUT.

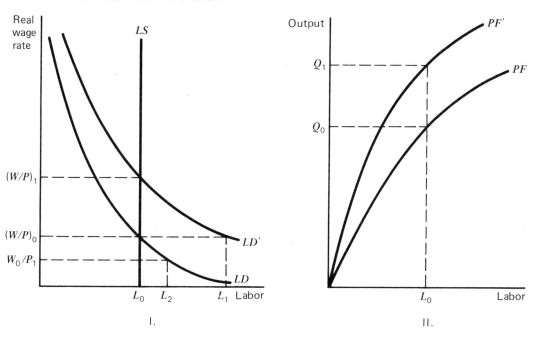

I.   II.

the labor supply schedule, *LS*, and the labor demand schedule, *LD*, the equilibrium real wage rate is $(W/P)_0$, and the quantity of labor is L_0. Now consider the effect of a technological advance that shifts the labor demand schedule from *LD* to *LD'*. The marginal product of labor now exceeds the real wage rate at $(W/P)_0$, and there is an excess demand for labor equal to $(L_1 - L_0)$. Firms attempt to hire more workers by offering a higher nominal wage rate. Thus, the nominal wage rate, *W*, rises. Given the price level, this raises the real wage rate and reduces the excess demand for labor. Because the labor supply curve is vertical, the real wage rate must rise until the same quantity of labor is hired as before. Equilibrium occurs at $(W/P)_1$.

Aggregate output rises even though the amount of labor input remains unchanged. This is shown in Panel II. The production function shifts from *PF* to *PF'*. With the technological advance, the fixed quantity of labor, L_0, can now produce aggregate output of Q_1 rather than Q_0. We conclude that the technological advance raises both the real wage rate and aggregate output. It is left to the reader to show that, for a given technology, (1) an increase in the quantity of labor supplied reduces the real wage rate and raises aggregate output; (2) an increase in the capital stock raises both the real wage rate and output.

Now consider the effect of a rise in the price level. As we shall see later in this chapter, a rise in P can come from a variety of sources. For present purposes, however, assume that an increase in aggregate expenditures produces a rise in the price level. Thus, P rises from P_0 to P_1. The nominal wage rate initially is unchanged at W_0. The real wage rate falls from W_0/P_0 to W_0/P_1. This produces an excess demand for labor. Firms attempt to hire more labor and bid up the nominal wage rate. The excess demand for labor is eliminated when the nominal wage rate rises to W_1, where the real wage rate is the same as before the rise in the price level; that is, $(W_1/P_1) = (W_0/P_0)$. If the price level falls rather than rises, the real wage rate initially increases. Firms want to hire less labor than before. The supply of labor exceeds the demand at the higher real wage rate. With an excess supply of labor, the nominal wage rate falls. The nominal wage rate falls until the real wage rate declines to its initial value.

We conclude that changes in the price level do not affect the real wage rate in the long run. The nominal wage rate adjusts to return the real wage rate to its initial value. Because the real wage rate is unchanged, real output is also unchanged. Thus, a change in the price level has no effect on real output in the long run. Technological advances, changes in the stock of capital, and shifts in labor supply affect the real wage rate and the level of output in the long run. Movements in the price level do not.

The relationship between the price level and aggregate output in the long run is shown in Figure 16.6. This gives us the vertical long-run aggregate supply schedule, AS_{LR}. As long as technology, the stock of capital, and the supply of labor are fixed, the economy produces the same quantity of goods and services in the long run no matter what the price level happens to be. Thus, aggregate supply, not aggregate demand, determines real output in the long run. This means that labor, capital, and technology are the ultimate determinants of the output that the economy produces. Aggregate demand affects the price level and the nominal wage rate, but it does not affect aggregate output or employment in the long run. There is no unemployment of labor, and there is no idle capacity in the long run.[5] Similarly, there are no labor shortages or unfulfilled desires of firms to produce more output.

Long-run equilibrium is important because it describes the position that the economy ultimately achieves following some disturbance such as a technological advance. Long-run equilibrium does not help us to understand much of what goes on in the shorter run, however. We know that recessions occur where there is substantial unemployment of labor and productive capacity. We also know that booms occur where there are shortages of labor, capital, and output. We even know that there can be rising unemployment coupled with rising wages and prices. In order to understand these phenomena, we have to study the behavior of aggregate supply in the shorter run.

---

[5] Even in the long run, some workers are temporarily unemployed because they are changing jobs. We abstract from this "frictional" unemployment and define long-run equilibrium in the labor market to be a condition of full employment.

FIGURE 16.6
LONG-RUN AGGREGATE SUPPLY.

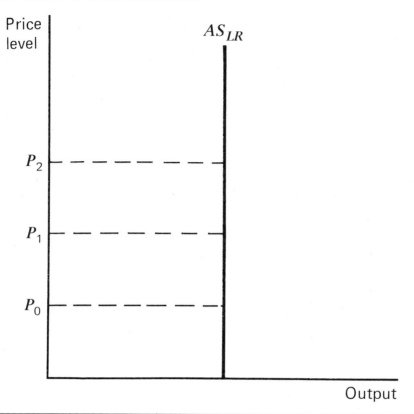

Aggregate Supply in the Shorter Run

The analysis of short-run aggregate supply is difficult because we are describing the behavior of the economy when it is out of long-run equilibrium. There is no clear consensus among economists concerning the behavior of short-run aggregate supply. Disagreements arise because real-world phenomena are subject to more than one interpretation. The approach used here is to rely on explanations of short-run aggregate supply for which there is widespread agreement among economists. The reader is cautioned, however, that the behavior of aggregate supply in the shorter run is only imperfectly understood. Furthermore, much of the analysis is dynamic and does not fit easily into the static framework used in this text. We shall attempt, however, to capture the dynamic character of short-run aggregate supply by comparing short-run static equilibria.

The economy behaves differently in the short run from the way it does in the long run. The most crucial difference is that wages and prices do not always adjust sufficiently in the short run to equate demand with supply. If wages and prices were completely flexible in the short run, there could never be any unemployment. The nominal wage rate and the price level would adjust immediately to produce a real wage rate that eliminates any imbalance between labor demand and supply. If the quantity of labor supplied exceeded the demand, the real wage rate would immediately decline to eliminate the excess supply. Similarly, the real wage rate would rise immediately to eliminate an excess demand for labor.

If the nominal wage rate were completely flexible, the labor market would behave like the markets for wheat or for securities. In these markets, prices change rapidly to eliminate any imbalance between demand and supply. The market for labor does not work this way. Nominal and real wage rates do change, but they often do not change enough to equate labor demand to supply. Workers do not face a different nominal wage rate every day or week. Rather, wages tend to change relatively infrequently. Sometimes the frequency with which the wage rate changes is set by union contracts, and sometimes less formal approaches are used. Whatever the situation, wages often do not change enough to equate labor demand with supply in the short run. When nominal wage rates are inflexible in the short run, situations can develop where the actual real wage rate differs substantially from its long-run equilibrium value. This means that over significant periods of time there can be either unemployment or labor shortages.

Consider the case where the economy is initially in long-run equilibrium and there is a fall in aggregate demand. Firms discover that they cannot sell their output at the old price, so they reduce their prices. As a consequence, the price level falls. Given the nominal wage rate, this means that the real wage, W/P, rises. The rise in the real wage rate induces firms to reduce their demand for labor. If the nominal wage rate were completely flexible, it would immediately fall as a result of the excess supply of labor, and the real wage rate would quickly decline back to its old equilibrium value. Labor demand would equal labor supply, so there would be no unemployment. This was the story we told earlier when discussing long-run equilibrium.

Now let us see what happens if the nominal wage rate does not adjust quickly. For simplicity, assume that the wage rate is fixed at $\overline{W}$.[6] The initial equilibrium is shown at the real wage rate $\overline{W}/P_0$ in Panel I of Figure 16.7. The decline in the price level from P_0 to P_1 raises the real wage rate to $\overline{W}/P_1$. Firms reduce the amount of labor they hire from L_0 to L_1. There is an excess supply of labor equal to $(L_1 - L_0)$. With the smaller use of labor, real output falls from Q_0 to Q_1 as shown in Panel II. As long as the nominal wage rate remains fixed at $\overline{W}$, firms

---

[6] Fixing the nominal wage at $\overline{W}$ allows us to simplify the story. It is possible to allow for a decline in the nominal wage rate. All that is needed for unemployment to develop is that the nominal wage rate does not fall sufficiently to prevent a rise in the real wage rate. More advanced texts deal explicitly with the disequilibrium that develops when the labor market does not clear. For example, see R. Barro and H. Grossman, *Money, Employment and Inflation,* Cambridge: Cambridge University Press, 1976.

FIGURE 16.7
EMPLOYMENT AND OUTPUT WHEN
THE NOMINAL WAGE RATE IS FIXED.

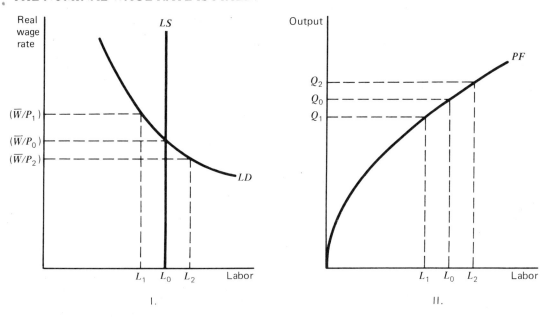

hire only L_1 of labor, and real output remains at Q_1. Note that there is now unemployment. At the real wage rate $(\overline{W}/P_1)$, the amount of labor that is available, L_0, is greater than the amount that is hired, L_1. There are people looking for a job who cannot find one.

Now assume that aggregate demand increases and the price level rises. With the wage rate fixed at $\overline{W}$, this lowers the real wage rate and increases the quantity of labor demanded.[7] Formerly unemployed workers can now get a job. Thus, as the price level rises relative to $\overline{W}$, the excess supply of labor is reduced, and unemployment declines. When the price level returns to P_0, the excess supply of labor is eliminated, and there is no unemployment. Everyone who is willing to work can find a job when the real wage rate is $(\overline{W}/P_0)$.

If the price level rises above P_0 to P_2, the real wage rate falls below $(\overline{W}/P_0)$, and there is an excess demand for labor equal to $(L_2 - L_0)$. Whereas we have assumed that the supply of labor does not exceed L_0, firms can raise their labor in-

[7] If workers knew in advance that the price level was going to rise, they would insist on a higher nominal wage rate to begin with. We are implicitly assuming that the rise in the price level comes as a surprise.

put in the short run by having their labor force work more intensively and by paying overtime. This raises labor costs, but the decline in the real wage rate makes the practice profitable. Similarly, firms use their capital equipment more intensively by delaying maintenance. Furthermore, in reality, the labor force is not homogeneous. Some workers are more skilled or highly motivated than others. At the initial equilibrium real wage, $(\overline{W}/P_0)$, there are workers for whom the value of their marginal products is less than the wage rate. They are unemployed even at $(\overline{W}/P_0)$.[8] When the price level rises above P_0, the real wage rate falls, and it becomes profitable to hire these workers. We conclude that in the short run real output can rise above the long-run equilibrium value Q_0. For example, if the price level increases from P_0 to P_2 output increases from Q_0 to Q_2 as shown in Panel II of Figure 16.7.

To summarize, if the nominal wage rate is fixed in the short run, a decline in the price level reduces aggregate output, and a rise in the price level raises aggregate output. This suggests the short-run aggregate supply schedule, AS_{SR}, as shown in Panel I of Figure 16.8. The short-run aggregate supply schedule is upward sloping, indicating that a rise in the price level increases aggregate output.

It is important to note that in deriving the short-run aggregate supply curve, we have assumed that the nominal wage rate is fixed. With the passage of time, the nominal wage rate adjusts, and the excess supply or demand for labor is eliminated. For example, at the price level P_1, there is unemployment, and real output is low. Over time, the nominal wage rate falls, which reduces the real wage rate. The reduction in the real wage rate reduces unemployment and raises real output. At the price level P_1, larger and larger quantities of output are produced as the real wage rate declines. Conversely, if the price level is P_2, there is an excess demand for labor. Firms attempt to hire more labor, and the nominal wage rate rises. This increases the real wage rate, which reduces the incentive of firms to pay overtime, to run their capital equipment so intensively, and to hire low-productivity labor. Furthermore, workers start to balk at continuing overtime and demand a return to normal working hours. Over time, the nominal wage rate rises, so at the price level P_2, smaller and smaller amounts of output are produced. As time passes, the aggregate supply curve rotates, that is, becomes steeper, as shown in Panel II of Figure 16.8. The economy moves from the short-run aggregate supply schedule, AS_{SR}, to the steeper aggregate supply schedule in the medium run, AS_{MR}. Thus, when the price level is P_1, the output Q_1 is produced in the short run, but output rises to Q'_1 in the medium run because the nominal wage rate falls. Similarly, when the price level is P_2, the output Q_2 is produced in the short run, but output falls to Q'_2 in the medium run because the nominal wage

---

[8] In the long run, one would expect the nominal wage rate paid to these workers to decline to the point that the value of their marginal products equals the wage. Factors such as minimum wage laws or social conventions against paying "starvation wages" may prevent the nominal wage from falling far enough. In this situation, these workers are unemployed even in the long run at $(\overline{W}/P_0)$.

FIGURE 16.8
SHORT-RUN AGGREGATE SUPPLY
AND THE TRANSITION TO THE
LONG RUN.

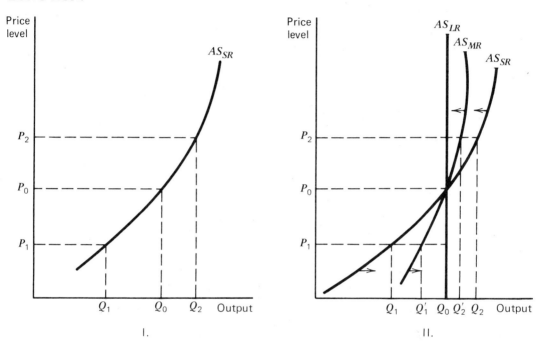

rate rises. Eventually, the vertical long-run aggregate supply curve, AS_{LR}, is reached, where, no matter what the price level, output is Q_0.[9]

We need to consider some further complications concerning short-run aggregate supply before turning to aggregate demand. The first complication arises because the prices of many products adjust slowly to excess demand or supply. The prices of some products such as agricultural commodities and raw materials are determined in organized markets. For these products, prices move rapidly to equate demand with supply. The prices of most manufactured goods are set by producers. These prices are changed relatively infrequently. As a result, excess demand or supply can exist for significant periods of time.

With sticky prices, changes in aggregate demand produce changes in the quantity produced. When aggregate demand increases, the prices of many kinds of

[9] We see in Figure 16.15 that the same adjustment can be described as shifts in the short-run aggregate schedule.

output do not rise immediately. Rather, firms raise their output.[10] This requires an increase in the employment of labor. The initial effect of a rise in aggregate demand is an increase in output and employment. Alternatively, when aggregate demand falls, many firms do not immediately reduce prices; they reduce output and employment instead.

The stickiness of many product prices suggests a flat aggregate supply curve for the very short run. In the very short run, the price level tends to be fixed, and output responds passively to changes in aggregate demand.[11] This very short run aggregate supply curve is shown in Panel I of Figure 16.9. There is a limit to the extent that firms can increase their output when there is an increase in aggregate demand. Thus, the very short-run aggregate supply curve is not horizontal indefinitely. Capacity and labor constraints determine the maximum amount that can be produced. For the sake of simplicity, we will ignore this complication and simply show AS_{VSR} as horizontal.

There is not a single, static aggregate supply curve. Rather, the curve becomes increasingly steep with the passage of time as prices and wages adjust. Thus, in the very short run we have the horizontal aggregate supply curve, AS_{VSR}, of Panel I of Figure 16.9; in the short run, we have the upward-sloping supply curve, AS_{SR}, of Panel II; and in the long run we have the vertical curve, AS_{LR}, of Panel III.

Another complication arises because in the short run many firms set prices as a markup over their costs of production. Thus, when nominal wage rates increase, these firms raise their prices. Similarly, when the prices of other inputs such as raw materials and energy rise, firms tend to raise their prices. This markup pricing does not mean that firms are indifferent to the demand for their products, however. If demand is low, they raise their output prices by less in response to increases in the prices of inputs than when demand is high. It does mean, however, that when the price of labor, oil, or some other input rises, firms tend to raise their prices. This implies, as shown in Panel IV of Figure 16.9, that the short-run aggregate supply schedule shifts up from AS_{SR} to AS'_{SR} when input prices rise. Firms are willing to produce the same output, Q_0, only if the price level rises from P_0 to P_1.

The upward shift in the short-run aggregate supply schedule can lead to a wage-price spiral. An initial increase in the price level, which may be caused by an increase in aggregate demand or an increase in factor prices, reduces the real wage rate. Labor responds by demanding a higher nominal wage rate. This produces a further increase in prices as the short-run aggregate supply schedule shifts up. The nominal wage rate then rises in response to the price increase. The wage-price spiral, and factors that limit it, are discussed after we analyze the effects of the price level on aggregate demand.

---

[10] Temporary increases in aggregate demand are met out of inventories with little or no change in production. Once inventories are run down, however, production must expand to meet demand and to rebuild inventories.

[11] In Chapters 13 through 15, we were implicitly assuming that firms were producing along a horizontal, very short-run aggregate supply curve.

FIGURE 16.9
AGGREGATE SUPPLY IN THE
VERY SHORT, SHORT, AND LONG RUN.

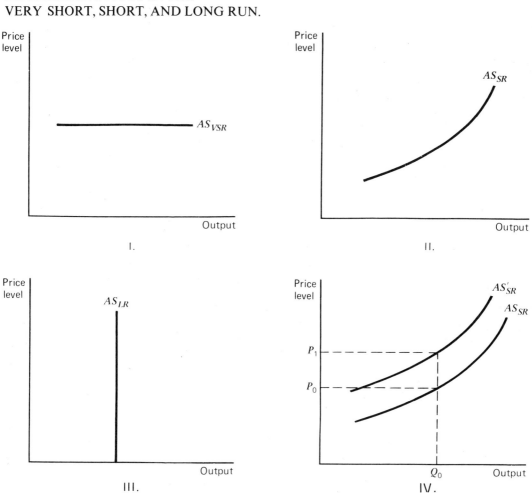

AGGREGATE DEMAND

In this section we analyze the effect of the price level on aggregate demand. It is shown that the financial sector of the economy plays a crucial role in transmitting the effects of changes in prices to aggregate demand.

In Chapters 13 through 15, where prices were held constant, it was shown that in equilibrium total output, Q, total income, Y, and total expenditures on currently produced output, $C + I + \overline{G}$, are equal: $Q = Y = C + I + \overline{G}$. When the price level is allowed to vary, it is necessary to modify this expression. The variable Q is the total (real) output of goods and services in the economy. Income and total expenditures are measured in dollar terms. As a consequence, if the prices of all factor services double, aggregate income doubles, and so does the equilibrium value of aggregate expenditures. A doubling of all prices, income, and expenditures does not mean that the economy is producing any more output. All nominal (dollar) magnitudes have doubled, but real output is unchanged. In order to get around this complication, one deflates nominal magnitudes by the price level to put them in "real" terms. This produces the new expression $Q = Y/P = C/P + I/P + \bar{G}/P$. Thus, aggregate output equals real income, and it equals aggregate real expenditures. A doubling of nominal income and of the price level leaves real income, Y/P, unchanged. Similarly, a doubling of nominal aggregate expenditures and of the price level does not affect real aggregate expenditures.

Real aggregate expenditures are affected by the price level, however. To see why this is the case, we must examine the determinants of real aggregate demand. Consumers are interested in the consumption of real goods and services. Similarly, firms are concerned with investment expenditures in real terms. Thus, the consumption and investment demand functions can be stated in real terms as

$$\frac{C}{P} = c_0 + c_1 \frac{Y_d}{P} + c_2 \frac{W}{P} - c_3 R$$

$$\frac{I}{P} = i_0 - i_1 R + i_2 \frac{Y}{P} . \quad [12]$$

Real consumption depends upon real disposable income, Y_d/P; real wealth, W/P; and the interest rate, R. Real investment depends upon the interest rate and real income.[13] It is assumed that government expenditures on goods and services are fixed in real terms. If prices double, nominal government expenditures also double in order to keep G/P unchanged.[14] Thus, we have:

$$\frac{G}{P} = \text{constant} .$$

The expressions for real consumption, investment and government expenditures imply an IS curve that shows the relationship between the interest rate, R, and real aggregate income, Y/P. The reader is spared the algebra, and the IS curve is shown in Figure 16.10. Because we assume that the economic decisions of the public and of the government are conditioned by real economic variables, the IS curve looks the same as in Chapter 12. Real income has simply replaced nominal income on the horizontal axis.

---

[12] The intercepts for the real consumption and investment functions, c_0 and i_0 respectively, should be interpreted as being in real terms.

[13] At this point, we do not distinguish between the nominal and the real interest rate. Later on in this chapter, we show the role of the real interest rate.

[14] For simplicity, we also assume that transfer payments are also constant in real terms and that the income tax rate is "indexed" by the price level.

FIGURE 16.10
THE *IS* CURVE USING REAL
RATHER THAN NOMINAL INCOME.

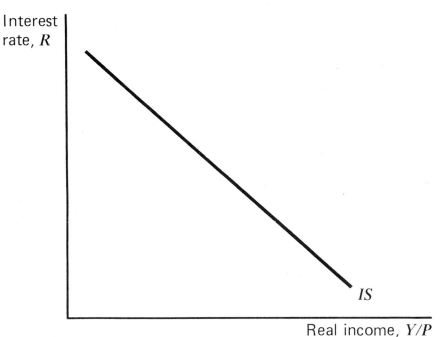

If it were not for the wealth term, W/P, in the consumption function, the *IS* curve would be unaffected by changes in the price level. Given real wealth, if the price level increases, nominal aggregate income and nominal disposable income also increase, leaving Y/P and Y_d/P unchanged. Thus, C/P and I/P remain unchanged, and the *IS* curve is unaffected by the increase in the price level. A change in the price level does affect real wealth, however. Both the monetary base (currency plus total reserves) and government bonds are fixed in nominal terms. When the price level changes, their real values change. The real value of corporate bonds also changes, but the capital gains of bond holders are offset by the capital losses to corporations and vice versa. Thus, for the private sector as a whole, there is no change in the real value of wealth from corporate bonds.[15] Put another way, the nominal value of the capital stock rises with the price level, so there is no real wealth effect from this source. We conclude that changes in the price level affect the real values of the monetary base and government bonds

---

[15] We neglect any effect on aggregate expenditures produced by the redistribution of wealth.

while leaving other components of real wealth unchanged. For example, if the price level doubles, the real value of the monetary base and of government bonds falls by one half. This reduces the real value of total wealth.

The expression for real consumption indicates that, given real disposable income and the interest rate, when real wealth falls, real consumption falls; and when real wealth rises, real consumption rises.[16] This implies that when the price level increases, real wealth falls, and the *IS* curve shifts to the left. When the price level falls, real wealth rises, and the *IS* curve shifts to the right.

Now let us turn to the *LM* curve. The money demand function can also be expressed in real terms. The demand for real money balances is

$$\frac{M}{P} = m_0 - m_1 R + m_2 \frac{Y}{P} + m_3 \frac{W}{P} . \quad [17]$$

This specification says that, given the interest rate, the demand for real money balances depends upon real income and real wealth. Leaving wealth aside for the moment, if the price level doubles, the public doubles its demand for nominal money balances. This leaves the demand for real money balances unchanged. A rise in the price level reduces real wealth, however. This means that when the price level increases, the demand for real money balances is reduced.

The real money "supply" function is

$$\frac{M}{P} = m_M \frac{\overline{TR}}{P} .$$

Here it is assumed that the Federal Reserve fixes the nominal quantity of total reserves, $\overline{TR}$.[18] When the price level increases, real total reserves and the real supply of money fall. When the price level falls, real total reserves and the real supply of money rise. Thus, though the Fed can control the nominal supply of reserves and money, it cannot control the real supply.

Panel I of Figure 16.11 shows the demand and supply for real money balances. The intersection of real money demand and supply gives the equilibrium interest rate R_0. When real income rises, from $(Y/P)_0$ to $(Y/P)_1$, the demand for real money balances shifts to the right from $(M/P)_0^D$ to $(M/P)_1^D$ and, the interest rate rises to R_1. Thus, when real income is high, the interest rate is high. This gives the *LM* curve of Panel II.

If the price level increases, with real income unchanged, real wealth falls, and the demand schedule for real money balances shifts to the left from $(M/P)_0^D$ to $(M/P)_1^D$ as shown in Panel III. If the supply of real money balances remained constant, this would reduce the interest rate to R_1. This does not occur, however, because real reserves decline, and the supply of real money balances shifts to the

---

[16] Even if government bonds are excluded from wealth, changes in the real monetary base still affect real consumption.

[17] The intercept m_0 should be interpreted as being in real terms.

[18] We could have assumed that the Fed sets the nominal monetary base, MB, rather than nominal total reserves. This would not materially affect the conclusions in the text.

FIGURE 16.11
REAL MONEY DEMAND, REAL
MONEY SUPPLY, AND THE *LM* CURVE.

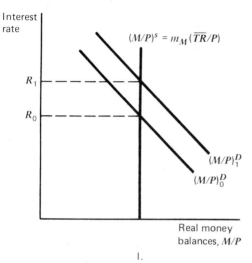

I.

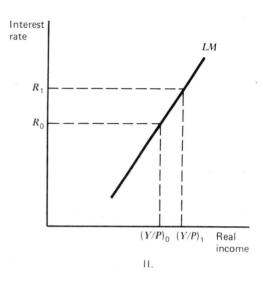

II.

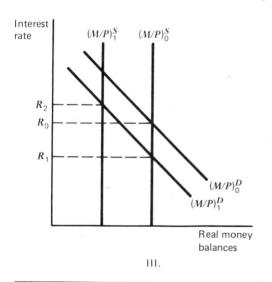

III.

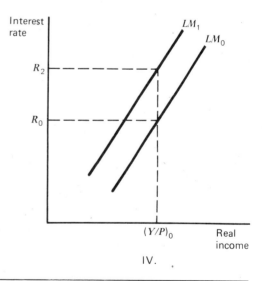

IV.

left when the price level increases. This is shown as the shift from $(M/P)_0^S$ to $(M/P)_1^S$. The shift in real money supply must be larger than the shift in real money demand because only part of the decline in real wealth is mirrored in real money demand. The remainder produces a decline in the real demand for other assets. All the decline in the real value of the money supply is reflected in the decline in actual real money balances. Thus, the real money supply shifts more than real money demand, and the interest rate rises from R_0 to R_2. We conclude that when the price level increases from P_0 to P_1, the interest rate increases when real income is constant at $(Y/P)_0$. This means that a rise in the price level shifts the LM curve up from LM_0 to LM_1 as shown in Panel IV.

We can now combine the IS and LM curves to show how changes in the price level affect real aggregate demand and real income. Panel I of Figure 16.12 shows the intersection of the IS and LM curves. The two curves are drawn under the assumption that the price level is P_0. Thus, $IS(P_0)$ is the IS curve, given P_0, and $LM(P_0)$ is the LM curve, given P_0. The two curves intersect at the equilibrium real income $(Y/P)_0$ and the interest rate R_0. Now consider the effect of a rise in the price level. With a higher price level, real wealth declines, so real consumption is reduced, and the IS curve shifts left to $IS(P_1)$, as shown in Panel II. The decline in real wealth also shifts the LM curve up to $LM(P_1)$. We see that, at the higher price level, real aggregate expenditures and income fall from $(Y/P)_0$ to $(Y/P)_1$. In the diagram, the shift in the LM curve is assumed to be larger than the shift in IS, so the interest rate rises to R_1. If the leftward shift in IS is larger than the shift in LM, the equilibrium interest rate could be lower than R_0. No matter what are the relative sizes of the shifts, real income falls, however.

We conclude that when the price level increases, real aggregate expenditures and income fall. This implies a relationship between the price level and aggregate expenditures shown in Panel III of Figure 16.12. This downward-sloping *aggregate demand schedule*, *AD*, indicates that when the price level is high, aggregate demand is low. Conversely, when the price level is low, aggregate demand is high.

DETERMINING REAL INCOME, OUTPUT, THE PRICE LEVEL, AND THE INTEREST RATE

By combining aggregate supply with aggregate demand, we can determine the equilibrium values for real income, the price level, and the interest rate. It is instructive to begin the analysis by looking at the long-run equilibrium of the economy. We then examine the economy in the shorter run.

It was shown earlier in this chapter that as long as technology, population, the capital stock, and the availability of raw materials and energy are constant, the economy produces a constant real output in the long run. Thus, long-run aggregate supply is not affected by changes in the price level or the interest rate.[19] This

---

[19] The interest rate does affect investment and, therefore, affects aggregate supply through that channel. Because investment is small relative to the total stock of capital, a substantial period of time must elapse before a change in investment has a significant effect on aggregate supply. For the time frame being considered here, we take aggregate supply as independent of the interest rate.

FIGURE 16.12
THE EFFECT OF THE PRICE LEVEL
ON AGGREGATE DEMAND.

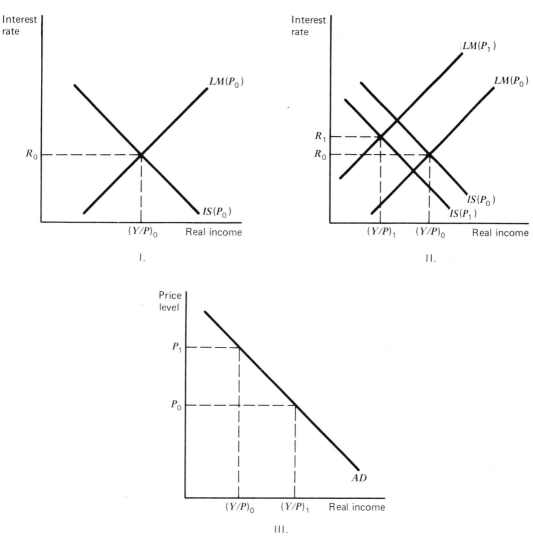

constant real output is shown as the vertical line in Panel I of Figure 16.13. No matter what the interest rate is, the economy produces the constant output $Q_0 = (Y/P)_0$. The interest rate does affect aggregate demand, however. The intersection of the IS and LM curves is shown in the same diagram. Real aggregate income equals real aggregate demand when the IS and LM curves intersect. For the price level to be at an equilibrium, aggregate demand must equal aggregate

FIGURE 16.13
THE PRICE LEVEL AND INTEREST
RATE ADJUST IN THE LONG RUN
TO EQUATE AGGREGATE DEMAND
TO LONG-RUN AGGREGATE SUPPLY.

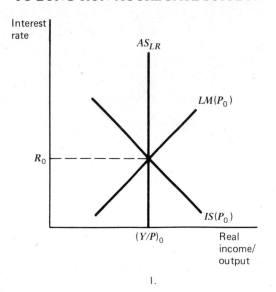

I.

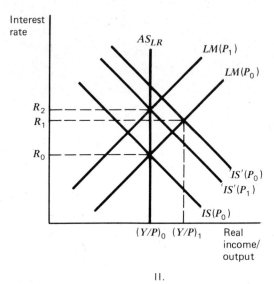

II.

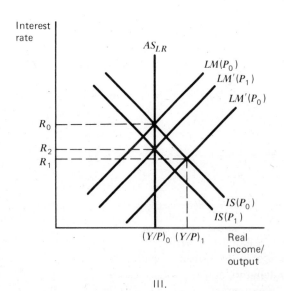

III.

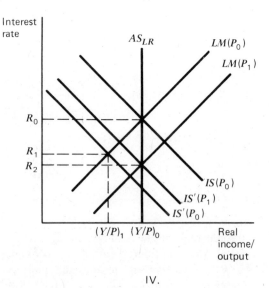

IV.

supply (output). Thus, the IS and LM curves must intersect on the vertical long-run aggregate supply schedule. The curves intersect the vertical line when the price level is P_0. The equilibrium IS and LM curves are $IS(P_0)$ and $LM(P_0)$. The equilibrium interest rate is R_0.

Now consider the effect of an increase in aggregate demand that shifts the $IS(P_0)$ curve to $IS'(P_0)$ as shown in Panel II. Given the price level, P_0, this produces an intersection of $IS'(P_0)$ with $LM(P_0)$ at the real income $(Y/P)_1$ and the interest rate R_1. Real aggregate demand now exceeds long-run real aggregate supply (output) by $(Y/P)_1 - (Y/P)_0$. This situation leads to a rise in prices and wages. As the price level rises, real wealth is reduced, so the IS curve shifts back to the left, and the LM curve shifts up. These shifts reduce aggregate demand. The price level continues to rise, and the IS and LM curves continue to shift until aggregate demand equals long-run aggregate supply. The adjustment is complete when the price level is P_1 and the interest rate R_2. Note that the price level and the interest rise until real aggregate demand and income adjust to the fixed long-run aggregate supply. At this point, $IS'(P_1)$ intersects $LM(P_1)$ at $(Y/P)_0$.

When there is a downward shift in the LM curve rather than a rightward shift in IS, the price level also rises to equate aggregate demand to the fixed supply. In this case, however, the equilibrium interest rate is reduced. As shown in Panel III, the LM curve shifts from $LM(P_0)$ to $LM'(P_0)$. This produces an intersection with $IS(P_0)$ at the higher real income $(Y/P)_1$ and the lower interest rate R_1. There is again an excess of aggregate demand over long-run aggregate supply. This raises the price level and reduces real wealth, which shifts the LM curve back up and the IS curve to the left. The new equilibrium occurs at the price level P_1 and the interest rate R_2. At this point $LM'(P_1)$ intersects $IS(P_1)$ at $(Y/P)_0$. Note that the new equilibrium interest rate R_2 is lower than R_0. The higher price level reduces consumption demand and allows a lower interest rate to prevail.

Now consider the case where a shift in the IS or LM curve reduce aggregate demand and income below long-run aggregate supply. Panel IV shows the situation when the IS curve shifts left to $IS'(P_0)$. The intersection of $IS'(P_0)$ with $LM(P_0)$ occurs at real income $(Y/P)_1$. Thus, long-run aggregate supply exceeds real aggregate demand and income by $(Y/P)_0 - (Y/P)_1$. With the low level of aggregate demand, firms are unable to sell all their output at prevailing prices. This leads to a reduction in prices and wages. When the price level falls, real wealth rises, so the IS curve shifts back to the right, and the LM curve shifts down. These shifts increase aggregate demand. The economy is in long-run equilibrium when the price level falls to P_1 and the interest rate is R_2. Again $IS'(P_1)$ intersects $LM(P_1)$ at $(Y/P)_0$. It is left to the reader to show that an upward shift in the LM curve produces excess supply, which is eliminated by a reduction in the price level and a rise in the equilibrium interest rate.

We conclude that, in the long run, aggregate demand adjusts to aggregate supply. Aggregate demand affects the price level and the interest rate, but it does not affect real output. In the long run, monetary and fiscal policy cannot affect real output through their influence on aggregate demand. These policies do affect real output, however, to the extent that they affect long-run aggregate supply. For example, a combination of monetary and fiscal policy that keeps the interest rate relatively low encourages capital formation. Over time, this increases the real output potential of the economy. Similarly, tax incentive plans for investment, and programs to promote research and development activities encourage capital formation and technological progress. Finally, programs directed to increasing the supply of labor and to increasing its efficiency also increase long-run aggregate supply. Thus, in the long run, government policies affect real output by affecting aggregate supply rather than aggregate demand.

Before we turn to the behavior of the economy in the shorter run, it is instructive to look more directly at the determination of the price level. Figure 16.14 relates aggregate demand and long-run aggregate supply to the price level. As shown earlier, the aggregate supply schedule is vertical, indicating that in the long run aggregate output is independent of the price level. The aggregate demand schedule is downward sloping, indicating that when the price level is high, aggregate demand is low. The initial equilibrium occurs at the price level P_0, where aggregate demand, AD_0, intersects long-run aggregate supply, AS_{LR}.

Now assume that aggregate demand shifts to the right. This shift can occur as a consequence of shifts in the consumption or investment function or as a result of an expansionary fiscal policy that raises spending or cuts taxes. These factors shift the IS curve to the right and increase aggregate demand, given the price level. Aggregate demand can also increase as a result of a decrease in the demand for real money balances, an increase in the money multiplier, or an increase in nominal total reserves. Any of these factors shifts the LM curve down, which lowers the interest rate and increases aggregate demand, given the price level. In Figure 16.14, the increase in aggregate demand is shown as the shift from AD_0 to AD_1. At the price level, P_0, aggregate demand exceeds long-run aggregate supply by $(Y/P)_1 - (Y/P)_0$. This excess demand leads to a rise in prices and wages. The rise in the price level lowers aggregate demand and reduces excess demand. Long-run equilibrium is achieved when the price level rises sufficiently to eliminate excess demand. This occurs as the price level P_1, which is the same result obtained in Panels II and III of Figure 16.13.

Determining Real Income, Output, the Price Level, and the Interest Rate in the Shorter Run

In discussing aggregate supply, we showed that in the very short run the supply curve is flat, in the short run it is upward sloping, and in the long run it is vertical. In this section, the interaction between aggregate demand and aggregate supply is studied for time intervals that are too short to allow the economy to achieve long-run equilibrium. In Chapter 18 it is shown that we should distinguish between short-run and long-run aggregate demand. In order to simplify the discussion in this chapter, however, we do not make the distinction.

FIGURE 16.14
DETERMINING THE PRICE LEVEL
IN THE LONG RUN.

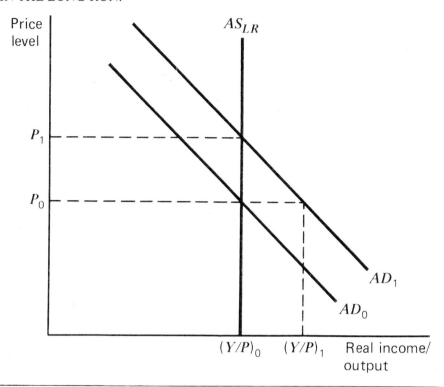

Let us begin by studying the effects of a fall in aggregate demand. Panel I of Figure 16.15 shows the response of real output and the price level to a decline in aggregate demand. Assume that the economy is initially in long-run equilibrium at the price level P_0 and real output $(Y/P)_0$. This equilibrium occurs where the aggregate demand schedule, AD_0, intersects the long-run aggregate supply schedule AS_{LR}. Now assume that the aggregate demand schedule shifts left from AD_0 to AD_1. Given the price level, aggregate demand falls from $(Y/P)_0$ to $(Y/P)_1$. In the very short run, prices and wages do not adjust, and firms reduce output to $(Y/P)_1$. Thus, the economy moves along the horizontal, very short-run aggregate supply schedule, AS_{VSR}. As long as prices and wages are fixed, real output falls, and unemployment occurs. In the very short run, aggregate supply adjusts to aggregate demand. This is the opposite of what happens in the long run where aggregate demand adjusts to aggregate supply.

With the passage of time, firms reduce the prices of their products. As long as the wage rate is unchanged, the real wage rate rises, and firms want to reduce out-

FIGURE 16.15
THE ADJUSTMENT TO LONG-RUN
EQUILIBRIUM FOLLOWING A
DECLINE IN AGGREGATE DEMAND.

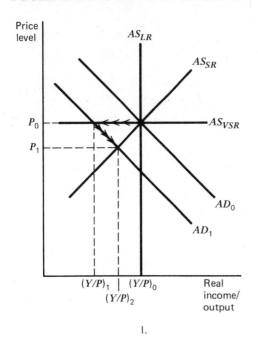

I.

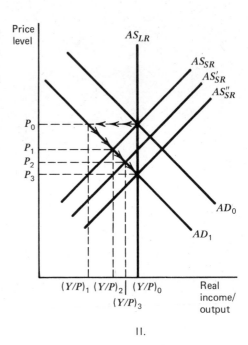

II.

put. With the adjustment in the price level, firms produce along the upward-sloping, short-run aggregate supply schedule AS_{SR}.[20] The decline in the price level increases aggregate demand, however, and the economy moves down AD_1. Short-run equilibrium occurs at the price level P_1 and real output $(Y/P)_2$. Thus, real output rises from $(Y/P)_1$ to $(Y/P)_2$ when sufficient time elapses for the price level to fall. The short-run equilibrium real output $(Y/P)_2$ is still below $(Y/P)_0$, however, and there is still unemployment in the economy.

As time passes, the nominal wage rate begins to decline which reduces the real wage rate. This produces a downward shift in the short-run aggregate supply schedule from AS_{SR} to AS'_{SR}, as shown in Panel II of Figure 16.15. With a lower

---

[20] In earlier diagrams, we showed the short-run aggregate supply becoming increasingly steep as the price level and real output increase. For simplicity, we use linear short-run aggregate supply schedules in the remainder of this chapter.

real wage rate, firms are willing to produce the same output at a lower price. The decline in the price level stimulates aggregate demand so output rises from $(Y/P)_2$ to $(Y/P)_3$. As long as there is unemployed labor, the nominal wage rate continues to decline, and the short-run aggregate supply curve continues to shift down. This produces further declines in the price level. With the passage of sufficient time, the short-run aggregate supply schedule shifts down to AS''_{SR}.[21] By that time, there is full adjustment of wages and prices. In the long run, the economy is back on AS_{LR} and real output returns to $(Y/P)_0$. The price level has fallen sufficiently to return aggregate demand to $(Y/P)_0$, and there is full employment. The long-run equilibrium occurs when the price level falls to P_3.

Note that the economy eventually returns to the full employment level of output $(Y/P)_0$. During the transition to the long-run equilibrium, however, there is a loss of real output, and there is unemployed labor. The lost real output and unemployed labor are the primary reasons for short-run stabilization policy. Expansionary monetary or fiscal policy, or both, can offset the effect of the original decline in aggregate demand. The policies shift aggregate demand back to the right. This allows full employment output to be achieved without putting the economy through the costly and painful process of adjustment illustrated in Figure 16.15.

There is an additional reason for using stimulative policies to avoid the deflation that accompanies a decline in aggregate demand. In the absence of stimulative policies, the economy suffers a decline in output, employment, and income. This produces the reduction in the price level required to stimulate aggregate demand and return the economy to full employment. There is no guarantee, however, that the decline in the price level will stimulate aggregate demand. Recall that the stimulus to aggregate demand arises from the increase in the real value of the monetary base and government bonds. Contrary to what we have assumed so far, the decline in the price level can, if large enough, produce a substantial decline in other components of wealth. Corporate bonds are contracts that require borrowers to pay a fixed, nominal amount of interest per year. As the price level falls, the real interest cost to borrowers rises. Nominal income receipts of business fall, but their interest payments remained fixed. If the decline in the price level is large enough, borrowers can be thrown into bankruptcy. At that point, the nominal value of the borrower's assets is not sufficient to cover the fixed nominal value of their liabilities. Holders of corporate bonds suffer a capital loss, and their wealth declines. Thus, the decline in the price level can reduce real wealth and actually reduce, rather than increase, aggregate demand.

It has not been proved theoretically that a decline in the price level produces a return to full employment when allowance is made for fixed nominal contracts

---

[21] It was shown earlier (Figure 16.8) that the process of adjustment can also be described as movements to ever steeper aggregate supply schedules as we move from the very short run to the short run to the medium run to the long run.

such as for corporate bonds.[22] As a result, it is dangerous to depend upon deflation as the method of returning the economy to full employment. Deflation could make the situation worse rather than better. It seems prudent to use monetary and fiscal policy to return the economy to full employment rather than rely upon the real wealth effect to spur aggregate demand. By the use of these policies, real output and employment can be maintained at their full employment levels, and possible economic instability is avoided.[23]

Let us now turn to the behavior of the economy when there is excess demand. Figure 16.16 shows an initial full employment equilibrium with real output at $(Y/P)_0$ and the price level at P_0. Assume that aggregate demand shifts right from AD_0 to AD_1. At the initial price level, P_0, aggregate demand exceeds long-run aggregate supply by $(Y/P)_1 - (Y/P)_0$. In the very short run, firms increase their output to $(Y/P)_1$ without raising prices. Thus, output rises to meet the increased aggregate demand along AS_{VSR}. As the increase in aggregate demand proves to be more than transitory, firms begin to raise their prices. This reduces the real wage rate, which encourages the use of overtime and leads to hiring of low-productivity workers. Thus, firms produce along the upward-sloping AS_{SR}. At the higher price level, P_1, aggregate demand is reduced relative to $(Y/P)_1$. Real income and output fall to $(Y/P)_2$. With the passage of time, the nominal wage rate rises as firms attempt to hire more labor and as workers seek to recover their reduced real wages. This increases the real wage rate and shifts the short-run aggregate supply schedule up from AS_{SR} to AS'_{SR}. Firms raise their prices, and aggregate demand is reduced. The price level rises to P_2, and real output falls from $(Y/P)_2$ to $(Y/P)_3$. Over time, there is a continuation of rising wages, upward-shifting short-run aggregate supply, and rising prices. The price increases continue to reduce excess aggregate demand. Eventually, short-run aggregate supply shifts up to AS''_{SR}, where excess demand is eliminated and there is long-run equilibrium. The price level rises to P_3, and real output returns to $(Y/P)_0$. The real wage rate also returns to its initial value.

We see that when aggregate demand rises above long-run aggregate supply, the consequence is a short-run increase in real output and a permanent rise in the price level. Because aggregate supply is a binding constraint in the long run, there cannot be a permanent rise in real output. There is a temporary increase in real output, however, and a temporary increase in the employment of low productivity workers.

It might appear that restrictive monetary or fiscal policy, or both, is not needed to offset the initial rightward shift in aggregate demand. After all, the economy gains real output and employment in the short run, and in the long run there are no real effects of the excess demand. All that happens is that the price level and

[22] For a forceful statement of this point see F. H. Hahn, "On Some Problems of Proving the Existence of Equilibrium in a Monetary Economy," in *The Theory of Interest Rates*, Hahn and Brechling (eds.), New York, Macmillan, 1965.

[23] As we shall see in Chapter 18, however, this is more easily said than done.

FIGURE 16.16
THE ADJUSTMENT TO LONG-RUN
EQUILIBRIUM FOLLOWING A RISE
IN AGGREGATE DEMAND.

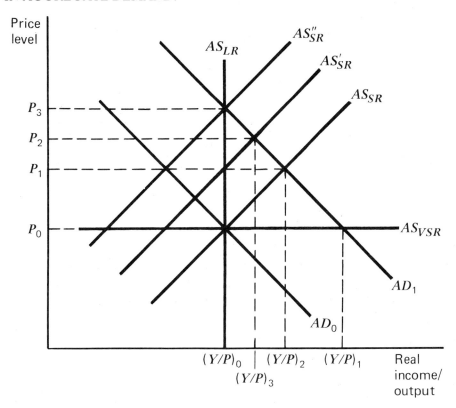

the nominal wage rate rise. Even assuming that no economic distortions occur as a result of the rise in the price level, potential problem still remain.[24] There are two problems that are particularly important for stabilization policy. One involves inflationary expectations and the other involves a wage-price spiral.

Inflationary expectations affect the adjustment to long-run equilibrium following an increase in aggregate demand. Because wages and prices tend to adjust slowly, a substantial period of time can elapse before the price level rises to its long-run equilibrium value. During this period, prices are rising (inflation). Dur-

---

[24] In the real world, distortions are created by a rise in the price level. For example, retired workers on pensions that are fixed in nominal terms suffer a loss of real income when the price level rises.

ing the transition to the higher price level, it is likely that economic agents expect prices to continue to rise. These inflationary expectations affect spending and portfolio decisions. In particular, if agents expect inflation to continue in the future, the real interest rate, which is approximately equal to the nominal interest rate less the expected rate of inflation, is less than the nominal interest rate. The behavior of the real interest rate affects the economy's adjustment to long-run equilibrium.

To see what is going on, let us look at the *IS-LM* diagram in Panel I of Figure 16.17. The initial long-run equilibrium is shown where real output is $(Y/P)_0$, the price level is P_0, and the nominal interest rate is R_0. At this equilibrium, $IS(P_0)$ intersects $LM(P_0)$ on the vertical long-run aggregate supply schedule. Assume for the moment that economic agents do not expect the price level to rise. In this situation, the nominal interest rate equals the real interest rate.[25] Now assume that there is an upward shift in the consumption function that shifts the *IS* curve from $IS(P_0)$ to $IS'(P_0)$. This produces excess demand of $(Y/P)_1 - (Y/P)_0$ at the price level P_0 and the interest rate R_1. With the excess demand, the price level starts to rise. As the price level increases, the real quantities of reserves and money decline. This shifts the *LM* curve up and the *IS* curve to the left. Long-run equilibrium is achieved when real income returns to $(Y/P)_0$. This occurs when the price level increases to P_1 and the interest rate rises to R_2.

In the absence of inflationary expectations, the rise in the nominal interest rate helps to eliminate excess demand. This affect is reduced, and possibly eliminated, when there are inflationary expectations. With the price level increasing, agents expect further price increases in the future. This means that the real interest rate is less than the nominal interest rate. For example, if the nominal interest rate is 10 percent and expected inflation is 8 percent, the real interest rate is approximately 2 percent. The real interest rate is important for investment spending. When the price level is expected to rise, there is more investment at any given value of the nominal interest rate than is the case when there are no inflationary expectations. Thus, with inflationary expectations, the *IS* curve shifts to the right. This shift tends to nullify the negative effect on aggregate demand of the rise in the price level and of the rise in the nominal interest rate. Thus, inflationary expectations add to excess demand and produce additional inflation.

Inflationary expectations also affect the *LM* curve. As explained in Chapter 5, the real rate of return on currency and on other forms of money that pay no interest is approximately equal to the negative of the inflation rate. For example, if expected inflation is 5 percent per year, the expected return on money is roughly −5 percent per year. The real rate of return on interest-bearing transactions ac-

---

[25] Thus, we are implicitly assuming that the increase in aggregate demand comes as a surprise to the private sector. If the increase in demand were anticipated, economic agents would expect rising prices, and the nominal interest rate would be greater than the real interest rate. An analysis of the implications of an anticipated shift in aggregate demand is provided in Chapter 18.

FIGURE 16.17
THE EFFECT OF INFLATIONARY
EXPECTATIONS ON AGGREGATE
DEMAND, THE PRICE LEVEL, AND
THE NOMINAL INTEREST RATE.

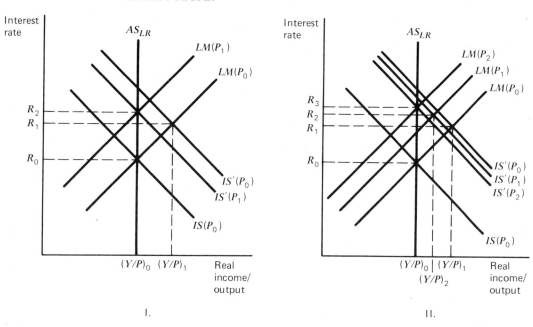

counts is the nominal interest rate less the expected rate of inflation. In all cases, an increase in expected inflation reduces the expected real rate of return on money. This reduces the real quantity of money demanded, given the nominal interest rate. Expected inflation also reduces the real expected return on bonds, given the nominal interest rate. In the two-asset model considered in this text, the choice between money and bonds is unaffected by the increase in inflationary expectations. In a more refined model, we have the demand for physical capital and other assets whose real rate of return is not affected by inflationary expectations. There is a shift out of both money and bonds into these assets when there is an increase in expected inflation. The *LM* curve shifts down. This adds to excess demand in the economy.

We conclude that when there are expectations of inflation, the *IS* curve shifts to the right, and the *LM* curve shifts down. These shifts tend to offset the leftward shift in *IS* and the upward shift in *LM* that are caused by the decline in real wealth resulting from the actual rise in the price level. Because it is the latter shifts that propel the economy to the new equilibrium, the process of adjustment is slowed down by inflationary expectations. Furthermore, the economy can overshoot equilibrium when there are inflationary expectations. Panel I of Figure 16.17 indicates that, in the absence of inflationary expectations, the economy is in equilibrium when the price level and interest rate rise to P_1 and R_2 respectively. Panel II of Figure 16.17 shows that with inflationary expectations there is still excess demand in the economy at this price level. Because there is expectation of further inflation, investment demand is stronger and money demand is weaker than if expected inflation were zero. Thus, at the nominal interest rate R_2, $IS'(P_1)$ intersects $LM(P_1)$ at $(Y/P)_2$, which exceeds $(Y/P)_0$; excess demand remains. The price level has to rise to P_2, and the nominal interest rate must rise to R_3 to offset the effects of inflationary expectations. At these values of the price level and the nominal interest rate, $IS'(P_2)$ intersects $LM(P_2)$ at $(Y/P)_0$. In this equilibrium, the nominal interest rate, R_3, exceeds the interest rate R_2 by the inflation that economic agents expect.

When the price level ceases to rise at P_2, the public reduces its expectations of inflation, and eventually no inflation is expected. As this occurs, the real interest rate rises, so the IS curve shifts left, and the LM curve shifts up. This produces excess supply, and the price level falls below P_2. The final equilibrium occurs at the price level P_1, where expected inflation is zero.

We see that when inflationary expectations enter the picture, the adjustment from one equilibrium to another is complex, and there can be overshooting of the price level and of the nominal interest rate. Thus, fluctuations in the price level and in real output can occur. These dynamic problems can be avoided if policy prevents excess demand from occurring in the first place.

Inflationary expectations are not the only complication. A wage-price spiral can develop that tends to destabilize the economy. As explained earlier, the short-run aggregate supply schedule is upward sloping because wages tend to lag behind prices. An increase in the price level reduces the real wage rate and induces firms to increase output. The nominal wage rate rises following the increase in the price level because there is an increase in the demand for labor and because workers demand a higher nominal wage rate to compensate for the decline in the purchasing power of their income. When the nominal wage rate rises, the short-run aggregate supply schedule shifts up. This leads to a further rise in the price level and then to a further increase in the nominal wage rate.

This interaction of wages and prices is part of the adjustment that occurs as the economy moves to a new equilibrium following an increase in aggregate demand. We know that equilibrium is achieved when aggregate demand equals long-run aggregate supply. This occurs when the price level rises sufficiently to reduce aggregate demand back into equality with long-run supply and when the nominal wage rate rises sufficiently to increase the real wage rate back to its original value.

It is possible, however, that the nominal wage rate continues to rise as workers demand higher wages to compensate for the last rise in the price level. If this occurs, the real wage rate rises above its equilibrium value, and the short-run aggregate supply schedule continues to shift up. In Figure 16.18 we have an initial long-run equilibrium at real output $(Y/P)_0$ and the price level P_0. Assume there is a rightward shift in aggregate demand from AD_0 to AD_1. The price level rises to P_1, and real output increases to $(Y/P)_1$ as the economy produces along

FIGURE 16.18
THE EFFECTS ON REAL INCOME
AND THE PRICE LEVEL OF A
WAGE-PRICE SPIRAL.

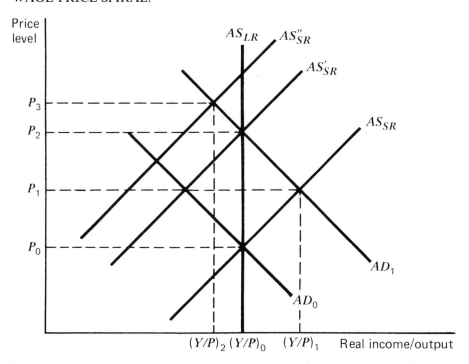

the short-run aggregate supply curve AS_{SR}. Wages rise and the short-run aggregate supply curve shifts up to AS'_{SR}. In the absence of a continuing wage-price spiral, this produces equality of aggregate demand with long-run aggregate supply. If the wage-price spiral continues, however, the short-run aggregate supply schedule shifts from AS'_{SR} to AS''_{SR}. This shift in short-run aggregate supply raises the price level to P_3, which is above its long-run equilibrium value. At this price level, aggregate demand is less than long-run aggregate supply; real income and output fall to $(Y/P)_2$. As long as wages continue to respond to past increases in prices and as long as the short-run aggregate supply schedule continues to shift up when the nominal wage rate increases, there is continued inflation[26] and rising unemployment.[27]

---

[26] This phenomenon is called cost-push inflation because prices are rising in response to increases in labor costs rather than to excess demand.
[27] As we shall see in the next section, the phenomenon of rising prices and rising unemployment is called stagflation.

Rising unemployment brings the wage-price spiral under control. With unemployment, workers are less inclined to demand higher wages. With declining sales, firms are less inclined to grant wage increases, and they are also less inclined to raise their prices if wages do increase. Thus, with unemployment producing smaller and smaller wage and price increases, the wage-price spiral eventually comes to an end. Unemployment remains, however. The unemployment can be eliminated either by expansionary policy or by deflation of wages and prices until the price level, P_2, is established.

We conclude that an increase in aggregate demand above long-run aggregate supply triggers a wage-price spiral that produces inflation and eventually can lead to unemployment coupled with inflation. We will have more to say about inflation and unemployment in the next section. For present purposes, it suffices to note that if policy allows aggregate demand to exceed long-run aggregate supply, a complex and potentially destabilizing adjustment of prices and employment may ensue.

Despite the complications of inflationary expectations and wage-price spirals, it still might appear that there is an economic cost to using stabilization policy to prevent aggregate demand from rising above long-run aggregate supply. If stabilization policy prevents excess demand from occurring, the temporary gain in output and employment is lost. Thus, it might be argued that policy should not offset excess aggregate demand. The problem with this strategy is that the economy has to live with a permanently higher price level and with the transitional problems created by inflationary expectations and the wage-price spiral. Furthermore, it is always possible to argue in favor of the transitory gains in output and employment. Thus, why not continue to stimulate aggregate demand to reap the temporary benefits? The answer is that the price level has to rise every time there is excess aggregate demand. This means that each time the temporary benefits are obtained, there is inflation. Continued pursuit of short-term output and employment gains obtained from an excess of aggregate demand over long-run aggregate supply would produce an ever higher price level, and it creates the potential for runaway inflation. Long-run aggregate supply is a constraint that limits output and employment. Though it may be possible to have gains in output and employment by moving up the short-run aggregate supply curve, the gains are temporary. It is dangerous to seek short-term gains in output and employment from a policy that tolerates, or even encourages, an excess of aggregate demand over long-term aggregate supply.

It is important to note that long-run aggregate supply is not a binding constraint during recessions. When there is a recession, aggregate demand is less than long-run aggregate supply; there is unemployment and idle capacity. In this situation, an increase in aggregate demand produces a sustainable increase in employment and output. As long as aggregate demand does not exceed long-run aggregate supply, measures to increase aggregate demand raise output and employment while avoiding the inflation problems that exist when aggregate demand exceeds long-run aggregate supply. We conclude, then, that policy should strive to keep aggregate demand equal to long-run aggregate supply. This allows the economy to produce as much output and employment as is possible, given the constraint of long-run aggregate supply. Such policy is consistent with the full employment and price stability. It avoids the inflationary pressures of excess demand and the unemployment of inadequate aggregate demand.

SUPPLY-SIDE SHIFTS, STAGFLATION, AND THE PHILLIPS CURVE

It is possible to have rising prices and high unemployment at the same time. This unhappy situation is called *stagflation*. With stagflation, price stability and full employment cannot be achieved simultaneously in the short run. We have already seen that a wage-price spiral can produce inflation and unemployment simultaneously. More generally, any factor that causes the short-run aggregate supply schedule to shift up is a potential source of stagflation. For example, a crop failure or a restriction on the supply of some key resource such as oil can lead to stagflation.

Oil has been a significant problem since the Organization of Petroleum Exporting Countries (OPEC) began to restrict oil supply in the 1970s. As we shall see in Chapter 19, increases in the price of oil in 1973 and 1979 were important causes of stagflation in the 1970s and early 1980s.[28] A change in the price of imported oil is used as the example of a source of stagflation. The reader should note, however, that any shift in the short-run aggregate supply schedule can produce stagflation.

The demand for oil is highly inelastic in the short run, so the price of oil rises sharply when supply is restricted. The rise in the price of oil increases production costs, and firms raise their prices. This produces an upward shift in the short-run aggregate supply schedule. The price level rises, aggregate demand is reduced, and unemployment develops.

The reaction of the economy to an increase in the price of imported oil is illustrated in Figure 16.19. The economy is initially in equilibrium at real output $(Y/P)_0$ and the price level P_0. The rise in the price of oil shifts the short-run aggregate supply curve from AS_{SR} to AS'_{SR}.[29] This leads to a higher price level, P_1, and to a lower level of output $(Y/P)_1$.

Given the increase in the price of oil, firms would be willing to produce the full employment output $(Y/P)_0$ only if the price level rose to P_2. The price level does not rise this much, however. Firms cannot sell the output $(Y/P)_0$ because as prices rise, aggregate demand is reduced. Aggregate demand equals the new

---

[28] Food and raw material shortages, along with changes in foreign exchange rates, were also important factors in the 1970s.

[29] For simplicity, we neglect the effects of the oil price increase on long-run aggregate supply.

FIGURE 16.19
EFFECTS ON REAL INCOME AND
THE PRICE LEVEL OF AN
INCREASE IN THE PRICE OF
IMPORTED OIL.

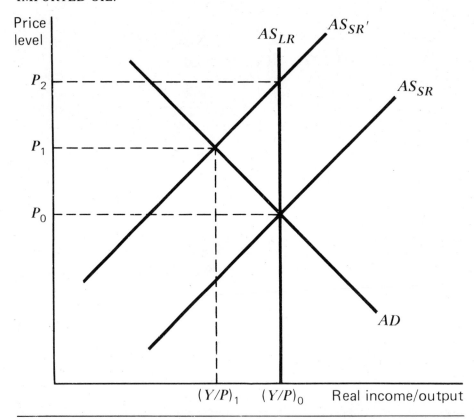

short-run aggregate supply when the price level is P_1.[30] Thus, real income and output fall below the initial value at $(Y/P)_0$. At the reduced output $(Y/P)_1$, there is lower demand for labor, so unemployment develops. The real wage rate declines when the price level rises to P_1, but, with the nominal wage rate fixed in the short run, the decline is not large enough to produce full employment. Given the nominal wage rate, the price level would have to rise to P_2 to achieve full employment. There is not sufficient aggregate demand to support the price level P_2, how-

---

[30] As we shall see in Chapter 17, the increase in the price of imported oil increases imports, which depresses aggregate demand. Thus, the aggregate demand schedule shifts to the left. We ignore this complication here.

ever. Thus, the increase in the price of oil simultaneously raises the price level and produces unemployment.

Before we turn to a discussion of the policy dilemma that is raised by a shift in aggregate supply, it is useful to discuss the transition to long-run equilibrium. In the long run, wages and prices adjust to produce full employment and price stability. This adjustment is a lengthy process. In the case of supply-side shifts, the adjustment period is even longer. In the absence of policy actions, long-run equilibrium is achieved when there is a sufficiently large decline in the real wage rate to return the economy to full employment. The rise in the price level to P_1 does reduce the real wage rate but not sufficiently to produce full employment. The remaining adjustment must occur as a decline in the nominal wage rate. It takes considerable time for this to occur. Because the price level increases when the short-run aggregate supply schedule shifts to the left, a wage-price spiral occurs that actually increases the nominal wage rate in the short run. Employed workers respond to the decline in the purchasing power of their nominal incomes by pressing for a higher nominal wage rate.[31] The rise in the nominal wage rate produces a further upward shift in the short-run aggregate supply curve. This leads to a further rise in the price level and to a further rise in the nominal wage rate. Thus, higher prices produce higher wages, and higher wages increase prices. This upward spiral of wages and prices is not endless, however. As prices rise, aggregate demand falls, and unemployment increases. Given enough time, rising unemployment eliminates the upward pressure on the nominal wage rate, and eventually there is a decline in the real wage rate. The period of transition can be lengthy, however. Substantial unemployment and inflation are required to force the nominal wage rate to decline.

Because stagflation involves both inflation and unemployment, monetary and fiscal policy face a dilemma. If policy eliminates inflation through reducing aggregate demand, unemployment increases. If policy eliminates unemployment through stimulating aggregate demand, inflation increases. Figure 16.20 illustrates the effects of two policy alternatives. Again we have an initial equilibrium where aggregate demand equals long-run aggregate supply at the price level P_0. The increase in the price of oil shifts the short-run aggregate supply schedule from AS_{SR} to AS'_{SR}. In the absence of policy action, this raises the price level to P_1 and reduces real income and output to $(Y/P)_1$. Now let us examine the effects of two policy extremes. At one extreme, we have a policy that tolerates no rise in the price level following the rise in the price of oil. This policy involves pursuing sufficiently restrictive monetary and fiscal policies to push aggregate demand to AD_1 following the rise in the price of oil. With AD_1, aggregate demand equals short-run aggregate supply at the original price level P_0. Note that this policy achieves its objective at the cost of a substantial reduction in real output and income to $(Y/P)_2$. At the opposite extreme we have a policy that tolerates no lost

---

[31] To the extent that labor contracts have cost of living adjustments, the rise in the nominal wage rate is automatic.

FIGURE 16.20
PRICE LEVEL ALTERNATIVES
FOLLOWING AN INCREASE IN THE
PRICE OF IMPORTED OIL.

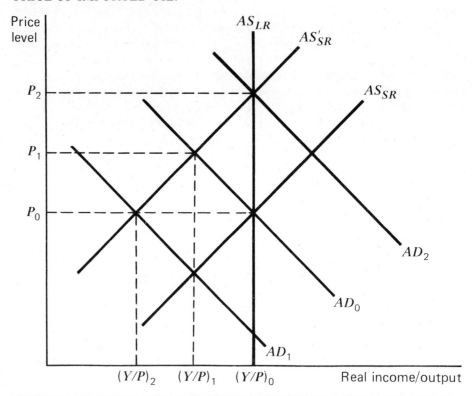

output and income. Here government policy is sufficiently stimulative to shift the aggregate demand schedule to AD_2. This policy maintains employment and output but at the cost of a rise in the price level to P_2. Because aggregate demand remains high, the nominal wage rate does not decline. The entire reduction in the real wage rate is achieved through a rise in the price level i.e., through inflation.[32]

These two extremes are limiting cases in the sense that one tolerates no rise in the price level and the other tolerates no lost output. Any policy that lies between the extremes must accept some rise in the price level and some lost real output. Thus, stabilization policy faces a dilemma during stagflation. It is not possible both to stabilize the price level and eliminate unemployment in the short run.

---

[32] As explained in the previous section, inflationary expectations and a wage-price spiral can produce substantial complications if this policy is pursued.

The more that policy attempts to stabilize the price level, the greater are lost employment and output. The more that policy attempts to stabilize employment and output, the greater is the rise in the price level. All that policymakers can do is to pick the combination of unemployment and inflation that best accords with the "national welfare." Unlike the situation where there is excessive or deficient aggregate demand, it is not possible to pursue a policy that is consistent with achieving full employment and price stability in the short run.

It is important to note that the policy dilemma created by stagflation is a short-run phenomenon. Irrespective of the source of stagflation, for example, oil prices, crop shortages, or the wage price spiral, the problem goes away in the long run.[33] Eventually, wages and prices fully adjust, so the economy returns to full employment. Stagflation can be a serious problem during the transition to this long-run equilibrium, however.

During the 1960s it was fashionable to express the trade-off between inflation and unemployment in terms of the *Phillips curve*.[34] This approach has been discarded by many economists because the Phillips curve can create the erroneous impression that the trade-off is invariant to the cause of stagflation or to the length of time between a policy change and the effects on inflation and unemployment. We shall use the Phillips curve to show why the trade-off depends upon the source of stagflation and upon the length of time being considered.

Panel I of Figure 16.21 shows a Phillips curve. It indicates that increases in the unemployment rate (unemployment as a percentage of the labor force) are associated with decreases in the inflation rate. This downward sloping curve illustrates the trade-off that policymakers face in the short run. For example, at point A the inflation rate is 10 percent and unemployment is 5 percent, and at Point B inflation is 8 percent and unemployment is 6 percent. Thus, a restrictive policy that moves the economy from point A to point B reduces the inflation rate by 2 percentage points and produces an increase in unemployment of 1 percentage point. Conversely, an expansionary policy can move the economy from point A to point C. This reduces the unemployment rate by 1 percentage point, but the inflation rate rises by 2 percentage points.

The extent of the trade-off between inflation and unemployment depends upon the source of inflation. Panel I shows the short-term trade-off when the source of

[33] As we shall see in Chapter 19, in the 1970s there was a seemingly unrelenting string of events that pushed policy from one dilemma to the next. This prevented the economy from achieving longer-run equilibrium. Government policies also contributed to the disequilibrium.

[34] It is called the Phillips curve in honor of A. W. H. Phillips, whose studies provided empirical evidence on the nature of the trade-off. See A. W. H. Phillips, "The Relationship Between Unemployment and the Rate of Change of Money Wage Rates in the United Kingdom, 1861–1967," *Economica*, November 1958, pp. 283–299. Phillips' study involved the relationship between unemployment and the increase in nominal wage rates. Economists later modified the original study to provide a relationship between unemployment and changes in the price level (inflation).

FIGURE 16.21
SHORT-RUN PHILLIPS CURVES.

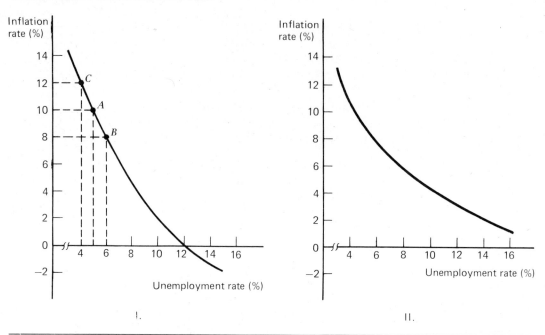

inflation is a wage-price spiral produced by excess demand in the economy. Panel II shows the trade-off when the source of inflation is an increase in the price of imported oil. The Phillips curve is flatter in Panel II. A larger increase in unemployment is required to reduce inflation in the short run. This occurs because depressing aggregate demand (increasing unemployment) does not have any short-run effect on the price of imported oil. Thus, the prices of other goods and services must bear the brunt of low demand. Because oil is the source of inflation to begin with, a large increase in unemployment is required to reduce inflation. In Panel I, excess demand produces the inflation, so a reduction in aggregate demand reduces the increase in the prices of all goods and services. We conclude that the extent of the short-run trade-off between inflation and unemployment depends upon the source of stagflation.

The trade-off also depends upon the length of time being considered. The relationship between inflation and unemployment is very different if we are talking about the trade-off that exists over the next few weeks or months versus the trade-off over the next year or longer. Because wages and prices adjust relatively slowly, it is difficult to affect the inflation rate over short periods of time. The aggregate supply schedule in the very short run is flat, indicating that an increase in aggregate demand raises output and employment with little or no effect on the price level. This gives a flat Phillips curve in the very short run as shown in Panel I of Figure 16.22. The Phillips curve in the very short run indicates that if policy

FIGURE 16.22
THE PHILLIPS CURVE IN THE
VERY SHORT, SHORT, AND LONG RUN.

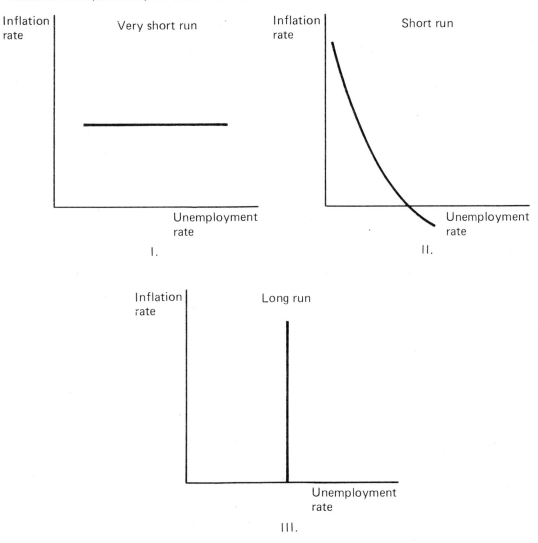

stimulates aggregate demand, the effect over the next few weeks or months is to lower the unemployment rate with little or no rise in the inflation rate. This suggests the favorable trade-off of a substantial reduction in the unemployment rate for a small increase in the inflation rate. Conversely, a reduction in the inflation rate requires a very large increase in unemployment. Thus, the trade-off is unfavorable in that direction.

When we consider time periods longer than just a few weeks or months following a policy change, the Phillips curve becomes steeper. This occurs because wages and prices adjust to shifts in aggregate demand. The short-run aggregate supply schedule is upward sloping, indicating that the price level must rise to induce firms to raise output and employment. As time passes following an increase in aggregate demand, prices rise. Thus, whereas a reduction of unemployment produces little additional inflation in the very short run (Panel I), it produces a larger increase in inflation as we move into the short run (Panel II).[35] Conversely, a reduction of inflation requires a larger increase in the unemployment rate in the very short run than in the short run. Finally, the aggregate supply schedule is vertical in the long run. This implies that eventually there is no trade-off between inflation and unemployment. In the long run, there is full employment no matter what the inflation rate is. Thus, in the long run, policy cannot affect employment, it only affects inflation. As shown in Panel III of Figure 16.22, the long-run Phillips curve is vertical.[36]

The changing slope of the Phillips curve as the economy moves from the very short run to the long run illustrates that patience has its rewards. An impatient policymaker might conclude that it is impractical to reduce inflation by pursuing restrictive policies. The Phillips curve is flat in the very short run, indicating that an unacceptably large increase in unemployment is required to reduce inflation appreciably. If the policymaker can be patient, however, restrictive policy does eventually reduce inflation without the cost of massive unemployment. Conversely, an impatient policymaker might conclude that aggregate demand should be stimulated. After all, the very short-run Phillips curve indicates that it is possible to reduce unemployment with little or no increase in inflation. This impatient policy causes problems later on because the stimulus to aggregate demand and employment does produce inflation. A year or two after stimulating aggregate demand, the policymaker might come to regret having stimulated aggregate demand so much.

We conclude that with the passage of time, the Phillips curve becomes increasingly steep and is eventually vertical. This does not imply that policy should avoid trying to trade inflation off against unemployment. Except in the long run, trade-offs are feasible. The extent of the trade-off does depend upon the period of time considered, however. Effective stabilization policy has to adjust in response to the changing Phillips curve. This is a difficult task at best. We shall have more to say about this in Chapter 18.

---

[35] The Phillips curve is shown as becoming steeper with the passage of time. We could reach the same conclusions by having the short-run Phillips curve shift up over time. The two approaches are equivalent. With either approach, expectations of future inflation by workers are an important part of the adjustment that occurs over time.

[36] Inflation can affect long-run aggregate supply. Inflation makes it difficult for economic agents to distinguish changes in relative prices from changes in the price level. This can lead to inefficiencies that adversely affect long-run aggregate supply. For simplicity, we abstract from this problem.

INFLATION IN THE LONG RUN

We now turn to the question of how an economy can sustain inflation over long periods of time. What factors make prices rise year after year? It is shown that only monetary policy can produce chronic inflation. Expansionary monetary policy produces the growth in money and credit needed to sustain inflation. If monetary policy stops being so expansionary, inflation is eliminated in the long run.

This text uses static models; long-run equilibrium involves a constant price level and, therefore, zero inflation. More advanced, dynamic models yield a long run, equilibrium inflation rate. Though dynamic models are beyond the scope of this text, we can use our static model to illustrate the crucial role that monetary policy plays in determining inflation in the long run. Figure 16.23 illustrates that chronic, sustained inflation occurs when aggregate demand continues to shift to the right by more than aggregate supply. Panel I shows a noninflation situation where aggregate demand shifts to the right over time by the same amount as long-run aggregate supply shifts.[37] In this situation, the price level is constant at P_0, and there is no inflation. Panel II shows the situation when aggregate demand shifts by more than aggregate supply. Here the price level increases over time in order to equate aggregate demand with supply. Thus, there is continued inflation.

Chronic inflation is not inevitable. After all, economic policies can reduce the shifts in aggregate demand, and they can increase the shifts in aggregate supply. For example, a combination of "tight" fiscal and "easy" monetary policy limits the growth in aggregate demand and stimulates expansion of aggregate supply. In principle, policy can achieve equality of aggregate demand and supply without chronic inflation. Put another way, chronic inflation must be the result of a failure of policy to do its job.

In the model we have used so far, chronic inflation can be produced by the *LM* curve, the *IS* curve, or both. Thus, either monetary or fiscal policy can cause and eliminate sustained inflation. In Panels I and II of Figure 16.24, it is shown that a given excess demand of $(Y/P)_1 - (Y/P)_0$ can be maintained either by the *LM* curve or the *IS* curve. In Panel I, the economy is initially in long-run equilibrium where IS_0 intersects LM_0 at $(Y/P)_0$ and R_0. Now assume that the *LM* curve shifts down to LM_1. This produces excess demand $(Y/P)_1 - (Y/P)_0$. With excess demand, the price level is rising. We have shown that when the price level rises, real reserves and real money balances decline, causing the *LM* curve to shift up. The decline in real wealth also shifts the *IS* curve to the left. The shifts in the *LM* and *IS* curves reduce excess demand. The process of adjustment is interrupted when the *LM* curve fails to shift up. A failure of the *LM* to shift up can be the result of a reduction in the public's demand for real money balances at the prevailing income, interest rate, and price level or the result of an increase in the quantity of nominal reserves.[38] We saw earlier that inflationary expectations do

---

[37] Recall that technical progress, labor force growth, and increases in the capital stock make the long-run aggregate supply schedule shift to the right.

[38] The money multiplier could also rise. For simplicity, we ignore this possibility.

FIGURE 16.23
THE GROWTH OF AGGREGATE
DEMAND RELATIVE TO
AGGREGATE SUPPLY
DETERMINES THE INFLATION
RATE IN THE LONG RUN.

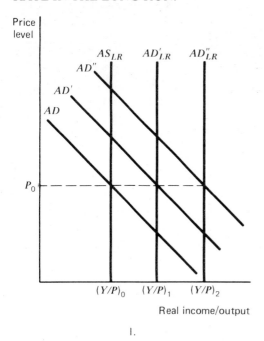

I.

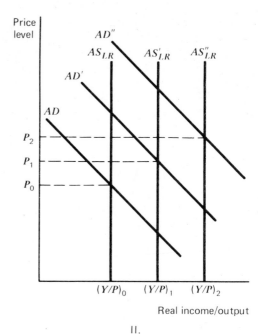

II.

induce the public to reduce its demand for real money balances and, therefore, to offset the upward shift in the LM curve. For reasons that will be explained later, we shall not use this explanation for fixing the LM curve at LM_1. Rather, it is assumed that expansionary monetary policy maintains LM_1. By providing additional reserves, the Fed sets the LM curve at LM_1 and fuels the inflation that results from excess demand. This inflation requires continued reserve growth to maintain the LM curve at LM_1.[39] Thus, excess demand is maintained and inflation continues.

The same excess demand can be achieved by the IS curve. In Panel II, the economy is initially in long-run equilibrium where IS_0 intersects LM_0 at $(Y/P)_0$ and R_0. Now assume that the IS curve shifts right to IS_1. This creates the same

[39] The increase in reserves prevents real wealth from falling and, therefore, prevents the IS curve from shifting up as prices rise.

FIGURE 16.24
MAINTAINING EXCESS DEMAND
THROUGH EITHER THE *LM* OR THE
IS CURVE.

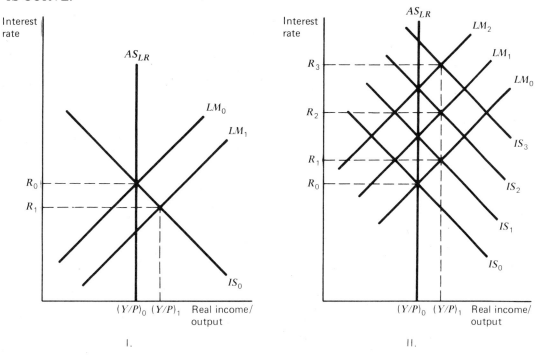

I.

II.

excess demand of $(Y/P)_1 - (Y/P)_0$. Now, however, as the price level rises, the *LM* curve shifts up to LM_1 because total reserves are fixed. This would reduce excess demand. Assume, however, that there is an offsetting rightward shift of the *IS* curve to IS_2. This maintains real income and output at $(Y/P)_1$, and it raises the interest rate to R_2. Several factors can shift the *IS* curve farther to the right. Inflationary expectations reduce the real interest rate and shift the *IS* curve. Alternatively, consumers might go on a spending spree, or firms might become so optimistic about the future, for whatever reason, that they generate an investment boom. Finally, fiscal policy can become more stimulative by cutting taxes or raising spending.[40] Note, however, that no matter what the source of the shift in the

[40] As we saw in Chapter 14, these fiscal policies affect the budget deficit and shift the *LM* curve upward if the deficit is bond financed. Thus, excess demand can be maintained only if monetary policy expands the quantity of reserves or if fiscal policy becomes increasingly expansionary.

IS curve, prices continue to rise, and the *LM* curve continues to shift up. This means that the *IS* curve has to continue to shift farther and farther to the right to maintain excess demand. The interest rate continues to rise. Only if the *IS* curve continues to shift to the right to offset the effects of the upward shifting *LM* curve does excess demand and inflation continue. Furthermore, it becomes increasingly difficult to sustain rightward shifts in the *IS* curve. As the price level rises, real wealth is reduced, which tends to make the *IS* curve shift to the left. Thus, the expansionary sources that are shifting the *IS* curve to the right must become larger and larger to offset the effects of declining real wealth on aggregate demand.

To summarize the argument, aggregate demand must exceed long-run aggregate supply for inflation to be sustained. If monetary policy is the cause of inflation, it must continue to expand the quantity of reserves and money. If either private spending or fiscal policy is the cause of inflation, the *IS* curve must continue to shift to the right to offset the effects of the upward shifting *LM* curve. Inflation is not necessarily a monetary phenomenon in this world. Fiscal policy or private spending can produce inflation even if monetary policy does not go along. The stimulus from private spending or from fiscal policy must become larger and larger, however, to offset the effects of the upward shifting *LM* curve. It is unlikely that the stimulus could be sustained for substantial periods of time. When monetary policy does not provide additional reserves, the decline in real money balances and real wealth provides a powerful brake that slows inflation. Furthermore, when we adopt a money demand schedule with a more realistic shape than the straight line used so far, the brake is even more powerful.

Straight lines simplify graphs and algebra, but at times they are not accurate characterizations of economic behavior. This is particularly relevant for the *LM* curve. A linear *LM* curve comes from the assumption that money demand is linear. Both theory and empirical evidence indicate that the money demand schedule is not linear. Panel I of Figure 16.25 shows a more realistic money demand schedule. As explained in Chapter 13, the demand schedule becomes flat at a low interest rate. This occurs because below R_0 the interest income from holding bonds is less than the transaction costs of purchasing and then selling bonds. Thus, at the interest rate R_0, the public wants to hold only money and no bonds. As a consequence, the interest rate cannot fall below R_0. The money demand schedule indicates that as the interest rate rises, the public reduces the real quantity of money demanded. It pays to economize on real money balances and hold bonds. The higher the interest rate, the greater the incentive to economize on real money balances. At very high interest rates, however, the money demand schedule becomes very steep. This indicates that when the interest rate rises, it is difficult for the public to economize any further on real money balances. A minimum amount of money is needed for day-by-day transactions. Even though the interest rate rises, real money holdings cannot be reduced below this minimum without interfering with the ability to conduct transactions. Thus, at a sufficiently high interest rate, the money demand schedule becomes vertical. Any further rise in the interest rate produces no further reduction in the real quantity of money demanded.

FIGURE 16.25
A NONLINEAR MONEY DEMAND
SCHEDULE AND *LM* CURVE.

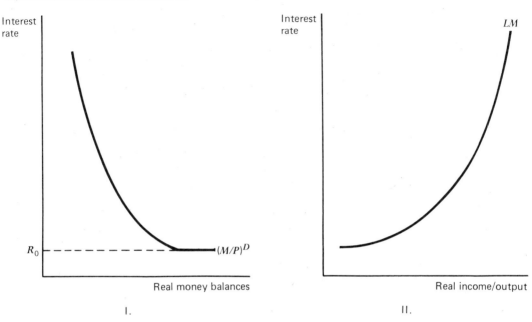

I. II.

A money demand schedule with this shape, combined with a fixed quantity of money, produces the *LM* curve shown in Panel II of Figure 16.25. The money demand schedule is flat when the interest rate is low. When real income rises, only a small increase in the interest rate is required to equate a fixed real money supply to the increased real money demand. Thus, when real income and the interest rate are low, the *LM* curve is relatively flat. When the interest rate is high, however, the money demand schedule is steep. A rise in real income requires a large increase in the interest rate to equate the fixed real money supply to the increased real money demand. This gives a steep *LM* curve at high values of real income and the interest rate.

We shall now show that this increasingly steep *LM* curve implies that sustained inflation can be produced only by monetary policy. Figure 16.26 shows the *LM* curve initially at LM_0 and the *IS* curve at IS_1. There is excess demand of $(Y/P)_1 - (Y/P)_0$. The excess demand makes prices rise and the *LM* curve shifts up to LM_1. This is offset by a rightward shift in the *IS* curve to IS_2, and excess demand is sustained. Prices continue to rise. This produces another upward shift in the *LM* curve to LM_2, which is matched by another rightward shift in *IS* to IS_3. Note that the shifting *IS* curves cross the shifting *LM* curves at points on the *LM* curves that are increasingly steep. This produces larger and larger increases in the

FIGURE 16.26
SUSTAINED INFLATION IS
IMPOSSIBLE UNLESS THERE IS
EXPANSIONARY MONETARY POLICY.

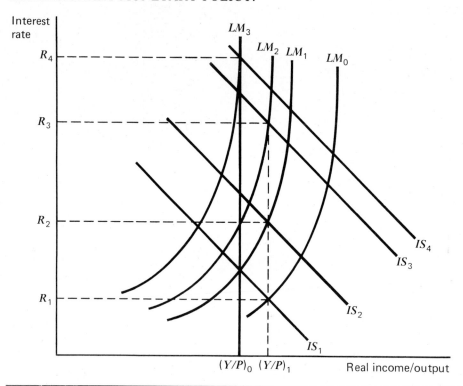

interest rate, which require larger and larger rightward shifts in *IS* to maintain $(Y/P)_1$. Eventually, the interest rate rises so high (above R_3) that aggregate demand and real output fall below $(Y/P)_1$. Thus, a shifting *IS* curve cannot sustain the excess demand. The *LM* curves continue to shift up, and the interest rate continues to rise, however, as long as there is any excess demand and inflation in the economy. Ultimately, the *LM* curve shifts up to LM_3. At this time, the economy returns to $(Y/P)_0$, the interest rate is R_4, and there is price stability.

We conclude that the *IS* curve cannot produce sustained inflation as long as the Fed refuses to allow reserves and money to grow. Although inflationary expectations or a spending spree by households, firms, or the government might produce rightward shifts in the *IS* curve, this is not sufficient to generate a chronic inflation. Monetary policy must be a coconspirator by providing additional reserves.

Chronic inflation does occur when monetary policy continues to make total reserves grow. The reserve growth prevents real money balances from falling as prices rise and, therefore, prevents the *LM* curve from shifting up. Thus, reserve and money growth maintains excess aggregate demand. Consumption, investment, or fiscal policy might be the initial source of inflation, but only monetary policy can keep it going. Alternatively, the *IS* sector might not be the initiating force. Monetary policy can initiate inflation by shifting the *LM* curve downward. It sustains inflation by preventing the *LM* curve from shifting back up.

Earlier it was argued that shifts in money demand can also produce inflation. We shall now show that these shifts cannot produce *chronic* inflation. Assume that the public decides that it wants to hold less real balances at the prevailing real income, price level, and nominal interest rate. This may be the result of a change in the public's tastes or the result of inflationary expectations. In either case, the demand for real money balances shifts down, and, given real income and the price level, the nominal interest rate falls. Thus, the *LM* curve shifts down. This produces excess demand, and prices rise. The real quantity of money declines when the price level rises. Thus, the *LM* curve starts to shift back up. Furthermore, with declining real wealth, the *IS* curve shifts to the left. Both of these shifts reduce excess demand. For excess aggregate demand to be maintained, it is necessary that the money demand schedule continues to shift down. This prevents the *LM* curve from shifting up and offsets the effect of the leftward shifts in the *IS* curve. If the downward shifts in money demand are large enough, they can sustain excess demand and inflation for a while. If the Federal Reserve does not supply additional nominal reserves, however, the public has to be satisfied with an ever-shrinking real quantity of money. This implies that the shifts in money demand must become larger and larger. After some point, it becomes impossible for the public to do any further economizing on real money balances. When this occurs, the *LM* curve must shift up.

We conclude that shifting money demand can cause inflation for a while, but the shifts cannot cause chronic inflation. If the nominal quantity of reserves is unchanged, real money balances are reduced as prices rise. It becomes increasingly difficult for the public to economize on shrinking real money balances. The *LM* curve shifts up, and interest rates rise sufficiently to reduce excess demand. Thus, eventually excess demand is eliminated and inflation disappears.[41]

We are led to the important conclusion that chronic inflation is impossible without an expansion in the quantity of reserves and money to support the inflation. An expansionary monetary policy is a necessary ingredient for sustained inflation. Consumers, firms, money demanders, or fiscal policy may get the inflationary process started, but monetary policy is needed to keep it going. Thus, chronic inflation is necessarily a monetary phenomenon because only expansionary monetary policy can sustain it.

---

[41] The same conclusion applies for increases in the money multiplier.

This section has dealt with unrelenting inflation. It is possible to have substantial periods of inflation that are not caused by monetary policy. For example, investment or consumption booms or expansionary fiscal policy can create excess demand and rising prices. Even if monetary policy fixes the nominal quantity of reserves, excess demand and rising prices continue until the *LM* curve shifts up to the point that the excess demand is eliminated. This takes time. Furthermore, inflationary expectations reduce the real interest rate and add to excess demand. Similarly, a wage-price spiral shifts the short-run aggregate supply schedule up and produces further inflation. These responses further delay the transition to stable prices. We have also seen that energy shortages, crop failures, and similar factors can produce rising prices. Though a determined monetary policy can eventually eliminate these inflationary pressures, the transition to price stability can be lengthy, and there may be substantial unemployment until equilibrium is reached.

The point of this section is not to demonstrate that all inflations are caused by monetary policy. Many factors can produce inflation. Rather, the point is that inflation can be brought under control and eliminated provided that monetary policy refuses to supply the reserves needed to sustain the inflation. We cannot blame all inflations on the Federal Reserve. We can point to the Fed as ultimately responsible for inflation that continues year after year. In Chapter 19 we shall discuss the political and policy dilemmas that led the Fed to fuel the inflation of the 1970s.

SUMMARY

Aggregate supply was introduced in this chapter. This allowed us to determine real output and the price level. It was shown that, in the long run, wages and prices adjust to give full employment. The price level is determined by the intersection of long-run aggregate supply with aggregate demand. Over shorter periods of time, however, there is not full adjustment of wages and prices. This can lead to unemployment of labor or to periods in which total output exceeds long-run aggregate supply.

Aggregate demand is affected by the price level. When the price level rises, the real values of reserves and government bonds decline. This reduces real wealth and increases interest rates. These effects reduce aggregate demand. Thus, when the price level is high, aggregate demand is low. Aggregate supply is also affected by the price level in the short run. When the price level rises, firms want to produce a larger output. Thus, when the price level is high, aggregate supply is high. In the short run, both the price level and real output are determined by the intersection of short-run aggregate supply with aggregate demand.

There is no dilemma for monetary and fiscal policy as long as recessions and booms are caused by aggregate demand. Policy eliminates these problems by adjusting aggregate demand to equal long-run aggregate supply. There is a policy dilemma when there are leftward shifts in short-run aggregate supply. These shifts can be produced by a wage-price spiral or by some exogenous force such as an increase in the price of imported oil. These shifts produce a dilemma because policy must trade unemployment off against inflation. It is impossible to achieve both price stability and high employment in the short run. This problem was encountered during the 1970s and early 1980s.

The chapter concluded with a discussion of the causes of chronic inflation. Many factors can produce spurts of inflation, but only monetary policy can produce chronic, sustained inflation.

SELECTED REFERENCES

Dornbusch, Rudiger and Stanley Fischer, *Macroeconomics* (2nd ed.), New York: McGraw-Hill, 1981.

Gordon, Robert, *Macroeconomics* (2nd ed.), Boston: Little, Brown and Company, 1981.

INTERNATIONAL TRADE AND FINANCE

17

This chapter is concerned with the effects of international trade and finance on the domestic economy. The international sector of the economy affects domestic interest rates, output, employment, and inflation. Furthermore, it can limit the ability of monetary and fiscal policy to stabilize the domestic economy. The issue of the mix of monetary and fiscal policy is particularly important when one is studying policy issues in an open economy. Most of the discussion focuses on the United States, but some of the problems faced by other countries are briefly covered. In order to keep the discussion manageable, we must gloss over much of the institutional and theoretical detail that makes international economics such an interesting and challenging topic.

The economy of the United States is less affected by international considerations than are most other economies. Even in the United States, however, the foreign sector is important. For example, in 1982 imports and exports of goods and services were about 11 percent of GNP. The ratio of imports to GNP understates the importance of international trade, however, because many domestic industries (e.g., autos, steel, and textiles) compete with imports. Furthermore, the domestic financial system is highly integrated with foreign financial centers. These economic linkages with the rest of the world allow the nation to enjoy a higher standard of living than would otherwise be the case. The linkages can pose significant problems for stabilization policies, however. Developments abroad affect domestic output, employment, inflation, and interest rates. Huge increases in the prices of imported oil and other materials are obvious examples of U.S. dependence on the rest of the world. Although other influences are less obvious and receive less publicity, their effects can be equally important. In order to describe the problems raised by international trade and finance, we must discuss some theoretical and institutional factors.

THE EFFECTS OF INTERNATIONAL TRADE ON THE *IS* CURVE

Expenditures by foreigners for our output, and expenditures by domestic residents for foreign output affect the domestic economy. Part of total domestic output is sold to foreigners as exports. Thus, part of total expenditures in the domestic economy is purchases by foreigners of our output. Part of the total expenditures of domestic residents is for output produced by foreigners. Thus, part of consumption, investment, and government expenditures is for imported goods and services.

The role of exports and imports can be seen in the following expression

$$Q = Y = C + I + G + EX - IM$$

where *EX* is the nominal value of exports and *IM* is the nominal value of imports. If the price level is held constant, total output of the economy, Q, equals total income, Y, which equals total expenditures. Now, however, total expenditures are affected by exports and imports. Exports, *EX*, add to aggregate expenditures in the domestic economy because they are purchases (by foreigners) of currently produced goods and services. Imports, *IM*, reduce aggregate expenditures in the domestic economy because they are purchases of goods and services supplied by other economies. The difference between exports and imports is called *net exports*, NX. Net exports are the net contribution that foreign trade makes to total expenditures in the economy. Because $NX = (EX - IM)$, we have:

$$Q = Y = C + I + G + NX$$

or

$$NX = Y - (C + I + G).$$

Consumption plus investment plus government expenditures on goods and services $(C + I + G)$ are the total expenditures of the economy's residents for goods and services. Net exports are the difference between total domestic output (income) and these total expenditures. Note that net exports can be either positive or negative. If net exports are positive, exports exceed imports. This means that the nominal value of output and income in the economy exceeds the aggregate expenditures of domestic residents. The economy is producing and selling a total output that is greater than domestic aggregate expenditures. The remaining output is exported to foreigners. If exports are less than imports, net exports are negative. In this case, output and aggregate income are less than the aggregate expenditures of domestic residents. The economy is producing and selling less than the amount that is spent by domestic residents. This occurs because part of aggregate expenditures is for goods and services produced in other economies.

Export and import demands affect the *IS* curve. Their role can be seen most easily by returning to the simple model of Chapter 13. In that model, consumption and saving depend only upon aggregate income. Investment depends only upon the interest rate. Furthermore, there is no government sector. We can add international trade to this model by introducing expressions that describe export and import demand. In order to simplify the algebra, we assume that export demand is exogenous to developments in the domestic economy. It is also assumed that the price of foreign output relative to domestic output is constant. We shall study more realistic cases later in this section.

With export demand fixed, or exogenous, changes in domestic income and interest rates do not affect exports. Export demand is affected by foreign income and interest rates, but these are assumed to be independent of domestic economic conditions.[1] With relative prices held constant, we do not have to worry about the effects on export and import demand of changes in the prices of domestic goods and services relative to the prices of goods and services produced abroad.

We approximate the relationship between income and import demand by the following relationship:

$$IM = im_0 + im_1 Y$$

where both im_0 and im_1 are positive. The intercept, im_0, allows us to account for changes in the tastes of domestic residents for imports. If im_0 increases, there is an increase in the demand for imports, given income. If im_0 decreases, there is a reduction in import demand, given income. The parameter, im_1, is the sensitivity of import demand to changes in income. It is called the *marginal propensity to import*.

We can now put the pieces together to derive the *IS* curve for the simple model. The model is given by the following equations:

$$C = c_0 + c_1 Y$$
$$S = s_0 + s_1 Y$$
$$I = i_0 - i_1 R$$
$$EX = \overline{EX} \ \ ^2$$
$$IM = im_0 + im_1 Y$$
$$Y = C + I + NX = C + I + EX - IM$$
$$Y = C + S \ .$$

We can solve this system of equations to obtain the expression for the *IS* curve. Solving for *Y*, the *IS* curve is

$$Y = \frac{c_0 - i_0 - im_0 + \overline{EX}}{(s_1 + im_1)} - \frac{i_1}{(s_1 + im_1)} R \ .$$

---

[1] This assumption is most realistic for an economy that is small relative to the rest of the world. It is a less reasonable assumption for the United States.

[2] The bar indicates that export demand is assumed to be exogenous.

Note that an upward shift in the consumption or investment functions (Δc_0, $\Delta i_0 > 0$) or an increase in exogenous export demand ($\Delta \overline{EX} > 0$) raises income, given the interest rate. Thus, the *IS* curve shifts to the right. The extent of the shift is determined by the income multiplier $m_Y(R) = 1/(s_1 + im_1)$. Note that the marginal propensity to import, im_1, reduces the multiplier. When domestic consumption expenditures rise in response to an increase in income, part of this rise goes for imported goods. Thus, when income rises, the demand for imports increases. In earlier chapters, there was no foreign trade, so increases in consumption and investment demand were for domestically produced output. Now, part of the increased demand is for output produced in foreign economies. This implies that a rise in income produces a smaller increase in the aggregate demand for domestic output when there is international trade. The multiplier is reduced. An increase in import demand has the same effect on the aggregate demand for domestic output as an increase in saving.

Import demand also makes the *IS* curve steeper. With income on the left-hand side of the expression, we have:

$$\frac{\Delta Y}{\Delta R} = - \frac{i_1}{(s_1 + im_1)}.$$

The graph of the *IS* curve implicitly has the interest rate on the left-hand side, so

$$\frac{\Delta R}{\Delta Y} = - \frac{(s_1 + im_1)}{i_1}.$$

Thus, the higher is the marginal propensity to import, im_1, the steeper is the *IS* curve.

To see the significance of this result, we will find it useful to recall why the *IS* curve is downward sloping. In a world without international trade, the *IS* curve shows the combinations of the interest rate and aggregate income for which desired saving equals desired investment. When income increases, there is more saving. The higher saving can be sustained only if desired investment rises to equality with the higher saving. Investment is increased as a result of a lower interest rate. Thus, income and desired saving can be higher if there is a lower interest rate. This gives the downward sloping *IS* curve.

With international trade, an increase in income produces a rise in both saving and imports. By setting aggregate expenditures equal to aggregate income, we observe that investment equals saving minus net exports, $C + I + (EX - IM) = C + S$, $I = S - (EX - IM) = S - NX$. With exports fixed at $\overline{EX}$, we have for a change in investment, $\Delta I = \Delta S + \Delta IM$. There must now be a greater increase in investment to equal the rise in saving *and* import demand. This requires a larger decrease in the interest rate. The more responsive import demand is to changes in income, the steeper the *IS* curve is.

The next step is to show how changes in the price of U.S. output relative to the price of output produced abroad affect aggregate demand. There are two ways that relative prices can change. The price level in the United States can change relative to the price levels in foreign countries, or the exchange rate between the dollar and foreign money can change. First, let us consider the effects of changes in the domestic and foreign price level. If the domestic inflation rate is different from the inflation rate in other countries, the price of domestic output changes relative to the price of foreign output. For example, if the United States is enjoying price stability while there is inflation abroad, the price of U.S. output falls relative to the price of foreign output. This induces foreigners to buy more goods and services in the United States, and it reduces the amount demanded by U.S. residents for goods and services produced abroad. Thus, the decline in the price of domestic relative to foreign output increase export demand and reduces import demand. At any given level of aggregate income, net exports are larger. This means that the *IS* curve shifts to the right. By a similar argument, if prices are rising faster in the United States than in the rest of the world, export demand declines and import demand rises. This shifts the *IS* curve to the left.

The second way that the price of domestic output can change relative to the price of output produced abroad is through a change in the exchange rate. Each country has its own monetary unit, that is, U.S. dollars, British pounds, German Deutsche marks, Japanese yen, and so on. Each country measures its prices in terms of its own domestic money. In foreign trade, the money of one country is exchanged for the money of another. This is accomplished in foreign exchange markets. An exchange rate is a price measuring the rate of exchange between money in two countries. For example, in 1981 the average exchange rate between dollars and German Deutsche marks (DM) was approximately 2.30DM per dollar. Thus, each dollar could be exchanged for 2.30 Deutsche marks (2.30DM/$). Equivalently, each Deutsche mark could be exchanged for $0.44. This is the reciprocal of the *DM* per dollar, that is, $1/(2.30DM/\$) = \$1.00/2.30DM = \$0.44/DM$. This reciprocal relationship can cause confusion, so we use the convention of measuring the exchange rate as the number of units of foreign currency that can be purchased for a dollar. Thus, we have 2.30DM/$ in our example. This can be thought of as the value of the dollar in terms of foreign exchange.

An exchange rate has little meaning unless we know the prices of goods and services in the two countries. Consider the example of automobiles produced in the United States and in Germany. Assume that similar cars cost $10,000 in the United States and 20,700DM in Germany. To compare the price of cars in the two countries, we must express the prices in terms of a single money. The relevant comparison for Americans is the number of dollars required to purchase 20,700DM. This gives the dollar price of a German car. Since $1 buys 2.30 DM, the dollar price is $20,700DM/(2.30DM/\$) = \$9000$. Because a similar automobile costs $10,000 in the United States, the price to a U.S. resident of a German car is $1000 lower than the price of a domestically produced car. Note that the dollar price of the German car, $\$P^G$, is obtained by dividing the Deutsche mark price, P^{DM}, by the exchange rate, e, or $\$P^G = P^{DM}/e$. Conversely, for a German resident, the relevant price is the number of Deutsche marks required to purchase $10,000. This gives the DM price of a U.S. car. In our example, each dollar costs 2.30DM, so the price is $\$10,000(2.30DM/\$) = 23,000DM$ for an American car. Thus, for Germans, the price of an imported American car is higher than the price of a car that is produced domestically. Given the relative prices of cars in the two countries, Americans will tend to import German cars, and Germans will purchase their own cars rather than import cars from the United States.

Now assume that the exchange rate falls, that is, the dollar depreciates. This means that a dollar can be exchanged for fewer DM than before. For example, after the decline of the exchange rate (depreciation of the dollar), assume that a dollar can now be exchanged for 2.00DM rather than 2.30DM. A German car now costs 20,700DM/(2.00DM/$) = $10,350 rather than $9000. After the depreciation of the dollar, German cars are more costly to Americans than are cars produced domestically. The relative price of German cars rises. It makes no difference to Americans whether the price increase is caused by a decline in the exchange rate or by a rise in the DM price. The effect is the same. For Germans, the opposite occurs. Each dollar now costs 2.00DM, rather than 2.30DM. The Deutsche mark has appreciated. A $10,000 car now costs Germans only $10,000(2.00DM/$) = 20,000DM whereas a domestically produced car costs 20,700DM. The relative price of U.S. cars falls. It makes no difference to Germans whether the price decline is caused by a reduction in the exchange rate or by a decline in the dollar price.

We conclude that the dollar price of German cars rises and the Deutsche mark price of U.S. cars falls when the dollar exchange rate falls. The decline in the exchange rate encourages the export of U.S. cars to Germany and discourages the imports of German cars into the United States.[3]

Both the exchange rate and the price level in each country affect import and export demand. For every country with which the United States trades, there is an exchange rate indicating the number of units of that country's money that can be bought for a dollar. These exchange rates in conjunction with the price level in each country relative to the price level in the United States affect the quantity of goods and services that the United States imports and exports. Rather than try to keep track of the exchange rate and price level for each country, we will combine all countries into one. For this foreign aggregate, there is a single exchange rate and a single price level. Thus, there is an exchange rate between the dollar and foreign money.[4] The exchange rate, e, is the number of units of foreign money that can be obtained for one dollar. There is also an average price level, P^F, in foreign countries expressed in terms of the foreign monetary unit. The amount of exports from the United States and the amount of imports into the United States are affected by the exchange rate, the foreign price level, and the price level in the United States.

The roles of the exchange rate and of the foreign price level can be seen by expressing the foreign price level in terms of dollars. The dollar price of foreign

---

[3] It is left to the reader to show that an increase in the exchange rate (appreciation of the dollar) reduces U.S. exports and increases imports from Germany.

[4] All foreign countries are lumped into one for ease of analysis. The single exchange rate is a weighted average (index) of the dollar exchange rates in each country using the relative amount of trade with the United States as weights.

goods and services, $\$P^F$ is the foreign price level divided by the exchange rate, or $\$P^F = P^F/e$. The dollar price of foreign goods and services relative to the price of goods and services produced in the United States, P, is $\$P^F/P$ or $[(P^F/e)/P]$. A rise in this relative price means that foreign goods and services are more costly to U.S. residents relative to domestically produced goods and services. Thus, when $[(P^F/e)/P]$ rises, the quantity demanded of imports declines. Conversely, when $[(P^F/e)/P]$ rises, goods and services produced in the United States are less costly to foreigners relative to goods and services produced in their own economies. Thus, when $[(P^F/e)/P]$ rises, the demand for U.S. exports rises. We conclude that when $[(P^F/e)/P]$ rises, export demand rises and import demand falls. Therefore, net export demand, $NX = (EX - IM)$, rises. By a similar argument, when $[(P^F/e)/P]$ falls, foreign goods and services are less costly relative to goods and services produced in the United States, so net export demand falls.

With the role of relative prices in mind, let us return to the effect of export and import demand on the *IS* curve. The demand for U.S. exports in real terms is approximated by the following export demand function:

$$\frac{EX}{P} = ex_0 + ex_1 \left[\frac{Y^F}{P^F} \right] + ex_2 \left[\frac{P^F/e}{P} \right].$$

Leaving the intercept, ex_0, aside for the moment, ex_1 and ex_2 are positive, indicating that the demand for U.S. exports varies positively with real income in foreign countries, Y^F/P^F, and positively with the foreign price level (in dollars), P^F/e, relative to the price level in the United States, P.

When real income rises abroad, foreigners increase their demand for U.S. exports. The parameter ex_1 is the sensitivity of real export demand to a change in real foreign income.

A rise in the price level abroad, measured in dollars, relative to the price level in the United States, also increases the demand for U.S. exports. The dollar price level in foreign countries is affected by both the exchange rate, e, and by the foreign price level measured in foreign money, P^F. Given the domestic and foreign price levels, a decline in the exchange rate raises the demand for exports, and a rise in the exchange rate lowers export demand. Given the exchange rate, a rise in the foreign price level, P^F, or a decline in the U.S. price level, P, increases export demand. A fall in the foreign price level or a rise in the U.S. price level reduces the demand for exports. The parameter ex_2 is the sensitivity of real export demand to a change in the dollar price of foreign output relative to domestic output.

Finally, the intercept, ex_0, is used to measure foreigners' tastes for U.S. exports, given real foreign income and given the foreign price level relative to the U.S. price level. The export demand function shifts, that is, ex_0 changes, when preferences for U.S. exports change.

We argued earlier that when real export demand rises, the *IS* curve shifts to the right; and when real export demand declines, the *IS* curve shifts to the left. The export demand equation explains why real exports change. An increase in ex_0 indicates that, given foreign real income and foreign prices relative to U.S. prices, foreigners demand more goods and services from the United States. This increases exports and shifts the *IS* curve to the right. A decline in ex_0 shifts the *IS* curve to the left. A rise in real foreign income increases export demand and causes the *IS* curve to shift to the right. A decline in real foreign income produces a leftward shift in the *IS* curve. A rise in the foreign price level (measured in dollars), P^F/e, relative to the U.S. price level, increases export demand and shifts the *IS* curve to the right. A decline in $[(P^F/e)/P]$ shifts the *IS* curve to the left.

In the earlier discussion of the effect of exports on the *IS* curve, we took export demand to be exogenous. This meant that exports were assumed to be unaffected by economic conditions in the United States. The term $[(P^F/e)/P]$ indicates that the assumption of exogenous exports must be abandoned. Given the exchange rate, e, the price level in the United States affects $[(P^F/e)/P]$ and, therefore, affects the demand for U.S. exports. Furthermore, as we shall see later in this chapter, economic conditions in the United States affect the exchange rate. Finally, the American economy is so large that income and interest rates in the United States affect real income in the rest of the world. Thus, we have another reason why export demand is affected by domestic economic conditions.

Now let us turn to real imports. The demand by U.S. residents for real imports is approximated by

$$\frac{IM}{P} = im_0 + im_1 \left[\frac{Y}{P} \right] - im_2 \left[\frac{(P^F/e)}{P} \right].$$

The intercept, im_0, indicates the taste for imports, given real income and the price of foreign output relative to domestic output. An increase in im_0 indicates that U.S. residents demand more imports, given Y/P and $[(P^F/e)/P)]$. With real income given, a rise in the demand for imports reduces aggregate demand. This produces a leftward shift in the *IS* curve. A decrease in im_0 produces a rightward shift in the *IS* curve.

The relationship between income and the demand for imports has already been discussed. Because real import demand varies positively with real income, part of the rise in (Y/P) leaks out of the domestic economy as imports. This has the same effect as saving and makes the *IS* curve steeper. High values of the marginal propensity to import, im_1, produce a steep *IS* curve.

Finally, the demand for real imports varies negatively with foreign prices relative to domestic prices. A rise in the dollar price of foreign output relative to U.S. output reduces the demand for real imports. Thus, given domestic real income, Y/P, a rise in $[(P^F/e)/P]$ reduces the demand for real imports as Americans substitute domestic goods and services for foreign goods and services. This means that aggregate demand increases, given Y/P, so the *IS* curve shifts to the right. A reduction in $[(P^F/e)/P]$ induces domestic residents to substitute imported goods and services for domestically produced goods and services. This means that a decline in $[(P^F/e)/P]$ shifts the *IS* curve to the right. The parameter im_2 is the sensitivity of import demand to a change in the price of foreign output relative to domestic output.

TABLE 17.1
EFFECT OF EXPORT AND IMPORT DEMAND
FACTORS ON THE *IS* CURVE

With Everything Else Held Constant, An Increase in	Makes Aggregate Demand,	So the *IS* Curve Shifts to the
ex_0	Increase	Right
im_0	Decrease	Left
Y^F/P^F	Increase	Right
P^F	Increase	Right
e	Decrease	Left
P	Decrease	Left

The combined effects of export and import demand can be seen in real net exports, $NX/P = (EX/P - IM/P)$. Subtracting the demand for imports from the demand for exports, we obtain

$$\frac{NX}{P} = \frac{EX}{P} - \frac{IM}{P} = \left[ex_0 + ex_1 \left[\frac{Y^F}{P^F} \right] + ex_2 \left[\frac{P^F/e}{P} \right] \right]$$

$$ - \left[im_0 + im_1 \left[\frac{Y}{P} \right] - im_2 \left[\frac{P^F/e}{P} \right] \right]$$

or

$$\frac{NX}{P} = (ex_0 - im_0) + ex_1 \left[\frac{Y^F}{P^F} \right] - im_1 \left[\frac{Y}{P} \right] + (ex_2 + im_2) \left[\frac{P^F/e}{P} \right].$$

Net exports are affected by the intercepts of the export and import equations. A rise in ex_0 or a decline in im_0 increases net exports and aggregate demand. Thus, when $(ex_0 - im_0)$ rises, the *IS* curve shifts to the right. When $(ex_0 - im_0)$ falls, the *IS* curve shifts to the left. A rise in real foreign income, Y^F/P^F, increases export demand and raises net exports. The *IS* curve shifts to the right. Conversely, a decline in Y^F/P^F lowers export demand and shifts the *IS* curve to the left. Given all other factors, a rise in real domestic income, Y/P, raises import demand and, therefore, reduces net exports. A decline in Y/P raises net exports. A rise in the dollar price of foreign output relative to domestic output increases export demand and decreases import demand. Thus, a rise in $[(P^F/e)/P]$ raises real net exports. Given Y/P, the *IS* curve shifts to the right. This means that a fall in e or P, or a rise in P^F shifts the *IS* curve to the right. Conversely, a decline in $[(P^F/e)/P]$ reduces export demand and increases import demand. When domestic prices rise relative to foreign prices, the *IS* curve shifts to the left. A rise in e or P or a decline in P^F shifts the *IS* curve to the left. Table 17.1 summarizes the effects of the several factors on the *IS* curve.

THE EFFECTS OF INTERNATIONAL FINANCE ON OUTPUT, INCOME, THE PRICE LEVEL, AND THE INTEREST RATE

International factors also affect aggregate demand through their impact on interest rates. International finance is a very large subject, and we can only scratch the surface in this section. It is possible, however, to show the basic mechanisms through which international finance affects output, income, and the price level in the economy.

The Effects of Net Exports on the *LM* Curve

When net exports are positive, the country is selling more abroad than it is purchasing abroad. This excess of export receipts over import expenditures means that there is a net flow of funds from foreigners to the domestic economy. When net exports are negative, the country is purchasing more from abroad than it is selling abroad. In this situation, there is a net flow of funds from the domestic economy to foreigners. Finally, when net exports are zero, export receipts equal import expenditures, and there is no net flow of funds between the domestic economy and the rest of the world. Note that it is the nominal value of net exports rather than real net exports that determines the net flow of funds from the domestic economy to the rest of the world. This net flow is affected by both the quantity of exports and imports and by the prices of exports and imports. Flows of funds also occur when foreigners purchase domestic assets and when domestic residents purchase foreign assets. These capital account transactions are discussed later.

The difference between the nominal value of exports and the nominal value of exports, that is, nominal net exports, is the flow of funds into or out of the country's trade account.[5] If net exports are positive, there is a surplus in the trade account; if net exports are negative, there is a deficit in the trade account. Finally, if net exports are zero, there is a balance in the nation's trade account.

In order to see how trade surpluses and deficits affect the financial sector of the economy, we must go through the mechanics of international payments. When goods and services are imported into the United States, importers obtain foreign exchange (money) to pay for the imports. When the United States exports goods and services, foreigners obtain dollars to pay for the goods and services. There is

---

[5] For simplicity, we identify net exports with the trade account. Strictly speaking, the trade account includes only trade in goods. The current account also includes services and transfer payments.

an organized market in which dollars are traded for foreign exchange and in which foreign exchange is traded for dollars.

The demand for exports and imports imply a demand and supply for dollars. Figure 17.1 shows the market. Imports and exports are flows of expenditures that are made per unit of time, for example, per year. Thus, the quantity of dollars demanded and supplied are also flows; these are shown on the horizontal axis. The exchange rate between dollars and foreign money is on the vertical axis. The demand and supply schedules are drawn under the assumption that real foreign income, real domestic income, and the foreign price level relative to the domestic price level are given. Thus, we are examining only the relationship between the exchange rate and the demand and supply of dollars.

The demand schedule shows the demand for dollars in exchange for foreign money. More dollars are demanded at a low exchange rate than at a high exchange rate. When the exchange rate is low, $[(P^F/e)/P]$ is high. Thus, the price of foreign output is high relative to the price of U.S. output. This means that the demand for U.S. exports is high.[6] Foreigners need dollars to pay for the exports, so the demand for dollars is high. The supply schedule indicates the supply of dollars to pay for imports. The schedule is upward sloping indicating that when the exchange rate is high, $[(P^F/e)/P]$ is low. This means that the price of foreign goods and services is low relative to the price of goods and services produced domestically. Thus, when the exchange rate is high, the demand for imports is high.[7] There is a large quantity of dollars supplied by domestic residents to pay for the imports.

When the exchange rate is free to fluctuate, an equilibrium occurs where the quantity of dollars demanded equals the quantity of dollars supplied. In Figure 17.1 this is shown as the equilibrium exchange rate e_0 and the quantity of dollars $\$_0$. Note that in equilibrium exports equal imports, so net exports are zero. The flow of dollars to pay for U.S. exports (demand) equals the flow of dollars to pay for imports (supply). Thus, when the exchange rate is free to clear the market for dollars, net exports are zero. International trade has no direct effect on aggregate income.

A Pegged Exchange Rate

Now let us consider the case where government intervention prevents the exchange rate from clearing the market for dollars. This case is important because prior to the early 1970s for most countries the exchange rate was fixed. Thus, the exchange rate was not free to clear the market. Though exchange rates are no longer rigidly pegged as they were in the past, governments continue to intervene in foreign exchange markets.

---

[6] We shall see later in the chapter that the demand for dollars schedule is steeply sloped if export demand is price inelastic.

[7] The supply of dollars is upward sloping only if import demand is price elastic.

FIGURE 17.1
THE DEMAND AND SUPPLY OF
DOLLARS DETERMINE THE
EXCHANGE RATE.

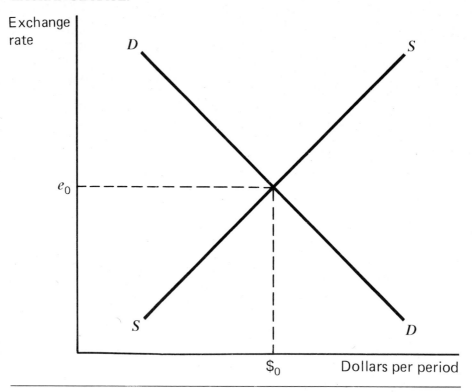

Assume that the foreign exchange market is initially in equilibrium at the exchange rate $\bar{e}_0$ as shown at Point A in Panel I of Figure 17.2. Now consider the effects of a rise in domestic income that increases import demand and shifts the supply schedule from S_0 to S_1. At the exchange rate $\bar{e}_0$ there is now an excess supply of dollars equal to ($\$_1 - \$_0$). This means that import demand exceeds export demand. There is a trade deficit, given $\bar{e}_0$. In the absence of government intervention, the excess supply of dollars would reduce the exchange rate to e_1. This would eliminate the excess supply of dollars and bring the trade account back into balance at Point B. Assume, however, that the government prevents the exchange rate from falling by standing ready to exchange foreign money for dollars at the exchange rate $\bar{e}_0$. Importers know that they can always exchange dollars for foreign exchange (money) with the government at the exchange rate $\bar{e}_0$. They will not accept any private offer of foreign exchange at a lower exchange rate. For example, if the official, that is, government-pegged, exchange rate is 4 DM per dol-

FIGURE 17.2
PEGGING THE EXCHANGE RATE.

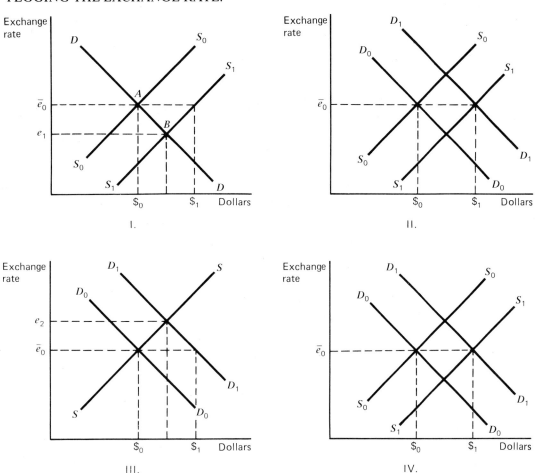

I.

II.

III.

IV.

lar, no importer will accept 3 DM per dollar from the market. Importers always have the option of exchanging one dollar for 4 DM with the government. Thus, all exchanges occur at the 4 DM-per-dollar exchange rate. Because the quantity of dollars supplied exceeds the demand at $\bar{e}_0$, the government buys the excess dollars. The government buys dollars with Deutsche marks to eliminate the excess supply of dollars. In effect, the government adds its demand for dollars to the private demand to produce a total demand schedule, D_1, that intersects S_1 at the exchange rate $\bar{e}_0$. This is shown in Panel II of Figure 17.2. The government is drawing down its holdings of Deutsche marks to buy the excess dollars.

Now consider the case when the exchange rate is initially in equilibrium at $\bar{e}_0$ and there is a rise in foreign income that increases export demand. The demand for dollars shifts to the right from D_0 to D_1 as shown in Panel III of Figure 17.2. This creates an excess demand for dollars of $(\$_1 - \$_0)$. With export demand exceeding import demand, there is a trade surplus at the exchange rate $\bar{e}_0$. In the absence of government intervention, the exchange rate would rise to e_2, which eliminates the excess demand and the trade surplus. The government maintains the exchange rate at $\bar{e}_0$ by standing ready to exchange dollars for foreign exchange at the fixed exchange rate. Again, consider the example of an official exchange rate of 4 DM for each dollar. Any rise in the exchange rate means that foreigners have to give up more than 4 DM to obtain a dollar. The U.S. government stands ready to exchange at four to one. This means that foreigners will make exchanges on the market only if they obtain the four-for-one exchange rate promised by the U.S. government. Thus, all transactions in the market occur at the four-for-one exchange rate. Note that the government buys enough Deutsche marks, that is, sells enough dollars, to eliminate the excess demand. Thus, the government is adding to its holdings of foreign exchange. In effect, the government has added its supply of dollars to the private supply to shift the supply schedule to S_1 as shown in Panel IV of Figure 17.2. This eliminates the excess demand for dollars and maintains the exchange rate at $\bar{e}_0$.

These two examples illustrate that the government can set (peg) the exchange rate. All that is required is the willingness and ability of the government to exchange dollars for foreign money, and foreign money for dollars, at the fixed exchange rate. All money exchanges then occur at the fixed exchange rate no matter what shifts occur in the private demand and supply schedules for dollars.[8]

With the mechanics of exchange rate pegging in mind, let us now turn to the effects that exports and imports have on the financial system. We will see that when the exchange rate is set at a value that is different from its equilibrium value, where the private demand for dollars equals the private supply, total reserves in the U.S. depository system are affected.

To see why this is the case, first consider the situation where the private demand and supply of dollars are equal. In this situation, net exports are zero; that is, exports equal imports. To keep the story as simple as possible, assume that U.S. importers supply dollars to foreign importers (buy foreign exchange) and foreign importers supply foreign exchange to U.S. importers (buy dollars). U.S. importers pay for foreign exchange by drawing down their dollar balances at U.S. depository institutions. These purchases of foreign exchange reduce deposit balances and reserves in the U.S. depository system. Foreigners use the dollars to purchase their imports from American exporters, who deposit the funds in depository institutions. This causes deposit balances and reserves in the United States to rise. As

---

[8] We will see later in this chapter that when there is a trade deficit and, therefore, an excess supply of dollars, the government may eventually run out of the foreign exchange needed to buy the dollars.

long as U.S. exports equal imports, the outflow of total reserves produced by imports equals the inflow of reserves from exports. Funds flow back and forth between the United States and foreign countries, but the net effect on total reserves is zero. Thus, when net exports are zero, there is no effect on total reserves in the United States.

Now let us consider the situation where exports and imports are not equal. Assume that exports exceed imports; that is, there is a trade surplus. This means that at the prevailing exchange rate, the demand for dollars by foreign importers exceeds the supply of dollars by U.S. importers. We saw earlier that, in the absence of government intervention, this causes the exchange rate to rise, which eliminates the trade surplus. The U.S. government prevents the exchange rate from rising by having the Federal Reserve sell dollars to foreigners. The amount of dollars that it sells equals the excess of U.S. exports over its imports. Foreigners use these dollars to purchase U.S. exports. The amount of dollars deposited into depository institutions by U.S. exporters is greater than the amount of withdrawals by U.S. importers. There is a net increase in total reserves in the U.S. depository system. The Fed has, in effect, engaged in an open market operation. It does not purchase government securities in this case; it buys foreign exchange. The effect on reserves in the U.S. depository system is the same, however; they rise.

We conclude that when net exports are positive and the exchange rate is pegged, total reserves rise. Unless the Fed takes offsetting action, this increases the quantity of money and credit in the economy and causes the *LM* curve to shift down. Note that net exports are a flow. This means that when net exports are positive and when, therefore, there is a trade surplus, the quantity of reserves continues to grow over time, and the *LM* curve continues to shift down.

Now consider the case where net exports are negative; that is, there is a trade deficit. With imports greater than exports, the supply of dollars by U.S. importers exceeds the demand for dollars by foreign importers. In the absence of government intervention, the exchange rate falls, and the trade deficit is eliminated. The U.S. government prevents the exchange rate from falling by having the Federal Reserve sell foreign exchange to U.S. importers. This foreign exchange is used to finance the excess of imports over imports. Because the U.S. importers use their balances in depository institutions to purchase the foreign exchange from the Fed, total reserves in the depository system fall. The sale of foreign exchange by the Federal Reserve has the same effect on total reserves as an open market sale of government securities.

We conclude that when net exports are negative and the exchange rate is pegged, total reserves in the depository system fall. This reduces the quantity of money and credit in the economy and causes the *LM* curve to shift up. As long as net exports remain negative, that is, there is a trade deficit, the quantity of reserves declines over time, and the *LM* curve continues to shift up.

Before going any further it is important to note that it is not necessary for trade surpluses and deficits to have an effect on the quantity of total reserves and the quantity of money. The Federal Reserve can engage in open market operations to offset or *sterilize* the effect on total reserves of trade surpluses and deficits. It will do so if it has a policy of maintaining a particular supply of money. Consider the case of a trade surplus. With exports greater than imports the Fed buys the excess supply of foreign exchange and there is an increase in the quantity of reserves in the depository system. The Fed can offset this effect by selling an amount of government securities equal to its purchase of foreign exchange (the trade surplus). The sale of securities reduces reserves by the amount that the trade surplus increases them so the net effect on reserves is zero. Conversely, with a trade deficit the Fed sells foreign exchange which reduces the quantity of reserves. It can offset the effect on reserves by purchasing an amount of government securities equal to the trade deficit. This keeps total reserves and interest rates unchanged.

The Effects of Trade Surplus or Deficits on Real Income, Output, the Price Level, and the Interest Rate

The effects of a trade surplus or deficit on real income, output and the price level depends whether or not the Federal Reserve offsets or sterilizes the effect on total reserves. Panel I of Figure 17.3 shows an initial equilibrium for the economy at $(Y/P)_0$ and R_0 where IS_0 intersects LM_0. Assume that at this equilibrium net exports are zero and, therefore, the trade account is exactly in balance. Because net exports are zero, there is no effect on total reserves. It is also assumed that the exchange rate is fixed and that aggregate demand equals long-run aggregate supply at $(Y/P)_0$.

Now assume that the IS curve shifts to the right from IS_0 to IS_1 as the result of some domestic event such as an upward shift in the consumption function. This raises real aggregate demand and income to $(Y/P)_1$. The rise in real income increases the demand for imports. Assume initially that the increase in aggregate demand does not affect the price level, so the price of domestic goods relative to foreign goods does not change. Because nothing has happened yet to affect exports, we assume that exports do not change. With exports unchanged and imports increased, net exports become negative. Because the exchange rate is assumed to be pegged, a trade deficit occurs, and total reserves fall as the Federal Reserve exchanges foreign money for dollars.

The relationship between net exports, or the trade deficit, and real income is shown by the downward sloping line, NX, in Panel II of Figure 17.3. Given the exchange rate, when income is high, import demand is high and, therefore, net exports are negative. When income is low, import demand is low, and net exports are positive. When real income is $(Y/P)_0$, net exports are zero.

If the Fed does not offset the effect on reserves of the trade deficit, the LM curve shifts up from LM_0 to LM_1 in Panel I. This produces an additional increase in the interest rate from R_1 to R_2, and real income only rises to $(Y/P)_2$ rather than $(Y/P)_1$. At real income $(Y/P)_2$, real imports and the trade deficit are less than at $(Y/P)_1$. This reduces the rate of decline in reserves. As long as real in-

FIGURE 17.3
THE EFFECTS OF NET EXPORTS ON
REAL INCOME.

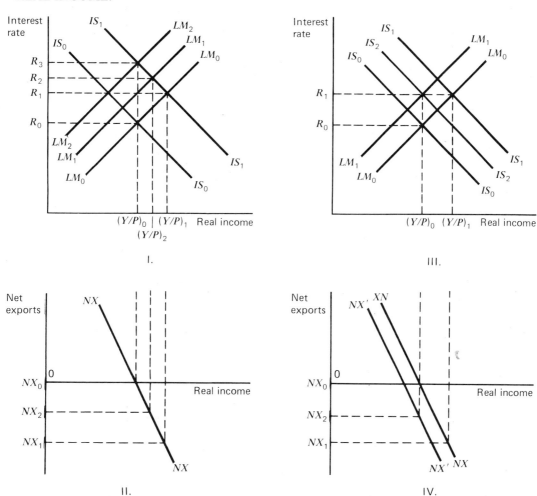

I.

III.

II.

IV.

come remains above $(Y/P)_0$, however, a trade deficit remains. Total reserves continue to decline, and the LM curve continues to shift up. This process continues until the LM curve reaches LM_2, where the intersection with IS_1 gives the initial income level $(Y/P)_0$. At this point, the trade deficit is eliminated.

Note that with a pegged exchange rate, the economy is brought back to equilibrium by having the Fed do nothing. Total reserves and the quantity of money fall by their own accord until the interest rate rises to R_3 and equilibrium is reached. In the absence of foreign trade, the Fed would have to sell securities and shrink the quantity of reserves in order to achieve the LM curve LM_2. The trade deficit eliminates the need to sell securities. The Fed sells foreign money instead.

Panel III of Figure 17.3 shows the case where the Fed sterilizes the effect on reserves of the trade deficit. Here we have the same shift in the IS curve from IS_0 to IS_1 and the same initial rise in income to $(Y/P)_1$. Now, however, the Federal Reserve offsets the financial effect of the trade deficit by purchasing government securities. Thus, the LM curve does not shift up. As long as aggregate demand and income remain at $(Y/P)_1$, the trade deficit continues, and the Fed continues to buy securities to offset the effect. We know, however, from Chapter 16 that real aggregate demand and income will not remain at $(Y/P)_1$. With real aggregate demand greater than long-run aggregate supply, prices and wages start to rise. With a higher price level, real wealth and the real quantity of reserves are reduced. This shifts the LM curve up and the IS curve back to the left. The adjustment continues until real output returns to $(Y/P)_0$.

The process of adjustment of the economy is influenced by the effect of the rise in the U.S. price level on exports and imports. As the price level in the United States rises, the price of U.S. goods and services increases relative to foreign goods and services. This reduces the demand for U.S. exports and increases import demand. Net exports decline, and the IS curve shifts further to the left. With a higher U.S. price level, net exports are reduced, but the trade deficit is not eliminated when real income and aggregate demand return to $(Y/P)_0$.

The adjustment of the economy is shown in Panels III and IV. At the initial price level, P_0, we have the net exports schedule NX (Panel IV) and net exports are zero when real income is $(Y/P)_0$. The IS curve initially shifts right from IS_0 to IS_1 in Panel III. The Fed maintains the quantity of money by sterilizing the reserve effect of the trade deficit. The LM curve remains at LM_0, and aggregate demand exceeds long-run aggregate supply. This produces a temporary rise of output to $(Y/P)_1$. At the higher output, $(Y/P)_1$, there is a trade deficit of NX_1 from the net exports schedule NX (Panel IV). With aggregate demand and output above long-run aggregate supply, the price level rises. An increase in the price level shifts the IS curve to the left and the LM curve up, as shown in Panel III. This reduces real aggregate demand and output below $(Y/P)_1$. The economy achieves long-run equilibrium when the price level rises to the point that real income and output return to $(Y/P)_0$. The rise in the price level produces more imports and less exports at $(Y/P)_0$, however. This means that the net exports schedule in Panel IV shifts to the left (down) from NX to NX'. There is now a trade deficit of NX_2 at $(Y/P)_0$.

In the case we just considered, trade was balanced at $(Y/P)_0$ before the expansion of aggregate demand. We now look at the case where there is a trade deficit when aggregate demand equals long-run aggregate supply (full employment output). Figure 17.4 illustrates the policy dilemma that occurs when the exchange rate is fixed and there is a trade deficit at full employment output. Panel I shows full employment output $(Y/P)_0$ where IS_0 intersects LM_0. Panel II indicates that at $(Y/P)_0$, there is a trade deficit of NX_0. In the short run, monetary policy can either reduce real output and income to $(Y/P)_1$, which eliminates the trade

FIGURE 17.4
THE POLICY DILEMMA WHEN
THERE IS A TRADE DEFICIT AT
FULL EMPLOYMENT.

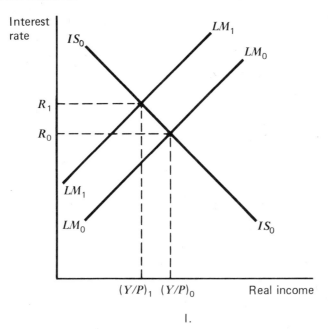

I.

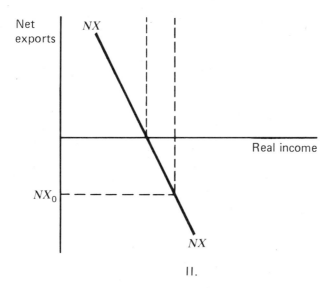

II.

deficit, but at the cost of unemployment, or it can maintain full employment output by keeping LM at LM_0, but at the cost of a continuing trade deficit.

Under a fixed exchange rate, output and employment fall when there is a trade deficit unless the Fed takes offsetting action. The trade deficit reduces the quantity of reserves in the depository system, which shifts the LM curve up. The interest rate rises, and aggregate demand and income fall below long-run aggregate supply. The decline in income reduces imports and the trade deficit. As long as real income is above $(Y/P)_1$, there is a trade deficit. Total reserves continue to fall, and the LM continues to shift up. This process continues until the LM curve shifts to LM_1, where the interest rate is R_1 and aggregate demand and income are reduced to $(Y/P)_1$. At this depressed level of output, net exports are zero, so there is a balanced trade account, and total reserves cease to decline.

With the economy at $(Y/P)_1$, there is unemployed labor and unused productive capacity. This eventually leads to a decline in the price level and wages. The decline in U.S. prices, relative to world prices, encourages exports and discourages imports. Though not shown in Figure 17.4, this shifts the net export schedule to the right. The increase in real export demand also shifts the IS curve to the right, which raises real income. The decline in prices not only stimulates export demand, but it also raises real wealth and the quantity of real reserves. Thus, with a lower price level, the IS curve shifts farther to the right, and the LM curve shifts down. This produces a further rise in real income. Because the price level is falling, the net export schedule continues to shift to the right. This means that the rise in real income and aggregate demand does not produce a trade deficit. The price level continues to fall as long as real aggregate demand is below real aggregate supply. This produces additional rightward shifts in the net export schedule and additional increases in real income. In the long run, the price level falls to the point that aggregate demand rises to $(Y/P)_0$, and the trade account is balanced.

We conclude that if the Fed is willing to put the economy through a period of unemployment and falling prices, real income can be brought into equality with long-run aggregate supply and the trade account will be in balance. By allowing total reserves to fall when there is a trade deficit, monetary policy produces the decline in domestic income and prices relative to world prices that is needed to bring the trade account into balance. This policy produces unemployment and lost output in the short run, however.

If the Fed does not allow the quantity of reserves to fall, unemployment and lost real output are avoided, but domestic prices do not adjust relative to foreign prices, so the trade deficit continues. At this point, it is relevant to determine the consequences of a chronic trade deficit. Note that net exports are a flow measuring the difference between the flow of exports and the flow of imports. This means that a constant trade deficit ($NX < 0$) requires the Fed to continue to pay out foreign exchange. At some point it will run out of foreign exchange. The United States can sell gold or other assets to foreigners and obtain additional foreign exchange, and it can borrow from other central banks and from the International Monetary Fund. If the trade deficit continues, however, these sources of foreign exchange dry up, and eventually the U.S. government can obtain no more foreign exchange. When this occurs, the Federal Reserve has to stop selling foreign exchange, and the exchange rate falls to bring the supply of dollars into equality with demand. The decline in the exchange rate reduces domestic prices relative to foreign prices, which stimulates net exports and eliminates the trade deficit.[9]

We conclude that the trade account can be brought into balance either by experiencing a domestic deflation and unemployment or by reducing the exchange rate. It is hardly necessary for the Fed to wait until it runs out of foreign exchange before the exchange rate is reduced. If there is a chronic balance of trade deficit at full employment, the exchange rate can be reduced as soon as the deficit develops.[10] The decline in the exchange rate shifts the net export schedule of Figure 17.4 to the right so that the trade account is in balance at $(Y/P)_0$.

The end effect of a policy that reduces the exchange rate is the same as a policy of depressing aggregate demand. Both policies reduce the price of domestic output relative to foreign output. The reduction in the exchange rate avoids the need to suffer unemployment. A policy of offsetting the reserve effect of the trade deficit and maintaining the exchange rate also avoids unemployment. This policy cannot be maintained indefinitely, however, because eventually the Fed will run out of foreign exchange. If foreign exchange deficits are temporary, however, it is possible to offset the reserve effect while pegging the exchange rate. We will have more to say about this topic when we discuss pegged versus flexible exchange rates. Before turning to that topic, however, let us first expand the analysis to include financial transactions across national boundaries.

INTERNATIONAL CAPITAL FLOWS

So far we have discussed only the monetary flows that result from imports and exports of currently produced output. Monetary flows also occur when foreigners purchase assets or borrow in the United States and when domestic residents purchase foreign assets or borrow abroad. Foreigners purchase stocks, bonds, and other financial instruments in the United States, they invest directly in American capital equipment, and they borrow in U.S. financial markets. U.S. residents engage in the same activities abroad. Financial markets in most industrialized nations are highly integrated with the financial markets in the United States. These markets allow funds to flow from one economy to another in response to changes in expected rates of return and risks in various economies. By having

---

[9] We will see later in this chapter that the positive response of nominal net exports to a decline in the exchange rate depends upon the price elasticity of demand for exports and imports. Here we assume that demand is sufficiently elastic to give the positive response.

[10] It is possible to use tariffs and export subsidies as means of increasing net exports. These policies can produce retaliatory measures from other countries and are usually unproductive.

access to foreign financial markets, economic agents are able to hold higher yielding and more diversified portfolios, or they can raise funds more cheaply than is possible by sticking to their own domestic financial markets. Because the financial systems of various economies are integrated, interest rates in each economy are affected by interest rates in the rest of the world. This has important implications for monetary policy in the United States and other countries.

The flows of funds among countries that are for purchases and sales of assets rather than for purchases and sales of currently produced goods and services are called *capital flows*. Capital flows occur when there is a change in the amount of assets that foreigners hold in the domestic economy or when there is a change in the amount of assets that domestic residents hold in foreign economies. Thus, capital flows occur when there are purchases and sales of assets across national boundaries.[11]

The mechanics of international payments for assets are the same as for purchases and sales of goods and services. When foreigners purchase assets in the United States, they demand dollars (and supply foreign money) in the foreign exchange market. When foreigners sell U.S. assets, they supply dollars (and demand foreign money). Similarly, when U.S. residents purchase foreign assets, they supply dollars; and when Americans sell foreign assets, they demand dollars. Thus, purchases and sales of assets across national boundaries affect the demand and supply of dollars in the foreign exchange market. Capital flows affect the quantity of reserves in the depository system when the exchange rate is fixed, or they affect the exchange rate when it is free to fluctuate.

Let us begin by looking at the effects of capital flows in a world of fixed exchange rates. The net value of financial transactions between the United States and the rest of the world determines whether the United States has a capital inflow, a capital outflow, or a balance on the capital account. When foreigners are purchasing more assets in the United States than Americans are purchasing abroad, there is a capital inflow. When U.S. residents are purchasing more assets abroad than foreigners are purchasing in the American economy, there is a capital outflow. The capital account is in balance, that is, there is no net capital flow, when purchases of foreign assets by U.S. residents equals purchases of U.S. assets by foreigners.

Capital flows occur when foreigners change the amount of U.S. assets that they hold or when Americans change the amount of foreign assets that they hold, or both. Thus, capital flows are determined by the portfolio decisions of both U.S. residents and of foreigners. These portfolio decisions are affected by the income and wealth of Americans and foreigners and by the expected rate of return and risk on U.S. assets relative to foreign assets.

Part of the saving of domestic residents is devoted to acquiring foreign assets. Given the expected rate of return and risk on domestic assets relative to foreign

---

[11] Purchases and sales of assets involve borrowing because the liability of the borrower is the asset of the lender.

assets, constant saving produces a constant capital outflow as domestic residents purchase foreign assets. When income rises, saving increases, and purchases of foreign assets rise.[12] Thus, a rise in domestic income increases the capital outflow. By a similar argument, part of the saving of foreigners is devoted to acquiring U.S. assets. Given the expected return and risk on U.S. assets relative to foreign assets, constant foreign saving produces a constant flow of capital into the United States. When foreign income and saving rise, foreigners increase their demand for U.S. assets. Thus, a rise in foreign income increases the capital inflow.

The share of wealth that U.S. residents want to devote to foreign assets and the share of wealth that foreigners want to devote to U.S. assets depend upon the expected rate of return and risk on U.S. assets relative to the expected return and risk on foreign assets. If we leave risk aside for the moment, a rise in the expected return on U.S. assets relative to foreign assets increases the flow of capital into the United States. With the higher expected return on domestic assets, U.S. residents devote a smaller share of saving to foreign assets and a larger share to domestic assets. This reduces the capital outflow. Domestic residents also reallocate their existing wealth by selling foreign assets and purchasing domestic assets.[13] This increases the capital inflow. Furthermore, a rise in the expected return on U.S. assets relative to foreign assets induces foreigners to devote a larger share of their saving and existing wealth to U.S. assets. This increases the flow of foreign capital into the U.S. A decline in the expected return on domestic assets relative to foreign assets has the opposite effect. There is an increase in the capital outflow.

In our discussion of the determinants of capital flows, the exchange rate was held constant. We will now show that an expected change in the exchange rate affects the expected return on foreign assets and, therefore, affects capital flows. We begin the analysis by noting that a change in the exchange rate affects the rate of return on foreign assets. When the exchange rate changes during the time that a foreign asset is held, the holder of the asset has a capital gain if the exchange rate falls and has a capital loss if the exchange rate rises.

Consider an American who has an amount of money (dollars), M_0, which is invested in a foreign asset for a year. In order to purchase the asset, the American must convert M_0 into foreign money, M_0^F. Let e_0 be the exchange rate at the time of conversion. The amount of foreign money is $M_0^F = M_0 \cdot e_0$. Furthermore, let R^F be the rate of return on the foreign asset measured in terms of foreign money. This is the rate of return that foreign residents earn on their country's assets. At the end of the year, the initial M_0^F grows to $(1 + R^F)M_0^F = M_1^F$. At that time, the American converts the amount of foreign money, M_1^F, into dollars at the prevailing exchange rate e_1. This gives the amount of dollars at the end of the year: $M_1 = M_1^F/e_1 = (1 + R^F)M_0^F/e_1$. The income to the American from investing in

---

[12] For simplicity, we assume that domestic and foreign saving are unaffected by interest rates.

[13] Note that a capital flow occurs only as portfolios are being adjusted. Once the adjustment is complete, there is no further capital flow from this source.

the foreign asset is the amount of dollars at the end of the year less the amount of dollars at the beginning of the year, $M_1 - M_0$. The rate of return on the foreign asset in terms of dollars, $R_\$^F$, is this income relative to the initial investment

$$R_\$^F = \frac{M_1 - M_0}{M_0}$$

or

$$(1 + R_\$^F) = \frac{M_1}{M_0} .$$

Now let us look more carefully at the role of a change in the exchange rate. The initial dollar investment, M_0, is $M_0 = M_0^F / e_0$, and the amount of dollars at the end of the year, M_1, is $M_1 = M_1^F / e_1 = (1 + R^F) M_0^F / e_1$. The amount of dollars received at the end of the year depends both on the rate of return on the foreign asset denominated in foreign money, R^F, and upon the exchange rate at the end of the year, e_1. We have:

$$(1 + R_\$^F) = \frac{M_1}{M_0} = \frac{(1 + R_F) M_0^F / e_1}{M_0^F / e_0}$$

so

$$(1 + R_\$^F) = (1 + R^F) \cdot \frac{e_0}{e_1} .$$

This expression indicates that the rate of return factor in terms of dollars, $(1 + R_\$^F)$, equals the rate of return factor for the asset in terms of foreign money, $(1 + R^F)$, times the ratio of the initial exchange rate, e_0, to the exchange rate at the end of the year, e_1. If the exchange rate does not change during the year, $e_1 = e_0$, and $(1 + R_\$^F) = (1 + R^F)$, so $R_\$^F = R^F$. There is no capital gain or loss from a change in the exchange rate, so the rate of return in terms of dollars, $R_\$^F$, equals the rate of return that foreign residents earn on their country's assets, R^F. If the exchange rate falls during the year, however, $e_1 < e_0$ and $e_0 / e_1 > 1.0$, so $(1 + R_\$^F) > (1 + R^F)$. The rate of return on the foreign asset in terms of dollars, $R_\$^F$, is greater than the rate of return on the asset in terms of foreign money, R^F. The decline in the exchange rate allows the investor to purchase a larger quantity of dollars at the end of the year. If the exchange rate rises, $e_0 / e_1 < 1.0$ and $(1 + R_\$^F) < (1 + R^F)$. With a rise in the exchange rate, the investor can purchase a smaller quantity of dollars.

An example should clarify the role of the exchange rate in determining the dollar rate of return on a foreign asset. Consider an American who invests $100 in Japan. The exchange rate when the asset is bought, e_0, is 200 yen per dollar. The investor exchanges the $100 for 20,000 yen and purchases a Japanese asset costing that amount. The asset earns a rate of return of 10 percent per year in Japan; that is, $R^F = .10$. By the end of the year, the investment has grown to $(1.10)20,000$ yen $= 22,000$ yen. The exchange rate does not change during the year, so $e_1 = e_0 = 200$ yen per dollar. The investor exchanges the yen into dollars, which provides

22,000 yen/(200 yen/\$) = \$110. The \$100 investment earns a return of 10 percent when converted back into dollars.

Now consider the case when the exchange rate falls during the year to 183.33 yen per dollar. The rate of return in Japan is still 10 percent so the investor again has 22,000 yen at the end of the year. Now, however, at the new exchange rate, the 22,000 yen can be exchanged for [22,000 yen/(183.33 yen/\$)] = \$120. This means that the \$100 investment earns an annual return of 20 percent when converted back into dollars. The investor earns a 10 percent return on the asset in terms of yen and has a 10 percent capital gain from the decline in the exchange rate. Alternatively, if the exchange rate rises to 220 yen per dollar, the 22,000 yen at the end of the year can only be exchanged for \$100. The rate of return on the Japanese investment when converted into dollars is zero. The 10 percent return on the asset in terms of yen is offset by a 10 percent capital loss from the rise in the exchange rate. We conclude that when the exchange rate falls, the rate of return on foreign assets to the American investor is increased. When the exchange rate rises, the rate of return falls.[14]

The rate of return that is relevant for portfolio decisions is the return that will be earned in the future. Because the future is uncertain, investors are concerned with *expected* rates of return and risks for foreign assets. This means that the expected dollar rate of return on a foreign asset, $E(R_\$^F)$, is affected both by the expected rate of return on the foreign asset in terms of foreign money, $E(R^F)$, and the exchange rate that is expected to prevail in the future, $E(e_1)$. This leads to the expression

$$[1+E(R_\$^F)]=[1+E(R^F)]\frac{e_0}{E(e_1)}.$$

The possibility of future changes in the exchange rate affect both the expected return and risk of holding foreign assets. If investors expect the exchange rate to decline, the expected return (in dollars) on foreign assets rises. If the exchange rate is expected to rise, the expected return on foreign assets falls. Thus, expectations of changes in the exchange rate affect the demand for foreign assets and, therefore, affect capital flows. The possibility of unexpected changes in the exchange rate is a source of risk when investing in foreign assets.[15]

For simplicity, we shall assume that the expected change in the exchange rate is zero, but that there is a risk that the exchange rate will change unexpectedly in

[14] The reader should verify that a Japanese investor who buys a U.S. asset has the yen return increase when the dollar exchange rate rises and the return decrease when the exchange rate falls.
[15] It is possible under certain circumstances for investors to avoid this risk by engaging in forward transactions in foreign exchange. There are transactions costs for these activities, however, and risk premiums can be substantial. The return on an investment that is "covered" on the forward exchange market may be substantially less than the expected return on an uncovered investment.

either direction. We shall see later in this chapter, however, that expectations of changes in the exchange rate can have a powerful effect on capital flows.

Although we will have more to say about the sources of special risks on foreign assets later in this chapter, at this point we are only concerned about the risk on foreign assets, however determined, relative to domestic assets. The riskiness of U.S. domestic assets relative to foreign assets affects capital flows. A rise in the riskiness of U.S. assets relative to foreign assets induces U.S. residents to hold more foreign assets, and it induces foreigners to hold fewer U.S. assets. This increases the capital outflow and decreases the capital inflow. A reduction in the riskiness of U.S. assets relative to foreign assets increases the capital inflow and decreases the capital outflow.

The net capital flow can be positive, negative, or zero depending upon the demand by foreigners for U.S. assets and the demand by Americans for foreign assets. We can summarize the several factors involved by the algebraic approximation.

$$CF = cf_1 Y^F - cf_2 Y + cf_3(R - R^F) - cf_4(\sigma_R - \sigma_R^F)$$

where

CF is the net capital flow

Y^F is aggregate foreign income

Y is aggregate domestic income

R is the interest rate on domestic assets

R^F is the interest rate on foreign assets[16]

σ_R is the risk on domestic assets

σ_R^F is the risk on foreign assets.

Foreign income, Y^F, exerts a positive effect on the flow of capital into the United States. A high value of cf_1 indicates that foreigners devote a relatively high proportion of their income to saving that is used to acquire assets in the United States. This exerts a positive effect on CF. Domestic income, Y, has a negative effect on the capital flow. A rise in domestic income produces additional domestic saving, part of which is invested in foreign assets. Thus, when Y rises, CF falls. A high value for cf_2 indicates that U.S. residents devote a relatively high proportion of their income to saving that is used to acquire foreign assets.

For simplicity, it is assumed that the expected return on U.S. assets equals the domestic interest rate, R, and that the expected return on foreign assets equals the interest rate on these assets, R^F. The capital flow for the United States is affected by the difference between the domestic interest rate and the foreign interest rate. When the domestic interest rate is higher than the foreign interest rate, domestic residents devote a relatively high proportion of their saving and wealth to domestic assets and a relatively low proportion to foreign assets. This increases the capi-

---

[16] Recall that we are assuming that the expected change in the exchange rate is zero.

tal flow into the United States. Similarly, when R is high relative to R^F, foreigners devote a relatively high proportion of saving and wealth to U.S. assets. This also increases CF. The greater the excess of R over R^F, the greater the capital inflow. When the foreign interest rate exceeds the domestic interest rate, there is a negative effect on CF as both domestic residents and foreigners move into foreign assets rather than U.S. assets. The parameter cf_3 is the sensitivity of the net capital flow to a change in the difference between the domestic interest rate and the foreign interest rate.

The difference between the risk on domestic assets, σ_R, and the risk on foreign assets, σ_R^F, also affects the net capital flow. When domestic assets are risky relative to foreign assets, both U.S. residents and foreigners place a higher proportion of their saving and wealth in foreign assets. This has a negative effect on the U.S. capital flow. Alternatively, if foreign assets have a high risk relative to domestic assets, there is a positive effect on CF. The parameter cf_4 is the sensitivity of the net capital flow to a change in the difference between the risk on domestic and foreign assets.

THE BALANCE OF PAYMENTS

A country's *balance of payments* is defined to be the sum of the flow of funds coming from its net exports (trade account) and from its net capital flow (capital account). Net exports and the net capital flow may either offset or reinforce each other. It is possible for a country to have positive net exports and a net capital outflow or negative net exports and a net capital inflow. In these situations, the flow of funds from the trade account tends to offset the flow of funds from the capital account. The country is borrowing on the capital account to finance its trade account deficit, or it is using its earnings from a trade account surplus to invest in other countries. Whether the balance of payments is negative, positive, or zero depends upon the size of net exports relative to the net capital flow. Alternatively, net exports and the net capital flow may be in the same direction, that is, positive net exports and a net capital inflow or negative net exports and a net capital outflow. In these cases, capital flows reinforce the effect of the trade account on the balance of payments.

When the balance of payments is negative, fewer funds are entering the country from exports and purchases of domestic assets by foreigners than are leaving the country from imports and purchases of foreign assets. This means that there is an excess supply of dollars on the foreign exchange market. The amount of dollars that U.S. residents are exchanging for foreign money exceeds the demand for dollars by foreigners. As we saw earlier, when the exchange rate is fixed, the Fed sells foreign exchange in an amount equal to the excess supply of dollars. The loss of foreign exchange by the Federal Reserve and the negative effect on the reserves of the depository system equal the balance of payments deficit. When the balance of payments is positive, there is a net flow of funds into the domestic economy. The positive effect on reserves in the depository system equals the balance of payments surplus.

The balance of payments, BP, is the flow from net exports, NX, (trade account), plus the flow from the capital account, CF: $BP = NX + CF$. Thus, in determining the net flow of funds into and out of the country, one must combine the trade and capital accounts. Because the determinants of NX and CF have been specified, we only need to combine these factors to determine the balance of payments.

In our discussion of the effect of net exports on aggregate demand, net exports were specified in real terms. This was appropriate because we were interested in determining the effect of net exports on real income and real output. When it comes to the balance of payments, however, nominal rather than real magnitudes are relevant. For the balance of payments, we are interested in the nominal flow of funds into or out of a country. It is the nominal flow that determines whether a country is gaining or losing reserves. Both quantities and prices determine the nominal flows. For example, a deficit on the trade account may be the result of an increase in the quantity of imports (real imports) with the price of imports unchanged or the result of an increase in the price of imports with the quantity unchanged. As far as the deficit in the trade account and the balance of payments are concerned, it does not make any difference whether price or quantity changes. It is the nominal value of net exports that is relevant for the balance of payments. Thus, we shall express net exports in nominal terms.

The expression for nominal net exports and for the capital flow are combined to determine the balance of payments

$$NX = (ex_0 - im_0) + ex_1 Y^F - im_1 Y + (ex_2 + im_2) \left[\frac{P^F/e}{P} \right]$$

$$CF = cf_1 Y^F - cf_2 Y + cf_3(R - R^F) - cf_4(\sigma_R - \sigma_R^F)$$

$$BP = NX + CF$$

so

$$BP = (ex_0 - im_0) + (ex_1 + cf_1) Y^F - (im_1 + cf_2) Y +$$

$$(ex_2 + im_2) \left[(P^F/e)/P \right] + cf_3(R - R^F) - cf_4(\sigma_R - \sigma_R^F).$$

The balance of payments depends upon all the factors that affect exports, imports, and capital flows. Thus, the intercepts of the export and import demand equations play a role.[17] An increase in ex_0 or a decrease in im_0 increases the balance of payments. Foreign income, Y^F, has two effects on the balance of payments. A rise in Y^F increases exports, and it increases foreign demand for U.S. assets. Both of these effects increase the balance of payments. Domestic income, Y, also has two effects on BP. A rise in Y increases imports, and it increases the demand for foreign assets. Both of these responses reduce the balance of payments. The

---

[17] The intercepts ex_0 and im_0 are now measured in nominal terms.

foreign price level, P^F/e, relative to the domestic price level, P, affects the balance of payments because it affects nominal net exports. Finally, the difference between the domestic interest rate, R, and the foreign interest rate, R^F, and the difference between the risk on domestic assets, σ_R, and the risk on foreign assets, σ_R^F, affect the balance of payments because these factors affect capital flows.

Given Y^F, P^F/e, P, R^F, σ^R, and σ_R^F, a rise in domestic income, Y, decreases the net flow of funds into the economy, and a rise in the domestic interest rate, R, increases the flow of funds into the economy. This suggests that there are combinations of Y and R for which the net flow of funds is zero. The values of Y and R for which the net flow of funds is zero are plotted as the upward-sloping schedule NFZ (net flow zero) in Figure 17.5. Point A indicates that if nominal income is Y_0, and the interest rate is R_0, there is a zero net flow in the balance of payments. This occurs because, given all other factors, the negative effect of domestic income on the balance of payments is just offset by the positive effect of the domestic interest rate. If domestic income rises to Y_1, the demand for imports and for foreign assets increases. Both of these factors produce a deficit in the balance of payments when the interest rate remains at R_0. The deficit is avoided at point B, where the domestic interest rate rises to R_1. At this higher interest rate, the demand by foreigners for our assets increases, and domestic residents reduce their demand for foreign assets. Both of these responses increase the capital inflow and increase the balance of payments. When the interest rate rises to R_1, the negative effective on the balance of payments from the rise in domestic income is just offset by the positive effect from the rise in the domestic interest rate. The balance of payments retains its zero value. By a similar argument, a decline in nominal income from Y_0 to Y_2 reduces the demand for imports and for foreign assets. This increases the balance of payments. There is a balance of payment surplus at the initial interest rate R_0. The surplus is eliminated when the domestic interest rate falls to R_2 at Point C. This increases the demand for foreign assets by domestic residents, and it decreases the demand for domestic assets by foreigners.

The expression for the slope of NFZ is easily derived. The general expression for a net flow of zero is

$$BP = (ex_0 - im_0) + (ex_1 + cf_1)Y^F - (im_1 + cf_2)Y$$
$$+ (ex_2 + im_2)\left[(P^F/e)/P\right] + cf_3(R - R^F) - cf_4(\sigma_R - \sigma_R^F) = 0.$$

We are holding everything but Y and R constant to determine the change in domestic income and interest that keeps the net flow equal to zero. Thus, $-(im_1 + cf_2)\Delta Y + cf_3 \Delta R = 0$, and the slope of NFZ, which is $\Delta R/\Delta Y$, is

$$\Delta R/\Delta Y = (im_1 + cf_2)/cf_3.$$

The NFZ line is steep when the marginal propensity to import, im_1, plus the income sensitivity of the capital outflow, cf_2, are large relative to the interest sensitivity of the capital inflow, cf_3. In this case, a large increase in the interest rate is required to produce a capital inflow of sufficient size to offset the negative effects on the balance of payments of the rise in income. Conversely, when im_1 and cf_2

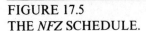

FIGURE 17.5
THE *NFZ* SCHEDULE.

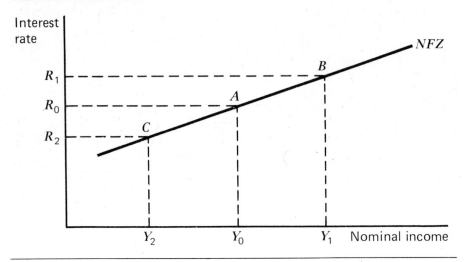

are low relative to cf_3, the *NFZ* line is relatively flat. Only a small rise in the interest rate is required to produce a capital inflow of sufficient size to offset the negative effect on the balance of payments of a rise in income.

A number of factors shift the *NFZ* line. For example, if the demand schedule for exports shifts up, that is, $\Delta ex_0 > 0$, foreigners demand more U.S. exports, given foreign income and relative prices. Exports rise, and there is a balance of payment surplus given domestic income and the domestic interest rate. This shifts the *NFZ* line down from NFZ_0 to NFZ_1 as shown in Figure 17.6. At the initial income and interest rate (Y_0, R_0) the United States would be running a balance of payments surplus after the shift in export demand. The surplus can be eliminated by adjustments in income and the interest rate. Given domestic income, Y_0, the domestic interest rate must fall to R_1 if the net flow of funds is to remain at zero. The increase in the flow of funds for greater export demand is just offset by the capital outflow caused by the decline in the domestic interest rate. Alternatively, given R_0, domestic income must rise to Y_1, which increases the demand for imports and for foreign assets. This also eliminates the surplus. Thus, NFX_1 must be below NFZ_0.

An upward shift in the import demand schedule has the same effect as a downward shift in export demand. If $\Delta im_0 > 0$, domestic residents demand more imports given domestic income and relative prices. Imports rise, and there is a balance of payments deficit at Y_0 and R_0. An upward shift in the import demand schedule shifts the *NFZ* line up from NFZ_0 to NFZ_2. Given income, Y_0, the deficit is eliminated by an increase in the domestic interest rate to R_2. This increases the capital inflow and eliminates the balance of payment deficit. Alter-

FIGURE 17.6
SHIFTS IN THE *NFZ* SCHEDULE.

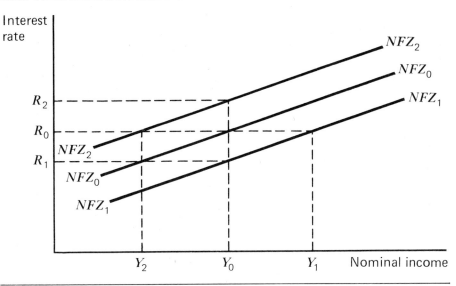

natively, given R_0, income must fall to Y_2. This reduces the demand for imports and for foreign assets, which eliminates the balance of payments deficit.

A change in foreign income also shifts the *NFZ* line. If foreign income rises, given Y_0 and R_0, the demands for exports and for domestic assets increase. This shifts the *NFZ* line down. If foreign income declines, given Y_0 and R_0, the *NFZ* line shifts up. Similarly, a change in the price of foreign output relative to domestic output shifts the line. If the price of foreign output, (P^F/e), rises relative to the price of domestic output, P, export demand increases and import demand decreases. This means that, given Y_0 and R_0, a balance of payment surplus develops. The surplus is eliminated by a fall in the domestic interest rate or a rise in domestic income. Thus, the *NFZ* line shifts down. A rise in the price of domestic output relative to the price of foreign output decreases exports and increases imports. This creates a balance of payment deficit at Y_0 and R_0. The deficit is eliminated by a rise in the interest rate or a decline in income. Thus, the *NPZ* line shifts up.

Changes in the foreign interest rate and in the risk on domestic assets relative to foreign assets also shift the *NPZ* line. If the foreign interest rate, R^F, rises given Y_0 and R_0, there is a capital outflow, and a balance of payment deficit develops. A rise in the risk on domestic assets, σ_R, or a decline in the risk on foreign assets, σ_R^F, also produce a capital outflow and a balance of payment deficit at Y_0 and R_0. Thus, an increase in R^F, σ_R, or a reduction in σ_R^F, shifts the *NFZ* line up. Given income, a higher interest rate is required to return the net flow of funds to zero.

Alternatively, given the interest rate, a lower income is required to return the flow to zero. A decline in R^F, σ_R, or a rise in σ_R^F produces a balance of payment surplus, given domestic income and the interest rate. The *NFZ* line shifts down. Table 17.2 summarizes the factors that shift the *NFZ* line.

FULL INTERACTION OF THE INTERNATIONAL SECTOR WITH THE DOMESTIC SECTOR OF THE ECONOMY

In this section we study the full interaction of the international sector with the domestic sector of the economy. We see the important role that imports, exports, and the balance of payments play in affecting domestic income, interest rates, and the price level. The effect of international factors on the efficacy of stabilization policies is also described.

Panel I of Figure 17.7 shows the *IS*, *LM*, and *NFZ* curves on one graph.[18] It is assumed that the exchange rate is fixed. Aggregate supply is omitted at this point for simplicity. The intersection of the three curves indicates the equilibrium for the economy. At real income $(Y/P)_0$ and the interest rate R_0, real aggregate demand and real income are equal. They in turn equal long-run aggregate supply (not shown). Furthermore, at $(Y/P)_0$ and R_0, the net flow of international payments is zero; the balance of payments is in equilibrium.

Now assume that aggregate demand falls below long-run aggregate supply. This is shown in Panel II as a leftward shift in the *IS* curve to IS_1. Given the shift in the *IS* curve, there is a new intersection with LM_0, where real income and the interest rate decline to $(Y/P)_1$ and R_1. At $(Y/P)_1$ and R_1, there is a balance of payment deficit when the exchange rate is fixed. In the diagram, the *LM* curve is steeper than the *NFZ* curve. We have shown *NFZ* as relatively flat on the grounds that the sensitivity of capital flows to changes in the domestic interest rate is large. The decline in income produces a net inflow from the trade account because imports fall. Only a relatively small decline in the domestic interest rate is required to produce a capital outflow that offsets the positive flow from the trade account.

The decline in the interest rate to R_1 produces a capital outflow that more than offsets the positive effect on the trade account of a reduction in imports. At the real income $(Y/P)_1$, the interest rate would have to be at the higher level R_2 rather than R_1 in order to have the net flow of funds equal zero. At the higher interest rate, R_2, the capital inflow eliminates the balance of payment deficit. Conversely

---

[18] We want to study aggregate income and demand in real terms and the balance of payments in nominal terms. The problem of mixing real and nominal magnitudes is dealt with by specifying the *NFZ* line in terms of the relationship between real output and the interest rate. The *NFZ* line shifts when the domestic and foreign price levels change even though relative prices do not change.

TABLE 17.2
SOURCES OF SHIFTS IN THE *NFZ* SCHEDULE

With Everything Else Held
Constant,

An Increase in	Makes the *NFZ* Schedule Shift
ex_0	Down
im_0	Up
Y^F	Down
Y	Up
P^F	Down
e	Up
P	Up
R^F	Up
σ_R	Up
σ_R^F	Down

at R_1, income would have to be $(Y/P)_2$ for there to be a balance of payments equilibrium. At this lower level of income, import demand is sufficiently small to eliminate the deficit. Because the equilibrium point where real aggregate demand equals real income is at $(Y/P)_1$ and R_1, there is a balance of payment deficit.

The effect of the balance of payment deficit depends upon the response of policy. One possibility is that the Federal Reserve does not offset the decline in total reserves produced by the deficit. In this case, total reserves fall, the *LM* curve shifts up, and real income falls below $(Y/P)_1$. As long as the balance of payments deficit remains, the *LM* curve continues to shift up, and real income continues to fall. Eventually, the *LM* curve, LM_1, intersects IS_1 at the point where the balance of payment deficit is eliminated. This occurs at real income $(Y/P)_3$ and the interest rate R_3 as shown in Panel III. Note that this policy eliminates the balance of payment deficit, but it also makes the recession worse. The higher interest rate R_3 chokes off interest sensitive spending and reduces real aggregate demand and income to $(Y/P)_3$. As we saw in Chapter 13, eventually prices and wages fall, and the economy returns to full employment. The reduction in total reserves produced by the balance of payments deficit makes the decline in prices even larger than is the case where the *LM* curve is not allowed to shift up.

This leads us to an alternative policy response. When the *IS* curve shifts left to IS_1, the Fed can offset the reduction in total reserves by purchasing an amount of government securities equal to the balance of payments deficit. This keeps the *LM* curve at LM_0. As long as real income and the interest rate remain at $(Y/P)_1$ and R_1, a balance of payment deficit remains (Panel II). When reserves are not allowed to fall, there is no increase in the interest rate to eliminate the deficit. Note that when monetary policy offsets the reduction in total reserves, real output does not fall by as much as when total reserves fall (Panel III). The Fed can only continue to offset the reserve effect of the balance of payments deficit as long as it has foreign exchange to pay out.

FIGURE 17.7
EFFECTS ON REAL INCOME, THE
INTEREST RATE, AND THE
BALANCE OF PAYMENTS OF A
LEFTWARD SHIFT OF _IS_.

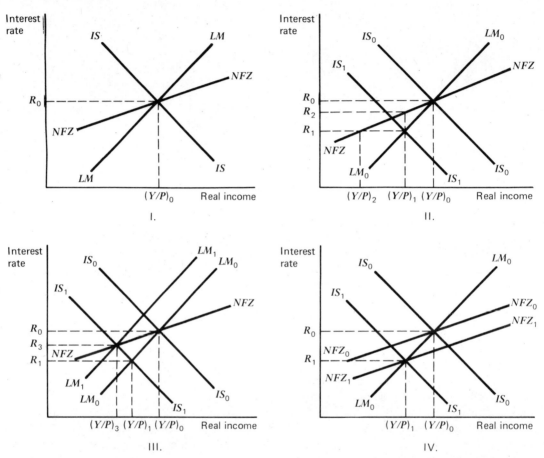

Another alternative is for the government to reduce the exchange rate.[19] This lowers the price of U.S. goods, relative to foreign goods which increases export demand and decreases import demand. A reduction in the exchange rate shifts the _NFZ_ line down from NFZ_0 to NFZ_1, as shown in Panel IV. The balance of payments deficit that occurs at $(Y/P)_1$ is eliminated at a lower interest rate, R_1. This means that the government can lower the exchange rate to the point that

---

[19] Assume that the fall in the exchange rate is unexpected, so there is no effect on capital flows.

NPZ_1 intersects IS_1 and LM_0 at the real output $(Y/P)_1$. The decline in the exchange rate eliminates any need for monetary policy to allow the interest rate to rise above R_1. At R_1, the balance of payments deficit is now eliminated.

The story does not stop here because the decline in the exchange rate increases net exports and shifts the IS curve to the right. Thus, aggregate demand is stimulated. The effects of this stimulus to aggregate demand are not discussed because there is a superior policy alternative available.

The policies discussed so far involve questions of how to deal with a balance of payment deficit that occurs when the economy is at the depressed level $(Y/P)_1$. None of the policies prevent the economy from experiencing unemployment. There is a policy that simultaneously eliminates the balance of payments deficit and unemployment. Fiscal policy can be used to increase aggregate demand by shifting the IS curve back from IS_1 to IS_0. The rise in the interest rate that occurs from this increase in aggregate demand eliminates the balance of payments deficit, and real output returns to its full employment level $(Y/P)_0$. Monetary policy keeps the quantity of reserves unchanged, and the exchange rate is not changed. All that is required is a stimulative fiscal policy that offsets the initial decline in aggregate demand.

Note that an expansionary monetary policy will not do the trick. A downward shift in the LM curve can return real income to $(Y/P)_0$, but the interest rate is reduced below R_0. At this low interest rate, a balance of payments deficit remains. Given the initial leftward shift in the IS curve, only fiscal policy can return the economy to full employment while simultaneously eliminating the balance of payments deficit.

This observation leads us to an important conclusion. A mix of monetary and fiscal policy is available that simultaneously achieves equality of aggregate demand with long-run aggregate supply and balance of payment equilibrium. The issues involved can be seen by studying Panels I and II of Figure 17.8. Panel I shows a situation where IS_0 and LM_0 intersect at $(Y/P)_0$. At this real income, real aggregate demand equals long-run aggregate supply. The NFZ line indicates, however, that at $(Y/P)_0$ and R_0 there is a balance of payment deficit. When real income is $(Y/P)_0$, the higher interest rate, R_1, is required to achieve balance of payments equilibrium. Monetary policy can be used to reduce total reserves, raise the interest rate, and eliminate the balance of payments deficit. This shifts the LM curve up to LM_1, however, which, given IS_0, reduces aggregate demand and income below $(Y/P)_0$. The depressing effect on aggregate demand can be offset by a stimulative fiscal policy that shifts the IS curve to the right to IS_1. Thus, a restrictive monetary policy raises the interest rate and achieves balance of payments equilibrium. An expansionary fiscal policy maintains aggregate demand at $(Y/P)_0$. Fiscal policy maintains aggregate demand at a level consistent with long-run aggregate supply. Monetary policy maintains an interest rate that achieves balance of payment equilibrium.

The case of a balance of payment surplus is shown in Panel II. Here IS_0 and LM_0 intersect at R_0 and $(Y/P)_0$, but now there is a balance of payments surplus. This surplus can be eliminated, and $(Y/P)_0$ maintained, if an expansionary monetary policy reduces the interest rate while a restrictive fiscal policy maintains aggre-

FIGURE 17.8
USING MONETARY AND FISCAL POLICY TO ACHIEVE FULL EMPLOYMENT AND BALANCE-OF-PAYMENTS EQUILIBRIUM WHEN THE EXCHANGE RATE IS FIXED.

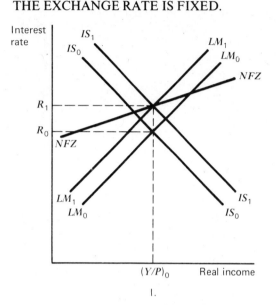

I.

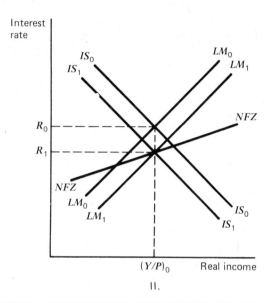

II.

gate demand at $(Y/P)_0$ despite the lower interest rate. This is shown as the intersection of LM_1 and IS_1. Again monetary policy achieves a balance of payments equilibrium, and fiscal policy maintains aggregate demand equal to long-run aggregate supply.

We conclude that the international sector of the economy need not interfere with achieving full employment and price stability. It is necessary that monetary and fiscal policy be coordinated, however. Monetary policy takes care of achieving balance of payments equilibrium, and fiscal policy takes care of equating aggregate demand with long-run aggregate supply. This means that the responsibility for stabilizing the domestic economy lies with fiscal policy and the responsibility for stabilizing the international sector of the economy lies with monetary policy.

PROBLEMS WITH FIXED EXCHANGE RATES

In this section, we describe problems that can develop with fixed exchange rates. These problems involve such factors as conflicting goals for monetary policy and foreign exchange crises. During the 1970s, the problems became of such magnitude that the industrialized nations moved away from fixed exchanged rates toward flexible, or market-determined, exchange rates.

When the exchange rate is fixed, monetary policy can be used to achieve balance of payment equilibrium, and fiscal policy is used to stabilize the domestic economy. We saw in Chapter 14 that, in an economy without international trade, fiscal and monetary policy can be coordinated to achieve economic stability and to determine the share of total output devoted to investment. Thus, if a high rate of capital formation is desired to increase future aggregate supply, a combination of easy monetary policy (low interest rates) and tight fiscal policy is used. If less capital formation is desired because the nation wants to enjoy a relatively high rate of current consumption, a combination of tight monetary policy and easy fiscal policy is used.

When monetary policy is used to achieve balance of payment equilibrium, it can not be used to achieve the desired rate of capital formation. The domestic interest rate is whatever value is needed to achieve balance of payments equilibrium. It is unlikely that this interest rate is consistent with the nation's goals concerning capital formation. The problem is illustrated in Figure 17.9. Panel I shows the equilibrium that emerges when a country is able to mix fiscal and monetary policies without any concern for the international sector. We have shown an equilibrium where aggregate demand equals long-run aggregate supply and in which the interest rate, R_0, is relatively low. By having a restrictive fiscal policy to limit aggregate demand and an easy monetary policy to achieve a low interest rate, the economy encourages capital formation.

Panel II introduces the balance of payment constraint. At the equilibrium $(Y/P)_0$ and R_0, there is a balance of payments deficit. The interest rate, R_0, is too low to achieve balance of payments equilibrium. The balance of payments can be brought into equilibrium by tightening monetary policy to raise the interest rate and by easing fiscal policy to maintain aggregate demand. This is shown by the upward shift in the LM curve to LM_1 and the rightward shift in the IS curve to IS_1. Balance of payments equilibrium is achieved at the new equilibrium interest rate R_1. This interest rate is too high to be consistent with the nation's capital formation goals, however.

This is an example of the general principle that an economy cannot achieve more goals than it has methods or instruments to achieve them. When there are the two goals of equating aggregate demand to long-run supply and of encouraging capital formation, a mix of monetary and fiscal policy can achieve them. Similarly, if there are the two goals of equating aggregate demand to long-run supply and achieving balance of payments equilibrium, monetary and fiscal policy can achieve these. It is not possible to achieve the three goals of equating aggregate demand to long-run aggregate supply, encouraging capital formation, and achieving balance of payments equilibrium with the two instruments of monetary and fiscal policy. There are three solutions to this problem: (1) a goal can be abandoned, (2) a compromise can be struck where none of the three goals is satisfied but some "least bad" combination is achieved, or (3) a third instrument is found.

FIGURE 17.9
CONFLICT BETWEEN CAPITAL
FORMATION AND BALANCE-OF-
PAYMENTS OBJECTIVES WHEN
THERE IS A FIXED EXCHANGE
RATE.

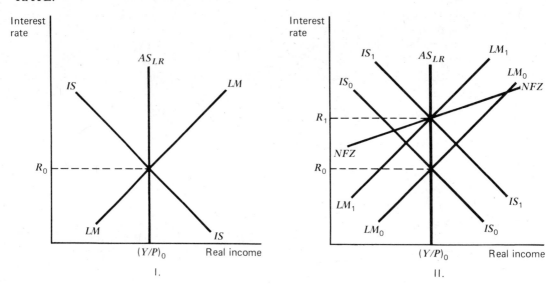

I.

II.

The third instrument is the exchange rate. A reduction in the exchange rate increases net exports and shifts the NFZ line down. This allows a balance of payments equilibrium to be achieved at a lower interest rate. Figure 17.10 shows an initial equilibrium where IS_0, LM_0, and NFZ_0 intersect at the real income $(Y/P)_0$ and the interest rate R_0. Real income and aggregate demand equal long-run aggregate supply at $(Y/P)_0$, and balance of payments equilibrium is achieved when real income and the interest rate are $(Y/P)_0$ and R_0. The interest rate R_0 is too high to be consistent with capital formation objectives, however. Thus, the initial equilibrium achieves two of the three goals of policy. The third goal concerning capital formation can be achieved by reducing the exchange rate while adjusting monetary and fiscal policy. A reduction in the exchange rate stimulates net exports and shifts the NFZ line down from NFZ_0 to NFZ_1 This implies that at the real income $(Y/P)_0$ there is now a balance of payments surplus. The surplus is eliminated by reducing the interest rate from R_0 to R_1. This is accomplished by having monetary policy increase the quantity of reserves, which shifts the LM curve down from LM_0 to LM_1. The larger quantity of reserves produces the lower interest rate R_1, which is consistent with capital formation goals and achieves balance of payments equilibrium at the lower exchange rate. The re-

FIGURE 17.10
USING MONETARY, FISCAL, AND
EXCHANGE RATE POLICIES TO
ACHIEVE THREE OBJECTIVES.

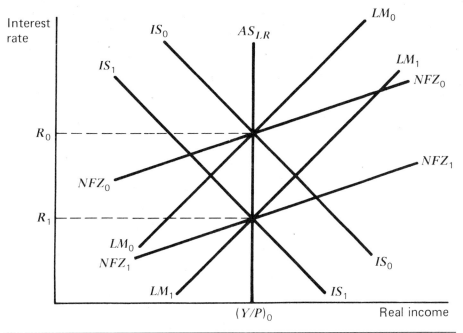

duced interest rate would push aggregate demand above long-run aggregate supply, $(Y/P)_0$, if fiscal policy remained unchanged. This excess demand is avoided by having fiscal policy shift the IS curve to the left from IS_0 to IS_1.[20]

We conclude that if the exchange rate is reduced, the quantity of reserves increased, and government spending reduced, the economy can achieve the three goals of full employment output, desired capital formation, and balance of payments equilibrium. Through the use of the three instruments of monetary policy, fiscal policy, and the exchange rate, the economy achieves its three goals.

The economy can continue to achieve the three goals only if the exchange rate is adjusted to compensate for shifts in the NFZ schedule. Shifts in the export and import demand schedules, changes in foreign income, as well as changes in foreign prices, interest rates, and asset risk relative to their U.S. counterparts, cause the NFZ schedule to shift. Any of these changes requires an adjustment in

___

[20] Fiscal policy must take into account the stimulative effect on net exports and aggregate demand of the reduction in the exchange rate.

the exchange rate if balance of payment equilibrium is to be maintained. As long as the factors affecting the *NFZ* schedule remain constant, no change in the exchange rate is required. If, however, those factors change frequently, the exchange rate must also change frequently if balance of payments equilibrium is to be maintained.[21] To the extent that policymakers are slow to change the exchange rate, significant problems can occur.

In order to appreciate the problems, we must understand the exchange rate policies of the major nations prior to the early 1970s. In 1945, these nations established the *Bretton Woods system* of fixed exchange rate.[22] The idea of the system was that nations only would adjust their exchange rates when some fundamental and long-lived development dictated a change. For example, different long-run rates of technological progress among economies affect relative prices and require occasional adjustments in the exchange rate to mirror the productivity differences. The presumption was that these productivity differences would be slow to develop and that infrequent changes in the exchange rate would allow countries to achieve balance of payments equilibrium.

The Bretton Woods system sought to avoid frequent and erratic changes in exchange rates. Individual countries pegged their exchange rates. This meant that short-term shifts in the demand and supply schedules for foreign exchange (the *NFZ* line) were accompanied by changes in foreign exchange holdings by central banks. Each nation was to have sufficient foreign exchange reserves to allow it to handle temporary deficits in the balance of payments.[23] If the fixed exchange rate system was correct on average, individual economies would have some periods of balance of payment surpluses and other periods of deficits as their *NFZ* schedules shifted around in the short run. On average, however, there would be balance of payments equilibrium. Thus, the objective was to achieve balance of payment equilibrium in the longer run but not necessarily in the shorter run.

There were several economic and political reasons for favoring a system of fixed exchange rates. Two economic reasons are most relevant for our discussion. First, nations wanted an international agreement that prevented the "beggar-thy-neighbor" policies that occurred in the 1930s. During the Great Depression of the 1930s, individual nations attempted to stimulate their economies by reducing their exchange rates. This increased net exports and aggregate demand, which helped to reduce unemployment. Imports fell and exports rose for the country that reduced its exchange rate, but exports fell and imports increased for other countries. Thus, aggregate demand was stimulated for the country that reduced its exchange rate but at the expense of a reduction in aggregate demand in other countries.

---

[21] As the discussion of Figure 17.10 indicated, monetary and fiscal policy must also be adjusted when the *NFZ* schedule shifts.

[22] Bretton Woods is a town in New Hampshire at which the conference was held where the exchange rate system was established.

[23] The International Monetary Fund was established to oversee the international system and to help channel funds from surplus to deficit countries.

These other countries responded by reducing their exchange rates. As a result, attempts to use a reduction in the exchange rate to stimulate aggregate demand in one country were not successful because other countries changed their exchange rates. When there is a worldwide depression, all countries have an incentive to stimulate aggregate demand through reductions in their exchange rate. If all countries attempt to reduce their exchange rates, there is no effect on aggregate demand because relative prices do not change. Considerable animosity is created, however, because a reduction in the exchange rate by one country is viewed as an attempt to "beggar" other countries, that is, to reduce unemployment in the country that reduces the exchange rate at the expense of increasing unemployment elsewhere.

The Bretton Woods system sought to eliminate these counterproductive beggar-thy-neighbor policies by having each country agree to abandon the practice. Thus, insufficient domestic aggregate demand was not viewed as an acceptable reason for reducing the exchange rate.

A second reason for adopting the Bretton Woods system was to avoid the uncertainty for exporters, importers, and international investors of frequent and erratic changes in exchange rates. The idea was that if exchange rates were allowed to fluctuate with short-term shifts in the *NFZ* schedule, exporters, importers, and international investors would be subjected to a high degree of uncertainty concerning relative prices among countries. For example, an American manufacturer makes a decision to produce steel for export to England based on a particular expectation concerning the exchange rate between the dollar and the British pound. If the exchange rate for the dollar rises unexpectedly before the steel is sold, the British may not make the purchase at the higher price. Similarly, importers of foreign goods are concerned that the exchange rate might fall unexpectedly, thus raising the price of imports.[24] To avoid these problems, the Bretton Woods system prevented frequent exchange rate adjustments.

The Bretton Woods system worked relatively well during the 1950s and the early 1960s. Individual countries experienced some difficulties from time to time in living with fixed exchange rates, but the system remained viable. Changes in exchange rates did occur, but the changes were infrequent. Beginning in the mid-1960s, a fundamental change occurred in the world economy that spelled doom for the fixed-rate system. Individual countries began to experience markedly different inflation rates. This meant that, given exchange rates, relative prices were changing relatively rapidly. For example, the United States and the United Kingdom had inflation rates that were far in excess of the inflation rates in Germany and Switzerland. The exchange rates for the German mark and the Swiss franc were raised relative to dollars and pounds (i.e., the exchange rates for dol-

[24] Markets exist that allow importers to purchase foreign exchange in the future at a known price and allow exporters to sell foreign exchange in the future at a known price. These forward contracts allow importers, exporters, and investors to avoid exchange rate risk. There are transactions costs in these markets, and risk premiums can be substantial.

lars and pounds were reduced). A one-time change in the exchange rate cannot compensate for differences in inflation rates, however. The exchange rates of the high-inflation countries must continue to decline relative to the low-inflation countries.

The Bretton Woods system was ill-suited to a world with differential inflation rates. In fact, it helped produce an unstable situation that led to the demise of the fixed-rate system. We shall focus on the United States and Germany in describing the end of the Bretton Woods system because these two countries played a crucial role. Beginning in the the mid-1960s, the inflation rate was substantially higher in the United States than in Germany. This meant that each year the prices of German goods and services fell relative to those in the United States. The exchange rate for the dollar had to decline to eliminate the excess supply of dollars relative to marks. The exchange rate for the dollar was reduced in 1969 and 1971. The United States continued to experience higher inflation than Germany did, and the excess supply of dollars was not eliminated. Market participants anticipated that a further decline in the exchange rate for the dollar was likely, if not inevitable. This led to heavy speculation against the dollar in favor of the mark.

If market participants can predict a change in an exchange rate, substantial profits can be made. It was shown earlier that the expected dollar return on a foreign asset is affected by both the expected rate of return in terms of foreign money and the expected future exchange rate.

$$[1 + E(R_\$^F)] = [1 + E(R^F)] \frac{e_0}{E(e_1)} .$$

Assume that the exchange rate is expected to fall from 3.20DM per dollar, e_0, to 2.30DM per dollar, $E(e_1)$.[25] This means that even if no interest is earned on German assets, $R_F = 0.0$, the expected rate of return, in terms of dollars, is $[1 + E(R_\$^F)] = e_0/E(e_1)$, $E(R_\$^F) = 3.20/2.30 - 1.0 = 0.39$, or 39 percent. At the initial exchange rate, e_0, a dollar purchases 3.20DM of German assets. After the expected change in the exchange rate, the 3.20DM of German assets can be converted into $1.39, (3.20/2.30), for a 39 percent expected rate of return. We see from this example that expectations of a decline in the exchange rate produced a powerful incentive for investors to switch from U.S. to German assets.

By late 1972 and early 1973 there was a widespread expectation that depreciation of the dollar relative to the mark was imminent. This led to a massive shift from dollar to mark assets. From the end of January to the beginning of March 1973 (five weeks), about $10 billion were converted into marks. The $10 billion that flowed into Germany raised its balance of paments surplus further and provided a massive injection of reserves into the German system. In order to maintain the exchange rate for the mark in the spirit of Bretton Woods, the Bundesbank, which is Germany's central bank, exchanged marks for dollars at the fixed

[25] These are the exchange rates that prevailed in December 1972 and July 1973, respectively.

exchange rate. This increased reserves in the German depository system by the mark equivalent of $10 billion. The Bundesbank was overwhelmed by a reserve movement of this size because it represented about 10 percent of the German money supply. The reserve inflow was not offset by sales of government securities, and total reserves rose dramatically. Rather than having their reserves and money supply continue to explode and, therefore, invite accelerating inflation, the Germans stopped buying dollars at a fixed exchange rate. The exchange rate between the dollar and the Deutsche mark was allowed to fluctuate freely in accordance with supply and demand. This spelled the end of the Bretton Woods system.[26]

The 1973 German experience was symptomatic of a fixed exchange rate system. Such a system is ill-equipped to deal with large-scale speculation concerning changes in exchange rates. The speculation was justified because exchange rates must eventually adjust to differences in inflation rates among countries. The longer the exchange rate adjustment is postponed, the greater is the speculation and the greater is the exchange rate adjustment.

FLEXIBLE EXCHANGE RATES

In a world with flexible exchange rates, the net flow of international payments is zero. The exchange rate adjusts to equate the demand to the supply of foreign exchange. Thus, the flow of funds into a country for exports and investments by foreigners equals the flow of funds out of the country for imports and for purchases of foreign assets. Because the government is not buying or selling foreign exchange in an effort to stabilize the exchange rate, international factors do not affect the quantity of reserves in the country's depository system.

The role of the exchange rate in achieving a zero net flow of international payments can be seen in Figure 17.11. Here we show the demand and supply of dollars. The figure indicates that when the demand and supply schedules are D_0 and S_0, respectively, equality of demand and supply is achieved at the exchange rate, e_0. At this exchange rate, the amount of dollars demanded by foreigners to pay for U.S. exports and assets equals the amount of dollars supplied by U.S. residents to pay for foreign imports and assets. This means that the flows of funds into and out of the country are equal. Thus, the net flow of funds is zero.

A rise in the U.S. interest rate relative to the foreign interest rate increases the amount that foreigners want to invest in U.S. assets. Thus, a larger quantity of dollars is demanded at any exchange rate; the demand schedule shifts to the right from D_0 to D_1. A rise in the U.S. interest rate relative to the foreign interest rate reduces the amount that U.S. residents want to invest abroad; they invest at home instead. This means that at any exchange rate, the quantity of dollars supplied

---

[26] The floating exchange rate system that has evolved since 1973 is described at the end of this chapter.

FIGURE 17.11
EFFECT ON THE EXCHANGE RATE
OF A RISE IN THE DOMESTIC
INTEREST RATE.

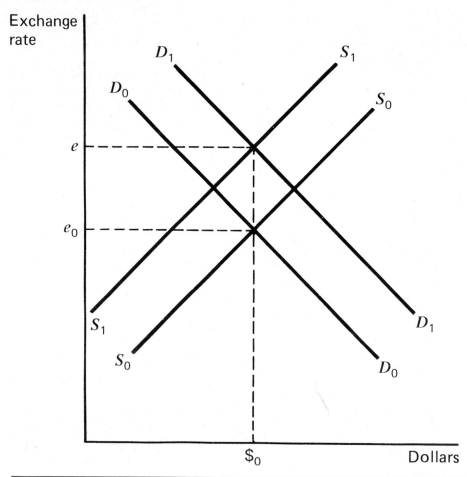

declines; the supply schedule shifts to the left from S_0 to S_1. The rightward shift
of demand and the leftward shift of supply produce a rise in the exchange rate.[27]
Thus, when the U.S. interest rate rises relative to the foreign interest rate, the exchange rate rises. When the foreign interest rate rises relative to the U.S. interest
rate, the demand schedule shifts to the left and the supply schedule shifts to the
right. In this case, the exchange rate falls.

[27] In the diagram, the shifts in demand and supply are of equal size. This need not be the
case. No matter what the size of the relative shifts, the exchange rate rises, however.

Domestic and foreign income, prices, and asset risk also affect the demand and supply for dollars and, therefore, the exchange rate. Furthermore, shifts in the demand schedules for imports and exports affect the exchange rate. Table 17.3 summarizes the factors affecting the demand and supply schedules for dollars and indicates the direction of the effect on the exchange rate.[28]

The exchange rate affects net exports and, therefore, affects aggregate demand and the price level. Aggregate demand and the price level, in turn, affect the interest rate and the exchange rate. This means that aggregate demand and income, the price level, the exchange rate, and the interest rate are determined simultaneously. A full analysis of the interaction of these variables is beyond the scope of this text. We shall, however, analyze one example that gives the reader some feel for the role of international factors in determining real output, the price level, and the interest rate.

We start the story at point A of Figure 17.12. At this point, the economy is in long-run equilibrium, where IS_0 intersects LM_0 at $(Y/P)_0$ and R_0, and $(Y/P)_0$ equals long-run aggregate supply. The exchange rate has adjusted to produce a balance of payments equilibrium. Now assume that an increase in investment or consumption spending shifts the IS curve from IS_0 to IS_1. The intersection of IS_1 with LM_0 occurs at point B, where real income rises to $(Y/P)_1$ and the interest rate increases to R_1. Point B cannot be maintained, however, because the exchange rate and the price level adjust. In the long run, increases in the exchange rate, the price level, and the interest rate drive aggregate demand and income back to equality with long-run aggregate supply at $(Y/P)_0$.

When real income and the interest rate rise following the shift in the IS curve, the exchange rate adjusts. The direction of the initial movement in the exchange rate is not obvious. The increase in real income raises the demand for imports. Given the interest rate, this reduces the exchange rate. The interest rate rises, however, which increases the demand for domestic assets relative to foreign assets. This tends to raise the exchange rate. Throughout the analysis that follows, we make the simplifying assumption that the positive effect on the exchange rate of the capital inflow produced by a rising domestic interest rate exceeds the negative effect on the exchange rate of declining net exports. This means that when there is excess aggregate demand and rising interest rates, the exchange rate increases.

With a higher exchange rate, the price of foreign output, relative to the price of domestic output, $(P^F/e)/P$, falls. This increases the demand for imports and reduces the demand for exports. Net exports fall, which shifts the IS curve back to the left. The leftward shift in IS reduces aggregate demand and real income relative to $(Y/P)_1$, but aggregate demand still exceeds long-run aggregate supply.

Because excess demand remains, domestic prices start to rise. Given the exchange rate, this further increases the demand for imports and further reduces the demand for U.S. exports. The decline in net exports and in real wealth produced by the rising price level causes the IS curve to shift further to the left.

---

[28] It is left to the reader to work through each of the cases summarized in Table 17.3.

TABLE 17.3
SOURCES OF CHANGES IN THE EXCHANGE RATE

With Everything Else Held
Constant,

An Increase in	Makes the Exchange Rate
ex_0	Rise
im_0	Fall
Y^F	Rise
Y	Fall
P^F	Rise
P	Fall
R	Rise
R^F	Fall
σ_R	Fall
σ_R^F	Rise

FIGURE 17.12
ADJUSTMENT TO LONG-RUN
EQUILIBRIUM FOLLOWING A
RIGHTWARD SHIFT IN *IS* WHEN
THE EXCHANGE RATE IS
FLEXIBLE.

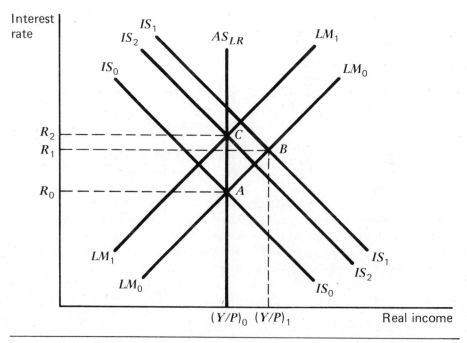

The rising price level also reduces the quantity of real total reserves and money. The *LM* curve shifts upward, and the interest rate rises. The rising interest rate further increases the demand for U.S. assets relative to foreign assets. Thus, rising interest rates in the U.S. produce further increases in the exchange rate. The rise in the exchange rate produces further leftward shifts in the *IS* curve.

Eventually, the *IS* and *LM* curves, IS_2 and LM_1, intersect at point *C*, where aggregate demand equals long-run aggregate supply. At this point the economy is in long-run equilibrium. The interest rate, the exchange rate, and the price level are all higher at point *C* than at point *A*. The higher exchange rate and higher domestic price level at Point *C* relative to point *A* imply that the price of foreign output relative to domestic output is lower, and, therefore, net exports are lower at *C* than at *A*. The lower net exports produce an outflow of funds from the United States. This outflow is offset by the capital inflow that occurs because the interest rate is higher at point *C* than at point *A*. It should be noted that the rise in the exchange rate reduces net exports and aggregate demand. This means that to achieve long-run equilibrium, the price level does not have to rise by as much as would be the case in the absence of an international sector.

With the mechanics of adjustment from one equilibrium to another in mind, let us look at monetary and fiscal policy in a world with flexible exchange rates. In terms of Figure 17.12, either monetary or fiscal policy can be used to offset the effects of the initial shift in the *IS* curve. A cut in government spending or an increase in the tax rate shifts the *IS* curve back from IS_1 to IS_0. Thus, fiscal policy can be used to avoid the rise in the interest rate, price level, and exchange rate that was produced by the initial rightward shift in *IS*. Conversely, monetary policy can reduce the supply of reserves and shift the *LM* curve up to the point that it intersects IS_1 at $(Y/P)_0$. This entails a rise in the interest rate, however. The rise in the interest rate increases the demand for U.S. assets by both U.S. residents and foreigners, so the exchange rate rises. The rise in the exchange rate reduces net exports, which shifts the *IS* curve back to the left. The final equilibrium gives negative net exports and a positive capital flow.

When monetary policy is used to contain excess aggregate demand, the interest rate rises, which crowds out domestic investment. If capital formation is a policy objective, it is better to use fiscal rather than monetary policy to offset the effect of the initial shift in the *IS* curve.

The general conclusion is that, with flexible exchange rates taking care of the balance of payments, monetary and fiscal policy can attend to domestic considerations. Fiscal policy can equate aggregate demand with long-run aggregate supply and monetary policy can be used to meet the nation's goals concerning capital formation.

THE SMALL COUNTRY CASE

The discussion of fiscal and monetary policy leads us to a problem that is faced in some economies. When an economy is sufficiently small, it may be unable to control the domestic interest rate. Attempts to raise the domestic interest rate produce such large capital inflows that the interest rate is forced back to its previous value. Attempts to reduce the domestic interest rate produce such large capital outflows that the interest rate rises back to its previous value. Thus, the domestic interest rate is outside the control of domestic policy.

Consider the case of a small country that wants to increase aggregate demand and income through fiscal policy. Panel I of Figure 17.13 shows a situation where aggregate demand and income are $(Y/P)_0$ and long-run aggregate supply is $(Y/P)_1$. The NFZ schedule is horizontal, indicating that the domestic interest rate cannot depart from the foreign interest rate. Thus, $R_0 = R^F$, and the foreign interest rate, R_F, is determined by economic conditions in other countries. Now assume that government spending increases, which shifts the IS curve from IS_0 to IS_1. In the absence of international considerations, real income rises to $(Y/P)_1$, and the interest rate increases to R_1. This reaction does not occur, however, because any increase in the interest rate is met by a capital inflow that raises the exchange rate. This prevents fiscal policy from achieving $(Y/P)_1$. The rise in the exchange rate reduces net exports and forces the IS curve back to IS_0. Thus, real income returns to $(Y/P)_0$, and the interest rate returns to R_0, as indicated by the arrows in Panel I. Fiscal policy is totally frustrated in its attempt to raise aggregate income. In the long run, wages and prices fall, which returns the economy to full employment. There is nothing that fiscal policy can do to speed up the process. however.

Now consider the case of monetary policy. An increase in total reserves shifts the LM curve to LM_1 as shown in Panel II. In the absence of an international sector, the interest rate falls, and real income rises. The decline in the interest rate starts a capital outflow that reduces the exchange rate. The fall in the exchange rate raises net exports and shifts the IS curve to the right from IS_0 to IS_1. This shift in the IS curve allows monetary policy to achieve the desired output level $(Y/P)_1$. This is not accomplished by a reduction in the interest rate, but rather by a fall in the exchange rate that shifts the IS curve to IS_1. Thus, monetary policy operates like fiscal policy in a closed economy in the sense that it shifts the IS curve. The stimulus to aggregate demand and output comes from the foreign sector, however, not from domestic spending as it does in a closed economy. Fiscal policy itself is ineffective in a small country when there are flexible exchange rates.

The small country case has received considerable attention by economists in recent years. The phenomenon is important to study, but one must be careful not to overstate its significance. First of all, when we take asset risk into consideration, it is unlikely that any economy faces the world interest rate independently of the amount of its liabilities that are held by foreigners. Investors hold diversified portfolios that are composed of assets from their own economies plus assets from other economies. If aggregate demand increases in a small country, its interest rate starts to rise, and foreign investors purchase its assets. This tends to reduce the interest rate back to its previous level. If aggregate demand continues to rise, foreigners buy more and more assets. This tends to cause an imbalance in their

FIGURE 17.13
FISCAL VERSUS MONETARY
POLICY IN A SMALL COUNTRY.

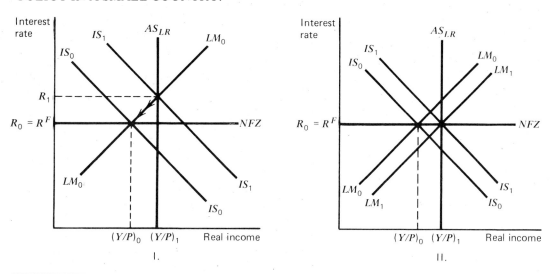

I. II.

portfolios because an increasing share is devoted to assets held in the small country. After some point, foreign investors demand a higher interest rate to compensate them for the additional risk of purchasing more of the assets. When this occurs, the interest rate in the small economy rises relative to the world interest rate. This means that fiscal policy can affect aggregate income and the interest rate.

Risk considerations are particularly important when it comes to international lending. Assets held in foreign countries have the conventional risk of unexpected fluctuations in rate of return plus other sources of risk that are not encountered when investors hold assets from their own economies. One source of risk involves unexpected fluctuations in the exchange rate. We saw earlier that the rate of return on a foreign asset is affected both by its own domestic rate of return and by changes in the exchange rate. This means that unexpected fluctuations in the exchange rate produce unexpected fluctuations in the rate of return. Though it is possible to eliminate this risk in some cases by using the forward market in foreign exchange, the practice involves costs. Furthermore, for long-term assets, it is typically impossible to arrange forward foreign exchange contracts sufficiently far in the future to eliminate exchange rate risk.[29]

---

[29] Under some circumstances it is possible to denominate long-term financial assets in dollars.

There are other risks as well. Investors can encounter substantial costs and difficulties in collecting on foreign loans that have defaulted. Foreign investors have to operate in a foreign legal system, and they can encounter hostility in the foreign country itself. In addition, foreign governments may impose capital controls to help keep financial capital in their country. Finally, the risk of foreign assets is affected by the relations between the home country and the foreign country. Hostilities between the two countries can result in the seizure of assets by the foreign government. Two recent examples of this situation are the seizing of assets held by Iranians in the United States when Iran held Americans hostage during the Carter administration and the seizing of assets held by Argentinians in the United Kingdom during the Falkland (Islas Malvinas) conflict. All these special risks prevent even a small country from inducing foreigners to hold an unlimited amount of its liabilities at a constant interest rate.

Even if there are some economies that are unable to affect their own interest rates, it is important to note that they must be small. The model surely cannot be applied to the United States. The financial system of the United States is so large that domestic interest rates are relatively unaffected by the activities of foreign investors. In fact, U.S. interest rates tend to push around world interest rates rather than vice versa.

A MANAGED FLOAT

When exchange rates are dictated purely by supply and demand, with no government intervention, there is a nonmanaged or "clean" float in exchange rates. When exchange rates are allowed to move but are affected from time to time by government intervention, there is a managed or "dirty" float.[30] When the industrialized nations abandoned the Bretton Woods system in 1973, they turned to a managed (dirty) float. Thus, governments intervene in foreign exchange markets, that is, buy and sell foreign exchange, when they want the exchange rate to behave differently from what is dictated strictly by supply and demand. As a result, exchange rates do move, but often not in exactly the same way as in a purely flexible system. The purpose of this section is to briefly describe some reasons why a clean float is not used.

Changes in exchange rates can have short-run effects that complicate the pursuit of national economic objectives. For example, a decline in the exchange rate raises the price of imports, which can produce a spurt of domestic inflation. If a country is already experiencing inflation, a decline in the exchange rate can make

---

[30] The terms *dirty* and *clean* are widely used to distinguish flexible exchange rates with government intervention from flexible exchange rates with no intervention. These adjectives are hardly neutral, and governmental institutions prefer the terms *nonmanaged* and *managed*.

the inflation worse for a while. In this situation, policymakers may resist a decline in the exchange rate by intervening in the foreign exchange market. Furthermore, because import and export demand are price inelastic in the short run, a balance of payments deficit can produce an increase rather than a decrease in the exchange rate. Over time, import and export demand becomes price elastic, and ultimately the exchange rate declines. This imparts a dynamic path to exchange rate movements that is difficult to interpret and evaluate. Policymakers may stabilize the exchange rate in an effort to reduce uncertainty. Developments in foreign countries also can lead to undesirable movements in a country's exchange rate. For example, unrest abroad can produce large inflows of funds into a "safe" country. This raises the exchange rate and tends to depress aggregate demand in that country. Furthermore, speculators may anticipate a further rise in the country's exchange rate. This produces additional capital inflows, which further raises the exchange rate. In order to avoid these developments and their potential reversal when international unrest diminishes, the country may decide to stabilize the exchange rate. Let us now look at each of these issues in more detail.

The Relationship Between the Exchange Rate and Domestic Prices

In Chapter 16, it was argued that in the short run many firms tend to set their prices as a markup over costs. Thus, increases in wage rates or energy prices are mirrored in increases in the price of output. This behavior means that changes in the price of imported goods and materials affect the prices that domestic firms charge for their output. For example, a decline in the exchange rate raises the price of imports. Many imports are used as inputs for domestic production. Increases in the price of these imports raise domestic prices. Furthermore, a rise in the price of imported consumption goods and capital equipment has a direct affect on the domestic price level. On top of all this, an increase in the price of imports shifts demand away from imports in favor of domestically produce substitutes. This tends to raise the price of these substitutes.

The response of domestic prices to the price of imports means that the short-run aggregate supply curve shifts when import prices change. Panel I of Figure 17.14 shows the effect of an increase in import prices on short-run aggregate supply, aggregate output, and the price level. The initial equilibrium is at point A, where short-run aggregate supply equals aggregate demand. Real output is $(Y/P)_0$, and the price level is P_0. For simplicity, assume that long-run aggregate supply is also $(Y/P)_0$. Now let the price of imports rise. This can occur as the result of a rise in the price level in foreign countries or as the result of a fall in the exchange rate. In either case, the price of imports rises, and the short-run aggregate supply curve shifts up to AS'_{SR}. The new short-run equilibrium occurs at point B, where the domestic price level rises to P_1 and real output falls to $(Y/P)_1$.[31]

---

[31] The effects of a change in P^F/e is already built into the aggregate demand schedule.

FIGURE 17.14
SHORT-RUN EFFECTS ON REAL
OUTPUT AND THE PRICE LEVEL OF
AN INCREASE IN THE PRICE OF IMPORTS.

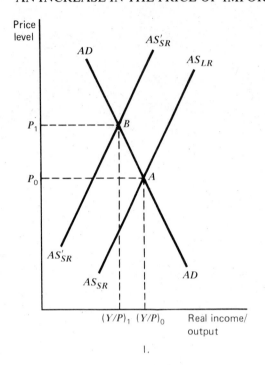

I.

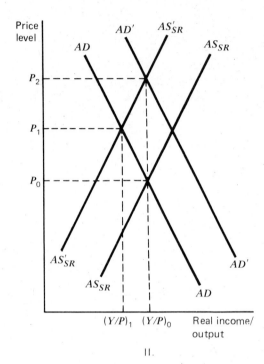

II.

With monetary and fiscal policy unchanged, the lower real output produces a decline in the domestic price level. In the long run, real output returns to its full employment value. The process takes time, however, and a recession is required to bring it about. Monetary or fiscal policy, or both, can stimulate aggregate demand to avoid the recession, that is, shift aggregate demand to AD' as shown in Panel II. This avoids unemployment, but it requires that the domestic price level be permanently higher at P_2 than it was prior to the rise in the price of imports. Thus, an increase in the price of imports is another source of the policy dilemma where unemployment must be traded off against inflation.

The prospect of this policy dilemma can make countries resist a decline in their exchange rate because domestic prices rise in the short run. There is a tendency among policymakers to avoid situations that raise prices. These concerns were important in the United States during the second half of the 1970s when stagflation produced inflation and unemployment.

Short-term Changes in Exchange Rates

In this section, we show that because import and export demand are price inelastic in the short run, changes in exchange rates can be difficult to interpret and evaluate. This complicates policy decisions and can induce policymakers to stabilize the exchange rate.

In the discussion of the effects of exchange rate changes on the balance of payments, we assumed that when the exchange rate falls, nominal net exports rise. A decline in the exchange rate raises the price of foreign output, (P^F/e), relative to the price of domestic output, P. This increases the demand for exports and decreases the demand for imports. Conversely, when the exchange rate rises, imports rise and exports fall, so net exports decrease. The inverse relationship between the exchange rate and net exports is an important factor in achieving balance of payments equilibrium. Net exports do move inversely with the exchange rate in the longer run, but this does not occur in the short run. In the short run, a fall in the exchange rate actually decreases nominal net exports, and a rise in the exchange rate increases nominal net exports.

To see why this is the case, we must recall that it is the *nominal* flows of expenditures on exports and imports that affect the balance of payments. When the exchange rate falls, the price of foreign output measured in dollars (P^F/e) rises. This induces domestic residents to reduce the quantity of imports demanded. Nominal dollar expenditures for imports equal the dollar price of imports times the quantity purchased. Because the price goes up and the quantity goes down, nominal expenditures on imports can either rise or fall. The response of nominal expenditures depends upon the price elasticity of demand for imports. If import demand is inelastic, a rise in the price of imports produces a small decrease in the quantity of imports demanded. This means that total expenditures on imports rise when the price increases. Thus, contrary to our earlier assumption, expenditures on imports may rise when the exchange rate falls.

We have a somewhat different situation when it comes to exports. A fall in the exchange rate decreases the price of exports in terms of foreign money. This increases the quantity of exports demanded. Thus, the price falls, and the quantity rises. If the demand for exports is inelastic, the reduction in the price produces a small increase in the quantity purchased. In this situation, total expenditures by foreigners of foreign money for U.S. exports fall. As long as the demand for exports is not totally inelastic, however, foreigners demand more dollars to purchase more of our exports. They can purchase more of our exports only if they spend more dollars. If demand is inelastic, they spend less of their own money, but they still buy more dollars. If export demand is totally inelastic, foreigners do not increase purchases of our exports when the exchange rate falls. In this situation, the quantity of dollars demanded does not change. Because there is some price elasticity of demand, we conclude that a reduction in the exchange rate increases total dollar receipts from exports.

A reduction in the exchange rate increases dollar expenditures on imports, and it increases dollar receipts from exports when import and export demand are inelastic.[32] It is shown later that this makes the exchange rate move in the "wrong" direction when the demand and supply schedules shift. Empirical evidence indicates that import and export demand are price inelastic in the short run.[33] It takes time for the quantity of exports and of imports to adjust to a change in price (exchange rate). With the passage of time, however, the quantities do adjust, and the elasticity of import and export demand rises. In the long run, the exchange rate does move in the "right" direction. A fall in the exchange rate does increase net exports, and a rise in the exchange rate decreases net exports.

Consider the case where a country starts to encounter a balance of payments deficit. This may be the result of an upward shift in the *NFZ* schedule or of an increase in domestic aggregate demand. We argued earlier that the balance of payments deficit implies an excess supply of domestic money in the foreign exchange market that produces a decline in the exchange rate. The decline in the exchange rate brings the balance of payments back into equilibrium. An important part of this process is the rise in net exports that occurs when the exchange rate falls.

If import and export demands are price inelastic, the excess supply of domestic money actually raises the exchange rate. This can be seen in Figure 17.15, which shows the market for dollars. In Panel I, the supply schedule for dollars is *downward* sloping, indicating that the dollar demand for imports is price inelastic in the short run. A decline in the exchange rate raises the dollar price of imports, which increases the dollar demand for nominal imports. Thus, when the exchange rate falls, a larger quantity of dollars is supplied by U.S. residents to pay for imports. Conversely, when the exchange rate rises, nominal import demand declines, and a smaller quantity of dollars is supplied.

The demand schedule for dollars is also downward sloping, but relatively steep, indicating that export demand is inelastic in the short run. The decline in the foreign-money price of U.S. exports produces only a small increase in the quantity demanded and, therefore, a small increase in the quantity of dollars demanded. Conversely, a rise in the exchange rate, which raises the foreign-money price of U.S. exports, produces only a small reduction in the quantity of dollars demanded.

Panel I shows an initial equilibrium for the exchange rate at e_0, where the downward-sloping, short-run demand schedule, D_0^{SR}, intersects the downward-sloping, short-run supply schedule, S_0^{SR}. Now assume that there is a rightward shift in the supply schedule from S_0^{SR} to S_1^{SR}. This indicates that Americans are supplying a greater quantity of dollars to pay for a large quantity of imports or for more foreign investments. As the diagram indicates, there is an excess supply of dollars of ($\$_1 - \$_0$) at the initial exchange rate e_0. All the dollars supplied cannot be sold at the initial exchange rate. Dollar demanders are willing to purchase more dollars if the exchange rate falls. A reduction in the exchange rate only

---

[32] It is left to the reader to work out the case for an increase in the exchange rate when import and export demand are price inelastic.

[33] For example, see H. Junz and R. Rhomberg, "Price Competitiveness in Export Trade Among Industrial Countries," *American Economic Review,* May 1973, pp. 412–418.

FIGURE 17.15
EXCHANGE RATE ADJUSTMENTS
IN THE SHORT AND LONG RUN.

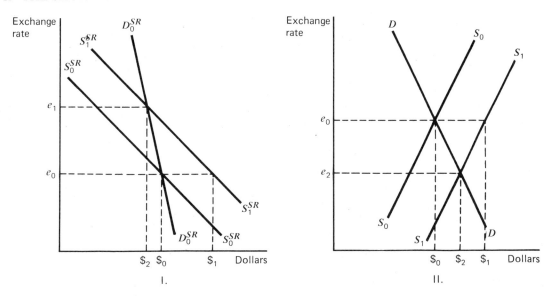

makes the situation worse, however. The quantity demanded does rise, but there is a larger increase in the quantity supplied along S_1^{SR}. Thus, a reduction in the exchange rate increases rather than decreases excess supply. The initial equilibrium at e_0 is unstable. The excess supply is eliminated by a rise in the exchange rate to e_1. This decreases both the quantity of dollars demanded and the quantity of dollars supplied relative to e_0. The reduction in the quantity supplied is large relative to the reduction in the quantity demanded when the exchange rate rises. The excess supply is eliminated at e_1. Thus, a rightward shift in the supply schedule must produce an increase in the exchange rate if a new equilibrium is to be achieved.

This result should be compared to Panel II, where we have the flatter downward-sloping demand and normal upward-sloping supply schedules that prevail in the longer run. In Panel II, a rightward shift in the supply schedule leads to a fall in the exchange rate to e_2. A comparison of Panels I and II indicates that a rightward shift in the supply of dollars can produce an increase in the exchange rate in the short run, and it produces a decline in the exchange rate in the longer run.

This analysis indicates that the exchange rate may move in the "wrong" direction in the short run following shifts in the demand and supply schedules for dollars. Eventually, however, the exchange rate does move in the "right" direction. The dynamic path of the exchange rate following shifts in demand or supply can produce considerable uncertainty and confusion on the part of both the public and policymakers.[34] Does a rise in the exchange rate mean that it will ultimately fall, or does it mean that there has been a permanent increase in the exchange rate? Policymakers may at times attempt to stabilize the exchange rate in an effort to eliminate the uncertainties that surround changes in exchange rates.

Vulnerability to International Unrest and Speculation

A country may have considerable control over its own income, inflation, and interest rates, but it has little or no control over developments abroad. This means that pursuit of domestic stabilization objectives are complicated by developments in foreign countries. We have shown that flexible exchange rates allow monetary and fiscal policy to pursue domestic objectives. There are times, however, when foreign developments can affect exchange rates to the point that it is in a country's interest to moderate fluctuations in exchange rates.

We have seen that movements in foreign income and foreign prices as well as changes in the expected return and risk on foreign assets affect exchange rates. A country has virtually no control over these factors, yet they affect its economy. Consider the example of an increase in the risk of holding a foreign country's assets. A particular country (or group of countries) may experience political and social unrest, be involved in a war, or experience large fluctuations in aggregate demand. When these situations occur, the risk of investing in that country rises. This can produce a large shift of funds out of that country into other countries that offer lower risk. When the particular disturbance disappears, funds may flow back into the country from which they left. This means that "safe" countries can experience substantial fluctuations in capital flows. These fluctuations affect the exchange rates and interest rates in those countries, which, in turn, complicates domestic policy. The domestic effects of foreign developments may induce these countries to stabilize their exchange rates. Vulnerability to foreign developments is particularly severe for Switzerland, which has stabilized its exchange rate from time to time and resorted to capital controls to insulate itself from disturbances in foreign capital markets.

Although we have used the example of changes in risk, fluctuations in foreign income, prices, and rates of return have the same effect. There is often a powerful incentive to stabilize exchange rates when the fluctuations are large. It may be good policy to stabilize transitory fluctuations in exchange rates, but we have seen that significant problems can arise when exchange rates are stabilized in the face of more permanent changes in foreign countries. One of the most difficult problems that policymakers face is to distinguish transitory from permanent changes in the economic environment. This topic is discussed in detailed in the next chapter.

---

[34] The problem is even more complex than indicated in the text because investor expectations of changes in interest rates and exchange rates also affect the demand and supply of dollars.

SUMMARY

This chapter examined the macroeconomic effects of international trade and finance. The international sector of the economy affects interest rates, output, employment, and prices. Export and import demand directly affect aggregate demand. Capital flows influence aggregate demand through their effects on interest rates. The short-run aggregate supply schedule is also affected by changes in the price of imports. Import prices can change either as a result of changes in prices in foreign countries or as a result of changes in the exchange rate.

The mix of monetary and fiscal policy in an open economy depends crucially on whether the exchange rate is fixed or flexible. If the exchange rate is fixed, monetary policy can sterilize the effects of a balance of payments deficit in the short run. If the balance of payments deficit continues, the government will eventually run out of foreign money to exchange for dollars. The country is forced either to let reserves in the depository system fall or to reduce the exchange rate. If the exchange rate remains fixed, the Fed allows reserves to fall and domestic interest rates to rise. The increase in interest rates eliminates the balance of payments deficit, but at the cost of reducing aggregate demand. Fiscal policy can eliminate deficient demand, but monetary policy must keep domestic interest rates high enough to eliminate the balance of payments deficit. This means that monetary policy cannot be used to promote full employment, price stability, and capital formation. It must be used to achieve balance of payments equilibrium. Fiscal policy can equate aggregate demand with long-run aggregate supply, but capital formation goals must be abandoned.

In a world with flexible exchange rates, monetary policy can return to pursuing capital formation goals. As long as a country has some control over its domestic interest rates, fiscal policy can be used to achieve equality of aggregate demand with long-run aggregate supply.

Flexible exchange rates can be a mixed blessing, however. Exchange rates change not only because of domestic economic conditions, but also in response to developments abroad. These changes in the exchange rate may have unpleasant effects on the domestic economy. Furthermore, if a country is experiencing inflation, a decline in its exchange rate will make inflation worse for a while.

International trade and finance allow the nation to enjoy a higher standard of living, but they can cause problems for stabilization policy. The problems are different depending upon whether exchange rates are fixed or flexible, but problems remain.

SELECTED REFERENCES

Branson, William, *Macroeconomic Theory and Policy* (2nd ed.), New York: Harper & Row, 1979.

Dornbusch, Rudiger and Stanley Fischer, *Macroeconomics* (2nd ed.), New York: McGraw-Hill, 1981.

Gordon, Robert, *Macroeconomics* (2nd ed.), Boston: Little, Brown and Company, 1981.

MONETARY POLICY IN THEORY AND PRACTICE

18

This chapter is concerned with the theory and practice of monetary policy. It is shown that it is difficult for monetary policy to offset short-term economic fluctuations. Lags in the response of the economy to changes in policy, errors in forecasting future economic events, and ignorance about the true structure of the economy make it difficult to pursue active stabilization policies. Indeed, there are situations when active stabilization policies are counterproductive. In these situations, a fixed policy that does not attempt to offset fluctuations is superior to a discretionary policy. The problems are compounded when there are more objectives for policy than there are instruments to achieve them. Attempts to jump from one problem to another can further weaken policy performance. There are circumstances, however, when it is appropriate to use policy actively to offset the effects of economic disturbances. The art of policymaking involves knowing when to change policy and when not to change policy.

The issues involved are first discussed in terms of theory and then in terms of how monetary policy is actually conducted. In the course of the discussion, we touch upon a number of issues that have sparked controversy in recent years. Among these are the use of the quantity of money as an intermediate target of monetary policy, the benefits and costs of stabilizing fluctuations in interest rates, the role of expectations, and problems posed by innovations that cloud the definition and measurement of money.

We shall start the discussion by considering both monetary and fiscal policy. This is appropriate because many of the same problems confront both policies. We then argue that the political process prevents fiscal policy from being used actively to stabilize the economy. As a result, monetary policy is the primary method used to achieve economic stability. This means that monetary policy often has the impossible job of achieving a number of conflicting objectives.

POLICYMAKING WHEN THERE IS COMPLETE KNOWLEDGE ABOUT THE ECONOMY

The last five chapters have covered a great deal of material. One reason for such a detailed analysis was to document the complexities of the interrelationships in the macroeconomy. Despite these complexities, policymaking would be relatively straightforward if there were complete knowledge about current and future aggregate demand and aggregate supply. With complete knowledge, policymakers could anticipate shifts in aggregate demand or supply and set policies that would produce the most favorable outcome. Thus, policy could always do the "right thing." For example, in a world of complete knowledge, if policymakers know that aggregate demand is going to rise above long-run aggregate supply, they can use restrictive policy to keep aggregate demand in balance with supply.

When there is complete knowledge, policy can always equate aggregate demand with long-run aggregate supply. Furthermore, proper coordination of monetary and fiscal policy can avoid any undesired crowding out of interest sensitive spending.[1] Thus, the economy can achieve equality of aggregate demand with long-run aggregate supply while obtaining the desired rate of capital formation.

Conflicts can arise even in a world of complete certainty when society has more objectives than instruments to achieve them. For example, if a stable exchange rate is desired, monetary policy must abandon its objectives concerning capital formation if it is to achieve balance of payments equilibrium. Thus, society must choose between a stable exchange rate and capital formation goals. Similarly, society may have objectives concerning income distribution that are inconsistent with its employment, inflation, capital formation, and exchange rate goals. Conflicting goals create important social and political problems that cannot be solved by monetary and fiscal policy. Conflicts of this kind can be eliminated only if more policy instruments are developed.

We conclude that in a world of complete knowledge, competent policymakers would never make mistakes. Policy would not be able to achieve all society's economic goals if the number of goals exceeded the number of policy instruments available to achieve them, but these "failures" are not policy errors. They are the result of too many goals or too few methods of achieving them, or both. Armed with complete knowledge of the economy's structure, with the ability to foretell the future, and with knowledge of society's wishes (including trade-offs of conflicting goals), policymakers should always be able to do the right thing.

There is clearly much more to policymaking than this! In reality, there is considerable uncertainty (ignorance) concerning the current and future behavior of aggregate demand and supply. Aggregate demand and supply cannot be ob-

---

[1] As we saw in the last chapter, crowding out can be avoided only if there is a flexible exchange rate.

served directly. When there is a change in real output or the price level, policymakers must try to infer whether the cause is a shift in aggregate demand, aggregate supply, or both. This is necessary because the appropriate policy response to a change in output or in the rate of inflation depends upon the source of the change. Furthermore, because the response of the economy to policy changes is distributed over time, policymakers must determine whether aggregate demand and supply shifts are transitory or of a more permanent nature. The appropriate policy response to a transitory shift in aggregate demand or supply is different from the appropriate response to a permanent shift. The problem of distinguishing between transitory and permanent shifts is compounded because the dynamic response of the economy to changes in policy is not well understood. There is considerable uncertainty concerning how the economy will respond to a change in policy. The problems are further compounded by the inability to predict future shifts in aggregate demand and supply accurately.

In the real world, there is considerable uncertainty about the sources of changes in real income and prices, about the permanence of the changes, and about how the economy will respond to policy changes. In this environment, reasonable people can disagree concerning how to conduct policy. Furthermore, policy errors do occur. It is the lack of complete knowledge that makes policymaking so difficult.

We shall now turn to the issue of how uncertainty affects policymaking. We start with a discussion of the relationship between forecasting errors and lags in the impact of a change in policy on the economy.

FORECASTING ERRORS AND POLICY LAGS

Perhaps the easiest way to see the relationship between forecasting errors and lags in the impact of policy is to consider a situation where there are no lags. In this case, monetary and fiscal policy have an immediate effect on aggregate demand. Assume that policymakers predict that there will be no shifts in aggregate demand or supply in the future. Policy is then set to achieve full employment output, price stability, and the desired rate of capital formation. Furthermore, assume that an unexpected, permanent shift in aggregate demand above long-run aggregate supply occurs. With this shift, real output rises above long-run aggregate supply, and prices rise unexpectedly. Because we are assuming that policy has an immediate effect, a tightening of monetary or fiscal policy can immediately offset the effects of the unexpected rise in aggregate demand. As soon as the need for a policy change is recognized, the effects of the shift on aggregate demand are offset. The same conclusions apply for an unexpected decline in aggregate demand or for an unexpected shift in aggregate supply. As long as policy has an immediate effect, forecasting errors cause no problem.

Now let us consider the more realistic situation where policy changes do not have an immediate impact. In this case, policy cannot immediately return the economy to its desired position following an unexpected shift in aggregate demand or supply. To see this, let us again consider a situation where there is an unexpected, permanent shift in aggregate demand. As we shall explain in detail later, it takes time for restrictive policies to reduce aggregate demand back to its previous level. Until policy has this effect, real output will be above long-run aggregate supply, and there will be increases in prices and wages. Thus, the lags in the impact of policy prevent monetary and fiscal policy from preventing inflation in the short run. Similarly, an unexpected decline in aggregate demand results in unemployment and deflation until the effects of stimulative policies are felt. The effects of unexpected shifts in aggregate supply also cannot be controlled immediately by policy.

Because unexpected shifts in aggregate demand and supply occur and because there are lags in the impact of policy, complete stabilization of the economy is impossible. The economy experiences fluctuations that are beyond the control of the policy maker.

It is important to note that policy lags are not sufficient to produce this lack of short-run control over the economy. If shifts in aggregate demand or supply, or both, could be accurately predicted sufficiently far in advance, policy could be changed in anticipation of the shifts. Thus, the effects of policy lags could be overcome by a forward-looking policy. In a world of perfect forecasts, lags do not prevent policy from stabilizing the economy.

Economic forecasts are subject to substantial error, however. There is some value in forecasts, but policies based on them can produce unfortunate consequences. For example, assume that a prediction of a future rise in aggregate demand produces a current tightening of policy. If the shift in aggregate demand does not occur, unemployment results. Conversely, the prediction of a future fall in aggregate demand calls for an easing of current policy. If the decline in aggregate demand does not occur, the policy produces inflation. Thus, there are dangers in basing current policies on forecasts of the future. Of course, if the forecasts are correct, policy can prevent unemployment and inflation from occurring. If the forecasts are wrong, however, policy can make the situation worse rather than better. The art of policymaking involves knowing when to respond to forecasts and when to disregard them. We shall return to this issue later in this chapter. At this point, it is useful to analyze the sources of policy lags.

Policy Lags

There are three sources of lags in policy: the recognition lag, the implementation lag, and the lag in the economy's response to a policy change. The sum of these three lags determines the total length of time that elapses between the need for a change in policy and its ultimate effect on the economy. The total lag spans a substantial period of time. The length of the lag significantly reduces the ability of monetary and fiscal policy to stabilize the economy in the short run.

The Recognition Lag

The recognition lag is the length of time between the time when there is a need to change policy and the time when policymakers actually become aware of the need. Ideally, policymakers predict shifts in aggregate demand or supply before they occur. This allows policy to change before the shifts occur so that the lags in the impact of policy can be overcome. Because economic forecasts are imperfect, a substantial period of time can elapse between when policy should change in anticipation of an aggregate demand or supply shift and when policymakers perceive the need for change. This lag can occur either because forecasts do not reveal the need to change policy or because policymakers are unwilling to base a policy change on forecasted shifts in aggregate demand or supply.

When policymakers do not anticipate a shift in aggregate demand or supply, the recognition lag can extend beyond the time when a shift actually occurs. Data on real output, employment and prices are not immediately available. A period of several months may elapse before policymakers are aware that there has been an unexpected change in the economic situation. Fragmentary data are available more quickly, but these data are not always accurate indicators of the movements in aggregate output, employment, and prices. As a result, a substantial period of time may pass following a shift in aggregate demand or supply before policymakers are convinced that a shift has occurred.

Policymakers must also determine whether the shift is transitory or more permanent. If the shift is transitory, its effect will quickly disappear without any policy action. If policymakers respond to a transitory shift in aggregate demand or supply as if it were permanent, the effects of the policy will remain in the system after the effects of the shift have disappeared. For example, if policymakers mistake a transitory decline in aggregate demand for a permanent decline, they will pursue an expansionary policy. This policy will create excess demand and inflation when aggregate demand shifts back to its previous position. Similarly, a transitory increase in aggregate demand can produce a restrictive policy and recession if it is mistaken for a permanent increase.

These considerations indicate that it is important for policymakers to distinguish transitory from relatively permanent shifts in aggregate demand or supply. This means that policymakers must forecast, either explicitly fo implicitly, the future course of aggregate demand and supply. It is not enough to know that a shift has occurred; the permanence of the shift must also be determined.

A substantial period of time can elapse between the time when a permanent shift in aggregate demand has occurred and the time when policymakers become convinced of its permanence. This adds to the length of the recognition lag. There are other times when the lag is short because the permanence is relatively easy to determine. This is the case, for example, when there is a shift in aggregate supply caused by a rise in the price of imported oil. Thus, the length of the recognition lag is not a constant; it depends upon the circumstances.

The Implementation Lag

The implementation lag is the length of time that elapses between the time when policymakers become convinced of the need to change policy and the time when policy is actually changed. It is at this stage of the policy process that monetary policy has a definite advantage over fiscal policy.

The Federal Reserve can change policy almost immediately. Although the Federal Open Market Committee meets only every six weeks, a telephone conference can be arranged almost immediately if circumstances warrant. This means that the implementation lag for monetary policy is very short.

In contrast, fiscal policy cannot move quickly. Proposed legislation must be drafted by the administration or Congress, hearings must be held before both houses of Congress, a final bill must be passed by both houses, and the legislation must be signed by the President. This process can take considerable time. Furthermore, with fiscal policy, it is necessary to decide what taxes to increase or decrease, or what spending programs to reduce or supplement, or all of these. These considerations can prompt considerable political debate, which slows the process. Finally, political realities can prevent fiscal policy from being used actively to stabilize the economy. Congress and the President often favor spending increases for national defense or for social programs, but they show less enthusiasm for reducing other forms of spending or for raising taxes. Similarly, tax cuts are more popular with politicians than are tax increases. These political factors make it relatively easy to pursue a stimulative fiscal policy and difficult to pursue a restrictive policy. Even when a more stimulative policy is appropriate, the implementation lag can reduce the ability of fiscal policy to be changed in a timely fashion.

Because of its short implementation lag and because it is less susceptible to political considerations, monetary policy is the primary tool for implementing stabilization policies in the United States.[2] Because monetary policy has the assignment of balancing aggregate demand with long-run aggregate supply, it cannot simultaneously pursue capital formation goals. This limitation has been offset to some degree by using fiscal policy, in the form of investment tax credits, rapid depreciation allowances, and other devices, to encourage capital formation.

Lags in the Impact of Policy

The third step in the policy process involves the lags in the impact of a change in policy on the ultimate objectives of policy, that is, real output, inflation, and capital formation. Here monetary policy probably suffers from a disadvantage compared to fiscal policy. Before discussing the disadvantage, however, we will find it instructive to analyze the general problem of lags.

Up to this point we have not discussed the dynamic response of aggregate demand to changes in monetary and fiscal policy. The response occurs only grad-

---

[2] We saw in Chapter 14 that because tax receipts vary positively with income and transfer payments vary negatively with aggregate income, fiscal policy does act as a built-in stabilizer.

ually, and this creates substantial lags. Just as there is a difference between long-run and short-run aggregate supply, there is also a difference between short-run and long-run aggregate demand.

In the short run, aggregate demand is not very sensitive to changes in income, the interest rate, or the price level.[3] For example, it takes time for the public to adjust consumption to changes in income. This occurs because consumers are concerned whether a change in income is transitory or relatively permanent. In the short run, a rise in income is likely to be perceived as transitory, so the public does not adjust its consumption very much. Thus, in the short run, when income rises, saving increases; and when income falls, saving declines. Furthermore, it takes the public time to change its consumption habits even when a change in income is perceived to be relatively permanent. For both these reasons, consumption adjusts relatively slowly to changes in income. This implies that the marginal propensity to save is relatively high in the short run.

Firms also adjust their investment expenditures relatively slowly to changes in income.[4] Firms have to be convinced that the change in income is sufficiently permanent to merit a change in their investment plans. Furthermore, it takes time to change investment expenditures physically even when a change in income is viewed as relatively permanent. For example, if income rises, firms first have to decide to increase their investment expenditures, and then they have to place orders for the capital goods and await delivery. Similarly, if income falls, firms must become convinced of the permanence of the decline before reducing their investment expenditures. Many firms have investment projects that are already being undertaken. They are likely to complete these projects because otherwise they will receive no return on the investments. Thus, investment remains relatively high for a while even though income declines.

Firms and households also respond slowly to changes in interest rates. This occurs because long-term interest rates respond with a lag to changes in short-term interest rates and because it takes time for consumption and investment demand to respond to changes in interest rates. We know from the discussion of the term structure of interest rates in Chapter 6 that if a change in short-term interest rates is perceived to be relatively transitory, there is little effect on longer-term interest rates. For example, when short-term interest rates rise, the public must become convinced that they will remain high in the future if there is to be a commensurate rise in the long-term interest rate. A substantial period of time may elapse before the public is convinced that a change in short-term interest rates is more than transitory. As the public becomes convinced of the permanence of the change long-term interest rates change.

Both long-term and short-term interest rates affect aggregate demand. Consumption and investment demand respond to changes in these interest rates with a

---

[3] The analysis that follows refers to unanticipated changes in income, interest rates, and prices.
[4] Here we are talking about investment in plant and equipment, not inventory investment, which changes quickly.

lag for much the same reasons that aggregate demand responds slowly to changes in income.

Empirical evidence indicates that the effects of fiscal policy are felt more quickly than the effects of monetary policy. Fiscal policy directly affects aggregate demand and income. Monetary policy affects aggregate demand and income indirectly through changes in interest rates and wealth. Furthermore, fiscal policy is changed relatively infrequently, and these changes are likely to be viewed by the public as permanent. Monetary policy is changed frequently, and it is more difficult for the public to distinguish transitory from more permanent changes. This also makes fiscal policy affect aggregate demand more quickly. The shorter lag for the impact of fiscal policy usually does not offset the much longer lag for the implementation of fiscal policy changes, however.

It must be emphasized that the time path of response of the economy to a change in either monetary or fiscal policy is strongly affected by the expectations of the public. If households and firms know that income and interest rates have changed permanently, they respond more rapidly than if they do not know that the changes are permanent. A relatively permanent change in monetary or fiscal policy that is not perceived to be permanent has a slower effect on the economy than a change that is perceived to be permanent. Thus, the expectations of the public concerning future policy affects the length of the lag. We shall return to this important issue later and first discuss policy issues when the lag in response is fixed and known to policymakers.

USING *IS-LM* CURVES TO ANALYZE POLICY-IMPACT LAGS

Although the lag in impact of policy is necessarily a dynamic concept, we can isolate the major issues by using the static *IS-LM* framework. When there are lags in the response of consumption and investment demand to changes in income and interest rates, the short-run income multiplier is reduced, and the short-run *IS* curve is relatively steep.

The basic issues involved can be seen by examining the simple *IS* curve derived in Chapter 13. This *IS* curve allows us to see the role of lags without having to deal with the complexities introduced by the government and international sectors, by wealth, by the price level, or by the dependency of investment on income and consumption on the interest rate. These complexities are important for analyzing lags, but their exclusion helps to simplify the analysis. The *IS* curve of Chapter 13 is

$$Y = \frac{c_0 + i_0}{s_1} - \frac{i_1}{s_1} R_{ST}$$

where

Y is GNP,

c_0 is the intercept of the consumption function

i_0 is the intercept of the investment function

s_1 is the marginal propensity to save

i_1 is the interest sensitivity of investment demand and

R_{ST} is the short-term interest rate.

The short-term interest rate, R_{ST}, is used because this interest rate is most directly affected by monetary policy. The relationship between short- and long-term interest rates is affected by the public's perception of the permanence of a change in the short-term rate.

The income multiplier for a shift in the consumption or investment function is $1/s_1$. We argued earlier that the marginal propensity to save, s_1, is higher in the short run than in the long run. This means that the multiplier, $1/s_1$, is relatively small in the short run. Shifts in the consumption or investment functions produce smaller increases in income, given the short-term interest rate, in the short run than in the long run.

The slope of the *IS* curve is relatively steep in the short run. This can be seen by rearranging terms to put the short-term interest rate on the left-hand side

$$R_{ST} = \frac{c_0 + i_0}{i_1} - \frac{s_1}{i_1} Y .$$

The slope of the *IS* curve is $\Delta R_{ST}/\Delta Y = s_1/i_1$. We have already explained that the numerator of the slope, s_1, is larger, and the denominator, i_1, is smaller, in the short run than in the long run. This means that $\Delta R_{ST}/\Delta Y$ is relatively large, and, therefore, the short-run *IS* curve is relatively steep.[5]

The short-run *IS* curve is steep because a rise in income requires a larger decline in the short-term interest rate to equate saving to investment in the short run than in the long run. This occurs because a rise in income produces a large amount of saving in the short run. The interest rate must fall by enough to encourage additional investment. This requires a large decline in the interest rate because investment is not very responsive to changes in the interest rate in the short run.

Now let us look at the *LM* curve. If we leave the price level and wealth aside for simplicity, the expression for the *LM* curve derived in Chapter 14 is

$$R_{ST} = \frac{m_0 - m_M \overline{TR}}{m_1} + \frac{m_2}{m_1} Y$$

---

[5] If we allow for government, wealth, net exports, and the price level and other factors, the *IS* curve is still relatively steep in the short run.

where

m_0 is the intercept of the money demand function

m_M is the money multiplier

$\overline{TR}$ is total reserves

m_1 is the interest sensitivity of money demand and

m_2 is the income sensitivity of money demand.

The interest sensitivity of money demand tends to be lower in the short run than in the long run. This occurs because the public tends to view a change in the short-term interest rate as transitory in the short run. As a result, the public does not change the quantity of money demanded very much. Thus, the money demand schedule is steep. With a permanently lower interest rate, the public finds it worth while to realign its portfolios to include more money and less of other assets. The low short-run elasticity of money demand implies that if total reserves and the quantity of money increase, the public can be induced to hold the increased quantity of money only if the short-term interest rate falls substantially.

We conclude that the interest sensitivity of money demand, m_1, is larger in the long run than in the short run. This means that the money demand schedule is less steep in the long run than in the short run. It follows, then, that a shift in the money demand schedule or a change in the quantity of reserves produces a larger change in the short-term interest rate in the short run than in the long run.[6] Thus, the shift in the LM curve is larger in the short run than in the long run.[7]

The effect of lags in adjustment on the slope of the LM curve is less clear. The slope, $\Delta R_{ST}/\Delta Y = (m_2/m_1)$, is the ratio of the income sensitivity of money demand to the interest rate sensitivity of money demand. Both m_2 and m_1 are smaller in the short run than in the long run, so one cannot predict on theoretical grounds what happens to the ratio. For simplicity, we shall assume that the slope of the LM curve is the same in the short run as in the long run.

With the discussion of short-run versus long-run IS and LM curves in mind, we can now examine the effect of lags in the impact of monetary and fiscal policy. Consider the case where the economy is initially in long-run equilibrium as shown at point A in Panel I of Figure 18.1, where the long-run IS curve, IS_{LR}, intersects the LM curve at $(Y/P)_0$ and $(R_{ST})_0$.[8] The short-run IS curve, IS_{SR} is also shown. Now assume that there is a permanent downward shift in the consumption or

---

[6] As explained in Chapter 14, recent deregulation of depository institutions allows a market interest rate to be paid on certain types of transactions accounts. This probably reduces the interest elasticity of money demand in both the short and long run. The extent of the change in the elasticities is uncertain. This has important implications that are discussed later.

[7] For simplicity, it is assumed that the money multiplier, m_M, is the same in the short run as in the long run.

[8] Recall that we assume that the slope of the short-run LM curve is the same as the slope of the long-run LM curve.

FIGURE 18.1
THE ADJUSTMENT OF
AGGREGATE DEMAND IN THE
SHORT AND LONG RUN.

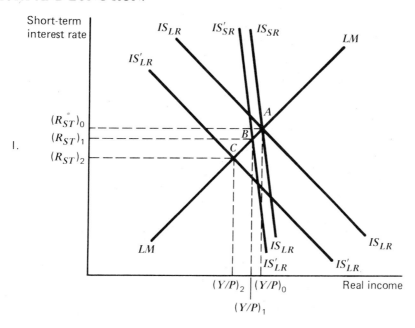

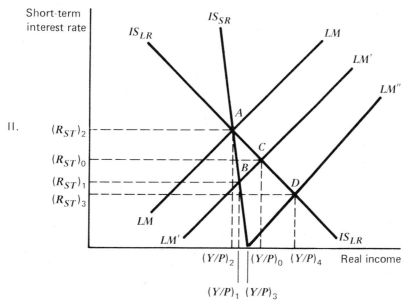

investment function. This leads to a relatively small leftward shift in the short-run IS curve from IS_{SR} to IS'_{SR} because the income multiplier is small in the short run. Thus, income falls to $(Y/P)_1$, and the short-term interest rate declines to $(R_{ST})_1$ at point B. With the passage of time, the multiplier increases, so the IS curve continues to shift to the left, and it becomes less steep. Eventually, we have the equilibrium at point C, where the long-run IS curve, IS'_{LR}, intersects the long-run LM at $(Y/P)_2$ and $(R_{ST})_2$. Though this is not a true long-run equilibrium because prices fall and the economy returns to $(Y/P)_0$ in the long run, we abstract from the price adjustment at this point. With monetary and fiscal policy unchanged, real income eventually falls from $(Y/P)_0$ to $(Y/P)_2$.

Now assume that the Fed decides to pursue an expansionary policy. The equilibrium at $(Y/P)_2$ and $(R_{ST})_2$ is shown as point A in Panel II of Figure 18.1. There is a short-run IS curve, IS_{SR}, that goes with the long-run curve, IS_{LR}. The Federal Reserve increases the quantity of reserves and the LM curve shifts down to LM'.[9] This policy shift eventually returns the economy to full employment at point C but the adjustment takes time. In the short run, real output rises only to $(Y/P)_1$ at point B. This occurs even though the short-term interest rate falls to $(R_{ST})_1$, which is lower than $(R_{ST})_0$. Though there is a large initial decline in the short-term interest rate, there is only a small response of aggregate demand, so income rises only to $(Y/P)_1$.

Note that IS_{SR} is sufficiently steep that no matter how much the LM curve shifts down and how much the short-term interest rate declines, full employment output, $(Y/P)_0$, cannot be achieved in the short run. Even if the LM curve is shifted all the way to LM'', where the interest rate is zero, real income only rises to $(Y/P)_3$.

Because there are lags in the response of aggregate demand to the reduction in the interest rate, monetary policy cannot return the economy to full employment immediately. Time is required for firms and consumers to expand their spending in response to lower short-term interest rates. During this time the economy operates below its potential.

The response of the economy in Panel II assumes that monetary policy provides a quantity of reserves that is consistent with achieving full employment once the lags have worked themselves out. Thus, the LM curve is shifted down to LM' to give an intersection with the long-run IS curve at point C. This is not the only policy strategy available. The economy can be returned to full employment more quickly if the LM curve is shifted all the way to LM''. This gives the largest decline in the interest rate and the largest initial increase in real income. In order to avoid having real income ultimately rise above $(Y/P)_0$, monetary policy must turn around and take some of the reserves back out of the system. The large initial injection of reserves gives the curve LM'', which produces excess demand

---

[9] We showed earlier that the shift in the LM curve is larger in the short run than in the long run. This implies that the Fed must increase total reserves over time to offset the upward shift in the LM curve and keep it at LM'.

once the lags have worked themselves out. If the reserves are kept in the system, the economy moves to point *D*. Real income rises to $(Y/P)_4$, and inflationary pressures develop. This can be avoided if the Fed shifts the *LM* curve up over time to compensate for the increasing response of firms and households to low interest rates. The dynamic path of monetary policy in this policy strategy is complex and may require temporary shifts of the *LM* curve above the long-run curve *LM'* to compensate for the lagged response of spending to low interest rates. Such a policy is difficult to execute in practice.

Two lessons emerge from this discussion of monetary policy strategies. First, when a leftward shift in the *IS* curve is not anticipated sufficiently far in advance, the presence of lags prevents policy from maintaining the economy at full employment. Unemployment and unused capacity prevail in the short run. Second, the Fed can speed the transition to full employment if it successfully pursues the complex strategy illustrated in Panel II of Figure 18.1. This strategy is feasible and desirable if the Fed has accurate and detailed knowledge of the dynamic response of the economy to changes in total reserves. Even with this knowledge, however, the Federal Reserve can only speed up the transition to full employment; it cannot eliminate unemployment in the short run. Full employment can be maintained only if the initial shift in the *IS* curve is anticipated sufficiently far in advance that the effects of lags in response to an easing of policy can be overcome.

In our story concerning the response of monetary policy to a leftward shift in the *IS* curve, it was assumed that the shift was permanent. The shift was not anticipated and unemployment had to develop before the Fed became convinced that the shift was permanent. The issue for monetary policy then became one of deciding how quickly to return the economy to full employment. This is a useful exercise, but it abstracts from the problem that the *IS* curve might continue to shift. If the *IS* curve continues to shift to the left, a monetary policy based on the assumption of a fixed *IS* curve will be headed in the right direction even though the expansion of total reserves will not be large enough to achieve full employment. If the *IS* curve shifts back to the right, however, monetary policy is providing too much reserves, and excess demand will ultimately develop.

These considerations illustrate the general proposition that successful stabilization policy must anticipate *future* shifts in aggregate demand. Given the limited success of economic forecasting, policy errors will occur. Uncertainty about the future coupled with adjustment lags can make stabilization policy extremely difficult. Our next task is to analyze the role of uncertainty in detail.

THE ROLE OF UNCERTAINTY

Uncertainty about the future is probably the greatest problem faced by policymakers. This uncertainty concerns unexpected shifts in aggregate demand and supply as well as unexpected changes in the response of the economy to policy. The role of unexpected aggregate demand shifts can be analyzed most easily by abstracting from adjustment lags. Thus, we will look at a world in which the economy responds immediately to a change in policy, but in which there are unanticipated shifts in aggregate demand. We will then look at the more realistic case where there are lags.

Unexpected shifts in aggregate demand result from unexpected shifts in the behavioral relationships underlying the *IS* and *LM* curves. The *IS* curve shifts when there are shifts in the consumption, investment, or net exports functions or when there are changes in the price level and real wealth.[10] The *LM* curve shifts when there are shifts in the demand or supply of money or when there are changes in the price level and real wealth. There are many reasons for unexpected shifts in the *IS* and *LM* curves. First, changes in tastes are unpredictable. Thus, changes in tastes for current consumption versus saving, as well as changes in the tastes of foreigners for our exports and of domestic residents for imports, produce unexpected shifts in the *IS* curve. Similarly, changes in the public's preferences for money relative to other assets affect the demand and supply for money and cause the *LM* curve to shift unexpectedly.

The second source of *IS* and *LM* curve shifts involves expectations. The public's preference for current consumption versus saving is affected by its expectations of the future. If the public expects steadily rising income, consumption will be high relative to income. Conversely, if the public is pessimistic and expects falling real income, consumption will be low relative to income. Thus, changes in expectations concerning future real income shift the consumption function, and they affect the demand for imports.

Business expectations have an important effect on investment. Firms make investment decisions based on their expectations of the discounted present value of the net income earned from new capital goods. We saw in Chapter 3 that this discounted present value depends both upon the expected flow of net income in the future and upon interest rates that are expected to prevail in the future. As explained in Chapter 15, given expected interest rates, if firms expect real income to rise in the future, investment demand will be high. Investment demand will be low when business expects real income to decline. Similarly, if interest rates are expected to be high in the future, there will be less investment than when interest rates are expected to be low. Finally, as we saw in Chapter 16, expectations of future inflation affect real interest rates. Thus, changes in inflationary expectations shift the investment function.

Expectations also affect the *LM* curve. When the public expects a deteriorating economic situation, asset risk is perceived to rise, and the public tends to shift its portfolio into money. Conversely, when the public expects a stable and growing economy, risk is perceived to be low, and the demand for money is relatively low. Furthermore, changes in inflationary expectations affect the real interest rate and shift the *LM* curve.

---

[10] Unexpected changes in fiscal policy also occur.

International developments can produce unexpected shifts in the *IS* and *LM* curves. Unexpected changes in foreign income and changes in the expectations of foreigners concerning their future income cause unexpected changes in the demand for our exports, which shift the *IS* curve. Furthermore, unexpected changes in foreign prices relative to domestic prices affect the demand for both exports and imports. These factors affect both the exchange rate and the *IS* curve. Finally, changes in expectations of foreign versus domestic rates of return and changes in perceptions of risk affect domestic interest rates, the *LM* curve, and the exchange rate.

An often major source of unexpected shifts in the *IS* and *LM* curves is fiscal policy. Though the President makes a budget proposal to Congress and Congress makes its own resolutions for spending and taxing, actual spending and tax programs can depart substantially from these plans. Unexpected changes in spending and tax programs affect the *IS* curve, and unexpected changes in budget deficits or surpluses affect the *LM* curve.

Finally, the recent financial innovations and deregulation described at various points in Chapters 8 through 12 have made the *LM* curve subject to substantial unexpected shifts. The public has made, and probably will continue to make, large portfolio shifts between money and other assets and between other liabilities of depository institutions and market securities as interest rate deregulation and financial innovation progress. These shifts affect money demand or the money and credit multipliers, or both, and, therefore, affect the *LM* curve.

Let us now turn to an analysis of how monetary policy should operate in this uncertain environment. To get the discussion started, we will initially look at the effects of unexpected *IS* shifts in a world where there are no unexpected shifts in the *LM* curve. Assume that the Federal Reserve expects the *IS* curve to be IS_E, as shown in Figure 18.2.[11] It sets the quantity of reserves to produce an *LM* curve that intersects the expected *IS* curve at point *A*, where aggregate demand equals long run aggregate supply. If the *IS* curve does not shift unexpectedly, this produces the desired real income $(Y/P)^*$ and the interest rate R^*. Further assume that the *IS* curve is subject to unexpected but transitory shifts, so it may be as high as IS_H or as low as IS_L. Thus, given the interest rate R^*, real income could be as high as $(Y/P)_H$ or as low as $(Y/P)_L$. Given total reserves and the *LM* curve, however, the interest rate rises when the *IS* curve is higher than expected, and the interest rate falls when the *IS* curve is lower than expected. This means that if the *IS* curve is IS_H, the equilibrium is at point *B*, where the interest rate increases to R_1 and real income rises only to $(Y/P)_1$. If the *IS* curve is IS_L, the equilibrium is at point *C*, where the interest rate falls to R_2 and real income declines only to $(Y/P)_2$. When total reserves are fixed, movements in the interest rate act like a built-in stabilizer that reduces excess aggregate demand and stimulates deficient

[11] Because we are dealing with a world that has no lags, it is not necessary to distinguish between short- and long-term interest rates. This allows us to deal with the single interest rate, *R*, in Figure 18.2.

FIGURE 18.2
FLUCTUATIONS IN REAL INCOME
WHEN THERE ARE TRANSITORY
SHIFTS IN THE *IS* CURVE.

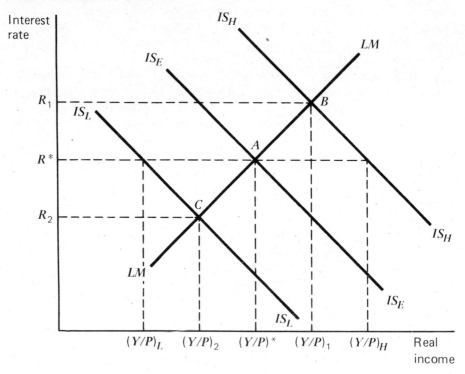

demand. Note that when the *LM* curve is steep and the *IS* curve is flat, the deviation of actual real income from its desired value is small. The deviations are large when the *LM* curve is flat and the *IS* curve is steep.

As long as the expected position of the *IS* curve, IS_E, does not change, monetary policy sets the *LM* curve to give an intersection with IS_E at the desired real income, $(Y/P)^*$. Unexpected fluctuations in the *IS* curve produce deviations of actual real income from $(Y/P)^*$, but these are unavoidable.[12] Sometimes real income exceeds $(Y/P)^*$, and sometimes it falls short of $(Y/P)^*$, but on average $(Y/P)^*$ is achieved.

---

[12] We will see presently that there is a policy that can reduce, but not eliminate, deviations of actual real income and output from $(Y/P)^*$.

When the shifts in the *IS* curve are unpredictable and transitory, it is counterproductive for monetary policy to chase after the shifting *IS* curve. This is illustrated in Figure 18.3. Monetary policy sets the quantity of total reserves to achieve the *LM* curve LM_0, which intersects IS_E at $(Y/P)^*$. Now assume that there is an unexpected rightward shift in the *IS* curve to IS_H. This produces an unexpected increase in real income and output to $(Y/P)_1$. When monetary policy reacts to the unexpected increase in real income, it reduces the quantity of reserves and shifts the *LM* curve up to LM_1. If the *IS* curve remains at IS_H, this raises the interest rate further and forces real income and output back to $(Y/P)^*$. There is no reason to expect the *IS* curve to remain at IS_H, however. It is no more likely to remain at IS_H than to shift left to IS_L. If the curve does shift to IS_L, real income and output fall all the way to $(Y/P)_2$. If policy responds to this shift, it pushes the *LM* down to LM_2. This would achieve $(Y/P)^*$ if the *IS* curve remains at IS_L, but if the *IS* curve shifts back to the right, the policy is overstimulative. The best guess of the new position of the *IS* curve is that it will return to its expected position IS_E. If this occurs and the *LM* curve is kept at LM_0, $(Y/P)^*$ is achieved. If monetary policy chases after transitory shifts in the *IS* curve, it increases the fluctuations in real income. Monetary policy reduces the chances of hitting $(Y/P)^*$ when it reacts to unexpected transitory shifts in the *IS* curve.

We conclude that if there are unpredictable and transitory shifts in the *IS* curve, monetary policy should set the *LM* curve at LM_0. This allows the interest rate to act as a built-in stabilizer that limits the fluctuations of actual real income from its desired value.

If the shift in the *IS* curve to IS_H in Figure 18.3 is permanent rather than transitory, however, monetary policy must change if $(Y/P)^*$ is to be achieved on average. In this situation, the expected *IS* curve has shifted to the right. What was previously an unusually high level for the *IS* curve is now the expected (average) level. This means that the *IS* curve now experiences transitory shifts that move it above or below the new, higher expected value. In this situation, the appropriate policy response is to shift the *LM* curve up to LM_1. This allows $(Y/P)^*$ to be achieved on average when the old IS_H becomes the new expected position of the *IS* curve.

This leads us to a dilemma that is faced by stabilization policy. Is an unexpected rise in real income and output the result of a permanent shift in the *IS* curve or the result of a transitory shift? If the shift is permanent, then policy should respond by shifting the *LM* curve to achieve $(Y/P)^*$. If the shift is transitory, policy should not respond. Mistaking a transitory shift for a permanent one or mistaking a permanent shift for a transitory one prevents the economy from achieving $(Y/P)^*$ on average.

Sometimes it is easy to distinguish a permanent from a transitory shift, as when there is a permanent change in the tax rate or some long-lasting development abroad that affects net exports. Usually, however, there are no clear signals indicating whether the shift in the *IS* curve is permanent or transitory. In these situations, policymakers can only guess and wait for further information. For

FIGURE 18.3
IT IS COUNTERPRODUCTIVE TO
CHASE AFTER TRANSITORY
SHIFTS IN AGGREGATE DEMAND.

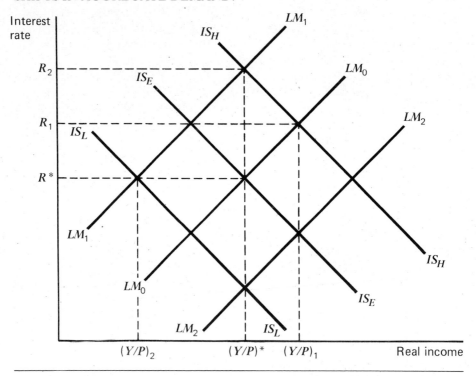

example, if an unexpected increase in real income and output is quickly reversed, it is likely that the shift is transitory. If the unexpected increase in real income and output continues month after month, it is likely that there has been a permanent shift in the *IS* curve.

Monetary policy should respond to expected shifts in the *IS* curve but not to transitory fluctuations. In effect, policy should treat the expected *IS* curve as if it were known with certainty. Assuming that the actual average position of the *IS* curve is the same as the expected position, this policy minimizes the deviations of actual income from $(Y/P)^*$. Because the expected *IS* curve is treated as though it is known with certainty, this is a policy of *certainty equivalence*.

Up to this point, we have assumed that the position of the *LM* curve is known with certainty. This was a convenient assumption for analyzing the role of fluctuations in the *IS* curve, but it is unrealistic. The *LM* curve is also subject to unexpected shifts. As discussed earlier, these come from unexpected shifts in money demand, unexpected changes in the money multiplier, and unexpected movements in the budget deficit or surplus. Even though total reserves are fixed, the *LM* curve fluctuates about its expected value.

FIGURE 18.4
FLUCTUATIONS IN REAL INCOME
WHEN THERE ARE TRANSITORY
SHIFTS IN THE *LM* CURVE.

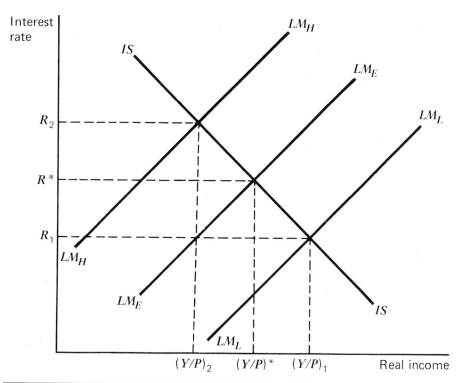

The role of shifts in the *LM* curve can be seen most easily by assuming that the *IS* curve does not fluctuate unexpectedly. This situation is depicted in Figure 18.4. The Federal Reserve sets total reserves so that the expected position of the *LM* curve is LM_E. This gives an intersection with the known *IS* curve at $(Y/P)^*$. Because of transitory shifts in money demand, the money multiplier, and the government budget, however, the *LM* curve can be as high as LM_H or as low as LM_L. This means that real income can be as high as $(Y/P)_1$ or as low as $(Y/P)_2$. Thus, even though the *IS* curve is fixed, real income and output fluctuate because the interest rate fluctuates as the *LM* curve shifts about its expected value.

This brings us to the issue of the interest rate as a built-in stabilizer or destabilizer. When transitory shifts in the *IS* curve are the source of fluctuations in real income and output, movements in the interest rate produced by a fixed *LM* curve limit the fluctuations in real income and output. In this situation, movements in the interest rate act as a built-in stabilizer. When transitory shifts in the *LM* curve occur, however, the fluctuations in the interest rate are responsible for the fluctuations in real income. In this case, interest rate fluctuations destabilize real income and output.

It might appear that the fluctuations in real income and output caused by unexpected shifts in the LM curve are unavoidable. It turns out that this is not the case. To see why this is so, let us look at the intersection of the fixed IS curve with the expected LM curve, LM_E in Panel I of Figure 18.5. Expected real income is $(Y/P)^*$, and the expected interest rate is R^*. When the LM curve is subject to transitory fluctuations, real income is higher than $(Y/P)^*$ when the interest rate is lower than R^*. Real income is lower than $(Y/P)^*$ when the interest rate is higher than R^*. The Fed can totally eliminate the fluctuations in real income by setting the interest rate at R^*.

The Federal Reserve can set the interest rate at R^* by standing ready to buy and sell government securities at a fixed price consistent with the interest rate R^*. Panels II and III of Figure 18.5 illustrate why this stabilizes the interest rate. Panel II shows how the Fed fixes the interest rate at R^* when there are unexpected shifts in money demand. When real money supply is $(M/P)_0^S$ and real money demand is at its expected value, $(M/P)_E^D$, the equilibrium interest rate is R^*. Now assume that the supply of money is fixed but the demand for money is subject to transitory fluctuations. Given real income, money demand might be as high as $(M/P)_H^D$ or as low as $(M/P)_L^D$. With a fixed quantity of total reserves, this gives possible interest rate fluctuations between R_H and R_L. It is these interest rate fluctuations that produce shifts in the LM curve.

Now let us see the implications of having the Fed stand ready to buy and sell bonds at a fixed price consistent with the interest rate, R^*. Consider the case where money demand is higher than expected at $(M/P)_H^D$. The public sells bonds in an effort to obtain additional money balances. In the absence of Fed intervention, this reduces the price of bonds and raises the interest rate. The public can avoid receiving a lower price by selling bonds to the Fed at the fixed price. When the Fed purchases bonds, the quantity of reserves and the quantity of money increase. The public continues to sell bonds to the Fed and adds to its money balances until the excess demand for money is eliminated. This occurs when the real quantity of money rises to $(M/P)_1^S$. The Fed has accommodated the increase in the demand for money by increasing the supply of money. Thus, the quantity of money rises, and the interest rate remains unchanged. This means that the LM curve does not shift even though there is an unexpected increase in money demand.[13]

Now consider an unexpected change in the multiplier linking total reserves to the quantity of money. Panel III shows the example where the money multiplier is higher than expected, so the real supply of money is $(M/P)_H^S$ rather than $(M/P)_E^S$. This produces an excess supply of money. In the absence of Fed intervention, money holders shift into bonds and bid up their price, that is, reduce

---

[13] It is left to the reader to show that an unexpected decline in money demand produces a decrease in the quantity of money and no change in the interest rate.

FIGURE 18.5
PREVENTING SHIFTS IN THE *LM*
CURVE.

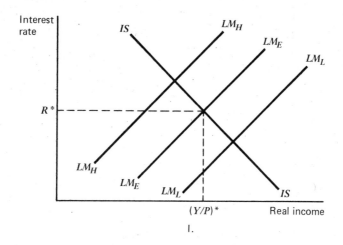

I.

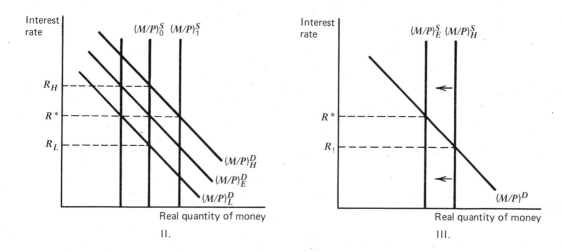

II.

III.

the interest rate, until the excess supply of money is eliminated. This produces a downward shift in the *LM* curve. When the Fed fixes the price of bonds, holders of excess money balances can buy bonds from the Fed at the fixed price rather than in the market at a higher price. Thus, they buy from the Fed. This is an open market sale of bonds by the Fed that increases the quantity of bonds and decreases the quantity of reserves. The Fed continues to sell bonds and reduce reserves until the excess supply of money is eliminated. In this case, the reduction in the quantity of reserves just offsets the rise in the money multiplier. After the smoke has cleared, the quantity of money has returned to its previous value, $(M/P_0)_E^S$. Again, the interest rate remains unchanged, and the LM curves does not shift.

We conclude that when the Fed sets the interest rate, the LM curve does not shift when there are unexpected shifts in money demand or supply. In fact, when the Fed sets the interest rate, the LM curve is horizontal, indicating that no matter what the value of real income and output, the interest rate is unchanged. An upward-sloping LM curve comes from the assumption that the quantity of nominal reserves is fixed. A rise in real income produces an increase in the demand for real money balances. With total reserves fixed, this raises the interest rate. When the interest rate is fixed, the rise in real money demand that accompanies an increase in real income produces an increase in reserves. This leads to an increase in money supply that equals the increase in money demand. The interest rate does not rise. We get the same interest rate no matter how high real income is because money supply rises with money demand. This gives a horizontal LM curve.

A horizontal LM curve eliminates fluctuations in real income and output when the source of the fluctuations is unexpected shifts in money demand or money supply. The horizontal LM curve amplifies fluctuations in real income and output, however, when the source of fluctuations is shifts in the IS curve. Panel I of Figure 18.6 shows a situation where the interest rate is set at R^* and there are transitory shifts in IS. With a fixed interest rate, R^*, the range of fluctuations in real income is $(Y/P)_H$ to $(Y/P)_L$. Because the interest rate does not rise when aggregate demand is unexpectedly high and does not fall when aggregate demand is unexpectedly low, there is a full multiplier effect from shifts in the IS curve. Panel II shows the situation when total reserves are fixed and the interest rate is allowed to fluctuate. When total reserves are fixed, the LM curve is upward sloping, and the range of fluctuations in real income is only $(Y/P)_1$ to $(Y/P)_2$.

We conclude that when the IS curve is subject to transitory fluctuations, but the LM curve is not, monetary policy gains closer control over real income and output by fixing total reserves rather than the interest rate. When the LM curve is subject to transitory fluctuations, but the IS curve is not, closer control is achieved by fixing the interest rate at a value consistent with the intersection of the fixed IS curve with the horizontal LM curve at $(Y/P)^*$.

The choice between reserves or the interest rate as the instrument of monetary policy depends upon the variability of the IS curve relative to the LM curve. This can be seen in Figure 18.7. In Panel I, there are fluctuations in both the IS and the LM curves, but the fluctuations in IS are large relative to LM. When total reserves are used as the policy instrument, the range of possible fluctuations in real income and output is $(Y/P)_1$ to $(Y/P)_2$. The low value, $(Y/P)_1$, occurs when the IS curve is at its low level, IS_L, and the LM curve is at its high level, LM_H. In this unfortunate circumstance, weak aggregate demand occurs at the same time that there is a high interest rate produced by a strong demand for money or a low money multiplier, or both. High real income and output, $(Y/P)_2$,

FIGURE 18.6
FLUCTUATIONS IN INCOME WHEN
THERE ARE TRANSITORY SHIFTS
IN THE *IS* CURVE: FIXING THE
INTEREST RATE VERSUS FIXING
TOTAL RESERVES.

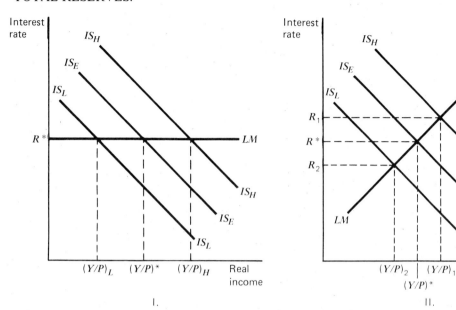

occurs when there is high aggregate demand coupled with a low interest rate. The range of possible values for real income is relatively large when both the *IS* and *LM* curves are subject to transitory shifts. Note, however, that the upward sloping *LM* curves still help to reduce the fluctuations in real income and output even though shifts in *LM* reduce the potency of the effect. This can be seen by observing the range of possible outcomes when the interest rate is fixed at R^*. In that case, the range of possible outcomes is $(Y/P)_3$ to $(Y/P)_4$, which is larger than $(Y/P)_1$ to $(Y/P)_2$.

Now consider Panel II of Figure 18.7. Here the shifts in the *IS* curve are small relative to shifts in the *LM* curve. In this case, it is preferable to use the interest rate as the instrument. When the interest rate is set at R^*, the range of possible fluctuations in real income and output is $(Y/P)_1$ to $(Y/P)_2$. When total reserves are the instrument, the range of possible outcomes is larger, $(Y/P)_3$ to $(Y/P)_4$.

We conclude that when there are unexpected shifts in both the *IS* and the *LM* curves, it is preferable to use total reserves as the instrument when the *IS* shifts are large relative to *LM* shifts. It is preferable to use the interest rate as the instrument when the *LM* shifts are large relative to shifts in the *IS* curve.

FIGURE 18.7
CHOOSING BETWEEN RESERVES
AND THE INTEREST RATE AS THE
INSTRUMENT OF MONETARY POLICY.

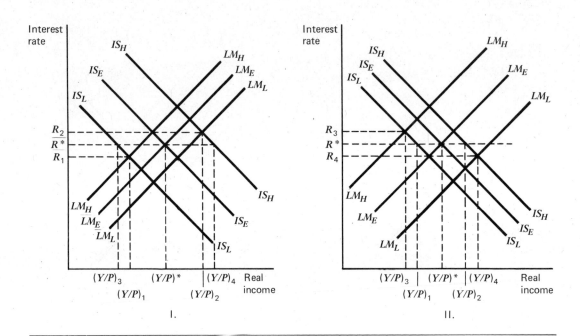

I.

II.

It is important to note that there is a policy strategy involving a combination of the interest rate and total reserves that is superior to using one instrument to the exclusion of the other. A full analysis of the combination policy is beyond the scope of this text, but two examples should make the point.[14] The superiority of the combination policy stems from the ability of the Fed to affect the slope of the LM curve. When total reserves are used as the instrument, the slope of the LM curve is the ratio of the income sensitivity of money demand to the interest rate sensitivity of money demand: $\Delta R / \Delta Y = (m_2 / m_1)$. Thus, the slope is determined by the behavior of the public. When the interest rate is used as the policy instrument, total reserves change when there is a change in real income and the transactions demand for money. This prevents the interest rate from changing when real income changes, so $\Delta R / \Delta Y = 0.0$. In this situation, the slope of the LM curve is determined by the Federal Reserve.

---

[14] For a full discussion, see W. Poole, "Optimal Choice of Policy Instruments in a Simple Stochastic Macro Model," *Quarterly Journal of Economics*, May 1970, pp. 197–216.

By pursuing a policy that changes both the interest rate and the quantity of reserves, the Fed can achieve any slope for the *LM* curve that it wants. Consider the case where there is an increase in real income and in the transactions demand for money. The Fed can decide how much of the increase in the demand for money to accommodate with an increase in the supply of money. If it accommodates all the increase in money demand, the interest rate does not increase, and the *LM* curve is flat, $\Delta R / \Delta Y = 0.0$. If it does not accommodate any of the increase in the transactions demand for money, $\Delta R / \Delta Y = (m_2 / m_1)$. The Federal Reserve can pick some intermediate point between these two extremes. In these situations, the quantity of reserves and money increase when the transactions demand for money increases, but the increase in money supply is less than the increase in money demand. The interest rate rises, but not by as much as when there is no accommodation.

Figure 18.8 illustrates the combination policy. When the interest rate is held constant, increases in money demand are completely accommodated by increases in money supply. This gives the horizontal *LM* curve, LM_0. When none of the increase in money demand is accommodated by an increase in money supply, we have the relatively steep curve LM_1. When half of the increase in money demand is accommodated by an increase in money supply, we have the intermediate position LM_2.

Now we must determine why the Fed might want to pursue a combination policy that produces the *LM* curve, LM_2. This policy provides some protection against situations where *LM* shifts are large relative to *IS* shifts *and* a risk exists that permanent shifts in the *IS* curve may be mistaken for transitory shifts. If there were no danger of undetected permanent shifts in *IS*, the best policy is a horizontal *LM* curve. This eliminates the large *LM* shifts that occur when total reserves are fixed. Conversely, If the transitory shifts in *LM* were not so great, a policy of fixing total reserves provides protection against undetected permanent shifts in *IS*. The combination policy yields the *LM* curve LM_2, whose relatively small slope insulates real income and output from transitory shifts in *LM*. With a relatively flat *LM* curve, the fluctuation in the interest rate are smaller when there are transitory shifts in *LM* and, therefore, the fluctuations in (Y/P) about $(Y/P)^*$ are reduced relative to the curve LM_1. The combination policy does yield a positively sloped *LM* curve, however, so undetected permanent shifts in *IS* do produce interest rate movements that reduce the change in real income and output. If the Fed is more concerned about the effects of transitory shifts in the *LM* curve than it is about undetected permanent shifts in *IS*, it can accommodate most of the unexpected transitory shifts in money demand with changes in money supply. This produces an upward sloping but quite flat *LM* curve. If the Fed is more concerned about undetected permanent shifts in *IS*, it will accommodate little of the unexpected transitory shifts in money demand. This produces a relatively steep *LM* curve.

A second example of the combination policy is provided by the situation where the transitory shifts in *IS* are large relative to the shifts in *LM*. We showed that in this situation the Fed should fix total reserves and let the interest rate fluctuate

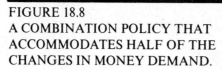

FIGURE 18.8
A COMBINATION POLICY THAT
ACCOMMODATES HALF OF THE
CHANGES IN MONEY DEMAND.

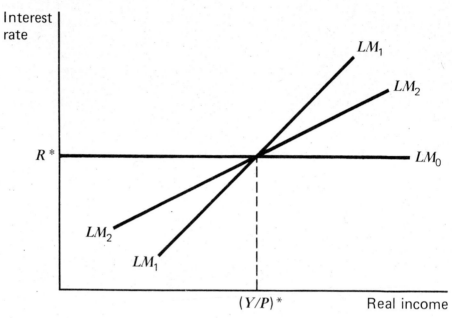

freely. Consider the extreme case where there are no shifts in the LM curve. By following a combination policy, the Fed can affect the slope of the LM curve and, therefore, affect the extent of the fluctuations in real income and output. Figure 18.9 shows the LM curve LM_0 that results from having the Fed fix the nominal quantity of reserves. The slope of the curve is (m_2/m_1), and the range of fluctuations in real output is $(Y/P)_1$ to $(Y/P)_2$. The Fed can achieve an LM curve with a steeper slope by reducing the quantity of reserves when the interest rate rises and by increasing the quantity of reserves when the interest rate falls. This combination policy produces the LM curve LM_1, which is steeper than LM_0 and, therefore, produces a smaller range of fluctuation of real output; that is, $(Y/P)_3$ to $(Y/P)_4$ versus $(Y/P)_1$ to $(Y/P)_2$.

In principle, the Fed can totally insulate real income and output from fluctuations in the IS curve by pursuing a combination policy that establishes a vertical LM curve. This is not desirable in practice, however, because the LM curve is also subject to unexpected fluctuations. Unexpected shifts in the LM curve have large effects on real output and income when the LM curve is vertical.

Transitory shifts in both the IS and the LM curves have little lasting effect on the economy. Permanent shifts have a more lasting effect. One of the most difficult policy problems involves distinguishing permanent from transitory shifts

FIGURE 18.9
A COMBINATION POLICY THAT
REDUCES THE QUANTITY OF
MONEY WHEN THE INTEREST
RATE RISES AND INCREASES THE
QUANTITY OF MONEY WHEN THE
INTEREST RATE FALLS.

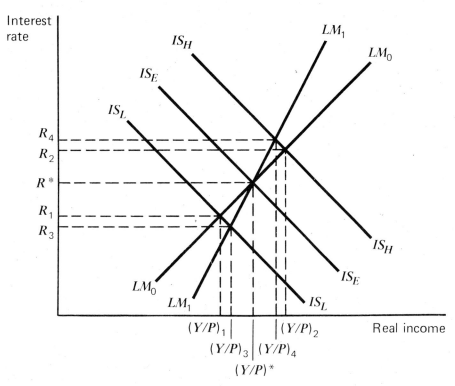

in the *IS* and *LM* curves.[15] When the *IS* curve shifts, is this just a transitory change in consumption, investment, or net exports; or have more permanent changes occurred? When the *LM* curve shifts, has there been a relatively permanent change in money demand or the money multiplier, or is the shift simply transitory?

There is no reliable way to distinguish transitory from permanent shifts quickly. With the passage of time, the permanence of shifts will be revealed, but policy decisions must be made before ultimate truth is revealed. We have seen that there

---

[15] Problems also arise in distinguishing transitory from permanent shifts in aggregate supply.

are costs of mistaking permanent shifts for transitory ones, and there are costs of mistaking transitory shifts for permanent ones. As we will see later in this chapter, the Federal Reserve expends considerable effort in attempting to determine whether *IS* and *LM* shifts are permanent or transitory. One important step is to determine which curve has shifted. It turns out that this is often a difficult question to answer.

An example makes the point. Assume that the Fed initially sets total reserves at a value consistent with achieving the expected real income $(Y/P)^*$ and the interest rate R^*. The interest rate starts to rise above R^*. This movement is consistent with either a rightward shift in the *IS* curve or an upward shift in the *LM* curve. There is no way to deduce from the increase in the interest rate which curve (or both) shifted. It is necessary to look for other information to help confirm which curve unexpectedly shifted. If data on real income or real output were available on a timely basis, it would be possible to isolate the cause of the increase in the interest rate. For example, a shift in the *IS* curve produces a rise in the interest rate and a rise in real income. A shift in the *LM* curve produces a rise in the interest rate and a fall in real income (or at least no rise). Data on real income or real output are available only with a substantial lag, however. It is necessary to use data that are available quickly that serve as indicators of real income. For example, data on retail sales are available relatively quickly, and retail sales are positively, but imperfectly, correlated with total income. If the interest rate is rising and retail sales are rising also, it is likely that the *IS* curve has shifted. This implies that the interest rate should be allowed to rise in order to reduce excess demand. If retail sales are not rising, it is likely that the *LM* curve has shifted. This implies that the interest rate should not be allowed to rise.

Because both the *IS* and *LM* curves can shift at the same time and because retail sales are not a perfect indicator of the behavior of aggregate demand, errors may be reduced by allowing the interest rate to rise, but not by as much as implied by sticking to a fixed quantity of reserves.[16] This means that the quantities of reserves and money are allowed to increase somewhat. Thus, monetary policy allows the interest rate to rise, but by less than what is implied by a fixed quantity of reserves. This is another example of a combination policy, but here the degree of monetary accommodation depends upon the behavior of the particular set of imperfect data that is observed.

The policy problem is made even more difficult by unexpected shifts in aggregate supply. We saw in Chapter 16 that shifts in aggregate supply directly affect real output and the price level. Movements in the price level affect aggregate demand through changes in real wealth and real reserves, and they affect net exports. An analysis of how policy should operate in a world where there are shifts in aggregate supply as well as in aggregate demand is beyond the

---

[16] For a full discussion of how policy should respond to imperfect information, see J. Kareken, T. Meunch, and N. Wallace, "Optimal Open Market Strategy: The Use of Information Variables," *American Economic Review*, March 1973, pp. 156–172.

scope of this text. It should be noted, however, that unexpected shifts in aggregate supply add a new source of fluctuations in real income and the price level.[17] The same is true of international developments that affect the exchange rate, net exports, and domestic interest rates.

THE THEORETICAL CASE FOR FIXED MONETARY POLICY RULES

This section presents the theoretical case for a fixed (unchanging) monetary policy as opposed to a discretionary policy that is changed in an effort to achieve greater economic stability. The issue is an important one because, as we shall see in Chapter 19, discretionary and highly active economic policies have been pursued in the United States during the past eighteen years. Because the performance of the economy has not been impressive, active discretionary policies may do more harm than good.

The discussion of shifts in the *IS* and *LM* curves in the previous section implies that discretionary policy is superior to a fixed policy. Given the expected position of the *IS* curve, monetary policy should provide a quantity of reserves that gives an expected level of the *LM* curve that is consistent with achieving $(Y/P)^*$. When the expected position of the *IS* curve shifts, monetary policy should change the quantity of reserves sufficiently to have an expected *LM* curve that is consistent with achieving $(Y/P)^*$. The same argument applies when the Fed sets the interest rate rather than total reserves. When the expected *IS* curve shifts, the interest rate should be changed to a value that is consistent with achieving $(Y/P)^*$. A combination policy is also guided by this strategy.

Consider the case in Figure 18.10, where the expected *IS* curve shifts right from IS_E to IS'_E. When the expected *IS* curve shifts, monetary policy should reduce the quantity of reserves and shift the expected *LM* curve up from LM_E to LM'_E. This policy reaction allows the economy to continue to achieve the desired output $(Y/P)^*$ on average. A policy that does not reduce the quantity of reserves and money enough to achieve LM'_E is counterproductive. If the quantity of reserves is left unchanged or if the quantity of reserves is not reduced sufficiently to shift the expected *LM* curve to LM'_E, aggregate demand exceeds $(Y/P)^*$ on average, and inflation results. A similar argument applies for a leftward shift in the expected *IS* curve. In all cases, monetary policy should not hold back. Rather, it should "go for it."

Discretionary policy is clearly desirable in the example summarized in Figure 18.10 because we have assumed a world of certainty equivalence. When there is

[17] For an analysis of the combined effects of unexpected fluctuations in aggregate supply and demand, see R. Craine and A. Havenner, "Choosing a Monetary Instrument: The Case of Supply-Side Shocks," *Journal of Economic Dynamics and Control*, 3:1981.

FIGURE 18.10
THERE IS NO HOLDING BACK IN A
WORLD OF CERTAINTY EQUIVALENCE.

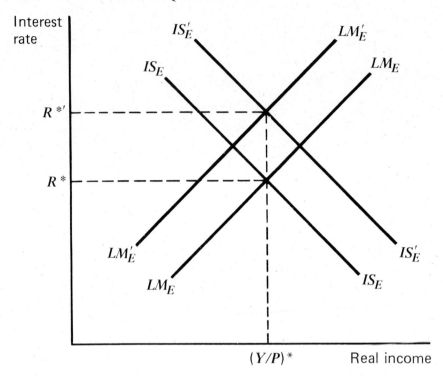

certainty equivalence, the optimal policy treats the expected positions of the *IS*
and *LM* curves as if they were known with certainty. With certainty equivalence,
the errors in predicting the *IS* and *LM* curves and, therefore, the errors in achieving $(Y/P)^*$, are not affected by the size of the policy change. The range of fluctuations in (Y/P) about $(Y/P)^*$ are minimized when the *LM* curve fully shifts
from LM_E to LM'_E.[18] There are irreducible errors in achieving $(Y/P)^*$ caused
by transitory fluctuations in the economy.

   We will now show that when we abandon the world of certainty equivalence,
the errors in achieving $(Y/P)^*$ are not independent of the size of the change in
policy. We will also show that this can make discretionary policies less attractive.
There are several reasons why certainty equivalence does not apply in the real

---

[18] We have shown that a combination policy is preferable to using either total reserves or
the interest rate alone. The conclusion in the text is not altered for a combination policy,
but the analysis is more complex.

world. One of the most important involves uncertainty about the parameters of the economic system. With certainty equivalence, it is assumed that the slopes of all the relationships in the economy are known. Thus, it is assumed that the slopes of the *IS*, *LM*, and aggregate supply schedules are known. This means for the *IS* curve, there is no uncertainty about the value of the marginal propensity to consume; the interest rate sensitivity of consumption demand; the interest rate or income sensitivity of investment demand; the marginal propensity to import; the effect of relative prices on net exports; or the effect of changes in real wealth and the price level on consumption, investment, and import demand. For the *LM* curve, it means that there is no uncertainty about the interest rate and income sensitivity of money demand, no uncertainty about the effects of changes in wealth on money demand, and no uncertainty about the effects of bond-financed deficits on interest rates. For the short-run aggregate supply curve, it means that the relationship between a change in the price level and a change in the quantity of output that firms want to produce is known exactly. Needless to say, there is no certainty about all these slopes. If follows, then, that the slopes of the *IS, LM,* and aggregate supply curves are not known with certainty.

It can be shown that when the slopes of the curves can change unexpectedly, a fixed policy may produce smaller fluctuations in real output and inflation than does a discretionary policy. This occurs because when the slopes of the curves are subject to unpredictable fluctuations, the effects on the economy of these fluctuations are not independent of the size of the change in policy. An example illustrates this point. Assume that there is a permanent, rightward shift in the expected *IS* curve above long-run aggregate supply. In the absence of a policy response, this is expected to produce excess demand and inflation. Assume that the Federal Reserve calculates, based on its best guess about the slopes of *IS* and *LM* curves, that a 5 percent reduction in the quantity of total reserves will raise interest rates and reduce aggregate demand back to equality with long-run aggregate supply. Now assume that the *LM* curve is steeper and the *IS* curve is flatter than the Fed thinks they are. In this situation, the 5 percent reduction in the quantity of reserves produces a decline in aggregate demand of such a large magnitude that, on average, real income actually falls below long-run aggregate supply.

The size of the error in achieving $(Y/P)^*$ depends not only upon the error in predicting the slopes of the *IS* and *LM* curves, but it also depends upon the size of the change in policy. The Fed has no control over the errors in predicting the slopes, but it does have control over the size of the policy change. Thus, the Fed may reduce the size of the fluctuations in real income by limiting the movements in total reserves.

The effect of the size of policy changes on the variability of real income can be shown by a formal but simple example.[19] Assume that there is a recession and the Federal Reserve wants to increase real income from $(Y/P)_1$ to $(Y/P)^*$. The

[19] For a more detailed and general treatment see W. Brainard, "Uncertainty and the Effectiveness of Policy," *American Economic Review,* May 1967.

Fed's staff estimates that the relationship between a change in total reserves and a change in real income is given by the expression

$$\Delta(Y/P) = \alpha \Delta TR + \epsilon.\ ^{20}$$

The Greek letter α is the Federal Reserve's estimate of the relationship between a change in total reserves and a change in real income, that is, $\Delta(Y/P)/\Delta TR = \alpha$. The estimated parameter α is a combination of the slopes of the *IS* and *LM* curves.[21] If the *LM* curve is relatively steep or the *IS* curve is relatively flat, or both, the parameter α is large. If the *LM* curve is relatively flat or the *IS* curve is relatively steep, or both, the parameter α is small. The Greek letter ϵ represents the errors caused by transitory shifts in the *IS* and *LM* curves. It is assumed that the average value of ϵ is zero. This implies that on average $\Delta(Y/P) = \alpha \Delta TR$.

If the parameter α is known with certainty, monetary policy can achieve its goals plus or minus the transitory error, ϵ. The change in total reserves ΔTR^* required to achieve the desired change in real income $\Delta(Y/P)^*$ is $\Delta TR^* = \Delta(Y/P)^*/\alpha$, so $(\Delta Y/P)^* = \alpha \Delta TR^*$. Because the change in real income is subject to transitory fluctuations, the actual change in income is $\Delta(Y/P) = \alpha \Delta TR^* + \epsilon$. The difference between the realized change and the desired change is $[\Delta(Y/P) - \Delta(Y/P)^*] = \alpha \Delta TR^* + \epsilon - \alpha \Delta TR^* = \epsilon$. Thus, the actual change in real income differs from the desired change by the transitory error ϵ. Note that the size of the error is not affected by the size of the change in total reserves. This means that policy should always change total reserves by the amount required to achieve $\Delta(Y/P)^*$. This policy will be successful except for the error ϵ. There is nothing that policy can do about this error, but the mean of ϵ is zero, so on average $\Delta(Y/P)^*$ is achieved. This is the lesson of certainty equivalence.

Now let us see what happens when the parameter α is not known with certainty. Recall that α is a combination of the slopes of the *IS* and *LM* curves. It is determined by the many factors that affect consumption, investment, net exports, money demand, and money supply. Policymakers attempt to estimate the parameter α, but this estimate can be in error. Changes in such factors as the marginal propensity to consume; the sensitivity of consumption and investment to interest rates; the sensitivity of investment to income; the effect of wealth on consumption and money demand; the effect of domestic income on import demand; the effects of domestic and foreign prices on net exports; the effect of the interest rate, income, and wealth on money demand; and the size of the money multiplier all affect the parameter α. This means that changes in any of these factors change α. Furthermore, as we saw in Chapter 14, the deregulation of interest rates for many transactions accounts makes the interest elasticity of money demand highly uncer-

---

[20] We will see later in this chapter that both econometric models and expert judgment are used by the staff to predict the relationship between a change in policy and changes in the goals of policy.

[21] The parameter α is also affected by the slope of the aggregate supply function. For simplicity, we will omit references to aggregate supply.

tain. It is unlikely that the parameter α can be estimated accurately or that it remains constant.

Changes in the parameter α influence the effectiveness of monetary policy. We can still write the expression for the change in real income as $\Delta(Y/P) = \alpha\Delta TR + \epsilon$, but now α is not a constant. It has an expected value of $\bar{\alpha}$, but the actual value fluctuates around that expected value. This means that the expected change in income is $E[\Delta(Y/P)] = \bar{\alpha}\Delta TR$ but the realized value is $\Delta(Y/P) = \alpha\Delta TR + \epsilon$. The difference between the realized and the expected change in real income is $\Delta(Y/P) - E[\Delta(Y/P)] = \alpha\Delta TR + \epsilon - \bar{\alpha}\Delta TR = (\alpha - \bar{\alpha})\Delta TR + \epsilon$. Now we see that when actual α differs from expected α, the size of the change in policy, ΔTR, affects the difference between realized and expected income. For a given change in total reserves, ΔTR, when actual α is larger than $\bar{\alpha}$, the change in income produced by the change in total reserves is larger than expected. When α is smaller than $\bar{\alpha}$, the change in income is less than expected. The variability of actual $\Delta(Y/P)$ about $E[\Delta(Y/P)]$ depends on (1) the transitory shifts of IS and LM embodied in ϵ, (2) deviations of actual α from $\bar{\alpha}$, and (3) the size of the change in total reserves.

There is nothing that policymakers can do about either ϵ or $(\alpha - \bar{\alpha})$. The effects that deviations of α from $\bar{\alpha}$ have on real output can be affected by policy, however. By limiting the size of the change in total reserves, the Fed reduces the effect that $(\alpha - \bar{\alpha})$ has on the realized change in income.

The issues involved are illustrated in Figure 18.11. In Panel I, the expected change in real income, E, is on the vertical axis, and the standard deviation of the change in income, σ, is on the horizontal axis. As explained in Chapter 5, the standard deviation is a measure of the variability of the actual change in real income relative to the expected change. It represents the risk that actual $\Delta(Y/P)$ will deviate from expected $\Delta(Y/P)$. This risk is affected by the variability of ϵ, the variability of α, and the size of the change in total reserves. Panel I shows an upward-sloping curve describing the trade-off between the expected change in real income, E, and the standard deviation of the change in income, σ. There is a trade-off because when there is a large change in total reserves, there is a large change in expected real income and also an increase in the standard deviation of real income. At point A, there is no change in total reserves, that is, $\Delta TR = 0$. With no change in total reserves, the expected change in income is also zero. Because of the transitory shifts in the IS and LM curves, ϵ, there are unexpected changes in real income even with an unchanged policy. Thus, the standard deviation of the change in income is σ_0. This equals the standard deviation of ϵ.

Now assume that the Fed wants to increase real income.[22] It accomplishes this by increasing total reserves. The expected increase in (Y/P) is E_1. The increase in total reserves also raises the standard deviation of the change in real income because of deviations of α from $\bar{\alpha}$. Thus, to achieve the expected rise in real income,

---

[22] As we are dealing with changes in real income, the argument that follows also applies to a desired decrease in real income.

FIGURE 18.11
RISK REDUCES POLICY
AGGRESSIVENESS.

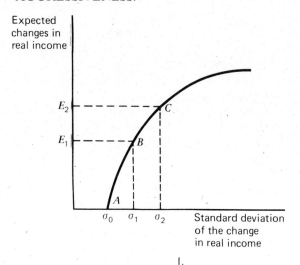

I.

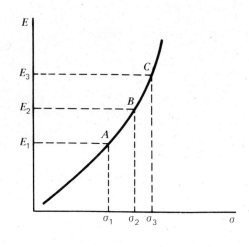

II.

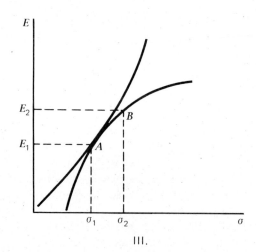

III.

E_1, the Fed has to accept the larger value of the standard deviation of real income, σ_1. This takes us to point B. By a similar argument, the Fed can achieve a larger expected rise in real income, E_2, by producing a larger increase in total reserves. This increases the variability of real income to σ_2 so we are at point C.

Assume that in the absence of risk the Fed would like to achieve the rise in real income indicated by E_2 because this increases expected real income to its desired value $(Y/P)^*$. The rise in expected real income can be achieved by an appropriate increase in total reserves. The Fed must determine, however, whether this policy change is worth the risk. Variability in α, the relationship between a change in total reserves and a change in income, implies that the variability of the change in real income rises to σ_2. The Fed may decide that the increased risk (variability) is not worth achieving the expected rise in real income, E_2.

Assuming that policymakers are risk averse, the trade-off between the expected value and risk that the Fed is willing to accept is shown in Panel II of Figure 18.11.[23] The Federal Reserve will accept additional variability in real income, that is, higher values of σ, only if there is a sufficiently large gain in the expected change in income, E. For example, the Fed is willing to move the economy from point A to point B. The rise in the expected change in income to E_2 just compensates for the increased risk, σ_2. The Fed is also willing to move to point C with its higher expected value and risk. The move from point B to point C involves a smaller increase in risk than the move from point A to point B. This occurs because the larger the amount of risk, the less additional risk the Fed is willing to accept. The trade-off curve in Panel II is the Fed's indifference curve describing the combinations of expected value and risk for which it is indifferent.

Panel III of Figure 18.11 combines the available trade-off between the expected change and risk of Panel I with the Fed's indifference curve of Panel II. At point A the Fed has done the best that it can do given its preferences and given the available trade-off between expected value and risk. In general, this optimal point involves a smaller expected change in real income than what would be dictated by certainty equivalence. Point B corresponds to the expected increase in real income, E_2, that the Fed would like to achieve if it did not have to worry about the effect of its policies on σ. This raises expected real income to $(Y/P)^*$. Because the increase in reserves required to achieve E_2 raises the variability of real income to σ_2, the Fed is not willing to increase reserves by this amount. It settles for a smaller increase in total reserves and a smaller increase in expected income to limit the variability in income. Thus, it only wants to achieve point A rather than point B.

We conclude that because the relationship between a change in total reserves and the change in real income is uncertain, the Fed will limit the change in total reserves. Thus, it changes total reserves by a smaller amount than would be dictated by a world where α is known with certainty. The more uncertain the Federal Reserve is about α, the smaller is the change in total reserves that it wants to produce. Because α is uncertain, the Fed pursues a more conservative policy in the sense that it avoids large changes in total reserves. This prevents the Federal Reserve from achieving the change it would otherwise like to have, but it limits the variability in real income. Thus, policy does not "go for" $(Y/P)^*$, but plans to fall short of this goals. The change in reserves required to hit $(Y/P)^*$, on average, involves too great a risk of overshooting the target.

So far we have only discussed the role of uncertainty in a static framework. When we introduce dynamic considerations, the case for conservative monetary

---

[23] A detailed discussion of risk aversion and the indifference curves implied by risk aversion is given in Chapter 5.

policy becomes even stronger.[24] We explained earlier in this chapter that because there are lags in the response of the economy to changes in monetary policy, the Fed must be forward-looking. For example, if there is a rightward shift in the *IS* curve, it takes time for monetary policy to offset the effects of the excess demand. There are two sources of uncertainty that are relevant for making policy in a dynamic environment. First, the Fed must forecast the future position of the *IS* curve. Will it permanently remain at its higher level, will it shift out even farther in the future, or will it return to its old position? Second, there is uncertainty concerning the lagged relationship between changes in monetary policy and changes in real income, inflation, and capital formation. The lags in the impact of monetary policy are long and variable.

Both of these forms of uncertainty call for a relatively conservative response to shifts in the *IS* curve. The reasons for this conservation are basically the same as for the static case discussed earlier. With the future difficult to predict and with long and variable lags, strong policy moves that are designed to return the economy to its desired state can increase the size of economic fluctuations. A strong response to what is perceived as a permanent shift in aggregate demand or aggregate supply can drive the economy farther away from $(Y/P)^*$ if the shift proves to be transitory. Because of the lags in the effect of policy, it is difficult to reverse the effects of an aggressive tightening or easing of policy. Furthermore, because the lags are variable and difficult to predict, strong policy moves can increase the variability of the economy.

FIXED RULES VERSUS DISCRETION IN MONETARY POLICY

The analysis of the effects of uncertainty on policymaking leads us to the continuing debate among economists concerning fixed rules versus discretion for monetary policy. One school of thought argues that monetary policy should make no attempt to offset the effects of fluctuations in aggregated demand or supply.[25] The lags in effect of changes in monetary policy are so long and variable and the future is so uncertain that attempts to offset economic fluctuations do more harm than good. It is argued that many economic fluctuations have been the result of policy changes rather than exogenous shifts in aggregate demand and supply. These fluctuations can be eliminated if monetary policy follows a fixed rule. In the absence of economic growth, this entails maintaining the amount of total

---

[24] For a more detailed and general treatment of dynamic considerations, see R. Craine, "Optimal Monetary Policy with Uncertainty," *Journal of Economic Dynamics and Control*, *1*:1979.

[25] This issue was raised initially in Henry C. Simons, "Rules Versus Authorities in Monetary Policy," *Journal of Political Economy, 44*:1946.

reserves (or monetary base) at a constant level. Under the implicit assumption that the money multiplier is stable, this translates into a constant quantity of money. Because of growth in the labor force, capital stock, and productivity, real output grows over time. A fixed policy in this environment means a constant rate of growth in total reserves and money. This school of thought argues that the Federal Reserve should not have the authority to engage in discretionary stabilization policy. It should be required to pursue a fixed policy rule.

There are other economists who believe that active stabilization policy is essential for maintaining economic stability. They argue that the Fed should be allowed to vary the growth in total reserves (or monetary base) in order to offset the effects of exogenous shifts in aggregate demand and aggregate supply. These economists argue that the Federal Reserve must have the authority to engage aggressively in stabilization policy, and they strongly oppose the imposition of a policy rule.

Although many economists reject both a fixed policy and a highly aggressive policy, it is useful to analyze the issues in terms of these extremes. One extreme is to keep policy unchanged (in terms of the rate of money growth) under all circumstances. This means that policy should make no attempt to offset fluctuations in real output, employment, or inflation. Policy should remain fixed irrespective of the size or source of the fluctuations. The other extreme involves aggressive use of monetary policy to push the economy back to its desired state. This involves attempts to "fine tune" the economy.

We have seen that in a world of certainty, fine tuning is always feasible and desirable. In this situation, an unchanged policy makes no sense when there are shifts in aggregate demand and supply. When we leave the world of certainty and of certainty equivalence, however, an unchanged policy begins to have some appeal. Because of uncertainty about the true parameters of the economic system, because of lags in the impact of policy, because the lags are variable (uncertain), and because the future is difficult to predict, aggressive policy may cause more harm than good.

There is no clear resolution to the debate on rules versus discretion because there is disagreement about the extent of uncertainty that policymakers face. Recent experience does suggest, however, that there is sufficient uncertainty about the future to make strongly aggressive monetary policy undesirable. This does not imply, however, that the Federal Reserve should slavishly follow a fixed rule irrespective of the circumstances.

The extent to which monetary policy should attempt to offset economic fluctuations depends upon the degree of uncertainty about the future and upon the degree of uncertainty about the dynamic response of the economy to policy changes. This uncertainty reduces the extent to which policy should attempt to offset economic fluctuations. It should be stressed, however, that uncertainty does not imply that policy should be totally unresponsive to economic fluctuations. An unchanged policy is only appropriate if there is complete ignorance of the future and complete ignorance about how the economy responds to policy.

Most economists conclude that neither a highly aggressive nor a fixed policy is desirable. The Federal Reserve should steer a middle course between these two extremes. There are times when some obvious event occurs, such as a massive increase in the price of oil by OPEC, or a war, when policy should move relatively aggressively to cushion the effects. Even in these cases, however, highly aggressive policy is probably not appropriate because of ignorance concerning how the economy will respond to the policy change. There are other times when the sources and permanence of economic fluctuations are difficult to identify and highly uncertain. In these cases, the policy response should be small and will be quite similar to an unchanged policy rule.

There is no getting around the fact that policymaking is more art than science. The degree of policy change depends upon the circumstances and upon the judgment of policymakers in an uncertain environment. It is argued in Chapter 19 that policy has moved too aggressively in recent years. Compared to the policies that were actually pursued, an unchanged policy has some appeal. There is a better alternative available, however. Less aggressive policy moves can improve upon an unchanged policy. Although attempts to "fine tune" the economy are inappropriate, so too is a policy that refuses to change no matter what the economic circumstances.

THE EFFECT OF MONETARY POLICY ON EXPECTATIONS

Up to this point, we have assumed that the expectations of households and firms are not affected by monetary policy. This assumption allowed us to simplify the analysis, but it is not realistic. In making their consumption and investment decisions, households and firms form expectations concerning future income, prices, and interest rates. Because income, prices, and interest rates are affected by monetary policy, the public explicitly or implicitly forms expectations about future monetary policy. This produces the situation where the Fed guesses about the expectations of the public in formulating its monetary policy and the public guesses about future monetary policy in formulating its consumption and investment plans. Thus, monetary policy is affected by the expectations of the public, and these expectations are, in part, affected by the public's perception of future monetary policy.

This interaction between the expectations of the public and the expectations of the Fed complicates monetary policy. In particular, when the Fed changes monetary policy, it must take into account the effect of the change on the expectations of the public.[26] For example, when the Fed reduces the growth of reserves and

---

[26] This important point is a reason why the "rational expectations" school favors fixed rules. Though the topic of rational expectations is beyond the scope of this book, the affect of monetary policy on the expectations is not. For an analysis of the implications of this effect, see R. Lucas, "Econometric Policy Evaluation: A Critique," in *The Phillips Curve and Labor Markets*, K. Brunner and A. Meltzer (eds.), Carnegie-Rochester Conference Series, Vol. 1, Amsterdam: North-Holland, 1976.

money, the public forms expectations of the permanence and degree of effect of the policy tightening. These expectations affect the extent to which the public reduces consumption and investment. Because expectations are difficult to predict, we have an additional reason for expecting a variable relationship between changes in total reserves and changes in real output, employment, and prices to exist.

A virtue of a policy rule is that it is predictable. This means that when the Fed follows a rule, the public does not have to figure out what monetary policy is doing. It is relieved of the task of figuring out the permanence and significance of policy changes. This eliminates at least one source of variability in the relationship between changes in reserves and change in real output.

It should be pointed out that the Federal Reserve could also reduce uncertainty by announcing what its policy is and how long it expects to pursue it. Historically, the Federal Reserve has been unwilling to make such announcements because it wants to retain "flexibility." This flexibility can produce considerable uncertainty in the minds of the public. This reduces the predictability of the relationship between a change in policy and changes in the ultimate objectives of policy.[27]

As we shall see in Chapter 19, over the last eighteen years monetary policy has taken some dramatic and unpredictable swings. This has increased public uncertainty, and it has produced a credibility problem for the Fed. Even when the Federal Reserve does announce its policy plans, the public is skeptical that the policy actually will be pursued. This reduces the chance that the policy will be successful, which, in turn, reduces the chance that the policy will be pursued for long. These complications reinforce the conclusion that monetary policy should avoid erratic changes in the pursuit of its objectives or erratic changes in its objectives.

MONETARY POLICY IN PRACTICE

Now that we have discussed some of the theoretical issues in designing effective stabilization policies, it is time to examine how monetary policy is conducted in practice. The discussion begins with a broad overview of how the Federal Reserve goes about making its policy decisions. We then turn to some specific issues in the practice of monetary policy. Among these are the use of growth of the quantity of money as an intermediate policy objective and the Fed's ability to control the quantity of money.

An Overview of the Policy Process

As explained in Chapter 12, the primary policymaking body within the Federal Reserve is the Federal Open Market Committee (FOMC). The FOMC deter-

---

[27] Some economists assert that monetary policy is powerful precisely because it surprises the public. These surprises are not productive, however, if they add to economic fluctuations.

mines the Fed's policies with respect to the quantity of reserves in the depository system, and it sets objectives for short-term interest rates. Policies concerning the discount rate and reserve requirements are coordinated with, and are largely subordinate to, the policies of the FOMC.

The FOMC meets approximately every six weeks in Washington, D.C., to review recent economic developments, to debate policy alternatives, and to determine the actual policy that will be pursued. Though only five of the twelve Federal Reserve Bank presidents vote on the FOMC, all twelve attend the meetings and take part in the discussion.

Only the members and the small staff of the FOMC are allowed to attend meetings. The content of the meetings is a tightly held secret. A few days following an FOMC meeting, a short summary is released describing the *previous* meeting. This summary, which is called the "record of policy actions," lists the FOMC's decisions at the previous meeting and provides a short discussion of the reasons for the decisions.[28]

At each meeting, the manager of the open market account (trading desk) in New York makes a presentation concerning the open market operations that have been conducted since the last meeting and gives an evaluation of the condition of financial markets. A report is also made about developments in foreign exchange markets and, when relevant, about the foreign desk's operations in the markets. The economic staff of the FOMC then makes a presentation concerning the current and prospective state of the economy.[29] A variety of topics is covered including recent developments for output, employment, and inflation as well as recent developments in financial markets, including the behavior of interest rates and of the growth in money and credit.

The staff also presents its latest economic forecast. Areas where there have been surprising developments or where there is greater than normal uncertainty receive particular attention. For example, uncertainty about the effects of financial innovation and deregulation may be discussed in detail. Similarly, if long-term interest rates have behaved strangely or if consumption or investment are unusually high or low relative to income, an analysis is made of these developments. Furthermore, if the future course of fiscal policy or international factors is

---

[28] The records of policy actions are issued initially as press releases. They are later published in the Federal Reserve *Bulletin* and in the *Annual Report* of the Board of Governors.

[29] The FOMC's staff is composed of staff members from the Board of Governors and the Federal Reserve banks. The chief economist to the FOMC is always a senior member of the Board's staff, and several other senior staff members from the Board serve as associate economists. The heads of research for the five Federal Reserve banks whose presidents serve as voting members are also associate economists. Economic presentations and advice during meetings are almost the exclusive preserve of the economists who are employed by the Board of Governors. This gives the Chairman of the Board of Governors and of the FOMC ability to influence the flow of economic information, and is an important source of power for the chairman.

particularly uncertain, the staff draws attention to these uncertainties and assesses the implications of alternative developments.

The FOMC's staff revises its forecasts continually as new information is received and as events develop. At least twice a year a major effort is made to rethink the forecast in preparation for the chairman's testimony before Congress concerning the FOMC's targets. At those times, a major portion of the FOMC's time is devoted to the new forecasts.

It should be noted that the forecasts produced for a policymaking body such as the FOMC are different from the forecasts produced by private forecasters. When private forecasters produce their projections of the economic future, they must forecast the future course of monetary policy. This is often not an easy task because monetary policy can and does change unexpectedly. This means that private forecasts have embodied in them the forecasters' best guesses concerning the future course of monetary policy. In contrast, the forecasts generated by the FOMC's staff are conditioned by specific assumptions concerning future monetary policy.[30] For example, one forecast is based on the assumption that monetary policy remains unchanged. Another forecast is based on the assumption that the FOMC either slows or accelerates the growth of reserves, money, and credit. These forecasts serve as a basis for the deliberations of the FOMC concerning the policies that it should adopt for the future.

In preparing its forecasts and analysis of policy alternatives, the FOMC's staff uses a variety of approaches. The staff uses econometric models of the entire economy, as well as detailed econometric models of the financial sector. The predictions from these models are modified to the extent that expert opinion and judgment by the staff dictate. The blending of the prediction from formal models with the judgment of seasoned staff observers is a means of dealing with uncertainties concerning the true structure of the economy and the future course of exogenous events.

The FOMC divides its decision-making process into two parts. The first part involves the ultimate policy objectives of real output, employment and inflation. Here the discussion is usually in terms of the growth in money that is required to achieve goals for these policy objectives. Because there are substantial lags between changes in the quantity of money and changes in output, inflation, and employment, the FOMC discusses the likely response over the next year or two of these variables to alternative money growth assumptions. It is during these discussions that unpleasant trade-offs between unemployment and price stability often surface and that the uncertainties about the future are most in evidence.

The ultimate objectives of policy and the money growth targets considered necessary to achieve them are subject to intensive evaluation twice a year in preparation for the chairman's congressional testimony required by the

---

[30] As explained in the previous section, the effects of the assumed monetary policy are affected by the public's expectations of what monetary policy will actually be.

Humphrey-Hawkins Act. In February a money growth target is determined for one year ahead. In July the current year's target is reevaluated, and a preliminary target is set for the next year. Implicit in the FOMC's money growth decision is an expectation of the relationship between money growth and the behavior of output, inflation, and employment.

The FOMC does not set a single target for money growth, such as 4 percent per year, but rather a range.[31] For example, it may determine that, between the fourth quarter of 1982 and the fourth quarter of 1983, the quantity of money should grow at between 3 and 5 percent. There are two reasons for this approach. First, the relationship between money growth and the ultimate objectives of policy is uncertain. By adopting a range for money growth, the FOMC retains flexibility to allow the growth to vary within the range as economic conditions develop. Second, adoption of a range for money growth rather than a single figure makes it easier for the FOMC to reach an agreement. The actual policy adopted is often the result of compromises that must be struck to achieve a majority vote among the twelve FOMC members. As explained in Chapter 12, the chairman of the FOMC has greater influence than the other members of the committee, but the chairman often has to modify his position to gain the votes of the other members. Substantial majorities are easier to reach when the FOMC is determining a range for money growth rather than a single value. Members who want slow money growth favor the low end of the range; members who favor more rapid growth favor the upper end. The ability to obtain substantial majorities is important because the FOMC likes to speak with a unified voice to the outside world and, therefore, attempts to achieve unanimous or near unanimous votes.

The second part of the policy process involves determining what growth in reserves and money and what range of fluctuations in short-term interest rates to allow until the next FOMC meeting. This involves projections of money demand and supply over the next six weeks or so. Shifts in money demand and supply can make the quantity of money grow more rapidly or more slowly than is consistent with the FOMC's longer-term objectives for money growth. Shifts in money demand and supply also affect short-term interest rates. When shifts occur, the FOMC must determine whether they are transitory or relatively permanent. If the shifts are transitory, money will return to its path with an unchanged policy. If the shifts are more permanent, a change in the growth of reserves is required to bring money back on target. In this situation, the FOMC must determine the speed with which it wants to return money growth to its desired path following a deviation. This is important because a rapid return of money growth to target requires a large change in reserves. This, in turn, produces large changes in short-term interest rates. The staff assists the FOMC in determining its short-run strategy by

---

[31] As we will see in the next section of this chapter, the FOMC sets target ranges for several different measures of "money."

providing predictions from formal econometric models that are modified by expert opinion and judgment.

The FOMC typically follows a short-run strategy that involves both the quantity of money (reserves) and the short-term interest rate. This approach is a means of dealing with uncertainty and is consistent with the combination policy discussed in the theoretical section of this chapter. If there is an unexpected increase in money demand, the short-term interest rate rises to equate the greater money demand with the fixed supply. When the money demand shift occurs, the Fed does not know whether the shift is permanent or transitory. Furthermore, it does not know the source of the shift. Has the public become more cautious and increased its demand for money, or is aggregate demand higher than expected and, therefore, the transactions demand for money has increased? If the public has become more cautious and if the shift in public preferences is more than transitory, the Fed should offset this upward shift in the *LM* curve by providing more reserves. This increases the quantity of money and pushes the short-term interest rate back to its previous value. If the cause of the shift in money demand is an unexpected increase in aggregate demand, the appropriate response is to keep reserves unchanged and let the short-term interest rate rise. Because the FOMC does not know either the permanence or the source of the shift, it compromises by allowing some increase in the short-term interest rate and some increase in reserves.

Much of the discussion of short-run operating strategy involves how much of a change in reserves and how much of a change in short-term interest rates should occur when there are unexpected shifts in either money demand or money supply. The end result of the discussion involves a directive to the trading desk in New York concerning the growth in money that is to be pursued until the next FOMC meeting. As was the case with the FOMC's longer-term objectives, the targeted growth in money is stated in terms of a range rather than as a single growth rate.

The directive also includes a range over which the FOMC will allow the federal funds rate to fluctuate.[32] If the federal funds rate rises above the upper limit or falls below the lower limit, the FOMC is consulted to determine whether or not to allow the federal funds rate to fluctuate outside the band. If it is determined that the federal funds rate should remain within the band, the trading desk is instructed to provide additional reserves or reduce reserves in order to push the interest rate back within the band.

A major short-run policy decision involves the width of the band for the federal funds rate. If the band is narrow, short-term interest rates are not allowed to change very much. This means that unexpected shifts in money demand or the money multiplier produce changes in the quantity of reserves and money. If the band for the Federal funds rate is wide, unexpected shifts in money demand or supply produce changes in short-term interest rates rather than changes in reserves

[32] As explained in Chapter 8, the federal funds rate is the interest rate on interbank loans.

and money. Choice of the width of the band is part of the FOMC's technical policy judgment concerning how to deal with current uncertainties.

It is important to note that when the FOMC controls the range of fluctuations in the federal funds rate, it also affects the range of fluctuations in other short-term interest rates as well. To see why this is so, consider the example of an unexpected increase in money demand. With a fixed supply of money, the interest rates on Treasury bills and other short-term securities rise until the public is willing to hold the same quantity of money as before the demand shift. With higher interest rates, depository institutions want to increase their holdings of securities. They attempt to obtain the funds, in part, by increasing their borrowing in the federal funds market. When the quantity of total reserves remains fixed, this pushes up the federal funds rate. If the rise in the federal funds rate is sufficiently large, it will exceed the upper limit set by the FOMC. When this occurs, the FOMC instructs the manager of the open market account to purchase securities. This increases the quantity of reserves and pushes the federal funds rate back down. The rise in the quantity of reserves produces an increase in the quantity of money. With a greater quantity of money, the interest rates on Treasury bills and other short-term instruments are pushed back down. Part of the increase in money demand is met by an increase in money supply. We conclude that by controlling fluctuations in the federal funds rate, the FOMC also limits the extent of fluctuations in other short-term interest rates.[33]

The Monetary Aggregates

We have defined the quantity of money in this text to be currency and transactions account balances held by the public. In fact, the Federal Reserve uses a number of different measures of money and liquid assets in formulating its policy. These measures are called *monetary aggregates.*

The definitions of the monetary aggregates are shown in Table 18.1. Our definition of money is M1. It includes media that can be used directly to conduct transactions. As shown in Table 18.1, M1 includes currency (actually, currency held by other than depository institutions), traveler's checks, demand deposit accounts, and other transactions accounts (NOWs, super NOWs, share draft accounts, and automatic transfer savings accounts). All the transactions accounts included in M1 are free of regulatory limits on the number of drafts that can be drawn or other third party payments that can be made. The M1 measure does exclude other financial assets on which unlimited drafts can be drawn, such as shares in money market mutual funds (MMMFs). Often there are minimum size restrictions on MMMF drafts, and the evidence suggests that a relatively small number of drafts are, in fact, drawn on such accounts. Also excluded from M1 are those

---

[33] It is left to the reader to work through the cases of reductions in money demand and shifts in the money multiplier.

TABLE 18.1
MEASURES OF THE MONEY STOCK AND LIQUID ASSETS SEPTEMBER 1983
(BILLIONS OF DOLLARS, SEASONALLY ADJUSTED UNLESS OTHERWISE NOTED)

Aggregates and Components	Amount
M1 Includes	$ 517
Currency (held by the public)	$ 143
Traveler's checks of nonbank issuers	5
Demand deposit accounts	243
Other transactions accounts at all depository institutions	126
M2 Includes[a]	$2,145
M1	$ 517
Overnight RPs issued by commercial banks and overnight Eurodollars held by U.S. residents at overseas branches of U.S. Banks NSA	53
Money market mutual funds shares (general purpose and broker/dealer, taxable and nontaxable) NSA	138
Savings accounts at all depository institutions	321
Money market accounts at all depository institutions NSA	367
Small denomination time accounts at all depository institutions[b]	758
M3 Includes[c]	$2,543
M2	$2,145
Large time accounts at all depository institutions[d]	318
Money market mutual funds (institution-only) NSA	39
Term RPS at all depository institutions NSA[e]	45
L Includes	$3,137
M3	$2,543
Other Eurodollars held by U.S. residents NSA	93
Bankers acceptances	43
Commercial paper	125
Savings bonds	70
Liquid Treasury obligations	263

[a] M2 is less than the sum of its components by a consolidation adjustment representing the amount of demand deposit accounts at commercial banks owned by thrift institutions that are estimated to be used in servicing their savings, MMA, and small time accounts.

[b] Time accounts in amounts less than $100,000. Includes retail repurchase agreements.

[c] M3 is less than the sum of its components by a consolidation adjustment that represents the estimated amount of overnight repurchase agreements held by institution-only MMMFs.

[d] Time accounts in amounts of $100,000 or more.

[e] Excludes retail repurchase agreements.

Note: NSA means "not seasonally adjusted."

Source: Board of Governors of the Federal Reserve System.

accounts for which there are regulatory limits on the number of permissible third party payments, such as money market accounts (MMAs) at depository institutions.

It should be noted that though MMAs and MMMFs are excluded from M1, some transaction accounts in M1 also are not very actively used for transactions purposes. Furthermore, other transactions accounts (OTCAs), which pay a market interest rate, evidently are viewed by many holders as both a transaction account and a repository of liquid assets much like a savings account. As a result, the public's demand for OTCAs, which have become a growing proportion of M1, may be responsive to different factors from those affecting the other more conventional components of M1. The growth of OTCAs adds to the difficulties of interpreting M1 and using it as a monetary policy guide during a period of rapid financial change.

The next monetary aggregate, M2, includes financial assets of the public that are liquid and can be converted into transaction balances with relative ease even though they cannot generally be used directly for transactions. As a way to minimize distortions to this measure produced by shifts among similar assets, instruments that are good substitutes for each other as liquid assets (such as MMAs and MMMFs) are included in M2, and those balances that are held for very long-term purposes (such as retirement accounts) are excluded from this aggregate.[34] For reasons of either limited data sources or because of the necessity of adopting relatively arbitrary dividing lines, M2 excludes certain important liquid assets (such as Treasury bills and commercial paper) but includes long-term time accounts that can be converted to transactions balances only at a relatively high cost (i.e., large early withdrawal penalties).

The components of M2 are shown in the second part of Table 18.1. In addition to M1, M2 includes savings accounts, MMAs, general purpose and broker/dealer MMMFs (both taxable and nontaxable funds), overnight repurchase agreements at commercial banks, overnight Eurodollars held by U.S. residents at overseas branches of U.S. banks, and small denomination (less than $100,000) time accounts (including retail repurchase agreements).

The broadest monetary aggregate, M3, is similar in concept to M2. It adds to M2 certain other liquid assets that are mostly held by large asset holders: large denomination CDs (those issued in amounts of $100,000 or more), term repurchase agreements (in denomination of $100,000 or more) at all depository institutions, and those MMMFs (taxable and tax-exempt) whose shares are restricted to institutions. The M3 measure thus contains, in addition to other financial assets, *all* account liabilities issued by depository institutions with the exception of those held by (1) other depository institutions (to avoid double counting), (2) the U.S.

[34] There is, for example, considerable evidence that most of the flows in and out of MMMFs and MMAs have come from or gone into other M2 assets. As a result, developments that have changed the relative importance of these assets have not significantly affected the M2 measures for more than a relatively short period.

government, and (3) foreign governments and official institutions (on the grounds that the behavior of such balances is largely unrelated to spending and economic activity in the United States).[35]

In addition to the above measures of the monetary aggregates, the Federal Reserve also publishes a measure of liquid assets, L. In addition to M3, L includes bankers acceptances, commercial paper, savings bonds, marketable Treasury and agency obligations with original maturities of less than 18 months, and other Eurodollar deposits held by U.S. residents. This series, the size of which is shown in the bottom panel of Table 18.1, is published with a relatively long lag because of delayed data availability.

All the monetary and liquid asset aggregates focus on the *asset* side of the public's balance sheet. Credit measures, in contrast, focus on the public's *debt*. In 1983 the FOMC indicated that it would pay attention to a broad measure of debt to augment and cross-check information conveyed by the monetary aggregates. This debt measure, D, is the borrowing of the domestic nonfinancial public, that is, the borrowing of all levels of government, nonfinancial business, and households. The debt series is positively correlated with aggregate expenditures and output, but is far removed from direct control of the Federal Reserve. The FOMC viewed the debt measure to be especially valuable as a source of information about financial markets and monetary policy pressures at those times when the monetary aggregates were being distorted by regulatory changes or innovations or by changes in the public's financial asset preferences.

Table 18.2 shows the size (as of the end of 1982) of total unadjusted debt (line 1), as well as the size of adjustments (line 2), to arrive at domestic nonfinancial debt, D (line 3). As indicated in the bottom panel of the table, commercial bank credit accounts for only about one fourth of domestic nonfinancial debt and other depository institutions another 15 percent. The bank and other depository credit flows fluctuate over a wider range than does total nonfinancial debt, and, therefore, the growth rate of such credit is often not representative of the growth rate of total nonfinancial debt.

Using the Monetary Aggregates

In practice, the FOMC sets long-term objectives for the three aggregates, M1, M2, and M3.[36] These objectives are stated in terms of desired growth ranges over the coming year for each aggregate. For example, the objectives for the period between the fourth quarter of 1982 to the fourth quarter of 1983 were 4.5 to 8.5 percent for M1, 7 to 10 percent for M2, and 6.5 to 9.5 percent for M3.[37]

---

[35] Balances held by all such parties are also removed from M1 and M2, where applicable.

[36] As mentioned earlier, the FOMC also looks at total liquid assets, L, and at total debt, D, but it does not set ranges for them.

[37] The ranges appear in the FOMC's record of policy actions.

TABLE 18.2
DERIVATION OF DOMESTIC NONFINANCIAL DEBT OUTSTANDING
DECEMBER 1982
(BILLIONS OF DOLLARS, SEASONALLY ADJUSTED)

1. Total credit market debt		$5,648.1
2. Less		
(a) Debt of foreigners	$ 224.8	
(b) Debt of financial business	677.8	
3. Equals: Domestic nonfinancial debt		$4,745.6
4. Which is made up of debt of		
(a) U.S. Government	$ 991.4	
(b) State and local governments	389.7	
(c) Nonfinancial business	1,696.2	
(d) Households	1,668.3	

Memorandum

5. Bank credit (loans and securities of commercial banks)	$1,443.8	
6. Less		
(a) Bank credit to financial business	$ 112.1	
(b) Bank credit to foreigners	37.1	
(c) Regulated security credit	26.2	
7. Equals: Bank holdings of domestic nonfinancial debt		$1,268.4
8. Credit extended by other depository institutions[a]	$ 816.3	
9. Less: Other depository institution credit to financial business[b]	$ 98.4	
10. Equals: Other depository institutions holdings of domestic nonfinancial debt		$ 717.9
11. Share of domestic nonfinancial debt held directly by		
(a) Commercial banks		26.7%
(b) Other depository institutions		15.1%
(c) All others		58.1%

[a] Savings and loan associations, mutual savings banks, credit unions.

[b] Securities of federally sponsored credit agencies and mortgage pools.

Source: Flow-of-funds accounts, Board of Governors of the Federal Reserve System.

The actual growth in the monetary aggregates is affected by the portfolio decisions of the public and of depository institutions. Sometimes all the aggregates remain within their desired ranges, sometimes they all exceed or fall short of the ranges, and sometimes one or two will remain within its, or their, range while the remaining aggregate or aggregates move outside its, or their, range. As long as all the monetary aggregates remain within their ranges, short-term policy is not changed. When one or more move outside the range, the FOMC must decide on the short-term strategy that it will employ. The considerations involve estimates of the source of the deviation and its permanence.

Historically, the FOMC has placed more emphasis on correcting deviations of M1 from its growth range than on correcting deviations of M2 and M3 from their ranges. The behavior of M2 and M3 did help guide the FOMC in determining the vigor with which it sought to return M1 to its ranges, however. For example, if M1 was growing more rapidly than desired and if M2 and M3 were also exceeding their upper limits, the FOMC would produce a relatively large decline in the growth of reserves. If M2 and M3 were within their ranges, the FOMC would reduce the growth of reserves by a smaller amount.

Since late 1982, when regulatory changes clouded the meaningfulness of M1, the FOMC has placed more emphasis on M2 and M3.[38] As before, however, reserves are changed more aggressively if both M2 and M3 move outside their ranges than if only one departs from its range.

The FOMC finds it useful to state its policy objectives in terms of several monetary aggregates, but the weight that it places on any or all of the aggregates depends upon the circumstances. Although this complex procedure is a means of dealing with uncertainty about the current and future state of the economy, it does have the unfortunate consequence of producing considerable public confusion.

Why Control the Monetary Aggregates?

The FOMC began to pay attention to the monetary aggregates in 1969. They received increasing emphasis since then, and in 1979 controlling the annual growth of the monetary aggregates became the FOMC's primary concern. Control over the monetary aggregates was deemphasized to some degree in 1982, in part, because deregulation of depository institutions and financial innovation was clouding the meaning of all the aggregates. Despite the deemphasis, the monetary aggregates are still an important consideration for monetary policy. The episode from 1979 through 1982 is discussed in Chapter 19. In this section, we explain why the monetary aggregates rose to prominence and why they are at times difficult to control.

During the 1950s and 1960s, the FOMC was not particularly interested in controlling the monetary aggregates. It was primarily concerned with setting short-term interest rates. Though short-term interest rates changed, they tended to move gradually. We saw earlier in this chapter that this policy strategy is appropriate when the transitory shifts in the *LM* curve are large relative to the shifts in the *IS* curve.

The strategy was fairly successful in the sense that the economy experienced relatively rapid growth of output, employment, and capital formation. There were

---

[38] It is impossible to predict whether M1 will continue to receive little attention by the FOMC in the future.

recessions in 1957-1958 and 1960-1961, however. During these episodes, the policy of stabilizing interest rates produced declining growth of the monetary aggregates. Declines in the demand for the aggregates were met by declines in the growth of reserves. By stabilizing interest rates rather than the growth of reserves, monetary policy prevented interest rates from falling rapidly and thus intensified the severity of these two recessions. Except for these periods, however, the policy of the 1950s and early 1960s of gradually adjusting the level of short-term interest rates was fairly successful.

In the late 1960s, the economic situation changed. The nation was involved heavily in the Vietnam War, and the government was simultaneously engaging in substantial social programs. Both of these factors led to rapid growth in government spending. The FOMC raised interest rates slowly and the economy boomed. Excess demand developed, and an inflationary spiral began.

As a consequence of criticism from both within the Fed and from outside, the FOMC began to change its operating strategy to place more emphasis on controlling the monetary aggregates. The idea was that shifts in the *IS* curve could be offset more easily and quickly if the FOMC set growth targets for the monetary aggregates rather than pursuing interest rate objectives. This would allow the interest rate to act as a built-in stabilizer, rising during booms and falling during recessions. Thus, if the *LM* curve were kept relatively fixed, shifts in the *IS* curve would produce smaller movements in output, inflation, and prices. Implicit in this strategy was the argument that the position of the *IS* curve was less predictable than the position of the *LM* curve.

An additional reason for focusing on the monetary aggregates was given at the end of Chapter 16. Unless the central bank provides additional reserves and money, it is difficult, if not impossible, for an economy to experience sustained inflation. Thus, if relatively low growth rates for the monetary aggregates were achieved, chronic inflation could be avoided.

While the FOMC adopted targets for the monetary aggregates during the 1970s, it also imposed narrow ranges of tolerance for movements in the federal funds rate. This prevented the monetary objectives from being achieved because money supply expanded with money demand. The transactions demand for money rose rapidly because of rapidly expanding nominal income. Reserves and money had to rise rapidly to keep the federal funds rate within its narrow band. Thus, the unwillingness to let the federal funds rate change very much contributed to high average growth in the monetary aggregates.[39]

In 1979, inflation was high, and the Fed was subject to increasing criticism. The FOMC changed its procedures in October 1979. It greatly widened the range of tolerance for the federal funds rate and made a serious effort to reduce the growth of the monetary aggregates. Though the policy was successful in the sense that

---

[39] It is shown in Chapter 19 that the FOMC did allow interest rates to move quickly from 1973 through 1975 in order to reduce money growth.

the growth decelerated substantially over the next three years, the monetary aggregates fluctuated erratically from month to month and quarter to quarter. Because of a deepening recession and increasing difficulty in controlling M1, the FOMC began to emphasize M2 in late 1982, and it narrowed fluctuations in the federal funds rate.

The experience from October 1979 through late 1982 indicated that the FOMC can control M1 and other monetary aggregates with some precision over horizons of six months or longer, but control over shorter periods of time is difficult. Several reasons for the lack of short-term control were given in Chapter 11, where it was shown that shifts in the portfolio holdings of both depository institutions and of the public affect the quantity of money in the economy. Unexpected shifts in these portfolios produce unexpected fluctuations in the growth of the monetary aggregates for a given growth in the quantity of total reserves. The magnitude of these shifts was increased by financial innovation and deregulation.[40]

Fluctuations in the relationship between reserves and the monetary aggregates indicate that all of the aggregates are determined endogenously within the economy. The FOMC can affect the average level of the monetary aggregates through open market operations, but it cannot control their short-term fluctuations. There are differences among the monetary aggregates in terms of their suspectability to short-term control by the Federal Reserve, however.

Except during times when there are portfolio shifts caused by regulatory factors, M1 can be controlled more easily and more quickly than the broader monetary aggregates. This occurs because most of M1 is transactions accounts that have a reserve requirement. Many of the components of M2, M3, and L do not have reserve requirements. These components are controlled only as monetary policy affects interest rates, income, and the price level.

Changes in interest rates, income, and prices affect the public's portfolio decisions concerning the demand for the various assets that constitute the broader monetary aggregates. They also affect the portfolio decisions of financial institutions, which affect the amounts of the monetary aggregates supplied. Income, the price level, and long-term interest rates change relatively slowly in response to a change in monetary policy. Furthermore, portfolios adjust relatively slowly in response to changes in these variables. As a result, the broader monetary aggregates respond slowly to changes in monetary policy.

In contrast, the presence of reserve requirements for transactions accounts provides quicker and closer control over M1. It is this consideration that led the FOMC to place heavy reliance on controlling M1 rather than the broader monetary aggregates. When regulatory factors exert unusual influence on M1, however, the FOMC put greater emphasis on the broader aggregates despite their reduced short-run controllability.

---

[40] As explained in Chapter 19, technical considerations relating to lagged reserve accounting also increased the problems of monetary control.

SUMMARY

Effective short-run stabilization policy is difficult because there is considerable uncertainty about the current and future status of the economy and about how the economy responds to changes in policy.

Policy lags create significant problems. There are three lags to contend with: the recognition lag, the implementation lag, and the lag in the impact of a policy change. Fiscal and monetary policy are similar when it comes to the recognition lag. Fiscal policy may have an edge over monetary policy with respect to the impact lag. It is with the implementation lag that monetary policy is often dominant. Monetary policy can be changed virtually on a moment's notice. It usually takes a long period of time to change fiscal policy. Changes in tax rates and spending have to go through the legislative process. Because of its short implementation lag, monetary policy is the government's major tool for actively pursuing economic stability.

Lags in response of the economy to policy changes, coupled with errors in forecasting the future, can lead to policy errors. When the response of the economy to policy changes is known, it is still desirable to pursue stabilization objectives actively. Errors will be made, but they are unavoidable. An active policy still promotes superior economic performance relative to a less active policy.

When both the real (IS) and the financial (LM) sectors of the economy are subject to unexpected fluctuations, monetary policy should allow both the quantity of reserves and short-term interest rates to move. This policy is superior to using either reserves or a short-term interest rate as the policy instrument to the exclusion of the other.

When there is uncertainty about how the economy responds to changes in policy, active policy is not necessarily best. For example, if the lags in response of the economy to a change in monetary policy are long and uncertain, active changes in policy instruments may actually make the situation worse. This is the basic message of the proponents of following a fixed policy rule. Though this position is extreme, it does illustrate the general principle that uncertainty about the effects of policy should reduce the aggressiveness with which policy is used. There are times, however, such as when the price of imported oil rises dramatically, that a relatively large change in policy may be justified.

SELECTED REFERENCES

Brainard, William, "Uncertainty and the Effectiveness of Monetary Policy," *American Economic Review,* May 1967, pp. 411–433.

Craine, Roger, "Optimal Monetary Policy with Uncertainty," *Journal of Economic Dynamics and Control,* 1, 1979, pp. 59–83.

Maisel, Sherman, *Managing the Dollar,* New York: Norton, 1973.

Friedman, Benjamin, "The Inefficiency of Short-Run Monetary Targets for Monetary Policy," *Brookings Papers on Economic Activity,* 2:1979, pp. 293–335.

Friedman, Milton, *A Program for Monetary Stability,* New York: Fordham University Press, 1959.

Kareken, John, Thomas Muench, and Neil Wallace, "Optimal Open Market Strategy: The Use of Information Variables," *American Economic Review,* March 1973, pp. 156–72.

Pierce, James and Thomas Thomson, "Some Issues in Controlling the Quantity of Money," in *Controlling the Monetary Aggregates II: The Implementation,* Boston: Federal Reserve Bank of Boston, 1973.

Poole, William, "Optimal Choice of Monetary Policy Instruments in a Simple Stochastic Macro Model," *Quarterly Journal of Economics,* May 1970, pp. 197–216.

THE AMERICAN ECONOMY 1965 THROUGH 1982

19

This chapter reviews economic developments from 1965 through 1982. This is an important period to study because the size of the fluctuations in real output, employment, and inflation were unprecedented in the post-World War II era. Furthermore, the fluctuations increased over time. This was also a period of stagflation; the economy experienced high unemployment and high inflation at the same time. Both monetary and fiscal policy were used aggressively during the 1965-1982 period in an effort to stabilize the economy. It is argued in this chapter that the problem from 1965 through 1982 was not that policies did too little; they did too much. Aggressive policy changes increased the amplitude of economic fluctuations and seriously worsened the economy's performance.

We begin our economic history with 1965 because it was the midpoint of a very long expansion, and it was the last year that the economy experienced relative stability. In 1966 and 1967 there were massive increases in government spending to finance the Vietnam War and ambitious social programs. This spending produced excess demand and rising inflation as the nation entered the 1970s.

A combination of bad luck and aggressive policies during the 1970s produced a decade of high inflation and high unemployment. It is often asserted that there are two competing explanations of the stagflation of the 1970s:

> *Many observers would explain the stagflation by the series of external shocks, unprecedented in their severity, that hammered the world economy during the 1970s: the depreciation of the dollar after Nixon proclaimed it inconvertible into gold in 1971, the worldwide commodity shortages and speculative booms in 1973, the two big OPEC shocks, 1973–1974 and 1979. Others blame over-stimulative monetary and fiscal policies in 1972–1973 and 1977–1978. The controversy is far from being resolved, . . .*[1]

---

[1] James Tobin, "Reaganomics and Economics," *The New York Review of Books*, 1981, p. 11.

We will argue in this chapter that actually both interpretations appear to be correct. It was the combination of aggressive policy and exogenous shocks that produced poor economic performance. During the decade of the 1970s, there was an unprecedented rate of inflation and two recessions, one of which was severe. The performance of the economy during the 1970s was hardly the result of the inactivity of government policies. In fact, the period was characterized by policies that were unprecedented in their frequency of change and in their vigor. Policies were pursued that produced deep, self-inflicted wounds on an economy that was reeling from the blows delivered by a number of external shocks.

External shocks were not an important factor in the early 1980s. A highly restrictive monetary policy reduced inflation substantially but at the cost of the largest decline in real output and the highest unemployment in the post-World War II period. That policy was eased in late 1982, and the economy began to expand in 1983.

This chapter chronicles the major economic developments from 1965 through 1982 and attempts to relate these developments to the specific policy actions that were taken. The object of this exercise is to draw some lessons for the future from previous policy failures and successes.

The history begins with a brief overview of U.S. economic performance for the period 1965 through 1982. We then consider specific episodes in greater detail with particular emphasis on the behavior of monetary and fiscal policy. The reader should be warned that the implications of external shocks and of policy actions are much clearer with the benefit of hindsight than they were at the time that they occurred. Furthermore, economic events are subject to more than one interpretation, and there is disagreement among economists concerning the causes of economic fluctuations. This is particularly true of the role of policy in worsening economic fluctuations.

1965 THROUGH 1982: AN OVERVIEW

Perhaps the easiest way to gain a perspective for the period is to examine Figures 19.1 through 19.5. These figures show the behavior of real GNP, unemployment, and prices for 1965 through 1982. Real GNP, which we will use as the measure of real output, is shown in Figure 19.1. The upward trend in real GNP over the period indicates the effects of growth in the labor force, the capital stock, and productivity that allow real output to grow over time. The growth is not steady, however. This indicates the effects of aggregate demand and supply shifts that produce fluctuations in economic growth. Real output expanded relatively rapidly from 1965 through 1968, fell in 1969 through 1970, expanded rapidly from 1971 through 1973, declined in 1974 through 1975, expanded rapidly in 1976 through 1978, and fell in 1980 and 1982. These fluctuations in real GNP may not look very large, but they were associated with large fluctuations in employment and inflation.

FIGURE 19.1
REAL GNP 1965–1982 (ANNUAL
AVERAGES IN BILLIONS OF DOLLARS).

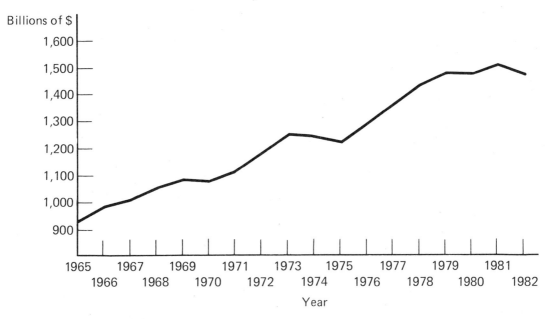

The magnitude of the fluctuations in real GNP can be seen more easily by look-ing at its annual growth for 1965 through 1982. Here we see that there were wide fluctuations in real GNP growth over the period and that the size of the fluctua-tions appear to be rising over time. Real GNP grew rapidly in 1965 through 1966, 1971 through 1972, and 1976 through 1978. These high rates of growth of real output were far in excess of the growth of long-run aggregate supply and, as we will see later, helped produce high rates of inflation. Figure 19.2 also shows the recessions of 1969 through 1970, 1974 through 1975, 1980, and 1982, where real output declined. The 1.8 percent decline in real output in 1982 is a post-World War II record. A decline in real output of 1.8 percent may not appear to be large, but, because the labor force continues to grow while economic activity is declin-ing, unemployment rose to nearly 11 percent of the labor force by the end of 1982.

Figure 19.3 shows the relentless rise in the price level that occurred in the 1965 through 1982 period. Though no one price index can capture all the effects on prices, the deflator for personal consumption expenditures is probably as good a single indicator as any, and we will use it in this chapter. The deflator is an index whose value is 100 in 1972. Because the price level was rising, the index is below 100 prior to 1972 and above 100 afterward. The index indicates that consumption

FIGURE 19.2
GROWTH OF REAL GNP 1965–1982
(PERCENTAGE CHANGE, YEAR
OVER YEAR).

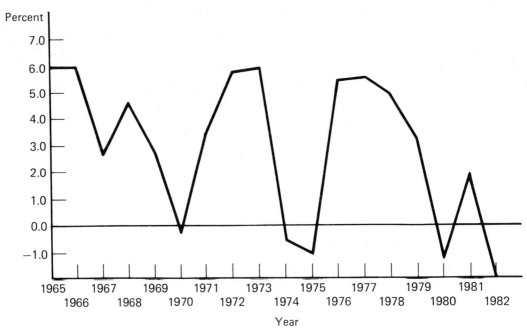

prices rose from an index value of 74 in 1965 to 206 in 1982 for a 280 percent rise over the period.

Figure 19.4 shows the inflation rate, measured as the annual percentage changes in the consumption deflator, for 1965 through 1982. Here we see that there were wide fluctuations in the inflation rate over the period and that the size of the fluctuations is increasing. The inflation rate in 1965 was at a low 1.8 percent for the year. Inflation accelerated in 1966 and fell again in 1967. Inflation started to increase in 1968, and in 1970 it peaked at 4.6 percent for the year. The rise in inflation in 1969 through 1970 is particularly important because, as Figure 19.2 indicates, real output declined over the 1969 through 1970 period. This was the first episode of stagflation. The inflation rate declined in 1971 and 1972 as a result of wage and price controls. From 1972 through 1974, inflation rose from 3.7 percent to over 10 percent. This was the nation's first experience with double-digit inflation since 1947. Real output fell sharply in 1974 as the effects of OPEC, food shortages, and the wage-price spiral reduced aggregate demand and supply. There were double-digit inflation and high unemployment. The inflation rate fell

FIGURE 19.3
THE PRICE LEVEL 1965–1982
(IMPLICIT DEFLATOR FOR
PERSONAL CONSUMPTION
EXPENDITURES, INDEX EQUALS
100 IN 1972).

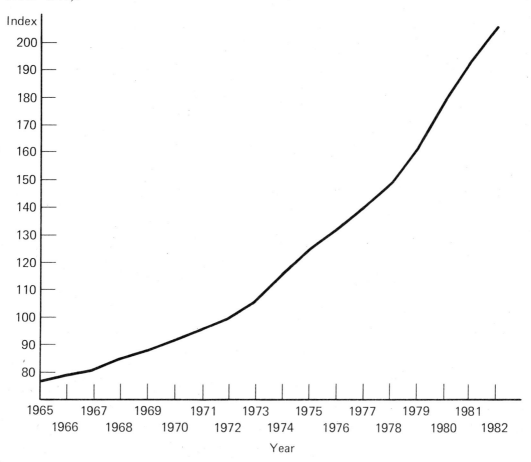

sharply in 1975 and 1976, reaching a low of 5.1 percent. This was a large reduction from the inflation in 1974, but it substantially exceeded the price increases of the 1960s and early 1970s. Inflation began another upward surge in 1977, and by 1980, following another large increase in the price of oil, the price level was again rising at over 10 percent per year. Inflation fell sharply in 1981 and 1982 as a consequence of the government's antiinflation policies that produced low real output and high unemployment.

FIGURE 19.4
INFLATION RATE 1965–1982
(YEAR-OVER-YEAR PERCENTAGE
CHANGE IN CONSUMPTION DEFLATOR).

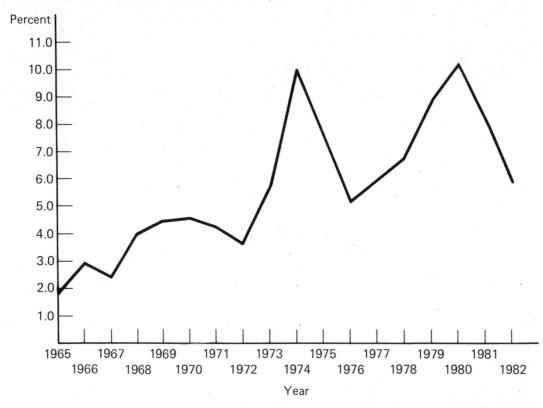

Figure 19.5 shows the behavior of the unemployment rate. Here, also, we see wide fluctuations, with the average unemployment rate rising over time. The unemployment rate fell from 1965 to 1969, reaching the low level of 3.5 percent of the labor force. Unemployment rose from 1969 through 1971 as the economy went through a recession.[2] The unemployment rate fell in 1972 and 1973 as the economy experienced a rapid expansion. Unemployment rose sharply in 1974 and 1975, when it peaked for the year at 8.5 percent of the labor force. At the time, this was the highest unemployment rate experienced since the 1930s. As Figure 19.4 indicates, this was also a time of very high inflation. The unemployment rate fell in 1976 through 1979 as the economy experienced another period of

---

[2] Recall that the inflation rate also rose in 1969 and 1970.

FIGURE 19.5
UNEMPLOYMENT RATE 1965–1982
(UNEMPLOYED AS A PERCENTAGE
OF CIVILIAN LABOR FORCE,
ANNUAL AVERAGES).

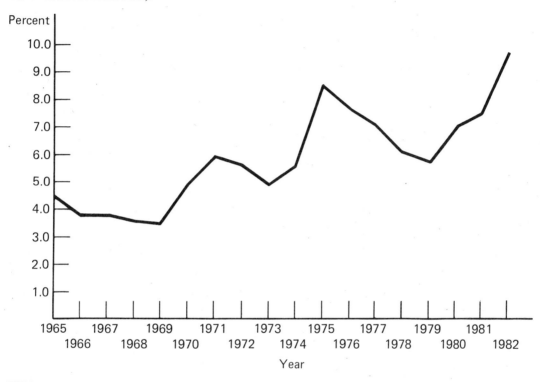

rapid expansion (see Figure 19.2). Unemployment rose sharply from 1980 through 1982. At the end of 1982, the unemployment rate stood at 10.8 percent of the labor force. A new record was achieved; 1982 replaced 1974 as the year with the highest unemployment rate since the Great Depression of the 1930s.

This brief review of the performance of real output, prices, and unemployment indicates that the 1970s and early 1980s were marked by large economic fluctuations. Furthermore, inflation and unemployment became worse with each cycle in economic activity. The reader might wonder what policy was doing during the period. Here we have the same record of wide fluctuations.

Figure 19.6 shows the annual growth of M1 for the 1965 through 1982 period as an indicator of monetary policy. It is important to note that growth in the quantity of money (M1) is a useful but imperfect indicator of monetary policy. We have seen in Chapter 11 and elsewhere in this book that the quantity of money depends upon the behavior of the public and depository institutions as well as upon the policies of the Federal Reserve. This means that the Fed cannot control

FIGURE 19.6
M1 GROWTH 1965–1982
(PERCENTAGE CHANGE,
DECEMBER OVER DECEMBER).

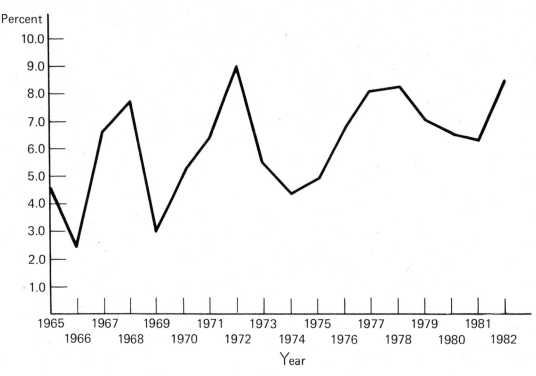

the quantity of money with precision. Furthermore, the quantity of money that is "appropriate" for promoting economic stability and growth depends upon the economic circumstances. For example, the effects of financial innovation and deregulation tend to shift the demand for money schedule and, therefore, affect the money growth that is appropriate for the economy. Furthermore, the stringency or ease of monetary policy as measured by money growth depends, in part, on the current rate of inflation. For example, 6 percent money growth may represent an expansionary monetary policy if there is no inflation, but a restrictive policy if inflation is 12 percent.[3]

Despite these reservations, M1 growth is still a useful indicator of monetary policy. Figure 19.6 indicates that M1 growth experienced wide fluctuations. The growth of M1 fell from 4.7 percent in 1965 to 2.5 percent in 1966. It then

---

[3] We will look at money growth relative to inflation later in this chapter.

accelerated to 6.6 percent in 1967 and 7.7 percent in 1968. The growth of real output slowed in 1967, largely as a result of the tightening of monetary policy in 1966. Following the return to more rapid money growth in 1967 through 1968, there was rapid expansion of real output and falling unemployment. The growth of M1 fell sharply in 1969, and the economy moved into recession. The growth of M1 then accelerated sharply in 1970 through 1972, reaching a peak rate of 9.2 percent for 1972. Inflation accelerated in 1973 and 1974, and M1 growth fell dramatically. Recall that 1974 was a year of severe recession and inflation. The growth of money increased substantially in 1976 through 1978. These were years of rapid economic expansion and, after 1976, of rising inflation. In 1979 through 1981, the growth rate of M1 declined, but rapid money growth followed in 1982.

Note that during most of the period, money growth tended to be procyclical. The growth of M1 accelerated during economic expansions and decelerated during recessions. This helped to increase economic expansions and to heighten recessions.

Figure 19.7 looks at interest rates as another indicator of monetary policy. As with money growth, interest rates are an imperfect indicator of monetary policy. Interest rates are affected by the behavior of the private sector of the economy, and not just by the Fed. Furthermore, as we will see later in this chapter, the significance of movements in nominal interest rates depends upon both actual and expected future inflation. Despite these problems, interest rates are a useful indicator of monetary policy.

We use the federal funds rate as a measure of short-term interest rates and the Aaa corporate bond rate as a measure of long-term interest rates. There were wide fluctuations in both short- and long-term interest rates during 1965 through 1982, with the size of the fluctuations increasing over the period. As we saw in Chapter 6, long-term interest rates are affected both by current short-term interest rates and by expected future short-term interest rates. Because short-term interest rates often fluctuate up and down with little net effect on their average level, long-term interest rates tend to fluctuate less than short-term rates. This difference in the size of the fluctuations in short- and long-term interest rates is apparent in Figure 19.7. Despite the difference in the size of the fluctuations, long-term interest rates tend to rise and fall with short-term rates.

Figure 19.7 indicates that the fluctuations in short-term interest rates were substantial. These interest rates rose in 1966 as the Fed slowed money growth, and they fell in 1967 as money growth accelerated sharply (see Figure 19.6). Short-term rates rose in 1968 despite a rise in money growth. This occurred because the growth in nominal income made the transactions demand for money grow more rapidly than the supply of money. Short-term interest rates rose sharply in 1969. This occurred because M1 growth slowed while nominal income continued to grow rapidly. Short-term interest rates peaked in 1969 and then fell during the 1969–1970 recession. A combination of falling real income and relatively rapid money growth in 1970 produced a decline in short-term interest rates in 1970. The transactions demand for money grew rapidly in 1971 and 1972, but short-term interest rates continued to fall. This occurred because money growth was very rapid during these years.

FIGURE 19.7
SHORT- AND LONG-TERM
INTEREST RATES 1965–1982
(ANNUAL AVERAGES, PERCENT).

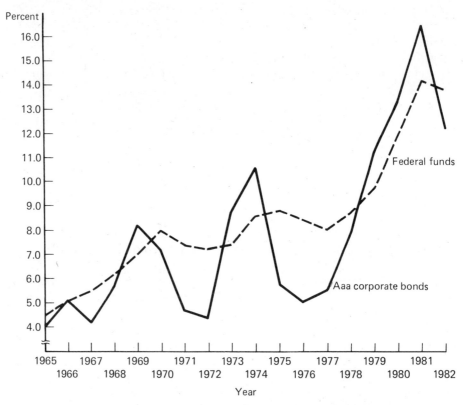

Long-term interest rate rose steadily from 1965 through 1970 and then fell in 1971 and 1972. This is in line with the upward trend in short-term interest rates for 1965 through 1969 and the decline in 1970 through 1972. Note that though short-term interest rates declined in 1970, long-term interest rates continued to rise. This is an indication that long-term interest rates tend to lag behind short-term interest rates. Even though 1969 through 1970 was a period of recession, long-term interest rates rose.

Short-term interest rates rose rapidly in 1973 and 1974, with the federal funds rate reaching a peak of over 10 percent. This occurred because nominal income was growing rapidly and money growth was reduced substantially. Long-term interest rates also rose during this period.

The 1974–1975 recession produced a dramatic decline in short-term interest rates because of the collapse in aggregate demand and income. As in the 1969-

1970 recession, long-term interest rates continued to rise after short-term rates fell. Long-term rates did fall in 1976, reaching a trough in 1977. Short-term rates reached their trough a year earlier, which is further evidence of the lag of long-term interest rates behind short rates. Money growth accelerated in 1976 and 1977, which helped keep interest rates relatively low.

After 1977, both the short- and the long-term interest rates began a rapid climb to extremely high levels in 1981. Long-term interest rates initially rose more slowly than short-term interest rates, but after 1979 they rose almost as rapidly. The phenomenal increase in interest rates from 1979 to 1981 was produced by the large reductions in money growth and the high rate of inflation that occurred during the period. Interest rates fell during 1982 with the decline becoming rapid toward the end of the year. This was a consequence of falling real output and inflation coupled with accelerating money growth.

Note that though long-term interest rates rose rapidly in 1979 through 1981, they were below short-term interest rates. This is consistent with the market expectation that the unusually high short-term interest rates in those years would not be sustained. The high level of the long-term interest rate was consistent with the expectation of high short-term rates in the future, however. In 1982 the sharp decline in short-term interest rates was accompanied by a much smaller fall in long-term interest rates. The relatively small decline in long-term interest rates suggests that market participants were still concerned about future inflation. Expectations of high inflation imply expectations of high future short-term interest rates. These expectations probably kept the long-term rate from falling much. Furthermore, uncertainty about future inflation (and short-term rates) probably produced a risk premium for long-term rates that also limited their decline. Finally, it is argued later in this chapter that large current and prospective budget deficits also probably contributed to the high long-term interest rates.

We conclude from this discussion that interest rates tend to rise during expansions and fall during recessions. Long-term rates lag behind, however. They continue to rise after the expansion has ended, and they continue to fall after a recession has ended. Short-term interest rates act more as a built-in stabilizer than do long-term rates. We also see that rapid money growth helped keep interest rates low in 1970 through 1972 and 1975 through 1977 despite the economic expansions that were occurring. During these periods, interest rates were not acting as built-in stabilizers. Finally, in 1979 through 1982 both short-term and long-term interest rates moved together. Their behavior was consistent with the tightening and then easing of monetary policy that occurred during the period. It proved easier to increase long-term interest rates in 1979 through 1981 than it did to reduce them in 1982, however.

As the final element in the overview of 1965 through 1982, let us turn to fiscal policy. Just as there is no one variable that is satisfactory for measuring monetary policy, there is no single variable that captures the thrust of fiscal policy. Government expenditures on goods and services, transfer payments, and tax rates all have important effects on the macroeconomy. We shall use total real spending and the high employment surplus or deficit as our measures. Real total spending by the federal government is measured by total spending, both on goods and services and on transfers, divided by the price level.[4] The high-employment deficit or surplus is a summary measure of the net contribution of discretionary fiscal policy to aggregate demand. Actual budget surpluses and deficits are deficient for this purpose because federal receipts and spending change automatically with fluctuations in economic activity. These automatic changes are not the result of a discretionary change in tax and spending programs but rather are a response of the budget to economic fluctuations under existing programs. The high-employment budget is a better measure than the actual budget of discretionary changes in fiscal policy because it removes the effects of economic fluctuations on the budget. This is done by measuring receipts and spending as they would be at high employment. Changes in the high employment budget are a consequence of discretionary fiscal policy changes and not of economic fluctuations. By examining both the growth of real total government spending and the behavior of the high-employment budget surplus or deficit, we get a fairly accurate measure of fiscal policy.

Figure 19.8 shows the annual growth in total real government spending (including transfers) for 1965 through 1982, and Figure 19.9 shows the annual high employment surplus or deficit. Both series moved erratically over the period. The highest growth rates for real spending occurred in 1966 and 1967, when there were large increases in spending for the Vietnam War and for the War on Poverty by the Johnson administration. Real government spending increased by 12.4 percent in 1966 and by 10.7 percent in 1967. We see in Figure 19.9 that there were high-employment deficits during these years. The policies of the Johnson administration played a major role in creating excess demand in the late 1960s.

Although the growth in government spending was reduced in 1968, it remained high, and there was only a small reduction in the high-employment deficit. In 1969 real government spending actually fell, and the high-employment budget moved into surplus as the Nixon administration teamed up with the Federal Reserve to reduce aggregate demand. Real spending started to grow rapidly in 1970, and by 1972 it was growing by over 6 percent per year. Largely as a result, the high-employment budget moved back into deficit during these years. Recall that the Federal Reserve was also pursuing an expansionary policy during the 1970–1972 period.

Real government spending fell sharply and the high-employment deficit was reduced in 1973 as the Nixon administration and the Fed pursued more restrictive policies. In 1974 fiscal and monetary policy continued to move in the same direction. The growth of real federal spending was relatively low, and the high-employment budget moved from a deficit to a near balance; monetary policy was restrictive. In 1975 fiscal policy turned stimulative with rapid growth of real spending and a tax cut that produced a large high-employment deficit. Monetary policy remained restrictive. In 1976 through 1979, fiscal policy was, in general, increasingly restrictive, with the growth of real spending declining and

---

[4] Here we use the GNP deflator rather than the consumption deflator.

FIGURE 19.8
GROWTH OF REAL FEDERAL
SPENDING 1965–1982 (YEAR OVER
YEAR GROWTH OF ANNUAL
AVERAGES, IN PERCENT).

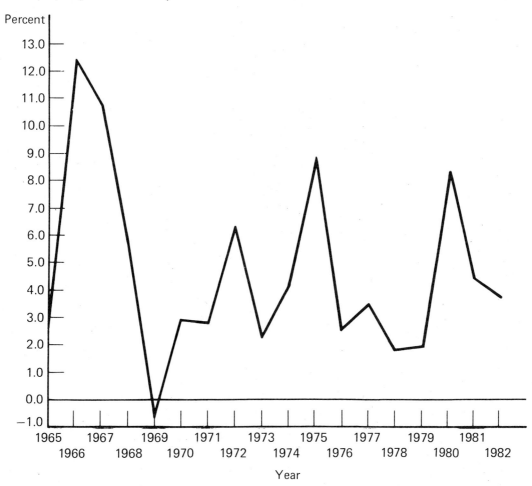

the high-employment budget moving from a substantial deficit in 1975 to a near balance in 1979. Monetary policy was expansionary until late 1979. Fiscal policy was stimulative in 1980, with rapid growth of real spending and a move to a substantial high-employment deficit. Real spending slowed in 1981 and 1982. The high-employment budget moved back toward balance in 1981 but had a large deficit in 1982 because of tax cuts. Restrictive fiscal policy in 1979 and 1981, cou-

FIGURE 19.9
HIGH-EMPLOYMENT BUDGET
SURPLUSES AND DEFICITS
1965–1982 (ANNUAL AVERAGES IN
BILLIONS OF DOLLARS).

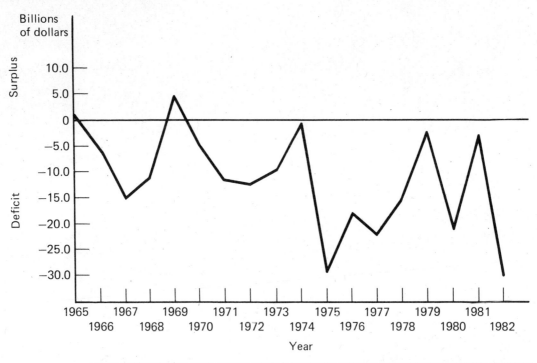

pled with highly restrictive monetary policy, produced record-high unemployment in 1982, but the policies reduced inflation.

This brief overview cannot do justice to the complex interactions of factors that produced the nation's economic history from 1965 through 1982. It is hoped that it gives the reader some impression of how poor economic performance was during the period. When we examine the charts for real output growth, unemployment, and inflation for the entire 1965–1982 period, two conclusions emerge. First, there is little indication of economic stability during the entire period. With minor exceptions, real GNP growth is either rising rapidly, or it is falling rapidly. There are few times during this eighteen-year period that real GNP is expanding at a steady rate that is consistent with the growth in long-run aggregate supply. After 1968, the unemployment rate is also either rising or falling rapidly. Inflation exhibits the same kind of instability, particularly after 1972.

The second conclusion involves the amplitude of the swings in real output, unemployment, and inflation. Each recession was larger than the one that preceded it, and each expansion was larger than its predecessor. Thus, the 1980–1982 recession was larger than the 1974–1975 recession, which was larger than the recession from 1969 through 1970. Furthermore, the expansions that followed each recession were more rapid with each cycle. The fluctuations in inflation also became larger with each cycle.

The period of 1965 through 1982 exhibited a high degree of economic instability. The reasons why this occurred and the implications for the future are the subject of the remainder of this chapter.

The analysis of why the economy performed so poorly is made easier by breaking the eighteen-year period into episodes. In describing these periods, we will continue to refer to the annual data charted in Figures 19.1 through 19.9. Because it is difficult to read specific numbers from charts, the data used to construct these figures are given in Table 19.1.

1965 THROUGH 1969

The year 1965 produced rapid economic expansion as well as low unemployment and inflation. Real output grew by 6 percent, unemployment was 4.5 percent, and inflation was about 1.8 percent. Policy was also moderate during the year. The quantity of money grew by 4.7 percent, the Federal funds rate averaged 4.1 percent, real federal spending grew by 2.5 percent, and the high-employment budget had a slight surplus. In 1966 and 1967 real government purchases of goods and services grew at a very rapid rate as a result of the Vietnam War. At the same time the Johnson administration engaged in ambitious social programs that greatly increased the growth of transfer payments. Total real government spending rose by 12.4 precent in 1966 and by 10.7 percent in 1967. This strong fiscal stimulus produced excess aggregate demand. The Federal Reserve attempted to reduce the excess demand by tightening monetary policy. The growth of money fell to 2.5 percent in 1966. This raised market interest rates above the interest rate ceilings at depository institutions, and they experienced deposit outflows (disintermediation).[5]

The disintermediation that occurred in 1966 was a surprise to depository institutions. In the past when market interest rates rose above interest rate ceilings, the regulators raised the ceilings. In 1966 this did not occur. Considerable disruption developed because depository institutions had loan commitments outstanding that they could not meet because of declining liabilities. Many firms were unable to obtain loans for investment expenditures. Similarly, many households were not able to obtain mortgage loans. As a consequence of these disruptions, real investment expenditures and real expenditures for housing construction fell in 1967.

---

[5] As explained in Chapter 8, virtually all accounts at depository institutions were covered by interest rate ceilings at that time.

TABLE 19.1
ECONOMIC VARIABLES 1965 THROUGH 1982 (PERCENTAGES) [a]

	Growth of Real GNP	Unemployment Rate	Growth of Consumption Deflator	Growth of Real Federal Spending	Growth of M1	Federal Funds Rate	High-Employment Surplus or Deficit (−)
1965	6.0	4.5	1.8	2.5	4.7	4.1	0.9
1966	6.0	3.8	2.9	12.4	2.5	5.1	−5.6
1967	2.7	3.8	2.4	10.7	6.6	4.2	−15.1
1968	4.6	3.6	4.0	5.6	7.7	5.7	−11.1
1969	2.8	3.5	4.5	−0.7	3.2	8.2	4.9
1970	−0.2	4.9	4.6	2.9	5.2	7.2	−4.6
1971	3.4	5.9	4.3	2.8	6.5	4.7	−11.3
1972	5.7	5.6	3.7	6.3	9.2	4.4	−12.1
1973	5.8	4.9	5.7	2.3	5.5	8.7	−9.5
1974	−0.6	5.6	10.1	4.2	4.4	10.5	−0.3
1975	−1.2	8.5	7.6	9.0	4.9	5.8	−29.1
1976	5.4	7.7	5.1	2.6	6.7	5.0	−17.4
1977	5.5	7.1	5.8	3.5	8.1	5.5	−21.7
1978	5.0	6.1	7.0	1.8	8.3	7.9	−15.1
1979	2.8	5.8	9.0	1.9	7.1	11.2	−2.1
1980	−0.4	7.1	10.3	8.5	6.6	13.4	−20.3
1981	1.9	7.6	8.6	4.5	6.4	16.4	−2.6
1982	−1.8	9.7	5.9	3.8	8.5	12.3	−29.8

[a] All data are for annual averages except for M1 growth, which is December over December.

Source: *Economic Report of the President*, Washington, D.C., U.S. Government Printing Office, various issues.

The rise in real consumption and real government spending in 1967 exceeded the decline in business investment and housing construction, so real GNP grew over the year. The rate of growth of real GNP growth fell from 6.0 percent in 1966 to 2.7 percent in 1967, however.

The Federal Reserve eased policy in 1967 largely because of the adverse effects of disintermediation. Money growth rose to over 6.6 percent in 1967, and short-term interest rates fell. Inflation rose from 1.8 percent in 1965 to 2.4 percent in 1967, whereas unemployment fell from 4.5 percent in 1965 to 3.8 percent in 1967. The decline in unemployment apparently came at the cost of a small rise in the inflation rate. This low cost was illusionary, however, because inflationary pressures were slowly building and there would be a stronger burst of inflation as the wage-price spiral gained momentum.

In 1968 the Johnson administration attempted to reduce excess demand by imposing a temporary income surtax. The surtax reduced the high-employment deficit somewhat, but it had little effect on consumption because it was temporary. Households reduced their saving rather than cut back on consumption. The effects of the surtax were also reduced by a monetary policy that accelerated M1 growth to 7.7 percent for the year. Short-term interest rates did rise somewhat during the year because of rapid economic expansion. Aggregate demand remained high during 1968 with real output rising by 4.6 percent and unemployment falling to 3.6 percent. The wage-price spiral picked up speed during 1968; inflation rose from 2.4 to 4.0 percent.

The Nixon administration took office in 1969, and Arthur Burns replaced William McChesney Martin as Chairman of the Federal Reserve Board. In response to the rising inflation rate, the Nixon administration, working in concert with the Federal Reserve, tightened policy and consciously produced a recession in 1969. It was argued that a short, sharp recession would convince the public that the government was serious about controlling inflation. The recession was expected to stop the wage-price spiral as the economy moved down a stable Phillips curve. The government's actions to limit expenditure and money growth were expected to reduce inflationary expectations and make the return to price stability smooth and rapid. Unfortunately, events did not conform to the policymaker's hopes.

Real federal spending declined by 0.7 percent in 1969 and rose by only 2.9 percent in 1970 despite the increase in transfer payments caused by the recession. The high-employment budget moved into surplus in 1969 and had only a small deficit in 1970. The growth of M1 slowed to 3.2 percent in 1969, and it was 5.2 percent in 1970. The federal funds rate averaged over 8 percent for 1969 and only fell to 7.2 percent in 1970. Because output and employment respond to policy changes with a lag, real output did not begin to fall until the fourth quarter of 1969, and unemployment did not rise until the first quarter of 1970. For 1969 as a whole, real output was 2.8 percent higher than in 1968. Unemployment in 1969 averaged only 3.5 percent of the labor force. The inflation rate rose to 4.5 percent.

The recession picked up momentum in 1970. Real output declined by 0.2 percent for the year, and unemployment, though averaging 4.9 percent for the year, rose to 6.0 percent in December. Inflation did not slow down, however. For the year as a whole, inflation averaged 4.6 percent, and prices were rising by 5.5 percent by the fourth quarter of 1970.

Policymakers seriously underestimated the amount of inflationary pressure that had built up in the economy. As a consequence, they were too optimistic about their ability to end the wage-price spiral quickly. In the late 1960s and early 1970s, there was little awareness that inflation could continue despite rising unemployment.

1971 THROUGH 1975

When inflation did not respond quickly to the government's policies, frustration mounted. The inflation rate continued to increase despite rising unemployment. Policymakers concluded that the conventional approach of reducing inflation through restrictive fiscal and monetary policies no longer worked. It was argued that inflationary expectations were causing the inflation and that these expectations were unaffected by the government's policies. Policymakers thought that the 1969–1970 recession "proved" that restrictive policies were no longer effective in reducing inflation. These policies only increased the unemployment rate.

The inflation and unemployment situation in the summer of 1971 was viewed by the Nixon administration and other politicians as unacceptable. The unemployment rate averaged 5.9 percent, and the rate of inflation was still in excess of 4.5 percent per year. Thus, inflation was still as high as it had been in 1969, when the restrictive policies were adopted, but the unemployment rate had risen from 3.5 percent to nearly 6 percent. It was decided that more direct methods were required to reduce inflationary expectations. The method was direct indeed: President Nixon imposed a price freeze in August 1971, followed by a program of wage-price controls. The dollar was also allowed to float on foreign exchange markets. Supply and demand would determine the exchange rate, and policy could turn to attaining domestic objectives.

In light of the performance of the economy during the remainder of the 1970s and into the 1980s, it is easy to lose sight of how strongly the public and policymakers felt about economic conditions in 1971. Republicans and Democrats alike were shocked by the "untenable" economic conditions of that year. There was agreement that something had to be done, and there was widespread political and public support for wage-price controls.

With wage-price controls in place and with the dollar floating to take care of the balance of payments problem, the administration and the Federal Reserve turned to the task of reducing unemployment. Fiscal policy turned expansionary, with total real federal spending increasing by more than 6 percent during 1972. Real federal expenditures on goods and services actually declined in 1972, but this was more than offset by a large increase in direct transfer payments and grants to states and localities. There was a small increase in the high-employment deficit. Monetary policy also turned highly expansionary, with M1 growing by more than

9 percent over the year. Money growth hit a peak of 9.9 percent in the fourth quarter of the year. Both short- and long-term interest rates fell despite the rapid economic expansion. With these stimulative policies, real output grew rapidly, and the unemployment rate fell. Wage-price controls did their job, and the rate of inflation averaged only 3.7 percent for the year.

By the end of 1972, the government's policies appeared to be successful. The old economics, which preached restrictive policies as the method of reducing inflation, had been replaced by a policy that suppressed inflation by controls and produced high employment by stimulating aggregate demand. The government "solved" the unemployment-inflation dilemma by using wage-price controls to control inflation and by simultaneously using monetary and fiscal policy to reduce unemployment. By matching the number of instruments to the number of targets, the government appeared to be able to achieve high employment and reduce inflation.

A great deal has been written about the policies that were launched in 1972.[6] It is often pointed out that 1972 was an election year and that stimulative policies combined with wage-price controls allowed the Nixon administration to "solve" the nation's economic problems just in time for the November elections. This is an oversimplification. It is important to note that there was widespread support for the policies. Democrats were particularly vocal about the unemployment-inflation situation, and they were supportive of wage-price controls. They were also highly critical of high interest rates and applied pressure on the Fed to expand money growth. Though the politics of presidential elections no doubt played a part in the policies, similar policies probably would have been pursued even if 1972 had not been an election year.

Price controls did "work" in 1972 in the sense that the measured rate of inflation was reduced dramatically. The reduction of inflation was only temporary, however. With expansionary monetary and fiscal policies, real output grew by 5.7 percent in 1972. The rapid increase in aggregate demand put intolerable strain on the wage-price program in terms of distortions in the production of output and the distribution of income. Eventually, controls had to be eliminated.

The inflation rate began to accelerate in 1973 as rising food prices and import prices worked their way through the system.[7] Rising aggregate demand and distortions from price controls also made other price increases difficult to contain as firms found ways to beat the system. The administration began to decontrol prices in 1973, and the inflation rate took off. The consumption deflator rose at an 8 percent annual rate by the second quarter of 1973.

---

[6] See for example, Alan Blinder, *Economic Policy and the Great Stagflation,* New York: Academic Press, 1979, pp. 29–35; and James Pierce, "The Political Economy of Arthur Burns," *Journal of Finance,* May 1979, pp. 485–496.

[7] Food and import prices were not controlled, and firms were allowed to "pass on" increases in these prices by raising their own prices. The exchange rate fell after the dollar was allowed to float, and this contributed to the rise in import prices.

The administration attempted a second price freeze in June 1973, but the effort had to be abandoned because of spiraling food and raw material prices. Despite the efforts to reintroduce rigid controls, the consumption deflator rose at a 7 percent annual rate in the third quarter of 1973. Beginning in August 1973, the process of decontrolling prices began in earnest, with general controls ending in April 1974. For 1973 as a whole, inflation was 5.7 percent. This was a higher rate of inflation than existed before price controls were introduced.

It is conceivable that wage-price controls could have made a more lasting contribution to reducing inflation if the growth of aggregate demand had been restricted. It was virtually impossible for price controls to work when aggregate demand was stimulated. It was not possible to use stimulative policies to reduce unemployment and wage-price controls to contain inflation. The rapid growth of aggregate demand made the controls program unworkable.

Wage-price controls did alter the timing of inflation. Inflation was lower in 1972 and early 1973 because of controls, but it was greater in late 1973 and in 1974, when controls were phased out and there was a "catchup" of wages and prices. Wage-price controls also probably produced a higher average inflation rate over the entire period than would have existed in the absence of controls.[8] Wage-price controls introduced distortions into the system that increased the costs of producing the nation's output. They also produced considerable uncertainty as the public attempted to assess the permanence of controls and their effect. Perhaps most importantly, the early success of the control program induced policymakers to pursue highly stimulative policies. It appeared that these policies would increase employment and output but not increase inflation. The growth of aggregate demand contributed to the inflation that occurred later. Had the price control program not been in operation, the inflation rate would have been higher in 1972, and it is likely that less stimulative policies would have been pursued during that year. As a result, inflation would have been lower in later years.

OPEC

As luck would have it, prices in the United States were increasing at a rapid rate when the oil embargo and then the increase of oil prices by OPEC hit. By pushing 1972's inflation into 1973, the wage-price control program helped to produce a high inflation rate, to which the effects of OPEC's price increase were added. Even in the absence of OPEC, 1973 would have been a bad year. The price level was rising rapidly as controls were lifted. This surge of inflation was compounded by the rise in food prices that resulted from worldwide food shortages and by the

---

[8] For a detailed discussion, see Alan Blinder, *Economic Policy and the Great Stagflation*, op. cit., pp. 107–132.

increase in import prices from the depreciation of the dollar.[9] To these shocks to aggregate supply were added the effects of OPEC.

The consumption deflator increased at an average rate of 7.5 percent in the second and third quarters of 1973. In the fourth quarter of that year, OPEC produced a fourfold increase in the price of oil. Furthermore, during the October war with Israel, Saudi Arabia imposed an oil embargo on the United States, which created production distortions quite apart from the effects of the oil price increase. The consumption deflator rose at an annual rate of 8.6 percent in the fourth quarter of 1973, and the increase hit 12.3 percent in the first quarter of 1974.

There have been many studies of the role of OPEC and other special factors in the inflation and recession of 1974 through 1975.[10] Several studies have also been made of the role of monetary policy during those years.[11] Though limitations of space do not allow a full discussion, we can draw together some of the common threads of various studies. There is a consensus that the increase in oil prices had real effects on the economy. As explained in Chapter 16, the short-run aggregate supply schedule shifted up, which accelerated inflation and reduced real output. The rise in the price of imported oil also meant that an increased proportion of total output and income had to be used to pay for imported oil.

The inflation that came from OPEC, depreciation of the dollar, and price decontrols was the process of adjustment to a higher level of prices. The speed of this move and the degree of adjustment of the price level depended crucially on the behavior of monetary policy. As explained in Chapter 16, if monetary policy did not accommodate the surge of prices from OPEC and elsewhere, the prices of other commodities ultimately would fall. This fall would occur only after a large and protracted decline in aggregate demand and employment. At the other extreme, if monetary policy attempted to offset all the aggregate demand effects, uncontrolled inflation could result. In this situation, monetary policy would be pushing up the prices of all commodities, so that relative prices could not adjust. This could produce excess demand and runaway inflation. The dilemma for monetary policy lay in deciding where to be between these two extremes. The decision was particularly difficult because there was no experience with such an external shock. There was great uncertainty about the effects of the oil price increase on aggregate demand and supply. There was also uncertainty about the income and price elasticities of oil demand and about the effects of the price increase on inflationary expectations.

[9] Between August 1971, when the United States stopped supporting the dollar, and the end of 1973, the dollar exchange rate fell by nearly 20 percent.

[10] For an excellent summary, see Blinder, *Economic Policy and the Great Stagflation*, op. cit., pp. 73–105.

[11] See James Pierce and Jared Enzler, "The Effects of External Inflationary Shocks," *Brookings Papers on Economic Activity*, 1974:1, pp. 13–54, and Alan Blinder, *Economic Policy and the Great Stagflation*, op. cit., pp. 184–194.

The Federal Reserve decided to put primary emphasis on limiting inflation. In fact, the FOMC pursued a policy that appeared restrictive even if OPEC had never raised oil prices. The average growth of M1 during 1974 was 4.4 percent, and during 1975 it was 4.9 percent. This was a low rate of growth relative to the rate of inflation; the consumption deflator rose by 10.1 percent in 1974 and by 7.6 percent in 1975. The result of this policy was a sharp reduction in real money balances.

In order to put monetary policy in perspective, we will find it useful to look at the behavior of money growth and interest rates during 1973 through 1975 in detail. Table 19.2 shows quarterly M1 growth, the inflation rate, and real money growth, which is measured as the growth of M1 minus the inflation rate. In the first quarter of 1973, monetary policy was expansionary. Money (M1) grew at an 8.6 percent annual rate, and inflation was 5.7 percent; real M1 grew at a 2.9 percent annual rate. From the second quarter of 1973 through 1975, monetary policy was restrictive in the sense that there was a substantial decline in the real quantity of money. During the final three quarters of 1973, M1 growth was approximately 5.0 percent. Inflation was 7.9 percent in the second quarter, 7.0 percent in the third quarter, and 8.6 percent in the fourth quarter. This meant that the real quantity of money declined at a 2.6, 2.1, and 3.8 percent annual rate in the second, third, and fourth quarters respectively.

During the first quarter of 1974, there was an acceleration in the growth of the nominal quantity of money. Prices rose at an annual rate of 12.3 percent, however, so the real quantity of money declined at a 5.5 percent annual rate during that quarter. The growth of the nominal money stock fell during the second and third quarters of the year whereas prices continued to rise rapidly. As a result, real money balances declined at over a 7 percent annual rate during the second and third quarters. Nominal money growth accelerated slightly in the fourth quarter to a 4.8 annual rate, but prices rose at a 10.5 percent rate so the real quantity of money declined at a 5.7 annual rate in that quarter.

The growth of nominal M1 fell to a 3 percent annual rate in the first quarter of 1975. Inflation was 5.7 percent, so the real quantity of money fell at "only" a 2.7 annual rate in that quarter. Nominal money growth accelerated in the second and third quarters of 1975, and the real money stock grew at annual rates of 1.5 and 0.1 percent during those quarters. Nominal money growth slowed to 3.3 percent in the fourth quarter of the year, however, and real money balances declined at a 2.8 percent annual rate during that quarter.

From the second quarter of 1973 through the fourth quarter of 1975, the real quantity of money declined by 8.7 percent. This is indicative of a severely restrictive monetary policy. The effects of the decline in the real quantity of money were partially offset, however, by a large downward shift in the demand for real money balances during the 1973–1975 period.[12] The shift in money demand lim-

---

[12] For evidence of the downward shift, see Steven Goldfeld, "The Case of the Missing Money," *Brookings Papers on Economic Activity, 3*:1976, pp. 683–730.

TABLE 19.2
QUARTERLY GROWTH OF M1, PRICES, AND REAL M1
1973 THROUGH 1975 (PERCENTAGES)

	Growth of M1	Growth of Consumption Deflator	Growth of Real M1
1973: I	8.6	5.7	2.9
II	5.0	7.9	−2.9
III	4.9	7.0	−2.1
IV	4.8	8.6	−3.8
1974: I	6.8	12.3	−5.5
II	3.8	10.9	−7.1
III	3.7	10.7	−7.0
IV	4.8	10.5	−5.7
1975: I	4.0	5.7	−2.7
II	6.4	4.9	1.5
III	7.7	7.6	0.1
IV	3.3	6.1	−2.8

ited the rise in nominal interest rates produced by the decline in real money supply. It also meant that monetary policy was less restrictive than the Federal Reserve thought. Targeting on the quantity of money is not a reliable way to execute policy when there are large money demand shifts.

Table 19.3 shows the quarterly behavior of the federal funds rate, the inflation rate and the real federal funds rate for 1973 through 1975. As before, the federal funds rate is used as an indicator of short-term interest rates in general. The nominal federal funds rate rose during 1973 from a low of 6.52 percent in the first quarter to 10.0 percent in the fourth quarter. The real federal funds rate was low in the first quarter, and it actually became negative in the second quarter. The real federal funds rate then rose sharply in the third quarter to 3.56 percent, only to fall to 1.40 percent in the fourth quarter of 1973 as inflation accelerated. The nominal federal funds rate fell in the first quarter of 1974 to 9.32 percent. Because inflation was 12.3 percent in that quarter, the real federal funds rate was −2.98 percent. The nominal federal funds rate rose sharply to 11.25 percent and 12.09 percent in the second and third quarters, respectively. Because inflation was nearly 11 percent in those quarters, the real federal funds rate was positive but low. The nominal federal funds rate fell sharply in the fourth quarter of 1974 to 9.35 percent. Inflation was 10.5 percent, so the real federal funds rate was −1.15 percent. Both the nominal federal funds rate and the inflation rate declined in 1975; the real federal funds rate remained low.

The Federal Reserve thought it was being highly restrictive in the 1973–1975 period because nominal short-term interest rates were the highest in the post-World War II era. The evidence in Table 19.3 indicates that short-term interest rates were not high during 1973 through 1975 in real terms. In fact, they were

TABLE 19.3
QUARTERLY NOMINAL AND REAL FEDERAL FUNDS RATES
1973 THROUGH 1975 (PERCENTAGES)

	Federal Funds Rate	Inflation Rate	Real Federal Funds Rate
1973: I	6.52	5.7	0.82
II	7.82	7.9	−0.08
III	10.56	7.0	3.56
IV	10.00	8.6	1.40
1974: I	9.32	12.3	−2.98
II	11.25	10.9	0.35
III	12.09	10.7	1.39
IV	9.35	10.5	−1.15
1975: I	6.30	5.7	0.60
II	5.42	4.9	0.52
III	6.16	7.6	−1.44
IV	5.41	6.1	−0.69

often negative. This is evidence of the large downward shift in real money demand that occurred during the period. This downward shift prevented nominal short-term interest rates from achieving the much higher levels that would have occurred in the absence of a shift. Table 19.3 illustrates that it can be dangerous to use nominal interest rates as an indicator of policy restrictiveness. Because the Fed used a money growth target during this period, the table also indicates that it can be dangerous to use money growth as an indicator of policy.

Measured in terms of the growth in the nominal and real quantities of money, monetary policy was highly restrictive from mid-1973 through 1975. Furthermore, the degree of restrictiveness was greatest during late 1974 and early 1975, when the recession was at its worst. When monetary policy is measured by real short-term interest rates, the policy does not seem harsh. It does appear, however, that despite the low and often negative real short-term interest rates during the period, monetary policy was restrictive. The quantity of real money balances declined, and real wealth shrank. The low real short-term interest rates did not stimulate investment spending because aggregate demand was low during the recession.

Several studies have been performed trying to devise monetary policies for 1974–1975 that would have helped moderate the deep recession of 1974–1975, though not accommodating the inflation.[13] The studies generally conclude that the

[13] See, for example, George Perry, "Policy Alternatives for 1974," *Brookings Papers on Economic Activity,* 1975:1, pp. 222–235; Pierce and Enzler, "The Effect of External Inflationary Shocks," *op. cit.*; William Poole, "Macro Economic Policy, 1971–1975: An Appraisal," in *Rational Expectations and Economic Policy,* Stanley Fischer (ed.), Chicago: University of Chicago Press, 1980, pp. 269–279, and Robert Solow, "What to Do (Macroeconomically) When OPEC Comes," in *Rational Expectations and Economic Policy,* pp. 249–264.

recession could have been moderated by a once-and-for-all increase in the nominal money stock followed by relatively low money growth thereafter. This would have prevented real money balances from declining so much. The increase in the quantity of money would not have added substantially to inflation because the economy was moving to a higher level of prices, not to a permanently higher inflation rate. A once-and-for all increase in the quantity of money would have helped cushion the shock to aggregate demand.

The Federal Reserve did not follow such a policy. The reason appears to be that the Fed was stung by the criticism of its expansionary policies in 1971–1972 and had resolved to reduce inflation quickly. In fairness to the Federal Reserve, there were great uncertainties surrounding the effects of price decontrols and of the oil-price increases. Furthermore, there was a public outcry over the rate of inflation. Neither the public nor Congress was interested in hearing that a good part of the inflation was simply the result of the earlier effort to use price controls. There was also little interest in hearing stories about how the effects of price decontrol and of OPEC would lead to a one-time increase in the price level, not to a permanent increase in the inflation rate. The public apparently feared that double-digit inflation would continue indefinitely.

Finally, there was no political leadership in Washington to deal with the crisis. Congress complained a great deal but offered little advice that was constructive. Following the oil embargo and the OPEC price increase in late 1973, the Nixon administration announced a nebulous program which it claimed would make the United States independent of imported oil by 1980. The lack of planning and the lack of feasibility of such an ambitious plan did little to ease the confusion and uncertainty under which the economy was operating.

In 1974 the attention of Washington was focused on the revelations of Watergate. When Richard Nixon resigned the presidency in August and was replaced by Gerald Ford, it was possible to have an effective presidency again, but Ford required time to establish and assert his policies. During much of 1974, the Federal Reserve was the only agency consciously affecting economic events. This was probably too large a burden to place on that institution.

Uncertainty and confusion in the economy were heightened by the Watergate scandal and the Nixon resignation. The situation was eased to some degree when Gerald Ford took office, but his initial policy pronouncements and proposals added to uncertainty in the economy. In October 1974 the Ford administration considered inflation to be the paramount problem and started a Whip Inflation Now (WIN) campaign, which included a proposal for an income tax increase for corporations and individuals. By January 1975, the administration abandoned the appeal for an increase in taxes and decided instead to propose a tax cut. This did lead to a tax reduction in 1975. Such a flip-flop on taxes is hardly conducive to public confidence in government policy.

There was a high degree of uncertainty and confusion among private citizens and policymakers during the mid-1970s. Hindsight allows us to clarify many of the issues that were unclear at the time that they occurred. Wage-price controls came as a surprise, and their implications were not easy to evaluate. The severity of the 1974–1975 recession also came as a surprise to the private sector and to policymakers. That recession was particularly confusing to many observers because there were rising unemployment and accelerating inflation at the same time. In 1974 many people concluded, once again, that the old economics did not work. It did work, however. Inflation fell sharply in 1975, reaching a low of 4.9 percent in the second quarter. Unemployment hit a peak of 8.9 percent in that quarter. Given enough unemployment, inflation could still be reduced.

1976 THROUGH 1982

The economy achieved some semblance of health in the first half of 1976. In the first two quarters of the year, real GNP growth averaged nearly 7 percent, and the inflation rate was about 4 percent. The unemployment rate had fallen from a high of 8.9 percent in the second quarter of 1975 to 7.5 percent in the second quarter of 1976. The growth of the money stock was a little over 6 percent in the first half of 1976, the federal funds rate averaged about 4.8 percent, and long-term corporate bond rates were at about 8.50 percent. By the fourth quarter of the year, however, inflation accelerated to 6.5 percent. Rapid growth of money kept the federal funds rate at low levels, and long-term interest rates fell.

In 1977 the Carter administration began, and G. William Miller was appointed as Chairman of the Federal Reserve Board. The new administration began on an expansionist tone. President Carter proposed a tax cut, and the Fed embarked on a expansionary monetary policy. Although the tax cut proposal was withdrawn, M1 grew by over 8 percent in 1977. The federal funds rate moved up slowly during the year, and long-term interest rates fell slightly. Real GNP grew rapidly during 1977, and the unemployment rate fell to 6.6 by the fourth quarter. Inflation rose from an average of 5.1 percent in 1976 to an average of 5.8 percent in 1977.

In 1978 there was a tax cut, and the quantity of money again grew by over 8 percent. Real GNP continued to grow rapidly, and inflation averaged 7.0 percent for the year. By the fourth quarter of 1978, the unemployment rate was below 6 percent, and the inflation rate was over 8 percent. Both long- and short-term interest rates moved upward. By late 1978, there was increasing concern about inflation, and President Carter called for "voluntary" wage and price restraint. This policy produced considerable uncertainty and fears concerning reinstatement of controls.

There was extensive discussion within the Carter administration during 1977 and 1978 about the "special factors" that were contributing to inflation. Rising food and energy prices and declines in the exchange rate were viewed as the primary sources of inflation. There was little discussion about the role of expansionary fiscal policy and rapid money growth, which stimulated aggregate demand and produced rapid growth of real GNP, as sources of inflationary pressures. The administration made additional contributions to higher prices through higher payroll taxes, increases in government salaries, and increases in the minimum wage.

The year 1979 saw the return to double-digit inflation in the United States. The effects of expansionary monetary and fiscal policies combined with a doubling of oil prices by OPEC and a large decline in the exchange rate, all added up to an inflation rate in excess of 10 percent. Money growth had slowed to 5.6 percent in the first quarter of 1979, but it soared to 10.5 percent in the second quarter and was 9.4 percent in the third quarter. The Federal funds rate rose from 6.70 percent in January to 8.45 percent in September of 1979. Long-term interest rates rose slightly. The inflation rate was 10 percent in the first quarter and varied between 8 and 9 percent in the second and third quarters of the year.

Paul Volcker replaced G. William Miller as Chairman of the Federal Reserve Board in August 1979. In October 1979 the FOMC announced new operating procedures that placed more emphasis on limiting the growth of the monetary aggregates and less emphasis on limiting short-term fluctuations in the federal funds rate. The FOMC also adopted low target rates of growth for the aggregates. These targets were thought to be consistent with a relatively rapid reduction in the rate of inflation.

The inflation rate was 10.7 percent in the fourth quarter of 1979, and it hit 12 percent in the first quarter of 1980. The quantity of money (M1) grew at an annual rate of 4.9 percent in the fourth quarter of 1979 and by 5.9 percent in the first quarter of 1980. Because the growth of money was far less than the rate of inflation, real money balances declined, and interest rates rose rapidly. The federal funds rate rose to over 17 percent during the period, and long-term interest rates moved up sharply.

In March 1980, President Carter announced an anti-inflation program. As part of the program, he declared an emergency under the Credit Control Act of 1969, and the Federal Reserve imposed credit controls on the economy. The imposition of credit controls created considerable public confusion, and they had a disruptive effect on economic activity. The controls also made it difficult to interpret the significance of movements in interest rates and the monetary aggregates.

The credit controls themselves were relatively mild, considering that the Credit Control Act granted the Fed nearly dictatorial powers once an emergency was announced. The controls were designed to limit the growth of total credit by restricting the growth of consumer and business loans. The controls were also intended to liberate credit for the use of farmers and small business by restricting the availability of credit to big business and to consumers. The major provisions of the credit control program were these: (1) all types of lenders (not just banks) were required to deposit with the Federal Reserve a percentage of increases in credit card lending and of other forms of unsecured consumer credit; (2) a marginal reserve requirement was imposed on large-denomination CDs and other managed liabilities of banks; (3) reserve requirements were extended to cover the liabilities of large nonmember banks and increases in the total assets of money market mutual funds;[14] (4) a "voluntary" program was established where com-

---

[14] The Monetary Control Act of 1980 had not yet been passed, so nonmember banks had no regular reserve requirements.

mercial banks and finance companies limited their growth in total loans. The Fed on its own also added a surcharge to the discount rate for large banks that were frequent borrowers at the discount window.

The expansion of money and credit slowed sharply after the credit-control program was imposed. The growth of business loans and consumer credit fell. The growth of all the monetary aggregates slowed, and M1 actually fell at a 2.6 annual rate in the second quarter of 1980. Interest rates collapsed with the federal funds rate declining from 17.61 percent in March to 9.03 percent in July. Long-term interest rates also fell sharply.

These developments and the general confusion about the nature and duration of credit controls helped produce a record decline in real GNP in the second quarter of 1980. Faced with the collapse in economic activity and the sharp declines in money, credit, and interest rates, the Federal Reserve abandoned the credit control program in July of 1980. Though the program lasted only four months, it had a great (and largely unexpected) impact on the economy.

The remainder of 1980 saw a sharp reversal of monetary policy. The growth of M1 was 14.6 annual rate in the third quarter and 10.8 in the fourth quarter. Inflation was 8.8 percent in the third quarter, and it rose to 9.7 percent in the fourth quarter. Nominal GNP grew at annual rates of 11.8 and 14.9 percent in the third and fourth quarters, respectively. This rapid growth of nominal GNP, coupled with an increase in money demand associated with fears of reimposition of credit controls and other uncertainties, produced a dramatic rise in interest rates. The federal funds rate rose from 9.03 percent in July to 18.90 percent in December. Long-term interest rates also moved up sharply. The swing in interest rates during 1980 was the largest in post-World War II history, and it was a major destabilizing force in the economy.

By any standards, 1980 was a terrible year for the economy. Despite the promise of the Carter administration to fight inflation, prices rose by over 10 percent for the year. The inflation was fueled by rising energy and food prices, but government policies were hardly consistent with controlling inflation and stabilizing the economy. For example, real government spending rose by 8.5 percent in 1980, and there was a large high-employment deficit. Furthermore, the experiment with credit controls made a bad situation worse. For the year as a whole there was a small decline in real GNP. As a consequence, unemployment rose to over 7 percent of the labor force.

Ronald Reagan took office in 1981, promising to put an end to inflation and to economic instability. His policies involved a large reduction in personal income tax rates (spread over three years), reductions in corporate taxes through accelerated depreciation allowances and investment tax credits, reductions in transfer payments, and increases in defense spending. Private saving and investment were to be stimulated by tax cuts for individuals and business and by reducing government interference in private decisions. The Reagan administration endorsed the low money growth targets set by the Fed but criticized the high variability of money growth that had occurred since October 1979.

The performance of the program did not live up to expectations. The administration and many of its supporters asserted that the tax and expenditure cuts would have a large and rapid effect on the "supply side" of the economy. Aggregate supply would grow along with aggregate demand so that the economy could enjoy rapid economic growth and price stability. Despite protests from most economists that there was no evidence from either historical experience or theory to support these claims, the "supply-siders" were confident of the wisdom of their plan.

Before we go any further, it is important to note that taxes and the size of government relative to GNP can have important effects on long-run aggregate supply. Many of the Reagan policies could ultimately add to the growth of aggregate supply. Long-run aggregate supply responds slowly to changes in investment and technology, however. Even if government policies are successful in stimulating investment and technical progress, years are required to affect long-run aggregate supply materially because net investment is small relative to the nation's capital stock. Furthermore, business will not invest much if aggregate demand is low and if real interest rates are high. The economy in 1981 and 1982 was depressed, and real interest rates were high. The optimistic predictions of the supply-siders were unrealistic.

Real federal spending slowed in 1981, and the high-employment budget deficit was reduced substantially. This tightening of fiscal policy had its effect, but restrictive monetary policy was largely responsible for the depressed economy in 1981 and 1982. The growth of the monetary aggregates slowed in 1981, with M1 growing by 6.4 percent for the year. Both short- and long-term interest rates rose sharply during the first two quarters of 1981, with the federal funds rate peaking at 19.10 percent in June. The federal funds rate began to fall in the third quarter, but long-term interest rates continued to rise. In September 1981 the long-term corporate bond rate (Aaa) stood at 15.5 percent. Real GNP fell sharply in the fourth quarter, and nominal interest rates also declined substantially. The inflation rate did slow somewhat to 8.6 percent in 1981 from 10.3 percent in 1980, but the average unemployment rate for the year rose from 7.1 percent to 7.6 percent. Real output growth was slow, but the 1.9 percent growth in 1981 was an improvement over the 0.4 percent decline in 1980.

The year 1982 saw a substantial decline in the inflation rate and a rise in unemployment to a post-Great Depression high. Real output continued to fall in the first quarter of 1982, and interest rates rose despite rapid growth in M1 during the quarter. Real output rose somewhat in the second quarter, and M1 growth was slow; short-term interest rates increased again. Interest rates declined during the remainder of the year as money growth accelerated. Real output growth was small in the third quarter and real GNP fell sharply in the fourth quarter. By the end of the year, inflation was about 5 percent, and unemployment was 10.8 percent.

HOW RESTRICTIVE WAS MONETARY POLICY DURING 1979 THROUGH 1982?

In discussing the monetary policy of the period 1973 through 1975, we showed that policy was restrictive in terms of the real quantity of money but that it was

TABLE 19.4
NOMINAL AND REAL VALUES OF MONEY GROWTH
AND THE FEDERAL FUNDS RATE (PERCENT)

		Annual Growth of M1	Federal Funds Rate	Annual Growth of the Consumption Deflator	Real M1 Growth	Real Federal Funds Rate
1979:	I	5.6	10.70	10.0	−4.4	0.70
	II	10.5	10.18	8.0	2.5	2.18
	III	9.4	10.94	9.4	0.0	1.54
	IV	4.7	13.58	10.7	−6.0	2.88
1980:	I	5.8	15.05	12.0	6.2	3.05
	II	−2.6	12.69	9.8	−12.4	2.69
	III	14.6	9.84	8.8	5.8	1.04
	IV	10.8	15.87	9.7	1.1	6.17
1981:	I	4.6	16.57	8.0	−3.4	8.57
	II	9.2	17.78	6.5	2.7	11.28
	III	0.3	17.58	9.0	−8.7	8.58
	IV	5.7	13.59	7.5	−1.8	6.09
1982:	I	10.4	14.23	3.8	6.6	10.43
	II	3.3	14.51	6.5	−3.2	8.01
	III	3.5	11.01	6.0	−2.5	5.01
	IV	16.2	9.23	4.9	11.3	4.33

not restrictive in terms of real interest rates. It is instructive to look at the 1979–1982 period from the same perspective. We shall see that there is no ambiguity about the thrust of monetary policy during this period. It was highly restrictive by any standard.

Table 19.4 shows the growth of M1, the level of the federal funds rate, and the inflation rate from quarter to quarter for the 1979–1982 period. The table also shows real money growth and the real federal funds rate from quarter to quarter.

The behavior of real money growth and the real federal funds rate for 1979 through 1982 do not tell the conflicting story that they did for 1973 through 1975. Although real money growth is not uniformly negative in 1979–1982, as it was from the second quarter of 1973 through the first quarter of 1975, there was a substantial decline in real money balances over the 1979–1982 period. The major difference between 1973–1975 and 1979–1982 is the level of real short-term interest rates. In the 1973–1975 period, the real federal funds rate was low and often negative. From 1979 through 1982, it was always positive, and it frequently was very high. The real federal funds rate rose from low levels in 1979 to 11.28 percent in the second quarter of 1981. This latter figure is higher than the *nominal* interest rates of the 1973–1975 period. Between the fourth quarter of 1980 and the third quarter of 1982, the real federal funds rate averaged 8 percent.

There was considerable discussion in the popular press and elsewhere during the 1979–1982 period about the effect that rising federal budget deficits played in

FIGURE 19.10
FEDERAL BUDGET SURPLUSES
AND DEFICITS 1965–1982 (ANNUAL
AVERAGES IN BILLIONS OF DOLLARS).

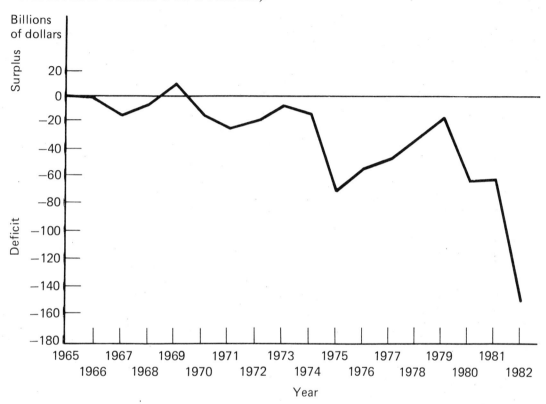

producing high interest rates over that period.[15] The budget deficit did rise substantially from 1979 through 1982. We saw in Chapter 15 that deficits can raise interest rates if they are not monetized. The growth of M1 during the period was relatively modest, and the quantity of government securities in the hands of the public rose substantially. This suggests that the rising deficits contributed to high interest rates.

Figure 19.10 puts the issue in perspective, showing the dollar size of federal budget deficits and surpluses from 1965 through 1982. We see that the deficits during the 1979–1982 period were very large by historical standards, reaching nearly $150 billion for 1982.

[15] Note that we are talking about the actual budget deficit here and not the high-employment deficit.

FIGURE 19.11
BUDGET DEFICITS AND
SURPLUSES RELATIVE TO GNP
1965–1982 (PERCENTAGES OF
ANNUAL AVERAGES TAKEN
WITHOUT REGARD TO SIGN).

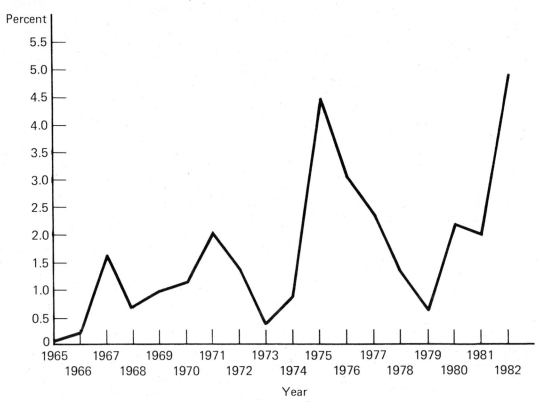

The deficits of 1979–1982 are so large by historical standards because the economy is much larger in nominal terms than it was ten or fifteen years ago. This occurred as the result of both growth of real output and inflation. As the nominal size of the economy becomes larger, a deficit of a given nominal size is less significant. Figure 19.11 adjusts for the growing size of the economy, showing the federal budget deficits and surpluses as a percentage of GNP for the years 1965 through 1982. Here a very different picture emerges. The 1975–1977 period had deficits as a percentage of GNP that were as high as the percentages in 1979 through 1982. Even 1971 had a percentage that was as high as in 1981. The deficits of 1979 through 1982 were large in nominal terms, but the economy during these years was also very large in nominal terms. There is little reason to believe that short-term interest rates were so high from 1979 through 1982 because of the budget deficits. If this were the primary cause, short-term interest rates would have been higher than they were in 1971 and 1975 through 1977.

The reason that real short-term interest rates were so much higher in 1979–1982 than in 1973–1975 is that money demand was strong in the later period, whereas there was a substantial downward shift in money demand in 1973–1975. A declining real money supply combined with strong real money demand produced very high short-term interest rates in the period 1979 through 1982.

The story is somewhat different when we consider long-term interest rates. We have already argued that long-term interest rates were so high from 1979 through 1982 because of inflationary expectations and market uncertainty that produced a substantial risk premium for long-term bonds. Part of the inflationary expectations and the uncertainty about the future involved projections of very large deficits throughout the 1980s. These projections implied a different pattern for future deficits from what occurred during previous expansions when budget deficits fell sharply. Concern over these future deficits probably helped produce high long-term interest rates.

The declining real quantity of money and high interest rates of 1980 through 1982 helps to explain why that recession was the largest since the Great Depression. With a recession of this magnitude, the inflation rate did fall sharply. The decline in inflation was the consequence of tight monetary policy and deep recession, not of supply-side economics.

The mix of monetary and fiscal policy and the deep recession were highly unfavorable to capital formation. Fiscal policy was expansionary in 1982. Cuts in personal income tax rates and rising transfer payments encouraged consumption expenditures. Monetary policy offset this effect by raising interest rates to the point that investment and other interest-sensitive forms of spending were reduced. The high interest rates crowded out the investment expenditures that are necessary for the growth of long-run aggregate supply. A fiscal policy that discouraged consumption, coupled with an easier monetary policy, would have been more consistent with expanding long-run aggregate supply.

Inflation was reduced by the low level of aggregate demand that was produced by a highly restrictive monetary policy. An unemployment rate of nearly 11 percent reduced inflation. It was not possible to have high investment and saving in a depressed economy, however. Even if fiscal policy had used tax increases or spending cuts, or both, to produce the deep recession, rather than relying on monetary policy, capital formation would have been low. Investment would be somewhat higher in this situation, but it would have been weak.

The primary objective of monetary policy was to reduce inflation. The policy was successful because it produced sufficient unemployment and unused capacity to break the wage-price spiral. Just as a large recession in 1973–1975 reduced inflation, the great recession of 1980–1982 also reduced inflation.

The inflation rate was also lowered by a substantial rise in the dollar exchange rate. With real U.S. interest rates at such high levels, there were large capital inflows that raised the exchange rate. This reduced the prices of imported goods and services and eased inflation. Foreign countries resisted declines in their exchange rates by raising their interest rates. This served to depress aggregate demand abroad and to produce a worldwide recession.

With the U.S. and the worldwide recession worsening and with massive domestic and foreign debt defaults resulting from recession and high interest rates, the FOMC relaxed its tight monetary policy in the fourth quarter of 1982. Interest rates fell, and money growth accelerated in the fourth quarter of 1982. The policy shift was too late to prevent the largest decline in real output and the highest unemployment rate since the Great Depression.

ATTEMPTING TO CONTROL THE MONETARY AGGREGATES: OCTOBER 1979 THROUGH NOVEMBER 1982

In assessing the role of monetary policy in the 1979–1982 period, we should note that between October 1979 and November 1982 the FOMC largely abandoned trying to limit short-term fluctuations in the federal funds rate and devoted its attention to controlling growth of the monetary aggregates. The change in policy emphasis and operating procedures was successful in restricting the average growth rate of the monetary aggregates. Violent fluctuations in interest rates occurred, however, and the growth of the monetary aggregates was highly erratic from month to month and from quarter to quarter. The wide fluctuations in both interest rates and money growth created considerable uncertainty and confusion in financial markets and in the economy as a whole. This may have contributed to the high real interest rates during the period.

To gain an appreciation of the degree of volatility of interest rates, we will find it useful to compare the monthly pattern of interest rates from 1973 through 1975 with the 1979–1982 period. Both were periods of high inflation followed by deep recession, and, in both periods, the Fed was actively attempting to limit money growth. The experience for interest rates on federal funds and long-term corporate bonds in 1973–1975 is shown in Panel I of Figure 19.12. The behavior of these interest rates in the period 1979–1982 is shown in Panel II. We see that the fluctuations in both short and long-term interest rates were substantially larger from 1979 through 1982 than they were from 1973 through 1975. It is important to note that the movements in short-term interest rates that occurred during the 1973–1975 period were large by historical standards. They seem small only in comparison to the 1979–1982 period.

One might conclude that the huge swings in interest rates during the 1979–1982 period were necessary for the FOMC to gain control over the monetary aggre-

FIGURE 19.12
MONTHLY INTEREST RATES ON
FEDERAL FUNDS AND
CORPORATE BONDS: 1973-1975
AND 1979-1982 (PERCENT).

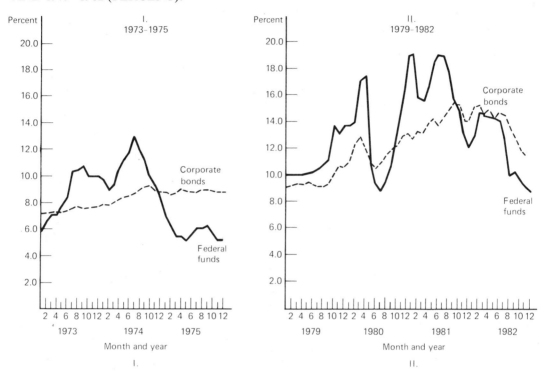

gates. Prior to October 1979, there were narrow limits on the fluctuations in the federal funds rate that could occur between FOMC meetings. Though the federal funds rate was changed when the Committee met, the interest rate fluctuated little between meetings. Beginning in October 1979, the limits for fluctuations in the federal funds rate between FOMC meetings were very large. For example, at the FOMC meeting of September 18, 1979, the range of fluctuations in the federal funds rate was 0.50 percentage points, that is, 11.25 to 11.75 percent. At the meeting of October 6, 1979, the range was 4.00 percentage points, that is, 11.50 to 15.5 percent. Over the next two years, the range was sometimes as large as 8.50 percentage points. By allowing greater variability in the federal funds rate between FOMC meetings, the Federal Reserve should have gained greater control over the monetary aggregates.

Inspection of Figure 19.13 indicates that this was not the case. Panel I shows the annual growth in M1 from quarter to quarter for 1973 through 1976. Panel II shows quarterly M1 growth for 1979 through 1982. The contrast is remarkable.

FIGURE 19.13
QUARTERLY M1 GROWTH:
1973–1976 AND 1979–1982 (ANNUAL
PERCENTAGE RATES).

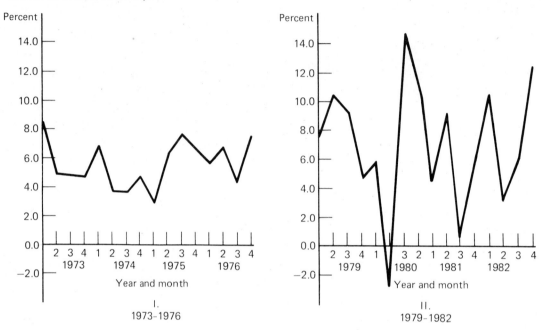

I.
1973-1976

II.
1979-1982

The quarterly growth of M1 from 1973 through 1975 is smooth compared to the wild fluctuations that occurred from 1979 through 1982. Money growth was under much better control, and interest rate fluctuations were smaller in 1973 through 1975 than in 1979 through 1982.

The wide fluctuations in interest rates and money growth that occurred from 1979 through 1982 are important because they produced great uncertainty in the economy. Interest rates rose to unprecedented heights only to plunge to relatively low levels and then take off for new record levels. This kind of behavior of interest rates was not conducive to public confidence or to promoting investment.

Furthermore, the public was informed that controlling the growth in the monetary aggregates was the Fed's number one priority for reducing inflation. As a result, the public paid considerable attention to the growth of the monetary aggregates. To a casual observer at least, the monetary aggregates appeared to be out of control. Swings from 10.5 percent in the second quarter of 1979 to −2.6 percent in the second quarter of 1980 to 14.6 percent in the third quarter of 1980 did little to build confidence in the Federal Reserve. This last big swing was largely the result of credit controls, but the Fed had promised to control money growth. Furthermore, the swings in money growth in 1981 and 1982, when there were no credit controls, were also very large. The growth of M1 was 9.2 percent in the second quarter of 1981, hardly a number consistent with containing inflation. Money growth then fell to 0.3 percent in the third quarter, only to be followed by growth of 5.7 percent and 10.4 percent respectively in the fourth quarter of 1981 and the first quarter of 1982.

We have argued repeatedly in this text that the Federal Reserve cannot closely control money growth in the short run. What we had in mind was the kind of fluctuations in growth rates that occurred from 1973 through 1975. We did not mean the kind of fluctuations that occurred from 1979 through 1982. Why was monetary control so poor during this latter period? There are several reasons, including the effects of financial innovations and deregulation, but an important factor was the change in the FOMC's operating procedures. The regulatory and institutional framework that worked fairly well under the old procedures worked poorly under the new one. This contributed significantly to the instability of both the monetary aggregates and interest rates in the 1979–1982 period.

Limitations of space do not allow a detailed account of why regulatory and institutional factors created problems, but a few comments are in order. In 1968 the Fed switched from a rule that required banks to hold required reserves against their current deposit liabilities to one in which required reserves were based on deposit liabilities two weeks in the past. This change from contemporaneous to lagged reserve accounting was made to ease the burden on small banks. They found it difficult to determine quickly the composition of their current liabilities and, therefore, their current required reserves. The two-week delay before reserve requirements were assessed allowed small banks time to determine the size and mix of the liabilities to which the reserve requirement apply.

Lagged reserve accounting did not cause substantial problems for monetary control when the FOMC had narrow bands for fluctuations in the federal funds rate. It did cause problems when the federal funds rate was allowed to vary over a substantial range. When the band of fluctuations in the federal funds rate was widened, the FOMC set a growth rate for reserves that was designed to achieve the desired growth rate for the monetary aggregates. With lagged reserve accounting, the FOMC could not use total reserves as its instrument; it could only use nonborrowed reserves. To see why this is the case, let us review some reserve identities.

Total reserves, TR, are comprised of required reserves, RR, and excess reserves, ER, or $TR = RR + ER$. Total reserves are also comprised of reserves borrowed from the discount window, BR, and reserves that are not borrowed, NBR. Thus, $TR = BR + NBR = RR + ER$. In any given week, the amount of required reserves is fixed because they are determined by the deposit liabilities that existed two weeks in the past. This means that when the FOMC engages in open market operations, it immediately affects nonborrowed reserves, borrowed reserves, and excess reserves but not required reserves. Open market operations pursued during a week affect the amount of deposit liabilities in the depository system for that week, but required reserves are not affected until two weeks later.

For simplicity, consider the case where there are no excess reserves in the system, so that total reserves equal required reserves. Assume the FOMC wants to reduce the amount of total reserves. This is not possible because an open market sale of securities reduces total reserves below the predetermined amount of required reserves. In this situation, depository institutions discover that they do not have enough reserves to satisfy reserve requirements. They attempt to obtain the reserves by selling assets and by borrowing in the federal funds market. The federal funds rate rises sharply in response to the increased demand, but there are not enough reserves available to meet reserve requirements. Note that with contemporaneous reserve accounting, deposit liabilities and required reserves are both reduced when depository institutions sell assets. The decline in required reserves reduces the excess demand in the federal funds market. This means that there is a smaller increase in the federal funds rate under contemporaneous than lagged accounting.

With lagged reserve accounting, depository institutions must turn to the discount window for reserves. Although, as explained in Chapter 12, the supply of credit through the discount window is rationed by the Fed, it must allow depository institutions to borrow enough to meet their reserves requirements when there is lagged reserve accounting. Thus, when nonborrowed reserves fall, borrowed reserves rise by the same amount, leaving total reserves unaffected. This is true only if there are no excess reserves in the system. If depository institutions have excess reserves, these can be used to satisfy reserve requirements. In this case, borrowed reserves do not have to rise by the full amount by which nonborrowed reserves fall. Because excess reserves are small, they do not provide much scope for adjustment. This means that virtually all adjustment to a decline in nonborrowed reserves occurs as a rise in borrowed reserves.

An open market sale of securities does not change total reserves by much; it primarily changes the mix of total reserves between borrowed and nonborrowed reserves. This change in the mix between nonborrowed and borrowed reserves does have an effect. Depository institutions are expected to repay their borrowing at the discount window quickly. They sell assets to obtain the funds. This produces a decline in deposit liabilities and a decline in required reserves two weeks later. With lower required reserves, they can repay their borrowing at the discount window.

Now let us consider the case where the system initially has no excess reserves and the FOMC wants to increase the quantity of total reserves during the week. The trading desk in New York purchases securities, which increases total reserves. Required reserves are determined by deposit liabilities of two weeks ago. This means that the additional reserves are held as excess reserves. Depository institutions do not want to hold any excess reserves, so they use the excess reserves to acquire loans and securities, and they lend in the federal funds market. This expands money and credit, and it reduces interest rates sharply, but it does not get rid of the excess reserves. Depository institutions get rid of the excess reserves by repaying debt at the discount window. This reduces borrowed reserves and total reserves.

A depository institution that has no borrowed reserves does not hold excess reserves. It lends its excess reserves to an institution that does have borrowed reserves to repay. Excess reserves rise substantially only when there is a small total amount of borrowed reserves outstanding. In this case, an open market purchase of securities by the Fed raises excess reserves during the week that the purchases occur.

There is always discount window credit outstanding, so when the FOMC purchases securities, total reserves are not increased. Nonborrowed reserves rise, but borrowed reserves fall. With this change in the mix of total reserves, there is a sharp decline in short-term interest rates and a substantial rise in money and credit.[16] When depository institutions purchase assets, the quantity of deposit liabilities rises. Two weeks later, required reserves rise.

We see from these two cases that open market operations during a week have no effect on required reserves and little effect on total reserves in that week. Open market operations primarily change the mix of total reserves between nonborrowed and borrowed. This can be shown algebraically. Because $TR = \overline{RR} + ER = NBR + BR$, we subtract BR to obtain

$$NBR = \overline{RR} + (ER - BR).$$

The bar over RR indicates that required reserves are predetermined. An open market purchase of securities raises nonborrowed reserves because excess reserves rise or borrowing falls.[17] An open market sale of securities reduces nonborrowed reserves because excess reserves fall or borrowed reserves rise, or both. Thus, open market operations affect nonborrowed reserves, excess reserves, and borrowed reserves during a week, but they do not affect required reserves.

We cannot end the story here, however. Open market operations do affect required reserves with a lag. An open market sale of securities reduces nonborrowed reserves and increases borrowed reserves. Depository institutions attempt to reduce the increased borrowing at the discount window quickly by selling assets. This raises market interest rates, and it reduces the quantity of deposit liabilities in the system. Two weeks later required reserves are lower. The opposite occurs when there is an open market purchase of securities. Depository institutions repay debt at the discount window, and they expand credit. This raises deposit liabilities, and required reserves rise two weeks later. As explained in more detail later, because required reserves do not rise and fall immediately with increases and decreases in deposit liabilities, there are larger changes in deposit liabilities and credit in response to open market operation when there is lagged reserve accounting.

Lagged reserve accounting builds a two-week lag into the system. This may not seem important, but it tends to create complex dynamic reactions that make control over the monetary aggregates more difficult. To see why this is the case, consider the example of an increase in loan demand. Depository institutions meet the demand by expanding loans, which produces an increase their deposit liabilities.

[16] If borrowed reserves were zero, the federal funds rate would plummet, stopping only at zero.

[17] The expression $(ER - BR)$ is called *free reserves.*

When there is contemporaneous reserve accounting, required reserves rise at the same time as deposit liabilities. This reduces the expansion in deposit liabilities and in credit. With lagged reserve accounting, required reserves do not rise at the same time as deposit liabilities rise. They increase two weeks later. The absence of a contemporaneous increase in required reserves means that credit and deposit liabilities initially increase by more than is the case of contemporaneous reserve accounting. Thus, for any given increase in loan demand during a week, there is a larger increase in loans and in deposit liabilities under lagged than contemporaneous reserve accounting.

Two weeks later required reserves rise. At that time, depository institutions must have enough reserves to cover the higher required reserves. There are two ways that the reserves can be supplied. If the FOMC does not increase the quantity of nonborrowed reserves, depository institutions borrow the reserves from the discount window. Alternatively, the FOMC can increase the quantity of nonborrowed reserves. In either case, total reserves rise to meet the increase in required reserves. If the quantity of nonborrowed reserves is unchanged, depository institutions borrow from the discount window. Total reserve rise to support the larger quantity of money in the system. Because depository institutions are not allowed to borrow from the discount window for substantial periods of time, they begin to sell assets and to shrink credit. This reduces deposit liabilities and eventually required reserves. This process takes time, however, and while the adjustment is taking place, the monetary aggregates remain above their desired levels.[18] If the quantity of nonborrowed reserves is increased rather than borrowed reserves, the monetary aggregates remain above their desired values until nonborrowed reserves are reduced.

The opposite phenomenon occurs when there is a decrease in loan demand. Loans and deposit liabilities fall, but required reserves do not decline at the same time. This produces a larger decline in money and credit relative to contemporaneous reserve accounting. Two weeks later required reserves fall. If the FOMC keeps the quantity of nonborrowed reserves unchanged, excess reserves start to pile up, and depository institutions repay debt at the discount window. Alternatively, the FOMC can decrease the amount of nonborrowed reserves. In either case, total reserves fall.

The adjustments that occurred with lagged reserve accounting produced larger fluctuations in both money and interest rates than would occur under contemporaneous reserve accounting. Interest rate fluctuations were made more complex and difficult to interpret by the interest rate speculation that occurred following the change in the FOMC's operating procedures. On each Friday the Federal Reserve announces the value of M1 for the week ending the previous Wednesday. Participants in the money market anxiously awaited this announcement because it gave them information on the future course of interest rates. If M1 increased

---

[18] Recall that, with lagged reserve accounting, the initial rise in money and credit is larger than under contemporaneous accounting.

sharply during the week, it was likely that interest rates would rise when the two-week lag for required reserves had passed. This raised current interest rates because the public increased its borrowing in an effort to avoid the higher interest rates in the future. Conversely, if M1 decreased, interest rates were likely to fall in the future. This led the public to postpone borrowing until interest rates fell, which lowered current short-term interest rates. Short-term interest rates fluctuated sharply as the speculative process developed.

Lagged reserve accounting was not the only cause of the erratic movements in short-term interest rates and in money growth during the 1979–1982 period. We have already pointed out that credit controls distorted the supply of credit and that they produced shifts in money demand. Furthermore, erratic shifts into and out of money market mutual funds and other "moneylike" assets produced erratic changes in M1 as financial innovation and deregulation had powerful effects during this period.

In November 1982, with the economy in disarray and with the newly authorized insured money market accounts and super NOW accounts for depository institutions, the FOMC abandoned M1 as a target. The FOMC switched to M2 as its primary monetary target, and it began to stabilize short-term interest rates. The experience gained during the 1979–1982 period did lead the Federal Reserve Board to adopt a form of contemporaneous reserve accounting to take effect in February 1984.

THE LESSONS OF 1965 THROUGH 1982

The poor performance of the U.S. economy during most of the 1965–1982 period was the result of a string of policy errors coupled with a number of large external shocks to the economy. The combination of policy errors and bad luck produced the large economic fluctuations as well as the high inflation and unemployment that characterized the period. There is no way for any economy to avoid exogenous shocks from food and oil scarcities; there are ways to guard against destabilizing policies.

In order to avoid destabilizing policies in the future, we must determine why policy performance was so poor in the past. There was not just a single policy error but a seemingly unrelenting string of errors. The fascinating question is, Why? The fiscal policies of 1965–1982 were formulated and executed under four different administrations, two Democratic and two Republican. The monetary policies were executed under four different chairmen of the Federal Reserve. One cannot point to a single political party, to a single president, or to a single chairman of the Fed as the source of policy errors. There was something more fundamental involved than a single personality or a single political philosophy.

Activism was the common element in the policies from 1965 through 1982. Conservatives and liberals alike actively used economic policy in an effort to solve pressing economic problems. Sometimes the problem was inflation, sometimes the problem was unemployment, and often the problem was both inflation and unemployment. Efforts to solve the problems quickly often made the situation worse. As an example of this phenomenon, one only has to refer to the inflation and unemployment rates that drove the Nixon administration to wage-price controls. By recent standards, an economy with 5 percent inflation and 6 percent unemployment looks good. Yet in 1971 the situation was considered so dire that drastic measures were taken. In an effort to reduce the "intolerable" rates of inflation and unemployment, the Nixon administration and the Fed unleashed a series of policies that worsened the situation. Later administrations and Federal Reserves responded to the effects of these policies by designing their own strong policies, which, in turn, helped to increase the size of economic fluctuations.

A policy cycle developed that exhibited signs of instability. When the inflation rate rose substantially, policy became very restrictive, and a recession developed. When unemployment rose substantially, policy became highly stimulative, and inflation was propelled to higher levels. This led to harsher policies to combat inflation, which produced even larger recessions. It appears that impatience and an unwillingness to assess the ultimate effects of policy changes caused the policy cycle.

At times, frustrations became so great that radical policies were tried. Thus, Nixon imposed wage-price controls, and Carter brought about credit controls. Not only were these policies harmful to the economy, but they are also examples of extreme policy activism. If conventional policies are not working, try something else—anything else!

It is remarkable that despite the worsening state of the economy over the 1965–1982 period, policy activism continued. Policy instruments continued to be used aggressively in an effort to correct economic wrongs. By pushing harder and harder on the economy to reduce inflation or unemployment and by underestimating the ultimate effects of these efforts, policymakers produced cycles in inflation and unemployment of increasing magnitude.

What can be done to bring the economy under control? The experience of the last eighteen years suggests that economic stability can be enhanced by stable and predictable policies. The public might be able to adjust to virtually any policy if given sufficient time. In order to make the adjustments, however, the public must know what the policy is. Frequent and erratic policy shifts make the adjustment process impossible. Some policy strategies are better than others and, therefore, can hasten the transition to stability. A stable and predictable policy is a necessary condition for the transition, however. The erratic and unpredictable policies over the last eighteen years made it virtually impossible for the economy to adjust to a rapidly changing world.

It is inconceivable that the public could have predicted the policies of the period. For example, who would have guessed that a Republican president would impose wage-price controls or embark on a scheme to achieve energy independence in six years? Who would have guessed that a conservative chairman of the Federal Reserve would have presided over an inflationary policy in 1972, then declare war on inflation in 1974, only to pursue expansionary policies in 1976?

Similarly, the policies of the Reagan administration and of the Fed are in flux, and future policy is difficult, if not impossible, to predict.

It is essential that the public knows the rules of the game and that the rules not be changed abruptly. The public needs to know how policy will respond to economic fluctuations and to stagflation. This requires a clear statement of policy objectives and policy strategy by the government. More importantly, it requires credibility.

SUMMARY

This chapter reviewed major economic events from 1965 through 1982. The period was marked by episodes of high inflation and high unemployment, with both often occurring at the same time. The poor performance of the economy was the result of some incredibly bad luck, coupled with what proved to be policy errors.

Bad luck in the form of OPEC, commodity and food shortages, and worldwide speculative booms is hardly the fault of monetary and fiscal policy. The highly stimulative policies surrounding the Vietnam War and the stop-go policies that followed were the responsibility of policymakers. Hindsight strongly suggests that policy was used too aggressively in pursuit of economic goals. This usually involved large changes in policy instruments to reduce inflation or to reduce unemployment. In the case of the 1974–1975 period, however, aggressive policy involved not responding to the massive external shock that came from OPEC.

As this section is written (early 1984), inflation has fallen to about 5 percent and real output is expanding. Unemployment is over 8 percent, however. The current situation presents a policy dilemma. If aggregate demand expands slowly, inflation should remain under control, but high levels of unemployment will continue. If aggregate demand expands rapidly, unemployment will be reduced, but at the risk of resurgence of inflation. There is terrible social, economic, and human waste in high unemployment. This argues for rapid growth in aggregate demand to reduce unemployment and excess capacity. If a stimulative policy is pursued for too long, however, inflation could take off again. This would continue the roller coaster ride that the economy began in 1965. There are few easy choices for policymakers.

SELECTED REFERENCES

Blinder, Alan, *Economic Policy and the Great Stagflation*, New York: Academic Press, 1979.

Fischer, Stanley (ed.), *Rational Expectations and Economic Policy*, Chicago: University of Chicago Press, 1980.

Goldfeld, Steven, "The Case of the Missing Money," *Brookings Papers on Economic Activity*, 3:1976, pp. 683–730.

Hester, Donald, "Innovations and Monetary Control," *Brookings Papers on Economic Activity*, 1:1981, pp. 141–189.

Perry, George, "Policy Alternatives for 1974," *Brookings Papers on Economic Activity*, 1975:1, pp. 222–235.

Pierce, James, "How Regulations Affect Monetary Control," *Journal of Money, Credit and Banking*, November 1981, pp. 775–787.

——, "The Political Economy of Arthur Burns, *Journal of Finance*, May 1979, pp. 485–496.

—— and Jared Enzler, "The Effects of External Inflationary Shocks," *Brookings Papers on Economic Activity*, 1:1974, pp. 13–54.

INDEX